ЛЕВЫЙ

Typographic Communications Today

Typographic Communications Today

by Edward M. Gottschall

EDITORS

Aaron Burns
Karl Gerstner
Allan Haley
Herbert Spencer
Victor Spindler
Maxim Zhukov

International Typeface Corporation
New York, NY

The MIT Press
Cambridge, Massachusetts
London, England

First MIT Press edition, 1989
Second printing, 1991

Printed and bound by Dai Nippon Printing Co., Japan

Library of Congress Cataloging-in-Publication Data

Gottschall, Edward M.
Typographic communications today / by Edward M. Gottschall; editors. Aaron Burns...[et al.]. – 1st MIT Press ed.
p. cm.
Bibliography: p.
Includes index.
ISBN 0-262-07114-2
1. Printing, Practical – Layout – History. 2. Type and type-founding – History. 3. Graphic arts – History. I. Burns, Aaron. II. Title.
Z246.G67 1989
686.2'2 – dc19

TYPOGRAPHIC COMMUNICATIONS TODAY

Table of Contents

TYPOGRAPHIC COMMUNICATIONS TODAY

Preface

TODAY, WITH THE introduction of personal computers and laser printers, hundreds of thousands and potentially many millions of people, with little or no knowledge or training in the typographic arts will soon be entering the field of typographic communications, and it is especially for this vast audience of untrained practitioners that TYPOGRAPHIC COMMUNICATIONS TODAY has been prepared.

Recording the most significant historical developments of typography in the 20th century will serve as a valuable educational source for all who would like to know more about how modern typography developed. When it began. Who the pioneers were. Where they came from. Why? How? And what their meaning is to us today, to the professional graphic designer and the many people who have recently entered the field of graphic design thanks to the design capabilities and availability of computers and software.

TYPOGRAPHIC COMMUNICATIONS TODAY was produced by *U&lc* under the sponsorship of International Typeface Corporation (ITC).

To produce this mammoth project, *U&lc* editor-in-chief, Edward Gottschall, spent five years traveling throughout the world, visiting such countries as Russia, Japan, Czechoslovakia, Italy, Germany, Switzerland, France, Great Britain, the Scandinavian countries and others. And where time could not permit, hundreds of letter and phone calls were made to others.

Ed met with some of the original pioneers such as Herbert Bayer, Max Bill, Max Huber, Josef Müller-Brockmann and many others whom you will read about in TYPOGRAPHIC COMMUNICATIONS TODAY. He spoke with them for hours and the results are all contained in what we believe will be a major contribution to recorded modern typographic history.

Aaron Burns
Chairman, ITC

Typographic Communications Today

Introduction

Today, typography is a vital element in making print or electronic communications more effective and more efficient. Until recently the choice of a typeface and specifying its parameters (size, weight, slant, line length, interline spacing, for example) was usually the province of art directors, graphic designers or others with appropriate sensitivity, knowledge and developed skills.

Today, thanks to computers and computer controlled devices, hundreds of thousands, perhaps millions, of people with little or no art/design training or experience are called upon to make typographic design decisions.

The aim of TYPOGRAPHIC COMMUNICATIONS TODAY is dual — to:

1. Develop in people new to communication design a respect for the power of typography to —

❧ make information more attractive, more noticed, more widely read;
❧ be more legible, more readable;
❧ save money by occupying less space than typewritten documents, and reducing reproduction, filing, distribution costs;
❧ enhance the tone of a message by employing the appropriate typeface and weaving it into a design well suited to the message, the medium and the audience;
❧ achieve the desired emphasis of key points in a message;
❧ improve message comprehension and retention.

2. Offer to art directors, designers and all type specifiers and users a one-stop review of some of the best typographic design work of this century and a pleasurable reminder of the many different and successful approaches to communication problems.

TYPOGRAPHIC COMMUNICATIONS TODAY *is not* a tutorial, not a how-to. It *is* a critical review of twentieth century typographic design. It aims to open eyes and minds to the potential power of typography when skillfully handled, and to do so by examining the roots of contemporary typographic design and the work of outstanding typographic designers all over the world.

TYPOGRAPHIC COMMUNICATIONS TODAY

Chapter I: The Many Faces of Typographic Design

Typographic characters are used pictorially to produce explosive graphics.

Vitality, Dynamism are supreme. Visual excitement dominates. Readability follows. Rules of grammar and design take a back seat. The graphic treatment is the primary message. The text details or supports the message. Typographic characters are used pictorially to produce explosive graphics.

The following is from the first futurist manifesto, published February 20, 1909, in the French newspaper, *Le Figaro.* Author Filippo Tommaso Marinetti believed that before one could build a new and better world one had to destroy the old. His philosophy extended to the way he used and extended the grammar of words and graphics.

"We declare that the world's splendor has been enriched by a new beauty; the beauty of speed. A racing motor car, its frame adorned with great pipes, like snakes with explosive breath…a roaring motor car, which looks as though running on shrapnel, is more beautiful than the Victory of Samothrace.

"We shall sing of the man at the steering wheel, whose ideal stem transfixes the Earth, rushing over the circuit of her orbit. The poet must give himself with frenzy, with splendor and with lavishness, in order to increase the enthusiastic fervor of the primordial elements.

"There is no more beauty except in strife. No masterpiece without aggressiveness. Poetry must be a violent onslaught upon the unknown forces, to command them to bow before man.

"We wish to glorify War…

"We wish to destroy the museums, the libraries, to fight against moralism, feminism and all opportunistic and utilitarian meannesses."

A futurist poem, *Bifszt 18 Simultaneità (Chimismi Iirici),* written in 1915 by Ardengo Soffici.

A powerful example of Futurist typography from *Bif§zf + 18 Simultaneità Chimismi lirici* by Ardengo Soffici, Florence, 1915.

VORZUGS-ANGEBOT

Im VERLAG DES BILDUNGSVERBANDES der Deutschen Buchdrucker, Berlin SW 61, Dreibundstr. 5, erscheint demnächst:

JAN TSCHICHOLD
Lehrer an der Meisterschule für Deutschlands Buchdrucker in München

DIE NEUE TYPOGRAPHIE

Handbuch für die gesamte Fachwelt und die drucksachenverbrauchenden Kreise

Das Problem der neuen gestaltenden Typographie hat eine lebhafte Diskussion bei allen Beteiligten hervorgerufen. Wir glauben dem Bedürfnis, die aufgeworfenen Fragen ausführlich behandelt zu sehen, zu entsprechen, wenn wir jetzt ein Handbuch der **NEUEN TYPOGRAPHIE** herausbringen.

Es kam dem Verfasser, einem ihrer bekanntesten Vertreter, in diesem Buche zunächst darauf an, den engen Zusammenhang der neuen Typographie mit dem **Gesamtkomplex heutigen Lebens** aufzuzeigen und zu beweisen, daß die neue Typographie ein ebenso notwendiger Ausdruck einer neuen Gesinnung ist wie die neue Baukunst und alles Neue, das mit unserer Zeit anbricht. Diese geschichtliche Notwendigkeit der neuen Typographie belegt weiterhin eine kritische Darstellung der **alten Typographie.** Die Entwicklung der **neuen Malerei,** die für alles Neue unserer Zeit geistig bahnbrechend gewesen ist, wird in einem reich illustrierten Aufsatz des Buches leicht faßlich dargestellt. Ein kurzer Abschnitt „**Zur Geschichte der neuen Typographie**" leitet zu dem wichtigsten Teile des Buches, den **Grundbegriffen der neuen Typographie** über. Diese werden klar herausgeschält, richtige und falsche Beispiele einander gegenübergestellt. Zwei weitere Artikel behandeln „**Photographie und Typographie**" und „**Neue Typographie und Normung**".

Der Hauptwert des Buches für den Praktiker besteht in dem zweiten Teil „**Typographische Hauptformen**" (siehe das nebenstehende Inhaltsverzeichnis). Es fehlte bisher an einem Werke, das wie dieses Buch die schon bei einfachen Satzaufgaben auftauchenden gestalterischen Fragen in gebührender Ausführlichkeit behandelte. Jeder Teilabschnitt enthält neben **allgemeinen typographischen Regeln** vor allem die Abbildungen aller in Betracht kommenden **Normblätter** des Deutschen Normenausschusses, alle andern (z. B. postalischen) **Vorschriften** und zahlreiche Beispiele, Gegenbeispiele und Schemen.

Für jeden Buchdrucker, insbesondere jeden Akzidenzsetzer, wird „Die neue Typographie" ein **unentbehrliches Handbuch** sein. Von nicht geringerer Bedeutung ist es für Reklamefachleute, Gebrauchsgraphiker, Kaufleute, Photographen, Architekten, Ingenieure und Schriftsteller, also für alle, die mit dem Buchdruck in Berührung kommen.

INHALT DES BUCHES

typ. tschichold

Das Buch enthält über 125 Abbildungen, von denen etwa ein Viertel zweifarbig gedruckt ist, und umfaßt gegen 200 Seiten auf gutem Kunstdruckpapier. Es erscheint im Format DIN A5 (148×210 mm) und ist biegsam in Ganzleinen gebunden.

Preis bei Vorbestellung bis 1. Juni 1928: **5.00** RM
durch den Buchhandel nur zum Preise von **6.50** RM

Bestellschein umstehend

Clarity and Order (but not boredom) are the primary objectives. Unessential elements (ornament, decoration) give way to functionalism. The elements are organized for easy eye-flow. A sans serif typeface focuses on basic, unadorned letter forms. Boldface type and rules introduce emphasis, direct the eye and mind of the reader logically and unemotionally. But, compared to symmetrical typographic designs of earlier centuries the dynamic symmetry (off center yet optically balanced) blends a degree of visual vitality with orderly presentation. This was a brochure with solid yellow background and black type, designed by Jan Tschichold in 1928, to promote his book, *Die Neue Typographie.*

"More matter is being printed and published today than ever before, and every publisher of an advertisement, pamphlet or book expects his material to be read. Publishers and, even more so, readers want what is important to be clearly laid out. They will not read anything that is troublesome to read, but are pleased with what looks clear and well arranged, for it will make their task of understanding easier.

"For this reason, the important part must stand out and the unimportant must be subdued…

"The technique of modern typography must also adapt itself to the speed of our times. Today, we cannot spend as much time on a letter heading or other piece of jobbing as was possible even in the nineties."

From *Asymmetric Typography* written by Jan Tschichold in 1935. The new typography (functional, visually streamlined and simplified) was an outgrowth of Russian constructivist ideas as applied by the Bauhaus in Weimar. Tschichold, in his practice, his teaching and his writings (notably *Die Neue Typographie* and *Asymmetric Typography*) enunciated most clearly, forcibly and effectively the need for unencumbered functionalism in typographic design.

This first state of modern typography, though often labeled as functional, is better described as elementary; going back to the elements was a direction that culminated in the Bauhaus. Sans serif typefaces were chosen by typographers because serifs were considered ornaments, unessential and decadent. At the begining of the century, in Vienna, architect Adolf Loos declared ornaments a crime.

Dada and Type Illustration

Disorder for Its Own Sake, calculatedly noncommunicative. Where futurists put vitality ahead of mere legibility, the dadaists' rejection of society's values (that lead to war and moral decadence) is expressed in their graphics and poetry. As in cubism, letterforms are fascinating visual shapes, not merely phonetic symbols. Items are randomly dispersed. In some dada pieces deliberate nonsense is the message. Spontaneity and planning collide in dada writings and graphics. Right, dada cover for *The Bearded Heart, 1922, by Ilya Zdanevitch.*

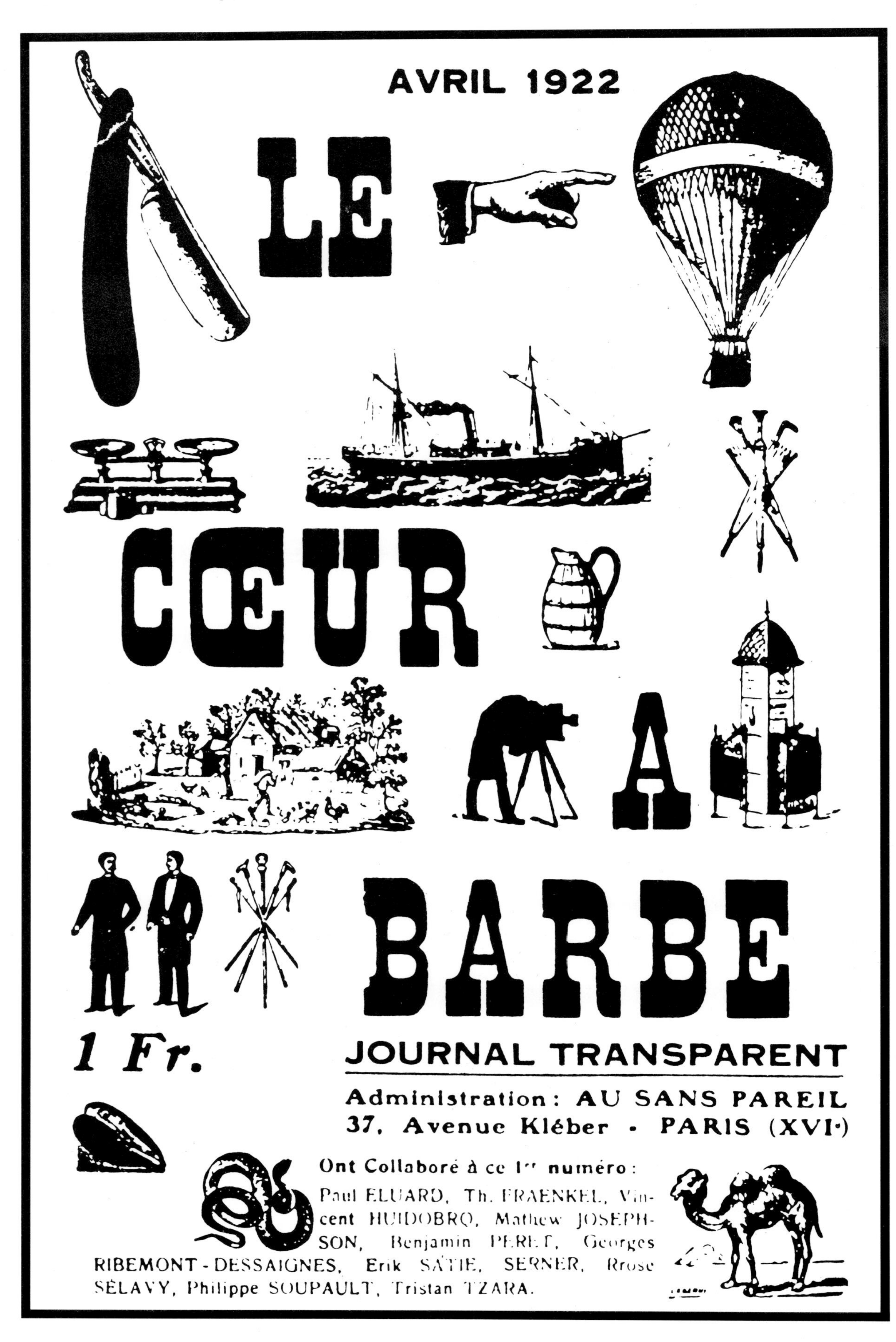

AND A LONG TALE.

so that her idea of the tale was something like this:——"Fury said to
a mouse, That
he met
in the
house,
'Let us
both go
to law:
I will
prosecute
you.—
Come, I'll
take no
denial;
We must
have a
trial:
For
really
this
morning
I've
nothing
to do.'
Said the
mouse to
the cur,
'Such a
trial,
dear sir,
With no
jury or
judge,
would be
wasting
our breath.
'I'll be
judge,
I'll be
jury,'
Said
cunning
old Fury:
'I'll try
the whole
cause,
and
condemn
you
to
death.

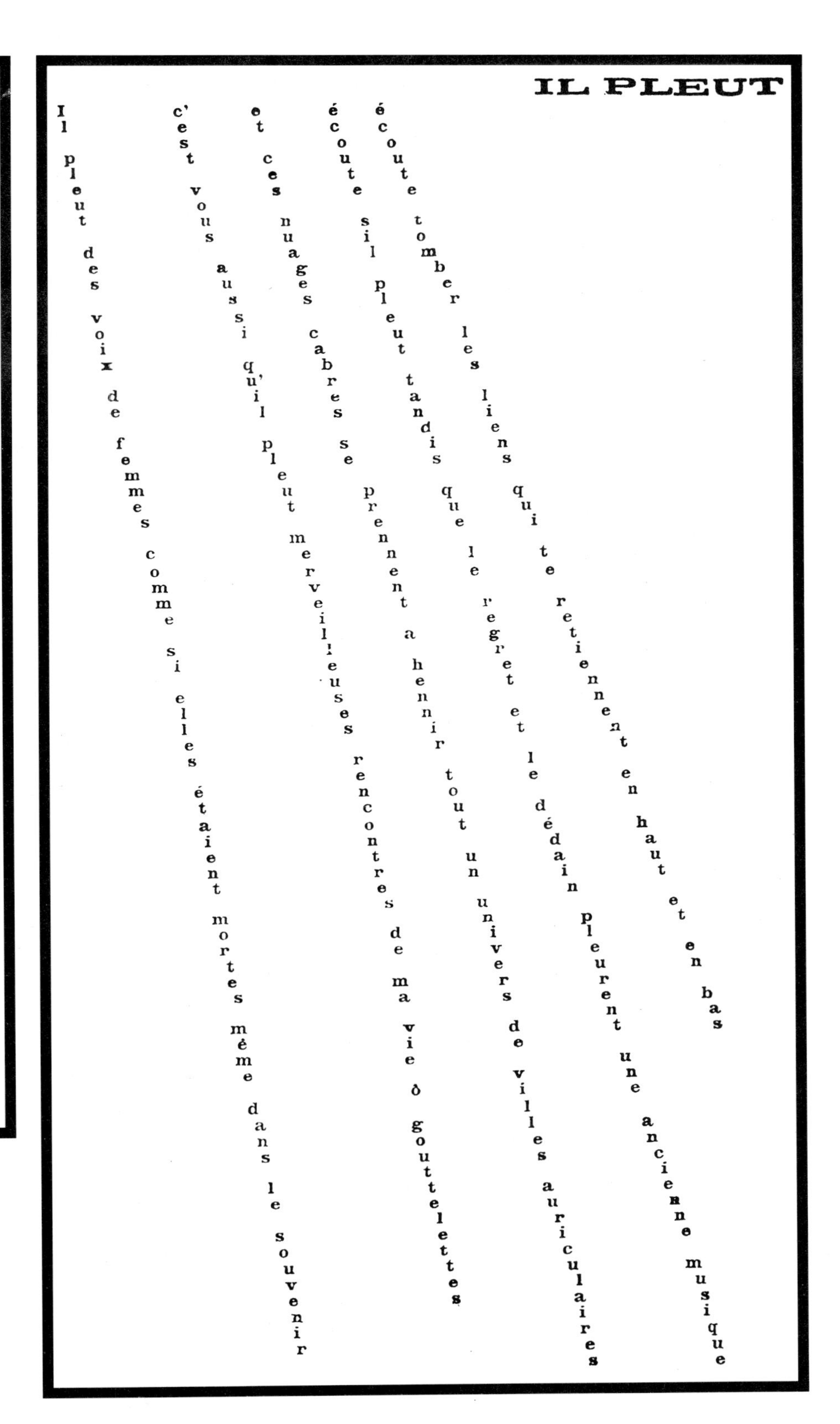

Typographic Irregularity with a Purpose. The mouse tells its long and sad tale in *Alice's Adventures in Wonderland.* Alice looks at the mouse and observes he has a long tail indeed, 1885. *Il Pleut* (It Rains) literally rains down the page, reads slantingly as the rain falls, in Guillaume Apollinaire's 1916 poem. This is one of the poems he called *Calligrammes* to express the unity of content and visual presentation. Type as illustration defies the "rules" followed for text typography, but with a purpose. In these examples the typographic illustration not only reinforces the text but is one with it.

TYPOGRAPHIC COMMUNICATIONS TODAY

Chapter I: The Many Faces of Typographic Design

Vigor and Order

Typographisches Bewußtsein ist engagiertes Experimentieren und kritische Distanz.

Oder:
Unter welchen Umständen diese Publikation zustande kam.

Beobachtungen Feststellungen Forderungen

Zur Verfügung stand eine typographische Werkstatt. Meine dringlichste Aufgabe, Typographie zu zeigen und weiterzugeben, sehe ich darin, dem Interessierten relativ alle Möglichkeiten zu zeigen, die in einer Werkstatt stecken. Das sind Materialien und technische Möglichkeiten. Besonders diejenigen, welche sich aus der wechselseitigen Beeinflussung gestalterischer Ideen, typographischer Elemente und technischer Verfahren ergeben. In diesem Zusammenhang ist es von Notwendigkeit, auf die weite Variabilität des typographischen Materials und die Dehnbarkeit seiner Bedeutungsfunktionen hinzuweisen. Leider bleiben entsprechende Untersuchungen meist auf das syntaktische, auf die Beziehung unterschiedlicher gestalterischer Elemente beschränkt. Es wäre daher von Notwendigkeit, die semantischen und pragmatischen Funktionen der Typographie, also die Bedeutung typographischer Zeichen und ihr Funktionieren in Kommunikationsprozessen stärker zu untersuchen und zu behandeln. Doch bereits jetzt reicht die Zeit nicht, mit gründlicher Methodik beizubringen, wie der Schüler mit den gegebenen Möglichkeiten fertig werden kann. **1**

Die ‹Typographen› waren Schüler mit verschiedenartigen Interessen. Und mit unterschiedlichem Niveau und Ausbildungsstand. Die erste Aufgabe im vorliegenden Heft wurde ausschließlich von Schülern gelöst, die am Anfang ihres Typographie-Unterrichtes standen. Dabei zeigte sich, daß größte Schwierigkeiten beim logischen Gliedern eines Textes auftraten. Diese Erfahrung machte ich mit Klassen der letzten Jahre ebenfalls. Das zeigt, welche komplexe Materie im Fach ‹Typographie› vermittelt wird und wie langwierig dieser Prozeß verläuft. Daher drängt sich immer stärker die Frage auf: Wie kann man Typographie innerhalb von zwei Jahren so vermitteln, daß der Schüler selbständig entscheiden lernt, ein gegebenes Manuskript in einen typographischen Entwurf umzusetzen? **Erste Voraussetzung** dafür scheint mir das Gefühl absoluter Entscheidungsfreiheit zu sein. Freilich eine Freiheit, unter der mehr die Verfügbarkeit der typographischen Möglichkeiten zu verstehen ist. Und Entscheidungen, die aus der Aufgabe **und** diesen Möglichkeiten abgeleitet werden. Da jede Entscheidung, die weitgehend durch Vorlieben, Unkenntnis und Unverständnis bestimmt wird, die also weitgehend schon zuvor feststeht, kann beim Umsetzen eines Textes in Typographie eine Fehlentscheidung sein. Auch das muß der Schüler lernen zu erkennen, um daraus vielleicht einen neuen Ansatzpunkt für seine Arbeit zu gewinnen. Deshalb wird in meinem Unterricht nicht skizziert. Die typographische Realität ist das abgesetzte Wort. Und nur die zeigt seine Länge, sein Verhältnis zu anderen Wörtern, zum gesamten Text und zum ihn umgebenden Raum mit seinen Begrenzungen. Wenn der Schüler diese didaktischen Motive verstanden und die vermittelten Kriterien begriffen hat, wird er im Sinne der oben geforderten ‹Freiheit› entscheiden können. **2**
Und nur wenn er die Funktion dieser Entscheidungsfreiheit in der typographischen Gestaltung verstanden hat, wird er auch die Grundfunktionen der Typographie begreifen. (Im Idealfall, muß ich einschränken). Ich bin überzeugt, daß wir die Ausbildung an diesen Idealen orientieren müssen.

Zur Verfügung stand jedem Schüler ein maschinengeschriebenes Manuskript. Unsere Schule kennt keinen Unterricht im Texten. Und auch keine Lehrfächer, in denen Textprobleme behandelt werden. Die Schüler können aus diesem Grund keine selbst konzipierten Texte in die Typographie-Werkstatt mitbringen. Das wäre zum Beispiel deshalb sinnvoll, damit die solchem Texte zugrunde liegende Konzeption auch für die Konzeption der Typographie verwendet werden kann. Was eine ausgezeichnete Hilfe für die logische Strukturierung des Textes und für die Bestimmung von Schrift und Satzart wäre. Ohne diese Kenntnis der textlichen Konzeption — also ohne Kenntnis der praktischen Aufgabe und geplanten Bedeutung eines Textes — bleibt die Typographie auf ihren syntaktischen Möglichkeiten beschränkt. Also: Wenn die semantische und pragmatische Funktion eines Textes erkannt und verstanden sind, können die vielfältigen syntaktischen Möglichkeiten sinnvoll eingesetzt werden. **3**
Ich betone das deshalb, weil ich mir davon eine entscheidende Objektivierung des Lehrprozesses verspreche. Einfacher ausgedrückt: Ein bißchen weniger auf Lehrmeinungen und Gefühlen gegründeten und damit letztlich für Schüler und Lehrer noch produktiveren Unterricht.

Zur Verfügung standen dem Schüler 4 Wochenstunden, um in der Typographie-Werkstatt zu arbeiten. Für das immer wichtiger werdende Kommunikationsmedium ‹Typographie› sind 4 Wochenstunden anachronistisch. Sie reichen kaum für die Vermittlung handwerklicher Fertigkeiten. Der vorliegende Druck entstand zwischen November 1970 und März 1971. Daran ist abzulesen, daß ein Viertel der Schulzeit dieser Aufgabe geopfert werden mußte. Nicht aus Ignoranz gegenüber anderen Aufgaben, sondern aus Gründen zeitlicher und didaktischer Not. Daran ist weiterhin abzulesen, daß andere dringende Probleme überhaupt nicht behandelt werden konnten. Ich denke beispielsweise an die Aufarbeitung der verschiedenen typographischen Theorien. An nicht-werbliche, sogenannte ‹technische Typographie›. An komplexe Typographie-Projekte als Teil visueller Erscheinungsbilder oder Orientierungssysteme. Oder, zum Beispiel weniger anspruchsvoll: Rasterprobleme und typographische Programme im Verlagswesen. Die Liste ließe sich beliebig fortsetzen. **4**

Zur Verfügung stand ein Lehrer, der (bei 20 Schülern) pro Schüler und Woche 10 Minuten investieren kann. Mit 10 Minuten pro Schüler und Woche ist es unmöglich, auf die natürlichen individuellen Probleme jedes Schülers einzugehen. Was im Hinblick auf die Probleme ‹kreativer› Gestaltung und die wirksame Vermittlung von Fertigkeiten mir unbedingt notwendig erscheint. Zudem waren die Klassen überfüllt, wodurch das Niveau der Ausbildung nicht verbessert wurde. Eine Beobachtung, die durch die Arbeiten in dieser Publikation teilweise bestätigt wird. Einheitsware entsteht, wenn die Möglichkeiten für Differenzierungen knapp sind. Das soll nicht heißen, daß das Niveau dieser Arbeiten hier ausschließlich von der Überfüllung der Klassen beeinflußt ist. Aber eine größere Variationsbreite von zeitlicher und thematischer Ausbildung hätte sich sicher positiver auf die Schüler und den hier gezeigten Arbeiten ausgewirkt. **5**

Diese Publikation sollte vor allem zur Diskussion beitragen. Arbeiten einfach abzubilden, um sie kommentarlos sich selbst zu überlassen — dazu ist der vorliegende Druck nicht gedacht. Er soll vielmehr Probleme zeigen, die bei der Reflexion über einen bestimmten Ausbildungszeitraum und die darin entstandenen Arbeiten aufgetaucht sind. Deshalb erlaube ich mir diese Beobachtungen, Feststellungen und Forderungen. Sie sollten im Einzelnen noch konkretisiert und diskutiert werden. Der Prozeß einer breiten Meinungsbildung erscheint mir hier wichtiger als die Vorstellung fertiger Meinungen. **W. Weingart, Basel im März 1971. 6**

Meine Unterrichts-Konzepte für die Typographie: **1. Versuch** einer Definition

Separatdruck aus ‹Beiträge zum typographischen Design› B 10. AGS Basel | Schweiz 1971

Customized, Non-Dogmatic Typographics by Wolfgang Weingart. Typographic Text Structure for a Book Preface.

"You see, I like to do everything in my field which I love very much. This open behavior makes me different from all the other dogmatic typographers like Tschichold, or Ruder, or Gerstner. These people are fantastic typographers but fanatical dogmats.

"The wonderful feeling which I have every time from twenties typography: These characters were not only typographers, they were hand-workers with heart and not only with cold heads, they were genius discoverers: El Lissitzky, Piet Zwart and many good persons more.

"What makes me so sad today is the fact, that nothing happens in the field of typography. We need new influences, which we can build on for this coming decade."

Wolfgang Weingart, December 23, 1979
Excerpted from his comments in *Idea Magazine* "Typography Today" issue.

VISIBLE LANGUAGE
VOLUME VIII
NUMBER 3 SUMMER 1974
THE JOURNAL FOR RESEARCH ON THE VISUAL MEDIA OF LANGUAGE EXPRESSION

Visible Language magazine cover, 1974, by Wolfgang Weingart.

Vitality/Clarity, a Blend. How much of each depends on the job. Wolfgang Weingart's typographics have that different look that won't be ignored while communicating the essential message. The typewriter type at the bottom of the cover is not text. It is an illustration derived from the manuscript of the table of contents. The collage of typewritten type was over-exposed and defaced to become a graphic symbol. The completely legible typeset table of contents appears inside the book. The sunburst symbol (for the summer issue) is repeated on the back cover.

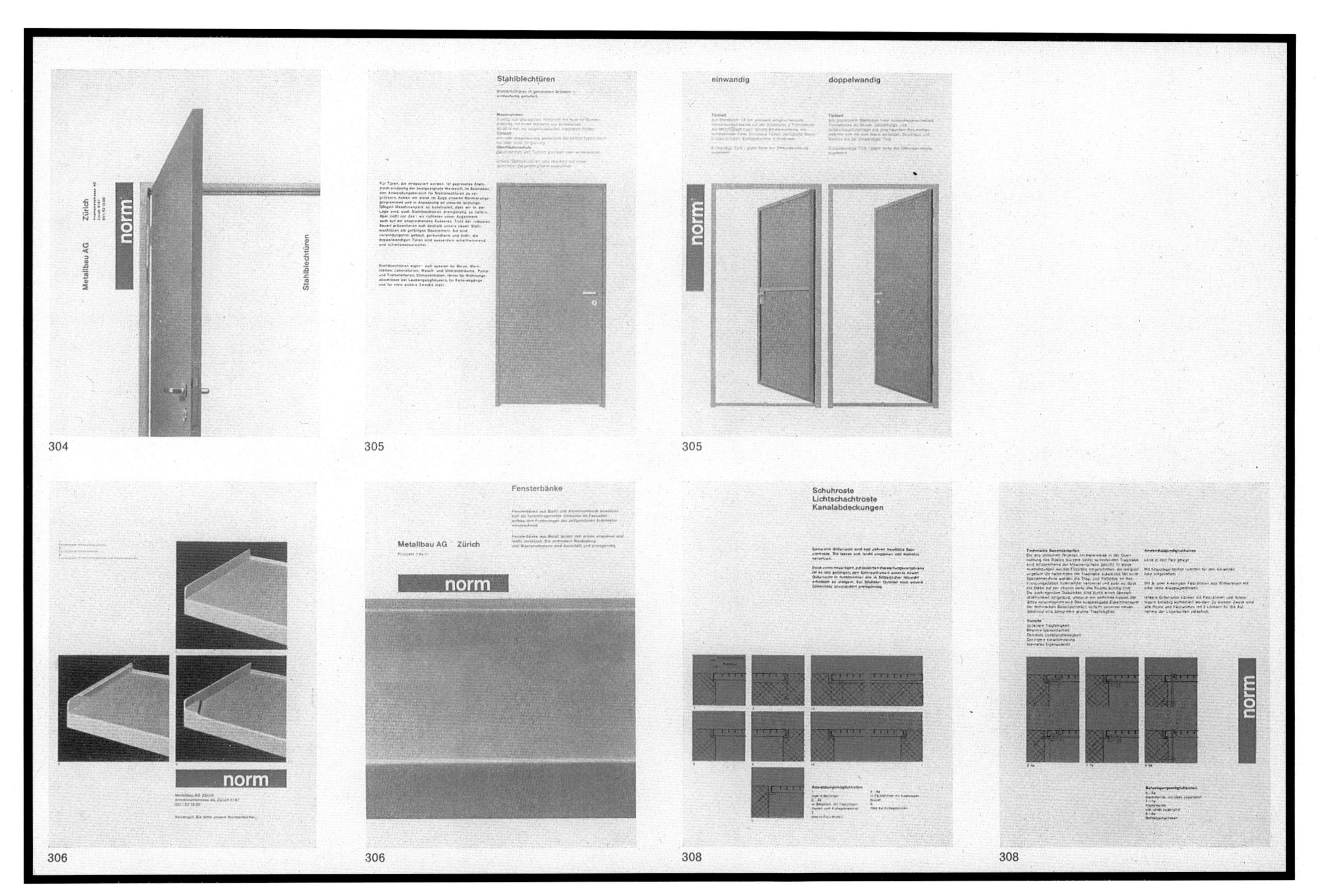

Order and Graphic Redundancy for clarity, continuity, referrability. Pages from an industrial prospectus, Carl B. Graf designer, Zurich.

Romance, Symbology, Appropriateness

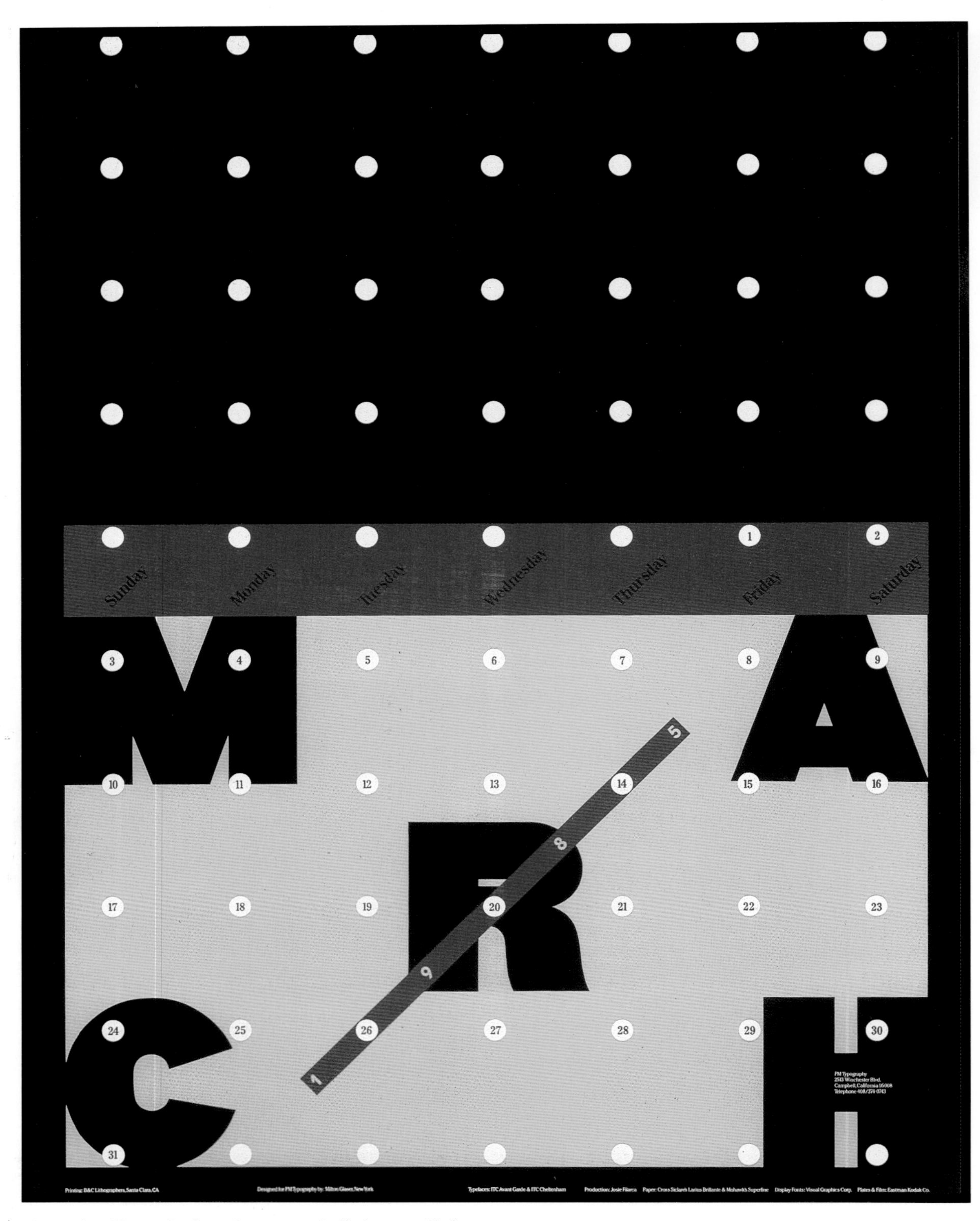

Symbology, Directness, Uniqueness and Appropriateness characterize these Herb Lubalin designs for Curtis Publications (1966) and Visual Graphics Corporation (1965). Often, in Herb Lubalin's work, the graphics don't simply organize the message, they help express it.

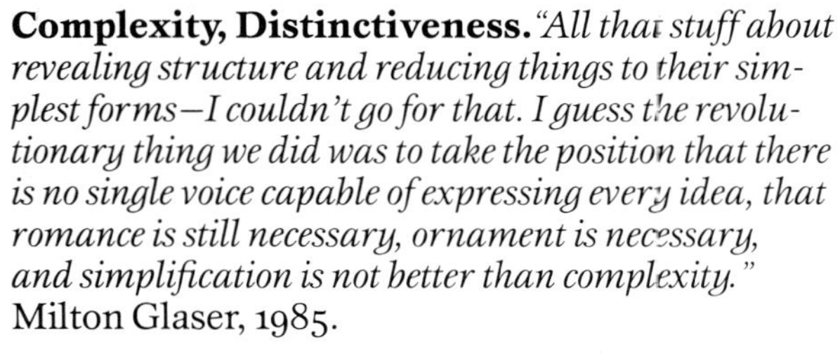

Complexity, Distinctiveness. *"All that stuff about revealing structure and reducing things to their simplest forms—I couldn't go for that. I guess the revolutionary thing we did was to take the position that there is no single voice capable of expressing every idea, that romance is still necessary, ornament is necessary, and simplification is not better than complexity."* Milton Glaser, 1985.

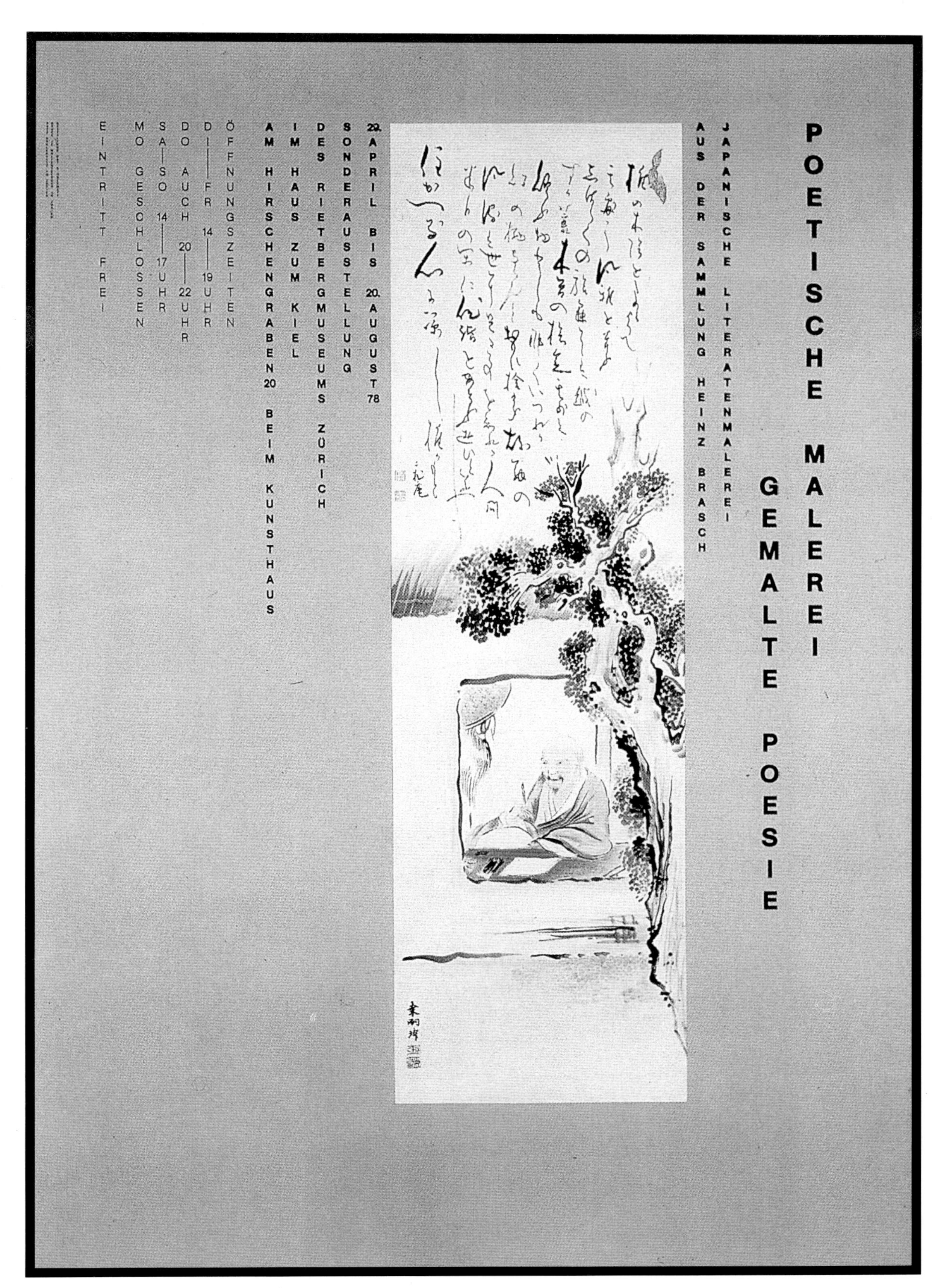

Appropriateness in typographic design grows from a clear understanding of the message problem and sensitively coordinating the graphic elements. The result is a blend of beauty and individuality, with no sacrifice in clarity or readability. Poster for an exhibition entitled *Poetic Painting, Painted Poetry*. The Japanese vertical writing is echoed in the typography. Designed by Siegfried Odermatt, Odermatt and Tissi, in Zurich.

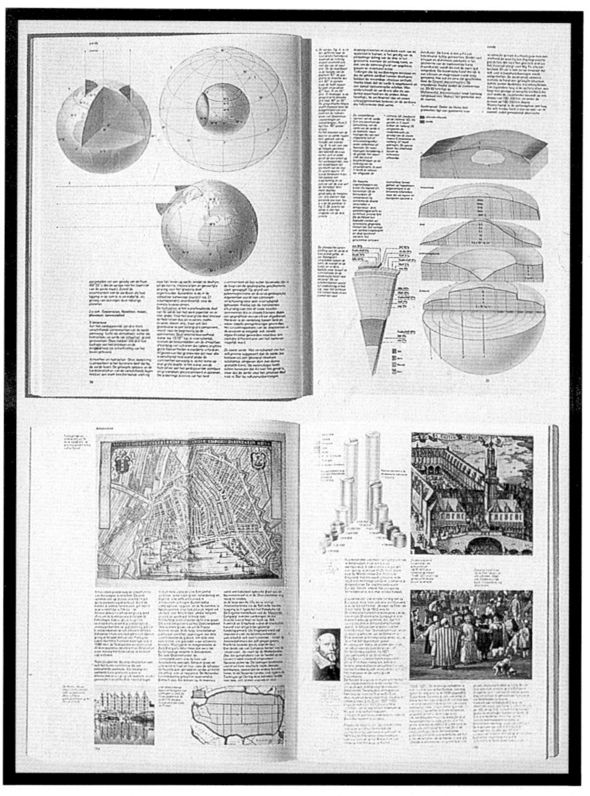

Organization of graphic elements on a suitable grid creates clarity out of complexity while producing colorful, eye appealing spreads in the *Spectrum Encyclopedia* designed in 1974 by Total Design in Amsterdam. The fixed matrix or grid controls the relation between text and illustrations. Total Design employs a grid for the layout of book pages because: *"The grid offers guarantees for a visual homogeneity from the first to the last page; simultaneously, it must be sufficiently flexible and finely meshed, to be able to clearly translate specific demands, such as footnotes, legends of illustrations, subheadings and references."**

Wim Crouwel, one of the founders of Total Design, once said in an interview:

"Design is genuine, that's to say pure designing, determined by the function which the object must have and the technical possibilities with which it can be produced...styling is adapting something to a certain fashion, determined by sales motives." TD's trademark is not fashion, trends or decoration, but solving a problem through research and analysis–that's designing.*

*From *Design: Total Design*, a catalog for an exhibition of the work of the Total Design studio.

TYPOGRAPHIC COMMUNICATIONS TODAY
Chapter I: The Many Faces of Typographic Design

Complexity, Simplicity, Appropriateness

Appropriateness. As the preceding pages show, there are many approaches to typographic design. In the 20th century many typographic designers broke away from formal center axis design and the typographically complex layouts of much work in the 19th century.

As the volume of printed material exploded, and radio and TV competed with newspapers, magazines, books and printed advertising and promotional material for time and attention, it was essential that printed pieces be at once more alluring, easier and faster to read, and more effective in making a message understood, believed, and acted upon.

L. SHAW,
HAIR AND BEAUTIFYING BAZAR,
No. 54 West 14th St., New York City.

The Fedora Elastic Spring Wave.
PERFECTION IN ITSELF,

AND SUPERIOR to any other, patent waves included. Clasps softly to the forehead, giving a beautiful shape and a perfectly natural appearance. No nets required, and not a single hairpin. Warranted of naturally curly hair, or money refunded. From $5 upward.

IMPORTANT TO LADIES.
My new Front Piece
THE EMPRESS
(patent applied for),
Shows ladies' own parting. No wig-like appearance. Fitted with my improved elastic spring.
Hair Cutting and Curling on the premises by best French artists. 50 cents.
Hair bought and exchanged.
Combings made up quicker, better, and cheaper than by any other house.
Front Pieces dressed while you wait. 25 cents each.
MARIE ANTOINETTE FEATHER-LIGHT SWITCHES,
Naturally wavy, from $5 upward; formerly sold at double the price.
GRAY HAIR A SPECIALTY.
The largest and most elegant stock of naturally Gray Hair Switches, &c., at fabulously low prices.
UNRIVALLED BEAUTIFYING COSMETICS.
EUGENIE'S SECRET OF BEAUTY
For the complexion. Produces a beautiful transparency. It is recommended by physicians. Price, $1 per box. Unrivalled VELOUTINE FACE POWDERS, 50c. and $1 per box. Amula, the great Tan and Freckle Lotion, $2 per bottle. Indelible SAFFOLINE Lip and Face Rouges, $1 and $1.50 per bottle. F. F. Marshall's ADONINE, for dyeing instantaneously the hair, the beard, the eyebrows, and eyelashes a beautiful light brown, brown, dark brown, or black, without injury to the hair, skin, or health, $1.50 per box. Applied on premises if desired.
Goods sent to all parts of the country, C.O.D., with privilege of returning.
For Hair Dyeing, Hair Dressing, Hair Cutting, Shampooing, &c., take Elevator.
NEW ILLUSTRATED CATALOGUE ON RECEIPT OF 3-CENT STAMP.
L. SHAW,
No. 54 West 14th Street, near 6th Avenue.

Clarity ↔ Vitality. Perhaps the most insistent theme in the mass of typographic design produced since the turn of the century is the tug-of-war between advocates of clarity and order in the design of printed communications and the advocates of visual vitality.

Dull, look-alike pieces are not inevitable when organizing material on a grid any more than confusion and poor readability must be accepted as the price of dynamic free-form layouts. The difference between the best examples of both approaches is one of degree and emphasis, not total negation of the opposite point of view. The best designers, as a reading of TYPOGRAPHIC COMMUNICATIONS TODAY will show, achieve a comfortable blend of the best of both worlds – a fresh, appealing design propelling a clear, emphatic message.

One can position much of the typographic design of this century on a clarity-vitality axis. You could put examples of futurism and dadaism at one extreme, and strict applications of a formal grid at the other.

No. 10. OCTOBER, 1869. Vol. 1.

Van Nostrand's
ECLECTIC
ENGINEERING
MAGAZINE

SELECTED FROM
THE HOME AND FOREIGN
ENGINEERING SERIALS.
Conducted by
Alex. L. Holley.

NEW YORK:
D. VAN NOSTRAND,
23 MURRAY STREET,
AND
27 WARREN STREET.
Up Stairs.

1869

Price Five Dollars per Annum. Single Numbers, 50 Cents.

Typographic Intricacy characterizes these Victorian-look advertisements, poster and magazine covers from the 1870s and 1880s.

What is Ideal? It is easy to ask, "Which extreme or what blend is best?" A message centered between the extremes on the hypothetical vitality-clarity axis? That's an easy answer but the wrong one. There is no universal rule for creating effective print communications. The key is appropriateness.

Appropriateness: the choice and execution of the graphics for propelling a message that are most suitable to the tone and content of the message, the nature and intent of the sender, the requirements of the medium, the needs, desires and orientation of the receiver.

A successful graphic design can be a multifaceted gem. Like a diamond, its beauty and value depend on the number of facets for its brilliant sparkle. Graphic designers, art directors, typographers – all who work with type are aware of graphics' many facets but often tend to focus on just a few.

Major aspects of graphic design include clarity (some elements of which are legibility, readability, order, emphasis), vitality (affected by such considerations as size, color, shape, position), craftsmanship (including letterspacing, word spacing, line spacing, character alignment, and more) and symbolism as well as appropriateness.

Some messages require maximal stress on clarity, others on vitality and still others some balance of the two. All messages deserve exquisite craftsmanship and psychologically well-targeted graphic symbols and all *must* be appropriately clothed typographically. Too many fail to meet these criteria.

Subjectivity and emphasis on esthetics come easily to many artists and designers. Analyzing a message and its purpose requires objectivity, often a pause in the creative surge, to ask not only if the design is exciting or strong or clear or beautiful, or if executed with skill and taste and employing lucid, effective symbols, but whether it is really the most effective way of saying what needs to be said to those we need to reach.

Typographic Noise. In communication theory noise is anything that reduces or interferes with comprehension of the message by its intended recipients. It might be static in a radio broadcast, wavy lines on a TV screen, volume too low, or someone speaking in a language not understood by a listener. In graphics it can be a confusion of elements with inadequate organization, or illegible type, or a picture that conveys the wrong impression, or a presentation too plain or too much like so many others that it fails to be noticed and read. One must remember that the role of typography is to present words to the eye.

It is the job of the person responsible for graphic design (by whatever job title) not only to avoid typographic noise but to give a printed piece the most appropriate blend of clarity, vitality and symbology.

But this is not solely the responsibility of the designer. Just as one would not choose pianist Arthur Rubinstein to perform Mendelssohn's violin concerto, so one should be careful to select for a given problem a designer whose past work is compatible with the problem at hand. Picking a designer well attuned to the problem is, as Saul Bass puts it, simply good casting. It is the first and often most overlooked step in starting a job toward a maximally effective solution.

A Myriad of Looks. A browsing through an Art Directors annual, a *Graphis* annual, or the yearbooks of the American Institute of Graphic Arts, or the yearbook of the Type Directors Club will show a wide range of solutions that work very well. In the best works, graphic vigor enhances, rather than obscures, the clarity of a message. One should also remember that beauty as well as utility are facets of function in communication design. It is the appearance that makes a message noticed, read, enjoyed, believed, remembered. It is the graphic look that makes the very important first impression.

Roots. What are the roots of today's typography? How did the variety of ways to achieve vitality and clarity develop and grow to their present state?

One need only go back to the beginning of this century to discover the roots of contemporary typographic design. TYPOGRAPHIC COMMUNICATIONS TODAY aims to help you discover these roots, to trace their growth and intertwining–and to develop an awareness of the many "looks" in today's design repertory. When you have finished reading TYPOGRAPHIC COMMUNICATIONS TODAY you may also have developed an appreciation for the communication power and the beauty, and often the joy involved in creating a truly effective typographic solution to a communication problem, as well as an appreciation of the sensitivity, taste, knowledge and skill that graphic designers contribute to the development of the most appropriate and most effective typographic design.

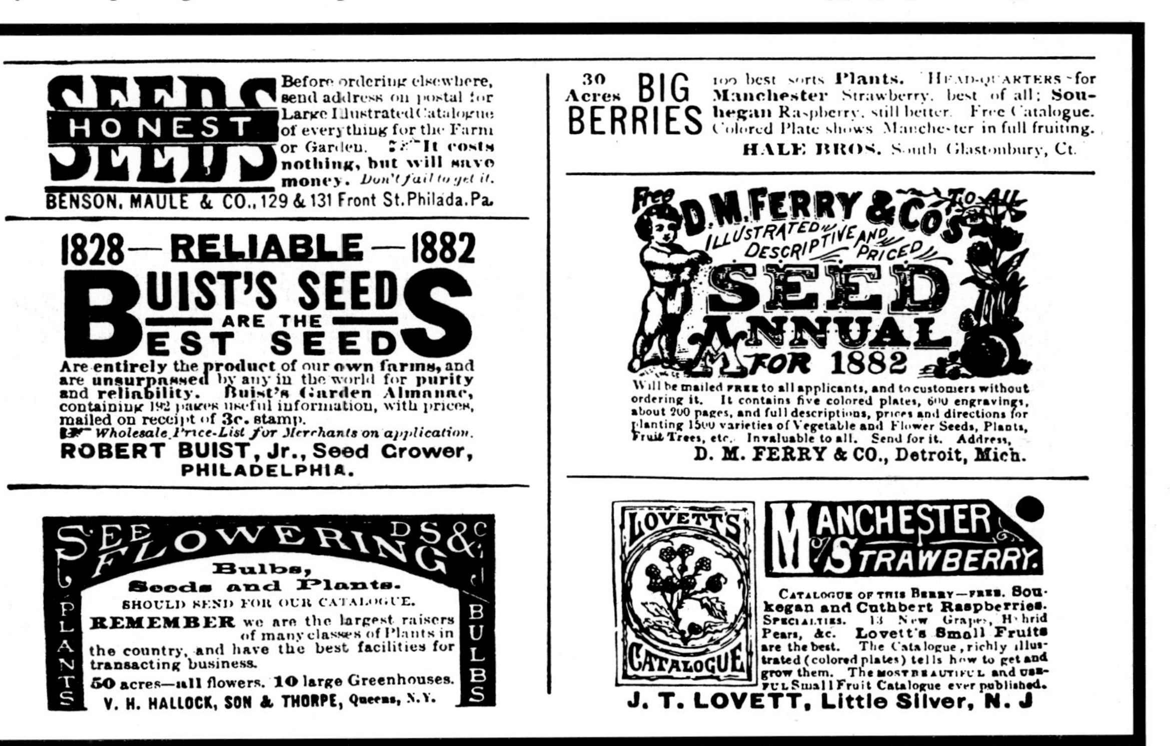

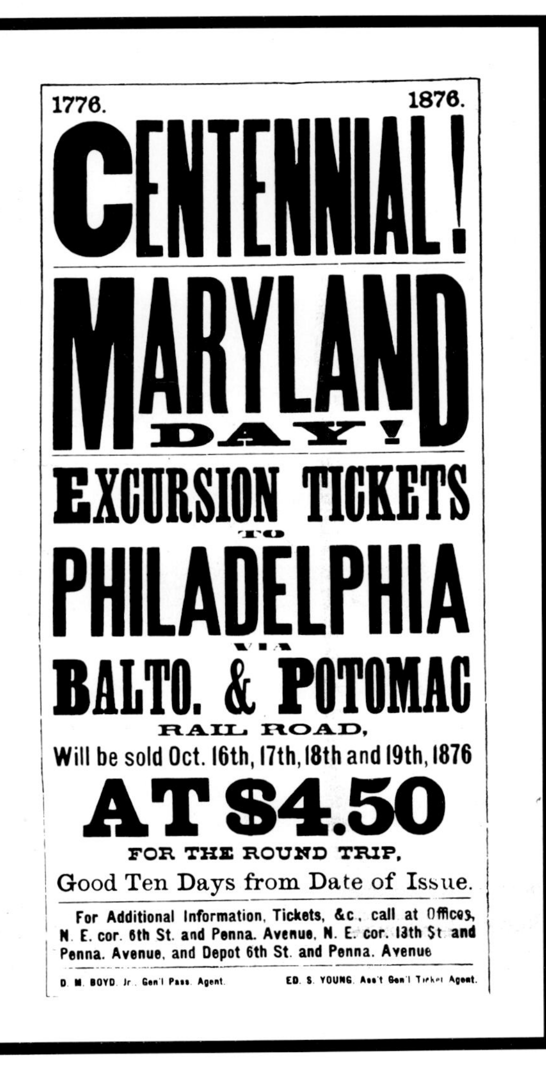

TYPOGRAPHIC COMMUNICATIONS TODAY

Chapter II: Roots – Evolution and Revolution from Constable to Kandinsky

"...the laws of creative typography are nothing but the practical application of the laws of creation discovered by the new painters."

THE GREAT BREAKTHROUGH period, a swath of almost 20 years, that separates modern typography from earlier typographics, started with the publication of the futurist manifesto in 1909 and peaked in the late twenties.

The roots of today's typography in the first half of the century trace back, more to early 20th century painting, poetry and architecture, than to changes wrought within the printing industry. As Swiss typographer and teacher Hans Rudolf Bosshard says, "...the laws of creative typography are nothing but the practical application of the laws of creation discovered by the new painters." The advent of photography, economic and social forces and new philosophical attitudes also contributed to the development of new attitudes toward communication design. The four or five decades from the 1880s into the 1920s were what Alvin Toffler, had he lived then, might have called Future Shock. Inventions, wars, economic upheavals, political revolutions changed not only the appearance of things but violently shook up people's attitudes and values. Formerly worshipped traditions became excess baggage or, worse, drags on progress or adaptation to the new world being formed. Just a few of the forces in these times were the advent of the motor car in 1885, wireless radio in 1895, motion pictures in 1896, and the airplane in 1903. The slaughter of wars and widespread poverty embittered people. The new inventions contributed to the feeling that "there must be another way." It was a time for revolution – cultural as well as political. If the primary direct forces affecting typographics in this period were the new approaches to painting, poetry and architecture, they in turn were driven by the technological-economic-social-political upheavals that were then brewing.

In the latter half of that century major forces affecting typographic design were new printing and typesetting technologies. Before the 1880s there was little graphic surprise. The 1880-1920s period was a time of artistic foment that changed art and design so they would never be the same. In this chapter we will review the changing art scene in the early decades and its affects on typographic design.

Throughout history man has established rules to bring order to the conduct of his affairs – governmental, financial, scientific, cultural, religious – whatever. It is an historical truism that no sooner are rules established than they are extended or bent or broken or replaced, not only to meet new needs but because of adventurous spirits, pioneers in new paths, improvisors. The arts have had many such creative geniuses, and often they have not been appreciated during their lifetimes.

Why Painting? What's the Connection?

What do Picasso, Mondrian, or Kandinsky, for example, have to do with the design of new typefaces and the way type and illustrations are deployed in a layout for an advertisement or a booklet?

Artists, architects and poets in the late 19th and early 20th centuries developed new ways of representing spatial relations, shapes, colors, textures. Their spirit of innovation, of presenting images and words in new ways, was contagious. Typographic designers saw the new art, read the new poets, had their eyes and minds opened to new ideas, and their spirit and sense of creativity stimulated to apply fresh thinking to their work.

But the influence of the fine arts was not as subtle and remote as that. Poets like Guillaume Apollinaire, artists like El Lissitzky and Theo van Doesburg, architects like Henri van de Velde used type and graphic elements in new ways and mingled and worked with typographic design students, teachers, and practitioners. Their ideas and enthusiasms were contagious. Designers were learning to rely less and less on previously accepted formats, and more and more on evolving customized solutions that were inspired and called for by a specific communication problem. We will consider these typographic developments in later chapters, but let's now take a look at the new ways painters saw and depicted the world.

From Constable to Kandinsky

Traditional concepts of painting from the Renaissance in the 15th century through the mid-19th century respected classic codes of composition, skilled execution and craftsmanship, harmonious colors, proper perspective, and often heroic subjects. If art had always been a little abstract, it was so within narrow limits. By the mid-19th century church and state patronage of the arts had declined, and artists became, or were allowed to become, more subjective. The grand landscapes and portraits that characterized much art of the time were challenged by Jean-Baptiste Camille Corot (1796-1875), Jean François Millet (1814-1875), and others who studied nature carefully and represented it in a relatively true-to-life manner, yet with a sense of visual poetry. Earlier, in England, John Constable (1776-1837) and Joseph Mallord William Turner (1775-1851) had brought what at that time was considered a romantic and often dramatic touch to their landscapes. But, from today's perspective, their break with traditional representational painting was slight.

By the 1870s painters became more daring, more subjective in the way they saw and represented life; notably French impressionists as Claude Monet (1840-1926), Camille Pissarro (1830-1903), Pierre Auguste Renoir (1841-1919).

Monet's landscapes (often the same scene at different times of day) revealed how he felt

"True-to-life" *was a guiding principle of the 19th century painters who studied nature carefully so as to render it realistically, yet romantically and often dramatically, as in* Salisbury Cathedral from the Bishop's Garden *by John Constable. Constable painted his landscapes on the site, not by synthesizing idealized bits and imagined scenes in a studio as some predecessors had done. From the Metropolitan Museum of Art, Bequest of Mary Stillman Harkness, 1950. (50.145.8)*

about a new scene. His eyes and hand were not mere scene recorders. They were painting personal impressions, not just landscapes. A new emotion, a new graphic/spiritual subjective vitality was maturing in his work. Impressionist painting marked the first major break with centuries-old traditional concepts. The impressionists represented a new bend in the trail from Constable to Kandinsky.

The progression from so-called traditional representational painting as epitomized by Constable, to totally abstract and then non-representational painting as developed by Kandinsky, can be summarized in these steps.

1. *A faithful picture of an object (scene, person, things, etc.). This is art as imitation of nature, human actions and passions, for example.*

2. *A picture of how one feels about, or what one sees, in an object. (Of course all paintings reveal how an artist feels about a subject. The difference is a matter of degree). This is art as self-expression of the artist, as an expression of emotions evoked by the object.*

3. *A picture of how one feels. (No object is involved.) Art as form.*

4. *A constructed picture that neither evolves from nor depicts an object (non-objective).*

5. *Non-objective, unconstructed, sometimes accidental, painting.*

Impressionism – A Freer Interpretation of the Subject

Who were the impressionists? How did they change our way of seeing things? What do they mean to us today?

Renoir, Pissarro, Monet, Manet (in some of his later work) and their followers used their brushes more freely than had been the custom. They made random spots of color. They put down strokes that did not always correspond to the object they were painting but formed coherent relationships among the parts of the paintings. The artist's eye was focusing on patterns in a subject, and on color impressions as well as on the obvious subject. The artists modified the representation of the subject to convey a sense of pattern and color and mood. They were especially fascinated with the effects of light and color on a subject at a given moment.

Other characteristics of some impressionists included:

- Two or more perspectives (for different picture elements) in one picture. An example would be Van Gogh's use of one perspective for a floor, another for a pair of shoes.
- Two dimensionality. A flattening of perspective.
- Zoom lens effect that created new relationships between parts of a scene.
- Asymmetrical composition. A new point of view for the artist.
- A dynamic sense of colors as variable. Not all leaves were the same green. There was color in shadows.
- Obvious brush strokes tend to make the subject less distinct and cause the viewer to see the painting surface as well as the scene.

Today we accept and admire their work, but that was not always so. Just as today some people disparage computer created art or the paintings of de Kooning or Motherwell, for example, so did the art followers in 1873 in France turn thumbs down to the impressionists. The paintings were rejected by the official Salon of 1873. Result, the disgruntled artists organized their own show in 1874. They called themselves *Societé anonyme des artistes, peintres, sculpteurs, etc.* An unfriendly critic called them "impressionists" (then a denigration) after Monet's "Impression: Sunrise," 1872. As a group, despite squabbles and differences, they held eight exhibits from 1874-1886. Their transitory visual impressions, although often painted directly from nature, used pure and broken color to achieve brilliance and luminosity.

The impressionists often met as a group at the Cafe Guerbois and one might find there Monet, Renoir, Sisley and Bazille, all students of the academic painter Marc Gleyre. Others in the group were Cézanne, Pissarro, Degas, Morisot and Manet (who would not exhibit with them). They rejected emotion as subject matter and sought visual realism in depictions of nature through their own eyes and style. They avoided the vulgar and the ugly. Monet, Sisley and Pissarro were particularly intrigued with the changing effects of light upon a scene. Renoir came to prefer pure, bright color to separate forms rather than using conventional outlines in black.

The net effect of the impressionist painters was to establish a separation or distinction between the subject and their image of it.

***Impressions of color** add a new dimension to representational paintings by Monet, Renoir, Pissarro and others. Monet painted 26 versions, for example, of the Rouen Cathedral at different times of day and conditions of sunlight, adding to each his personal vision of the light and color. He painted more than 100 versions of the lily pond in his garden. Here are two variations of the same scene by Claude Monet,* The Manneport, Etretat, I *and* The Manneport, Etretat, II. *Both are from the Metropolitan Museum of Art. No. I is from the Bequest of William Church Osborn, 1951, (51.30.5) and No. II is from the Bequest of Lillie P. Bliss, 1931, (31.67.11). For the Rouen Cathedral Monet sometimes worked simultaneously on 6 to 14 canvases to catch the changing light.*

TYPOGRAPHIC COMMUNICATIONS TODAY

Chapter II: Roots – Evolution and Revolution from Constable to Kandinsky

"A mind, once opened to a new idea, does not return to its original condition..."

Post-Impressionism and Expressionism – A Further Departure from Absolute Realism

Bolder departures from painting merely what the eye sees characterized the paintings of the German expressionists as well as of Van Gogh, Cézanne and Gauguin. Seurat developed a technique of putting down his colors dot by dot rather than by conventional strokes. Van Gogh and Gauguin used bold masses of color to bring unprecedented excitement and emotional intensity to their work. Their images were as much created in their minds as they were observed by their eyes. Likewise Cézanne, striving for something beyond the observed image, employed subtle nuances of tones and colors. Seeking a structural clarity in his paintings he often flouted the laws of perspective and extracted geometrical forms from nature. New spatial patterns characterized many of his landscapes and still lifes.

Cézanne's later paintings verged on cubism. He, as did Rodin, treated the human form freely. Artist and critic Amédée Ozenfant felt that fauves, cubists, and all succeeding schools were indebted to them.

Cézanne's extreme distortion of the human form derived from his studies of El Greco. The dominance of verticals and the elongation of forms in El Greco's murals are not examples of distortion for effect but were due to the position of the murals high up on altar walls. When viewed from the floor, as intended, the distortion largely disappears. Ozenfant says that "El Greco distorted above all to defeat distortion." Nevertheless, photographic reproductions of El Greco taught Cézanne the power of expression that lay in distortion.

Where is reality? *Van Gogh and many other post-impressionists still aimed to represent reality in their paintings, but to them reality was not on the surface of things. Their minds and spirits looked beyond the apparent to discover and depict the reality as they saw it.* The Starry Night *by Vincent Van Gogh. The Museum of Modern Art, New York. Acquired through the Lillie P. Bliss Bequest.*

In the early years of the 20th century in Europe there was considerable disillusionment with previously accepted institutions and ways of life. A revulsion, not unlike that in the United States during the Vietnam war years, set in. By 1905, faith in society and slogans of progress had so deteriorated that a new climate permitted questioning all things, all values in society, human relations and the arts.

Van Gogh's early work was almost Courbet-like realism. Later a number of his landscapes were impressionistic. But at Arles his work took on a new and daring look. Van Gogh was one of the first to look beyond the surface appearance of things, to remodel reality. He wanted to create images that would be "...truer than the literal truth." Van Gogh and other artists not only blended their images of a scene or portrait or still life with what their eyes beheld, to create a better structured or designed painting, but began to question whether surface appearance was a true and full expression of reality.

Consequently, these artists were not content to merely record what they saw. They also expressed in their painting how they felt about the subject. They were expressing personal emotions and passions. Subjectivity was gaining an upper hand in their work. Expressionism in painting took many forms as different painters brought their personal reactions and attitudes into their work.

Sometimes refined lines were replaced by bold lines and planes clashing with others dramatically as harmony gave way to drama. Many of these artists were impressed and influenced by the art of primitive races which was expressed in strong and contrasting colors, and where lines suggested rather than precisely depicted reality.

To these artists color and form not only described an object but also conveyed an emotion. The path from Constable to Kandinsky, from essential realism to non-representational art, had passed another milestone.

Expressionism implies an aversion to refinement. It is a simplification of language and content that often aims to interpret social attitudes toward life and thus appeal to circles wider than those of artists and art lovers. Van Gogh also wrote, "If one were to make the color correct or the drawing quite exact, one would not be able to convey these emotions."

Fauvism – Exuberant Colors, Distorted Forms

A group of French painters in 1904-1908 went further in distorting forms and using bold colors. They were called "fauves," wild beasts. They held three exhibitions, including one at the Salon d'Automne in 1906. Although the movement was short-lived, its impact was great. Other artists, notably Kandinsky, had their eyes opened to innovative use of color and to color dissonance. Kandinsky, who later taught at the Bauhaus, attended the 1906 exhibition, and by 1908-09 his paintings showed the direct impact of the fauve paintings of Rouault, Braque, Matisse and others.

To understand the full social force of these artists' attitudes one must appreciate that writers and musicians in many countries were going through similar metamorphoses. Old ideas were being modified and often discarded completely. The spirit that drove these changes of attitudes pervaded all walks of life; not just the arts, but also the social, economic and political facets of life. And, of course, they affected other disciplines such as architecture, graphic design, and typographics. The famous armory show in New York introduced cubism and fauvism to the United States in 1913. The March 16 *New York Times* headlined, "Cubists and Futurists Make Insanity Pay." The United States was slow to accept the new kinds of art.

◀ ***Exuberant colors, distorted forms*** *employed by the fauves widened the gap between the subject and the artist's image of it.* Nasturtiums *and the* Dance, II *by Henri Matisse. The Metropolitan Museum of Art, Bequest of Scofield Thayer, 1982. (1884.433.16)*

Before turning our attention to typographic developments, let's continue to trace the evolution in the art movements in the 20th century. Keep in mind that typographers and designers in the early and ensuing decades of this century, right up to today, were very aware of the movements in the fine arts and very affected by them. A mind, once opened to a new idea, does not return to its original condition, and the developments in the fine arts opened the minds of those engaged in the communication and applied arts. Today's typographic designer, choosing a typeface, controlling its size and shape and color in mass, positioning typographic and pictorial elements in relation to each other, and manipulating white space, is really composing a scenario of balances or imbalances of masses and lines, and tones and colors. The orderliness of some typographic designs, the dynamism of others, and the large pool of design approaches available, owes much to the lessons learned from the various art movements of this century.

Art Nouveau – Art as Decoration

Some artists in the 1890-1910 period turned their paintings and drawings into sinuous linear decorations. Where impressionist and expressionist painters were departing from sheer realistic portrayal in order to convey an emotional reaction to the subjects, art nouveau artists focused on the subject's decorative facet. Art nouveau pervaded all the applied arts including architecture, product design, glassware, textiles, posters, bookbinding and typographic design. It was a resurgence of the romantic, baroque style that exploited the ornamental character of curved lines. Interlacing lines and floral forms became common. Tiffany's favorite glassware, Yale & Towne hardware, and the still existing Coca-Cola logo, Hector Guimard's entrances to the Paris Métro, René Lalique's (Austria) creations, Antonio Gaudi's structures in Barcelona, Victor Horta's *Hôtels,* and Henri van de Velde's graphics, are but a few examples of how art nouveau penetrated many aspects of our life and environment.

Gismonda ***poster,*** *1894, by Alphonse Mucha. Line plate in blue. Gentle greens and golds elsewhere, plus pink flowers. Library of Congress Poster Collection.*

Typography shaped around illustrations *which fade out under the type. Eugène Grasset,* Histoire des Quatre Fils Aymon, *1983. By permission of the Houghton Library, Harvard University.*

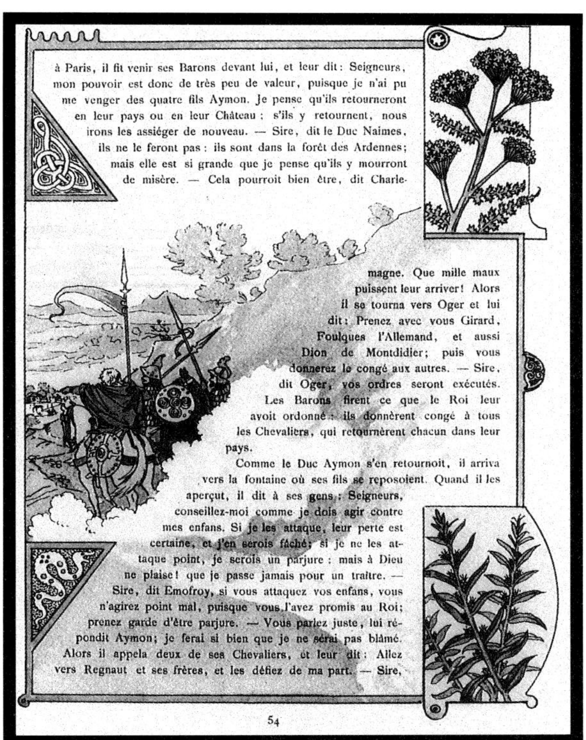

à Paris, il fit venir ses Barons devant lui, et leur dit: Seigneurs, mon pouvoir est donc de très peu de valeur, puisque je n'ai pu me venger des quatre fils Aymon. Je pense qu'ils retourneront en leur pays ou en leur Château ; s'ils y retournent, nous irons les assiéger de nouveau. — Sire, dit le Duc Naimes, ils ne le feront pas : ils sont dans la forêt des Ardennes; mais elle est si grande que je pense qu'ils y mourront de misère. — Cela pourroit bien être, dit Charlemagne. Que mille maux puissent leur arriver! Alors il se tourna vers Oger et lui dit: Prenez avec vous Girard, Foulques l'Allemand, et aussi Dion de Montdidier; puis vous donnerez le congé aux autres. — Sire, dit Oger, vos ordres seront exécutés. Les Barons firent ce que le Roi leur avoit ordonné : ils donnèrent congé à tous les Chevaliers, qui retournèrent chacun dans leur pays.

Comme le Duc Aymon s'en retournoit, il arriva vers la fontaine où ses fils se reposoient. Quand il les aperçut, il dit à ses gens : Seigneurs, conseillez-moi comme je dois agir contre mes enfans. Si je les attaque, leur perte est certaine, et j'en serois fâché; si je ne les attaque point, je serois un parjure : mais à Dieu ne plaise! que je passe jamais pour un traître. — Sire, dit Emofroy, si vous attaquez vos enfans, vous n'agirez point mal, puisque vous l'avez promis au Roi; prenez garde d'être parjure. — Vous parlez juste, lui répondit Aymon; je ferai si bien que je ne serai pas blâmé. Alors il appela deux de ses Chevaliers, et leur dit : Allez vers Regnaut et ses frères, et les défiez de ma part. — Sire,

54

VOL. I. NO. 1. APRIL, 1893.

THE STUDIO

AN ILLUSTRATED MAGAZINE OF FINE AND APPLIED ART.

Artists as Craftsmen. No. I.
Sir Frederic Leighton as a Modeller.
The Growth of Recent Art. By R. A. M. STEVENSON.
A New Illustrator : Aubrey Beardsley. By JOSEPH PENNELL.
Spitalfields Brocades. By LASENBY LIBERTY.
Designing for Book-plates.
Spain as a Sketching Ground. By FRANK BRANGWYN.
The Newlyn Point of View.
The Grafton Gallery. By C. W. FURSE.
News of the Month. Reviews. &c. &c.

With Auto-lithograph (33 × 15), "WEED BURNERS IN THE FENS." By R. W. MACBETH, A.R.A.

SIXPENCE — OFFICES: 16 HENRIETTA ST., COVENT GARDEN, LONDON — MONTHLY

Annual Subscription, Seven Shillings and Sixpence, Post Free.

The Studio, *1893. Cover by Aubrey Beardsley. Beardsley's exotic imagery and strong black-and-white contrasts and predominant use of curved lines made him a strong figure in the art nouveau scene in England.*

TYPOGRAPHIC COMMUNICATIONS TODAY

Chapter II: Roots – Evolution and Revolution from Constable to Kandinsky

"If necessary, we will use three or four different colors and 20 different typestyles on the same page."

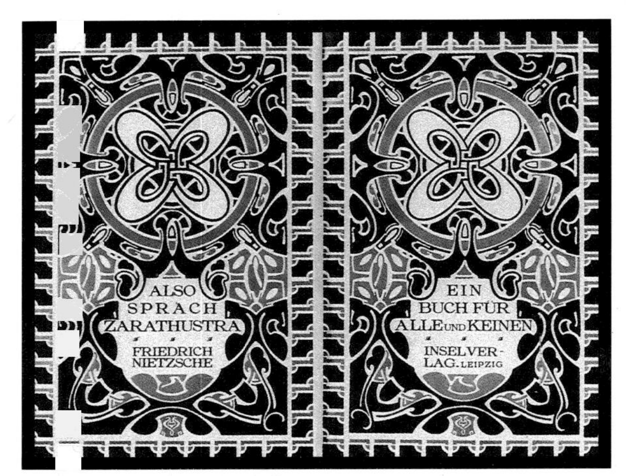

Also Sprach Zarathustra. *A most important art nouveau book designed in 1908 by the Belgian, Henri van de Velde. His use of symbolic forms, although often inspired by plant motifs, became abstract. By permission of the Houghton Library, Harvard University.*

Ecce Homo, *designed by Henri van de Velde in 1908. By permission of the Houghton Library, Harvard University.*

Art Nouveau in America. *Cover design by Will Bradley, 1894.*

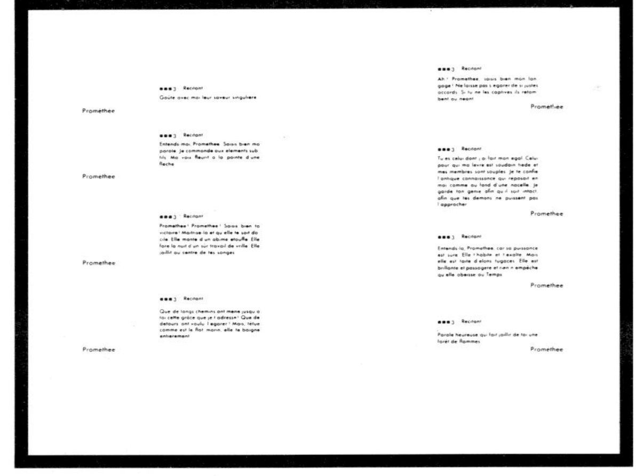

Futura type *was used for the text by designer Henri van de Velde.* Promethée *by H. H. Dubois, 1929. Institut Superieur des Arts Decoratifs, Brussels. Contrast this contemporary handling of type with* Also Sprach Zarathustra *and* Ecce Homo *by the same designer.*

ABCDEFGHIJKLMNOPQ
RSTUVWXYZ
abcdefghijklmnopqrſßst
uvwxyz
1234567890
ABCDEFGHIJKLMNOPQRSTUVWXYZ
abcdefghijklmnopqrſßstuvwxyz
1234567890
BEHRENS

Jugend *was designed by Peter Behrens in 1904. Stylized peacock feathers and lotus designs embellish the page. A graphic designer, Behrens also designed Behrens Roman, issued by Klingspor around 1900.*

Artistik *released by Bauer & Co. in Stuttgart, and H. Berthold in Berlin.*

Initials *by William Morris.*

A B C D E F G H

Jubilaums *– Initials, Bauer'sche Giesserei, Frankfurt.*

ABCDEFGHIJK

Culdee, *American Type Founders Co., Philadelphia.*

ABCDDEEFGHIJ

Alphabet *by Georges Lemmen.*

nomme vulgairement p a i n d e s o r c i è r e s, et il est bleu. Les sages, qui en ont mangé, ne sont pas morts, comme on croyait ; ils se sont endormis d'un sommeil si long, si fabuleux qu'on l'a cru éternel.

– Mène-moi dans cette prairie, dit le prince. Nous mangerons du p a i n d e s s o r c i è r e s, puis nous nous enfermerons dans quelque grotte pour y dormir en paix.

– Oui, maître, mais cette prairie est à une journée d'ici. Si nous voulons y arriver avant le soir, il faudra partir sur l'heure.

Aussitôt le prince se leva et tous deux s'apprêtèrent ; Saturne fit son sac pour le voyage du long sommeil. Il y mit, en perspective du lointain réveil plutôt, son vêtement de dimanche, qui était de satin, couleur de soleil ; il emporta sa flûte, une épée, un pain, des nourritures terrestres, toutes choses inutiles, déclara le prince, et dont il prétendait se passer. Quant à lui, il ne voulut rien emporter de la terre, il resta en chemise et pieds nus, pour mieux marquer son dédain du monde.

Aussitôt ils sortirent secrètement du palais et prirent, par des rues détournées, le chemin des champs. Personne ne fit attention à eux, les croyant fous ou lunatiques, ce qui pour les gens de Porqueville était la même chose.

Vers la tombée du jour, ils sortirent de la ville par le vieux pont en bois, dit le p o n t d e l a S i r è n e. Il menait dans une vaste prairie solitaire et humide. D'énormes quantités de champignons y croissaient, précisément de ceux dont avait parlé Saturne, qui étaient bleuâtres et vénéneux et auxquels personne, ni bêtes, ni gens, ne touchait par crainte de la mort. Toute la vallée que la lune inondait en ce moment semblait phosphorescente, comme un jardin magique ou un site d'un autre monde.

Voici la P r a i r i e d u S o m m e i l, dit Saturne, et le P a i n d e s S o r c i è r e s, et voilà tout proche la grotte où nous nous retirerons pour dormir.

Sur quoi tous deux se mirent à cueillir des brassées de champignons et les emportèrent dans la grotte.

Elle était profonde, obscure et fraîche. Saturne roula à l'entrée une énorme pierre, semblable à la porte d'un tombeau. Tous deux se mirent à manger en silence. Puis ils s'endormirent. Les champignons bleuâtres luisaient comme du phosphore dans les ténèbres. Ils avaient un goût laiteux dans leurs bouches et s'y éteignaient lentement, comme de petites étoiles. Une obscurité d'or se fit dans l'obscurité azurée. Puis leur âme se détacha du monde, devint infiniment lointaine, nébuleuse. Ils dormaient.

Since no Futura italic was available then, *van de Velde added letter and/or word spacing for emphasis. This was in accordance with what the Germans did when using blackletter. From* Les Sorciers De Borght, *by Georges Eckhoud, 1927. This was the first book produced by van de Velde at the Institut des Arts Decoratifs en l'Abbaye de la Cambre.*

Henri van de Velde's *personal logo.*

In the United States the art nouveau period saw the development of new advertising media such as bus and car cards, posters, billboards, direct mail and catalogs from mail order firms such as Sears, Roebuck and Montgomery Ward.

An advertising executive of this era, wearing an Arrow collar no doubt, commenting on the rapidly changing fashion in lettering wrote: "New styles in lettering are created in order that attractive variety may be added to the world of commerce." It seems that to be progressive, the advertiser felt he had to use new alphabets before they become ancient history.

Art nouveau was inspired by many things, including William Blake's book illustrations, Japanese calligraphy, Van Gogh's swirling forms, celtic ornament, the rococo style and Paul Gauguin's flat colors and stylized contours. Ornament and curves were part of the basic design, not merely added elements. The art nouveau period marked a transition from the past, characterized by the repetition of classic forms, and the experimental movements of the early 20th century.

Art nouveau typographic designers had fine arts schooling, with its esthetic emphasis, and were knowledgeable regarding printing's requirements of art. Thus they were instrumental in upgrading the quality of illustration and typographic design in mass communications. Different sources claim art nouveau first appeared in France and in England. In any event it spread throughout Europe and across the Atlantic. In Germany it was called *Jugendstil* (youth style). In Austria it was known as *Sezessionstil* and *Modernismo* in Spain.

One of its leading practitioners, the Belgian Henri van de Velde, was called to Weimar by the Grand Duke of Saxe in 1902. He reorganized the Weimar Arts and Crafts Institute and the Weimar Academy of Fine Arts. This work eventually led to the formation of the Bauhaus by Walter Gropius in 1919.

Van de Velde was one of a number of important artist/designers of the time whose work and thinking influenced that of the Bauhaus masters and students. El Lissitzky from Russia and Theo van Doesburg from Holland were other key forces at the Bauhaus, although, like van de Velde, they were not on the faculty.

All three men's work also demonstrates the linkage among the art disciplines. Van de Velde, for example, was an architect, a teacher, a book designer, an industrial designer, and he frequently designed ornamental and display letters. He was the first, in Belgium, to use Paul Renner's Futura for setting literary texts.

Cubism – Shifting Volumes and Planes

Another major departure from straight realistic painting was the development in the early 1900s of cubism. This art represented objects (so that it was not totally abstract) in a new way. The artists envisioned a still life, for example, as comprised of shifting volumes and planes.

As cubism evolved, concave and convex volumes were also used. The cubist painter abstracts or isolates certain attributes or qualities from the object being represented. In *Les Demoiselles d'Avignon* we principally see the volumes and planes that comprise the women, yet we can discern the women. The result is a considerable but partial abstraction.

The development of cubism by Pablo Picasso, Georges Braque, Juan Gris and others, was a strong departure from the 400 years old Renaissance tradition of pictorial art. Impressionists had modified pure representation by introducing new ways of handling light and color. Post impressionists had carried this one step further and often distorted classic concepts of perspective to achieve a desired art effect. Art nouveau artists focused on the decorative aspects of the object represented. But always the subject was obvious and paramount. In cubism, technique and style overwhelm the subject. Cubist painters were greatly influenced by the geometric stylizations of African sculpture and by Paul Cézanne who said that "the painter should treat nature in terms of the cylinder, the sphere, and the cone." This statement inspired Apollinaire to baptize the style "Cubisme." Cubism is really an art of invented forms. It results from analyzing the planes of a subject from different points of view and constructing a painting by creating visual rhythms by the way the planes were composed. This is not what-you-see-is-what-you-get art. It challenges and involves the viewer to interpret it.

Les Demoiselles d'Avignon, *1907. Here is design derived from, but independent of, nature. Five figures are the starting point but they have been abstracted into geometric planes. Pablo Picasso. The Museum of Modern Art, New York. Acquired through the Lillie P. Bliss Bequest.*

Cubists regarded letter forms as concrete visual shapes to be manipulated rather than merely phonetic symbols. One can find the influence of cubism in graphic design in the work of E. McKnight Kauffer, A. M. Cassandre, Jean Carlu and others.

Futurism – Energy, Dynamism and a New Sense of Reality

Futurism provided the big bang that brought the changing approaches to painting, sculpture, architecture and literature together under the umbrella of a new understanding of reality, and in so doing exploded the conservatism that characterized much typographic design. Most artists through the 19th century assumed reality was essentially unchangeable. But the revolution in social thinking that was fomenting, disillusionment with life and governments and accepted ways of doing things, affected attitudes toward reality as well as toward society. Thus the climate was ripe for the proliferation of new approaches to the arts and to communication design.

But no one was prepared for the bang that rocketed out of Italy in 1909. Typographically, words were placed wildly on the page to express sensations and evoke ideas. Sheer legibility and graphic order took a back seat to rhythm, intonation and startling emphasis. Sometimes large letters were used as visual grabbers while diagonal rules connected reading units to provide visual rhythm and content continuity. The futurists ignored the constraints of metal typography and letterpress printing. Horizontalism was out. Type at any angle was in, and this long before the advent of phototypesetting or transfer lettering. The big thing in futurist design was shock and contrast, in type size, the angles at which words or phrases were placed, oversize letters or numbers or other characters seemingly randomly enlarged and dropped on the page. Nevertheless there was reason behind the seeming chaos as Filippo Tommaso Marinetti wrote in the magazine, *Lacerba*.

"I am making a typographical revolution which is directed, most of all, against the idiotic, sickening notion of the poetry book with its hand made paper, its 16th century style, decorated with galleys, Minervas, Apollos, tall initials, florid ornaments and mythological vegetables with its 'motti' and roman numerals: A book must be the futuristic expression of our futuristic thoughts. Better yet: my revolution is, among other things, against the so-called typographical harmony of the book page which is in opposition to the flow of style manifest on the page. If necessary, we will use three or four different colors and 20 different type styles on the same page."

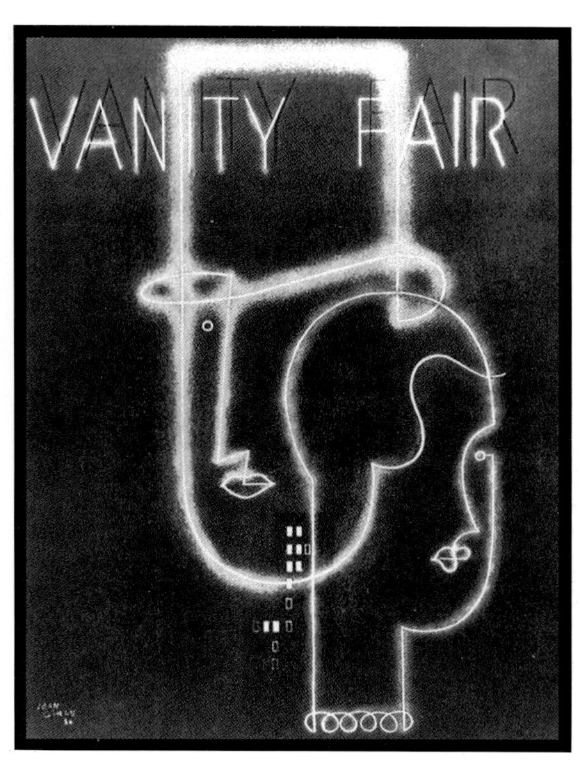

Stylized drawing *shows cubism's influence on 1930 cover for* Vanity Fair *by Jean Carlu.*

Cubism in Advertising. *Poster for the* Daily Herald, *1918. By E. McKnight Kauffer. Courtesy of Her Majesty's Stationery Office, Norwich, England.*

TYPOGRAPHIC COMMUNICATIONS TODAY

Chapter II: Roots – Evolution and Revolution from Constable to Kandinsky

"Typography was considered an important carrier and impeller of facts and ideas..."

"The 'heroic' period of modern typography may be said to have begun with Marinetti's Figaro manifesto in 1909." (Herbert Spencer, in *Pioneers of Modern Typography*.) Futurism was a violent reaction by artists and writers against the status quo which symbolized failure to make life worth living. The early cubist paintings of Braque and Picasso and the bold use of colors of the fauves were harbingers of the deeper breaks to come. The development of futurism was spurred by new social attitudes and resentments and influenced by the earlier and concurrent art movements. But futurism immediately became a more powerful force propelling the developments of modern typography. Typographics, like painting, was ready to shed many of its conventions and constraints to score a deeper impression.

Emilio Filippo Tommaso Marinetti was an Italian poet. Seething at inequities and injustices, he published in the French newspaper, *Le Figaro*, February 20, 1909, a strident call for a new concept of art and design. As reported in the previous chapter, the manifesto glorified the modern – speed, revolution in many aspects of life, even strife and war and the destruction of museums and libraries that were considered repositories of a failed past. Politically, Marinetti was a fascist. Many of his typographic followers were not.

Adherents sprang to Marinetti's side. A year later five painters published a manifesto of futurist paintings. It condemned "all forms of imitation, harmony, and good taste." The signers were Umberto Boccioni, Carlo Carra, Giacomo Balla, Gino Severeni, and Luigi Russoclo. Two months later, April 11, 1910, the *Technical Manifesto of Futurist Paintings* called for the "universal dynamism which must be reproduced in painting as dynamic feeling."

Typography was considered an important carrier and impeller of facts and ideas, and by 1914 the Florentine, Giovanni Papini, linked thoughts with the futurist painters. Papini was editor of the periodical *Lacerba*. In it he published the first experiments in *Tipografia in liberta*. In 1914 Carlo Carra published the first of a series of "parole in liberta," (free-word compositions).

***"Not literally readable** but intended to be a joyous celebration possibly heralding the end of the war. Une assemblée tumultueuse," 1919. F. T. Marinetti. From* "Les mots en liberté futuriste."

Just as street-corner orators often shout and wave their arms to get attention and be heard and, hopefully, believed, so did futurist typographers scream with large black type waving in all directions. In futurism, social protest, new ideas, and new ways of expressing them came together explosively. The world of typography was blown on to a new course. All over Europe artists and designers were to take note of the futurists and seek in their own way to bring the right combination of vitality and clarity to their creations.

The gentle stream of artistic revolt seeking new, freer, better ways of communicating, epitomized by a Monet, a Van Gogh, or a Picasso, became a torrent in the hands of the early futurists.

A later futurist, seeking more order while retaining vigor, was the painter, designer and poet, Fortunato Depero. His typographic style influenced Italian advertising typography of the 1920s and 1930s.

The typographic bursts of the early futurists and the partial calming down as exemplified by Depero's work is characteristic of the waxing and waning of the typographic order vs. typographic vitality throughout the 20th century.

One might think of typographic design as passive (center axis, symmetrical, with minimal contrasts), active (asymmetrical, dynamically balanced, with clear contrasts for emphasis and to control eye flow), and aggressive (unbalanced, blatant with contrasts).

Typographic Communications Today will trace the development of these typographic streams as they have flowed, sometimes uneasily and concurrently through the 20th century.

***A futuristic free-word composition.** By F. T. Marinetti, 1919. The text tells of the route taken by Marshal Joffre's automobile on a visit to the front after the battle of the Marne. Sounds of the automobile on its journey are symbolized and blended with the text. Marinetti intended this to be read aloud; performed, in fact.*

A word of caution. Sometimes a piece that at first glance seems aggressive, typographic overkill, hard to read, is employing typographic elements as symbols or illustrations, and the area carrying the message that is to be read is quite readable, even passive by itself. As will be observed, active typography not only brings a message to life, it can aid visual fluency and clarity as the imaginative yet controlled use of contrast and asymmetry provide desired emphasis to the various elements of the design.

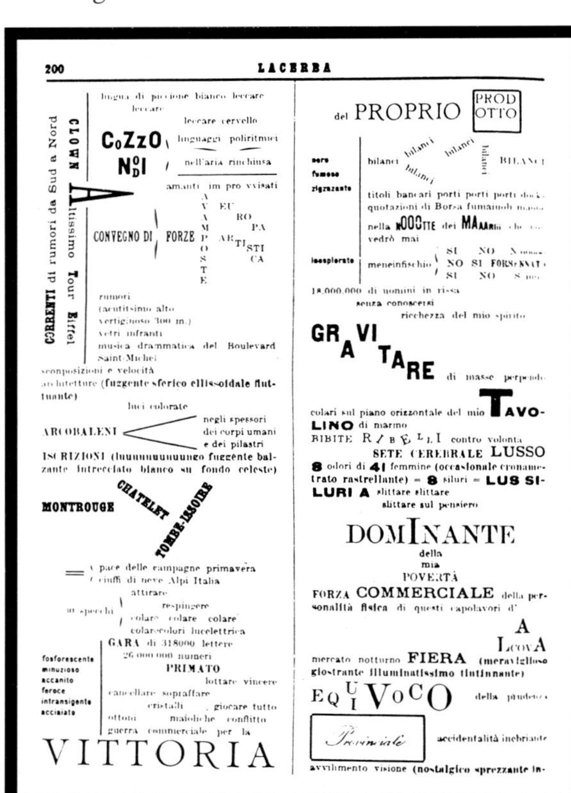

***Different type sizes and styles** blend elements of a free-word composition. Carlo Carrà felt they added beauty to a message. 1914.*

***A blend: Futurism's explosiveness plus some order,** 1927. A page from* Depero Futurista, *a 234-page book of innovative typographic design and illustrations for manifestos and proclamations. Text was often in the form of calligrams and free-word compositions. This page advertises Depero's office, "Dinamo-Azari," and highlights the many talents/services available there.*

From Evolution to Revolution

With the outbreak of futurism the evolution in painting, poetry and prose became a revolution. The split between what the artist's eyes saw and the poet's mind understood and what and how they painted and wrote became a chasm. Several other art movements continued this break with realistic representation by image or word. They were dadaism, surrealism, and non-representational art. Concurrent with the development of these extreme art forms was the development in Eastern and Western Europe of attempts to capture the vitality of the new art forms while bringing some order and clarity to it for purposes of effective communication. These latter movements will be reviewed in the next chapter.

Why Irrationality?

Some artists and writers in Western Europe in 1916-1923 felt it was necessary to destroy failed traditions before a sane world could be built.

The assault on straight representational art reached its zenith, or perhaps its nadir, in dadaism. It started as a literary movement in Zurich. The guiding spirit of dadaism was Tristan Tzara, a young Hungarian. Young poets, painters, musicians met with him at the Cabaret Voltaire. Tzara edited their publication, *Dada,* which first appeared in 1917. Some of the others in the group were poet Hugo Ball, also the cafe proprietor, artists Hans Arp, Max Ernst, Kurt Schwitters, Francis Picabia, Theo van Doesburg (more of him later) and poet André Breton.

For them the world had gone mad and the only valid art was non-art and the only sense nonsense. Their work appears as playful meaninglessness but it was purposeful. Their pleasure in nonsense and anti-seriousness was their way of mocking, deriding, destroying the decadence of European society and its social injustice. The horrors of war, to them, were only followed by the horror of a blind faith in technology to make everything right. They scorned absence of effective religious/moral codes. Behind all their non-serious manner was the serious aim to employ comic derision to put an end to the role of chance, intuition and irrationality in determining the direction of culture and society. Typographically they dealt a final blow to sterile typographic design and reinforced cubism's concept of letter form as a concrete visual shape (not merely a phonetic symbol) with style and communicative value inherent in its shape.

Hans Arp wrote that "The logical nonsense of man is to be replaced by illogical no-sense. Dada is without sense, like Nature. Dada is for Nature and against Art."

Make no mistake. These young men, some fleeing from their homelands and war and conservative do-nothing societies were gifted artists and writers. To them art and writing had a role to play in reforming society and so they opposed art for salons as being just toys for the rich and the elite. Such art to them was bourgeois (a pejorative) and anti-humane. They wanted to de-estheticize art, to knock it off its pedestal of beauty, and use art to oppose the greed of a commodity culture. Dadaism developed adherents, during its lifespan from 1916 to about 1923, in various countries. In Berlin its political overtones were exemplified by the caricatures of George Grosz. In France the emphasis was also literary and centered around Tzara and Breton. Two French artists, Marcel Duchamp and Francis Picabia and the American, Man Ray brought the spirit of dada to New York City. Man Ray invented the photogram (first called a Rayogram), and Picabia blended painting and collage.

No. 4 DER·BLUTIGE·ERNST PREIS 60 PFENNIG

Arbeiten und nicht verzweifeln!

SONDERNUMMER IV. DIE SCHIEBER

Der Blutige Ernst, *1919. George Grosz's cover for the magazine comments on decadence in post-war Germany and employs a typographic collage for background.*

Other important dada artists or those who contributed to its development include:

Stéphane Mallarmé (1842-1892). A French symbolist poet, his poem *Un Coup de Dés* (A Throw of the Dice), ran to 700 words on 20 pages. It employed different type sizes, caps, lowercase, roman and italic type to give typographic change of pace and emphasis. Some pages had only a few words seemingly scattered (but set horizontally) in the white space. Phrases and thoughts had much air around them. This was a forerunner of expressive typography that later cropped up in various periods and several countries.

John Heartfield founded the dada group in Berlin in 1919. He changed his name from Helmut Herzfelde as part of his protest against German militarism. With vigorous typography on book jackets and posters and his political illustrations and cartoons and use of photomontages he fought militarism and Nazism until forced to flee first to Prague and then to London. Shortly before his death in 1968 his posters were protesting the Vietnam War.

By 1924 the principles of dadaism had been modified and became the basis of surrealism.

Nude Descending a Staircase, *1912. Duchamp explains this is "an organization of kinetic elements, an expression of time and space through the abstract presentation of motion." Philadelphia Museum of Art. The Louise and Walter Arensburg Collection.*

TYPOGRAPHIC COMMUNICATIONS TODAY

Chapter II: Roots – Evolution and Revolution from Constable to Kandinsky

"...when abstraction is total the end result appears non-objective."

Behind the Real – Surrealism

As the enthusiasm for ridiculing art and social conventions to death waned, the young artists and poets became more positive minded. They sought a "more real than real world behind the real." They sought a true reality in dreams, in intention, in Freudian psychology, in the unconscious and the subconscious. Former dadaists moved in different directions. French writer André Breton founded the surrealist movement. His manifesto in 1924 gave new expression to the rebellion against conventional ways of thinking and expression (visually or verbally). Some of surrealism's roots trace to the French poets Baudelaire, Rimbaud and Apollinaire (See P. 5) and the Italian painter, Giorgio de Chirico. Jean Cocteau's surrealist films baffled many but caused a considerable stir in art circles. The movement was particularly strong in the 1920s and 1930s. It took many forms of expression as practiced by Salvador Dali, Yves Tanguy, Max Ernst, René Magritte, Joan Miro, Hans Arp, and others.

MUSJK JM LEBENDER VÖLKER AM 2.JULJ
20 UHR DJRJGJERT JM OPERNHAUS
WARSCHAUS BERÜHMTER DJRJGENT WERKE
POLNJSCHER MEJSTER PREJSE 1–5MK.

Single alphabet phonetic type designed by Kurt Schwitters, *1927. Schwitters, 1919 Merz pictures were "disparate elements merged into a work of art with the help of nails and glue, paper and rags, hammers and oil, paint, parts of machinery and bits of lace." Later he became a concerned typographer, after associating with Theo van Doesburg and El Lissitzky.*

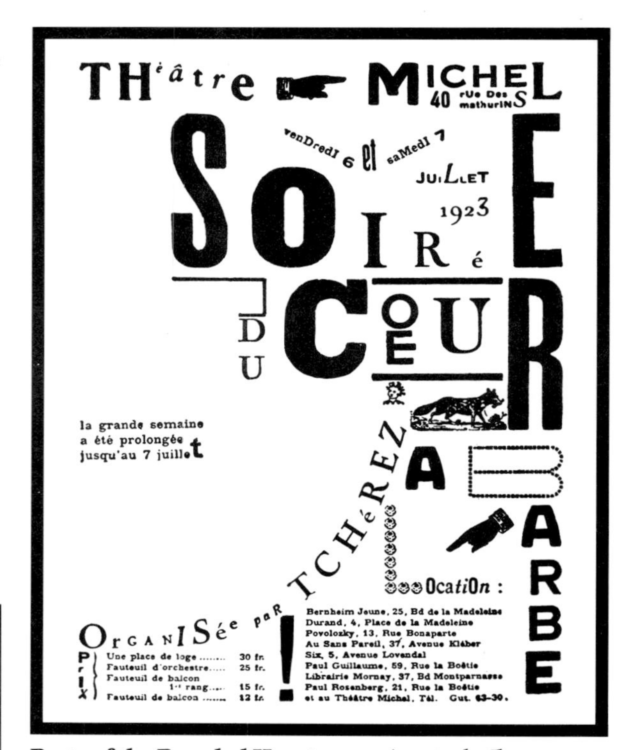

Party of the Bearded Heart, *1923. A poster by Ilya Zdanevitch for the play. Over 40 fonts of type are used. The essential data is legible on the full size poster. (Some sources attribute this work to Tristan Tzara.)*

Early expressive typography. *Guillaume Apollinaire. From his* Calligrammes, *1917. The type is a bird, a water fountain, and an eye.*

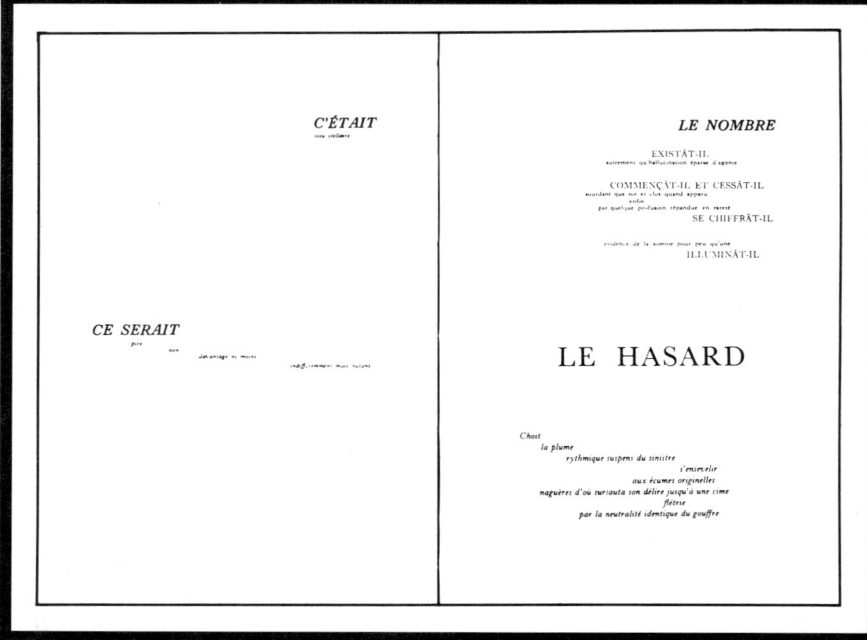

Early expressive typography: *From Stéphane Mallarmé's* Un Coup de Dés.

Giorgio de Chirico, The Departure of the Poet, *1914 verges on the supernatural. Museum of Art, Rhode Island School of Design, Providence, Rhode Island.*

Dada poem by Hugo Ball, *1917. Plenty of sight and sound and "illogical nonsense." Meaningless in its lack of real words but meaningful in its decisiveness.*

Dynamism of a Dog on a Leash. *By Giacomo Balla. Motion, speed, energy on a flat surface. Albright-Knox Gallery, Buffalo, New York. Bequest of A. Conger Goodyear and gift of George F. Goodyear, 1964.*

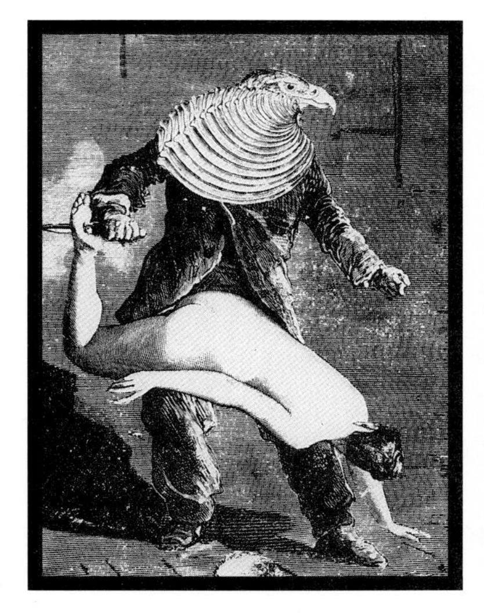

Max Ernst, *(far left) from* Une Semaine De Boute, *1934. Fantastic imagery, startling combinations of real but incongruous elements painted with almost photographic realism characterized much of Ernst's work. In this collage the cut edges of the elements are obscured, giving unity to the whole.*

René Magritte, *(middle left)* The Blank Signature, *1965. An impossible scene depicted with realistic detail. National Gallery of Art, Washington. Collection of Mr. & Mrs. Paul Mellon.*

Salvador Dali, *(left)* Le Grand Paranoiac, *1936. Dreamlike version of space and dream-inspired symbols like melting watches characterized by Dali's paintings. Museum Boymans-van Beuningen, Rotterdam.*

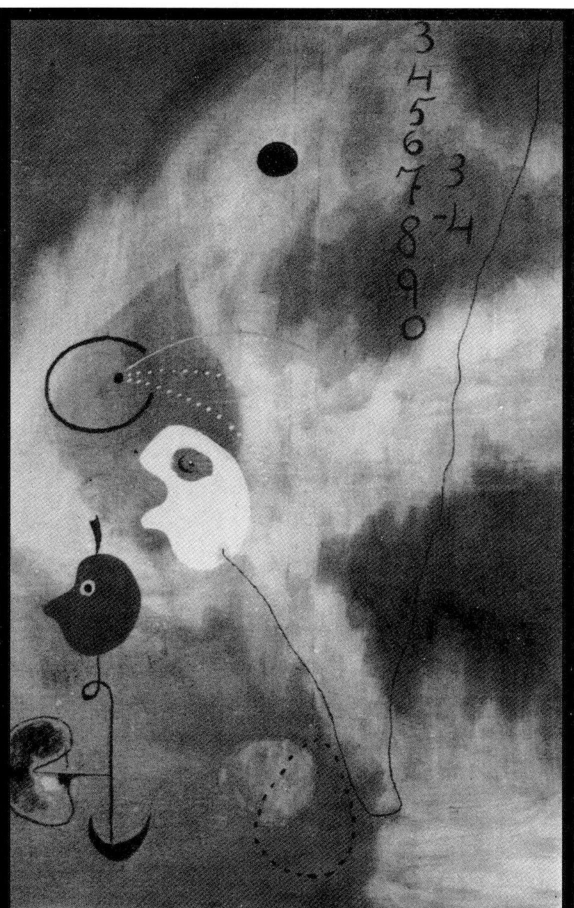

Joan Miro, Peinture (Dite l'addition), *1925. Spontaneous thought rather than conscious plan drove Miro's brush. Pierre Matisse Gallery, New York.*

Images Without Objects – Non-Objective Art

The gentle break with absolute realism in painting, recording faithfully what the eye sees, that started with Constable and Turner, Corot and Millet and others has been traced in the preceding pages through various art movements that also had an impact on typography and graphic design.

The ultimate, the other-end-of-the-line, if you will, from absolute realism, is reached in non-objective art which has manifested itself several ways. Whereas all other art forms deal with an object – a landscape, a portrait, a still life, for example – and record its surface appearance faithfully or permit the artist's mind or spirit to see beyond the surface impression, non-objective art as the term makes explicit, does not depict a real life object. Sometimes the shapes that comprise a picture are derived or abstracted from an object, a landscape, for example, but the viewer may not be aware of this. Abstraction may be in the creative process but when abstraction is total the end result appears non-objective. Through the early decades of the 20th century the distinction between the object as seen and the image recorded became greater and greater. Slight abstraction became virtually total abstraction in some cubist art. But abstraction, by definition, is "the process of isolating an attribute or quality from a particular object." Thus, as with cubism, the starting point is an object although it may not be readily apparent when heavily abstracted.

Kinds of Non-Objective Art

For the purpose of this discussion we will consider three kinds of non-objective art:

1. *Image evolved by total abstraction of object(s).*
2. *Calculated construction of images with no real life object as a point of departure.*
3. *Spontaneous and accidental art.*

In order to briefly but clearly explain each of these we will focus on the work of one major artist in each category.

Wassily Kandinsky (1866-1944) – From Abstraction to Non-Objective Art

Wassily Kandinsky was a pioneer of abstract art whose later work was object-free. He was a tremendous force not only in painting but in graphic design as well because of his innovativeness, the great volume of his work, his writings which articulated clearly, forcefully, convincingly, what he was trying to do, and his long sojourns from his native Russia to Munich, Berlin, Weimar, and Paris. He met and interchanged ideas with many of the artists of the time and taught at the Bauhaus in Weimar where he also mingled with the faculty and students in and outside the painting department. The following phrases from *Kandinsky at the Guggenheim* (Abbeville Press, N.Y.) although excerpted in order to present a concise explanation of the artist's attitudes, reveal the essential nature of his approach to painting and how his vision of art evolved "from an idiom in which themes are recognizable to an object-free pictorial language."

❧ "painting is…an attempt to render insights and awareness transcending the commonly descriptive as well as the explicitly logical."

❧ He "…saw music as the spiritual, non-objective art form par excellence" and felt that "painting may enter its musical phase by existing independently of the recognizable object."

❧ "…The object as reflected in painting constituted a disturbing or at least irrelevant element in his search for the spiritual in art." He seeks "images freed from the burdensome object."

❧ "Kandinsky transcends traditional links with subject matter in favor of a pictorial language that dilutes and eventually eliminates the object while enhancing its meaning."

❧ "Kandinsky starts with an abstract form and he endows it with a purely pictorial meaning."

❧ "Kandinsky speaks of 'abstract' as meaning the same as 'non figurative' in French and what is called 'non-objective' in America." His own preferred word to describe his art, expressed in 1937, was "concrete." "Art Concret" was a term suggested by Theo van Doesburg and others in 1930.

In his own words:

❧ "Abstract or non-figurative or non-objective art (which I myself most prefer to call concrete) differs from older forms of expression and from Surrealism today by reason of the fact that it does not set out from nature or from an object, but itself 'invents' its forms of expression in very different ways. A subdivision of this general form is Constructivism, which operates with 'exact,' 'strict,' or, as is often said, 'mathematical' forms and rejects 'free' forms on principle…"

Kandinsky – A Mini Bio

Wassily Kandinsky was born in Moscow in 1866. He decided on an art career when he was 30 years old and pursued it for the next 48 years. In 1896 he went to Munich to study art, and that was his home base until 1914. He returned to Russia in 1921 but came back to Germany (to Berlin in 1921 and Weimar and the Bauhaus in 1922). He followed the Bauhaus to Dessau in 1925. In 1933 he moved to Neuilly-sur-Seine on the outskirts of Paris and there he spent the rest of his life.

His early paintings are loosely structured, intensely colored, employ free forms with blurred edges that blend together, and contain identifiable forms – houses, trees, horses, people, for example. By the time he returned to Germany in 1921 his colors were clearer and the shapes more defined. Geometric forms as triangles, circles, squares and their derivatives appear in his work. These were his basic grammar in that period but they play a smaller role in his later work.

Major influences on Kandinsky as an artist (he had been a law student and law teacher in Moscow when he left for Munich in 1896) included:

❧ Claude Monet's painting of *The Haystack.*

❧ Richard Wagner's *Lohengrin.*

❧ Fauvist artists in Paris and their daring use of color.

❧ His work was not influenced by the cubism of Picasso and Braque. This was a style and a kind of abstraction that he rejected.

❧ The suprematist paintings of Kasimir Malevich (reviewed in the next chapter).

❧ Surrealism.

❧ "Art Concret" or geometric abstraction as epitomized by the work of van Doesburg and Mondrian (reviewed in the next chapter).

Kandinsky taught painting at the Vkhutemas and Svomas schools in Russia during his return in the World War I period. His subsequent return to Germany coincided with the new and strong interest there in the Russian avant garde art movements. His most important books were *On the Spiritual in Art,* 1912, and the Bauhaus book, *Point and Line to Plane,* 1926.

Chapter II: Roots – Evolution and Revolution from Constable to Kandinsky

"The work of these modern painters... contributed to the development of freer forms of typographic design so much in evidence in the 1980s."

Kandinsky, Klee, Malevich, and Mondrian among others completely banished the subject (object) from their later art just as Ballanchine banished the story in his pioneering work. They wanted their art to be absolute, like music. Their work was derived from color and line, not objects nor people or nature. That cameras could do. Thus painters were developing a new approach to visual language.

Landscape With Factory Chimney, *oil, 1910. A wide range of high keyed and pastel colors – blue, violet, red, pink, yellow – show the influence of the fauvist painters on Kandinsky's work. One has to look carefully to see buildings, trees, and hills. Wassily Kandinsky. The Solomon R. Guggenheim Museum, New York.*

Striped, *oil with sand on canvas, 1934. Fine-grained painted sand adds texture to the painting. Here geometric shapes give way to freer forms in glowing colors. Rectangular zones contrast with the overlying curving biomorphic forms of surrealism. Wassily Kandinsky. The Solomon R. Guggenheim Museum, New York.*

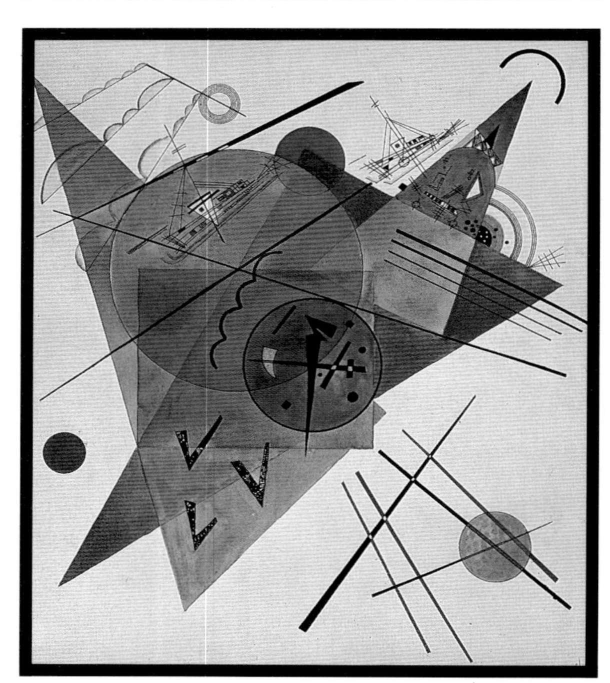

Dream Motion, *Watercolor, india ink, pencil, 1923. There is no real-life object here. Now Kandinsky is concerned with circles, squares, triangles, lines, their interplay with each other and with color. Wassily Kandinsky. The Solomon R. Guggenheim Museum, New York.*

View from the Window, *oil, 1904, records a specific impression: The view from Amsterdam's American Hotel on the Leidesplein. It has vivid yet realistic colors. He was starting to experiment with various techniques and was already familiar with the work of Monet and Van Gogh. The scene is clear yet blended with the artist's impression of it. Wassily Kandinsky. The Solomon R. Guggenheim Museum, New York.*

Number 10, *1950, Mark Rothko Collection, The Museum of Modern Art, New York. Gift of Philip Johnson.*

Spontaneous and Accidental Art

Many artists in recent years and today, each in their own way, can be categorized under the umbrella term "non-objective." Many, unlike Kandinsky, or Mondrian or Malevich, for example, neither pre-plan nor construct their art. Two art movements worth mentioning in this connection are abstract expressionism and post-painterly abstraction.

Abstract expressionism is essentially an American movement that first developed in New York City in the 1940s. It has also been called action painting and the New York school. A broad range of styles are included in its largely but not exclusively non-objective or non-representational framework. Jackson Pollock's turbulent works were created by spattering paint on a large canvas on the floor. Much cooler was the work of Mark Rothko. A common denominator to these paintings was the surface qualities given a painting by brush stroke and texture. Often accidents that occurred in the act of painting would be retained in the finished work. Other artists of this movement at some point in their career include Arshile Gorky, Willem de Kooning, Hans Hofmann, Robert Motherwell and Franz Kline.

Post-painterly abstraction is a term used by art critic Clement Greenberg to distinguish paintings of the 1960s from the abstract expressionist work of the 1940s and 1950s. The 1960s painters were more impersonal and intellectual in the work which focused on such fundamental formal elements of abstract or non-objective painting as pure, unmodulated color areas; flat (two dimensional) space; huge scale and varying shapes of the canvas. In this movement were Ellsworth Kelly, Jules Olitsky, Kenneth Noland, Frank Stella, and Morris Louis.

The work of these modern painters in so freely working with colors and sizing, shaping and positioning of elements contributed to the development of freer forms of typographic design so much in evidence in the 1980s.

An Exchange of Vitality

A successful painting, according to Frank Stella, must effect a convincing exchange of vitality between the viewer and the painting. This is true of representational art – a Caravaggio, a Monet, a Winslow Homer – or of abstract or non-representational art as in a Kandinsky, a Pollock, a Stella. In the latter, pictorial dynamics and elements may take the place of human dynamics in figurative or landscape paintings.

In today's non-representational art, motion can be a pictorial element. In place of faces, or leaves, or a recognizable bowl of fruit the pictorial elements are lines, shapes, planes, volumes, shading, color and texture, with motion created by an unbalance of forms, by the direction of the various elements. This art also derives its energy from the freedom of its forms sometimes floating and rotating in space, and its freedom from conventional scale. The aim of such art is not to depict an object but to express it, or, totally free of an object, to create an exchange of vitality without representing or abstracting from real objects.

Calculated Construction of an Image with No Real Life Object as a Point of Departure

At the same time that the various directions in painting described above were driving artists from the representations of nature of a Constable to the non-representational or non-objective work of Kandinsky, other movements and artists were seeking order and organization, blended with visual vitality and sometimes message symbolism. These movements, as will be explained in a later chapter, had great impact on typographic design. They included the constructivist and suprematist artists in Russia and the Russian schools, Vkhutemas, Svomas and the school in Vitebsk, the De Stijl group in the Netherlands and the Bauhaus in Germany.

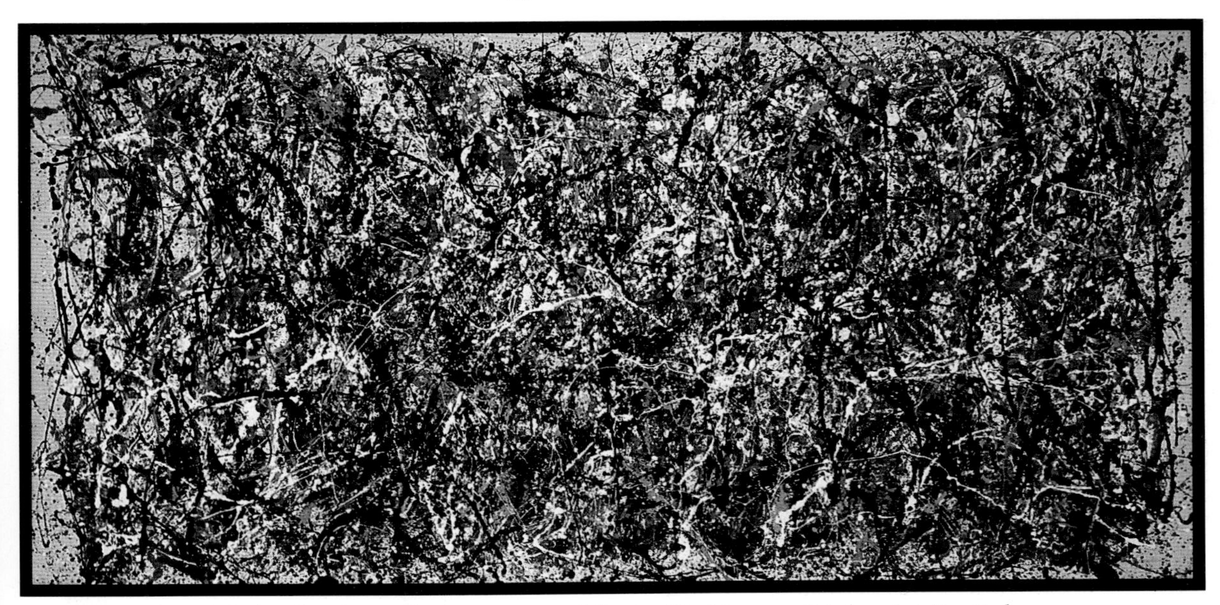

One, *1950, Jackson Pollock. Oil and enamel paint on canvas. Collection, The Museum of Modern Art, New York. Sidney and Harriet Janis Collection Fund.*

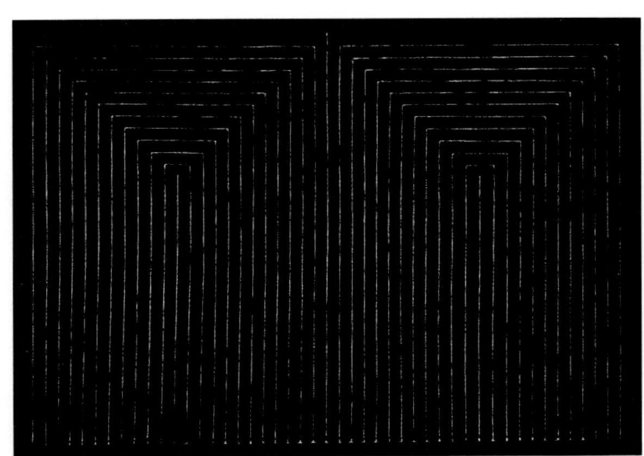

The Marriage of Reason and Squalor, *1959, Frank Stella. Collection, The Museum of Modern Art, New York. Larry Aldrich Foundation Fund.*

TYPOGRAPHIC COMMUNICATIONS TODAY

Chapter III: Order Out of Chaos

"The criterion is not which one is best in a general sense but which is most appropriate *as a design solution to a specific problem."*

TYPOGRAPHY, after all, is primarily concerned with aiding the communication of ideas and information. The art movements of the late 1800s and early 1900s awakened not only painters but typographic designers to the excitement and visual vitality inherent in the blank canvas or the white page. But some of the most exciting and screaming works of the futurists and dadaists caused a counter reaction among non-futurist, non-dadaist designers. Many such thoughtful graphic communicators sought to blend the newly rediscovered power of the printed message with a disciplined presentation that might improve message readability and comprehension. The object was to achieve the best of both worlds – graphic beauty, charm, excitement that would command attention and graphic structure that would contribute message clarity and impact. To keep these developments in a proper perspective, one should know that the traditionalist typography rejected by the avant garde was neither messy nor chaotic.

Victorian and art nouveau typography, for example, were both fully-developed esthetic systems with their peculiar structures, elaborate vocabularies, consistent grammars, and a sense of order of their own. The same is true for the esthetics of the Anglo-American and German "Typographical Revival" movement (Morison, Rogers, Warde, Gill, Goudy, Mardesteig, et al.) which, having developed from the pre-Raphaelite Morris' venture brought the Renaissance tradition back into use.

The point is that the very avant garde (especially in its most extremist and radical manifestations, such as futurism, dadaism, Merz, and the like) did do away with what its adherents called bourgeois rationalism and common sense, neatness and decency, asserting deliberate absurdity and irrationality, nonsense and chaos instead.

The key movements, schools and players in this blending of visual excitement and formalism in painting and in applied and communication arts were:

❧ Russian avant garde artists, including the constructivists and suprematists and particularly El (Lazar Markovich) Lissitzky.
❧ The Bauhaus, where all the art and cultural forces taking place throughout Europe in the first two decades of the century came together and developed a coherent platform for both fine and applied arts.
❧ The De Stijl movement in the Netherlands and particularly the work and influence of its founder, Theo van Doesburg.
❧ New Objectivity in Germany and its art of social protest.
❧ Art Deco and its expression of industrial forms. There was nothing avant gardeist about Art Deco. It was, rather, a reaction against the radicalist tendencies, an opportunistic and conformist trend in art and design.

The schools, groups, individuals striving to bring some order to what was, from the viewpoint of communication effectiveness, graphic chaos, grew, lived, and flourished alongside the art movements (not primarily concerned with conveying articulated messages) that still exist and seek new forms of expression today.

One might summarize the flow of typographic design over the past 100 years as follows:

❧ All too often a choice of graphic confusion or a kind of sterile, orderly clarity.
❧ A striving for graphic vitality influenced by experiments of painters and poets.
❧ A striving for vitality plus order, influenced by painters and typographic designers.
❧ An overwhelming focus on presentation orderliness and clarity.
❧ A coexistence of extreme forms of precisely ordered design, wildly alive design, and many intermediate forms striving for the best of both worlds in a period when technology rather than fine art is the great modifier of typeface and typographic design. This is where we are today, a time in which widely diverse approaches to typographic design are accepted. The criterion is not which one is best in a general sense but which is most *appropriate* as a design solution to a specific problem.

The Russian Avant Garde – Abstraction, Vitality, Order

In 1913, the year the Armory Show introduced cubism and fauvism to New Yorkers, Wassily Kandinsky was nearing the end of his stay in Munich, where his painting had become highly abstract. The same year, an issue of *Lacerba* in Florence called for a typographic revolution against classicism, the first major exhibition of post-impressionist art had been shown, and painters, typographers and book designers in Russia were taking new approaches. The Russian avant garde movement was well under way when the futurist Filippo Marinetti lectured in St. Petersburg in 1910 and again in that city as well as in Moscow in 1914. Cubism and futurism were changing the way Russian artists painted and the way typographic designers manipulated graphic elements and white space. The avant garde in Russia changed the face of both painting and typographic design. The major movements, which deeply affected typographic design, were suprematism and constructivism. Some of the best and most innovative Russian painters, such as El Lissitzky and Alexander Rodchenko, were also the great innovators in typographic design.

A second wave of Russian avant gardeists included such designers as Solomon Telingater, Faik Tagirov, and Varvara Stepanova. Many of them had their primary background in typographics rather than in painting. (For some examples of their work see Chapter XIII.)

Commenting on the two waves of typographic avant gardeists in Russia and the early years of the USSR, graphic designer Maxim Zhukov notes that "The functionalism of the Lissitzky and Rodchenko projects was much more declarative than real. They did not really seek it but were rather looking for a *new visual language* in order to better express the values and ideals of the 'machine age,' admiring and aestheticizing all of its revelations both material and spiritual. That was, as Vladimir Favorsky put it, an aesthetically sophisticated 'play at engineer' in art.

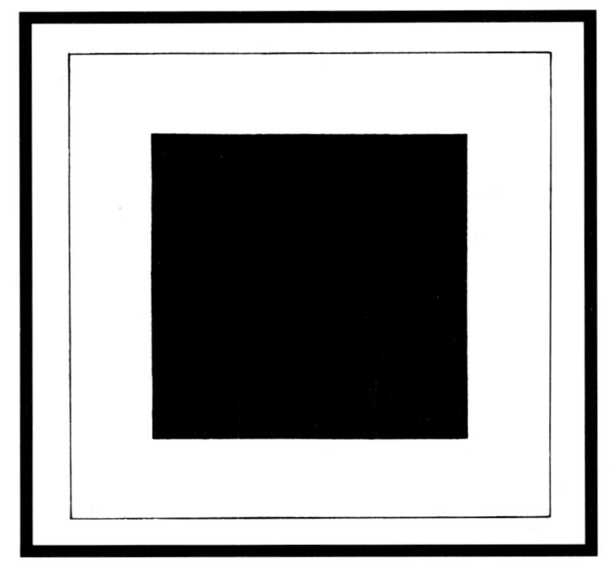

***Kasimir Malevich*, Black Square,** *1913. Non-objective art in which the* supreme *expression of feeling is achieved by eliminating any real object from the composition. This painting heralded the beginning of the suprematist painting movement.*

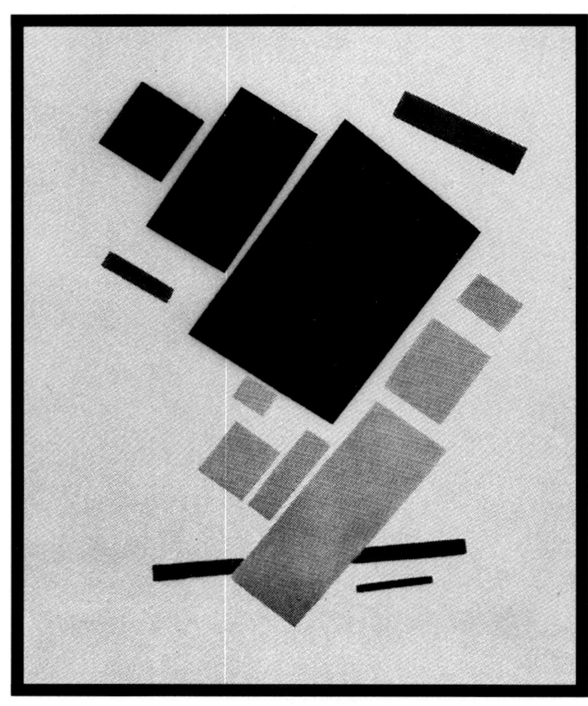

***Kasimir Malevich*, Suprematist Composition,** *1915. A construction of elements of color and shape. The visual form is the content. Stedelijk Museum, Amsterdam.*

"Does a book of poetry *really* need an index tab?

The Isms of Art, designed by El Lissitzky in 1925, although not an antecedent of the Swiss Grid System, seems to anticipate it. Note the three-column vertical grid structure used for the text, the three-column horizontal grid structure used for the title page. A two-column structure was used for the contents page. Note also the use of sans serif type and of bars for emphasis and organization.

III

DIE KUNSTISMEN

HERAUSGEGEBEN VON EL LISSITZKY UND HANS ARP

LES ISMES DE L'ART

PUBLIÉS PAR EL LISSITZKY ET HANS ARP

THE ISMS OF ART

PUBLISHED BY EL LISSITZKY AND HANS ARP

1924 1923 1922 1921 1920 1919 1918 1917 1916 1915 1914

EUGEN RENTSCH VERLAG
ERLENBACH-ZÜRICH, MÜNCHEN UND LEIPZIG
1925

Is a rapid search and/or quick reference really crucial in using it? Of course not. The famous frontispiece pictures facing the text pages in *Dla Golosa* (For The Voice) are of no functional value at all: they are merely beautiful typographic illustrations, symbolic in context and suprematist in form. Also remember a bizarre (though unfulfilled) idea of the same Lissitzky of printing poetry in the form of index cards (collections of poems disguised as indices, open to additions). There was a certain trend to present impractical objects (like works of art, fiction, literature, poetry, etc.) shaped as functional structures. It wasn't without reason that one of the traditionalist critics of the avant garde called their new publication *Veshtch* (Object), an art magazine shaped as a catalog of bicycle spare parts.

"Those 'functional' concepts were also *unnatural and uneasy* for the typographic technique at that time of metal composition. Following the early constructivist layouts in typesetting and make-up required all the skill and contrivance of the tough pros of hand (jobbing) composition trained on the late 19th century eclectical *Akzidenzsatz.* The very handling of material by the avant garde was actually as untrue and unnatural as one of its most contemptible predecessors who really forced the stiff and unflexible lead type for the sake of their fanciful inventions. Though the avant garde did vow fidelity to the 'truth to material.' It is also well known that the 'typographic' *LeF* covers designed by Rodchenko were printed from the wood blocks (just like the mediaeval block books!) engraved by a certain obscure craftsman called Andreyev.

"Though Lissitzky's and Rodchenko's oeuvre was rather doubtful an implementation of their own principles, it (or rather they) did rouse a ready and broad response in the graphic community and, what was much more significant and fruitful, among printers. The younger, revolutionary minded, type people carried through the innovative spirit of the pioneers of Russian Constructivism. Through the efforts of such people as Telingater et al. those ideas got a proper application in print and beyond, finding both due relevance and appropriate ways of production. Isn't it significant that the successors of Constructivists called themselves 'Productivists' (*Proizvodstvenniks*) and were much more of the functionalists than the founding fathers themselves?"

Suprematism

Kasimir Malevich had been painting in cubist and futurist styles. He was fully aware of Kandinsky's expressionist and abstract art. In 1913 Malevich exhibited the pencil drawing of his later oil painting, *Kvadrat.* He described it as, "nothing more or less than a black square upon a white ground." Here was, to use the critic's term, pure abstraction. Other paintings of simple squares, circles and geometrical compositions followed. Malevich felt that his first square "was no empty square...but rather the experience of non-objectivity."

Artists such as El Lissitzky and Alexander Rodchenko were attracted to suprematism. This non-objective art consisted of geometrical shapes flatly painted on pure canvas. It sought to "liberate art from the ballast of the representational world." As later disseminated and applied at the Bauhaus in Germany it was to influence the development not only of modern art but of architecture, industrial and graphic design as well. The movement's name, suprematism, grew from Malevich's belief that art can achieve the supreme expression of feeling by avoiding practical values and ideas. Suprematism reconsidered such formal values as paint, line, surface, space, color, etc. It cultivated a new spiritualism based on the management of the very layout of pictures and graphic elements.

If Malevich had carried abstraction to the extreme of non-objectivism, Kandinsky (who had been a lawyer and law professor before turning to art at the age of 30) clearly articulated the meaning of the term abstraction to himself. It was "a visualization of the interior of things." He was impressed with the power of pure color. He sought "a composition purely, infinitely and exclusively based on the discovery of law, of the combination of movement, of consonance and dissonance of forming a composition of drawing and color." Art was no longer to represent the material but the spiritual as is the case with music.

A Split – Art for Art's Sake vs. Art for Society

The Russian revolution of October 1917 brought about a split in the art movement. Malevich and Kandinsky maintained their art-for-art's-sake position and continued to create abstract and non-objective paintings. To them art was spiritual and must be kept distinct from utilitarian matters.

But by 1921 many artists disagreed. Five among them, led by Alexander Rodchenko, switched from their art-for-art's-sake attitudes and focused their talents and energies on industrial design, visual communication and other applied arts to better serve the new communist society. They designed everything from more efficient stoves to propaganda posters. Their $5 \times 5 = 25$ exhibition (five works by each of five artists) rejected studio art in favor of industrial design. Art became utilitarian and these artists became industrial and typographic designers.

The viewpoint of the constructivists was perhaps best articulated by Aleksei Gan in a 1922 brochure, *Konstruktivizm.* Practical applications of art were advocated and those who disagreed were put down as too tied to the past. The basic princi-

TYPOGRAPHIC COMMUNICATIONS TODAY

Chapter III: Order Out of Chaos

"Printed words are seen and not heard."

El Lissitzky, *cover of* For the Voice, *a book of poems by Mayakovsky, 1923. The circles and the diagonal lines relieve the rigidity of the orderly right angle design.*

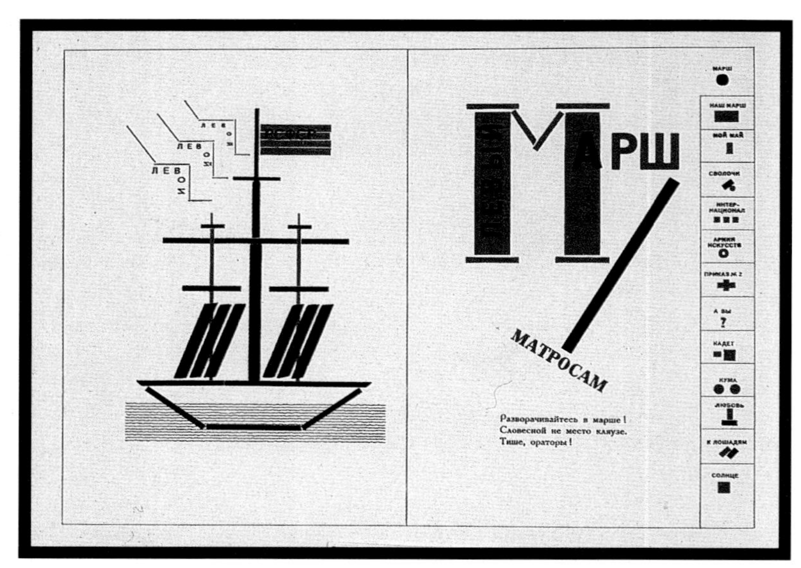

El Lissitzky, *pages from* For the Voice, *1923. Note the die-cut tabs that index the poems for easy reference. The poems were written to be read aloud. The designer comments: "To make it easier for the reader to find any particular poem, I use an alphabetical index. The book is created with the resources of the compositor's type-case alone. The possibility of two-color printing... [has] been exploited to the full. My pages stand in much the same relationship to the poems as an accompanying piano to a violin."*

ples of constructivism were defined as tectonics (visual form employed to express communist ideology), texture (a study of materials and how they could best be put to use by industry), and construction (the creative process and the development of the laws of visual organization).

It is here, especially in the work of El Lissitzky and Rodchenko, that the many forces of the arts that strove for more vitality in visual expression, were harnessed by typographic designers to bring back the order and organization necessary to communication effectiveness without sacrificing the graphic excitement and vigor needed to attract, lure and retain readers.

The development of the new art forms and their application to social needs including typographic design was hastened, not only by idea exchanges among the artists, but in two important art/design schools, Svomas and Vkhutemas. Kandinsky, at both schools, expressed his thoughts on modern art and modern art education. He was, later, to bring his ideas to the Bauhaus in Germany where there was a growing interest in the Russian avant garde, not only in the suprematists and the constructivists, but also in the work of Marc Chagall (cubist, expressionist, early surrealist) and the sculptor Alexander Archipenko. Tatlin and El Lissitzky were among the teachers at the Vkhutemas in Moscow. Vkhutemas was founded in 1921. Its purpose was to find a way to depart from the old art school approach, to create new art forms suited to contemporary life. There was a printing department and critical studies were made of color, shape, form, and space. A key figure in the school was Vladimir Favorsky who taught wood engraving. El Lissitzky and Malevich also taught at the art school in Vitebsk headed by Marc Chagall.

Constructivism as a pure art form was founded in 1913 by Vladimir Tatlin. In 1921, Tatlin and others, as noted above, applied their art technique to the needs and objectives of the new society.

Some constructivist artists, as Naum (Pevsner) Gabo and Antoine Pevsner, chose exile. In the early days of the movement the focus was on glass, sheet metal and other industrial materials used to create non-representational, often geometric, objects. There was more concern with volume than with plane and with non-art materials in their existing forms and colors.

The Major Links Between Fine Art and Graphic Design: El (Lazar Markovich) Lissitzky and Alexander Rodchenko

El Lissitzky, who had studied architecture and the structural properties of materials in Darmstadt, introduced the third dimension in his compositions. Unlike Malevich, who focused on planes, El Lissitzky represented depth by using receding and advancing planes. His paintings known as "Prouns" illustrate this. Prouns, by the way, is a shorthand expression for "project for the establishment of a new art." El Lissitzky's later typographic designs, especially those for books, drew many of their visual ideas about balance, space, and form from his oil paintings. El Lissitzky was also an early rebel against the limitations of metal typesetting. He used drafting instruments and pasteups to achieve the effects he wanted. In this he foresaw the era of pasteups for photo-mechanical reproduction processes that would replace metal type and form composition for letterpress printing.

As you can see from the accompanying illustrations, his books were not decorated with typographic ornaments. Their visual beauty and vigor grew from the designer's construction plan, his placing of typographic elements in dynamic balance relative to each other. But he sought more than vigor to attract readers. He sought clarity and order to encourage reading. He also used sans serif typefaces.

To understand the extent to which the constructivist painter had become a designer in the service of his country one need only read his own words. In 1921 Lissitzky said, "It is time to transform our intellectuals' meetings from idea bazaars into action factories." His words were not mere declarations. He put them into practice. In this sense he was more of a revolutionary in Russia than William Morris had been in 19th century England. Morris, a Utopian Socialist, urged English workingmen to beautify their homes but he would not employ machines to produce wallpapers, chairs, fabrics; thus his designs were expensive, high fashion and were found only in the homes of the rich. He preached but did not adequately practice economic democracy. El Lissitzky practiced what he preached with the result that today's communication effectiveness in reaching mass audiences owes much to him.

El Lissitzky's own words help us understand his role as a typographic designer.

"For modern advertising and for the modern exponent of form, the individual element – the artist's 'own touch' – is of absolutely no consequence."

"Printed words are seen and not heard."

"Concepts are communicated by conventional words, by letters they are designed."

Alexander Rodchenko, *cover for* Novyi LeF, *No. 2, 1923. Early use of photomontage. A red "x" over the pictures crosses out the old order including the old capitalist in the circle. The children above the circle represent the new social order.*

Alexander Rodchenko, *cover for* Novyi LeF, *No. 1, 1923. A magazine about the left front of the arts. The top of the logo (at bottom of the cover) is red, the bottom black.*

"Concepts should be expressed with the greatest economy – optically not phonetically."

"The layout of the text on the page, governed by the laws of typographical mechanics, must reflect the rhythm of the content."

"The new book demands new writers."

El Lissitzky was one of the first typographic designers to understand that white space is not left over space but something to be manipulated. He recognized white space as a vital design element equal in importance to the pictures or the areas of black type. His fine arts background, in washing away formal and sacred rules of artists of the past, was applied to architecture, book design, product design, posters, typography. The advent of photography also helped him organize the page in new ways to in effect, fragment the page. With masses of people wanting information, he knew books had to be attractive, exciting, yet readable. Just as stage design was no longer mere decoration but an integral part of a performance, so book design went beyond ornament and became an integral part of the reading experience.

In 1921 the Russian government sent El Lissitzky to Berlin to establish contact with Western designers. We'll consider this phase of his career in later pages when we discuss the Bauhaus.

Alexander Rodchenko applied geometrically constructed designs to his posters and typographic designs. He, too, used sans serif types and, along with El Lissitzky, was an early user of photomontages. This was at a time when photomontage was developing as a cinematic form. At the Vkhutemas he ran the metal-working department and soon concentrated on typographic design. In 1922 he became the art director and typographer for the constructivist magazine *LeF,* and collaborated with the poet Mayakovsky on a series of posters, books of poetry and more than a dozen Mayakovsky anthologies.

The painters, El Lissitzky and Rodchenko, had become typographic designers, and through them all the forces of the new art forms from Constable to Kandinsky were harnessed to graphic discipline and order, to lay the foundation for typographic design as we know it today. If all these forces came into focus when Russian constructivist artists became typographic designers, they were to come into still sharper focus when El Lissitzky, with Theo van Doesburg, founder of the De Stijl movement in the Netherlands mingled with the Bauhaus students and masters. The De Stijl artists and designers like the constructivists, were to create a new blend of graphic vigor and order for art and for typographic design.

Order, Type in Rectangular Blocks, Asymmetrical Balance

The De Stijl (The Style) artists of the Netherlands were painters and graphic designers, architects, sculptors, poets. At about the time that El Lissitzky, Rodchenko and other constructivists were bringing a kind of geometric order to painting and typographics in Russia, the De Stijl group was founded (1920) in Leyden, in the Netherlands, by Theo van Doesburg. In 1917, as an artist in Zürich, he had been a dadaist and continued to produce dada art and poetry into the 1920s. But in De Stijl he was seeking to make graphic sense of paintings, books and typographic communications. Later he was to go to Germany, as did El Lissitzky, there to mingle with Bauhaus students and masters (but not to serve on the faculty), and considerably influence the typographic directions that were to develop there. Constructivist typography emerged in Russia about three years after De Stijl was founded.

Others in the De Stijl group in 1917 were the painters Bart van der Leck, Piet Mondrian, and Vilmos Huszar, the sculptor Georges Vantongerloo, the writer Anthony Kok and architects J. J. P. Oud, Robert van't Hoff and Jan Wils. Through their journal, as well as through their art, the De Stijl group made their philosophy known. Its chief ingredients were harmony, equilibrium, primary colors, straight lines, and right angles. As with some other movements of the time they sought art within art rather than with subjects or reality. These World War I years were years of tragedy and the De Stijl approach was one way of eliminating tragedy from art. Emotion in art, as expressed in curves, diagonals, fading and intensifying colors, was out. Even the name De Stijl was written in capital letters made of vertical and horizontal strokes and rectangular elements.

The totally abstract or non-objective art evolved by van Doesburg, Mondrian and others evolved from the cubism of Picasso, Braque, and Gris. As ultimately refined by the De Stijl artists the same attitudes towards line, space, color and volume carried over into their typographic design. The most strict adherents, in typographic design, to De Stijl theory were van Doesburg and Mondrian. Others, such as Piet Zwart, were more innovative, less rule-bound. Zwart never formally joined the De Stijl group. He, Paul Schuitema and H. N. Werkman brought their personalities to bear on typographic design in the 1920s but were really independents, influenced by the De Stijl group and other art movements of the time but not clearly identified with any group.

Manifesto of "De Stijl," 1918

As with other art movements, leaders of the movement got together and issued a proclamation of their aims and attitudes. These artists declared that "The object of nature is man...the object of man is style." Their 1918 manifesto makes clear what they were trying to do, and how and why.

1. There is an old and new consciousness of time. The old is connected with the individual. The new is connected with the universal. The struggle of the individual against the universal is revealing itself in the world war as well as in the art of the present day.
2. The war is destroying the old world with its contents: Individual domination in every state.
3. The new art has brought forward what the new consciousness of time contains: a balance between the universal and the individual.
4. The new consciousness is prepared to realize the internal life as well as the external life.
5. Traditions, dogmas and the domination of the individual are opposed to this realization.
6. The founders of the new plastic art therefore call upon all who believe in the reformation of art and culture to annihilate these obstacles of development as they have annihilated in the new plastic art (by abolishing natural form) that which prevents the clear expression of art, the utmost consequence of all art notion.
7. The artists of today have been driven the whole world over by the same consciousness and therefore have taken part, from an intellectual point of view, in this war against the domination of individual despotism. They therefore sympathize with all who work for the formation of an international unity in Life, Art, Culture, either intellectually or materially.
8. The monthly editions of *De Stijl,* founded for that purpose, try to attain the wisdom of life in an exact manner.

Cooperation is possible by:
Sending, with entire approval, name, address and profession to the editor of *De Stijl.* Sending critical, philosophical, architectural, scientific, literary, musical articles or reproductions. Translating articles in different languages or distributing thoughts published in *De Stijl.*

Signatures of the present collaborators:
Theo van Doesburg, Painter/Robt. van't Hoff, Architect/Vilmos Huszar, Painter/Anthony Kok, Poet/Piet Mondrian, Painter/G. Vantongerloo, Sculptor/Jan Wils, Architect.

Theo van Doesburg

Van Doesburg, as did El Lissitzky, Rodchenko and other Constructivists in the USSR in 1921, believed as early as 1917 that art was a social function and existed to serve the welfare of society. He was extraordinarily multi-talented and energetic. He lectured, wrote, taught, organized Congresses and meetings, formal and informal, where ideas

"The more uninteresting a letter, the more useful it is to the typographer."

were exchanged and such disciplines as architecture, painting, typographics, sculpture, furniture and product design intermingled. He also published, under the pseudonyms of I. K. Bonset and Aldo Carmini, dadaist poems.

On the surface it would appear that his expressions of Dadaism, which movement was dedicated to ridiculing and destroying the arts as they had existed, and his concern that art serve the needs of society were inconsistent, especially since they coexisted in the same years of his career. But Van Doesburg's dynamism was such that, while part of him was tearing down what he felt was outmoded and socially unviable art, he could not wait to start building a new and meaningful art. Hence De Stijl. In the magazine *De Stijl* he advocated the absorption of pure art by applied art.

From 1921-1923 he lived in Weimar where, although not of the faculty of the Bauhaus, he ran a series of lectures on De Stijl that were chiefly attended by Bauhaus pupils.

Although he founded De Stijl, and he and Mondrian painted within its strict guidelines – horizontals, verticals, right angles, etc., he was the first to depart from this rigidity. He sought more dynamism in painting, and later in typographic design, and developed the theory of elementarism which admitted oblique effects. Mondrian did not agree. Van Doesburg, in his way, was trying to combine dynamism and order in his paintings and in his typographics.

Commenting on book design and typography Van Doesburg wrote that, "A book is read from left to right and from top to bottom, one line after the other. But at the same time it is seen one entire page at a glance. This simultaneous process (acoustical-optical) has given the modern book a new 'plastic' dimension. The old setting was passive and frontal, while the new setting is active and spatial-temporal. The modern book is no longer just a cinematographic running of different processes. 'Intensity' has replaced 'direction' and because of this intensity we demand a typographic support of the text which, however, does not mean an ornamental effect or the kind of typographic illustrations which is so popular with the Russians today, but a complete new command of the means of typography. These are: white space, text, color and, lastly, the photographic picture… In the design of both a book and architecture we encounter a double problem: both the book and the house should not only be useful but beautiful and nice to look at…"

Piet Mondrian

Although Piet Mondrian's activities did not expand to typographic design, his painting, architecture and interior designs, his teaming of art and jazz as when his *Boogie Woogie* was displayed with accompanying music, and his relating of his non-objective art to atonal music, made him a powerful force in heightening the world's awareness of the interrelationship among the arts. In 1940 he came to New York where he had studios in the East Fifties through early 1944. Because of his presence in the United States the De Stijl principles were seen and adapted by many typographic designers, artists and art directors. His ways of dividing space, with geometric order yet vigor and beauty, greatly influenced advertising and graphic design in the United States.

Piet Zwart

Although he knew and met with van Doesburg, Mondrian and others of the De Stijl group, he was not a member of the group and his typographics are freer and more individualistic. He used diagonals, curved shapes, photographs and photomontages. An examination of his work shows the sense of order he derived from the De Stijl principles, plus visual excitement that was his personal contribution. As with so many who changed the course of typography in this era, he started his career as an artist and architect. In 1911 he designed furniture and interiors. World War I and mobilization interrupted his studies and work for a while. His first contact with the De Stijl artists came in 1919. From then until 1921 he worked with the De Stijl architect Jan Wils. In 1921 he moved to the architectural office of H. P. Berlage. While there he produced the first of his advertisements, for a flooring manufacturer. By 1925, at the age of 40, he was primarily a typographic designer producing many catalogs and advertisements. By 1928 he became deeply interested in photography and photomontages. His ads used them but he adhered to the primary red, yellow and blue colors characteristic of the De Stijl artists and designers.

Piet Mondrian, Composition II. *1929. The Museum of Modern Art, New York. The relationship between Mondrian's painting and Vilmos Huszar's title page for* De Stijl *(Fig. 2) is obvious.*

Zwart was his own copywriter, and a good one. His novel handling of type and rules, the contrast in his designs in the size and color of the type and its positioning, the contrast in the photographs, the juxtaposing of straight lines with curved and circular forms, vitalized the printed page with power and tension. His was a new blend of readability and typographic excitement. Typographically, he focused on simple letter forms. The excitement came from how he used – sized/positioned – the type. He wrote, "The more uninteresting a letter, the more useful it is to the typographer." He also regarded white space as a graphic element, not merely a canvas to be filled, and considered

ABONNEMENT BINNENLAND 4.50 BUITENLAND 5.50 PER JAARGANG BIJ VOORUITBETALING. VOOR ANNONCES WENDE MEN ZICH TOT DE ADMINISTRATIE.

DE STIJL

MAANBLAD GEWIJD AAN DE MODERNE BEELDENDE VAKKEN EN KULTUUR REDACTIE: THEO VAN DOESBURG.

ALLE STUKKEN DE REDACTIE BETREFFEND: K. GALGEWATER 3, LEIDEN. ALLE STUKKEN VOOR DE ADMIN. ADRESSEERE MEN MORSCHWEG 20, LEIDEN, HOLLAND.

2e JAARGANG. DECEMBER NEGENTIENHONDERDACHTTIEN. NUMMER 2.

GUILLAUME APOLLINAIRE +

PARIJS. NOVEMBER 1918.

13

ABONNEMENT BIJ VOORUITBETALING BINNENLAND 4.50 BUITENLAND 5.50 PER JAARGANG. VOOR ANNONCES WENDE MEN ZICH TOT DEN UITGEVER.

DE STIJL

MAANDBLAD VOOR DE BEELDENDE VAKKEN. REDACTIE THEO VAN DOESBURG. UITGAVE X. HARMS TIEPEN.

ADRES VAN REDACTIE: KORT GALGEWATER 3 LEIDEN. ADMINISTRATIE: X. HARMS TIEPEN, HYPOLITUSBUURT 37 DELFT, INTERC. TEL. 729 EN 690.

1e JAARGANG. APRIL NEGENTIENHONDERDACHTTIEN. NUMMER 6.

Vilmos Huszar, *title pages for* De Stijl*. Compare this with Mondrian's* Composition*. The logo, constructed from an open grid of squares, was designed by van Doesburg. Even the text type forms neat rectangles.*

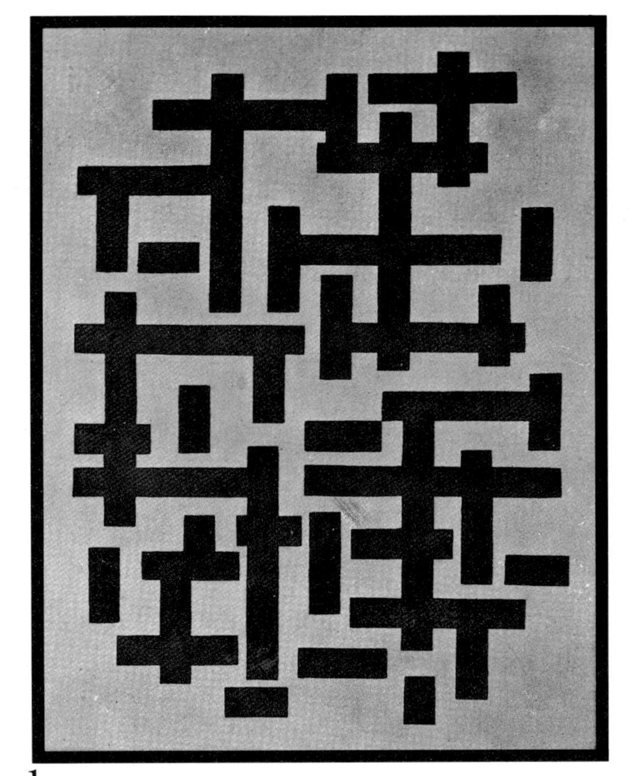

1

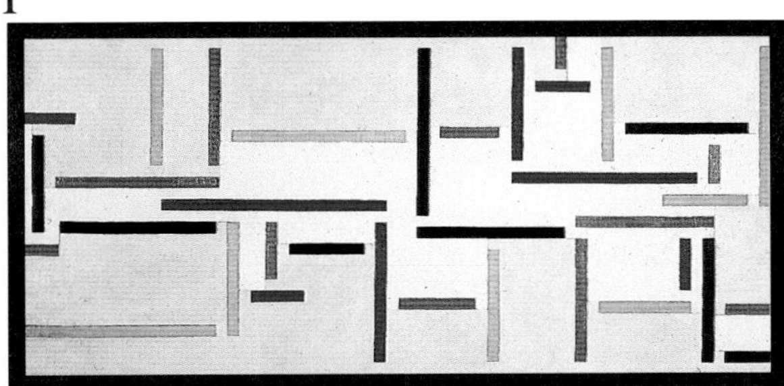

2

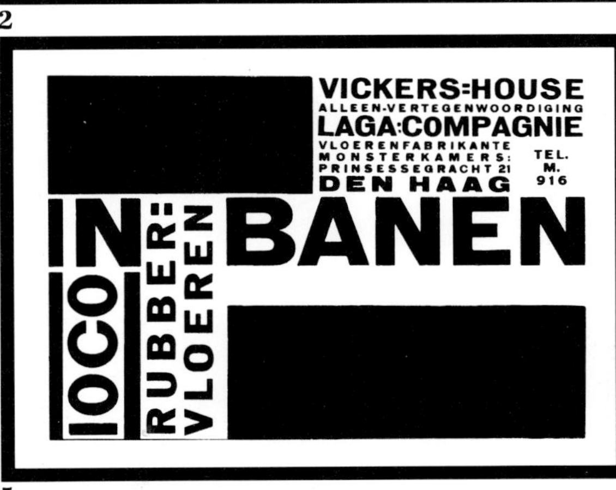

VICKERS-HOUSE
ALLEEN-VERTEGENWOORDIGING
LAGA-COMPAGNIE
VLOERENFABRIKANTE
MONSTERKAMERS:
PRINSESSEGRACHT 21
DEN HAAG
TEL.
M.
916
IN
BANEN
IOCO
RUBBER-
VLOEREN

5

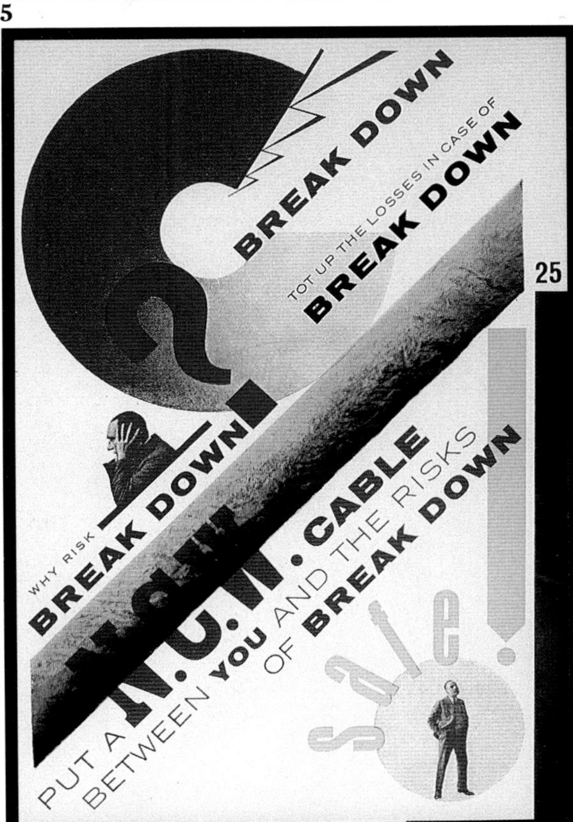

BREAK DOWN
TOT UP THE LOSSES IN CASE OF
BREAK DOWN
25
WHY RISK
BREAK DOWN
PUT A N.C.W. CABLE
BETWEEN YOU AND THE RISKS
OF BREAK DOWN
sale!

6

A composition in black and white, *1918 (1); an oil on canvas,* Rhythm of a Russian Dance, *1918, (2); an exhibition poster, 1920, (3); and an alphabet based on the square, and free of curves, 1919 (4), all by Theo van Doesburg. This is a clear example of how modern art affected not only typographic, but typeface design also. As with the Russian constructivists, the avant garde painters were often also typographic designers. Paintings (1) from the Kunstmuseum Basel, Emanuel Hoffmann Stiftung, and (2) the Museum of Modern Art, New York, Lillie P. Bliss Bequest.*

KUBISTEN
LA
EN
SECTION
INTERNATIONALE
TENTOONSTELLING
SECTION
NEO
D'OR
KUBISTEN

3

ABCDEFGHIJKLM
NOPQRSTUVWXYZ

4

7

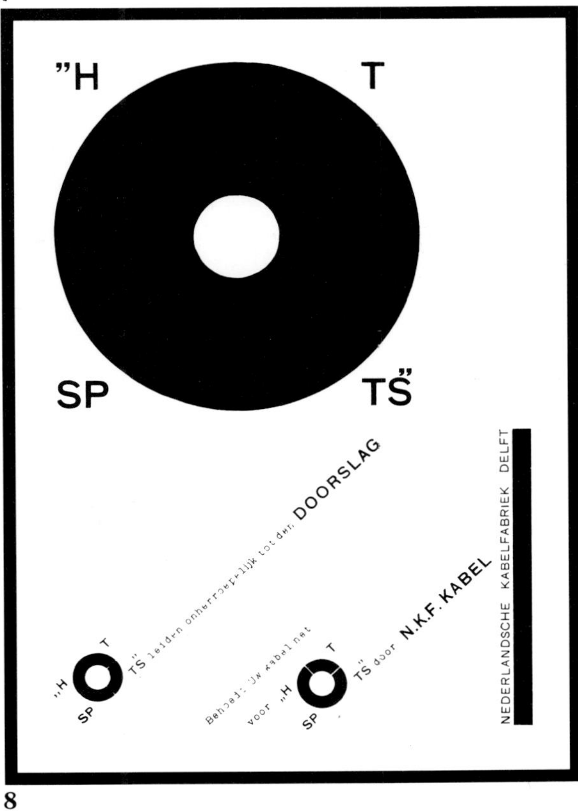

8

Piet Zwart's *advertisements (5-9) often followed De Stijl principles but just as often departed from them, using diagonals, curves, circles, freely handled photographs. He, as did De Stijl artists and designers, preferred the primary colors of yellow, red and blue.*

9

"Color is a creative element, not a trimming."

In 1937 Piet Zwart wrote that "It is the task of functional typography to create the typographical look of our time, free from tradition, to activate as far as possible typographic forms to find clear and ordered visual ways of expression, to define the shape of new typographic tasks and methods such as machine setting, photo typesetting and to break the guild mentality."

Peter Althaus, commenting in 1966 wrote, on Piet Zwart, "Whereas in the past a page used to be composed to achieve an even, harmonious, 'decorative' look, Zwart called for an asymmetrical, function oriented and 'brutal' legibility, a tension in the distribution of the basic elements that was to appeal to the reader's awareness: the given type material (he regretted the lack of an 'ideal' typeface for his time) with all the corresponding signs, the white spaces (pauses), the parts of a sentence and finally, as a signal and eye catcher, even color."

H. L. C. Jaffe wrote of him, "Piet Zwart, a man of eminent social conscience, saw the problem as a social problem: the renewal of typography was as much a problem of the reader as it was of reading. Zwart took the factor 'space' into his typography by contrasting the white page with the black type material, emphasizing it with screened photos in the text which often made the third dimension come shockingly alive. Maybe more important is his integration of the 'time' factor into the function of typography, because through the signal-like use of letters and oversized or diagonally positioned lines the text is scanned in a new, lively way. It is no longer the even, inorganic beat of linebreaks that distributes the text, but a living rhythm which springs from its very content."

Chapter III: Order Out of Chaos

"A letter was to serve the function of reading, nothing else."

WITCH DENAR

In this typeface, *Bifur, by A. M. Cassandre, the angularity was compatible with much of the poster design and illustration of the 1920-30 period. It is a typographic form of abstraction, omitting but suggesting some parts of the letter.*

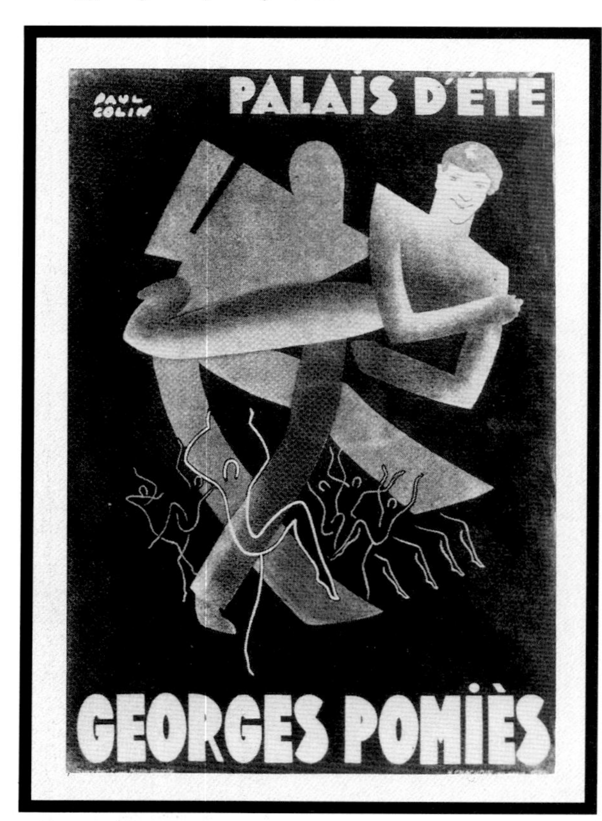

The angular figures *and the sharply lined type for* Palais D'Été *are characteristic of art deco posters. By Paul Colin for dancer Georges Pomies in 1932.*

Flat shapes *and sharp letter forms in 1924 poster by Joseph Binder for the Vienna Theatre and Music Festival.*

Sleekness and Modern Technology – Art Deco

In the 1920s, artists, illustrators and typographic designers, influenced by modern technology, sought to express its visual aspects in their work. Angularity and a reduction of natural images to basic geometric forms such as cubes, spheres and cones resulted. Flat tones also contributed to a machine-like sleekness, a streamlined rather than a natural image, a zig-zag line rather than a graceful curvilinear feeling. Art deco, as it came to be known in the '60s, was not a major movement but a design style of the 1920s and 1930s with a revival of sorts in the 1970s. Some of art deco's chief practitioners were Paul Colin in France, Jean Carlu in France and the United States, Joseph Binder in Vienna, Austin Cooper and Abram Games in London. The typefaces and lettering they used were often angular and compatible with the geometric aspect of the accompanying illustrations.

A 1924 poster *for the London Electric Railway by Austin Cooper.*

Industrial Production and Modern Design In Poland – Mechano-Faktur

Functional typographics in Poland in the 1920s was greatly influenced by Henryk Berlewi. In 1924 in Warsaw, he founded the "Group of abstract constructivist art." He also opened an advertising agency. Through Berlewi the art and the applied design movements developing in Russia, Italy, Germany and the Netherlands reached Poland. Berlewi, in Berlin, had met with El Lissitzky, van Doesburg, Moholy-Nagy, Raoul Hausmann and others. El Lissitzky's influence at the Bauhaus, in fact, grew from this Berlin group. There, Moholy-Nagy blended his own sense of creativity with type and other graphic elements with El Lissitzky's sense of typographic design, and it was this blend he brought to the Bauhaus a little later.

In 1924 Berlewi expressed his attitude toward fine and applied art as follows: "Art must break with all the practices of the perfumed, perverse, hypersensitive, hysterical, romantic, individualis-

Advertising brochure *by Henryk Berlewi, 1924. Red and black on yellow paper. Inside page from booklet, cover shown below. Yellow paper was used for inside pages.*

Cover *of* Reklama Mechano, *a booklet designed by Henryk Berlewi, 1924. It was printed in red and black on white paper.*

***Paul Schuitema** designed this advertisement for Berkel in 1927. It is clear, organized, yet eye-catching and alive.*

tic, boudoir-type art of yesterday. It must create a new language of forms, available to all and in harmony with the rhythm of life." Berlewi made an important and original contribution to standardized elements in art and in the applied arts he called "Mechano Faktur."

An Art of Social Protest

Much of the art and design of the early decades of the 20th century was at least partially an expression of cultural and social protest. In Germany the exponents of what was called "New Objectivity," were most obvious in their social protestations. Leading the protests were George Grosz, Otto Dix, and Max Beckmann. Such cultural/political artists were not confined to Europe. In Mexico, for example, during the rise of fascism and the period of the great economic depression in the early 1930s, there were Diego Rivera, José Orozco and David Siqueiros. While these artists did not directly change the face of typographic design they did focus the minds and hearts of many artists and designers on the need for graphic communications to be socially significant.

The Fine Art Connection

Many fine artists in the 1900-1930 era also were, or became, typographic designers. Some, already mentioned, were El Lissitzky, Theo Van Doesburg, and Filippo Marinetti. Each was identified with an important art or design movement. Two of the Netherlands' artists, not so clearly a part of any group or movement, also produced typographic work of significance, work that helped break with past traditions and sought new ways of blending order and vitality in visual communications. They were Paul Schuitema and Hendrik Nicolaas Werkman.

During World War I, Schuitema studied painting, but by 1920 he was attracted to graphic design and soon was designing booklets, folders, advertisements, trademarks, stationery, showrooms, exhibits. In the mid-twenties he was attracted to photographs as a communications medium but was turned off by the formal approaches most photographers followed. He experimented with motion effects, photomontages as well as motion picture films. As with many great designers, he also was a teacher, at the Royal Academy in The Hague, from 1930 until 1963.

Paul Schuitema, commenting on earlier days, wrote in 1961 that "Every thing, every letter, every picture, every sound, every color should have its function. Artists too should have their function in society. One did not think of success, only of the essential values. Everything else was denied. A letter was to serve the function of reading, nothing else. It had to have distinct, objective, and clear forms, it was not supposed to be elegant, beautiful, feminine. Its beauty is its function, there should not be anything mysterious behind or beside it.

"What we make should be full of tension. Red was the first and most important color, the signal color. Then yellow and blue were added. Always primary colors, never mixed colors. For type, grotesque (sans serif): condensed and expanded, bold and light. Those were the working principles; just as important for us was the photo montage. The photo was mounted freely on the plane of the rectangle. No section area, no drawing, because that was 'painterly.' When we did draw it was abstract or a simplified form of a symbol, direct and without romantic *side ideas*."

The Next Call 4 *was an occasional publication of eight pages limited to 40 copies. It was produced as a tribute to Lenin, upon his death in 1924. These pages are forerunners of the expressive typography of recent decades in the United States and elsewhere. The columns of type, if sounded, become a graphic dirge. H. N. Werkman. The two pages shown here were not facing pages in the original publication.*

H. N. Werkman, like Paul Schuitema, was born in Groningen in Northern Holland. He was a journalist and a printer. As a printer he had a type shop. In 1917, when he was 35, he started painting. By 1923 he had a workshop in his home and his skills with painting, type and printing came together. He made prints with printing ink, hand-rollers, type, rules, and a hand-press. He often printed lightly on colored paper. Later, using a stencil technique, he disciplined the shapes in his prints. He usually produced only one copy of each picture. His prints often included typographic elements purely as art forms. In 1945 he was arrested and executed by the Nazis, just three days before the allied armies reached northern Holland. Many of his oil paintings and prints were destroyed during the battle of liberation.

Also highly influential in the 1920's in Holland was Gerrit Rieffeldt.

TYPOGRAPHIC COMMUNICATIONS TODAY
Chapter IV: The Focal Point – The Bauhaus

"Typography must be clear communication in the most vivid form... clarity is the essence of modern printing."

IT ALL CAME TOGETHER in Weimar, Germany, in 1919. A new kind of school opened its door there. It was an interdisciplinary blending of fine and applied arts. It was at once pragmatic and idealistic. It emphasized crafts and excellence of craftsmanship. It was a blend of hands-on, learn-by-doing workshops and new attitudes towards artistic expression of all kinds. In architecture, painting, sculpture, product and graphic design, it sought to blend order in presentation with vigor and relevance in expression.

The Bauhaus quickly became a powerful cultural magnet. Artists and designers from all over Europe came to it and exchanged ideas, became teachers or students, then migrated and spread Bauhaus thinking throughout the civilized world. Typographic design, one of the concerns at the Bauhaus, metamorphosed there, never to be the same again. Although the surface appearance of today's communication design often bears little resemblance to the typographics produced at the Bauhaus, many of today's approaches to typographic design are offshoots of the work done under the influence of Bauhaus masters Johannes Itten, Laszlo Moholy-Nagy, Herbert Bayer and Joost Schmidt as well as the influence of Theo van Doesburg and El Lissitzky. Because the Bauhaus was both the focal point of all the new thinking about art and design that had been developing since the 1880s and the launching platform for typographic design in the subsequent decades, it is worth careful scrutiny. We will consider how it came into being, the overall philosophy and the key figures, the development of the typographic program, typefaces of the periods, what the Bauhaus really accomplished, how Jan Tschichold became its great apostle, and its significance today.

Origins

In 1902 the Grand Duke of Saxe-Weimar recognized the need to modernize the Weimar Arts and Crafts Institute and the Weimar Academy of Fine Arts. To do this he called on Henri van de Velde, the distinguished Belgian art nouveau architect and designer. Van de Velde became principal of the school, and the curriculum and concepts that he evolved there laid the groundwork for what was to become the Bauhaus. In 1914, with war between Germany and Belgium imminent, van de Velde resigned his post and returned to Belgium. He recommended three possible successors, one of whom was a young but already distinguished architect, Walter Gropius, who had used glass and steel innovatively in a factory he had designed. But, with war on the horizon, the Grand Duke closed the school and the academy. After the war the two institutions were merged and Gropius was appointed principal of the new school, which was named, in March 1919, Das Staatliches Bauhaus. As early as 1910 Gropius had ideas about how such a school should be organized and run, and he presented them in a memorandum to Berlin industrialist Emil Rathenau. His ideas were partially compatible with van de Velde's but he modified van de Velde's curriculum and organization of the school to create the new Bauhaus. When Henri van de Velde returned to Belgium he did not forget his commitment to art and design education. In 1925 he established in the Abbey of LaCambre, the Institut Superieur des Arts Decoratifs which is still an outstanding art/design school in Brussels.

The Bauhaus was established in the wake of defeat in World War I. This was a time of economic, political, and cultural decades-old yearning and quest for a new social order, and new approaches to many aspects of life. The Bauhaus was born in the right place and at the right time for a school aiming to explore new ways of applying art and design.

The Big Idea

Published in a German newspaper, the *Bauhaus Manifesto* explained the philosophy of the school. It was the first official publication of the Bauhaus and, also published as a four-page leaflet, it contained a woodcut by Lyonel Feininger and Gropius' manifesto and program. Key points were:

❧ Emphasis on architecture, and the need of all kinds of artists (painters, sculptors, handcrafters, designers, etc.) to relearn their role in creating a building. The Bauhaus strives to reunify all disciplines of practical art as inseparable components of the architecture. "The complete building is the ultimate aim of all the visual arts."

❧ To explore a unity of art and technology. (Aren't we going through this now in the early years of the computer era?)

❧ Gropius felt that the mass production age needed artists and brilliant ideas so that mass produced and distributed products would be visually appealing and satisfying. Where William Morris and the 19th century English Arts and Crafts movement emphasized the superiority of handicrafts to machine produced goods, the Bauhaus people felt the opposite was now true. Gropius had been educated in the Deutsche Werkbund in Munich, which emphasized the esthetic qualities and potentials for low cost consumer goods.

❧ To seek a functional architecture while exploring the use of new building materials.

❧ Art training must include workshops. Artists should learn a trade to be productive. The school is the servant of the workshop.

❧ Workshops were to be run by two masters, one an artist without craft experience, and the other a master craftsman. Thus form, theory and skilled execution were to be co-emphasized.

❧ Craft skills should be fully developed in order to achieve artistic excellence. Art is not a profession. There is no essential difference between the artist and the craftsman. The artist is an exalted craftsman whose rare moments of inspiration may cause his work to blossom into art.

❧ Avoidance of all rigidity. Emphasis on creativity and individuality combined with strict study discipline.

❧ Constant contact with leaders of crafts and industries and with the public through exhibitions.

❧ Research new techniques for displaying art in architecture.

❧ There were to be no teachers or students as such. The Bauhaus was to be organized like a craft guild with masters, journeymen, and apprentices.

❧ Encourage extracurricular friendliness between masters and apprentices by attending lectures, poetry readings, musical performances and costume parties.

The program outlined in the manifesto covered a wide range of art disciplines including lettering, but not typography. Typography became an important part of the curriculum with the arrival of Moholy-Nagy.

Like Kandinsky, Gropius had a vision of an international community of artists, and this the Bauhaus became. Talents in many disciplines and from many countries came to the Bauhaus and made it truly the focal point for all the art/design forces of the young century. Later, when Hitler closed the school, these talents would radiate out around the world and spread the influence of the Bauhaus, especially to the United States.

One can understand the international flavor of the Bauhaus just by considering where some of its masters came from. Kandinsky came from Russia as did El Lissitzky, who, though not affiliated with the Bauhaus, was a tremendous influence on its typographic program. Paul Klee came from Switzerland and Moholy-Nagy and Marcel Breuer from Hungary. Theo van Doesburg, who, like El Lissitzky, was not officially part of the Bauhaus but was a tremendous influence in it, came from the Netherlands. Lyonel Feininger came from the United States. He had studied painting in Berlin, Hamburg, and Paris.

The Bauhaus, not at first, but later, became nonbourgeois. As the Arts and Crafts movement in 19th century England showed, only the rich could afford handmade objects. Art, to be nonbourgeois, must be machine made. Curves in art were not easily handled by machines but the linear art of the De Stijl artists was made-to-order for mechanical devices. Curves, van Doesburg felt, were voluptuous and luxurious and for the elite. Gropius understood van Doesburg's point, and the straight lines in architecture and graphic design for which the Bauhaus became famous had much to do with van Doesburg's influence, which

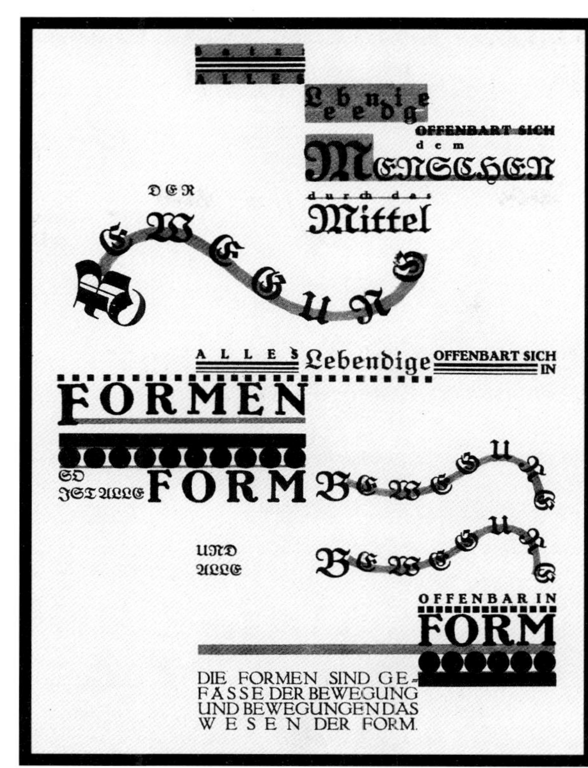

Johannes Itten: *Typographical design. Page from* Utopia. *1921, an example of early Bauhaus typography showing Itten's stress on self-expression rather than communication clarity.*

Gropius articulated as "Art and technology – a New Unity!" This way emphasis on functionalism in art at the Bauhaus could be read as "non-bourgeois!" The political implications of this point of view had much to do with its eventual closing in 1933 by the Nazis. Even in its early days in Weimar there were local officials who felt the school was bolshevistic.

Typography at the Bauhaus

As the preceding information makes clear, the Bauhaus was not a graphic or typographic design school. Typography was not even included in its original manifesto and program description. Yet typography soon played an important role in the program and in its posters and publications. Here, as never before, typographics was achieving a new, effective, and exciting balance between orderly, clear presentation and vigorous, eye-appealing treatment. The transformation can be traced through the 14 years of the institution's life by examining the roles of four masters and two outside forces. The masters were Johannes Itten, Laszlo Moholy-Nagy, Herbert Bayer, and Joost Schmidt. The outsiders were El Lissitzky and Theo van Doesburg.

Johannes Itten

One of Gropius' first appointments to the staff, Itten conducted a six-month obligatory course to be taken prior to selecting specialized training in one of the workshops. Itten had run a private art school in Vienna and Gropius admired his teaching methods. At the Bauhaus he gave his obligatory preliminary course informally, playfully, so that the students were free to develop their tactile and visual powers. For Itten, art was essentially a psychic means of expression and in this respect he was in conflict with Gropius' pragmatism. Itten's focus on self-expression eventually provoked an ideological crisis, and in 1923 he resigned his post. Typography was about to be recognized as an important communications art form, and, under Moholy-Nagy, a constructivist approach would replace Itten's expressionism.

Laszlo Moholy-Nagy

In Weimar the Bauhaus was not equipped to teach typography, but students did experiment on their own. Early Bauhaus typography used the same typefaces available to everyone and its look was not distinguishable from work done elsewhere. But, with the departure of Itten in 1923 and the arrival of Moholy-Nagy, who took over the preliminary course, typography became an important area. Until the Bauhaus moved to Dessau in 1925 much of the typography and design and production of Bauhaus literature was produced on the outside. The stimulus in this area was Moholy-Nagy whose most important contribution, aside from running the preliminary course, was the designing of the "Bauhaus Books." A Bauhaus style developed. The dadaist, Kurt Schwitters, the De Stijl leader, Theo van Doesburg and some students, including Herbert Bayer and Joost Schmidt, contributed to this effort.

Typographical signs were used as eye catchers. A De Stijl sense of asymmetry became a Bauhaus trademark. Although graphic design was not yet on the curriculum, it was studied and practiced unofficially and in contact with such designers, living elsewhere, as Jan Tschichold, Ladislav Sutnar, Piet Zwart, Paul Schuitema, Henryk Berlewi and others.

Moholy-Nagy, in Berlin prior to coming to Weimar, had much contact with El Lissitzky and blended the Russian designer's ideas of vitality and order with his own and brought much of El Lissitzky's thinking to his Bauhaus teaching. He also invited El Lissitzky to conduct seminars for the students even though he was not part of the faculty.

He used modular, simple letters rather than pre-existing styles. His strong preference was for sans serif typefaces. A dynamic symmetry with elements positioned for their relative importance replaced the conventional center-axis, formal design of pre-Bauhaus graphics.

Moholy-Nagy, a Hungarian, studied law, then turned to painting. He soon developed into a non-objective painter, influenced by Malevich's work. He had met El Lissitzky in Dusseldorf. In 1921, in Berlin, his studio became an avant garde meeting place for people like van Doesburg, El Lissitzky and Kurt Schwitters. In 1922, inspired by Man Ray's "Rayograms," he experimented with photography and started his creation of photograms. He was an infectiously enthusiastic man and brought to his Bauhaus students and to Bauhaus Books his talents which were a blend of those of the artists with whom he had mingled. He resigned from the Bauhaus when Gropius did in 1928. In 1937 he founded the School of Design in Chicago known as the "New Bauhaus."

Moholy-Nagy's commitment to typographic clarity and his sense of the importance of photography to graphic communication is made clear in these brief quotations from his writing.

"Typography must be clear communication in its most vivid form... clarity is the essence of modern printing."

Commenting on the new role of typographic design in an age in which posters and other media were finding it necessary to attract and hold and impress readers as well as to inform them, he wrote:

"Whereas typography, from Gutenberg up to the first posters, was merely a [necessary] intermediary link between the content of a message and the recipient, a new stage of development began with the first posters. ... One began to count on the fact that form, size, color, and arrangement of the typographical material (letters and signs) contain a validity to the content of the message as well; this means that by means of printing, the content is also being defined pictorially... This ...is the essential task of visual-typographical design."

He also wrote, *"Typography is a tool of communication. It must be communication in its most intense form. The emphasis must be on absolute clarity... legibility. Communication must never be impaired by* a priori *esthetics. Letters must never be forced into a preconceived framework, for instance a square."*

In 1924 he wrote that *"The harmonic arrangement of space, the invisible yet clearly noticeable tense linear relationships which allow not only a symmetrical but other kinds of balances form an essential part of typographical order. Instead of the century old static-concentric balance we are trying to create today a dynamic-uncentric balance. In the first case the typographic objective in the central relationship of all, even the peripheral, parts is seen at a glance; in the second case, the eye is gradually guided from one point to the next without losing the correlation of its parts..."*

To Moholy, photography (including photograms and photomontages) offered a new way of seeing, and thus a new way of understanding and believing. Moholy's photo assemblages remind one of El Lissitzky's Proun paintings. Moholy's paintings also show the influence of constructivism, but neither in his photography, his paintings, nor in his typographics was Moholy a pure constructivist. Of photography he wrote,

"The knowledge of photography is just as important as that of the alphabet. The illiterate of the future will be the person ignorant of the camera as well as of the pen."

Where dadaists were satirists and constructivists social idealists, Moholy was an unusual blend of a romantic and a pragmatist. He was equally concerned with visual vigor that would attract and hold readers and viewers and with communication clarity. To achieve these ends he blended photography and typography in what was then a new way. His thoughts on this are expressed in his book, *Painting, Photography, Film,* as follows:

"What is typophoto?

"Typography is communication composed in type.

"Photography is the visual presentation of what can be optically apprehended.

"Typophoto is the visually most exact rendering of communication.

TYPOGRAPHIC COMMUNICATIONS TODAY
Chapter IV: The Focal Point – The Bauhaus

"Communication↔Typography↔Person"

"Every period has its own optical focus. Our age: that of the film; the electric sign, simultaneity of sensorily perceptible events. It has given us a new, progressively developing creative basis for typography too. Gutenberg's typography, which has endured almost to our own day, moves exclusively in the linear dimension. The intervention of the photographic process has extended it to a new dimensionality, recognised today as total. The preliminary work in this field was done by the illustrated papers, posters and by display printing.

"Until recently type face and typesetting rigidly preserved a technique which admittedly guaranteed the purity of the linear effect but ignored the new dimensions of life. Only quite recently has there been typographic work which uses the contrasts of typographic material (letters, signs, positive and negative values of the plane) in an attempt to establish a correspondence with modern life. These efforts have, however, done little to relax the inflexibility that has hitherto existed in typographic practice. An effective loosening-up can be achieved only by the most sweeping and all-embracing use of the techniques of photography, zincography, the electrotype, etc. The flexibility and elasticity of these techniques bring with them a new reciprocity between economy and beauty. With the development of photo-telegraphy, which enables reproductions and accurate illustrations to be made instantaneously, even philosophical works will presumably use the same means – though on a higher plane – as the present day American magazines. The form of these new typographic works will, of course, be quite different typographically, optically, and synoptically from the linear typography of today.

"Linear typography communicating ideas is merely a mediating makeshift line between the content of the communication and the person receiving it:
COMMUNICATION↔TYPOGRAPHY↔PERSON

"Instead of using typography – as hitherto – merely as an objective means the attempt is now being made to incorporate it and the potential effect of its subjective existence creatively into the contents."

Moholy goes on to advocate (and experiment with) what he calls the "typophoto" in which in some instances pictures in the text replace words.

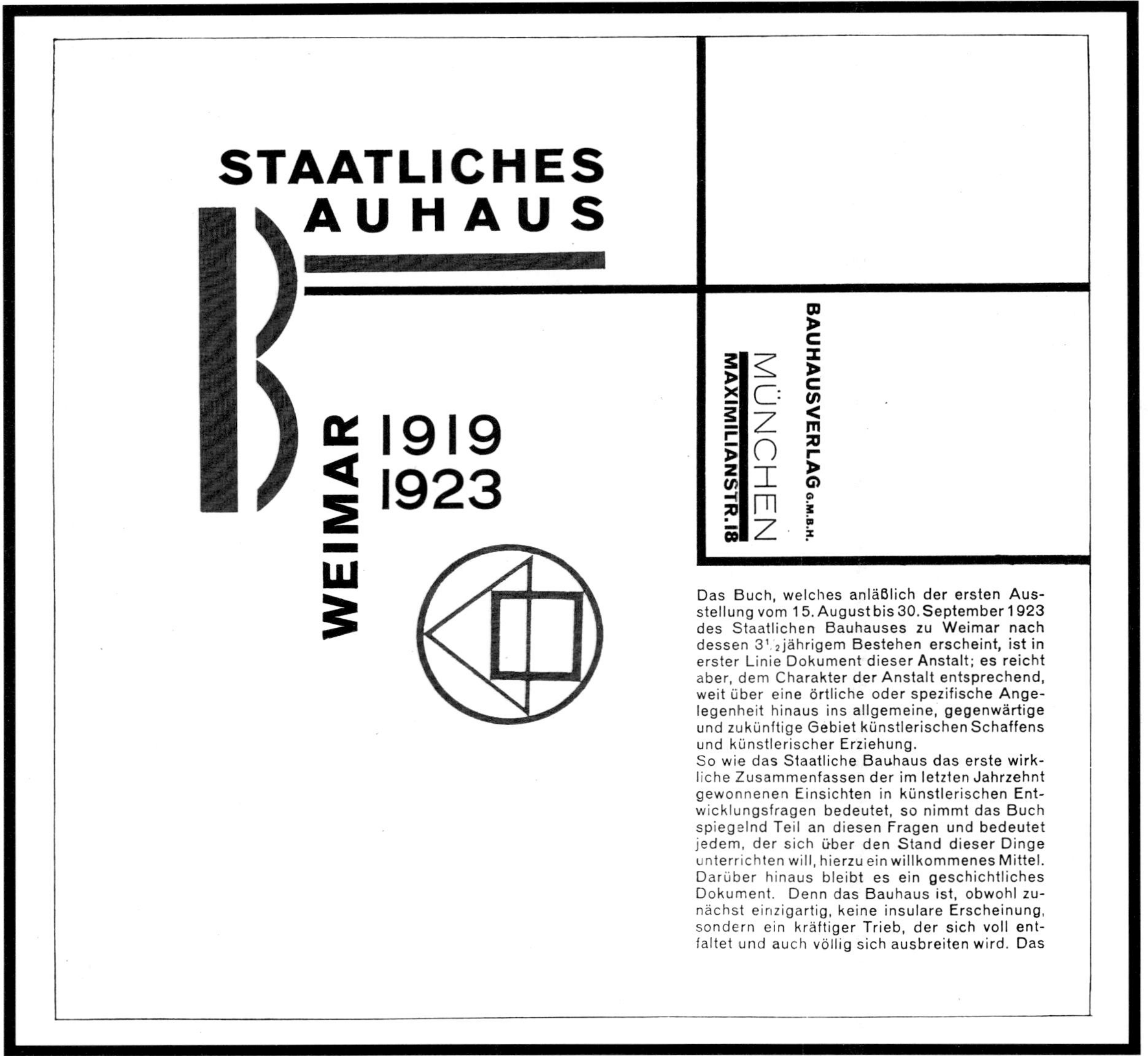

Das Buch, welches anläßlich der ersten Ausstellung vom 15. August bis 30. September 1923 des Staatlichen Bauhauses zu Weimar nach dessen 3½jährigem Bestehen erscheint, ist in erster Linie Dokument dieser Anstalt; es reicht aber, dem Charakter der Anstalt entsprechend, weit über eine örtliche oder spezifische Angelegenheit hinaus ins allgemeine, gegenwärtige und zukünftige Gebiet künstlerischen Schaffens und künstlerischer Erziehung.
So wie das Staatliche Bauhaus das erste wirkliche Zusammenfassen der im letzten Jahrzehnt gewonnenen Einsichten in künstlerischen Entwicklungsfragen bedeutet, so nimmt das Buch spiegelnd Teil an diesen Fragen und bedeutet jedem, der sich über den Stand dieser Dinge unterrichten will, hierzu ein willkommenes Mittel. Darüber hinaus bleibt es ein geschichtliches Dokument. Denn das Bauhaus ist, obwohl zunächst einzigartig, keine insulare Erscheinung, sondern ein kräftiger Trieb, der sich voll entfaltet und auch völlig sich ausbreiten wird. Das

Prospectus *for the Bauhaus, designed by L. Moholy-Nagy in 1923.*

BAUHAUSBÜCHER
SCHRIFTLEITUNG:
WALTER GROPIUS
L. MOHOLY-NAGY

L. MOHOLY-NAGY:
MALEREI, PHOTOGRAPHIE, FILM

8

L. MOHOLY-NAGY:
MALEREI
PHOTOGRAPHIE
FILM

ALBERT LANGEN VERLAG MUNCHEN

Title-spread *of* Painting, Photography, Film. *1925. This was the eighth volume in the series of 14 Bauhaus books designed and edited by Moholy-Nagy and Gropius. At a time when the Bauhaus still did not have a graphic design workshop these books, by their teaching and by their design were creating a Bauhaus style.*

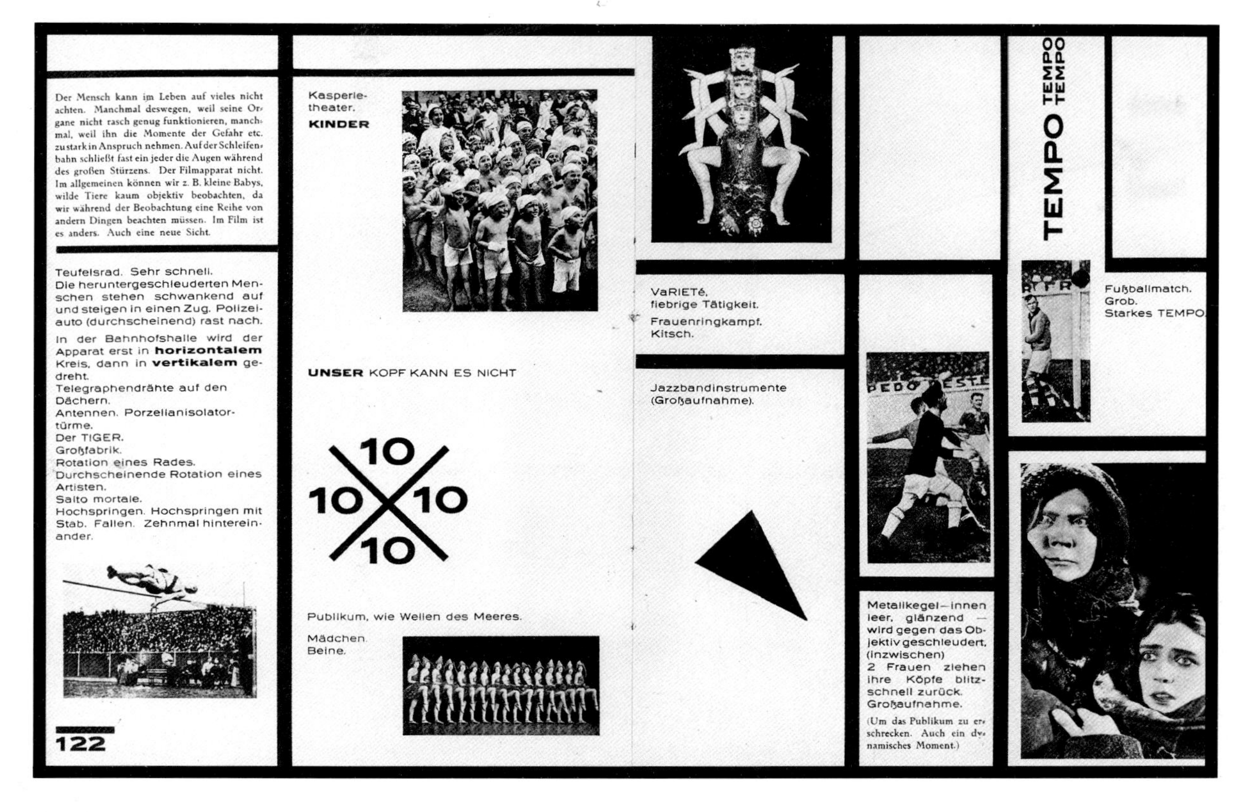
Der Mensch kann im Leben auf vieles nicht achten. Manchmal deswegen, weil seine Organe nicht rasch genug funktionieren, manchmal, weil ihn die Momente der Gefahr etc. zu stark in Anspruch nehmen. Auf der Schleifenbahn schließt fast ein jeder die Augen während des großen Stürzens. Der Filmapparat nicht. Im allgemeinen können wir z. B. kleine Babys, wilde Tiere kaum objektiv beobachten, da wir während der Beobachtung eine Reihe von andern Dingen beachten müssen. Im Film ist es anders. Auch eine neue Sicht.

Teufelsrad. Sehr schnell.
Die heruntergeschleuderten Menschen stehen schwankend auf und steigen in einen Zug. Polizeiauto (durchscheinend) rast nach.

In der Bahnhofshalle wird der Apparat erst in **horizontalem** Kreis, dann in **vertikalem** gedreht.
Telegraphendrähte auf den Dächern.
Antennen. Porzellanisolatortürme.
Der TIGER.
Großfabrik.
Rotation eines Rades.
Durchscheinende Rotation eines Artisten.
Salto mortale.
Hochspringen. Hochspringen mit Stab. Fallen. Zehnmal hintereinander.

122

Kasperletheater.
KINDER

UNSER KOPF KANN ES NICHT

10
10 10
10

Publikum, wie Wellen des Meeres.

Mädchen.
Beine.

VaRIETé,
fiebrige Tätigkeit.
Frauenringkampf.
Kitsch.

Jazzbandinstrumente
(Großaufnahme).

Metallkegel—innen leer, glänzend — wird gegen das Objektiv geschleudert, (inzwischen)
2 Frauen ziehen ihre Köpfe blitzschnell zurück.
Großaufnahme.
(Um das Publikum zu erschrecken. Auch ein dynamisches Moment.)

TEMPO TEMPO TEMPO

Fußballmatch.
Grob.
Starkes TEMPO.

A double spread *from* Painting, Photography, Film. *Replace the text blocks and photographs with rectangles of the primary colors and you have a van Doesburg or Mondrian De Stijl painting. Laszlo Moholy-Nagy.*

Herbert Bayer

1925 was a year of major change for the Bauhaus. It moved from Weimar to Dessau. It dropped its organization based on the medieval hierarchy of master, journeyman, and apprentice. It became known as the Hochschule für Gestaltung (University of Design).

It was also in 1925 that Jan Tschichold published *Elementare Typographie* and thus spread the understanding of Bauhaus typography throughout Europe and eventually to the United States.

Five major additions were made to the teaching staff: Joseph Albers, Joost Schmidt, Marcel Breuer, Hinneck Scheper and Herbert Bayer. And, most significantly from the viewpoint of this story, graphic design was added to the curriculum, and former Bauhaus student Herbert Bayer was put in charge of the workshop for graphic design and printing. Bayer brought a new blend of vitality and order to Bauhaus typography. He had studied under Kandinsky and Moholy-Nagy.

Bayer's typography was orderly and functioned along constructivist lines. Vigorous and innovative, it featured:

❧ Sans serif type.
❧ Circles, squares, rectangles, triangles, bars, and rules, to unify or separate elements and for emphasis but not for decoration.
❧ Primary colors.
❧ Typography without capitals was introduced.
❧ Type rules subdivided the area in a De Stijl-like manner with contrast deriving from the varying direction, length and thickness of the rules.
❧ Extreme contrasts of type size and weight to achieve various degrees of emphasis.
❧ Type and pictures sized to the same column width.
❧ Horizontals and verticals were dominant.
❧ He introduced a flush left, ragged right typography in a trade magazine ad for the Bauhaus. His studies of the needs of stationery led logically to the use of ragged right typography.
❧ Color tints emphasized key words.
❧ Photographs printed in uncommon colors caught the eye (from Moholy-Nagy he developed an enthusiasm for photography's value in communication).
❧ Some copy elements were rotated through 90 degrees.
❧ In some work a single-alphabet type (no capital letters) was used. Bayer designed such an alphabet in 1925. All the letters were based on a few arcs and straight lines. Only structurally essential parts were used. In 1933 Bayer designed a geometrical serif typeface called Bayer-type. In his work at the Bauhaus he went one step beyond Moholy-Nagy's teaching by emphasizing the psychological aspects of typography and advertising.

Bayer felt that, "We must overcome the dreadful notion that the artist is a luxury. His role in society is equally needed as that of the laborer." He felt that a designer must also be an artist, yet he clearly knew the difference between a painter and a typographic designer. He wrote, "The first step at the inception of any project or problem is always to analyze it thoroughly as to its functions, purpose, size, proportions, materials and structures. Out of such analysis there always develops a direction of thought and subsequently a concept for a project. The painter does not have to deal with such..."

Bayer left the Bauhaus in 1928 and became Art Director of Vogue in Berlin, then Art Director of the Dorland Advertising Agency there. In 1938 he came to the United States.

He became a consultant to John Wanamaker, J. Walter Thompson and Container Corporation of America, and for the cultural development at Aspen, Colorado. Aside from his many achievements and great influence in the typographic world Bayer was an outstanding photographer and painter and designer of three-dimensional constructions.

If Bayer's typographic work could be characterized by key words one would choose: carefully proportioned, balanced elements, internal harmony among numerous elements, precision, clarity, rhythm.

To Bayer, typography was a service art, not a fine art. Typography was more than a medium for making language visible, it had distinctive optical properties...pointing toward specifically typographic expression. And he knew that "graphic design will more than ever be determined by its purpose. The designer-typographer can find new impetuses from research in vision..."

At the Dessau Bauhaus, Bayer established the DIN standards (Deutsche Industrie Norm) for paper sizes which are still used.

Although not a strict grid designer he was a forerunner of grid typographics in that he carefully organized elements to control eye-flow.

Thinking back over the great influences on his approach to typography, Bayer once cited the poems of Mayakovsky. He said they were a revelation to him with their free artistic treatment of typography, the way type and pictures were blended, and the use of type characters as decorative elements. The book, *For the Voice,* had been designed by El Lissitzky (See illustrations from it in chapter III.)

Another major influence on Bayer was the book, *Sprach und Schrift* (Speaking and Writing), by Dr. W. Porstmann. It analyzed the written word and how it communicated. This awakened Bayer's concern with making typographic communications more effective. It started him analyzing and rethinking typographic design and led him in the direction of serifless type and all-lowercase alphabets.

On October 2, 1985, painter, architect, philosopher, typeface-graphic-industrial designer, sculptor and tapestry maker Herbert Bayer died at his home in Montecito, California, at the age of 85.

abcdefghijkl
mnpqrstuvw
xyzag dd

abcdefghi
jklmnopqr
stuvwxyz
a dd

Bayer's *Universal type (narrow face bold, 1925)*

TYPOGRAPHIC COMMUNICATIONS TODAY

Chapter IV: The Focal Point – The Bauhaus

"Jan Tschichold became the Johnny Appleseed of typography who carried the seeds planted in Weimar, Dessau, and Berlin, far and wide."

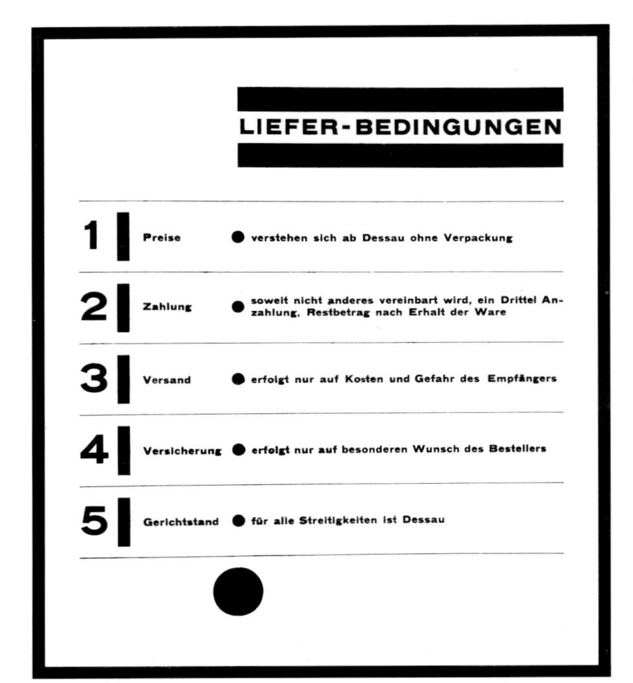

A Bayer design *for a Bauhaus publication. Rules organize the content elements.*

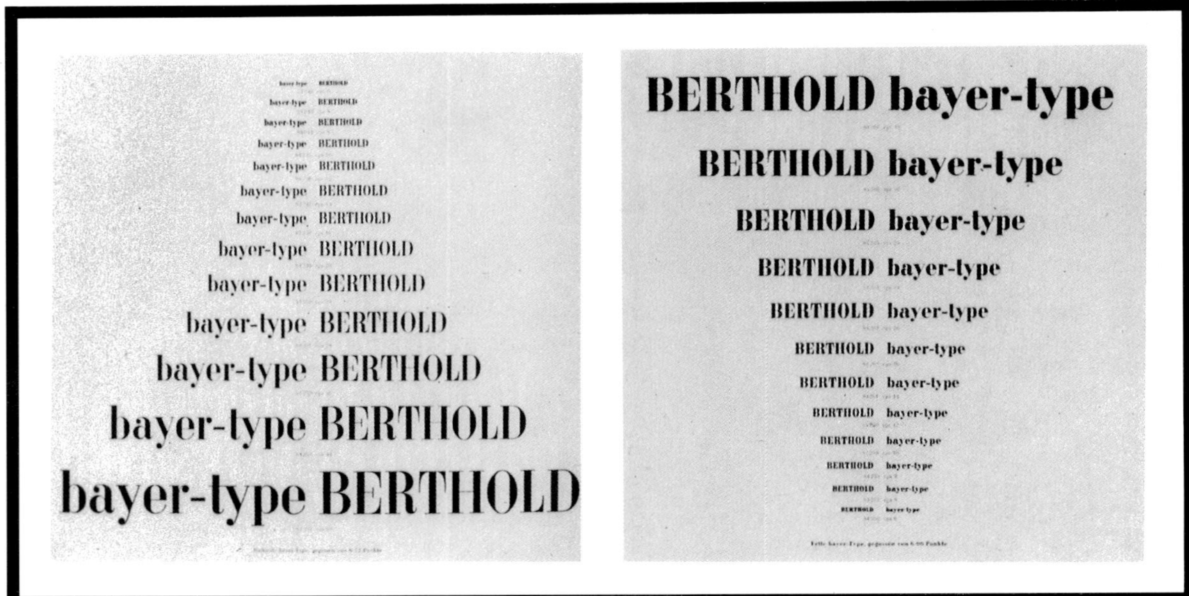

Double page *from Berthold prospectus for Bayer-type (1933).*

A Bayer cover *for product catalog of the Bauhaus, 1925.*

Herbert Bayer, *1923. One of a series of banknotes designed for the State Bank of Thuringia.*

Two *of Bayer's functionally organized letterheads for the Bauhaus.*

Magazine cover, *1940, by Herbert Bayer for Harper's Bazaar.*

One of Herbert Bayer's pieces *in the series of Great Ideas of Western Man institutional advertisements, which he developed for Container Corporation of America, 1952. Readable, organized, but free-form rather than rigid.*

BAUHAUS DESSAU
DRUCKEREI U. REKLAME-ABTEILUNG

ES IST AN DER ZEIT, AUF DIE
BESONDERE LEISTUNGSFÄHIG-
KEIT UNSERER ABTEILUNG FÜR
DRUCKEREI UND REKLAME
HINZUWEISEN.
AUSGEHEND VON ELEMENTARER
GESTALTUNG, ÜBERNIMMT SIE
DIE HERSTELLUNG VON
ENTWÜRFEN JEDER ART,
AUSARBEITUNG VON
WERBEPLÄNEN UND
DRUCKAUSFÜHRUNGEN:
GESCHÄFTSPAPIER, NORM-
VORDRUCK, PROSPEKT, PLAKAT,
KATALOG, GELEGENHEITSDRUCK.
DIE WERBEKRAFT DER
ERZEUGNISSE BERUHT AUF
PSYCHOLOGISCHER WIRKUNG
DER KÜNSTLERISCHEN FORM.

This was Bayer's *first use of ragged right text typography. It resulted from his study of the needs of stationery. Note also the absence of rules. He was departing from the typography of Moholy-Nagy.*

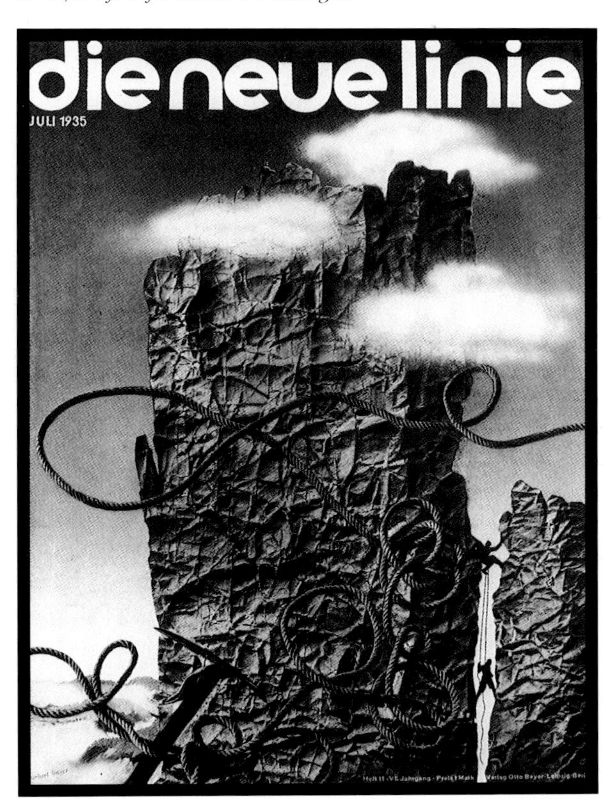

Photomontage *cover by Herbert Bayer for the monthly periodical* die neue linie, *1935.*

Joost Schmidt

Like Herbert Bayer, Joost Schmidt was a Bauhaus student in Weimar and became a member of the faculty in Dessau in 1925. He taught lettering, commercial art, life-drawing, and sculptural composition. When Bayer left the Bauhaus in 1928 Schmidt took over the graphic design and printing workshop. He dropped the constructivist typographics of his predecessor and worked with a wider range of typefaces. He also brought more photography into the type shop. He was a born teacher, had many pupils, and through them, his writings and his exhibition techniques he greatly influenced typography in Europe. Under Schmidt typographic design was more grid-based than under Bayer. Schmidt experimented a great deal in this area, with remarkable results.

El Lissitzky and van Doesburg

El Lissitzky's great influence on Bauhaus typographics was primarily through his meetings with Moholy-Nagy in Berlin and only secondarily through his visits to the school at Weimar.

El Lissitzky was the great innovator. It can be said that he established modern typography. Where Marinetti had liberated typography by making it visually exciting, El Lissitzky, retaining visual vitality, brought order and clarity and controlled emphasis to graphic communication. Educated as an architect, El Lissitzky combined an analytical mind with a passion for the new art forms. He was exposed to futurism, cubism, to Malevich's non-objective art, to Kandinsky's abstracts. He was the right man at the right place at the right time. His sense of graphic organization

ORT DES ERSCHEINENS MELLE IN HANNOVER

JUNGE MENSCHEN

MONATSHEFTE
FÜR POLITIK, KUNST, LITERATUR UND LEBEN
AUS DEM GEISTE DER JUNGEN GENERATION
HERAUSGEGEBEN VON WALTER HAMMER

SCHRIFTLEITUNG: WERTHER B. BIELEFELD • VERLAG: HAMBURG 13, JOHNSALLEE 54.
POSTSCHECK HAMBURG 31941

HEFT 8
SONDERHEFT

Bauhaus
WEIMAR

5. JAHRGANG
NOVEMBER 1924
HEFTPREIS 0.50 G.-M.
356

Title page *of the November 1924 issue of the magazine* Junge Menschen, *dedicated to the Bauhaus. Copy in the Bauhaus-Archiv, Darmstadt. By Joost Schmidt. Schmidt did not restrict himself to sans serif typefaces but the strict horizontal/vertical plan and the use of rules carry out the Bauhaus typographic sense of graphic organization.*

influenced the grid system that was to be formally developed in Switzerland. Everyone he came into contact with changed their point of view, not because of his charisma (he was a quiet man) but because his unusual far-out work made much sense. You knew you were in the presence of an extraordinary talent. He influenced such key figures as Moholy-Nagy, Kurt Schwitters, Herbert Bayer, Theo van Doesburg, and Jan Tschichold. If he was the great innovator, the Bauhaus was the great proving ground for a new typography and Jan Tschichold became the Johnny Appleseed of typography who carried the seeds planted in Weimar, Dessau, and Berlin, far and wide.

El Lissitzky believed that typographics should do for a reader what tone of voice does for a listener. The free way he positioned and treated typographic elements would be more easily executed today with film or digital typography but he did not let the constraints of metal typography limit his typographic expressiveness.

Van Doesburg, on the other hand, although like El Lissitzky not on the Bauhaus faculty, divided his time between Weimar and Berlin. Students would visit with him outside of the school and thus absorb directly much of his emphasis on clarity and discipline in style in typographics as well as in architecture.

Van Doesburg had wanted to be on the Bauhaus faculty but Walter Gropius felt he was too style oriented, geometrically. Nevertheless van Doesburg's influence was profound, even more in the area of design philosophy than in actual design.

Summarizing his influence at the Bauhaus, van Doesburg wrote in 1921, "In Weimar, I have radically turned everything upside down. This is the famous Academy with the most modern teachers! Every evening I have spoken to the students and have scattered the poison of the new spirit. De Stijl will soon reappear in a more radical form. I have mountains of strength and I now know that our ideas will triumph over everything and everybody."

TYPOGRAPHIC COMMUNICATIONS TODAY

Chapter IV: The Focal Point – The Bauhaus

"Typography today would not be the same had there been no Bauhaus."

The End and The Beginning

The Bauhaus. Born in Weimar, April 11, 1919. Died in Berlin, April 11, 1933, when Nazi storm troopers and police searched it, unsuccessfully, for "illegal propaganda materials." Nevertheless they seized 15 students and nailed the doors shut. So the brief chronology reads like this: Weimar 1919-1925; Dessau 1925-1932; Berlin 1932-1933. Local rightist politicians in Weimar had refused to renew the school's subsidies in 1925. In 1932 the Nazis took control of the Dessau town council and moved the Bauhaus to Berlin where it existed briefly as a non-subsidized private enterprise.

At Dessau the Bauhaus Corporation was formed to handle the sale of workshop prototypes to industry. In 1926 the *Bauhaus Journal* was started. It was an early example of type/photo integration. Along with the Bauhaus Books it spread Bauhaus ideas about art theory, architecture and design. It was in Dessau that several former students joined the faculty, including Josef Albers, Herbert Bayer, Marcel Breuer, and Joost Schmidt.

From the viewpoint of typographic design the Dessau period was most crucial to the development of a functional yet vigorous typography. The nailing of the school's doors in 1933 marked not so much the school's death but its birth as an international force. The evolution and spread of this force was largely the result of three developments which will be described later in this story: (1) the emergence of Jan Tschichold as an apostle of Bauhaus typography; (2) the fine tuning of functional typography by a group of Swiss typographic designers, and (3) the emigration from Germany to the United States of many key Bauhaus figures.

Preliminary study *for Bayer-type, 1930/32 (top) and an experimental test drawing for it. Herbert Bayer.*

The Impact, the Meaning, Then and Now

Bauhaus typography, for all the innovations and new looks Moholy-Nagy, Herbert Bayer and others brought to it, was not a style. Superficially, momentarily, it was a style. But then and in the long run its real importance lay, and continues to be, in a new way of thinking about typography as a powerful, malleable, communication tool. It brought everyone's mind and eyes to a new appreciation of functionalism, of letting a design solution grow from a communication problem into an appropriate and effective format.

Every form of printed media was affected by Bauhaus thinking. Books, magazines, posters were the first to blend a new typographic clarity with visual vitality. On the surface one sees simple, asymmetrical layouts, dynamic balance, sans serif typefaces, much use of white space, use of typographic characters, rules, squares, and the like, not for ornament but to bolster perception, to function on a psychological level, to guide the eye, to control emphasis. The specific devices introduced to achieve these ends matter less than the new focus on using typography to propel, not merely present or adorn a message. Typography today would not be the same had there been no Bauhaus. Today's most effective typographic designers might use different devices and bring different personalities to bear on a message problem; but the emphasis on using typography to literally propel a message that came into focus with the Bauhaus, endures.

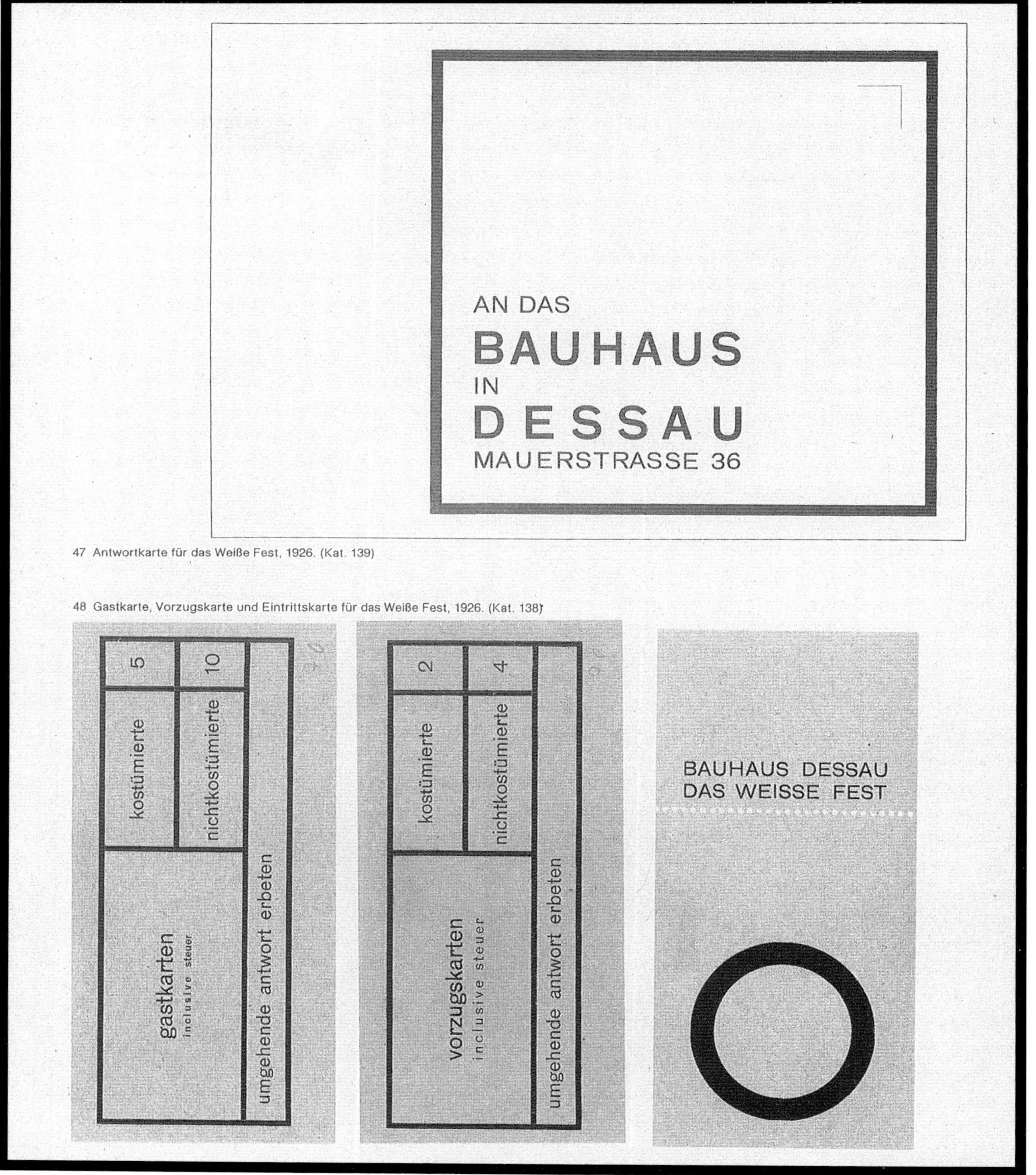

Reply card *for the White Festival, 1926 (top) and guest ticket, priority ticket and admission ticket for the event. Herbert Bayer.*

(Above left) Design *for a Bauhaus poster. 17″ × 12½,″ Herbert Bayer. 1923. Collection of Busch-Reisinger Museum, Cambridge, Massachusetts.*
(Above) Book cover *for The Bauhaus. Laszlo Moholy-Nagy. 1923.*
(Left) Title page *of a prospectus for the Bauhaus books. Laszlo Moholy-Nagy. 1924.*

TYPOGRAPHIC COMMUNICATIONS TODAY
Chapter V: Spreading the Word – Jan Tschichold

"The new typography differs from the old in that it tries for the first time to develop its form from the function of the text."

It has been said that every cause, to be successful, needs a passionate advocate. If the Bauhaus was the focal point where new ideas and new practices in painting and typographic design came together, the passionate advocate, the apostle for spreading the gospel of the new typography was Jan Tschichold. This is ironic considering that he was neither a student nor a teacher at the Bauhaus.

He was born in Leipzig, Germany, in 1902. He studied at the Leipzig Academy of Book Design where, 1926-1933, he became a lecturer. In addition to his awareness of all the art movements of the time, he understood what the constructivist's sense of the "utilitarian aspects of artistic order" meant to typographic design, and he was impressed by De Stijl's attempt "to create a style appropriate for every aspect of contemporary life" from tea cups to typography. He absorbed practical lessons from traditional designers such as Edward Johnston of England and Rudolf von Larisch of Germany, but he was greatly stimulated by the innovators of his time, including Kurt Schwitters, Theo van Doesburg, and El Lissitzky, as well as the typographics of Moholy-Nagy and Piet Zwart. With this eclectic background absorbed and blended it is no wonder he was able to write several classic books that shook up the typographic world.

His major book, *Die Neue Typographie* (The New Typography), was published in 1928. It was a challenge to "The general mediocrity of German typography in the 1920s," a result of too many badly designed typefaces and "undisciplined arrangements." In his book, Tschichold advocated, as had El Lissitzky and the Bauhaus, a complete break with traditional typography. His book was widely read and extremely influential. Of it he wrote,

"I thought the solution to be in a single type face only, for all purposes, namely that which is called in German 'Grotesk,' in English 'sans serif,' and in the United States 'Gothic.' For the arrangement, I suggested total asymmetry instead of centering the lines."

He favored sans serif typefaces, not for their novelty but for their function. Nevertheless he recognized their growing popularity was due to their fashionableness and that their "success has less to do with merit than their association with a prevailing fad, a kind of 'pop' art."

Earlier, in 1925, in *Elementare Typographie,* Tschichold, who was young (23), enthusiastic, and full of new ideas had first advocated asymmetrical typography. It had first appeared as an article in the October 1925 issue of the Leipzig magazine, *Typographische Mitteilungen.* He wrote it as "a protest against the enfeebled printing of the pre-war period." Another major work was his *Typographische Gestaltung,* published in 1935. The English version, *Asymmetric Typography,* was translated by the Scot, Ruari McLean, in 1967. He criticized the gray typography of the early 19th century, followed by successive styles of ornament, and resultant low legibility.

In his eyes the "freie richtung" (free typography) movement of the late 1890s and the jugendstijl (art nouveau) movement in the early 1900s attempted to free typography from its grayness, its disorder, its illegibility, but failed to make typographics more readable and more effective because they only replaced old restrictive rules with a clutter of their own (non-functional) rules and ornaments. The period of 1910-1925 in Germany saw a proliferation of new, more expressive, fancy, but not widely used typefaces.

This is an example (1922) of the typography that disturbed Tschichold and impelled him to eradicate it.

As Tschichold saw it, the classic, center axial typography with its classic ornaments dominated typography in the 1900-1920 period. If it was too rule-bound, much of the reaction in the 1920s was chaotic, "wilder and wilder," a period when too many rules gave way to no rules. Tschichold believed that "What was badly needed was a new typography which would not depend on ready-made layouts and would express the spirit, the life and the visual sensibility of its day." The pre-war attempt to improve typography had failed because it focused on designing new typefaces, whereas the real problem was with layout and design, how typefaces were used. He wrote:

❧ "In centered typography, pure form comes before the meaning of words."
❧ "Contrast is perhaps the most important element in all modern design."
❧ "Sans serif is the type of the present day."
❧ "The new typography is not a fashion."

The purpose of the new, or functional, typography was to make reading easy, as well as to appear easy, to read. This was considered essential to avoid loss of readership as printed matter proliferated.

As a corrolary, important parts of the message must be graphically emphasized and the rest subdued. Therefore:

"The rules of the old typography contradict the principles of fitness for purpose in design... Unsymmetrical arrangements are more flexible and better suited to the practical and aesthetic needs of today... A work of typography must be not only suitable for its purpose and easy to produce, but also beautiful."

Tschichold felt that with the freeing of typography from ornament, every element in a job takes on a new importance as does the interaction of their visual relationship. Since the harmonious relation of the elements of each job is always different, every job has an individual appearance.

Of simplicity in design, he wrote, "We aim at simplicity: we therefore require simple and clear typefaces." He found sans serif typefaces the best all-purpose typefaces for his time. Not only were the new sans serifs simple in design then, some were full family designs with four roman weights and corresponding italics, whereas many traditional faces were not that complete. This encouraged designing within one type family and mixing of light and bold typefaces of the same family; thus making possible the contrast that Tschichold felt was crucial to effective typographic design.

He also opposed letterspacing of lowercase copy, whether to justify lines or for emphasis. He felt that letterspacing of text matter made for irregular white spots, broke up the color of a type block uncontrollably, was less pleasing and less legible. For emphasis he turned to medium or bold weights or italics. He felt words should rarely be set in all caps. Of course much of this thinking dictated the use of ragged-right typography.

Tschichold's writings, teaching, and his own typographic designs spread El Lissitzky's constructivist typography and the typographic thinking of the Bauhaus through Western Europe and eventually across the Atlantic to the United States and Canada. Years later, commenting on Tschichold's impact, Herbert Spencer wrote, "Asymmetry and contrast provide the basis of modern typography."

Tschichold was the voice and the conscience of the new typography and his own consummate, refined typography did as much to impress the combined vitality and order of the new typography as did his teaching and writing. His more than 50 books include some that have been published in five languages.

Comparing the new typography with the old he wrote:

"The essence of the new typography is clarity. This puts it in conscious contrast to the old typography which aimed for 'beauty' but did not have the ultimate degree of clarity demanded today.

"However, not only the preconceived form idea of an axial order but also all others – such as the pseudo-constructive idea – are contrary to the essence of the new typography. Each typography which is based on a preconceived form idea — no matter of what kind — is wrong.

"The new typography differs from the old in that it tries for the first time to develop its form from the function of the text. When looking at the text from such a point of view we find in most cases a different rhythm than the dual symmetry used up to now: the rhythm of asymmetry. Asymmetry is the rhythmical expression of functional design. Thus the predominance of asymmetry in the new typography."

A Typeface Designer

Tschichold was also a typeface designer, and in this respect is best known for his design of the Sabon family. It was the first typeface family designed specifically for several different methods of setting type. It was jointly developed (1964–1967) by Linotype, Monotype, and Stempel, in response to a common need of German master printers for a type face to be made in identical form for mechanical composition by linecasting and single-type methods, and for hand composition in foundry type. Tschichold designed Sabon years after discovering the new typography described above. When Sabon was designed he was defending symmetrical typography and classical typefaces.

The sources for the design are to be found on a specimen sheet of the Frankfurt typefounder, Konrad Berner, who married the widow of another typefounder, Jacques Sabon – hence the name of the face. The roman is based on a typeface engraved by Garamond and the italic on a Granjon typeface, but Tschichold introduced many refinements to make these models suitable for the typographic needs of his day and for the varying mechanical requirements of the three manufacturing companies.

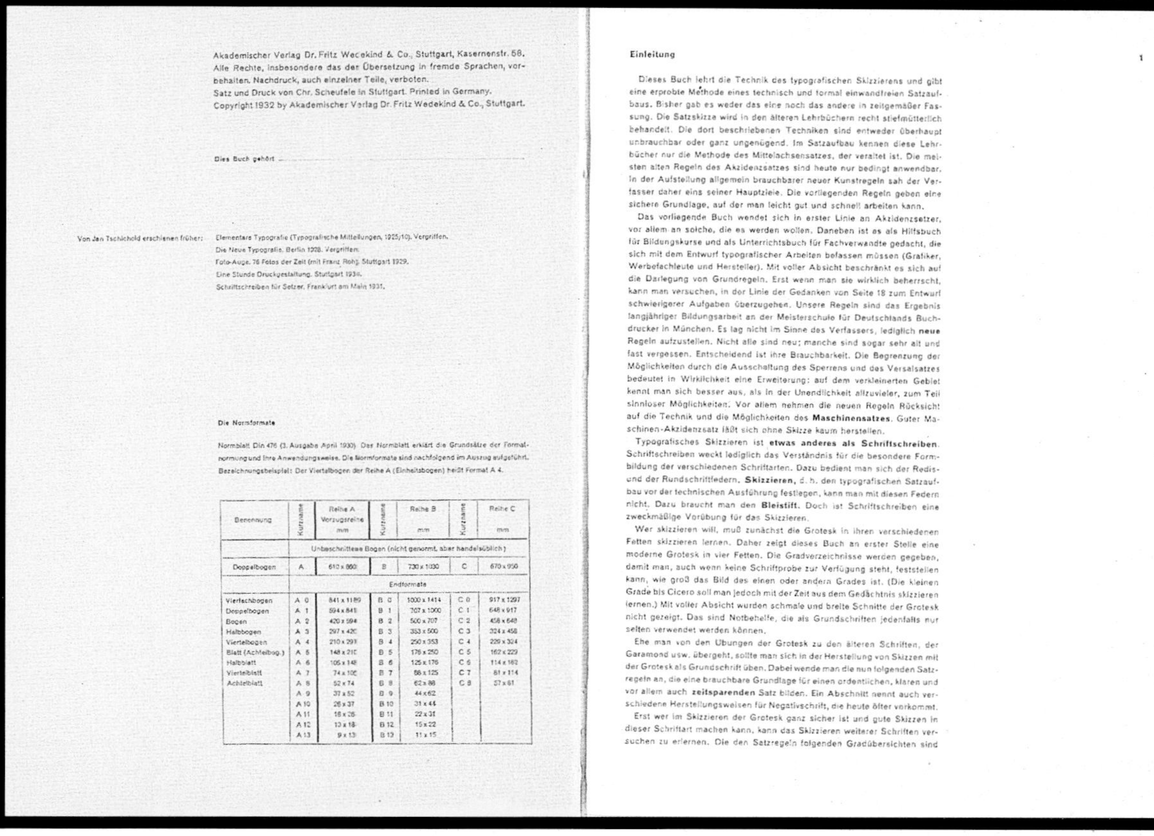

Akademischer Verlag Dr. Fritz Wedekind & Co., Stuttgart, Kasernenstr. 58.
Alle Rechte, insbesondere das der Übersetzung in fremde Sprachen, vorbehalten. Nachdruck, auch einzelner Teile, verboten.
Satz und Druck von Chr. Scheufele in Stuttgart. Printed in Germany.
Copyright 1932 by Akademischer Verlag Dr. Fritz Wedekind & Co., Stuttgart.

Dies Buch gehört ______

Von Jan Tschichold erschienen früher:
Elementare Typografie (Typografische Mitteilungen, 1925/10). Vergriffen.
Die Neue Typografie. Berlin 1928. Vergriffen.
Foto-Auge. 76 Fotos der Zeit (mit Franz Roh). Stuttgart 1929.
Eine Stunde Druckgestaltung. Stuttgart 1930.
Schriftschreiben für Setzer. Frankfurt am Main 1931.

Die Normformate

Normblatt Din 476 (3. Ausgabe April 1930). Das Normblatt erklärt die Grundsätze der Formatnormung und ihre Anwendungsweise. Die Normformate sind nachfolgend im Auszug aufgeführt.
Bezeichnungsbeispiel: Der Viertelbogen der Reihe A (Einheitsbogen) heißt Format A 4.

Benennung	Kurzname	Reihe A Vorzugsreihe mm	Kurzname	Reihe B mm	Kurzname	Reihe C mm
	Unbeschnittene Bogen (nicht genormt, aber handelsüblich)					
Doppelbogen	A	610 x 860	B	730 x 1030	C	670 x 950
	Endformate					
Vierfachbogen	A 0	841 x 1189	B 0	1000 x 1414	C 0	917 x 1297
Doppelbogen	A 1	594 x 841	B 1	707 x 1000	C 1	648 x 917
Bogen	A 2	420 x 594	B 2	500 x 707	C 2	458 x 648
Halbbogen	A 3	297 x 420	B 3	353 x 500	C 3	324 x 458
Viertelbogen	A 4	210 x 297	B 4	250 x 353	C 4	229 x 324
Blatt (Achtelbog.)	A 5	148 x 210	B 5	176 x 250	C 5	162 x 229
Halbblatt	A 6	105 x 148	B 6	125 x 176	C 6	114 x 162
Viertelblatt	A 7	74 x 105	B 7	88 x 125	C 7	81 x 114
Achtelblatt	A 8	52 x 74	B 8	62 x 88	C 8	57 x 81
	A 9	37 x 52	B 9	44 x 62		
	A 10	26 x 37	B 10	31 x 44		
	A 11	18 x 26	B 11	22 x 31		
	A 12	13 x 18	B 12	15 x 22		
	A 13	9 x 13	B 13	11 x 15		

Einleitung

1

Dieses Buch lehrt die Technik des typografischen Skizzierens und gibt eine erprobte Methode eines technisch und formal einwandfreien Satzaufbaus. Bisher gab es weder das eine noch das andere in zeitgemäßer Fassung. Die Satzskizze wird in den älteren Lehrbüchern recht stiefmütterlich behandelt. Die dort beschriebenen Techniken sind entweder überhaupt unbrauchbar oder ganz ungenügend. Im Satzaufbau kennen diese Lehrbücher nur die Methode des Mittelachsensatzes, der veraltet ist. Die meisten alten Regeln des Akzidenzsatzes sind heute nur bedingt anwendbar. In der Aufstellung allgemein brauchbarer neuer Kunstregeln sah der Verfasser daher eins seiner Hauptziele. Die vorliegenden Regeln geben eine sichere Grundlage, auf der man leicht gut und schnell arbeiten kann.

Das vorliegende Buch wendet sich in erster Linie an Akzidenzsetzer, vor allem an solche, die es werden wollen. Daneben ist es als Hilfsbuch für Bildungskurse und als Unterrichtsbuch für Fachverwandte gedacht, die sich mit dem Entwurf typografischer Arbeiten befassen müssen (Grafiker, Werbefachleute und Hersteller). Mit voller Absicht beschränkt es sich auf die Darlegung von Grundregeln. Erst wenn man sie wirklich beherrscht, kann man versuchen, in der Linie der Gedanken von Seite 18 zum Entwurf schwierigerer Aufgaben überzugehen. Unsere Regeln sind das Ergebnis langjähriger Bildungsarbeit an der Meisterschule für Deutschlands Buchdrucker in München. Es lag nicht im Sinne des Verfassers, lediglich **neue** Regeln aufzustellen. Nicht alle sind neu; manche sind sogar sehr alt und fast vergessen. Entscheidend ist ihre Brauchbarkeit. Die Begrenzung der Möglichkeiten durch die Ausschaltung des Sperrens und des Versalsatzes bedeutet in Wirklichkeit eine Erweiterung: auf dem verkleinerten Gebiet kennt man sich besser aus, als in der Unendlichkeit allzuvieler, zum Teil sinnloser Möglichkeiten. Vor allem nehmen die neuen Regeln Rücksicht auf die Technik und die Möglichkeiten des **Maschinensatzes**. Guter Maschinen-Akzidenzsatz läßt sich ohne Skizze kaum herstellen.

Typografisches Skizzieren ist **etwas anderes als Schriftschreiben**. Schriftschreiben weckt lediglich das Verständnis für die besondere Formbildung der verschiedenen Schriftarten. Dazu bedient man sich der Redis- und der Rundschriftfedern. **Skizzieren,** d. h. den typografischen Satzaufbau vor der technischen Ausführung festlegen, kann man mit diesen Federn nicht. Dazu braucht man den **Bleistift.** Doch ist Schriftschreiben eine zweckmäßige Vorübung für das Skizzieren.

Wer skizzieren will, muß zunächst die Grotesk in ihren verschiedenen Fetten skizzieren lernen. Daher zeigt dieses Buch an erster Stelle eine moderne Grotesk in vier Fetten. Die Gradverzeichnisse werden gegeben, damit man, auch wenn keine Schriftprobe zur Verfügung steht, feststellen kann, wie groß das Bild des einen oder andern Grades ist. (Die kleinen Grade bis Cicero soll man jedoch mit der Zeit aus dem Gedächtnis skizzieren lernen.) Mit voller Absicht wurden schmale und breite Schnitte der Grotesk nicht gezeigt. Das sind Notbehelfe, die als Grundschriften jedenfalls nur selten verwendet werden können.

Ehe man von den Übungen der Grotesk zu den älteren Schriften, der Garamond usw. übergeht, sollte man sich in der Herstellung von Skizzen mit der Grotesk als Grundschrift üben. Dabei wende man die nun folgenden Satzregeln an, die eine brauchbare Grundlage für einen ordentlichen, klaren und vor allem auch **zeitsparenden** Satz bilden. Ein Abschnitt nennt auch verschiedene Herstellungsweisen für Negativschrift, die heute öfter vorkommt.

Erst wer im Skizzieren der Grotesk ganz sicher ist und gute Skizzen in dieser Schriftart machen kann, kann das Skizzieren weiterer Schriften versuchen zu erlernen. Die den Satzregeln folgenden Gradübersichten sind

The inner cover *and the facing page of a small textbook by Jan Tschichold.*

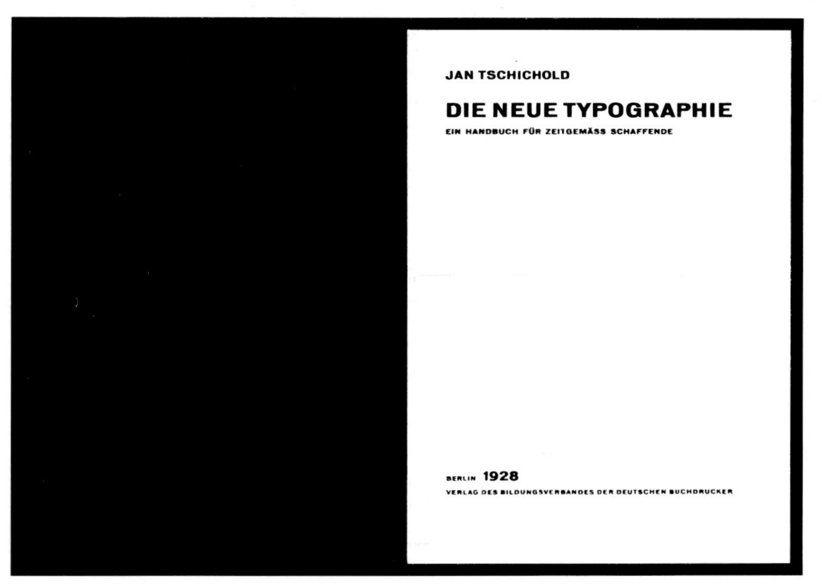

JAN TSCHICHOLD

DIE NEUE TYPOGRAPHIE

EIN HANDBUCH FÜR ZEITGEMÄSS SCHAFFENDE

BERLIN 1928

VERLAG DES BILDUNGSVERBANDES DER DEUTSCHEN BUCHDRUCKER

Title spread *for* Die Neue Typographie. *Berlin, 1928.*

TYPOGRAPHIC COMMUNICATIONS TODAY

Chapter V: Spreading the Word – Jan Tschichold

"The aim of typography must not be expression, least of all self-expression, but perfect communication."

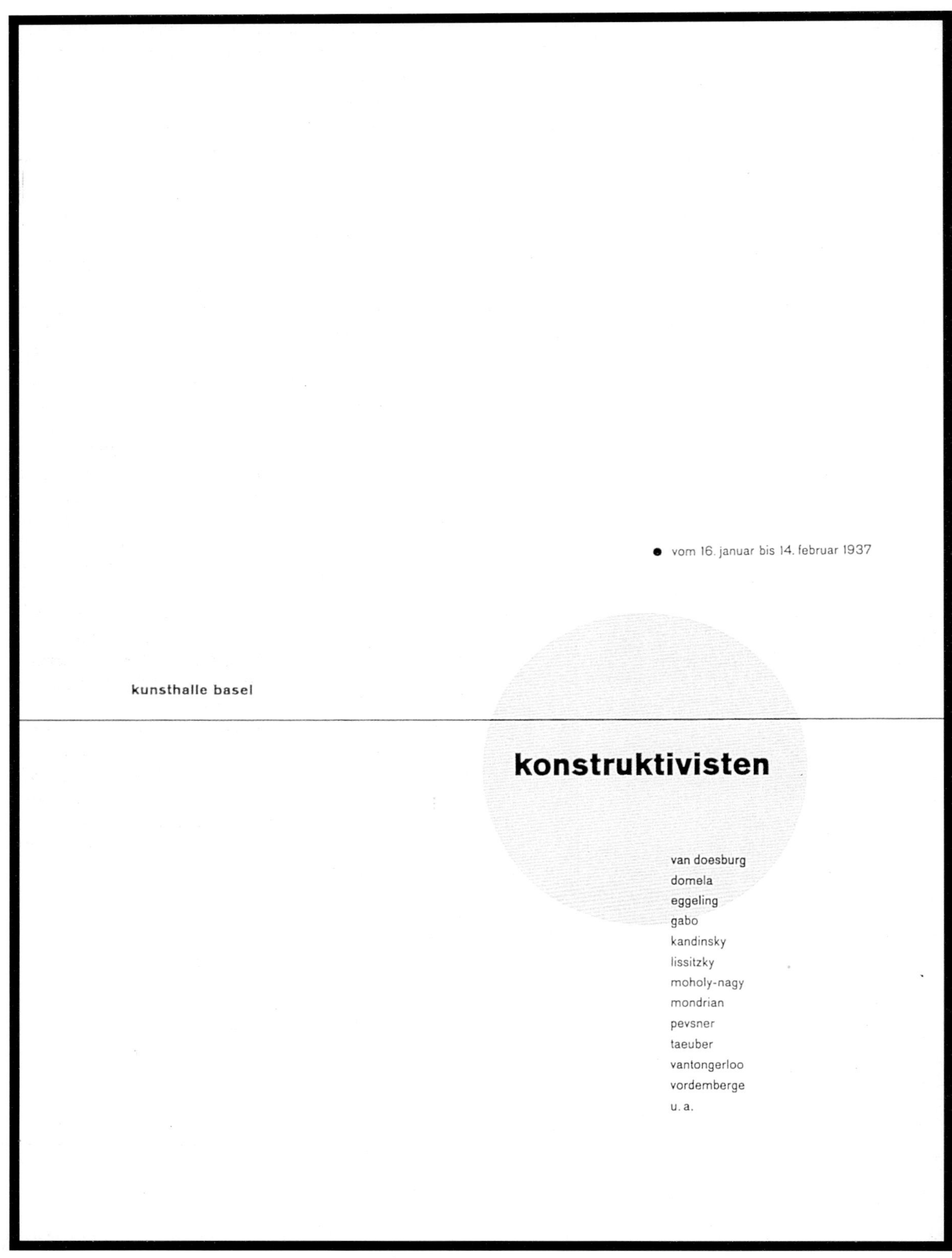

vom 16. januar bis 14. februar 1937
kunsthalle basel
konstruktivisten
van doesburg
domela
eggeling
gabo
kandinsky
lissitzky
moholy-nagy
mondrian
pevsner
taeuber
vantongerloo
vordemberge
u. a.

Poster *by Tschichold, 1937. Dynamically balanced. All lowercase. White space used generously as a design element.*

1933 — An Emigré

In 1926 Tschichold was appointed by Paul Renner (the designer of Futura) to teach typography and lettering at the Munich Meisterschule für Deutschlands Buchdrucker. In 1933 the Nazi government accused him of "kulturbolschevismus" and of creating un-German typography. He promptly moved to Basel, then as now a superb center for studying and teaching typographic design. It was there, in 1935, that *Typografische Gestaltung* was published. While in Switzerland he rethought his attitudes towards typography and resumed a classical style. In 1947 he was invited to England where he redesigned Penguin books. He returned to Switzerland in 1950. Tschichold's repudiation of his advocacy of the new typography was due to political as well as graphic considerations. He felt he had been used by the Nazis, and equated the new typography with fascism. In any event, his powerful advocacy of the new typography was a tremendous force in spreading its influence and acceptance; and his later, more conservative work, shows how effective conservative typography can be when exquisitely executed. His work became symmetrical and employed roman, Egyptian (square serif), and script typefaces. Sans serif typefaces now seemed militaristic and inhuman to him and he decided that long passages set in sans serif were too difficult to read.

Der Neue Tschichold

His latter day thinking is best revealed in a letter addressed to the Typography U.S.A. seminar sponsored by the Type Directors Club in New York City in 1959, in which he reviews the considerations that led to his advocacy of a new typography and to his later form reversal.

"In Switzerland, a few years ago, there was a rumor ...about the possibilities of a 'Swiss' typography. I do not believe in the value of any 'national' typography. The attempt to create a 'national' typography is certainly, to my mind, a fallacy. Still, even when such an approach is expressly avoided, it is in practice often the casual result of work. In general, we should consider the typography of the western world as one and the same thing. True, we can no more overlook the English approach than the American one, and probably nobody will be doubtful that there is a certain Swiss approach of today. The latter, for which I do not feel responsible, is the exemplar of a most inflexible typography which makes no distinction between the advertising of an artistic performance or of a screw catalog. Nor does this typography allow for the human desire for variety. It has an entirely militaristic attitude.

"What I do today is not in the line of my often-mentioned book, 'Die Neue Typographie,' since I am the most severe critic of the young Tschichold of 1925-28. A Chinese proverb says, 'In haste there is error.' So many things in that primer are erroneous, because my experience was too small.

ABCDEFGHIJKLMNOPQRSTUVWXYZ
abcdefghijklmnopqrstuvwxyz
1234567890
ABCDEFGHIJKLMNOPQRSTUVWXYZ
abcdefghijklmnopqrstuvwxyz
1234567890
SABON
ABCDEFGHIJKLMNOPQRSTUVWXYZ
abcdefghijklmnopqrstuvwxyz
1234567890
SABON BOLD

Sabon *was designed late in Tschichold's career (he died in 1972) after he had abandoned his advocacy of sans serif typefaces. Earlier, he had designed a single-alphabet (all lowercase) typeface, including a phonetic version. In 1932 his design of Saskia was released. It featured a large x-height and was a thick and thin sans serif italic.*

"In Germany in 1925 (and the present situation there is not too different from what it was in that period), far too many typefaces were used and, with a few exceptions, only bad ones. (I still remember the deep satisfaction of the moment when I saw, by chance, at the tender age of seventeen, English magazine pages set up in Caslon.)

"Those German typefaces appeared in undisciplined arrangements, not at all 'traditional' in the present-day meaning of this word. Those unacquainted with it can hardly imagine the mediocrity of German typography of that period. As a letterer, I felt insulted, day after day, by the ugly appearance of the newspapers, magazines, and the many sorts of advertisements. To cure these weaknesses I suggested two remedies, one for the type and one for the arrangement.

"In order to reduce the number of typefaces... I thought the solution to be in a single typeface only, for all purposes, namely that which is called in German 'Grotesk,' in English 'sans serif,' and in the United States 'Gothic.' For the arrangement, I suggested total asymmetry instead of centering the lines.

"Now I have to reveal what I think is wrong with these juvenile ideas and with the situation of 1924. It was not the great number of typefaces in fashion then, but the poor quality of practically all these typefaces, and it was not the general unsuitability of a centered order but the lack of the compositor's skill in such arrangements. Had I been more experienced then than could be expected at the age of 23, and had I been instructed in arranging type (of which I never heard lectures in my youth or later, because there weren't any available), then perhaps I should have thought over my immature ideas more carefully.

"So far, in this haste there was certainly error. Yet, very often, error is creative. My errors were more fertile than I ever imagined. Certainly, the typography of the time shortly before 1925 was, in general, ailing, and in urgent need of a doctor. The treatment was heroic but healthy. Yet one cannot live by abstinence and pharmaceutics. The weakness of the period before 1925 was the lack of at least one good type. It would have been better to look out for a good type or, better, for a greater number of useful typefaces, than to reduce their number to a single typeface of doubtful utility. In the light of my present knowledge, it was a juvenile opinion to consider the sans serif as the most suitable or even the most contemporary typeface. A typeface has first to be legible, nay, readable, and a sans serif is certainly not the most legible typeface when set in quantity, let alone readable. Nor does a centered arrangement of too many different and even ugly letters prove the inappropriateness of line centering in general, but rather is evidence of lack of skill and artistic intelligence.

"A few years after 'Die Neue Typographie,' Hitler came. I was accused of creating 'un-German' typography and art, and so I preferred to leave Germany. Since 1933 I have lived in Basle, Switzerland. In the very first years I tried to develop what I had called 'Die Neue Typographie.' In 1935 I wrote another textbook, 'Typographische Gestaltung,' which is much more prudent than 'Die Neue Typographie' and is still a useful book! In time, typographical things, in my eyes, took on a very different aspect, and to my astonishment I detected most shocking parallels between the teachings of 'Die Neue Typographie' and National Socialism and fascism. Obvious similarities consist in the ruthless restriction of typefaces, a parallel to Goebbels' infamous 'gleichschaltung' (political alignment), and the more or less militaristic arrangement of lines. Because I did not want to be guilty of spreading the very ideas which had compelled me to leave Germany, I thought over again what a typographer should do. Which typefaces are good and what arrangement is the most practicable? By guiding the compositors of a large Basle printing office, I learned a lot about practicability. Good typography has to be perfectly legible and, as such, the result of intelligent planning. The classical typefaces such as Garamond, Janson, Baskerville and Bell are undoubtedly the most legible. Sans serif is good for certain cases of emphasis, but is used to the point of abuse. The occasions for using sans serif are as rare as those for wearing obtrusive decorations...

"Typography should be allowed individuality; this is to appear as different as the people around us, just as there are girls and men, fat and thin, wise and stupid, serious and gay, easily-pleased and fussy.

"The aim of typography must not be expression, least of all self-expression, but perfect communication achieved by skill. Taking over working principles from previous times or other typographers is not wrong but sensible. Typography is a servant and nothing more. The servant typography ought to be the most perfect servant..."

Tschichold notwithstanding, there are those today who preach and practice that at times communication effectiveness can be enhanced by properly harnessed and directed graphic expressiveness.

Paul Rand, writing about Tschichold in *Print*, January 1969, said,

"Typography, no matter how it is looked at, remains a difficult, subtle, and exacting art. And even though a certain degree of technical skill is relatively common, typographic mastery is the province of the perceptive and the prerogative of the few.

"For his vision,
his sensitivity
and his dedication,
for being a pioneer typographer,
a master of his craft
and a typographic historian,
for teaching us awareness of the
new and respect for the old,
for giving us Saskia and Sabon,
for pointing out those subtleties
and refinements without which
we would be the poorer,
for his integrity, his restraint,
and for his quality,
I salute Jan Tschichold."

TYPOGRAPHIC COMMUNICATIONS TODAY

Chapter VI: Fine Tuning – Clarity and Grid Systems

"A printed work which cannot be read becomes a product without a purpose."

THE striving for order and organization in communication graphics that was initiated by El Lissitzky, further developed by van Doesburg, Moholy-Nagy, and Bayer, and broadcast throughout Western Europe, and eventually the United States and Canada by Jan Tschichold, reached its zenith in the 1930s in Switzerland. There, in schools in Zürich and Basel, what had been an emphasis on functionalism in communication typography became an overriding concern, with the emphasis on communication clarity and systematically orderly typography. Typographic functionalism of the 1920s was fine-tuned to become typographic clarity in the 1930s. Just as painting had run the gamut from Constable to Kandinsky, so typographics, an art for aiding communication, ran a reverse gamut from the explosiveness of futurism to the orderliness of the grid systems.

What is a Grid?

A grid system as such is a very old method. One can trace its roots to the classical architecture of Japanese Zen-Buddhism. In our century, major contributors to its development were made by the architect, Le Corbusier with his "Modular" system. It was first introduced into typography circa 1930. Major contributors to the typographic grid system include Herbert Bayer, Max Bill and Richard Paul Lohse. Today's grid is a development of the well-known column-typography of newspapers. Whereas the columns produce a vertically oriented typographic structure, the grid adds to it a horizontally oriented structure, a kind of coordinate structure. It produces modules, but not necessarily square ones. A major step in giving the grid the potential to add vitality and originality to clarity and order in typographic communication was Karl Gerstner's development of the "mobile grid," a less rigid, less stereotyped plan facilitating designer creativity without sacrificing control of order and clarity.

The grid system is a very basic and timeless useful system (or method). It can be applied for what typographic task ever. But actually it makes sense above all for complex tasks like newspapers, catalogues, magazines, illustrated books and so on.

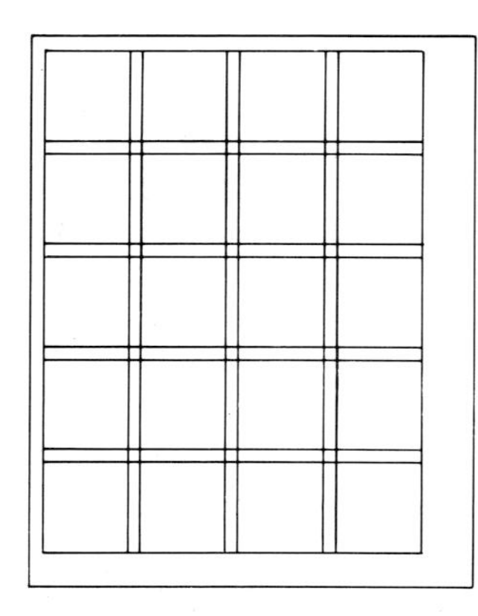

***A grid** with 20 grid fields. The examples show only six (1–6) of many typography solutions possible with such a grid. Empty spaces, as between title and text are equal to one line of type to assure that columns align with each other. Lines can be set centered, flush left and right, or ragged. **The same grid** is here applied to text/graphics pages (at right). Here, too, only a few of the possible variations are shown. Note how the position of all the elements is controlled by the grid.*

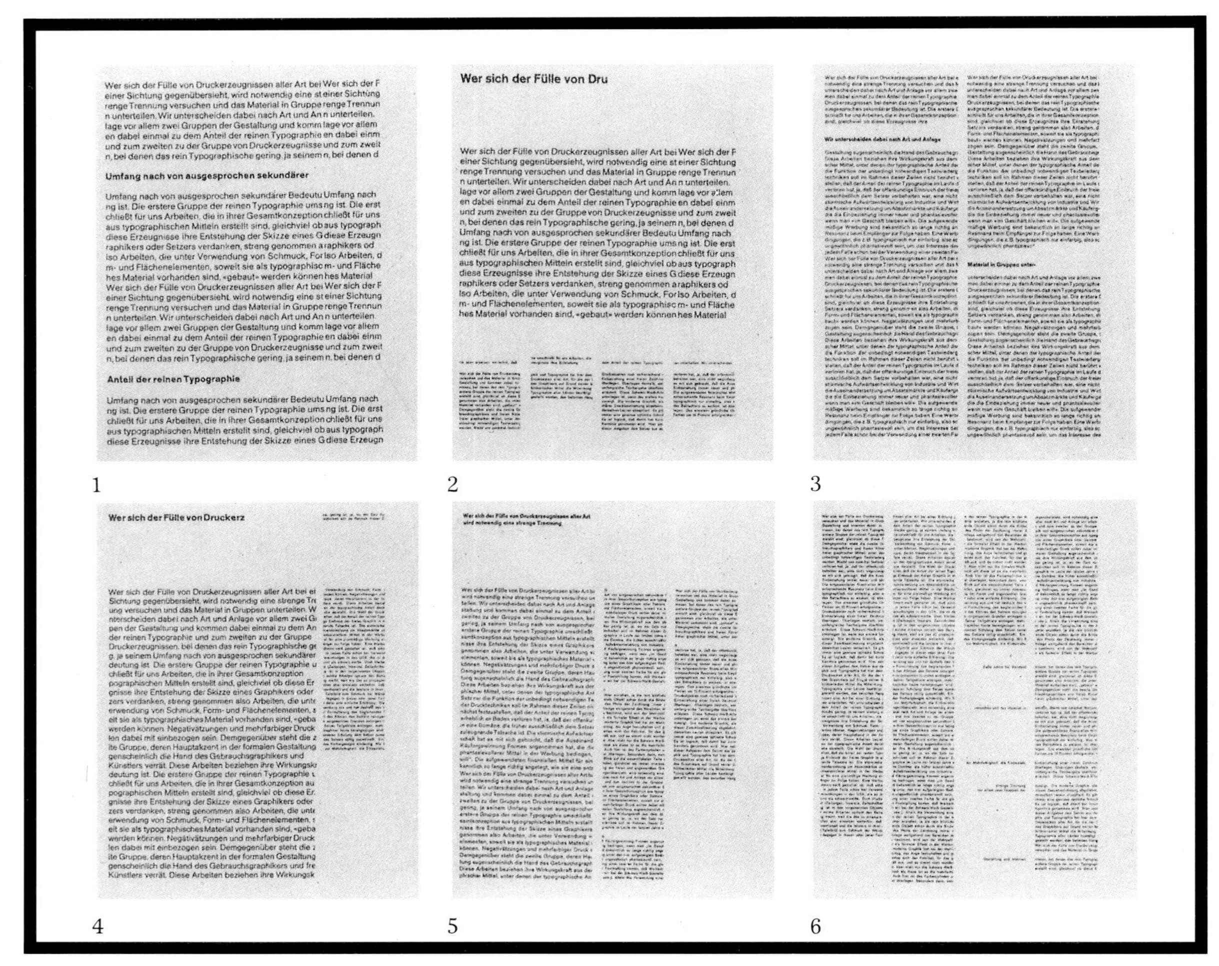

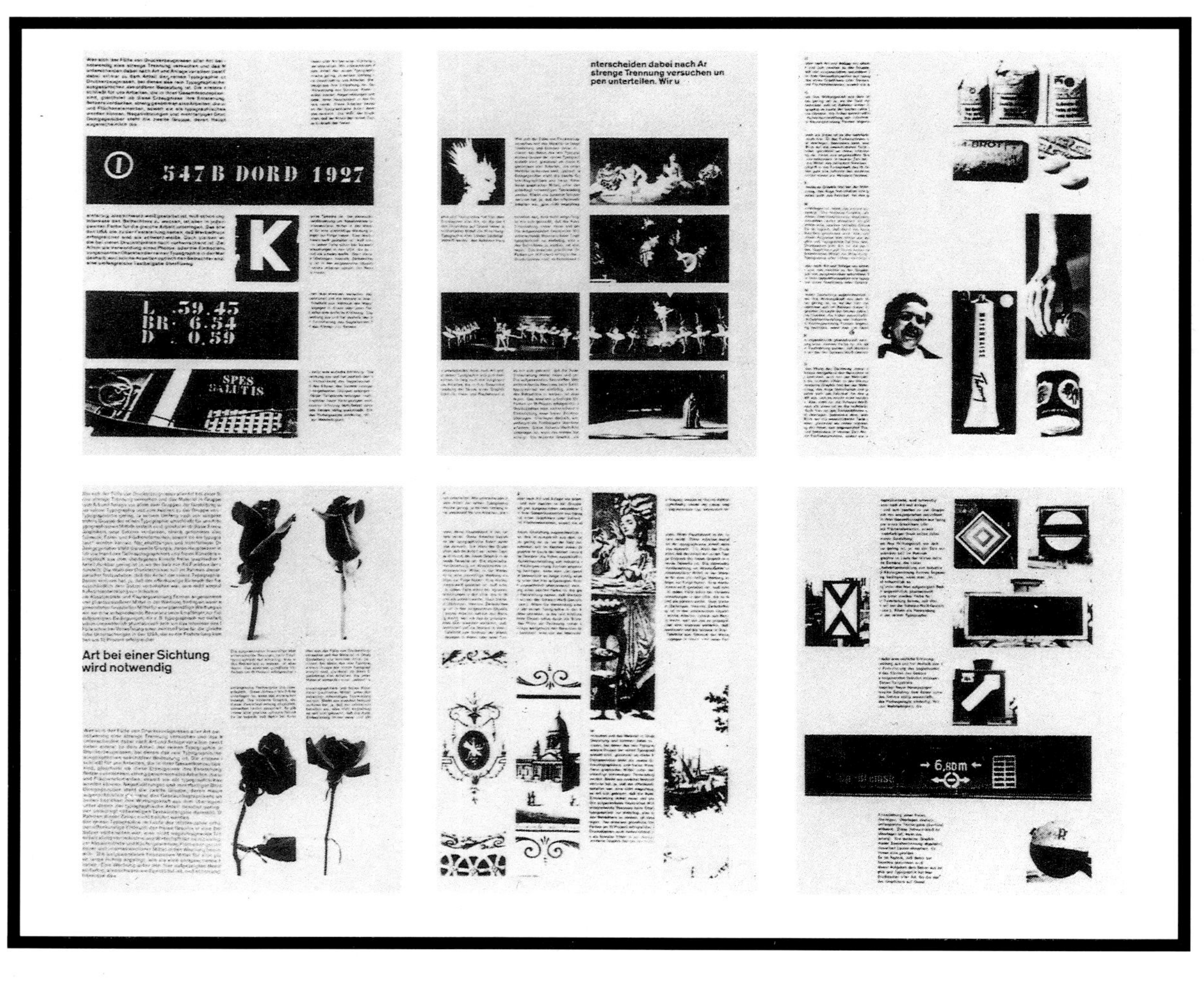

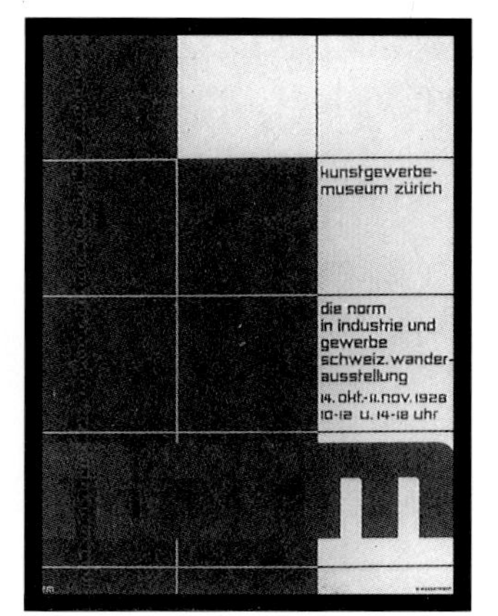

***Two posters** by Theo Ballmer show how he used a grid to organize the typographic elements. The orderliness aimed to enhance message impact and clarity. Whereas De Stijl artists used asymmetrical rectangles for variety in their paintings, Ballmer worked with squares. His aim was absolute control, and his method was mathematically precise. Some critics feel that Ballmer did not use the grid to its best advantage.*

***Three pieces** by Max Bill. Note the alignment of letters down the center axis of the book jacket. Irregular branching out left and right achieves a dynamic balance. The type is Akzidenz Grotesk, a forerunner of many later popular typefaces and a type widely used by Swiss designers in the 1940s and 1950s. The two posters were created in 1945 and 1951 and are in the Library of Congress, Washington, D.C., Poster Collection.*

Albert Einstein said of the module: "It is a scale of proportions that makes the bad difficult and the good easy." The typographic and pictorial elements for a given area are lined up with the grid lines (which are invisible on the finished job although they serve to position and align the elements of the job).

A casual grid may identify only margins, column measures, and major spaces within a design. There are stock grids one can apply to many jobs. Many designers custom create a grid to fit the needs of a specific job. Others employ an implied grid, one in which no rules are actually drawn on the layout surface but which, consciously or subconsciously, exist in the designer's mind. And, of course, many designers use no grid at all. A grid can be applied to any graphic design problem but is most useful in multi-page work such as newspapers, magazines, books, annual reports, and catalogs.

The Early Days of the Grid

No one could have known, in 1918, when Ernst Keller, at the age of 27, started teaching advertising layout at the Kunstgewerbeschule (School of Applied Art) in Zürich, what a profound effect he would have. His emphasis on professionalism and adherence to high standards showed in his own work and that of his students. He developed a course in design and typography and taught it until 1956. He did not advocate any style. He believed the solution to a design problem derived from an understanding of the message and its intent. He was also a great poster designer. The typographic genius of the Zurich school was Alfred Willimann.

The De Stijl way of dividing space with horizontal and vertical lines influenced graphic designers Theo Ballmer and Max Bill. Ballmer studied under Ernst Keller and in 1929/30 in the Bauhaus.

Max Bill studied at the Bauhaus. There he studied under Gropius, Moholy-Nagy, Josef Albers, and Kandinsky among others. He was to become distinguished as both an architect and a typographic designer. The Bauhaus' stress on functionalism, the De Stijl manner of organizing space, and Theo van Doesburg's *Manifesto of Art Concret* (1930), which advocated a universal art of absolute clarity, made great sense to him and were to come together in his work and his teaching. He knew that the planes and colors of a Mondrian or van Doesburg painting had no meaning beyond themselves but that the opposite was true in communication design. He realized that the graphic elements had to be used to organize and propel ideas and information. He executed his work with precision. His text type could be ragged-right. He favored sans serif typefaces and line space for paragraphs rather than indenting paragraphs. In 1949 he wrote, "I am of the opinion that it is possible to develop an art largely on the basis of mathematical thinking." Despite this seemingly rigid concept Bill's work was graphically alive. He was not afraid of diagonals or vertical lines of type but used such devices with great purpose and care.

In 1950 Max Bill brought his De Stijl, Bauhaus, Zürich grid background to the Hochschule für Gestaltung, in Ulm, where he helped develop the school's buildings and curriculum. There, until 1968, he focused on design problems and featured a scientific and methodological approach to developing a solution.

"...A Product Without a Purpose"

"Typography has one plain duty before it and that is to convey information in writing. No argument or consideration can absolve typography from this duty. A printed work which cannot be read becomes a product without a purpose." Emil Ruder

Emil Ruder (1914–1970), teacher and typographer, apprenticed as a compositor at the age of 15 at the Zürich School of Arts and Crafts. Thirteen years later he became a teacher of typography at the Basel school, Allegemeine Gewerbeschule.

Although he focused on the need for clarity and order in typography, Ruder felt that the typographic designer must be receptive to novelty. He advocated experimental workshops and stressed the need to produce vital work reflecting the spirit of the times while avoiding the excessively modish.

The typographer, he explained, must work with type, paper, ink, tools, machines not of his own making, with ready made typefaces. A typographic design is not merely aesthetic and the forms that can be created are largely determined by technical factors. Nevertheless the typographer has an almost infinite number of ways of arranging type.

Ruder advocated avoidance of idiosyncrasies as far as possible. He also wrote, "There is hardly any warrant for using five different alphabets such as lower case roman and italic, small caps, and upper case roman and italics to set an ordinary text." He particularly admired the Univers typeface family for its enormous range and for its being well graded, weight to weight.

The following excerpts from his book, *Typography* not only reveal his teaching and practice in the Basel of his day but contain sound advice for all of us and for all time.

Emptiness as a Design Element

The importance of purposefully manipulating white space in developing a typographic design was stressed by Ruder. He wrote:

"The oriental philosophers hold that the essence of created form depends on empty space. Without its hollow interior a jug is merely a lump of clay, and it is only the empty space inside that makes it into a vessel. Thus we read in the eleventh aphorism of Lao-Tse:

'Thirty spokes meet the hub,
but it is the emptiness between them that makes the essence of the wheel.
'From clay pots are made,
but it is the emptiness inside them that makes the essence of the pot.
'Walls with windows and doors form the house,
but it is the emptiness between them that makes the essence of the house.
'The principle: The material contains usefulness,
the immaterial imparts essence.'

"These are considerations which can and should be transferred to typography. Unlike the Renaissance when the unprinted blank was merely a background for what was printed thereon, contemporary typographers have long recognized the empty space of the unprinted surface to be an element of design. The typographer is familiar with white as a value in design and he is familiar with the visual changes of white."

Without Rhythm There Would Be No Life

"Without rhythm there would be no life, there would be no creation at all... And in the twentieth century... artists have again become alive to the significance and power of rhythm in design.

"In typography there are many opportunities of working with rhythmic values. Take a typeface for instance. The straights and curves, verticals and horizontals, sloping elements, starts and finishes work together to produce a rhythmic pattern. There is an abundance of rhythmic values in an ordinary piece of composition: ascenders and descenders, round and pointed forms, symmetry and asymmetry. The word spaces divide the line and type matter into words of unequal size, into a rhythmic interplay of varying lengths and values of different weight. Break and blank lines also add accents of their own to the pattern of composition, and finally the graded sizes of the type are another excellent means of bringing rhythm into the typographer's work. If a simple piece of text is well composed, it will of its own accord give the work a rhythmic appeal.

"The format of the paper is another rhythmic pattern, whether it is the symmetry of the equilateral square, or the stressed rhythm of the edges and sides of the rectangle. The typographer has endless possibilities of creating rhythms by the way he disposes his composition on the page. The shape of the composition can harmonize or contrast in its rhythm with the format

Chapter VI: Fine Tuning – Clarity and Grid Systems

"Each problem calls for a grid specially suited to itself."

of the paper. In designing composition, the typographer should examine every possible means of getting away from rigid systems and dull repetition, not merely for the sake of vitalizing the form but also in the interests of legibility."

Pure Functionalism Not Enough

"Masterpieces of typography show perfect unity between word and typographical form... Form must be developed as benefits purpose... but pure functionalism is not itself enough for good form."

Ideal Line Length

"A line containing 50–60 characters is easy to read." But longer lines degenerate in a gray mass and finding the next line becomes difficult. Too narrow a line causes too much eye travel and poor word spacing. Unlike some of his contemporaries, Ruder advocated justified typography because, to him, the ragged-right slows down reading, results in a too gray mass for the text block, is contrary to what the reader has grown up with.

Some of Ruder's other concerns were:

❧ Be careful of excessive leading that creates white ribbons which distract the reader and reduce legibility.
❧ Take great care in designing such white space elements as the space between letters, words, lines, paragraphs, the elements in a layout and even the counters within the letterforms.
❧ White space can create tension, emphasis, control eye flow, as in the advertisement for Delft Cable Factory by Piet Zwart.
❧ Typographic contrasts are needed to avoid monotony. He cites the example of the Univers type family with its many degrees of contrast of color, slant, letter width, etc., as a way to achieve contrast control by working with a single type family.
❧ As concerned as he was with legibility, he advised that in advertising it is the visual impact on the public that matters and not so much the legibility. Of course this should not be interpreted as condoning illegibility.
❧ "Consistency of design can also be achieved by devising an underlying grid pattern to which all the elements must comply."

Typefaces Are Essentially Active Forms

"Paul Klee's demand, 'We do not want form but function,' is satisfied in typography. True, a few of the individual letters are static forms devoid of movement like A, H, M, O and T, but most typefaces are built up around movement, and movement from left to right: B, C, D, E, F, K, L, etc. When composed into words and lines, even the static letters are carried along in the direction of reading, first from left to right, then from right to left as the eye travels back to the start, and then from top to bottom as line is added to line. There is always a reading process involved in typography, and hence there can never be a static typography."

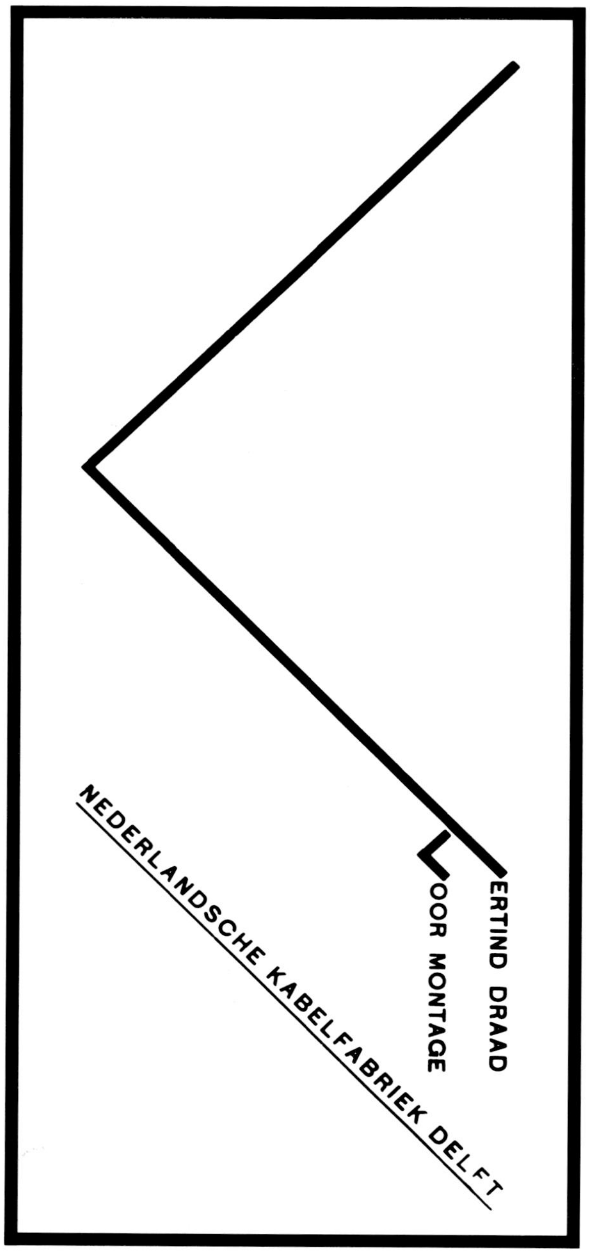

In his book, Typography, *Emil Ruder comments on form and counter-form as follows.*

"The modern artist, unlike his counterpart of the Renaissance, raises empty space to be an element of equal value in design. Instead of space flowing round the surface we have surface tension. The white surfaces are enriched with tensions and the white is activated up to the edge of the format."

"Twentieth century typography, as here in the advertisement for the Delft Cable Factory by Piet Zwart, gives the unprinted area the same importance as the printed. The dominant right angle produced a pronounced white effect as an inner counter-form."

Picture/Type Harmony

Ruder established two ways of harmonizing type with pictures: by "The closest possible format combination" and by contrast between them. "A mixture of the two should be avoided."

Typography in Advertising

Josef Müller-Brockmann, through the excellence and pervasiveness of his designs and through his several books was a major influence in spreading understanding and acceptance of the grid system and functional, clarity-focused typographic design throughout the world.

In his book, *The Graphic Designer and His Design Problems,* he sets down no-nonsense rules as follows:

"The designer must know and accept the technical possibilities of modern typography and, instead of striving for ornamental effects, he must be able to see his plan as a formal conception. This economic, time-saving and practical method of composition is consonant with our age of technical perfection and clarity and has led to the following postulates:

*"**a)** The arbitrary, fortuitous and individual composition of typographical elements is to be replaced by an objective design in accordance with typographical principles.*

*"**b)** The paramount requirement is an unadorned typographical form serving purely the needs of communication.*

"Used in this way, typography becomes functional, objective and informative. Functional in respecting the technical premises of the art, objective in the logical composition of letters to form words and of words to form sentences, in the arrangement of sentences according to their contents and, finally, in the formal organization of the contents according to its inner coherence. Typography of this kind is informative because all its groups of sentences are clearly laid out for good legibility and the message can thus be readily understood.

"Apart from considerations of principle and practice, the rules of thumb briefly stated below are of importance for typography in graphic art.

*"**a)** Never combine different type families.*

*"**b)** Never use different forms of the same family, e.g., the sans serif, in the same piece of composition.*

*"**c)** Do not use a lot of different type sizes, but make sure those used are clearly distinguishable.*

*"**d)** Try to achieve a compact effect in the type arrangement (type area).*

*"**e)** Never attempt to set a word apart in the text by spacing its letters, instead set it in bold or extra bold type or isolate it.*

*"**f)** Attempt to relate the picture and copy, i.e., the type matter should be arranged in relation to the photograph or drawing employed so that there is a link with the picture that compels attention and is visually and aesthetically satisfying. Type matter and picture become a harmonious composition.*

*"**g)** The lead between the lines should be chosen so that it leaves a space between the descender height of one line and the ascender height of the next line without, however, creating the impression that they are isolated lines. The compactness of the composition must be preserved so that the typography is easily read and remains aesthetically effective.*

*"**h)** The distance between words should be uniform; white interspaces of varying size give rise to a form of composition that is disturbing to the eye.*

*"**i)** As figures are equivalent to capitals, it may be necessary, so as not to disrupt the appearance of the composition, to set the figures a size smaller than the rest of the type, particularly when a large number of figures have to be accommodated."*

***Shown here** are a few concert posters by Müller-Brockmann for the Tonhalle Gesellschaft Zürich. They illustrate not merely his design orderliness but his ability to make each piece beautiful and exciting as well as readable. Rich colors not only give these posters eye appeal but help organize the message and the reader's eye-flow.*

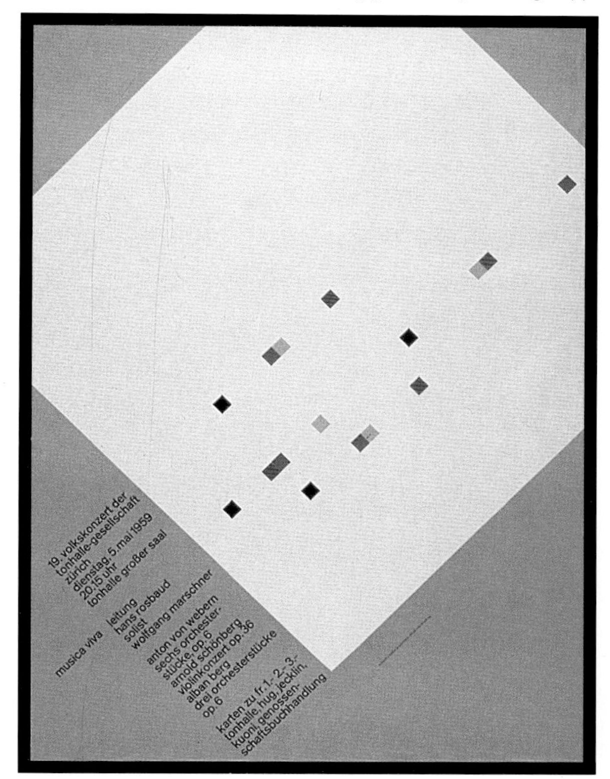

Müller-Brockmann also felt that lettering, and thus typography, were an expression of the spiritual and cultural atmosphere of the time, as are painting, architecture, sculpture, music and literature. The right kind of letter for the time (1960s) was a sans serif letter because it was essentially functional and free of the ornamental, decorative characteristics of roman letters with their varying weight strokes and decorative feet. He wrote, "Almost any typographical job can be done just as well with sans serif as with roman."

Of the grid, he wrote: *"Each problem calls for a grid suited specially to itself. It must enable the designer to arrange the captions, photographs and drawings so that they are as visually effective as their importance warrants and yet form an ordered whole."*

Besides *The Graphic Designer and His Design Problems* other major books by Müller-Brockmann are *A History of Visual Communications* and *Grid Systems.*

Typographic Communications Today is essentially an analytical look at objective (functional, formalistic, anonymous) design and the subjective (spontaneous, illustrative) approach. Josef Müller-Brockmann has been and is a leading practitioner and spokesman for objective typographic design. Designers of the subjective school often accuse the Swiss designers and their followers of being excessively rigid, cold, static, visually antiseptic, and advocates of objective design have labeled subjective designs as illegible, ineffective and graphic horrors.

This kind of talk makes little sense. A study of the best work done today, as a later chapter in this work shows, makes clear that a piece can be both well organized and graphically beautiful and vigorous. There need not be an either-or choice. Much depends on the nature of the problem and what design solution is most appropriate, as well as on the skill and personality of the designer. There is nothing inherent in a grid developed design that makes it sterile nor in a subjective illustrative design that makes it illegible or confusing. Of course, poor execution can make either approach fail.

Josef Müller-Brockmann's application of objective design has been expressed in a wide range of applications, including book jackets, books, posters, advertisements, packages, stage settings, exhibitions. He is best known, perhaps, for his poster designs.

TYPOGRAPHIC COMMUNICATIONS TODAY
Chapter VI: Fine Tuning – Clarity and Grid Systems

"Dullness is not inherent in a striving for clarity nor in the grid system."

Contrasting Elements Plus Integration
Armin Hofmann studied in Zürich with Ernst Keller and was a staff designer for studios there until 1947 when he started teaching at the Basle School of Arts and Crafts and opened his own studio. In Basel he had much contact with Emil Ruder. To their focus on typographic clarity he brought his own sense of blending vigor with order. He worked painstakingly with spatial relationships so as to bring the vitality of contrasts into a design while properly integrating all the elements into a graphic whole. He employed contrasts of scale between elements, mixed soft or active photography with static or hard-edged type elements. He also contrasted light and dark areas, curves and straights, forms and counter forms, dynamic and static elements, and colors. His dynamic harmony of the elements in a design created unity with liveliness.

***A 1916 Herman Miller ad** by Armin Hofmann illustrates his way of blending order and vitality in a typographic design. This newspaper ad captures the vigor of a poster.*

Focus on Coordinating Photography and Typography
Alfred Willimann taught the class in photography at the Zürich School of Industrial Design in the 1930s, '40s, and '50s. His concern was with photography as a communications aid. It had to be printed successfully and was nearly always combined with type and had to fit an allotted space. For Willimann the photograph was not complete until it was effectively combined with type. His intense focus on this aspect of typographics made many students, designers-to-be, particularly sensitive to the type-photo relationship.

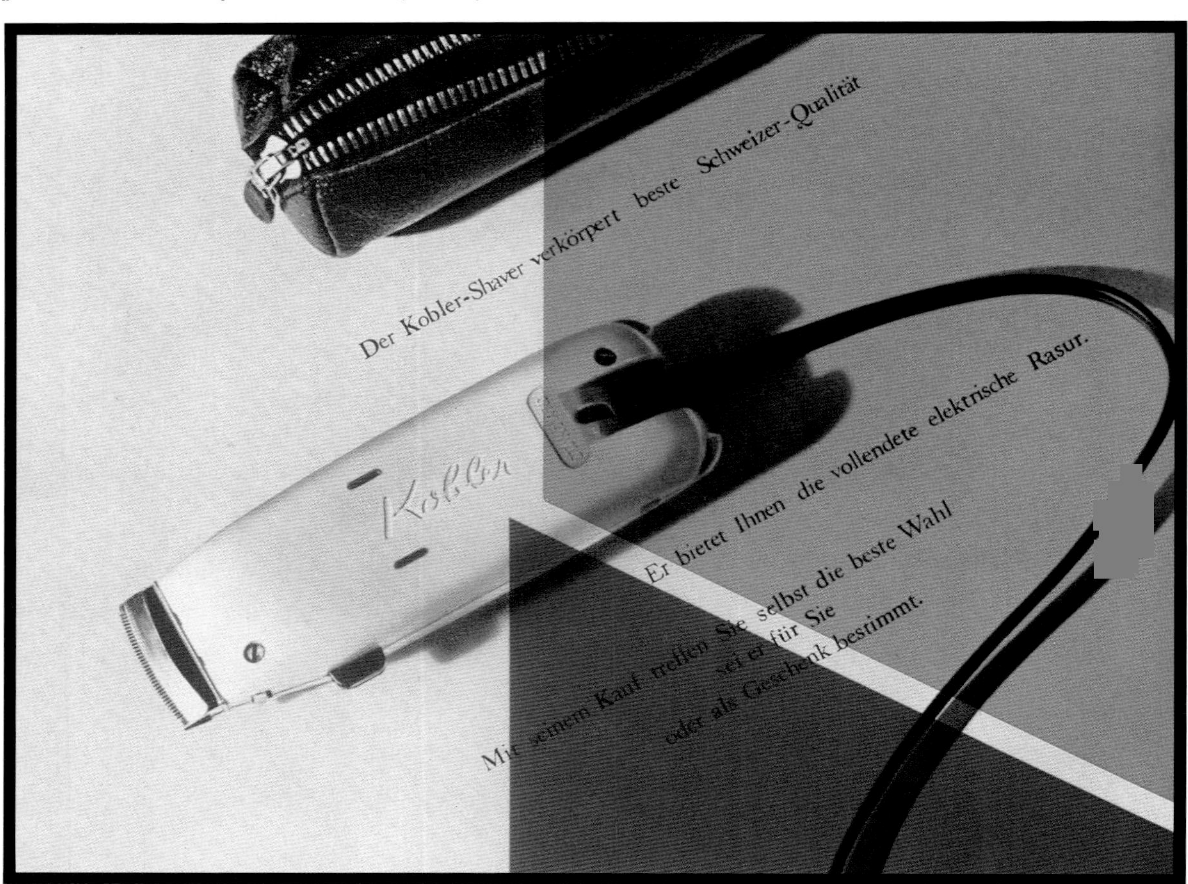

***Prospectus** for Kobler & Co., Zürich, 1953, designed by Alfred Willimann's class in photography at the Zürich School of Industrial Design. The left panel is in black, the upper part of the right panel has black copy surprinting a green background. The bottom right solid color panel is an orange-red.*

***How typography** and photography could reinforce each other was also evident in the powerful and widely circulated Swiss Tourist Office posters of the 1930s and later. These two, by Herbert Matter, throw elements out of scale with each other, employ dramatic colors and exaggerated perspective for dynamic effects. Angled type suits the active nature of the posters yet the message is clear and powerful.*

***Perhaps** the earliest example of organized yet dynamic typographics in Italy was the publication* Campo Grafico *that was introduced in 1933. This cover, (below) December 1934, was designed by Studio Boggeri.*

***The mark of Studio Boggeri** was designed by Deberny & Peignot.*

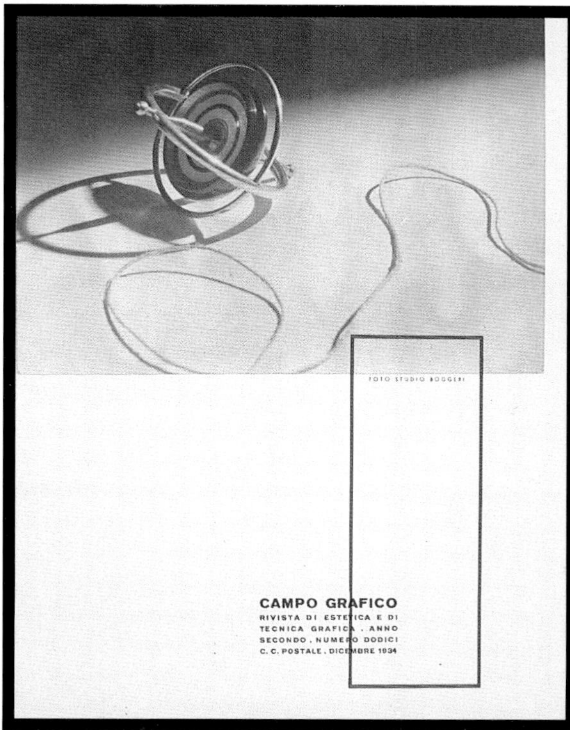

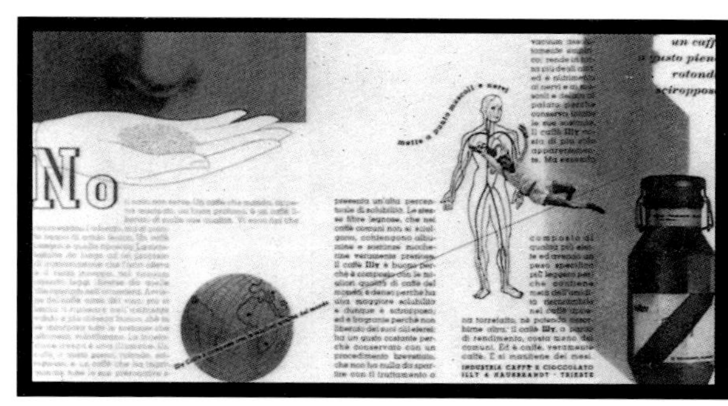

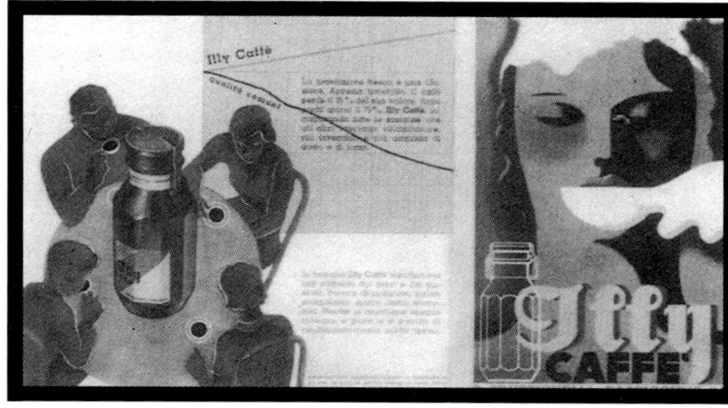

***Pharmaceutical piece,** 1934, by Xanti Schawinsky, Studio Boggeri.*

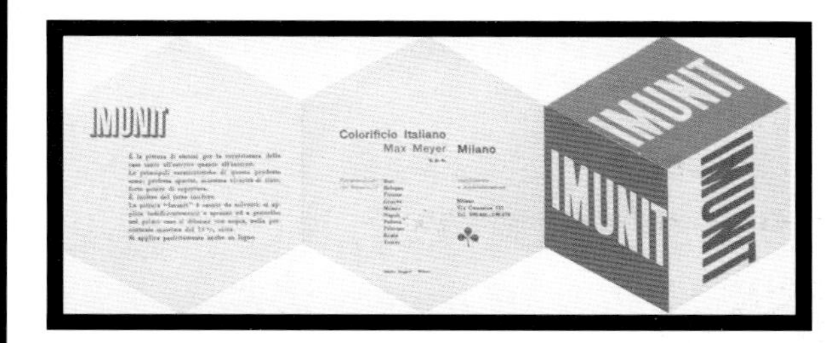

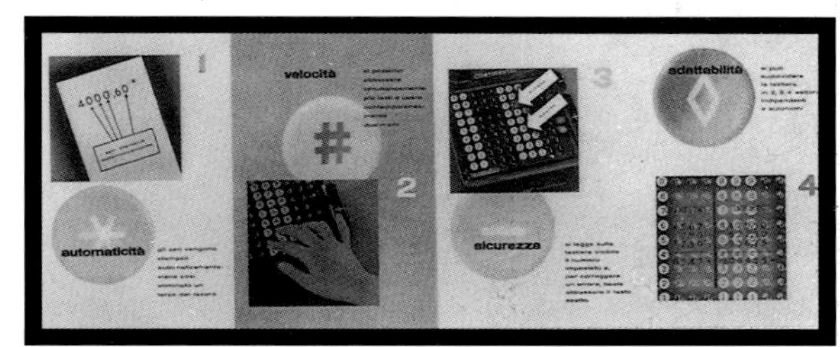

***Designed by Max Huber** in 1940, the year he joined Studio Boggeri.*

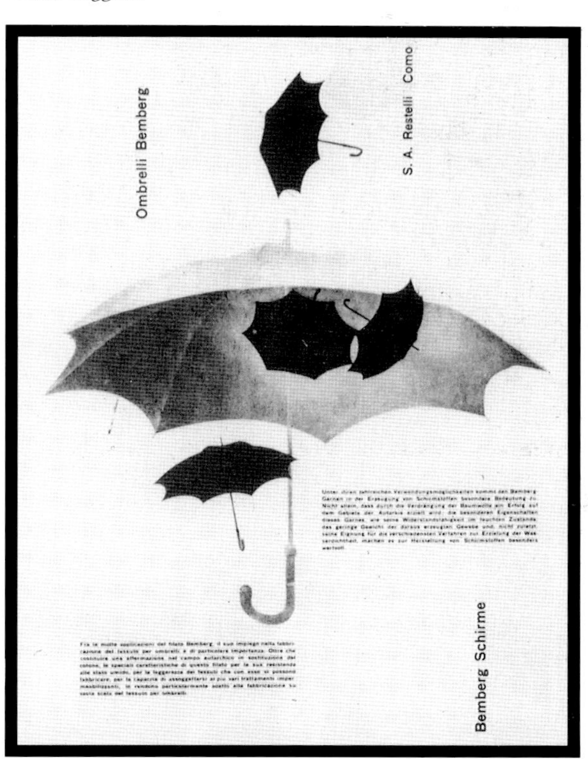

***Designed by Albe Steiner** (Studio Boggeri). 1942.*

Walter Herdeg, a Zürich based designer, in his work for the St. Moritz ski resort, also brought his graphics to life with his cropping and blending of pictures with type. Today some people claim that Swiss typography is dull and look-alike. A study of the work of the Swiss typographic design pioneers shows this need not be so. Dullness is not inherent in a striving for clarity nor in the grid system. Dullness is a product of poor execution.

The Grid System Emigrates

The grid system was developed and fine-tuned in Zürich and Basel but it didn't take long for it to be adopted in other countries. Anton Stankowski came from Germany to study in Zürich where, from 1929–1937, he mingled with such grid oriented designers as Max Bill and Richard P. Lohse. In 1937 he moved to Stuttgart, Germany, and has been a graphic designer and painter there ever since. Max Huber had studied Bauhaus theories and worked in Zürich. He collaborated with Max Bill on exhibition designs. He brought a blend of Swiss design orderliness and the use of bright, clear colors, photographs in unusual and complex juxtapositions, and overlapped images to his work in Milan, Italy.

In 1959 the journal *Neue Grafik* (New Graphic Design) was born. Its editors were four Zürich based graphic designers, Richard P. Lohse, Josef Müller-Brockmann, Hans Neuberg, and Carlo L. Vivarelli. Printed in German, English, and French, it effectively made Swiss typography an international style. It told the world about the viewpoints and accomplishments of Swiss typography. This made sense to many designers abroad who adopted its tenets, and students from many countries were attracted to the Basel and Zürich schools.

The Italian Connection

Italian typographics, although somewhat toned down from the flamboyance of the early futurist era, were not noted for orderliness, clarity, beauty, or communication effectiveness when Max Huber and other Swiss designers came to already famous Studio Boggeri in Milan, in the early 1940s.

The groundwork for a new era of typographic design in Milan was laid in 1933 with establishment of Studio Boggeri. Antonio Boggeri was born in Pavia in 1900. He studied in Turin, and in 1924 joined the staff of Alfieri and Lacroix, a large Milanese printer and publisher of art books. At that time Herbert Bayer was a design consultant for their magazine, *Natura,* with which Boggeri was concerned. Boggeri was a photographer but he sensed the need for a full-service art/design studio and opened one. He became the first real art director in Italy. One might say he and an associate, Kathe Bernhardt, invented the profession there. He was a self-taught photographer, but in his studies and through the publications he helped produce at Alfieri and Lacroix, he absorbed the thinking of Moholy-Nagy, El Lissitzky, Piet Zwart, Ladislav Sutnar, Herbert Bayer, Jan Tschichold and others. The studio became a magnet for German and Swiss designers and was the key force in bringing effective contemporary typographics to Italy. In 1933 when Studio Boggeri was established, Xanti Schawinsky also came from the Bauhaus to Milan. He stayed with the studio for a year. In 1935 Boggeri went to Zürich with Schawinsky. At this time he met Bayer, Breuer, Gropius and Moholy-Nagy. From 1935–1939 Boggeri worked with outside collaborators but he sought a full-time design director. Others who came from Switzerland to Milan and influenced the typographic touch of the young studio were Carlo Vivarelli, one of the editors of *Neue Grafik,* Imre Reiner, Walter Ballmer and, in 1940, Max Huber, who became the design director. Vivarelli's stay was brief, but Ballmer and Huber stayed in Milan. In the 1940s (except for 1941–1945 when, because Italy was at war, he returned to Switzerland) and for many years thereafter Max Huber became a major force in changing the face of Italian (Milanese) typographics, bringing to it the orderliness and focus on clarity of Bauhaus and Swiss typography. Huber's sense of communication design was less dogmatic than that advocated and practiced in Zürich and Basle. His use of colors and photography combined an eye-catching drama with a non-static sense of organization to make his work alive and effective. In the '30s, Huber had studied at the Kunstegewerbeschule in Zürich with Willimann, where he also met Müller-Brockmann, Carlo Vivarelli and others. Later there he met Max Bill and Hans Neuberg. It is no wonder that when he joined Studio Boggeri he brought modern and avant garde graphics to Italy. He also attended night courses at the Accademia de Brera, where he met Albe Steiner, Bruno Munari, Giovanni Pintori and other leading designers and artists. Franco Grignani was another leading designer in the Milano scene.

Chapter VI: Fine Tuning – Clarity and Grid Systems

"The problem, not a theory nor a style, determines the solution."

***Max Huber** integrated type with photography in this 1940–41 pharmaceutical piece.*

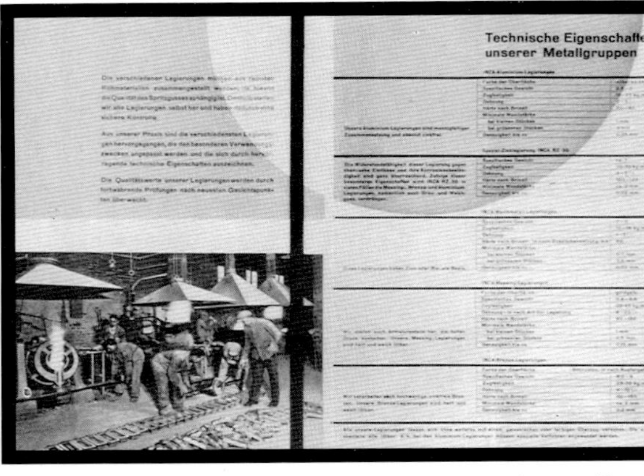

***Two-color pages** from a catalog for MCA spray, designed by Anton Stankowski, Stuttgart, c. 1930.*

Formalism With Flexibility

Anton Stankowski's schooling and his early work for Max Dalang, Ltd., a Zürich advertising agency, left him respectful of the need for organization and clarity in communication graphics. When he went to work in Stuttgart, Germany, he blended this training with his sense of bringing imagination and graphic vigor to his work. He handled type freely but kept it highly readable. He could organize a chart or a table meticulously but experimented with photographs and rotated planes rhythmically in a design. He used sans serif types when he could, but blended type and pictures creatively. He took most of the pictures he used. If his work in Stuttgart brought a sense of Swiss typography there, he showed that a varied approach, solving each job in a style appropriate to it, was the wave of the future and that no one approach, a Swiss grid or whatever, was the answer to all design problems. Even when his type was cleanly organized he would silhouette and tilt a photograph or use color strips or obliqued headlines to bring a design to life without compromising its readability.

The strict Swiss designers rejected personal expression in design in favor of a mathematical/scientific/objective approach on the grounds that a designer is primarily not an artist, but a communicator. Stankowski, while striving for clarity of communication, merged this effort with a personal expression and pointed a new way to reaching the best of both worlds in graphic design.

In 1920, in Stuttgart, Germany, Professor Ernst Schneidler, considered one of the foremost type designers, calligraphers and typographic designers of the first half of the 20th century, started teaching at the Stuttgart Kunstgewerbeschule. He

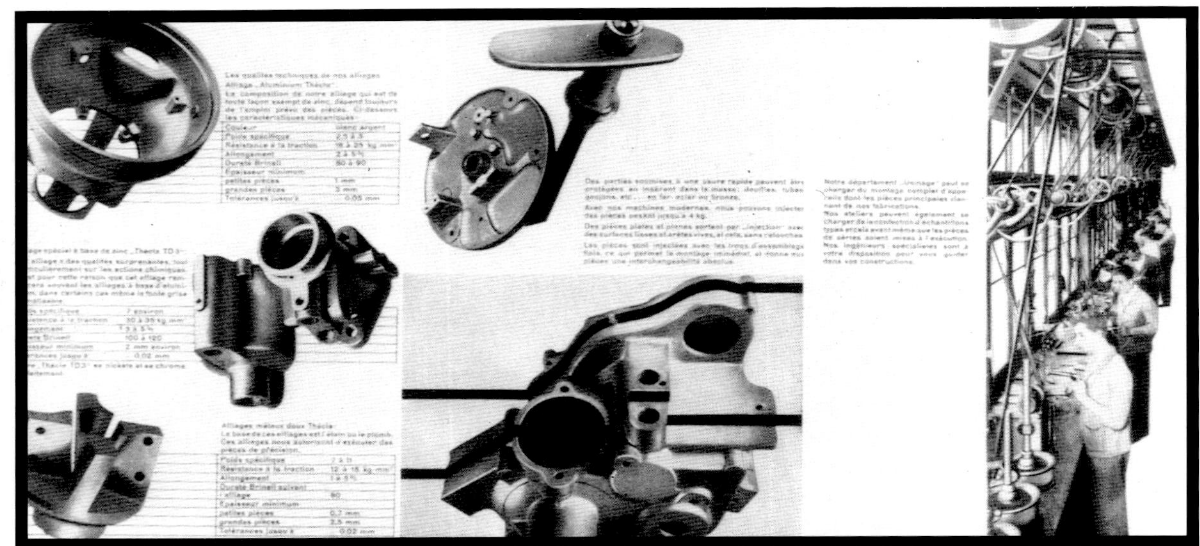

***Two-color pages** from a brochure for Thecla, designed by Anton Stankowski, c. 1934.*

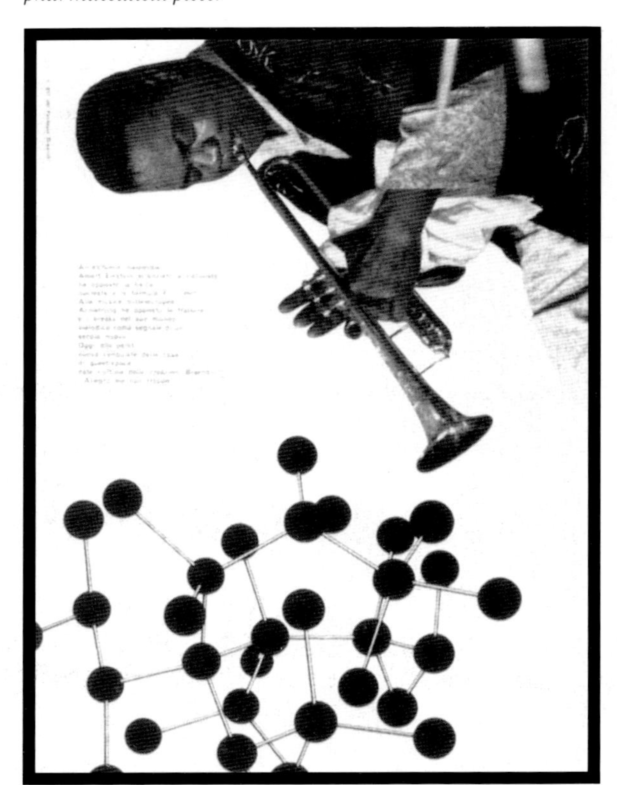

***An advertisement** that appeared in* Domus *magazine in 1947. Designed by Max Huber.*

***Designed** by Max Huber. 1943.*

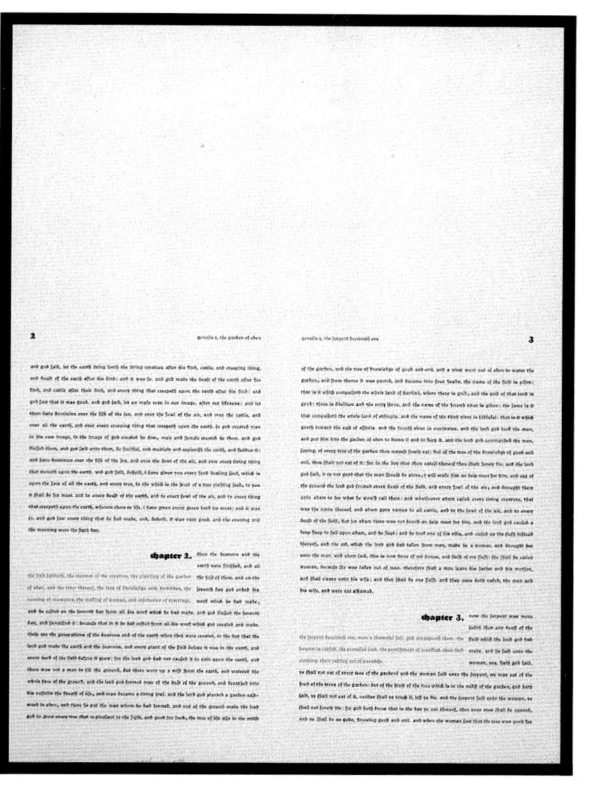

Shown here *are a selection of specimens from* Der Wassermann, *a rare collection of Professor Schneidler's personal typographic and calligraphic works, which he produced at his private press.*

taught for 30 years and influenced generations of designers with his pure approach to typographic excellence.

In the mid 1920s and early 1930s important and innovative work in typography was also being done in Czechoslovakia by Ladislav Sutnar and Karel Teige.

To Guard Against Being Merely Fashionable

In 1959 a young Swiss designer, Karl Gerstner, took a critical look at the work of the typographic pioneers and the isms of the 'teens, '20s, '30s, and '40s and recognized that:

❧ The stress on functionalism and clarity, the chain of developments from El Lissitzky's innovations through the Bauhaus workshop and publishing, through the work and writing and teaching of the likes of Max Bill, Emil Ruder, Jan Tschichold, Josef Müller-Brockmann and others "are no longer controversial...they are accepted..."

❧ But, "If most of the pioneers' theses have become self-evident, the aesthetic criteria have been generally outlived."

Such specific manifestations of the striving for order and clarity as the following tend to become fashions, outmoded or at least less than hard and fast rules. Some examples:

❧ The stress on sans serif typefaces. Not only did Tschichold back off of this but he and many others came to realize that both sans serif and roman typefaces had their place.

❧ It was also appreciated that asymmetry was not the only contemporary, genuinely functional mode of typographic expression.

❧ Ragged-right, it was realized, had its place, but so does flush right and type set diagonally or vertically.

Gerstner, in his work, *Integral Typography,* noted that "either-or" typographic thinking, the idea that only one way is the right way, had had its time. "Today everything is stylistically allowable." The key of course, is what is best for the job at hand. The problem, not a theory nor a style, determines the solution.

Two magazine cover *designs by Ladislav Sutnar. The triangle in the cover for* Zeneni a Vdavani *(1929) was in red. Both covers show Sutnar's Bauhaus approach to design and his focus on communication clarity, especially in using graphic elements to draw the eye and mind to a particular spot first, and then to direct eye-flow through a design. He was to advocate this principle strongly in later years in the United States in both his work and his writings. In Czechoslovakia, in addition to being design director for the publishing house of Druzstevni Prace he designed toys, furniture, silverware, dishes, and fabrics.*

"...and integral typography in which the marriage of language and the type results..."

Integral Typography

Gerstner considers text and typography "not so much two consecutive processes on different levels as interpenetrating elements." He strives for an integral typography in which the marriage of language and type results "in a new unity, in a superior whole." It is the designer's role to integrate signs and letters into words, words into sentences, sentences into the "reading time dimension" and to relate all the graphic elements to the function of the piece.

In his work and in his writings Gerstner stresses the need to understand the message problem thoroughly so as to derive from it the single graphic solution that is best for it. He cautions against imposing a style on a message and warns that "the knowledge and experience of the pioneers, what has already been done and is generally recognized, will degenerate into mere formalism, become fashionable."

◀ ***Two advertisements*** *designed by Karl Gerstner. The type literally expresses, illustrates, the message. The Sinar lens features excellent depth of field. Voll (full) and leer (empty) makes the message instantly clear and memorable.*

Gerstner's ability *to derive a graphic solution from the problem to apply a grid strictly or loosely, is illustrated (below and right) in the accompanying pictures. "Unsere Kaffeemaschine" (Our Coffee Machine) is an advertisement for Nescafe. The copy advises no roasting apparatus, no filters, no machines, nothing is needed but a spoon. Conservative, organized text type, crisp message, support the picture that catches the eye while it tells the story. The newspaper ads for the reopening of a department store following alterations has the vitality and excitement and graphic enthusiasm the message requires.*

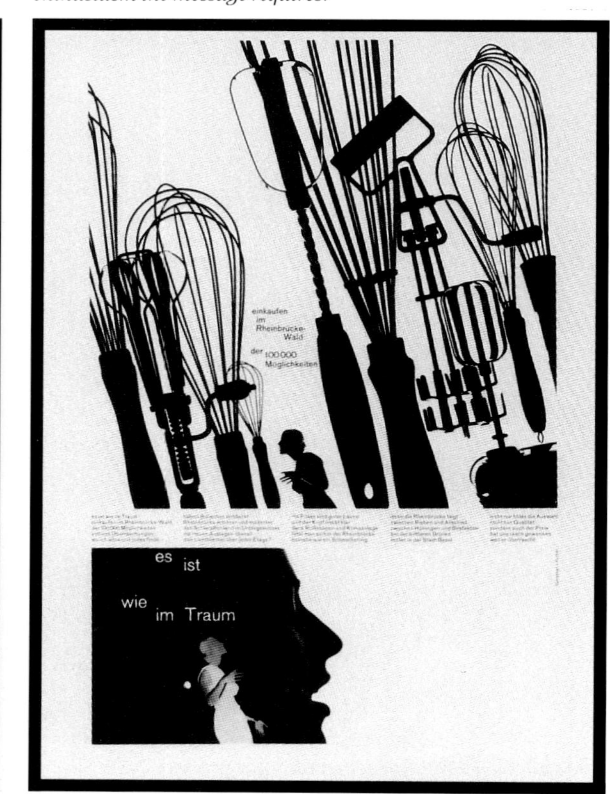

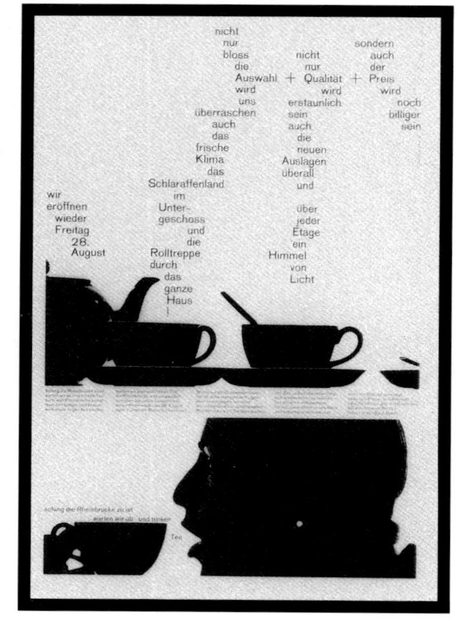

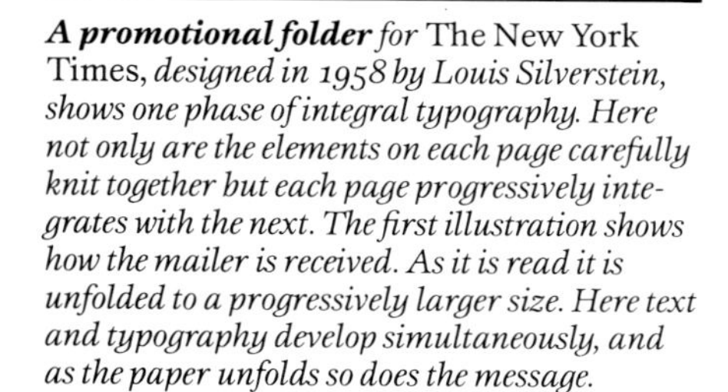

A promotional folder *for* The New York Times, *designed in 1958 by Louis Silverstein, shows one phase of integral typography. Here not only are the elements on each page carefully knit together but each page progressively integrates with the next. The first illustration shows how the mailer is received. As it is read it is unfolded to a progressively larger size. Here text and typography develop simultaneously, and as the paper unfolds so does the message.*

Karl Gerstner is a protagonist of Swiss typography, of its orderliness, its stress on function and clarity, if not a hard-line follower of its every rule. Today he is primarily concerned with the role of color in communication, as his book, *The Spirit of Colors,* indicates. Earlier and influential writings include *Compendium for Literates,* a system of writing with typefaces and typographic specifications appropriate to different kinds of messages, as well as *Designing Programs* and numerous magazine articles. His first book, which appeared in 1957, *Cold Art,* was an analysis of the development and status of a form of painting committed not to mathematics but rather to mathematical thinking, meaning: logic in art.

If the pioneers of the Swiss grid system fine-tuned typographics into an impersonal and almost exact science, as has been demonstrated, some followers fine-tuned it further by saying, in effect, here we will use a grid, here we won't, here we will apply it loosely.

In the 1930s and 1940s the combined influence of all the art and design movements described heretofore made itself felt across the Atlantic in the United States and in Canada. The scene in the United States (with and without the grid) is our next concern.

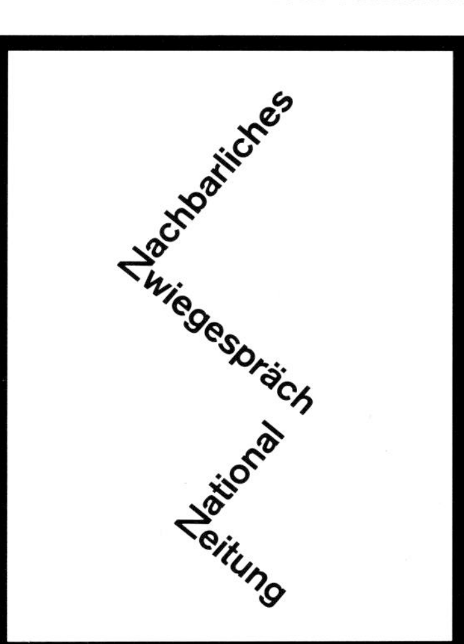

These designs *are for postal wrappers to fit folded newspapers for the dispatch of sample copies of* National Zeitung. *The use of the letters N and Z as one common character lend a distinct identity to this design. All the samples were created in the Agency Gerstner, Gredinger and Kutter, founded in 1959.*

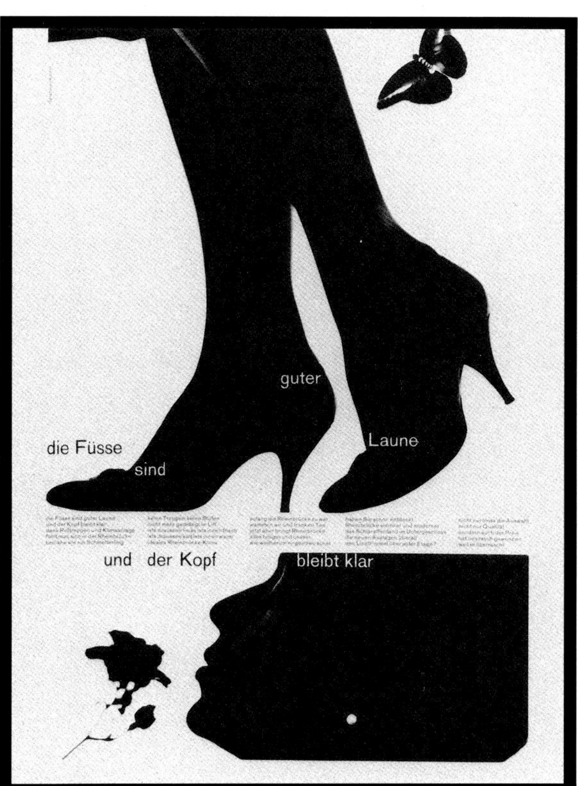

Here Gerstner *married typography, essentially a two-dimensional element, with photography, essentially a three-dimensional medium. To do this he employed two-dimensional silhouette-like photography.*

TYPOGRAPHIC COMMUNICATIONS TODAY

Chapter VII: The New Typography Crosses the Ocean

"The roster of European design talent that came to the United States in the 1930s and 1940s is a notable 'who's who' of that era."

THE WRITINGS OF Tschichold, the publication *Neue Graphik,* the exodus from Europe to the United States of many leading European typography designers, and the influence of the pocket-size magazine, *PM,* introduced American designers to what was then the best contemporary design thinking and practice.

The Exodus

The roster of European design talent that came to the United States in the 1930s and 1940s is a notable "who's who" of that era. Following is an impressive, albeit partial, list. It includes just a few who crossed the ocean more recently.

Mehemed Fehmy Agha. Born in the Ukraine, he studied art in Kiel and was a graphic artist in Paris in the 1920s. Condé Nast, publisher of *Vogue* and other magazines, met him in Berlin in 1920. Agha became Vogue's art director in Paris and later in New York where his work and his lucid and entertaining lectures charmed, and opened the eyes of many young American art directors and designers. In 1935 he was President of the New York Art Directors Club; in 1953 and 1954 he was President of the AIGA.

Josef Albers. Came to the United States in 1933 and propagated the ideas of the Bauhaus in his work, lectures and courses. He was particularly concerned with color theory, its physical and psychological effects. Albers taught at Black Mountain College in North Carolina. This was an experimental school based on the then new teaching theories of John Dewey. The school, at that time, was influential and Albers' teachings there were heard across the land. He left Black Mountain College in 1949, and from 1950 to 1959, when he retired, he was a professor at Yale University and a lecturer at Harvard University and elsewhere.

Walter Allner. A former Bauhaus student. An artist and a designer, he was also art director of *Fortune* magazine.

Herbert Bayer. Came to the United States in 1938. In 1946 Walter Paepcke, President of the Container Corporation of America, named him his art adviser and chairman of the design conferences at Aspen, Colorado. The International Design Conference in Aspen was a focal point for progressive designers. He has also been design consultant to the Atlantic Richfield Oil Company. In the United States Bayer became less constructivist-oriented but remained concerned about using design effectively to solve communication problems. He had originally taken an interest in typography because he realized that the way type was being set was antiquated, not so much in a fashion sense but in terms of type's function, to facilitate communication. Bayer was a forerunner of many great graphic designers who followed him because he combined a highly creative mind and spirit, with a sense of beauty and a keen analytical ability.

Lucian Bernhard. A self-taught German graphic designer and innovator. His minimal posters, often consisting of one word and one illustration that focused on the primary statement of the message, was a major force in the simplification of poster design. In the 1920s he came to the United States, and in 1929 started to design the first of a number of typefaces he created for the American Type Founders Company.

Joseph Binder. Studied and started his career as a poster designer in Vienna. Came to the United States in 1930, where he also lectured and conducted workshops.

Marcel Breuer. Came to the United States in 1937. He had been head of the furniture workshop at the Bauhaus, and the inventor of tubular steel furniture. In 1937, at Harvard, he taught architecture. In the United States he continued to design furniture and even the exterior and interior of railway cars for the New York, New Haven and Hartford Railroad.

Alexey Brodovitch. Born in St. Petersburg, Russia. In 1930 Brodovitch came to teach at the School of Industrial Art at the Philadelphia Museum. In 1934 he came to New York as art director of *Harper's Bazaar* where he reigned until 1958. In that time he influenced such students as Henry Wolf, Otto Storch, Richard Avedon, Irving Penn, Art Kane, Louis Danziger, Howard Zieff, Sam Antupit, Robert Gage, Helmut Krone, and Stephen Frankfurt. He also commissioned work from such innovative photographers as Man Ray and Martin Munkacsi as well as from artists such as Salvador Dali, Marc Chagall and Saul Steinberg (other emigrés) and Jean Cocteau, Raoul Dufy, Erté, and Henri Cartier-Bresson. He developed new ways of cropping and juxtaposing pictures. He used white space generously as a design element and insisted on sharp, highly readable type. Brodovitch also ran design laboratories at Richard Avedon's studio and at the Young & Rubicam advertising agency, and designed sets for the Ballet Russe de Monte Carlo.

Will Burtin. From 1927 to 1938, in his native Cologne, Germany, he ran a graphics design studio known not only for its print graphics but for its exhibition and display designs and films. He came to the United States in 1938, and his contributions to the New York and national design scenes were many. For seven years he was design consultant to the Upjohn Company and art editor of its publication, *Scope.* He taught at Pratt Institute, New York; wrote, lectured, operated a distinguished design studio serving major corporations; was art director of *Fortune* magazine, chaired a number of major design conferences, including Vision 65 and Vision 67, "The Art and Science of Typography" sponsored by the Type Directors Club in Silvermine, Connecticut in 1958, and played a major role in the International Design Conferences in Aspen, Colorado, in 1956, 1957 and 1958. Will Burtin was a philosopher of design. In conferences and writings and teaching he was never satisfied with merely looking at current work or identifying trends. He was concerned with the why as well as the how of design and with its role in communication effectiveness. An unique and major contribution was his work in making scientific information visual by means of large-scale structural models. His model of a human brain, for example, was large enough for people to walk inside. His genius was to reduce complex processes and data to an understandable visual form. In a booklet, *Visual Aspects of Science,* he stated his graphic communications credo. "Simplicity to assist perception (recognition) and recall (memory); logic in the relationship between content and appearance; emphasis on the basic idea of the message." Burtin found beauty in science and truth in art, and expressed both sensitively and dramatically. "Beauty," he wrote, "is not necessarily a matter of form or style, but a result of order achieved." To him simplicity of statement was a major element of beauty in communication.

Will Burtin went well beyond making layouts of material brought to him. He brought an editorial as well as a visual mind to his work, and analyzed just how the information could be presented most effectively. This often led him away from illustration to creating charts, diagrams, and models and using microscopic photography.

Jean Carlu. One of a number of outstanding European artists who came to the United States and did work for the Container Corporation of America. His posters for the U.S. Office of War Information (OWI) were powerfully effective and won top recognition from the New York Art Directors Club. His posters were not only graphically forceful, their copy was telegraphically simple and direct, with words and images completely integrated. In his native France, Carlu had become sensitized to the modern art movements and their lessons for visual communication, as well as for the need for brief, clear text. He was also sparing in his use of lines in illustrations, striving for clarity and force through simplicity. Carlu was also a student of new technologies and of graphic symbols.

A. M. Cassandre. His focus on broad surfaces, graphic symbols, abstract design, two-dimensional art, and his integration of type and art, gave his posters and other work great importance. His love of letterforms led him to use typefaces with great care and to design several mentioned earlier in this work. He came to the United States for a few years in the late 1930s and did work for *Harper's Bazaar,* Container Corporation of America, and the N. W. Ayer advertising agency. He was born in Kharkov, Russia, studied painting in Paris, where, except for his three-year visit to the United States, he worked until his death in 1968.

***Herbert Bayer's** type was always readable, yet blended with illustration or photography to create a live, arresting, memorable whole. Often the type itself became an illustration, yet retained its readability.*

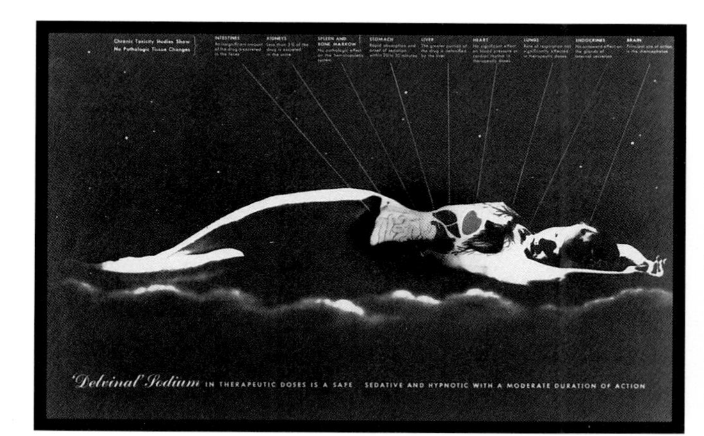

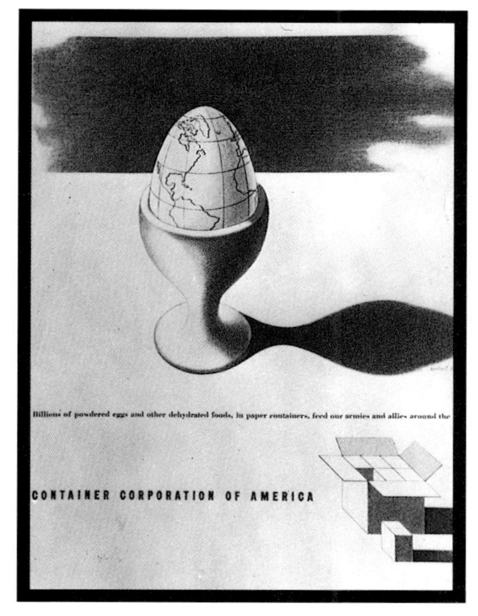

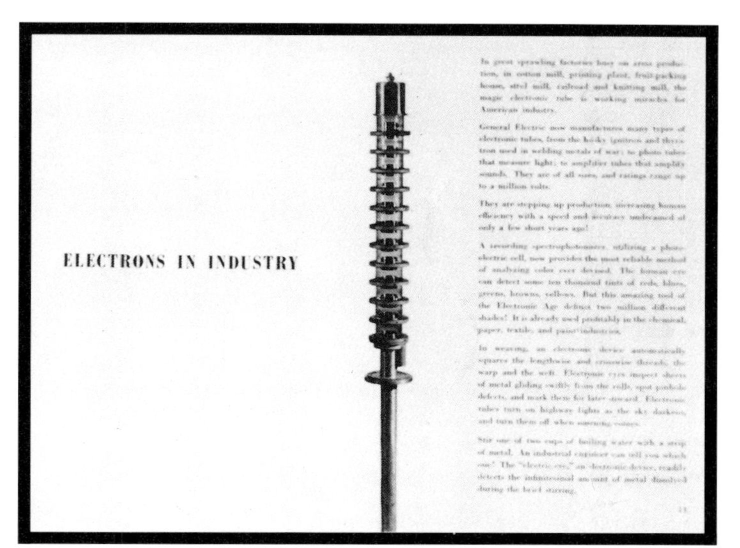

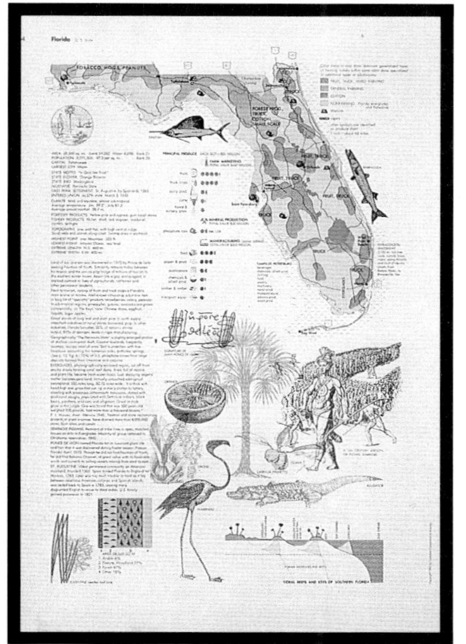

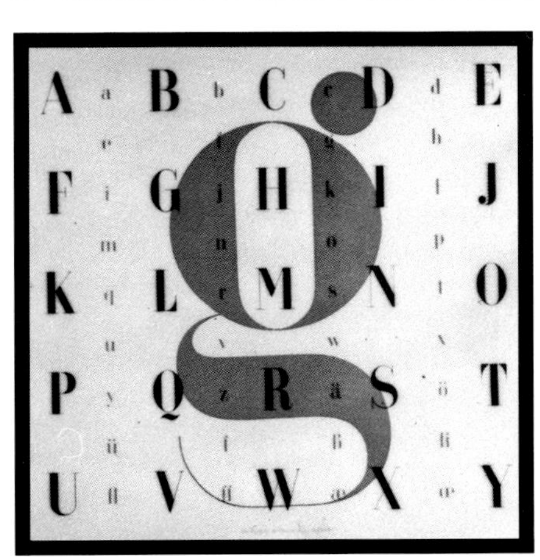

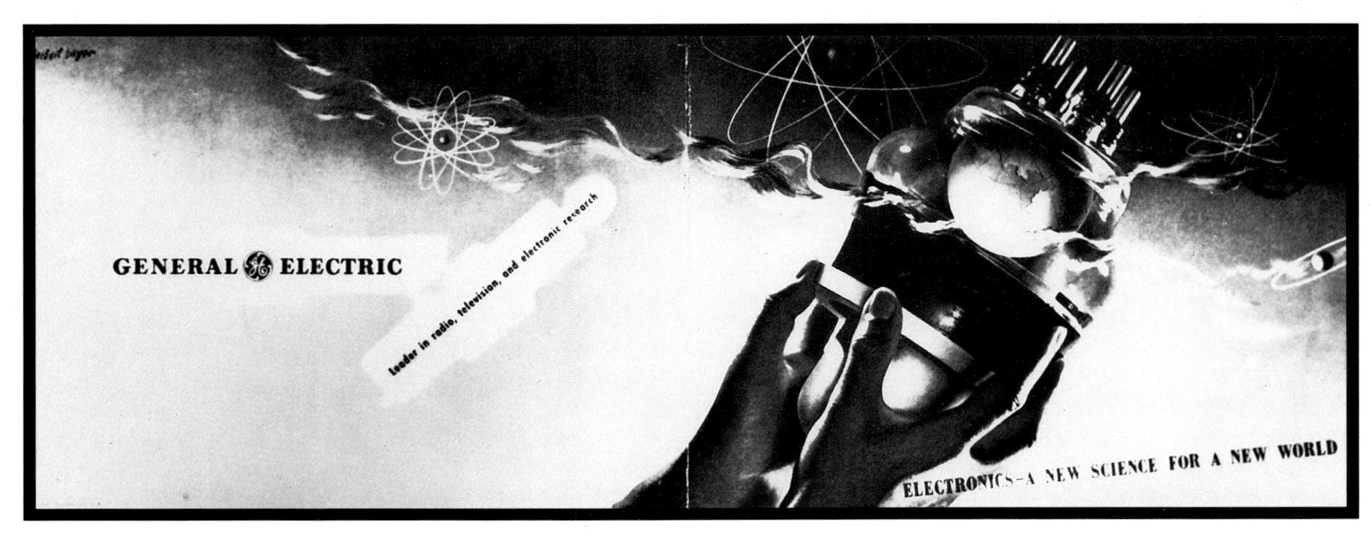

TYPOGRAPHIC COMMUNICATIONS TODAY
Chapter VII: The New Typography Crosses the Ocean

"...their influence, as well of that of their students, accelerated the spread of a new kind of typographic design that rapidly replaced the traditional graphics of preceding decades."

George Giusti. Worked in Italy and Switzerland before coming to New York in 1938, where he opened a design office. His covers and designs for special features for *Fortune* and *Holiday* magazines set a new pace for bold yet simple graphic images and fresh uses of color.

Walter Gropius. Resigned his Bauhaus post in 1928 to re-establish his architectural office in Germany. After the closing of the Bauhaus in 1933, Gropius came to the United States where, in 1937, he began his tour as professor of architecture at Harvard University.

Gyorgy Kepes. Hungarian born and educated, was an assistant to Moholy-Nagy in the 1920s. Kepes came to the United States where his writings and teaching were most influential. He conducted a seminar and taught visual design at the Massachusetts Institute of Technology and authored the widely studied *Language of Vision.*

Albert Kner. In 1940 Albert Kner came to the United States from Hungary. He went to Chicago where he became the first staff package designer for the Container Corporation of America. Kner led the department for more than 20 years. A research laboratory was established to measure the sales effectiveness of package design, and an ocular camera to study eye movements while a person looked at a design, was developed. Walter Paepcke, who had founded CCA in 1926, was a new breed of industrialist. He sensed the value of good design in products, in advertising and promotion, and in projecting a corporate image. He also appreciated the cultural value of good design, as well as its force in communications. He had hired Egbert Jacobson as CCA's design director, supported Moholy-Nagy at Chicago's Institute of Design (known then as "The New Bauhaus"), and brought a number of European talents to CCA, including Albert Kner, Cassandre, Herbert Bayer, Herbert Matter, Fernand Leger, Man Ray, and Jean Carlu.

Fernand Leger. This French cubist painter used geometric letterforms in some of his work as well as stylized human figures, flat color planes, and hard-edge forms. His pictorial elements often seemed machine made, and his then modern and synthetic imagery were an "in" style for a while. His work was commissioned by CCA, as noted above.

Leo Lionni. Born in Holland in 1910, went to Italy at the age of 12, where he studied photography and accounting, and received a doctorate in economics. He painted during his student years and got to know some of the futurist artists and designers. In the United States he taught at Black Mountain College in North Carolina, became an art director at the N. W. Ayer & Son advertising agency and later at *Fortune* magazine. He returned to Italy where he continues to distinguish himself as an artist and illustrator. Today he divides his time between his New York and Italian offices.

Herbert Matter. Swiss born, he was a photographer, graphic designer, and painter of international fame before coming to New York. He was a partner in Studio Associates, and his design work for Container Corporation of America, the New York, New Haven and Hartford Railroad, and other clients was widely acclaimed, as was his photography for *Vogue, Fortune,* and *Harper's Bazaar.* He was also graphic design and photography consultant to Knoll Associates (designer and manufacturer of furniture) and creator/producer of a number of outstanding films interpreting works of art, notably a film about Calder, and the photography for the Charles and Ray Eames film, *A Communications Primer.*

Laszlo Moholy-Nagy. Came to the United States in 1937, and founded the School of Design in Chicago, where he taught until his death in 1946. He advocated the ideas of the Bauhaus. His most influential writings in this period were *The New Vision,* 1946, and *Vision in Motion,* 1947, published posthumously.

Erik Nitsche. Born in Lausanne. Studied there, in Munich and in Paris; came to New York in 1934 as art director for Saks Fifth Avenue and other stores, and continued his career in the United States with, among others, Dorland International and General Dynamics.

Cipe Pineles. Came to New York from her native Austria at the age of 13. Attended Pratt Institute in Brooklyn, and in 1933 became assistant to Dr. M. F. Agha at Condé Nast Publications. In 1936 she went to London as associate art director for *Vogue* and in 1938 returned to New York as art director of *Glamour.* In later years she was art director of *Seventeen, Charm,* and in 1959 of *Mademoiselle.* Since 1963 she has been on the faculty of Parsons School of Design.

Ladislav Sutnar. He left Prague, Czechoslovakia, in 1939, to design the Czechoslovakian New York World's Fair exhibit. In Prague he had been an advocate of functional, Bauhaus design. He put his theories into practice designing exhibits, graphics, toys, furniture, silverware, dishes, and fabrics. In the United States he taught advanced advertising design at Pratt Institute, co-authored *Catalog Design,* and wrote *Controlled Visual Flow* and *Shape, Line, and Color.* He became consultant art director for Sweets Catalog in 1941, and operated a design studio in New York. His design work, teaching and writing added up to a considerable force, impressing many with the need for informational design to be carefully structured to control reader eye-flow, to synthesize function, flow, and form. In his eyes the function of design was to make information easy to find, read, understand and recall. By flow he meant the logical sequence of information and control of the reader's eye path through a message. He used many bleed pages and rejected traditional margins. He thought in terms of visual units (such as a spread) rather than pages. He used shape, line and control to achieve the desired eye-flow, and not merely for decoration. Underscores, changes in typeface size and weight, white space, reverses, colors, were manipulated to maximize communication effectiveness. He often reorganized conventional text into simple charts to present complex information in findable, digestible units. His sense of visual coding of information even affected the way catalog information was written. Copy became more concise, more factual. "Gimmicks and Gadgets," he wrote, "do not make for good design." His sense of visual simplicity was an example of the "less is more" philosophy. The strength of simple design lies in its ability to communicate directly to meet the demand for rapid perception.

And More, and More, and More

There were many more European designers, architects, and artists who came to the United States and to Canada, and whose presence gave design west of the Atlantic a new functionalism, a new sense of order, a new vitality, a new personality, or, more accurately, new personalities. One could write whole books about each of them and many such have been written. But enough has been said here to convey and impress the importance to design of the emigrés of the 1930s and 1940s from across the ocean. There were others then and since, and the following is only a partial listing of them. The work of some will be reviewed in later chapters of this work.

Marc Chagall, Serge Chermayeff, Marcel Duchamp, Fritz Eichenberg, Max Ernst, Erté (Romain de Tirtof), Steff Geissbuhler, Albert Gleizes, Fritz Gottschalk, George Grosz, Jacques Lipschitz, Piet Mondrian, Martin Munkacsi, Amadeo Modigliani, Francis Picabia, Man Ray, Mies van der Rohe, Saul Steinberg, Xanti Schawinsky, Yves Tanguy, George Tscherny, Massimo Vignelli, Henry Wolf.

The influx of European designers to the United States in the 1930s and 1940s worked in many ways to change the face of, and the thinking behind, designs. At first the newcomers were commissioned by a few key people for particular projects. Then they secured positions of high visibility and became teachers and lecturers, and their influence, as well as that of their students, accelerated the spread of a new kind of typographic design that rapidly replaced the traditional graphics of the preceding decades.

But the international status that typographic design in the United States was to achieve did not develop solely as a result of the arrival of European designers. Partly influenced by the new typography, a number of American-born designers, each with his/her own strong personal way of treating visual communications, brought new vigor and new blends of communication clarity and power and freshness to the scene. Key pacesetters at this time and in the early 1950s include: Paul Rand, Bradbury Thompson, Lester Beall, Matthew Leibowitz, Herb Lubalin, Saul Bass, Gene Federico, William Golden, Louis Dorfsman, Jerome Snyder, Milton Glaser, and Rudolf deHarak; many of whom are professionally active today.

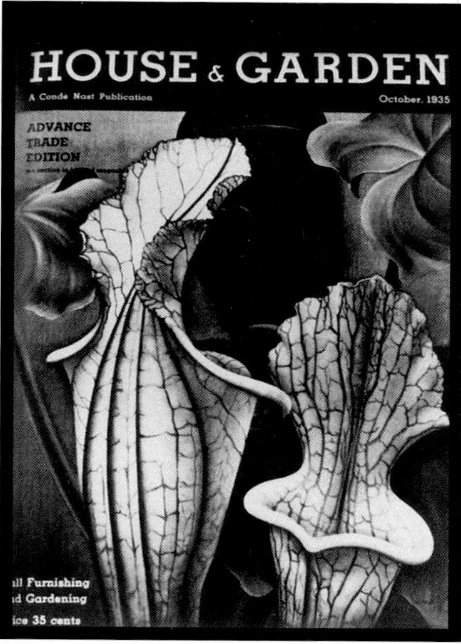

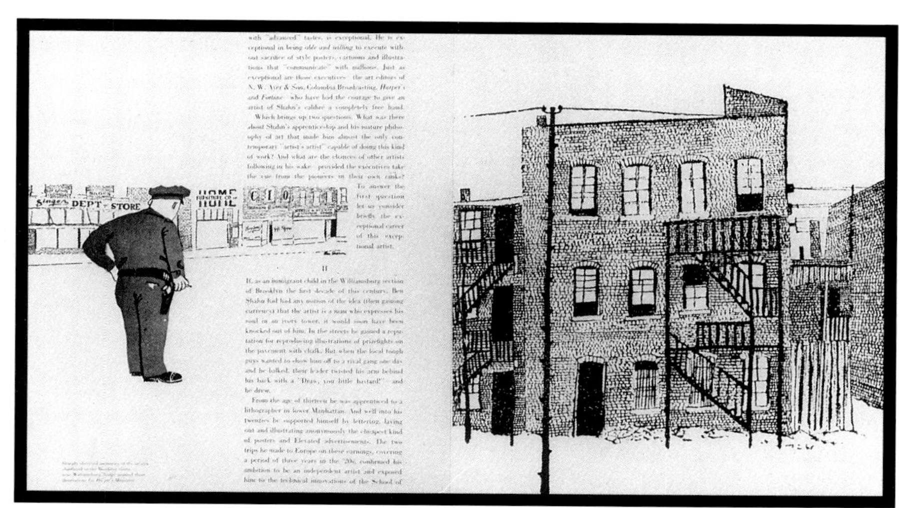

FASHIONS BY RADIO

MAN RAY'S PHOTOGRAPHIC IMPRESSION OF A NEW FASHION "COMING OVER" THE SHORT WAVES. IN THIS ISSUE FIVE PAGES OF FASHIONS FROM THE NEW COLLECTIONS WERE RADIOED FROM PARIS TO NEW YORK.

ALL COLLECTIONS VIOLENTLY PICTURESQUE
LOOK 1880 ONE MINUTE, 1950 THE NEXT
THE MOST FANTASTIC MODERN MATERIALS
STIFF AS INFANTAS IN THE EVENING
EVERYONE IS CUTTING WHOOPSY BANGS
DO NOT BELIEVE THAT DERRIERES ARE FLAT
CROWNS ZOOM HIGH AS HUSSARS
WONDERFUL NEW SHADE OF VIOLET BLUE

Spread *from* Portfolio *magazine and* Harper's Bazaar *cover by Alexey Brodovitch.*

The typography *picks up the rhythm of the Man Ray photograph in this* Harper's Bazaar *page by Alexey Brodovitch.*

Magazine covers *designed by Dr. M. F. Agha. Agha found many ways to build drama into his graphics—by exaggerated perspective, a pattern built of multiple images, stylized art, extreme close-ups for example, in a simple composition that the eye and mind could grasp at a glance.*

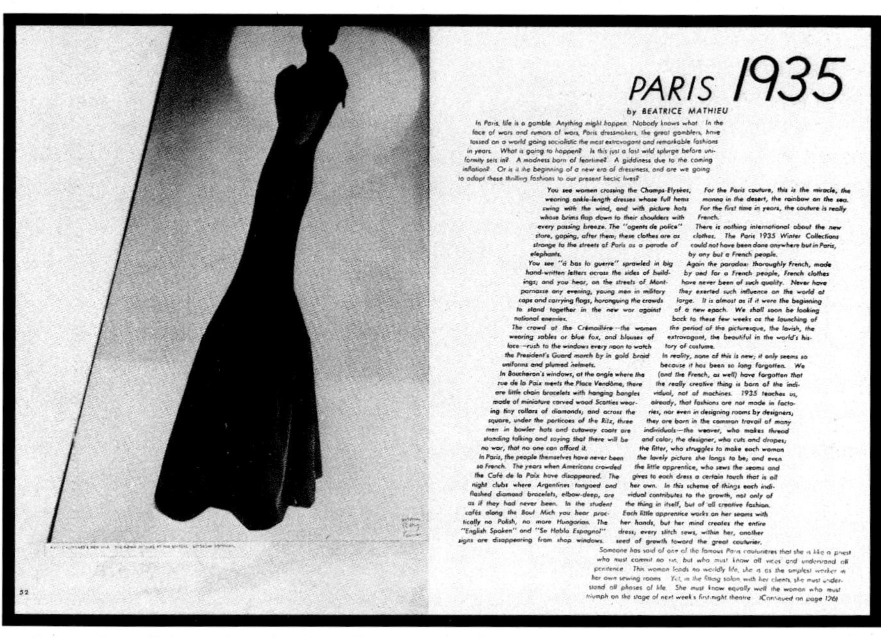
PARIS 1935

by BEATRICE MATHIEU

In Paris, life is a gamble. Anything might happen. Nobody knows what. In the face of wars and rumors of wars, Paris dressmakers, the great gamblers, have tossed on a world going socialistic the most extravagant and remarkable fashions in years. What is going to happen? Is this just a last wild splurge before uniformity sets in? A madness born of feartime? A giddiness due to the coming inflation? Or is it the beginning of a new era of dressiness, and are we going to adopt these thrilling fashions to our present hectic lives?

You see women crossing the Champs-Elysées, wearing ankle-length dresses whose full hems swing with the wind, and with picture hats whose brims flap down to their shoulders with every passing breeze. The "agents de police" stare, gaping, after them; these clothes are as strange to the streets of Paris as a parade of elephants.

You see "à bas la guerre" sprawled in big hand-written letters across the sides of buildings; and you hear, on the streets of Montparnasse any evening, young men in military caps and carrying flags, haranguing the crowds to stand together in the new war against national enemies.

The crowd at the Crémaillère—the women wearing sables or blue fox, and blouses of lace—rush to the windows every noon to watch the President's Guard march by in gold braid uniforms and plumed helmets.

In Boucheron's windows, at the angle where the rue de la Paix meets the Place Vendôme, there are little chain bracelets with hanging bangles made of miniature carved wood Scotties wearing tiny collars of diamonds; and across the square, under the porticoes of the Ritz, three men in bowler hats and cutaway coats are standing talking and saying that there will be no war, that no one can afford it.

In Paris, the people themselves have never been so French. The years when Americans crowded the Café de la Paix have disappeared. The night clubs where Argentines tangoed and flashed diamond bracelets, elbow-deep, are as if they had never been. In the student cafés along the Boul Mich you hear practically no Polish, no more Hungarian. The "English Spoken" and "Se Habla Espagnol" signs are disappearing from shop windows.

For the Paris couture, this is the miracle, the manna in the desert, the rainbow on the sea. For the first time in years, the couture is really French.

There is nothing international about the new clothes. The Paris 1935 Winter Collections could not have been done anywhere but in Paris, by any but a French people.

Again the paradox: thoroughly French, made by and for a French people, French clothes have never been of such quality. Never have they exerted such influence on the world at large. It is almost as if it were the beginning of a new epoch. We shall soon be looking back to these few weeks as the launching of the period of the picturesque, the lavish, the extravagant, the beautiful in the world's history of costume.

In reality, none of this is new; it only seems so because it has been so long forgotten. We (and the French, as well) have forgotten that the really creative thing is born of the individual, not of machines. 1935 teaches us, already, that fashions are not made in factories, nor even in designing rooms by designers; they are born in the common travail of many individuals—the weaver, who makes thread and color; the designer, who cuts and drapes; the fitter, who struggles to make each woman the lovely picture she longs to be; and even the little apprentice, who sews the seams and gives to each dress a certain touch that is all her own. In this scheme of things each individual contributes to the growth, not only of the thing in itself, but of all creative fashion. Each little apprentice works on her seams with her hands, but her mind creates the entire dress; every stitch sews, within her, another seed of growth toward the great couturier.

Someone has said of one of the famous Paris couturieres that she is like a priest who must commit no sin, but who must know all vices and understand all penitence. This woman leads no worldly life, she is as the simplest worker in her own sewing rooms. Yet, in the fitting salon with her clients, she must understand all phases of life. She must know equally well the woman who must triumph on the stage of next week's first-night theatre. (Continued on page 126)

As he so often did, *Brodovitch relates the type to the illustration, here capturing the obliqueness of Man Ray's model. Note use of sans serif type in various weights and sizes.*

The blue and white areas *dominate this cover. Erte's illustration is accented by scarlet fish earrings, and the type echoes the flavor of the stylized head. A 1929 cover by Alexey Brodovitch.*

TYPOGRAPHIC COMMUNICATIONS TODAY
Chapter VII: The New Typography Crosses the Ocean

"Beauty is not necessarily a matter of form or style, but a result of order achieved."

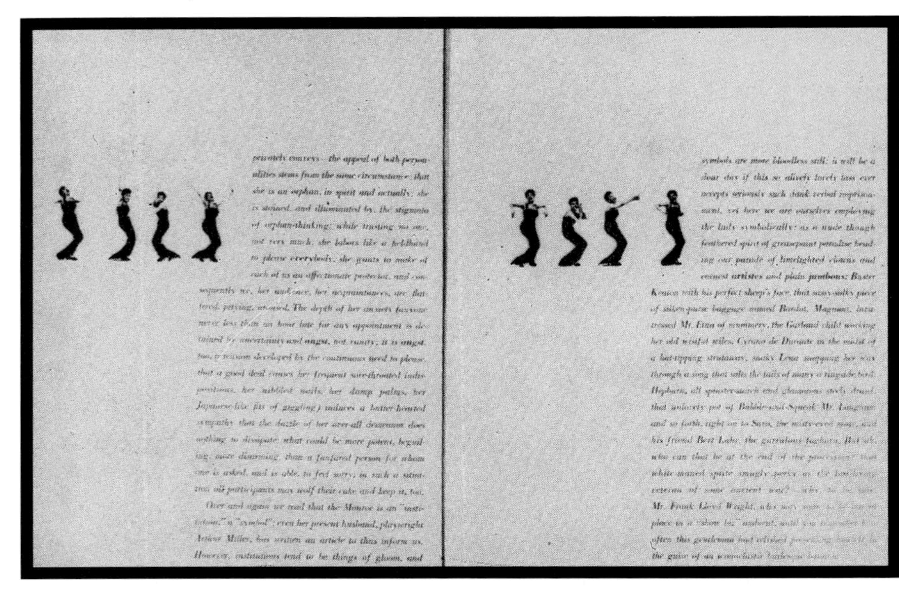

In 1958 *Brodovitch became less active at* Harper's Bazaar *and spent more of his time and energy teaching and designing special books. One such book was* Observations, *published in 1959, created in collaboration with Richard Avedon and Truman Capote. These three spreads show how he was able to achieve vigor, elegance, and clarity simultaneously. Capote wrote of Brodovitch, "What Dom Perignon was to champagne, Mendel to genetics, so this over-keyed and quietly chaotic but always kindly mannered Russian-born American has been to the art of photographic design and editorial layout, a profession to which he brings boldness bordering on revolution, an eye unexcelled, and in educated terms a taste for vanguard experiment that has been for thirty-plus years the awe, just possibly the making, of all who have ever had the privilege of his guidance."*

This Brodovitch layout *for* Arts et Metiers Graphiques *is one of the first to use typewritten type. c. 1928.*

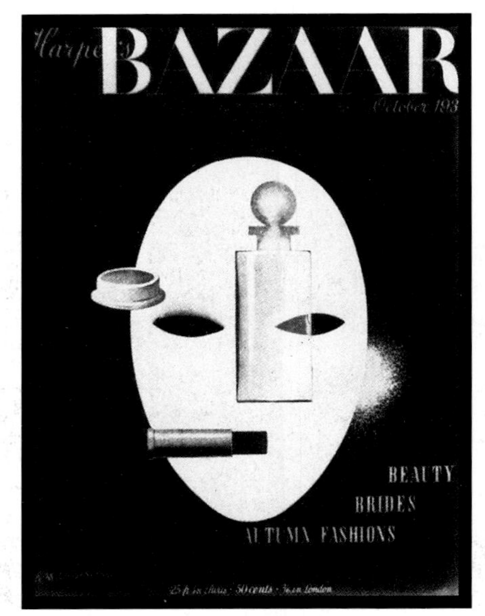

Graphic symbols *and two-dimensional art were trademarks of A. M. Cassandre. This 1939 cover features a pink perfume bottle (the nose), lipstick for the mouth, a puff of powder on the cheek.*

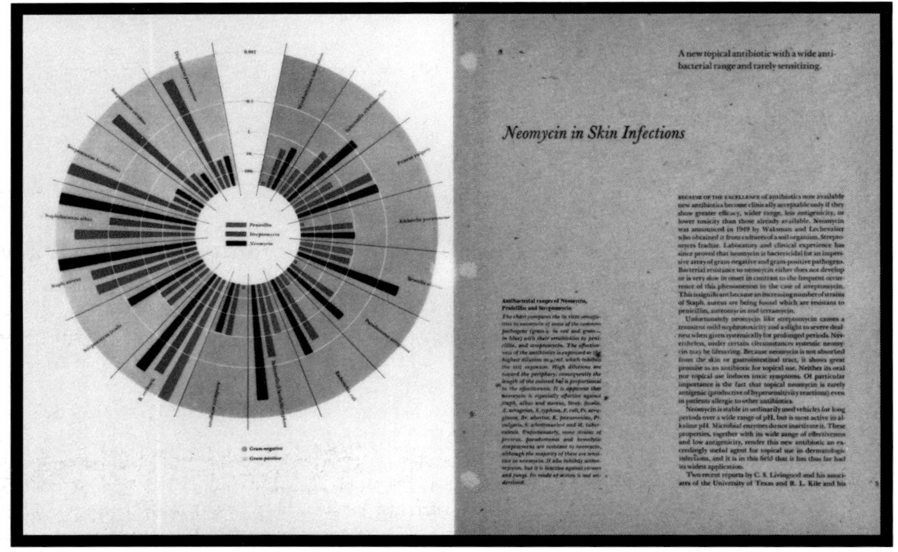

Will Burtin *went well beyond making layouts of material brought to him. He brought an editorial as well as a visual mind to his work, and analyzed just how the information could be presented most effectively. This often led him away from illustration to creating charts, diagrams and models, and using microscopic photography. Above is a typical diagram, in color, flanked by a typographically simple page containing a detailed caption and related text.*

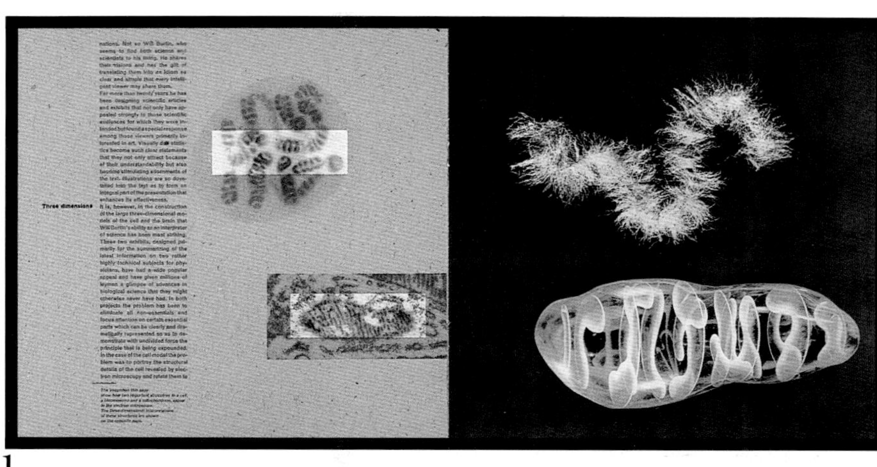
1

2

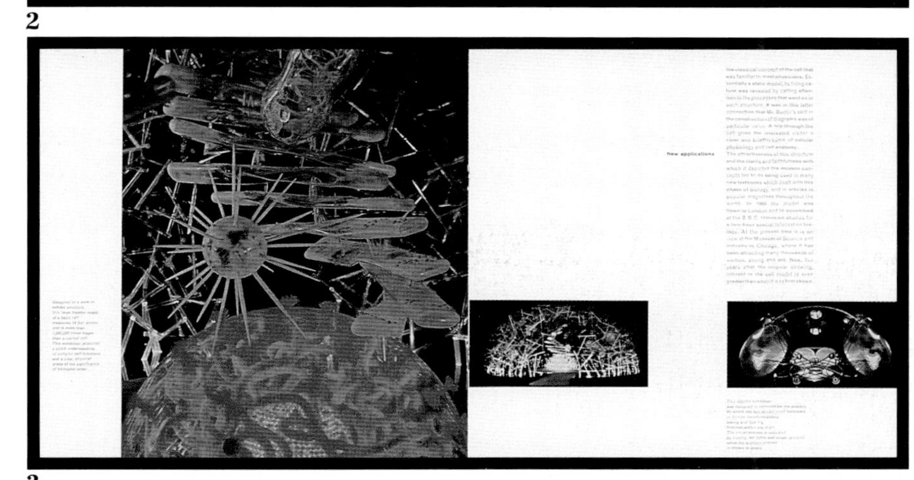
3

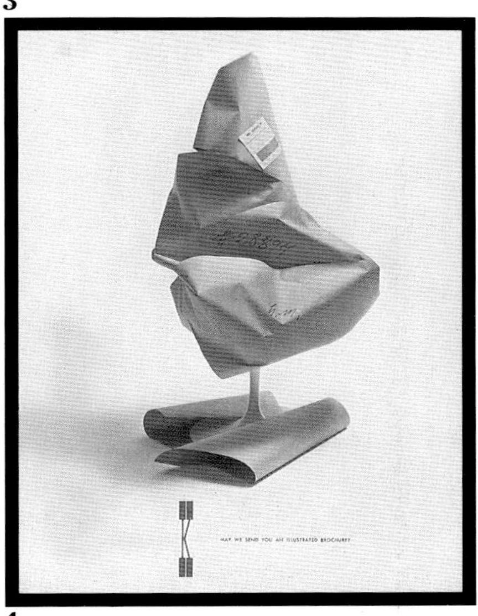
4

5

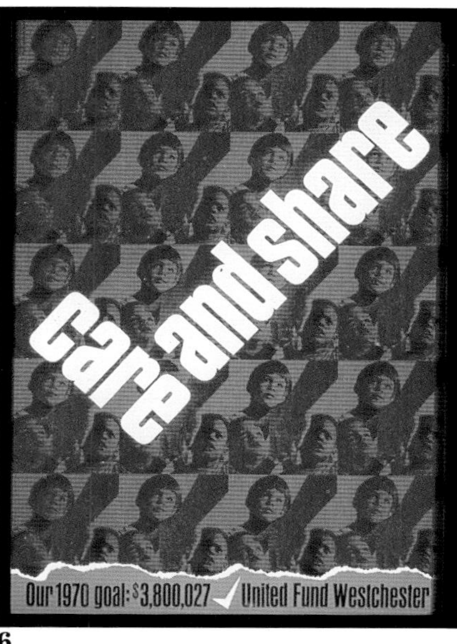

6

7

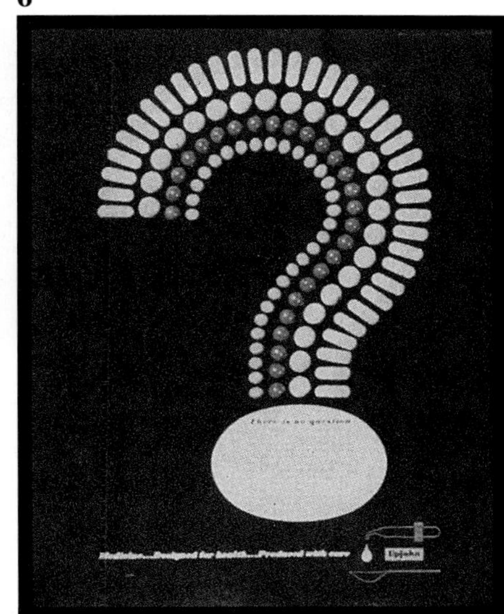

8

9

10

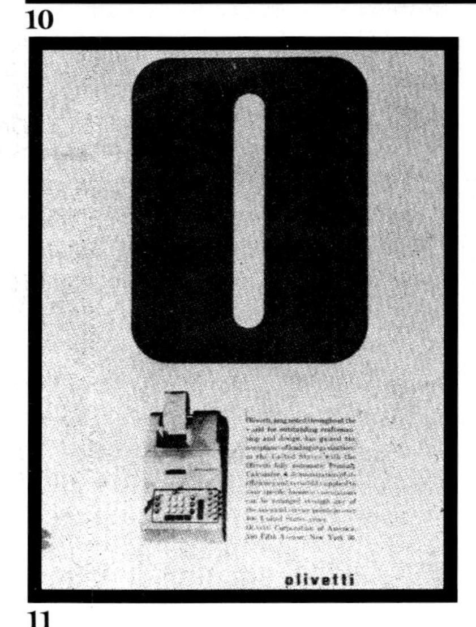

11

12

1–3. ***Will Burtin's*** *pages were always alive, yet orderly. These spreads are from a booklet for the Upjohn Company. It is about the visual aspects of science, and includes photographs by Ezra Stoller of mammoth, walk-in scientific exhibit structures of a human blood cell and a human brain.*
4, 5. ***From a brochure*** *for a new Knoll chair. Herbert Matter, 1956.*
6. ***Poster*** *for United Fund of Westchester. Will Burtin, 1970. From the Graphic Design Archive, Rochester Institute of Technology, Rochester, New York.*
7. ***Brochure*** *cover for Vision 67 Conference. Will Burtin, 1967. From the Graphic Design Archive, Rochester Institute of Technology, Rochester, New York.*
8. ***Will Burtin*** *designed this ad for Upjohn in 1959.*
9. ***Cover*** *by George Guisti illustrates his fresh touch with illustrations.*
10. ***Spread*** *for* Seventeen *magazine. Cipe Pineles. Illustrations dance through the type.*
11. ***Huge initials*** *are effectively used by many designers to get attention, to provide drama a mandatory illustration may lack, to tie the elements of a piece together while providing a focal point. Here Leo Lionni took the Olivetti "O" and put it to work in this advertisement.*
12. ***Ad*** *for American Type Founders. Will Burtin, 1958. From the Graphic Design Archive, Rochester Institute of Technology, Rochester, New York.*

TYPOGRAPHIC COMMUNICATIONS TODAY
Chapter VII: The New Typography Crosses the Ocean

"...the art director and designer moved from a stool and a drawing board to the executive-client conference room."

The 1940s, '50s and '60s were decades when art directors and graphic designers were asserting their talents for evolving graphic statements to powerfully, and sometimes subliminally, make statements formerly reserved for words. Copy became more concise, more supportive of a psychologically aimed illustration or design, and the art director and designer moved from a stool and a drawing board to the executive-client conference room, so that he or she should hear the message-marketing problem first hand, and make a more intelligent, more fundamental contribution to its solution. The designers whose works are illustrated in this section of Typographic Communications Today were key figures (along with the activity of the Art Directors Club of New York) in establishing the importance of the art director and graphic designer in communication and, as a by-product, the importance of expertly handled typographics.

A spread *from Cipe Pineles' cookbook that won an Art Directors Club medal. The illustrations weave into and around the text to create a total picture. The type columns flow irregularly to create an appealing yet thoroughly readable whole.*

This piece *by Cipe Pineles was a book cover for a Parsons editorial design class project.*

Seventeen *magazine spread by Cipe Pineles with a moody portrait by Kunyoshi. The type supports but does not upstage the illustration.*

Few designers *matched Cipe Pineles' blend of vigor and readability and graphic freshness derived from a keen understanding and feeling for the message problem. Formula-free, her work has many faces. Here she works totally with type in a powerful cover for the* Lincoln Center Journal.

Dynamic balance *is one method used to combine order and vitality in a graphic design. In this title page for* Catalog Design Progress, *1950, Ladislav Sutnar uses bars and rectangles enclosing type as elements to be dynamically balanced. The design is asymmetrical but the elements are balance-related to each other, not freely scattered.*

Other U.S.-Europe Typographic Bridges

The influence of the emigré designers in the United States was reinforced by two other developments: (1) the publication *PM*, (later renamed *AD*), and the role of Aaron Burns and others in arranging seminars, exhibits and various contacts between American and overseas designers. Furthermore, several trade journals were starting to broadcast design developments nationally.

PM

Volume I, Number 1 appeared in September 1934. It was a 5¼″ x 7¾″ monthly gold mine of ideas and information. It described itself as "An Intimate Journal for Advertising Production Managers, Art Directors and their Associates." The principals of the publishing company were owners of a New York typographic service, The Composing Room, Inc. The masthead of Volume I, Number 1 lists the following: Editor, Percy Seitlin; Art Director, Martin J. Weber; Contributing Editors, H. E. Cooke, Herbert Holzer, Robert L. Leslie, Irving B. Simon. Later Percy Seitlin and Robert Leslie were *PM*'s editors. Essentially *PM*, as its title implies, covered the concerns of production managers, with information about paper, plates, presswork, estimating, mechanical methods, etc. But there were also articles about William Morris, Frederic Goudy, Aldus Manutius, Theodore Low De Vinne, Giambattista Bodoni and others. Issue by issue *PM* was informing and sensitizing its readers to the work of the typographic giants of the past. With articles on Joseph Blumenthal and Bruce Rogers, for example, it also called attention to the work of contemporary American typographic innovators and expert craftsmen. But *PM*'s importance, from the viewpoint of TYPOGRAPHIC COMMUNICATIONS TODAY, was in its articles dealing with European designers and the recent emigrés. One of the first of these, on Lucian Bernhard, appeared in March 1936, Volume XI, Number 7. May 1936 featured a report on cubism and abstract art. Other early issues featured articles on A. M. Cassandre, E. McKnight Kauffer, Swiss born Amberger, and Marcel Jacno, French typographer and poster designer. The first of its series on the Bauhaus focused on Walter Gropius (then at Harvard) and the essentials for architectural education. Subsequent features were devoted to L. Moholy-Nagy, of the New Bauhaus American School of Design, Chicago; and to Josef Albers and Xanti Schawinsky, then teaching at Black Mountain College in North Carolina. A major report in 1938 covered *The Bauhaus Tradition and The New Typography*. This was a thorough examination of the roots of the then contemporary typography and like TYPOGRAPHIC COMMUNICATIONS TODAY, covered the work, influence, and inter-connections of various artists and schools including Wassily Kandinsky, sculptor Alexander Archipenko (then in Chicago), the history and role of the Bauhaus, the typography of the Czechoslovakian, Karel Teige, futurism, dadaism, the influence of El Lissitzky and Jan Tschichold, the significance to typographics of Guillaume Apollinaire (pseudonym of Wilhelm von Kostrowitzki). the typographics of L. Moholy-Nagy, the role of the De Stijl group and especially of van Doesburg and Mondrian, the relationship between constructivism and the Bauhaus philosophy, the advent of Paul Renner's Futura type and Herbert Bayer's experimental Universal type. Also included was a thoughtful review of the roles of Gropius, Moholy-Nagy and Herbert Bayer in the development of the new typography at the Bauhaus, and of Tschichold's role in telling the world about the Bauhaus. Bayer, at this time, had left the Bauhaus and was with Dorland Studios in Berlin. The *PM* report concluded with comments on the opening of the New Bauhaus in Chicago. Other *PMs* in the 1937-1939 period reviewed the work of Dr. Agha and Stanley Morison. Later there were additional features on Herbert Bayer, Joseph Binder, Lucian Bernhard, Gyorgy Kepes, George Guisti, Herbert Matter and Will Burtin. In mid-1942 the final issue of the magazine appeared, and then became a casualty of the war. But the pocket-sized publication had done a giant-sized job of bringing to American art directors and designers the work of leading designers at home and abroad.

Bringing People Together

After World War II, with *PM* no longer on the scene, and with many former European designers established in the United States, trade magazines, professional societies and art directors club annuals continued to call attention to the current typographics, but something was missing: personal contact among designers from all over the world.

Aaron Burns, now President of International Typeface Corporation, then an active graphic designer/typographer and member of the Type Directors Club, spearheaded a number of projects that further acquainted designers with each other's work and enabled more designers to meet each other than had been the custom.

In 1956 he conceived, organized and supervised, for the Type Directors Club, an evening lecture series, Inspired Typography 26-66. This series brought to the attention of American designers the work in typographic design done from the De Stijl and Bauhaus periods up to the mid-'50s. It documented the work of the pioneers, innovators, and design and typography leaders, and was the beginning of what was to become a growing interest and concern for typographic design throughout the world.

Two years later, also for the Type Directors Club, Burns, together with Will Burtin, put together The Art and Science of Typography. Held in Silvermine, Connecticut, it was the first world typographic design seminar. It brought together designers from all over the world. The seminar, the exhibition, the personal interchanges not only shed light on state-of-the-art typography, but lit a flame of international enthusiasm and cultural exchange that has burned brightly ever since. And again in 1959, for the Type Directors Club, Aaron Burns organized the symposium, Typography USA, which assembled a panel of 20 of the foremost designers in the United States to review and evaluate the state of contemporary typography in America.

In 1960 Burns founded the International Center for the Typographic Arts. He traveled throughout Europe lecturing and organizing ICTA, and bringing together collaborators from all over the world. This was the first significant banding together, for educational purposes, of designers from all over the world. Examples of typographic art were gathered from many countries and made available as exhibitions and lecture programs for schools and interested groups. This was the beginning of a worldwide exchange of typographic knowledge.

In 1964, under ICTA sponsorship, Burns organized Typomundus 20, a worldwide exhibition of the most significant typography of the 20th century. More than 12,000 pieces were judged by a jury of designers from ten countries. Typomundus 20, as both a traveling exhibition and a book, reached lovers of typography everywhere and was a major force in spreading knowledge about the origins and evolution of modern typographic design. It also introduced and reinforced standards of excellence and quality among students, teachers, and practicing designers.

The bringing together of designers gathered momentum as Aaron Burns, together with Will Burtin again, spearheaded three world seminars sponsored by ICTA, Vision 65, Vision 67, and Vision 69. These explored all aspects of visual design in all disciplines of art, and further contributed to the continuing growing body of knowledge of design and its role in communications.

In 1977 the International Typeface Corporation sponsored Vision 77. This was the first international conference addressed to graphic designers and typographers, concerning the then new typesetting technologies and their impact on typefaces, typesetting and design. Aaron Burns had proposed the conference. It was organized and chaired by Edward Gottschall.

The TDC Exhibitions

In 1955 the Type Directors Club, at the suggestion of Edward Gottschall, sponsored the first of its annual exhibitions. In the more than three decades since then the exhibition has become the premier showcase for typographic excellence. Multiple sets of the show now travel to key cities in Europe and Japan as well as throughout the United States and Canada. Work in the show also comes from all over the world, so the show is now a medium enabling designers all over the world to see much of the best work done, internationally, year after year.

TYPOGRAPHIC COMMUNICATIONS TODAY

Chapter VIII: American Design Pioneers

"...one can see how they blended the best of European and American art developments to evolve typographic design that was vigorous yet clear, derivative yet original, beautiful yet functional."

Although the émigrés from Europe numerically dominated the field of distinguished designers in the United States, in the late 1930s and the 1940s there were a small number of American-born-and-educated designers whose work equaled the best created anywhere in the world. Their influence was to be profound and enduring, and their ranks were to be swelled until the number of topflight typographic designers in the United States transformed the country from a Johnny-come-lately in contemporary design, to the position of leadership it enjoys today. Two of these American design pioneers, Paul Rand and Bradbury Thompson, are still active in the mid-1980s as designers and teachers. In this chapter we will look at some of their early work, and the work of Lester Beall and William Golden. Together they helped set a new tone and personality for American typographic design in the '40s. The later work of these designers and the work of other American designers in this and subsequent decades will be reviewed in Chapter XIII, where we will survey the typography of the past several decades worldwide.

American born and bred designers like Beall and Golden, Rand and Thompson, though deeply influenced by the 20th century European art movements and European designers, were also influenced by contemporary American culture – by Thomas Hart Benton, Reginald Marsh, Edward Hopper, Alfred Stieglitz, Georgia O'Keeffe, to name just a few. With hindsight one can see how they blended the best of European and American art developments to evolve typographic design that was vigorous yet clear, derivative yet original, beautiful yet functional.

Paul Rand

Paul Rand was born in Brooklyn, New York, in 1914. He studied art and design at Pratt Institute, Parsons School of Design and The Art Students League. In 1937, at the age of 23, he became art director for *Apparel Arts* magazine and then of *Esquire* magazine. In 1941 he became art director of the William H. Weintraub agency where he stayed until 1954, in which year he was voted one of the ten best art directors in the United States and his work was exhibited at the Museum of Modern Art. His first book, *Thoughts on Design,* was published in 1946. It contained crisp yet profound statements and over 80 examples of his work. Generations of designers have been inspired by it. In the 1940s he taught at The Cooper Union and at Pratt Institute. In 1956 he became Professor of Graphic Design at Yale University and graphic consultant to IBM and Westinghouse. Over the years he has won all the important honors in the field and through his design work, his books and magazine articles, and his teaching, he has vastly influenced the direction of typographic design in the United States and in the world. His own design thinking was greatly influenced by George Grosz (his teacher at the Art Students League), *Gebrauchsgraphik* magazine (which brought the work of the best European graphic designers to him), Jan Tschichold (and his advocacy of Bauhaus typography), Le Corbusier, Moholy-Nagy, and A. M. Cassandre. His creation of freely invented shapes grew from his appreciation of the works of Klee, Kandinsky, and the cubists. He knew such fresh shapes could be symbolic and communicative as well as arresting.

Herb Lubalin once wrote, in *Print* magazine, "Paul Rand's influence on so many of us was really the beginning of the 'New School' of graphic design. Paul was the first to break the mold so adamantly adhered to by typographic traditionalists. He showed me and others there was a different way to create graphic images, a new way to break up space and, in spite of overwhelming opinion to the contrary, it was O.K. to use quantities of so-called 'illegible' typefaces – the gothics. Single-handedly Rand was responsible for the revival of Futura... He was also influential in popularizing News Gothic and Alternate Gothic... Paul Rand was the Pablo Picasso of graphics. His innovativeness encouraged our inventiveness."

Although Rand is not characterized as a grid designer or a Bauhaus designer, he uses grids expertly and innovatively when the job calls for such an approach, and even in his most playful and casual seeming work the simplicity and communication orientation stressed in Bauhaus design is apparent. He arrives at these goals in his own way. The combination of playfulness and visual dynamism linked to a communication objective, epitomized by Rand's work, Herb Lubalin called "The American School of Graphic Expressionism."

The Beautiful and the Useful

In *Thoughts on Design* Rand wrote:

"Graphic design –
which fulfills esthetic needs,
complies with the laws of form
and the exigencies of two-dimensional space:
which speaks in semiotics, sans-serifs,
and geometrics;
which abstracts, transforms, translates,
rotates, dilates, repeats, mirrors,
groups, and regroups –
is not good design
if it is irrelevant.
"Graphic design –
which evokes the symmetria of Vitruvius,
the dynamic symmetry of Hambidge,
the asymmetry of Mondrian;
which is a good gestalt;
which is generated by intuition or by computer,
by invention or by a system of co-ordinates –
is not good design
if it does not co-operate
as an instrument
in the service of communication.

"Visual communications of any kind, whether persuasive or informative, from billboards to birth announcements, should be seen as the embodiment of form and function: the integration of the beautiful and the useful...

"Ideally, beauty and utility are mutually generative. In the past, rarely was beauty an end in itself. The magnificent stained glass windows of Chartres were no less utilitarian than was the Parthenon or the Pyramid of Cheops. The function of the exterior decoration of the great Gothic cathedrals was to invite entry; the rose windows inside provided the spiritual mood. Interpreted in the light of our own experiences, this philosophy still prevails."

When Paul Rand became the art director of *Esquire* magazine in 1937, the term "Graphic Design" was little known and rarely used. Art directors made layouts based on an understanding of a problem fed to them by a copywriter. The key element in advertising was the illustration, and the art directors selected the illustrator, bought the lettering and typography, but did not have input at the concept development stage, nor full control over the total ad. Rand, probably more than any other designer of his time and place, helped change the role of art directors from layout artists and art buyers to that of a graphic designer who helped conceive, as well as execute, the message and graphic concepts. Art directors knew how to use graphic symbols. They knew they were communicators first, then artists. Ads could apply Bauhaus values of simplicity in fresh ways. He knew that getting attention was only a preliminary to holding attention. He knew that form and function are intertwined and in this context employed contrast, humor, asymmetric balance, rhythm, texture, color, and surrealistic juxtaposition of elements. He applied this design sense to typographic elements. To him type was not simply a bland vehicle for text but a vital graphic part of a total design. Not only graphic design and typography but the very role of the art director and graphic designer were greatly vitalized by Rand's work, writing and teaching.

In the AIGA *Journal* in the Spring of 1951, he articulated his approach to design as follows:

"1. *Designing is not capricious arrangement.*
2. *Freedom of expression is not anarchy.*
3. *Understanding of the nature of new materials is not an exercise in novelty.*
4. *Functional form is not streamlining.*
5. *Order, discipline and proportion are not a Greek monopoly.*
6. *Simplicity is not nudity.*
7. *'Space' does not mean empty space, nor is 'space articulation' the arbitrary placement of things in a void.*
8. *Sensitivity is not fussiness nor is it preciousness.*
9. *Glass bricks do not a modern house make.*
10. *Lower case letters and sans serif do not make modern typography.*
11. *Montage is not synthesized confusion.*
12. *Cropping and bleeding are not the prerogative of a Bluebeard.*
13. *Texture is not exclusively a physical experience."*

Shown here is some of Rand's earlier work. Later pieces are shown in Chapter XIII.

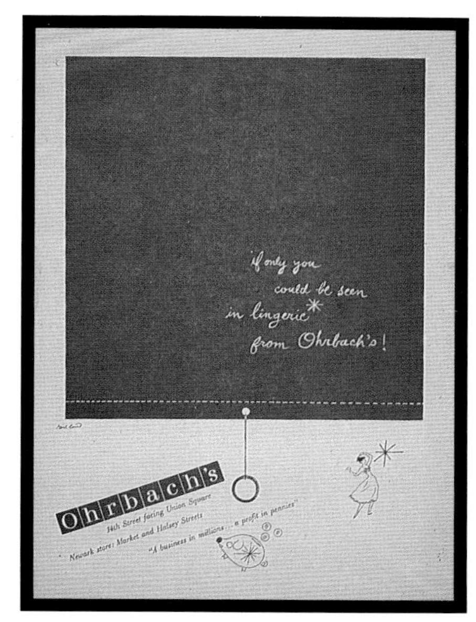

Newspaper ad *for Ohrbach's department store, 1946.*

Westinghouse trademark, *1960. The symbol came to life as it moved in an animated film.*

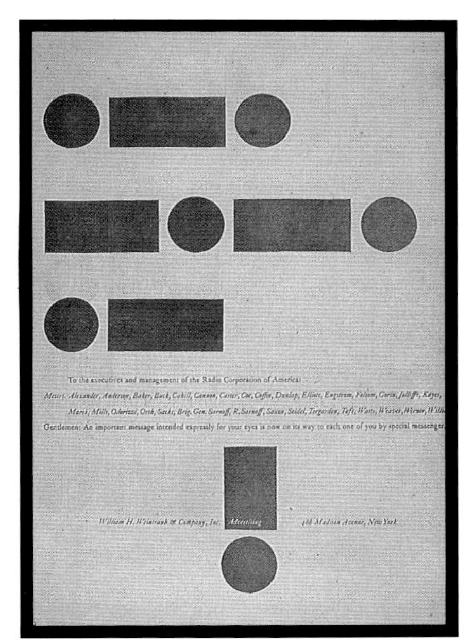

Newspaper ad *for* RCA, *1954.*

Box *for G. H. P. Cigar Co., 1957.*

One of a series of ads *for Stafford Fabrics showing how a single symbol can be exploited in a variety of ways to give identity, vibrancy, and continuity to a campaign.*

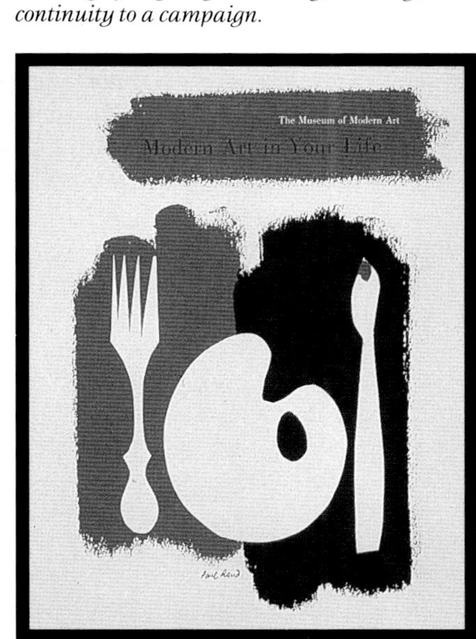

Museum catalog *cover, 1949.*

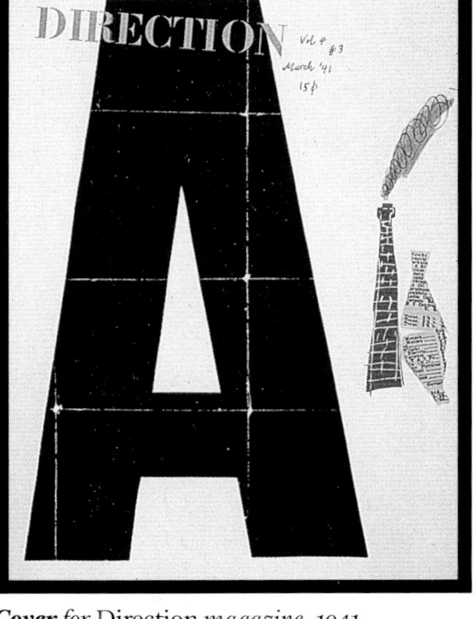

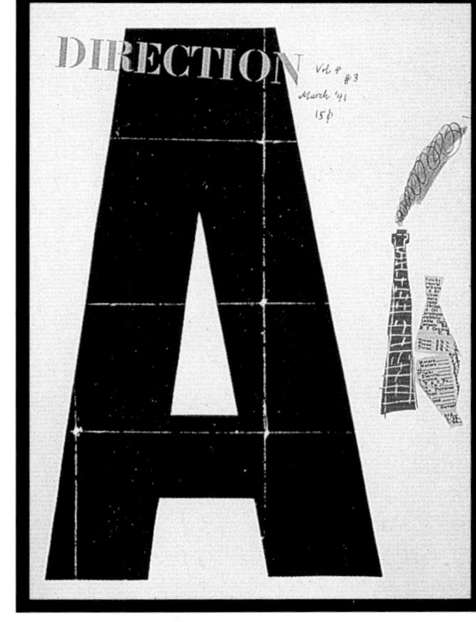

Cover *for* Direction *magazine, 1941.*

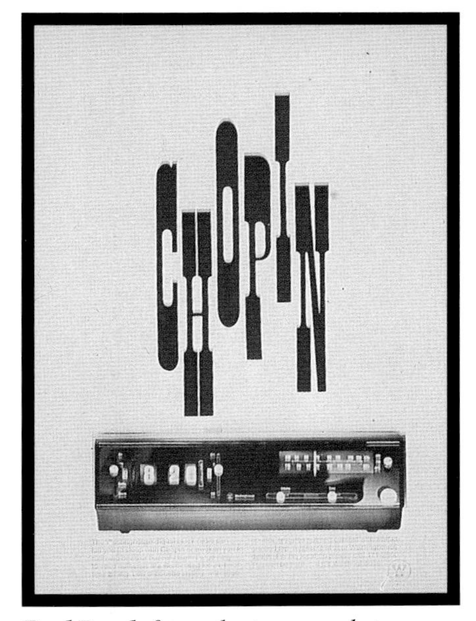

Paul Rand *often makes type move, but always with a reason and without sacrificing readability.*

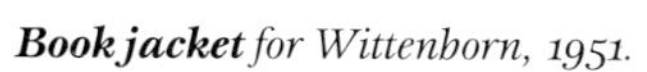

Book jacket *for Wittenborn, 1951.*

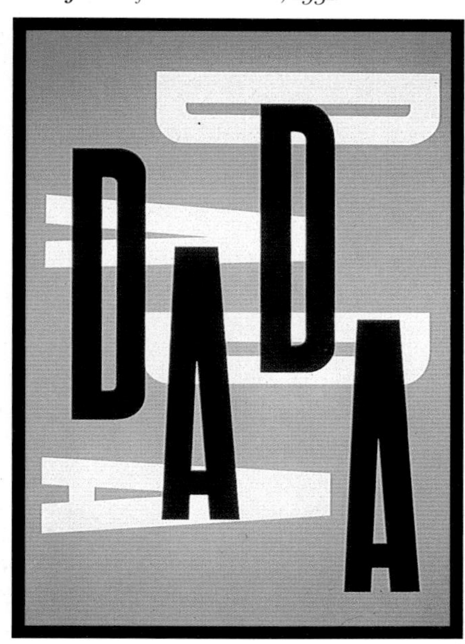

The famous Dubonnet man *created by Cassandre was ingeniously adapted in more recent advertising by Paul Rand. The simplified, two-dimensional treatment of this figure and other elements help create an appropriate, forceful symbol. Filling in the man and the letters gradually as the man fills himself with wine is a graphic and friendly, humorous way of getting the message across.*

All *the work shown on this page was designed by Paul Rand.*

TYPOGRAPHIC COMMUNICATIONS TODAY
Chapter VIII: American Design Pioneers

"His experiments made other designers rethink the conventional way of making layouts."

Bradbury Thompson

Typography today is more exciting and more effective than it was 50 years ago, and one of the great forces that propelled it as a mighty communications tool was Bradbury Thompson. His early work was innovative, colorful, dynamic, visually exciting and alerted designers of the 1940s and 1950s to new ways of using type both dramatically and effectively. In his more recent work, reviewed in Chapter XIII, we see a more classical typography exquisitely, yet still vibrantly executed.

Thompson was born in Topeka, Kansas, in 1911 He studied economics at Washburn University in Topeka. He designed and supervised the engraving and printing of the college's yearbook. After graduating he designed books and magazines at Capper Publications in Topeka. In his spare time he read in the local library about artists and designers in Europe and New York. In 1938 he came to New York and became art director of the printing firm, Rogers-Kellogg-Stillson. Perhaps his most influential graphics contributions were made in the 1939-1961 period when he was designer-editor of *Westvaco Inspirations.* Just a few other highlights from his ongoing career include: 1945, he introduced The Mono Alphabet, an innovative, simplified alphabet; 1945-59, art director, *Mademoiselle* magazine; 1950, created Alphabet 26, a simplified alphabet (see Chapter X). Brad Thompson has redesigned numerous national magazines, been a faculty member, board member, consultant or lecturer at the Philadelphia College of Art, Yale University (where he is presently senior visiting critic in the School of Design), Cornell University, and Harvard University. As might be expected, he has received the top honors from the profession's leading clubs and societies.

A New Way of Seeing...New Ways of Showing

The tremendous impact of Thompson's typographics developed through the pages of *Westvaco Inspirations,* a four-color magazine demonstrating the capabilities of printing papers. Thompson combined a hands-on knowledge of typography and printing with an adventurous spirit. He wasn't going to do what had been done, yet his innovations would be purposeful, appropriate to the communication problem. With a limited budget, he would work with existing color plates (these were the great days of letterpress printing) and cut them apart, reassemble them, team them up with tint plates, overprint to create action and new colors. He used large shapes for their symbolism and power, often greatly enlarged letter forms, blended old art (such as prints from the Diderot encyclopedia) with new color combinations and symbolic shapes. Pattern, movement, color, excitement, were combined and harnessed to reinforce the message. No obscurity, no blatancy for its own sake here. Thompson strove for and achieved a wonderful blend of vitality and clarity. He employed dynamic balance, often avoiding the usual columns of type. He did not hesitate to mix several typefaces when he thought doing so would strengthen the message. He used white space generously and judiciously. He grouped graphic elements by units (message related) rather than in conventional columns or blocks. When others were busy making certain four-color plates were precisely registered, Thompson would throw the colors obviously off register to focus attention on a given spot or achieve a sense of action. He often used simple and inexpensive line art, perhaps printed in one of the primary colors, to extend the size and impact of a small four-color process plate. He used tint plates of unusual shapes to add color economically to otherwise color-dull areas and to counter the staticism of square halftones. But always his type was not only compelling but very legible and readable.

Yet, for all the flare and vigor, the result was a design unit with graphic coherence and controlled eye-flow. Twice he introduced new alphabets to advocate a simpler form of typographic expression. And occasionally he advocated and demonstrated phrased typography, as in *Westvaco Inspirations* No. 127 and in the Washburn Bible published in 1979. In phrased typography, type lines end or break at rhythm points or between thought units. When economics permit such functional, ragged-right margins, the ease and joy of reading is greatly improved. The Washburn Bible, using the King James version, is a dramatic example of this. (See Chapter XIII)

Unlike most art directors of the 1930s and 1940s Thompson did not simply make layouts. He blended type and pictures into a free-form unit. He avoided the preconceived format into which any layout could be poured.

Thompson was the first typographic designer, the innovator, of most of the techniques described above. His innovations with type and plates and graphic elements reached a well-targeted and receptive audience via the pages of *Westvaco Inspirations,* that included advertising agencies, printers, art studios and related schools.

In experimenting with type and attempting to simplify the alphabet by using only lowercase letters he would begin new sentences with ellipses, underscore a lowercase letter that normally would be capitalized, or use a boldface or larger size lowercase letter instead of a capital letter. His experiments made other designers rethink the conventional way of making layouts.

When he came to New York, Thompson chose the position at Rogers-Kellogg-Stillson, the printer of *Westvaco Inspirations,* over an opening at *Vogue* with Dr. Agha. His work on the Westvaco account led to his ultimate role on the latter publication. The budget for the Inspirations precluded commissioning art, but facilitated borrowing of plates from museums, publishers and advertisers. Thompson's creative touch made a virtue of this necessity. His work, starting in 1945, for *Art News* gained him entrée to the Metropolitan Museum of Art, a prime source of press plates.

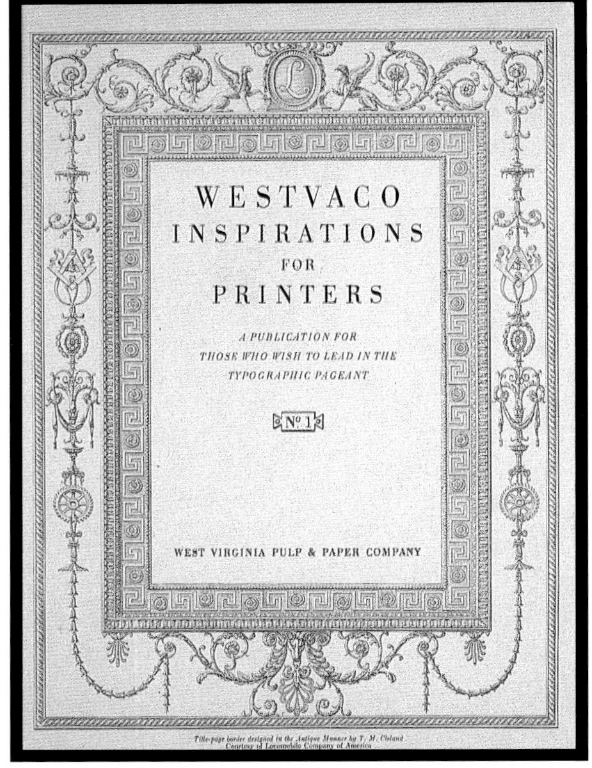

Title-page border *designed in the Antique Manner by T.M. Cleland for the first issue of* Westvaco Inspirations, *1925. Courtesy of Locomobile Company of America. Here exquisite use of ornament and precise handling of center axis type give this page life and charm. Contrast this 1925 page with the later* Westvaco Inspirations *work of Bradbury Thompson, using dynamic balance and freely positioned type and pictorial elements to achieve beauty and vitality while reinforcing the message.*

A key consideration in all of Thompson's work is appropriateness. Perhaps no other designer carries this concern to the lengths he does. Excellent examples of his concern for appropriateness are the exquisite books he has designed for Westvaco since 1958. These are American classics inspired by different periods of the country's history. In each the typeface, paper selection, illustration style and design are appropriate to the period of the subject matter. The result is not merely a beautiful book but a total reading experience in which the clothing of the text and the text itself are one.

Whether in his early experimental work or his more traditional later work, he always used his graphic touch to make a message be seen, read, understood, felt and remembered. His work is consistently appropriate to the problem and always powers but never overpowers the content.

Bradbury Thompson's mark is impeccable taste applied with great elegance, an elegance frequently of simplicity, wit, vast learning, and an intimate knowledge of the process of printing. His feeling for type is best expressed in his own words spoken at *Inspired Typography,* '26-'66, a symposium sponsored by the Type Directors Club of New York, in New York City, in 1956.

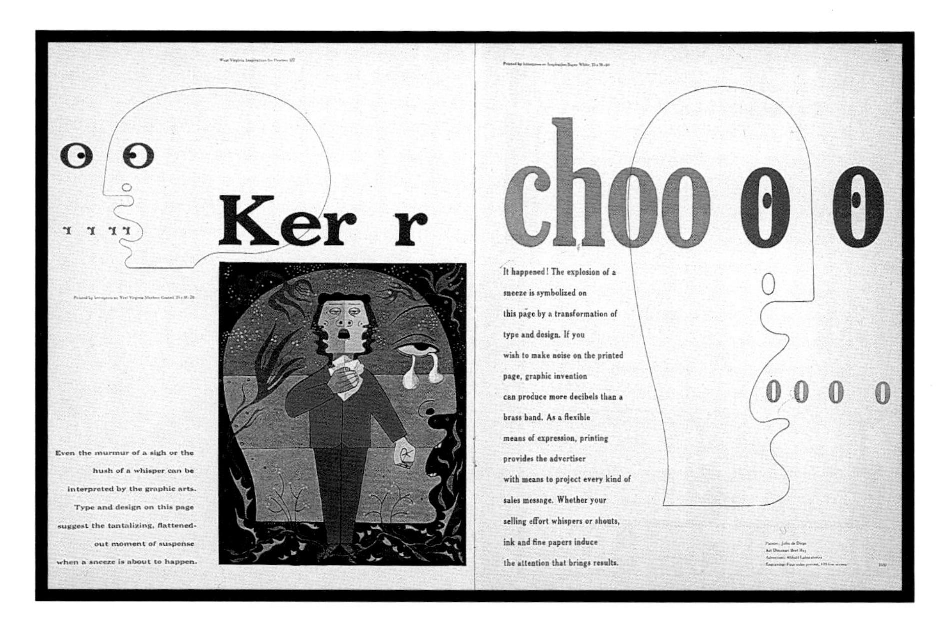

***Here** Thompson catches the evolution of a sneeze in a powerful and witty spread that borders on great surrealistic art, as it brings sound to the printed page.* Westvaco Inspirations, *No. 177, 1949.*

***A series of Os** in a crescendo/diminuendo baseball-flight arc make the typographics alive.*
Westvaco Inspirations, *No. 210, 1958.*

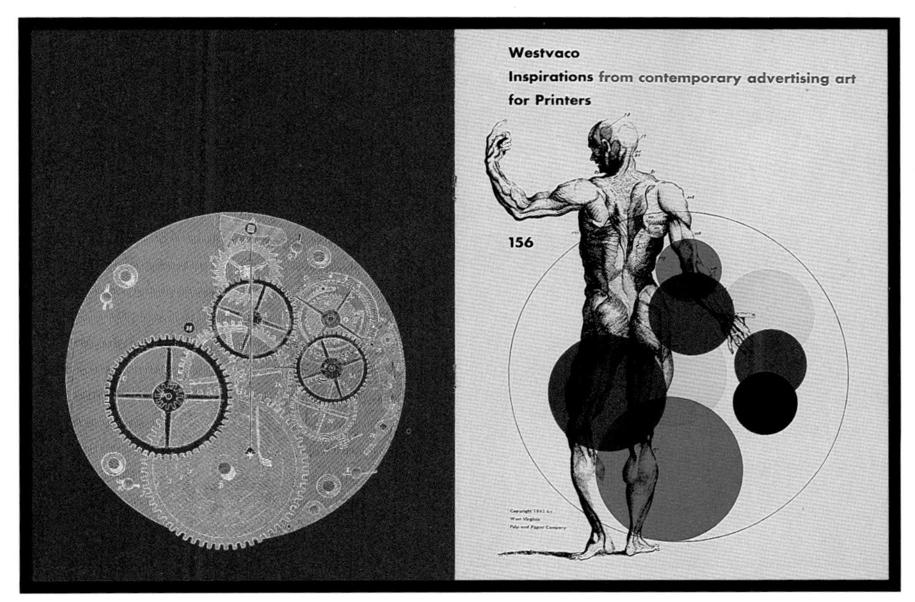

***This spread** from* Inspirations, *No. 156, 1945, brings alive man's concern for time as the colorful motion of clockworks becomes surrealistically fused within his inner self.*

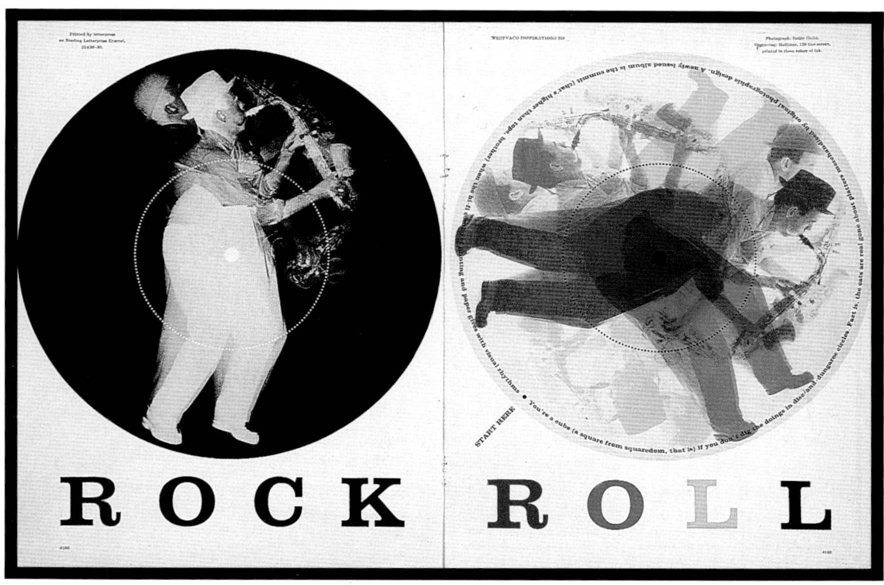

***A multiple exposure** of a saxophone player and off-register over-printing in primary colors vitalizes the image. Bradbury Thompson,* Westvaco Inspirations, *No. 210, 1958.*

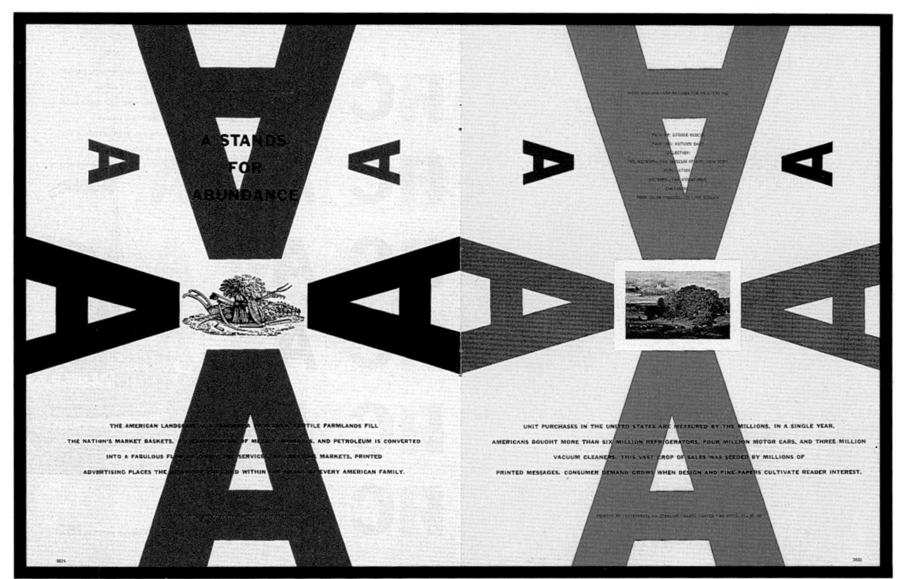

***Typographic letters** are the pure basis for the design of an entire issue of* Westvaco Inspirations, *No. 192, 1952. Bradbury Thompson. Here the alphabet becomes the* visual *component.*

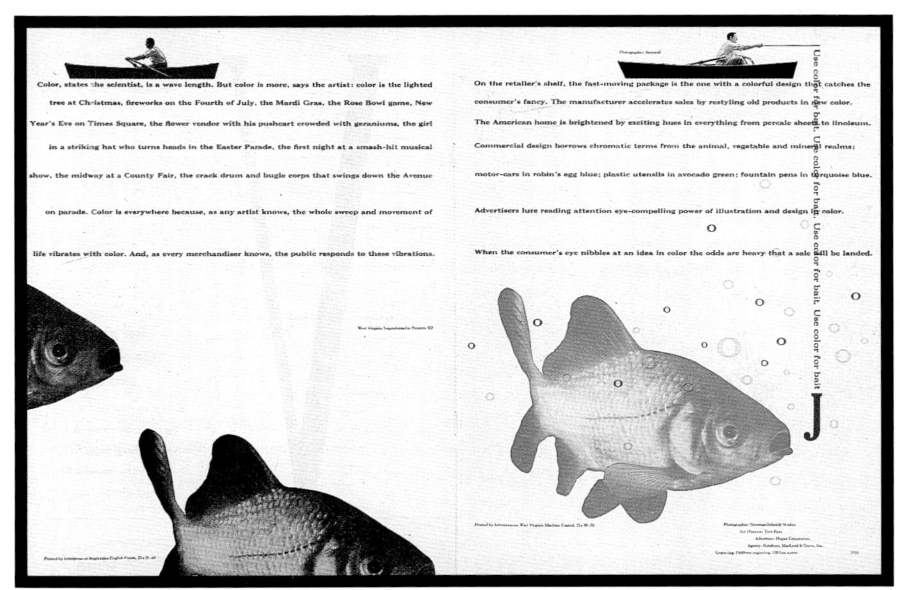

***Fish** in a sea of type.* Westvaco Inspirations, *No. 177, 1949. Bradbury Thompson.*

"He was acutely aware of the effects of graphic design on the human environment and the social responsibilities of the designer."

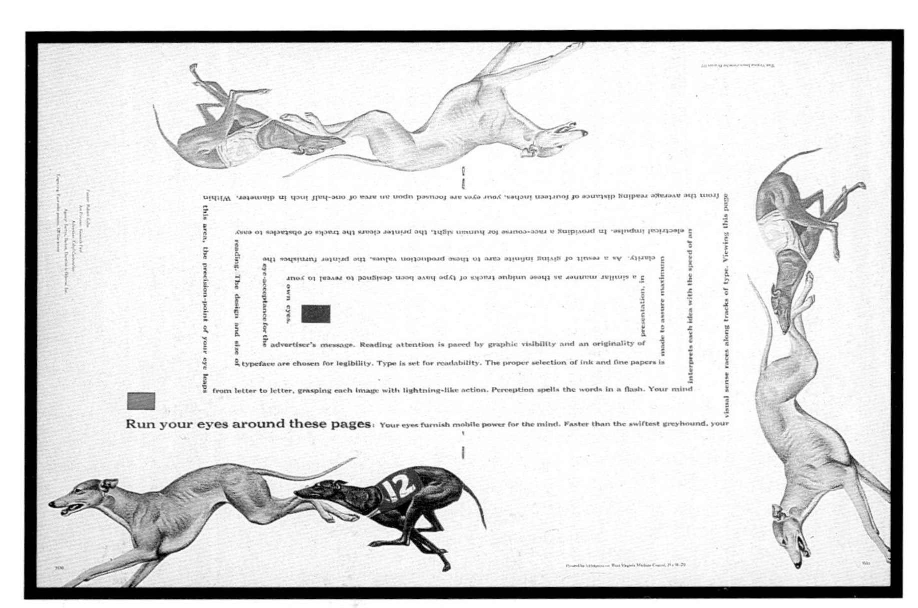

***Dog** on a racetrack of type,* Westvaco Inspirations, *No. 177, 1949. Bradbury Thompson.*

***This** is from* Westvaco Inspirations, *No. 216, 1961, on the 100th Anniversary of the American Civil War. In this spread the chug-chug puff-puff type brings the spread alive to both the eye and the ear.*

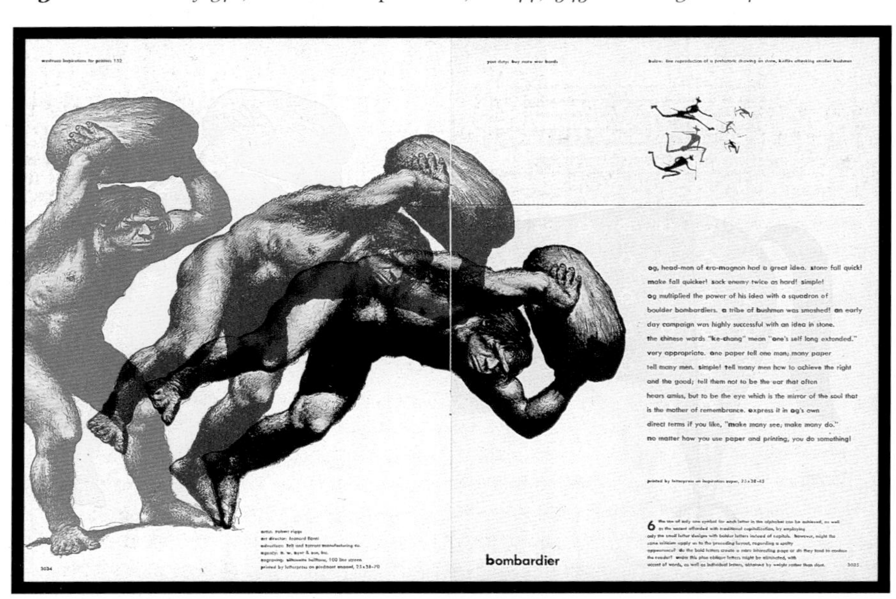

***Whimsically labeled** "bombardier," this spread springs the primitive man into action via off-register process color plates. Color is economically extended with line plates at upper right. This issue of Inspirations introduced Mr. Thompson's ideas for an alphabet of 26 characters, with the same designs used for the "capital" letters. The type is all lower case with boldface lowercase replacing caps. Bradbury Thompson,* Westvaco Inspirations, *No. 152, 1945.*

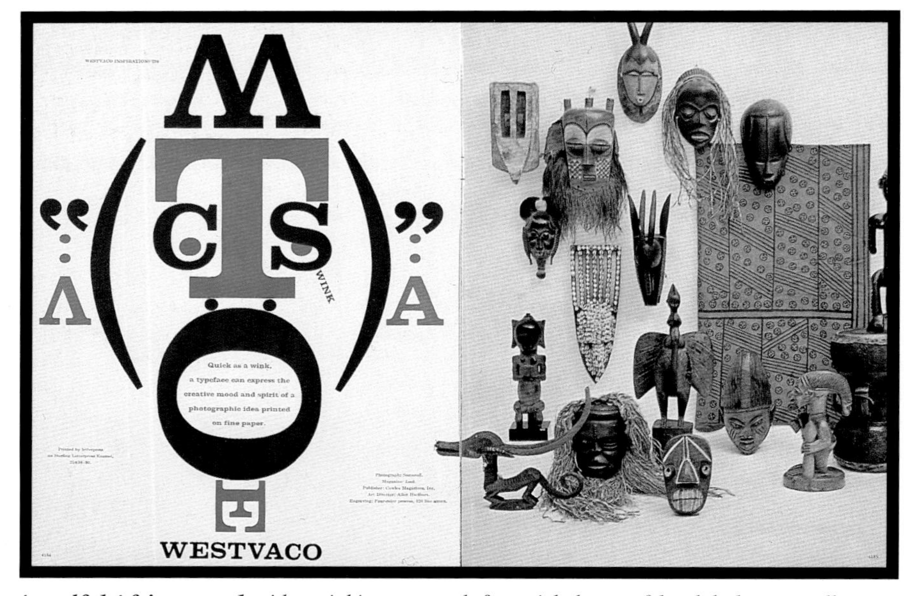

***A soulful African mask** with a winking eye, made from eight letters of the alphabet. Actually, an idea that originated when a six-year-old child brought home from school the drawing of a large face with her first printed words placed in her mouth where words usually belong.* Inspirations, *No. 210, 1958. Bradbury Thompson.*

"Type is a thing of constant interest to me.
It is sometimes a serious and useful tool,
employed to deliver a message,
sell a specific article,
or give life to an idea.
"At other times it is a plaything
that affords personal amusement
and recreation.
It is fun to produce fresh designs
and spontaneous ideas with letters and numbers –
by themselves,
or together with other graphic objects.
"Type is a medium of philosophical enjoyment.
It is interesting to discover typographic rules
containing inconsistencies in logic,
which are in use only because of tradition.
It is also interesting to ponder
the origin of these errors,
the practical reasons for their perpetuation,
and to suggest remedies.
"An interest in Type
provides a broader knowledge of history,
including the appreciation of such related arts
as painting, architecture and literature –
and even business and politics.
This affords opportunity for pleasant romantic
indulgence.
At the same time,
it develops confidence
in one's practical ability
to specify appropriate type faces
to accompany creative works of specific periods.
"In short,
Type can be a tool, a toy and a teacher;
it can provide a means of livelihood,
a hobby for relaxation,
an intellectual stimulant –
and a spiritual satisfaction.
"I believe an avid interest in Type
necessarily includes
a zest for everyday life."

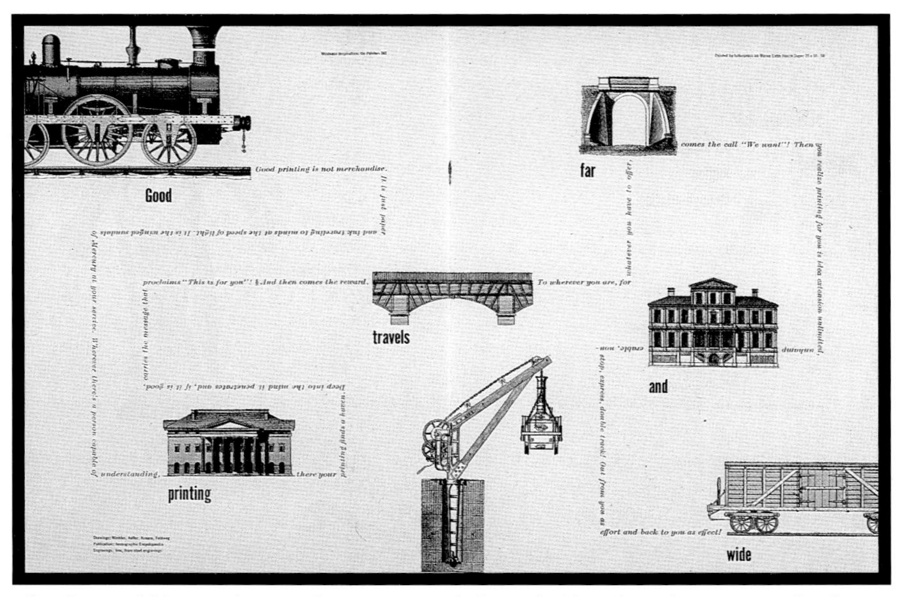

***The theme** of this spread is "Good Printing Travels far and wide." The train runs on tracks of type as it goes over trestles and through tunnels. Bradbury Thompson,* Westvaco Inspirations, *No. 161, 1946.*

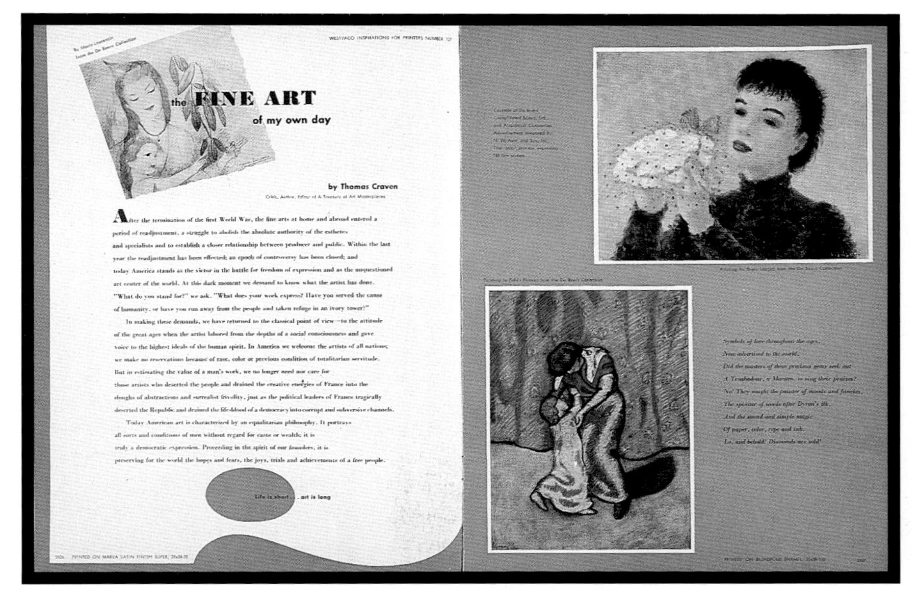

***The phrased typography** on the lower right permits each line to break at the end of a thought unit or at a natural rhythmic pause. Reading is easier, faster, more understandable, more enjoyable. Prose almost becomes poetry.* Westvaco Inspirations, *No. 127, 1941. Also used in Bible, 1969-1979.*

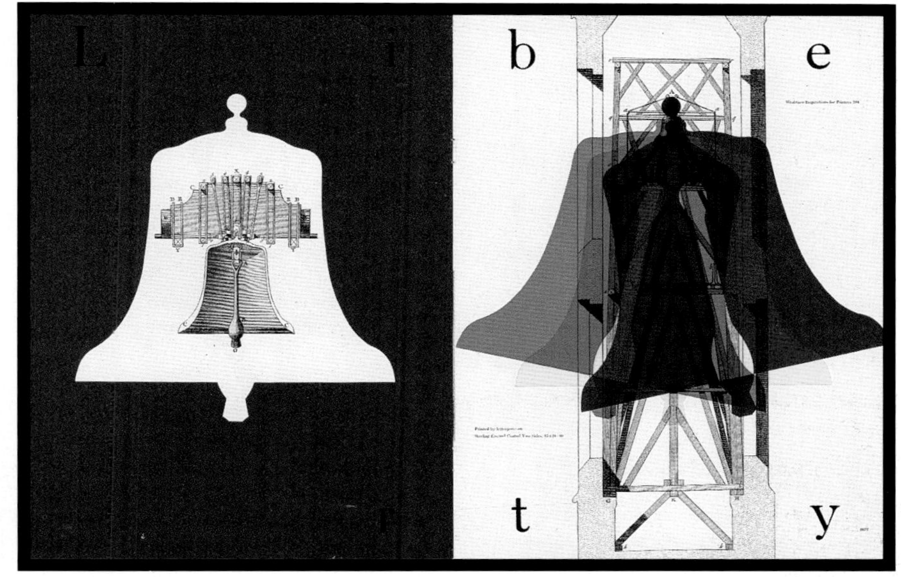

***This bell** swings in process colors and the type comes alive with it. Bradbury Thompson,* Westvaco Inspirations, *No. 194, 1953.*

Lester Beall

"Lester was first of all an artist, not only because of a vital and important talent, but because of an emotional spiritual quality, a very special attitude. He was a pioneer in his application of graphic design to advertising, publishing and related creative activities. He was acutely aware of the effects of graphic design on the human environment and of the social responsibilities of the designer."
Dorothy M. (Mrs. Lester) Beall

It was not until the mid and late 1930s that the graphic innovativeness and vitality in Europe made an impact on graphic design in the United States. Traditional illustrations dominated the scene. An early exception to this situation was Lester Beall (1903-1969). Born in Kansas City, he earned a doctorate in art history at the University of Chicago in 1926. He was a self-taught designer. Beall had studied the European art movements, as outlined in the earlier chapters of Typographic Communications Today at Chicago's Art Institute and in 1931 he met Fred Hauck, who had studied with Hans Hofmann and visited the Bauhaus before becoming an art director at BBD&O. They freelanced together, and from Hauck, Beall learned more about the avant garde artists and typographers of Europe. In 1935 he moved his studio to New York, and in 1951 to his country home, Dunbarton Farms, in Connecticut. Of his years in Chicago he wrote:

"Because of the depression of 1929, I shortly found myself much too frequently without work, and rather then spend all my time just pushing doorbells, I began to visit the Ryerson Library of the Chicago Art Institute. It was there in 1931 that I discovered Cahiers d'Art *for the first time. Previous to this I had found a few copies in a local bookstore of* Arts et Metiers Graphiques. *It was in* Arts et Metiers Graphiques *and* Cahiers d'Art *that I first saw the work of El Lissitzky, L. Moholy-Nagy, Jan Tschichold, Tristan Tzara, Piet Zwart, Mondrian and Man Ray. Simultaneously, and also at the Art Institute, I found copies of books on Picasso, Dufy and Klee. In a period where I was perhaps more interested in drawing than I was in design, Dufy was probably the most positive influence. But, it is difficult for me, even now, to underestimate the stimulation and excitement that both* Cahiers d'Art *and* Arts et Metiers Graphiques *gave to us in the thirties."*

He fully appreciated the need for organized yet strong, clear yet exciting, design. He developed a sense for random organization and intuitive selection and placement of graphic elements without creating graphic chaos. He blended in his work his sense of European graphics with a feeling for American wood types, flat planes of color, old woodcuts, photograms and original typographic effects, and simple signs and symbols combined with photographs. By the 1950s-1960s Beall was one of country's best known designers and a leader in the development of corporate design.

Beall took pleasure in the unusual in illustrations, juxtaposing and angling of elements, contrasts in scale, color, texture, and mixing of line and tone art and photography. Yet all were knit together to form a coherent entity.

His work was recognized in Europe and in *Gebrauchsgraphik* in the 1930s. In 1937 the Museum of Modern Art in New York dedicated a special exhibition to his graphics. He was the first commercial designer to be so honored. By 1941 his innovative graphics had won him the title "typographic surrealist." Throughout his career Beall won many honors, and magazines in the United States and abroad reviewed his work. Exhibitions of his designs took place all over Europe, in the United States, the USSR, and in Japan.

Ugliness Is a Form of Anarchy

Beall's attitude toward his profession was best summed up by himself, *"A genuine knowledge and love of great design is the first requirement of the professional designer, the second requirement is a sound knowledge of the principles and techniques of business communication."* He believed, too, that anyone interested in design, *"... must necessarily be interested in other fields of expression – the theatre, ballet, photography, painting, literature, as well as music, for from any of these the alert designer can at times obtain not only ideas related to his advertising problem, but genuine inspiration."* He felt very strongly that, *"Good design is also good citizenship. Ugliness is*

TYPOGRAPHIC COMMUNICATIONS TODAY
Chapter VIII: American Design Pioneers

"...the anarchy that ugly cities, ugly advertising and ugly books breed cannot be separated from the life of the individual."

a form of anarchy that must be stamped out wherever it is evident, for the anarchy that ugly cities, ugly advertising and ugly books breed cannot be separated from the life of the individual. Ugly lives makes bad citizens. Bad citizens, whether clothed in a senatorial mantle or a Brooks Brothers shirt, can part us all, businessman and designer alike, from some of the freedoms of expression we so dearly strive to maintain."
(From AIGA *Journal* 11, 1969.)

A Statement of Strength

At the 1959 symposium sponsored by the Type Directors Club, Typography USA, Lester Beall spoke of the roots of the new typography. He said:

"...In appraising the influence of the typographical design of the dadaists and the pioneers of "Die Neue Typographie" on American typographical design, as it unfolded in the early thirties, it would be a serious mistake not to also evaluate the influence of American political, county fair, and recruiting posters of the Civil War, and American and English children's books. For the American political posters, the recruiting posters of the Civil War and "Die Neue Typographie" all had one factor in common...a statement of strength! In the early thirties, the desire to meet the challenge of a new period in our economic and social history was reflected by the designer's search for forms that were strong, direct, and exciting!

"Esthetic as well as mechanical standards vary – the designer matures – he becomes interested in areas that for him hitherto have been unexplored. No longer are the mechanical standards of the type founder confused with the personal standards of the designer... and those standards must be in the heart. Mr. Robin Boyd, writing on the 'Engineering of Excitement' in the November 1958 issue of Architectural Review, *says in part, 'But today architecture's main weakness is not in the science of design practice, but in the belief that this is all there is to architecture... The lack is not of technique or technology or science of design, but of heart in the center of design...*

"So yes, there is a New Typography USA *tradition – a tradition of ever-constant examination of new as well as traditional forms – a tradition of experimentation in application – a constant searching for new forms that will better man's system of communication...all with heart!"*

Double-spread *from the* Production Yearbook, *Colton Press, Inc., New York. One in a series of spreads by different designers on the theme, "Printing: the art preservative of all the arts." Lester Beall.*

Front and back *cover for* Scope *magazine, the Upjohn Company, Vol. II, No. 9, December, 1948. Illustration is graphically integrated with text and relates to it literally as well. Text begins, "Unicaps, a fiber in the thread of life." Lester Beall.*

Spread *from* Scope, *house organ of the Upjohn Company. Lester Beall, 1948. Each issue of* Scope *had a different format, yet Beall gave them a consistent personality.*

One of a series *of posters for the Rural Electrification Administration exhibit at the Museum of Modern Art in New York, 1937. Lester Beall.*

Brochure *in a series for Sterling Engraving Co., 1938. Lester Beall.*

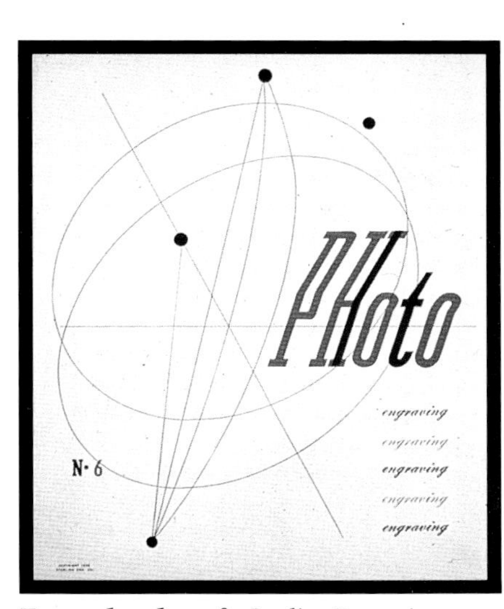

From a brochure *for Sterling Engraving Company. Lester Beall.*

Poster *for the Rural Electrification Administration. Lester Beall. 1930. From the Graphic Design Archive, Rochester Institute of Technology, Rochester, New York.*

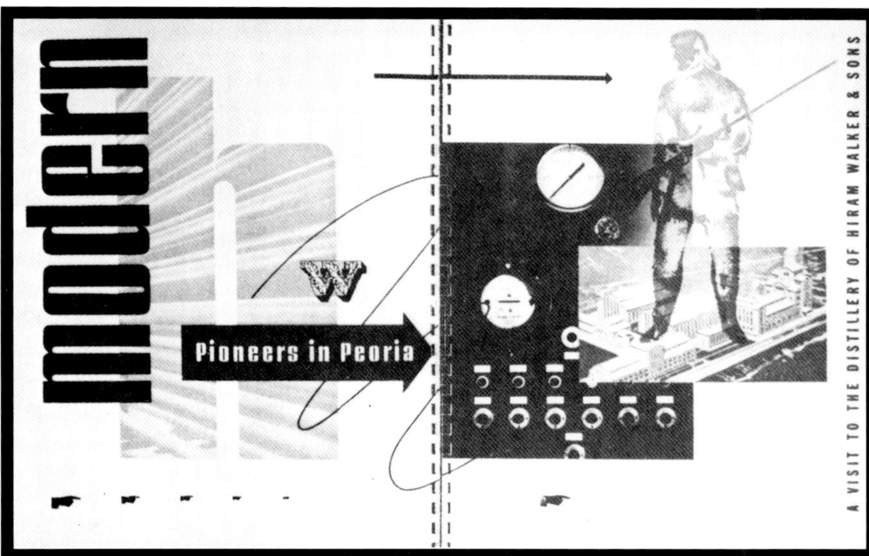

Promotional brochure *for Hiram Walker Distillers, c. 1935. Contrast of wood type and sans serif type, photography and drawing, with horizontal and vertical thrusts. Lester Beall.*

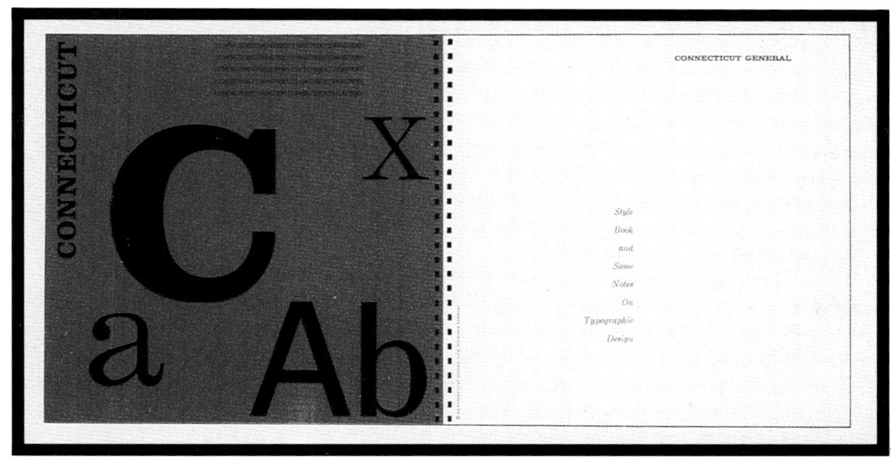

Style book *for Connecticut General, 1959. Lester Beall.*

Cover *for a 1948 issue of* Scope*, published by the Upjohn Company. Lester Beall.*

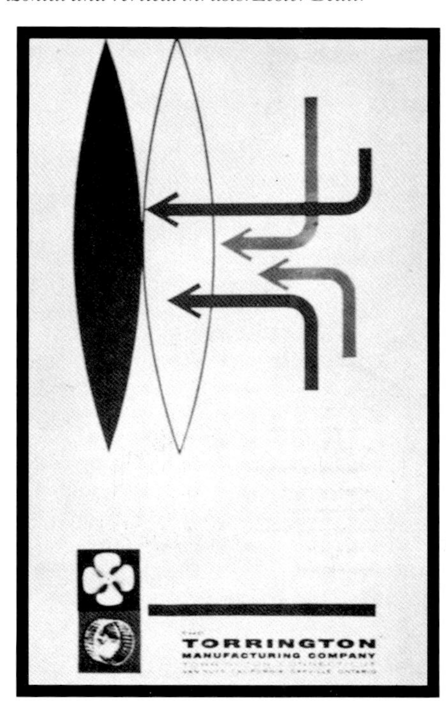

Advertisement *for Torrington Manufacturing Company. Lester Beall.*

Cover *for Connecticut General Identity Brochure. Lester Beall. 1950s. From the Graphic Design Archive, Rochester Institute of Technology, Rochester, New York.*

One of many *Lester Beall posters for the Rural Electrification Administration, c. 1940. Library of Congress, Washington, D.C., Poster Collection.*

The egg-shaped *copy block discusses the life cycle of malarial parasites. Red superior numbers in the text key the copy to the pictures. For* Scope *magazine, the Upjohn Company, No. 7, June 1944. Lester Beall.*

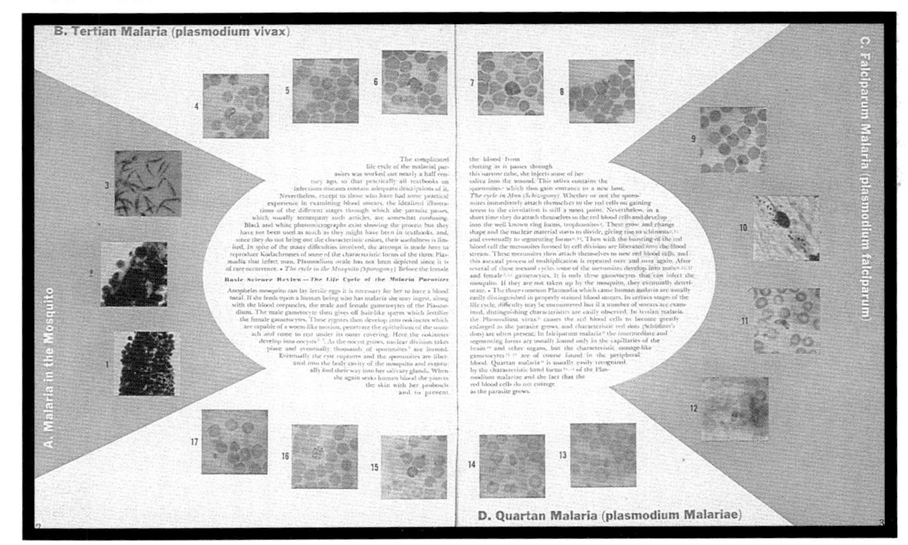

TYPOGRAPHIC COMMUNICATIONS TODAY

Chapter VIII: American Design Pioneers

"Graphic fashions were not his guiding star, communication effectiveness was. He had no fixed style to impose on problems."

William Golden

In the 1940s corporations in the United States became "corporate identity" conscious. They were concerned with the image they projected to their markets, their stockholders, their employees, the public, and they became aware that typographic design played a role in helping them project the desired image.

Stepped-up competition and a new economic scene accelerated the development of corporate image programs. Products and services with negligible real distinction proliferated, so that competing ads stressing product features tended to say the same things. Furthermore, the number of products and services offered by many companies mushroomed. These and other conditions made the development of a corporate image, one that could benefit all of a company's products and services and distinguish them from the competition, a valid concept.

In the early days of corporate image awareness three companies set a fast pace: Container Corporation of America (art oriented ads and the Great Ideas of Western Man series by key designers), IBM (projecting itself as the extremely advanced technology leader), and Columbia Broadcasting System.

In each case the corporation head set the tone for the program: Walter Paepcke at CCA, Thomas Watson, Jr. at IBM, and Frank Stanton at CBS. Stanton initiated the CBS approach and in 1937 brought in William Golden to execute it. This Golden did supremely for 23 years.

He was born in 1911 in New York City. He studied photography and commercial design at the Vocational School for Boys. In Los Angeles he worked in printing plants and art departments from 1928-1932. In 1933 he returned to New York and for three years was in the promotion department of the newspaper, the *Journal-American.* In 1936 he joined *House and Garden* magazine and worked for Dr. M. F. Agha, art director of the Condé Nast publications. A year later he joined CBS, and in 1940 was named art director.

William Golden was totally devoted to his work, days, nights, seven days a week, and to every detail of every project. He felt responsible for the communication effectiveness of every project he undertook. This attitude took him well beyond the conventional role of an art director and greatly influenced not only other art directors but management's attitude toward art directors and the role of graphics in a corporation. Golden needed to be involved at the very outset of a project, not only to hear the problem stated first hand but to contribute to the development of the communication concept as well as the graphic concept. He applied his standards to the copy and edited and rewrote text and headlines when he felt that was required. Graphic fashions were not his guiding star, communication effectiveness was. He had no fixed style to impose on problems. For Golden, a solution derived from a problem and should be appropriate to it. He felt that fine art and good design and the highest artistic standards would enhance communication effectiveness. Golden not only concerned himself with concept development and copy, as well as art and design but followed through every production step to assure that the execution of the concept and design achieved the finest reproduction obtainable.

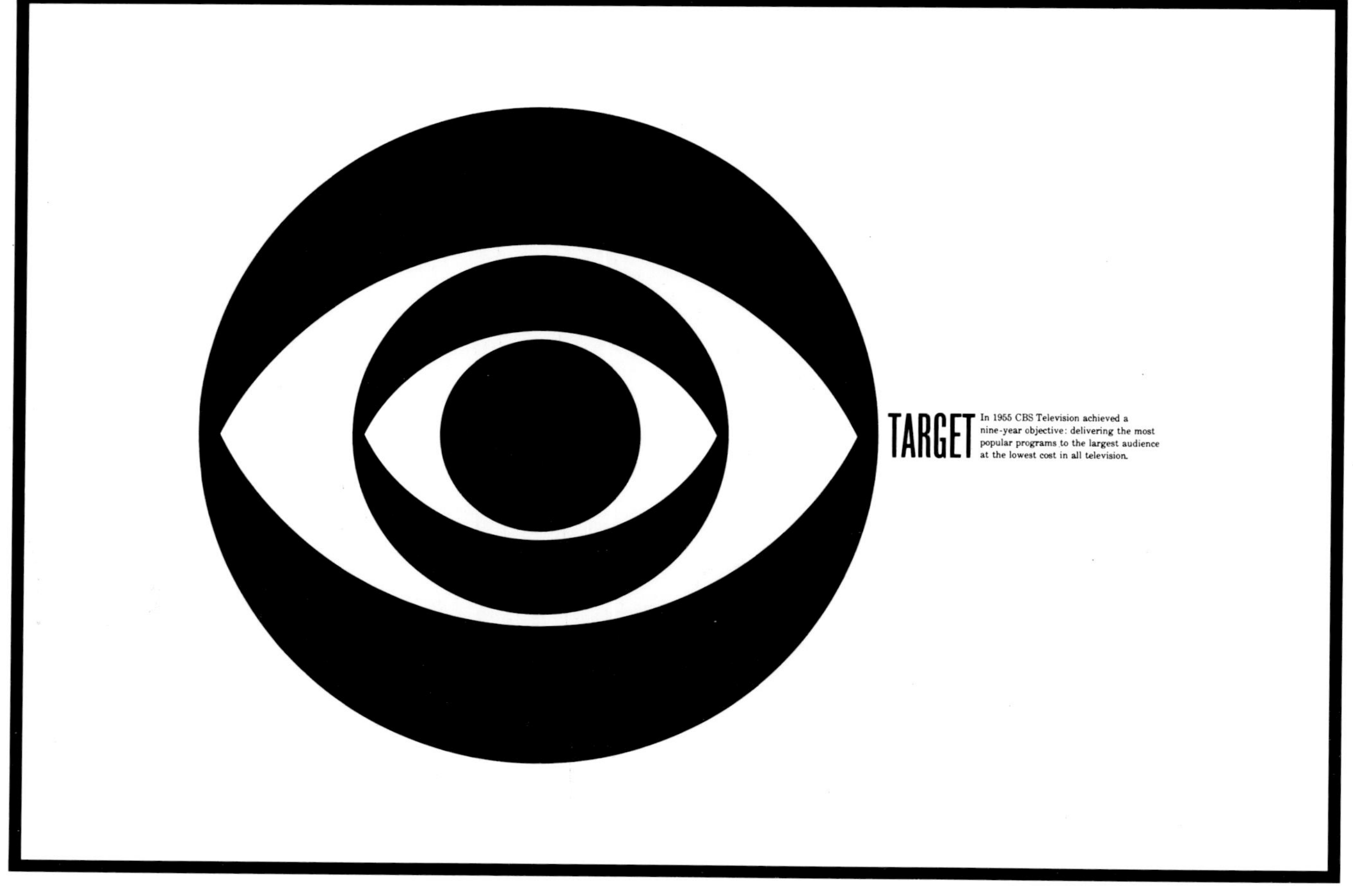

TARGET
In 1955 CBS Television achieved a nine-year objective: delivering the most popular programs to the largest audience at the lowest cost in all television.

***Two versions** of the CBS Television symbol. Above, as it appeared on-air in 1951. Right, in a 1955 trade show.*

Advertisement *for* CBS *Television. William Golden. 1954. From the Graphic Design Archive, Rochester Institute of Technology, Rochester, New York.*

Network ad. *Illustration, Ludwig Bemelmans. Art Director, William Golden.*

Trade *advertisement for* CBS *Television, 1957. Ben Shahn illustration. Designed by William Golden.*

TYPOGRAPHIC COMMUNICATIONS TODAY

Chapter VIII: American Design Pioneers

"...Americans were striking new design chords with new personalities and their fresh approaches to blending vigor and clarity for communication and typographic design."

At a time when much advertising was visually cluttered and unappealing, CBS was showing the design community as well as its own market, just how effective better organized, more tasteful, ads could be.

Unlike the IBM approach, in which a typographic style was developed by Paul Rand and others, CBS did not adhere to a specific typeface family or design approach. The common denominator that affected the unity of a corporate look was the consistent use of fine art and design carefully crafted to propel the message.

Among the fine artists whom Golden brought to CBS were Ben Shahn, Feliks Topolski, Ludwig Bemelmans, and René Bouché. Of course Golden's influence went far beyond the company's advertising. It covered a wide range of promotional material and kits for CBS, and all the things an affiliate station might require for local promotion. The kits were sent to CBS advertising agencies and to potential clients to show how CBS supported its advertisers.

The famous "CBS eye," still in use, was developed by William Golden. It first appeared on November 16, 1951, and it remains one of the most enduring and effective corporate symbols. But Golden realized, as not everyone did in those days, that even such a strong mark does not by itself a corporate image make. He wrote, "A trademark does not in itself constitute a corporate image. As I understand the phrase...it is the total impression a company makes on the public through its products, its policies, its actions, and its advertising effort." The CBS eye was initially developed for on-the-air use. It first appeared as a still composite photo of the "eye" and a cloud formation. It was originally conceived of as a symbol in motion and had several concentric "eyes." The pupil became an iris diaphragm shutter. When it clicked open it revealed the network identification. The "eye," in a way, was an obvious symbol, since CBS Radio used an ear for its symbol. Over the years the "eye" has been used many ways: in trade ads, on curtains, matchboxes, cuff links, to frame station call letters, on cameras, on brochures and packaging, on studio marquees and building exteriors, on stationery and many kinds of business forms.

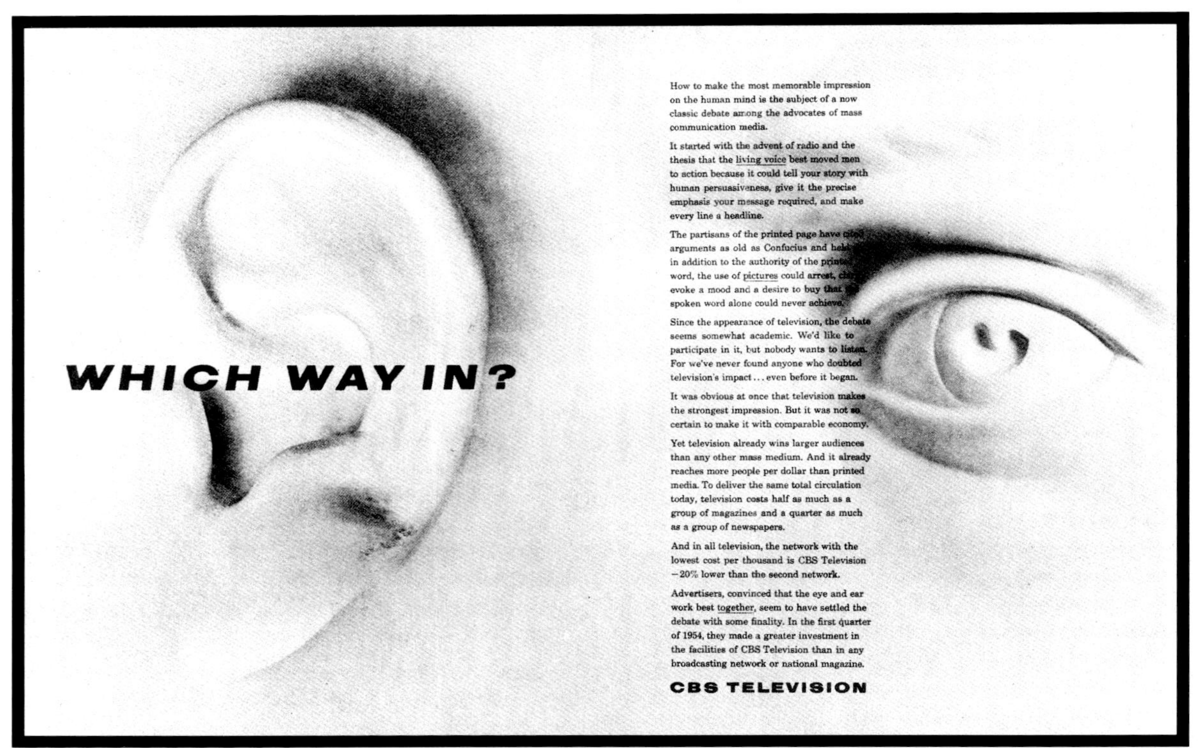

CBS *trade ad*, 1954. *William Golden.*

Bill Golden died in 1959, and that year Mrs. Golden (Cipe Pineles Golden) accepted a special memorial award from the Art Directors Club naming him Art Director of The Year. At the same awards dinner another great tribute was paid to Golden's profound and enduring contribution to graphic design and graphic designers: of the pieces honored with awards, 34, including six gold medal and distinctive merit award winners, were designed by people who used to work for Golden at CBS.

Golden Words

Perhaps the best way to understand Bill Golden is through his own words. He was as fluent with words as he was with graphic elements. In April 1959, the Type Directors Club of New York sponsored a forum, Typography-USA. Panelist-designers contributed statements to a booklet issued as part of the seminar. Following are excerpts from Golden's statement.

"Type is to read.

"If there is such a thing as a 'New American Typography' surely it speaks with a foreign accent. And it probably talks too much. Much of what it says is obvious nonsense. A good deal of it is so pompous that it sounds like nonsense, though if you listen very carefully it isn't—quite. It is just over-complicated.

"Some 30 years ago the rebellious advertising and editorial designer in America was engaged in a conspiracy to bring order, clarity and directness to the printed page. He fought against the picture of the factory, the company logotype, and the small picture of the package that invariably accompanied it. He protested that the copy was too long, and that he was obliged to set it so small that no one would read it. He argued that the normal ad contained too many elements (He even invented the 'busy page' in some effort to accommodate himself to it.) He insisted that this effort to say so many things at once was self-defeating and could only result in communicating nothing to the reader.

"He was essentially picture-minded, and only reluctantly realized that he had to learn something about type. It was and still is a damned nuisance, but when he realized how thoroughly its mechanical and thoughtless application could destroy communication of an idea, he had to learn to control it—to design with it.

"More and more typography was designed on a layout pad rather than in metal. Perhaps the greatest change in American typography was caused by this simple act—the transfer of the design function of the printer to the graphic designer.

"The designer was able to bring a whole new background and a new set of influences to the printed page. He could 'draw' a page. There was more flexibility in the use of a pencil than in the manipulation of a metal form. It became a new medium for the designer.

"Under the twin impact of the functionalism of the Bauhaus and the practical demands of American business, the designer was beginning to learn to use the combination of word and image to communicate more effectively.

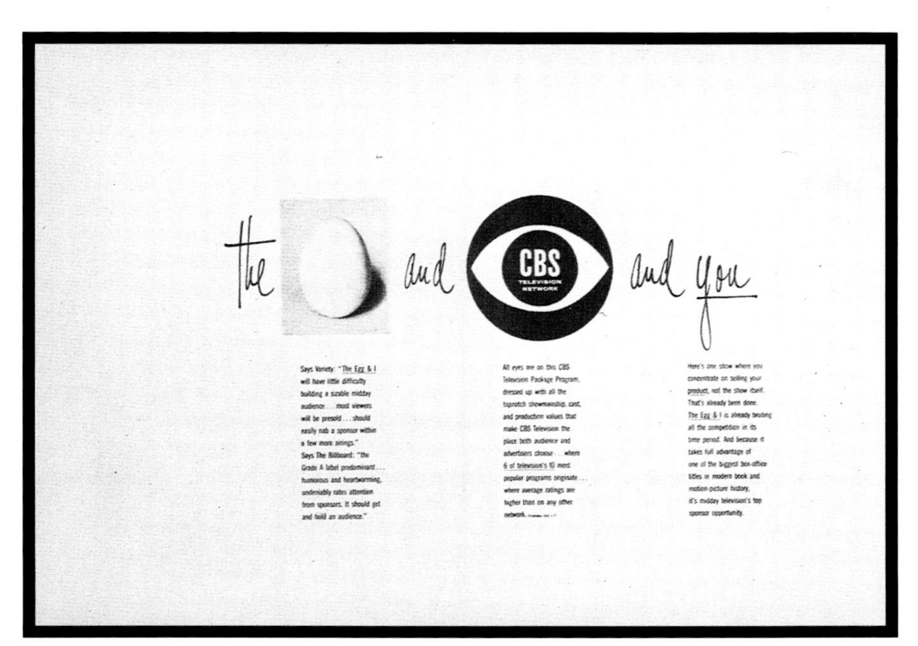

Trade advertisement *for* CBS *Television. William Golden. Photo by Midori. Kurt Weihs, Design Assistant. 1951. From the Graphic Design Archive, Rochester Institute of Technology, Rochester, New York.*

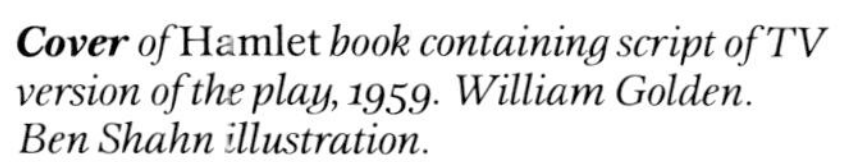

Cover *of* Hamlet *book containing script of TV version of the play, 1959. William Golden. Ben Shahn illustration.*

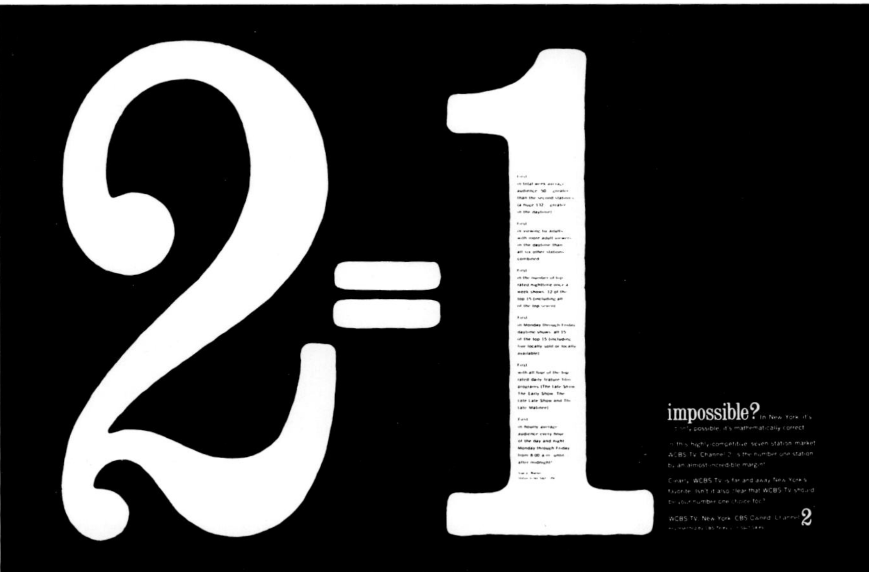

Ad *for* CBS *Television. William Golden. Kurt Weihs, Design Assistant. 1956. From the Graphic Design Archive, Rochester Institute of Technology, Rochester, New York.*

"Under the influence of the modern painters, he became aware (perhaps too aware) of the textural qualities and color values of type as an element of design.

"And surely a dominating influence on American typography in the pre-war years was exerted by the journalists…

"The skillful development of the use of headline and picture was a far more prevalent influence than the European poster. The newspaper taught us speed in communication…

"The magazine communicated at a more leisurely pace and could be more provocative since it addressed a more selective audience. Because the magazine dealt more in concepts than in news it was far more imaginative. There was more opportunity here to design within the framework of the two-page spread. But still, the devices that bore the main burden of interesting the reader were the 'terrific headline' and the 'wonderful picture'…

"But what gave it a new direction and style was not so purely American. I think it was men like Agha and Brodovitch. These importations from Europe set a pace that not only changed the face of the magazine and consequently advertising design, but they changed the status of the designer. They did this by the simple process of demonstrating that the designer could also think.

"The 'layout man' was becoming an editor. He was no longer that clever, talented fellow in the back room who made a writer's copy more attractive by arranging words and pictures on the printed page in some ingenious way. He could now read and understand the text. He could even have an opinion about it. He might even be able to demonstrate that he could communicate its content better and with more interest than the writer. He could even startle the editor by suggesting content. It wasn't long before he began to design the page before it was written, and writers began to write to a character count to fit the layout…

"I have no quarrel with the abstract movement – except with its vociferous intolerance of any other school. But I think the effect on the minds of young designers is a matter of concern. To regard the blank rectangle on a layout pad with the same attitude that the abstract painter confronts his blank canvas is surely a pointless delusion.

"The designer will find that the most satisfying solutions to a graphic problem come from its basic content. He will find it unnecessary and offensive to superimpose a visual effect on an unrelated message… he will want to be sure that what he has to say will be clearly understood – that this is his primary function…

"I do not argue for the return to any form of traditionalism. I do argue for a sense of responsibility on the part of the designer, and a rational understanding of his function.

"I think he should avoid designing for designers."

The Follow-Up Was Fast and Powerful

Lester Beall, William Golden, Paul Rand and Bradbury Thompson were the first of the American design pioneers in the '30s and '40s. Just a few years after their careers had started, and while the emigré designers from Europe were establishing themselves in the United States, a larger group of Americans were striking new design chords with new personalities and their fresh approaches to blending vigor and clarity for communication and typographic design. Their work, the later work of Paul Rand and Bradbury Thompson, and the work of many other designers in the United States and abroad will be reviewed in Chapter XIII.

Chapter IX: The Influence of the Private Press

"...their willingness to experiment and innovate, have affected the courses of both typeface and typographic design."

A private press has a primarily esthetic objective. It caters to a limited market. Whether or not the press has to pay its way, it is more interested in producing a good book (booklet, or whatever) than in a fat profit. The printer prints what he likes, not what someone else pays him to print.

Some private presses, although outside the mainstream of commercial printing, because of their adherence to high standards of design and production, and their willingness to experiment and innovate, have affected the courses of both typeface and typographic design.

Many books have been written about private presses and anyone interested in more than the brief report we can give about them here, should refer to *The Private Press* by Roderick Cave. It includes an extensive bibliography. The second edition was published in 1983 by R. R. Bowker Company, New York and London. Cave's book focuses on the English speaking world.

Here we will focus on just a few presses, those that have had the greatest influence, from the 1890s through the 1960s, on the design of printing and typefaces.

When one considers private presses, one is concentrating on fine letterpress printing, which in those days was essentially limited edition book printing.

Perhaps the first press to undertake raising the standards of book printing was the Kelmscott Press, founded by William Morris in 1891. Morris had been one of a jury selecting examples of the best commercial printing a few years earlier. He became aware of the inferiority of contemporary books to the incunabula. Morris wanted to produce better books than the available commercial printers were turning out. He noticed that currently available typefaces did not harmonize well with woodcuts, the prevalent illustration technique. He concerned himself with papers, binding materials and every aspect of book manufacture.

Morris also developed new typefaces, the first known as the Golden Type. His designs were based on the 15th century Venetian types, especially those of Nicholas Jenson. Some critics found the Golden Type blacker and less elegant

ſua ruina cipare uno
che lementi degli huomin
eglino poſſino rimunerar
do che epremii ſono alle u
fficulta non e appreſſo ed
iamo quegli

Drawings *for the Kelmscott Golden Type. Photograph: The Pierpont Morgan Library, New York,* PML 76945.

than the old Jenson types; others admired the new type. Perhaps more important than the actual design was the fact that it reawakened people to the need for good, new typefaces. Variations of Morris' type were produced by foundries in the United States. Morris later developed Troy type, a version of which, known as the Chaucer type, was used to set the Kelmscott Press edition of Chaucer. It, too, influenced new type designs by the American Type Founders Company and other foundries. The Chaucer was considered at the time the greatest triumph of English typography. Certainly it awakened the English typographic world to the beauty and power of a good typeface properly used.

Morris' books, not universally worshipped, were faulted for their old-fashioned look, their appeal to the elite, pomposity and pretentiousness. Others accused him of being too obsessed with decoration, and guilty of "typographic impertinences." Nevertheless the work of the Kelmscott Press, by focusing on beauty and high standards of manufacture, changed for the better the course of printing and typographic design.

Other influential presses of the 20th century, in Britain, some of which had typefaces specially designed for them, were: Vale Press, Eragny Press, Ashendene Press, Doves Press, Essex House Press, and the Caradoc Press. Many of the Ashendene Press books used Subiaco type, its proprietary design, which had been projected for but not cut for the Kelmscott Press. Ashendene also developed the Ptolemy type which it used in a number of its books.

in the fable of the fat baron or
the barbarian barber a fatal rain
of hot beer or herb tea on the
northern hill left one another to
tolerate the entire fare or to alter

and that othur knight hight
palamon nat fully quyk nes
fully deed they were buf bye
here cooki armure and by her
g pilouis som and folk town
joy saturne constellacioung
heraudes knew hom wyl ing
bon jour mon fight dwyk m
dyk fgbqwx jpbz vpf

Top: ***Trials*** *for the Kelmscott Golden Type and (bottom) for the Subiaco type, never used by the Kelmscott Press but used in many Ashendene Press books. Photograph: The Pierpont Morgan Library, New York,* PML 76897.

Unlike Morris' work, the output of the Doves Press was free of ornament. Ruari MacLean considered this a most devastating criticism of Morris' highly ornamented work at Kelmscott Press. Ornament-free, Doves Press books derived their beauty from the clarity of the type, their layout, and excellent presswork. Cobden-Sanderson (Dove's founder/proprietor) felt that "The whole duty of typography...is to communicate without loss by the way, the thought or image intended to be communicated by the author."

between the seen and the unseen, the finite and the infinite, the human and the superhuman, and is a monumental work of the eighteenth as distinguished from the seventeenth century, the century of the Bible and of Milton. Finally, in the nineteenth century, Sartor Resartus, the Essays of Emerson, and Unto this Last, are related & characteristic attempts to turn back the Everlasting Nay of scepticism into the Everlasting Yea of affirmation, & in the presence of the admittedly inexplicable & sublime mystery of the whole, to set man again at work upon the creation of the fit, the seemly, and the beautiful. Browning's Men & Women, now in the press, conceived about the same time, is a more direct presentment of the same positive solution.

¶ These Books printed, as a first essay, the whole field of literature remains open to select from. To-day there is an immense reproduction in an admirable cheap form, of all Books which in any language have stood the test of time. But such reproduction is not a substitute for the more monumental production of the same works, & whether by The Doves Press or some other press or presses, such monumental production, expressive of man's admiration, is a legitimate ambition and a public duty. Great thoughts deserve & demand a great setting, whether in building, sculpture, ceremonial, or otherwise; & the great works of literature have again and again to be set forth in forms suitable to their magnitude. And this

3

352. *Doves Type: Doves Press*

***Doves Press**, London. Doves type.*

***Kelmscott Press**, London. Wayzgoose, Menu, second dinner. Photograph: The Pierpont Morgan Library, New York,* PML 76941.

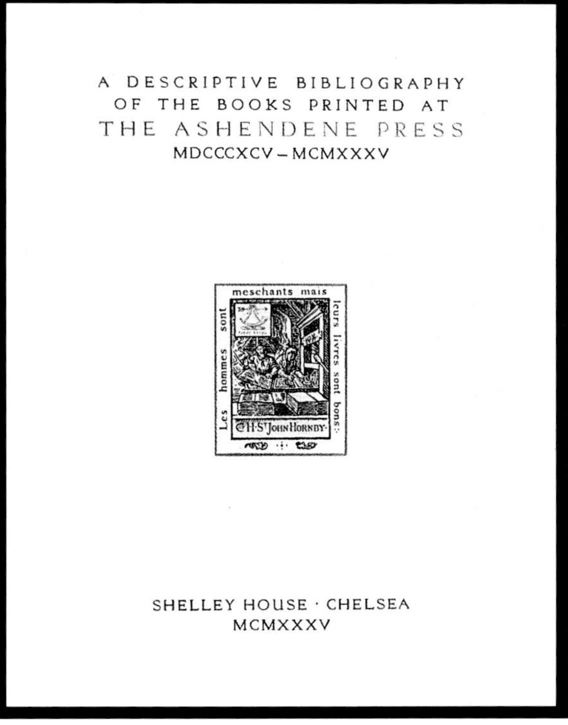
A DESCRIPTIVE BIBLIOGRAPHY
OF THE BOOKS PRINTED AT
THE ASHENDENE PRESS
MDCCCXCV – MCMXXXV

SHELLEY HOUSE · CHELSEA
MCMXXXV

***Title page** for a Descriptive Bibliography of the Books printed at the Ashendene Press,* MDCCCXCV–MCMXXXV. *1935. The Pierpont Morgan Library, New York,* PML 31855.

Presses in the United States that helped emphasize the role of typefaces and good typography in adding beauty to printed matter while increasing communication effectiveness include the Roycroft Press (New York) of Elbert Hubbard. As with Morris, Hubbard's typography and printing were castigated by knowledgeable critics who found his books guilty of unappropriate and derivative design, poor presswork on the wrong kind of paper, cheap bindings, and high prices. Yet, paradoxically, as with the Kelmscott Press, The Roycroft Press had its admirers and helped focus minds on the importance of good typography.

In the early years of the 20th century Chicago was becoming a printing center. There Frederic W. Goudy met Will Ransom. Goudy's Village type gave the press its name in 1903. From 1904 on, Fred and Bertha Goudy ran the Village Press, and moved it to Hingham, Massachusetts, where it was located for two years. In 1906 it was moved to New York. In 1921 Will Ransom established the Golden Cockerel Press which had a short life. Among those in Goudy's circle in Chicago were Oswald Cooper, designer of the Cooper type family, and W. A. Dwiggins, designer of the Electra, Caledonia, Eldorado, Falcon and Metro type families. When Goudy moved to New York, Dwiggins, who had followed him to Hingham, stayed on in Hingham.

TYPOGRAPHIC COMMUNICATIONS TODAY

Chapter IX: The Influence of the Private Press

"Typographers and printers (and in those days they were often the same person) loved their art and their craft."

These presses were influenced by Kelmscott books that had reached America. Other American presses similarly influenced include the Bandarlog Press, the Blue Sky Press, the Alderbrink Press, the Cranbrook Press, the Elston Press, Alwil Shop, Hillside Press and Philosopher Press.

Typographers and printers (and in those days they were often the same person) loved their art and their craft. Then, as now, they met and talked shop. Their combined influence on the world of typographic design was considerable.

After World War II

New private presses dominated the scene in the 1920s and 1930s. Notable among them were the Nonesuch Press and the Golden Cockerel Press, both in Britain. These presses as well as the Fleuron Society, founded in 1922, aimed to show that machine-set books (Linotype, Monotype) could be as beautiful as their handset pre-war counterparts. Although the society was short lived, *The Fleuron,* an English typographical journal, was most influential in this regard. Stanley Morison of Times Roman fame, and a prominent typographer, Oliver Simon, produced *The Fleuron* from 1923 to 1930.

Unlike its American namesake, London's Golden Cockerel thrived from 1920 to 1923. Its Golden Cockerel typeface was designed by Eric Gill. This was a slightly heavier and rounded version of Gill's Perpetua design. The Press' books combined clean typography with minimal ornamentation and exquisite illustrations, often wood engravings by Eric Gill and others.

Other influential presses of this period include the Mall Press, the Romney Street Press, both in Britain, in Wales the Gregynog Press, and at Stratford-on-Avon, The Shakespeare Head Press. In the United States during the between-the-wars decades several presses were noted for their fine design, typography and manufacture. Among these was Dard Hunter's Mountain House Press. Hunter had seen Kelmscott and Doves books, and in 1903 joined the Roycrofters for whom he designed some books. Most of the books produced at The Mountain House Press dealt with studies of paper and papermaking methods and history.

Among the presses catering to collectors of fine books was Arthur K. Rushmore's Golden Hind

IT WAS THE TERRACE OF
God's house
That she was standing on,—
By God built over the sheer depth
In which Space is begun;
So high, that looking downward

Goudy's Village Type. *Drawn entirely freehand, it was a private type for his and Will Ransom's Village Press in 1903. Not to be confused with his later designs of Village No. 2, Village Italic, or New Village Text.*

Press, established in 1927. Many of the Press' books were given away, not sold. Many of its 200-plus books were honored by being included in the prestigious Fifty Books of the Year Show, sponsored by the American Institute of Graphic Arts.

The American Institute of Graphic Arts is the national, nonprofit organization of graphic design and graphic arts professionals. Founded in 1914, AIGA conducts an interrelated program of competitions, exhibitions, publications, educational activities, and projects in the public interest to promote excellence in, and the advancement of, the graphic design profession.

Members of the Institute are involved in the design and production of books, magazines and periodicals, as well as corporate, environmental and promotional graphics. In addition to the role of some private presses producing fine books, many commercial printers in America produced beautiful books. In the 1920s these included Pynson Printers, W. E. Rudge, C. P. Rollins, the Spiral Press headed by Joseph Blumenthal, and the Peter Pauper Press run by Edna and Peter Beilenson. The Peter Pauper Press books were usually small and inexpensive, and brought beautiful books into thousands of homes not previously penetrated by the private presses or the large fine commercial printers. The quality tradition of the private and semiprivate presses flourished in California, notably at the Grabhorn Press. Later California private printers include Adrian Wilson, Sherwood Grover, Jack W. Stauffacher and Andrew Hoyem.

By the 1930s few private presses were developing proprietary types. One exception was Aries, designed by Eric Gill for London's Stourton Press in 1932. The need for new typefaces was being met by the commercial foundries, such as the American Type Founders Company, D. Stempel AG, Bauer/Neufville, the Klingspor type foundry, and by The Monotype Corporation Ltd. Most of the private presses used the typefaces from these sources.

A number of typefaces of interest to private presses were developed in Italy. These include Victor Hammer's Hammer-Unziale and Pindar-Uncial, both cut by Klingspor, and his later American Uncial.

At the Officina Bodoni in Italy, Giovanni Mardesteig developed Griffo type. He also

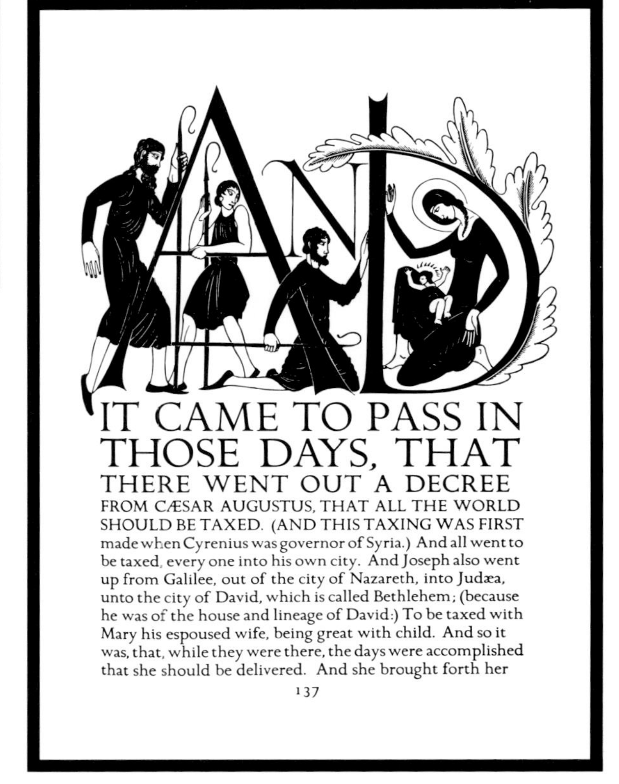
AND IT CAME TO PASS IN THOSE DAYS, THAT THERE WENT OUT A DECREE FROM CÆSAR AUGUSTUS, THAT ALL THE WORLD SHOULD BE TAXED. (AND THIS TAXING WAS FIRST made when Cyrenius was governor of Syria.) And all went to be taxed, every one into his own city. And Joseph also went up from Galilee, out of the city of Nazareth, into Judæa, unto the city of David, which is called Bethlehem; (because he was of the house and lineage of David:) To be taxed with Mary his espoused wife, being great with child. And so it was, that, while they were there, the days were accomplished that she should be delivered. And she brought forth her

137

Golden Cockerel Press. The Four Gospels. *Wood engraving by Eric Gill, in perfect harmony with his Golden Cockerel type. The Pierpont Morgan Library, New York,* PML *63922.*

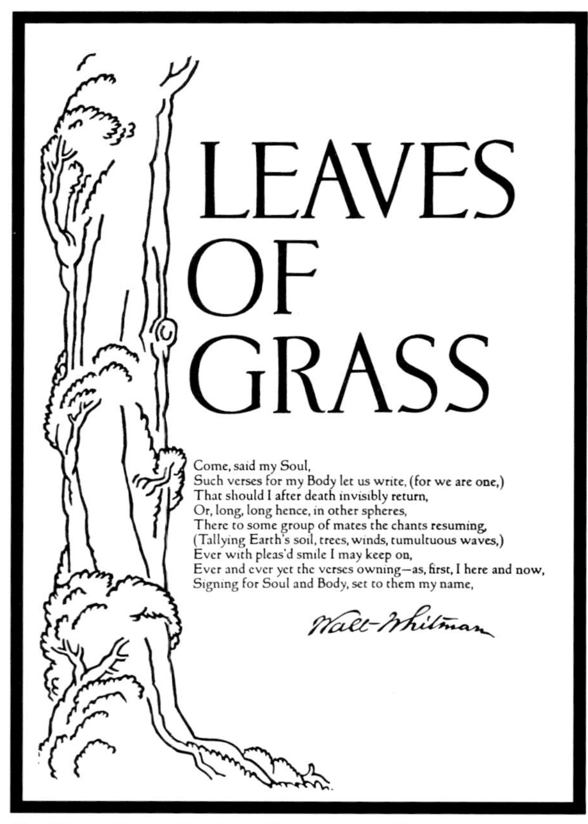
LEAVES OF GRASS

Come, said my Soul,
Such verses for my Body let us write, (for we are one,)
That should I after death invisibly return,
Or, long, long hence, in other spheres,
There to some group of mates the chants resuming,
(Tallying Earth's soil, trees, winds, tumultuous waves,)
Ever with pleas'd smile I may keep on,
Ever and ever yet the verses owning—as, first, I here and now,
Signing for Soul and Body, set to them my name,

Walt Whitman

Grabhorn Press. *San Francisco.* Leaves of Grass, *1930. Photograph: Courtesy of the Rare Books and Manuscripts Division, The New York Public Library, Astor, Lenox, Tilden Foundations.*

HOW EDITH McGILLCUDDY MET

R·L·S

A STORY BY JOHN STEINBECK

THE ROWFANT CLUB : CLEVELAND
1943

***Title page** for* "How Edith McGillcuddy met RLS." *A story by John Steinbeck. The Rowfant Club, Cleveland, 1943. The Pierpont Morgan Library, New York,* PML *55567.*

***Mardersteig's** Griffo type.*

montis rupe viatoribus late prospicitur,
unde illud devectum Ovidianum
Nisiades matres sicelidesque nurus.
Incolae vallem etiam omnem, quae subest, Nisi regionem vocant.
B.P. Erit isto sane modo etiam aliquid infra Taurominium memorabile. Nam de hoc poetae versu, si recte memini,

designed Zeno, Dante, and Pacioli for the Press.

Today, with film and digital typography taking over the commercial type-making world, there are few sources of metal type for private presses and the development of proprietary designs for them is a thing of the past (but not for periodicals or corporations). For a while, at least, some private printers are still able to buy type abandoned by commercial typesetters, to supplement what can be obtained from the few sources catering to them. Some presses, with Monotype casters, can have a continuing supply of type as long as they keep the casters operating. Eventually, as private presses follow the commercial trend and move from letterpress to offset printing, they will be able to take advantage of the many typefaces available in film and digital fonts manufactured by today's typesetter manufacturers and typeface development companies.

THE
HANSOM CAB AND
THE PIGEONS
BEING RANDOM REFLECTIONS UPON
THE SILVER JUBILEE OF
KING GEORGE V
by
L. A. G. Strong

Printed in Great Britain at the
GOLDEN COCKEREL PRESS
Ten Staple Inn, London
1935

***Golden Cockerel Press,** London.* The Hansom Cab and the Pigeons, *1935. Wood engraving by Eric Ravilious; set in Gill's Golden Cockerel type.*

second of the three miracles. The third was the healing of Gallienus' daughter, whose body the demon vacated amidst much clamour at the Saint's command. When the grateful Gallienus presented San Zeno with a valuable crown, the Saint at once broke it into small pieces which he distributed among the poor. Nevertheless, a demon who had twice offered resistance could not be allowed to go unpunished; San Zeno therefore compelled him to carry from Rome to Verona a large porphyry basin, another gift of the Emperor. This task the demon accomplished in an instant, but in his fury he scratched the surface of the stone; the

11

***Officina Bodoni,** Italy. The Zeno type.*

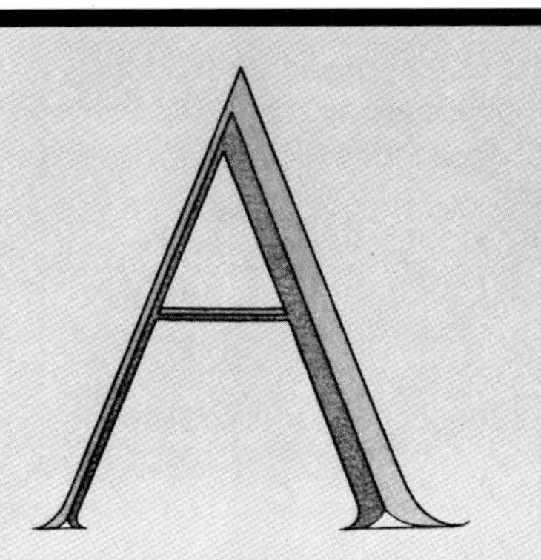

Suole l'usanza antiqua cauare la littera di tondo e quadro, la summa de le qual forme ascende al n. lij, del qual si caua il numero perfecto che è X. E cossi uol esser la tua littera grossa la X^a. parte de l'alteza et per questo modo hauerà tanto del tondo quanto del quadro; et uolsi causare la soprascripta littera doue si tagliano le linie .x. con la circonferentia. Et questo è quanto per misura io, Felice Feliciano, habia nelle antique caractere ritrouato per molte pietre marmoree, cossi ne l'alma Roma quanto negli altri [luoghi].

Amid accumulated pollen and massed flowers the two phoenixes droop their wings. The colour is confined to that prized by the Yin dynasty (i.e., white, which was the Imperial colour in that dynasty), simple and unadorned. It is not till we come down to the Chu dynasty of Hsüan [Tê] and Ch'êng [Hua][1] that we get elaborate painting and the employment of five colours.

Composed by Ch'ien Lung in the spring of the cyclical year *ting yu* (A.D. 1777), and inscribed by Imperial order.

Seal: *t'ai p'o*, 'Great Unpolished-gem'.

Now the hungry lion roars,
And the wolf behowls the moon;
Whilst the heavy ploughman snores,
All with weary task fordone.
Now the wasted brands do glow,
Whilst the screech-owl, screeching loud,
Puts the wretch that lies in woe
In remembrance of a shroud.

(Far left) ***Officina Bodoni,*** *Italy. Page from Felice Feliciano, 1960, showing use of Mardersteig's Dante Type.*
(Top left) ***Eric Gill's*** *Aries type.*
(Bottom left) ***Olivieri's*** *cursive characters for Dante Italic.*

TYPOGRAPHIC COMMUNICATIONS TODAY

Chapter X: Typeface Milestones, 1896-1969

"Typefaces give personality and power and direction to a message.... Typography is the only art which can recall all others."

In visual communications, when you get to the bottom line, what the reader/viewer/prospect sees are words or images or both, so arranged as to make an impression, convey information, and/or entertain. This is true of print and electronic media.

Typographic Communications Today is particularly concerned with typographic design, the way the words (in type) are integrated with each other and with other graphic elements. Previous chapters have explored the seeds and roots of today's design by looking at fine art and applied design movements. This and the next chapter will focus on typeface designs, how they evolved and adapted to the needs of typographic designers.

Typologia

Frederic W. Goudy, the great American typeface designer, wrote several thoughtful books about typography. In his *Typologia** he expressed his feelings about typefaces and their role in fine printing. His thoughts help one to appreciate the beauty, the power, the utility, the importance of typefaces, their design and their intelligent use. Here are a few of his observations.

❧ Goudy refers to Gutenberg's leaden types, which "made the thoughts and imaginations of the soul visible to all."

❧ He quotes Lemoine, who called typography, "the only art which can recall all others."

❧ On the effects of technology on typefaces and typographic design he wrote:

"When writers on the crafts deprecate the displacements of hand-cut punches by the machine-cut ones, what they say often betrays their ignorance. Much that they write is based, indeed, on theory and not on fact. I agree with them up to a certain point, but I would direct their attention to the atrocities produced in the first half of the 19th century, when all types were hand cut; there certainly must be something else besides 'hand cutting' to give distinction to a type. Too often they confuse the thing itself and the method of its production. The machine has not killed good craftsmanship; the machine in the hand of the craftsman is merely a more intricate tool than any that was available to the earlier worker, and enables him to carry out his own creative idea more exactly than can be done when the work is passed into the hands of artisans employed to perform the various processes singly: they obviously cannot realize fully just what was in the type creator's mind, and therefore cannot carry out the work absolutely in the spirit in which he worked.

"I hold that if the final printed result is satisfactory to the creator of it, and to the viewer of it as well, the method of its production is in a sense immaterial."

❧ *"Type, after all, is merely handwriting divested of the exigencies and accidents of the scribes."*

❧ *"The designers of the first types...shaped their type forms so that the letters combined insensibly into words – the sole elements which the reader should be conscious of."*

❧ *"Types of distinction are created by artists only, and not by engineers or artisans – by craftsmen with a knowledge of the technical limitations and requirements of the craft, and by designers who place feeling above the cut-and-dried effect which comes from slavish adherence to workshop traditions."*

❧ *"The types of Garamond, Bodoni, Didot, Caslon, Baskerville and other well-known faces (or type founders' imitations of them) have been available for years to printers generally, and practically any piece of printing required can be done adequately and satisfactorily with one or another of them, old as they are. It is no less true, however, that the wearing apparel of the citizen of Shakespeare's time was adequate and suited to his times, and might, so far as practicality is concerned, be just as suitable for our own. But there is the matter of 'style' to consider, and just as in the matter of clothes, styles in types change capriciously."*

❧ *"...tradition is not to be followed solely for its own sake...to accept medieval tradition, however, without adding something of ourselves to it, is mere affectation; it is no longer tradition if servilely copied. Genius cultivates old fields in new ways."*

❧ *"If a design has character it is in spite of its imperfections, not because of them."*

❧ *"When a type design is good it is not because each individual letter of the alphabet is perfect in form, but because there is a feeling of unbroken harmony and rhythm that runs through the whole design, each letter to every other and to all."*

❧ *"It is hardly possible to create a good typeface that will differ radically from the established forms of the past; nevertheless, it is still possible to secure new expressions of life and vigor."*

❧ *"Today it remains only for the artist, by modification and new expression, to beautify the classic forms fixed for us by years of evolution and the stress of necessity."*

With these thoughts in mind, let's now review the role of typefaces in today's communications and the typeface design milestones of the past century.

Why Typefaces?

When you listen to a great public speaker or performer, a Bob Hope or a Helen Hayes, or a Laurence Olivier, or watch a Marcel Marceau, the information, the entertainment, the stimuli are enhanced, propelled, by a smile, a wink of the eye, a pause, a whisper or a shout, the tone of voice, a gesture of hands or feet or the body. And sometimes, as with Marceau, the facial and body expressions not only convey the message, they virtually are the message.

And so it is with typefaces. They give personality and power and direction to a message. A large library of typefaces has matured over the years enabling the knowledgeable and sensitive designer to choose those most appropriate for almost any kind of communication problem.

What is Best?

How does one get to know which is best, or at least right, for a particular job? Not only by reading books or taking courses on typography. These will give you the basics, the ABC's of selecting and specifying typefaces. To go beyond the basics, to get a real feeling for type so that you know in your bones what is called for, there is no substitute for working with type, specifying it and using it again and again.

Most of the typographic designs we are concerned with aim to inform and/or entertain, to impress, to move people. To be successful typographic messages must be noticed, read, understood and remembered long enough to achieve the intended result. The design must effectively allocate emphasis to the different graphic elements and guide the flow of the eye and the mind through the message. The best typeface for a particular job is the one that is most appropriate to the message, the medium and the audience, and is most effective in working with the other graphic elements to achieve the objective of the message's sponsor.

Just as you buy a suit or a dress, a car or a chair, as much if not more for its appearance as for its utility, so are typefaces often chosen at least in part for their style. In today's society, in much of the world, almost every business is to some degree a part of the fashion business. Thus changes, sometimes subtle, in the look of a car, a chair, an electric razor or a typeface, can make a big difference in its appeal.

An Explosion of New Typefaces

For all these reasons, and because there are many manufacturers of typesetting machines that require typeface libraries for their machines, the 20th century has been an era exploding with new typeface designs.

Often the same or a very similar typeface is brought out by more than one manufacturer, sometimes with different names. In this chapter we will look at the more significant type families introduced from the late 1890s through the 1960s. In the next chapter we will review the more recent typeface introductions spurred by the shift from metal typefaces to film and then to digital font masters. In most cases we will note only the first version of a specific design and will explain in what typeface design category it falls, as well as note the date of its public introduction, its designer (where known) and its original manufacturer.

**TYPOLOGIA: Studies in Type Design & Type Making with Comments on the Invention of Typography, the First Types, Legibility and Fine Printing.* Frederic W. Goudy, 188 pages. $3.95 paperback; $15.00 cloth. University of California Press, Berkeley, CA.

Many of these faces developed over the years into full families of several weights and with condensed or extended versions. Today, of course, faces are usually introduced as full families. The captions for the typeface showings will list the family name only, i.e., Garamond (not Garamond Light).

Typefaces and Type Families

Just a few terms should be defined now. A type family is a group of typefaces with shared design characteristics, but with each typeface or member of the family varying from each other in weight (as light, book, medium, bold, black) or slant (roman, italic), or proportion (as normal, condensed, extended). In common practice, however, the term "typeface" is often used to refer not only to a specific typestyle within a family, but also to the family as a whole.

Typeface Categories

Most text typefaces can be divided into two categories: those with serifs and those without serifs. Over the years, to further classify typeface design traits, several more definitive systems have been developed – some with over a hundred different categories.

Classification systems can be helpful in facilitating the identification of a type design and, where necessary, selecting suitable substitutions when the typeface of first choice is not available. While two categories of type are inadequate for any meaningful work, hundreds become self-defeating. What is presented here is hopefully a valuable compromise between these two extremes. The following utilizes nine basic categories, some of which have been further subdivided for added clarity.

While there may be some differences between this and other systems, or even some disagreements concerning the placement of a typeface or two, the intent here is to provide a working guideline for both the typographic professional and the neophyte. (Few things typographic can be confined to "black or white," "either/or" regulation.)

Old Style

These are typefaces which were originally created between the late 15th and mid 18th century. (Or are patterned after typefaces which were originally designed in this time period.) In these designs the axis of curved strokes is normally inclined to the left, and the contrast in stroke weight is not dramatic. Some versions, like the earlier Venetian old style designs, are distinguished by the diagonal cross stroke of the lowercase e. Serifs are almost always bracketed and headserifs are often angled.

Reoi

Category: Old Style/Venetian

Features:

These are the first of the old style faces, created in Venice around 1470; and take their style from handwritten letters drawn with an obliquely held broad pen. Venetian old style designs are normally distinguished by the diagonal cross stroke of the lowercase e and very minor contrast in stroke thickness.

abcdefghijklmnopqrstuvw
xyzABCDEFGHIJKLM
NOPQRSTUVWXYZ

*1897/**Cloister Old Style**/ M.F. Benton/ATF. This was one of the first modern revivals of the Old Style Venetian type forms. The typeface immediately became popular and sparked a long and diverse list of similar designs to be created.*

abcdefghijklmnopqrstuv
wxyzABCDEFGHIJKLM
NOPQRSTUVWXYZ

*1911/**Kennerley**/F. W. Goudy/Lanston Monotype.*

abcdefghijklmnopqrstuvw
xyzABCDEFGHIJKLM
NOPQRSTUVWXYZ

*1914/**Cloister**/M. F. Benton/ATF.*

abcdefghijklmnopqrstuv
wxyzABCDEFGHIJKLM
NOPQRSTUVWXYZ

*1924/**Italian Old Style**/F. W. Goudy/Monotype. (or Nicolas Jenson)*

Goudy writes that his Italian Old Style, "…is not an adaption or copy of any of the early Italian faces, though of course it shows a study of them. The individual letters are quite full and round…" Speaking of earlier types, he observed that "The old fellows stole all of our best ideas."

*abcdefghijklmnopqrstuvw
xyzABCDEFGHIJKLM
NOPQRSTUVWXYZ*

*1929/**Arrighi**/Frederic Warde/Monotype.*

abcdefghijklmnopqrstuvw
xyzABCDEFGHIJKLM
NOPQRSTUVWXYZ

*1929/**Centaur**/Bruce Rogers/Monotype.*

Based on Rogers' 1914 design of a titling font for the Metropolitan Museum of Art, 1929 Centaur is similar to, but lighter and more modeled than Cloister Old Face. It is derived from Jenson's roman. Monotype's italic companion face is known as Arrighi Italic. Once, when Rogers was asked to list the ten typefaces he would choose to equip an ideal printing office, he replied, "I don't believe there are any ten best types – anymore than there are 100 best works of fiction – etc., etc. A type design can only be considered in relation to the use to which it is to be put – in the period when (and for which) it was designed."

abcdefghijklmnopqrstuvw
xyzABCDEFGHIJKLM
NOPQRSTUVWXYZ

*1929/**Deepdene**/F. W. Goudy/Lanston Monotype.*

Deepdene was the name of Goudy's "modest estate" in Marlboro, New York. The typeface was developed for Goudy's own use and for such private printers as Peter Beilenson and William Edwin Rudge. Goudy later sold the reproduction rights to the Lanston Monotype Machine Company.

abcdefghijklmnopqrstuv
wxyzABCDEFGHIJKLM
NOPQRSTUVWXYZ

*c. 1936/**Bauer Text**/F. H. E. Schneidler/Bauer/Neufville. (Also known as Schneidler Old Style)*

Reoi

Category: Old Style/Aldine
Features:
Aldine old style designs are based on the original work of Aldus Manutius in the early 1490s. During the 16th century this model was adopted and followed first in France, then in all of Europe. These typefaces generally have more contrast in stroke weight than Venetian old style design and the lowercase e crossbar is horizonal.

abcdefghijklmnopqrstuv
wxyzABCDEFGHIJKL
MNOPQRSTUVWXYZ

*1914-1923/**Garamond**/M. F. Benton, T. M. Cleland/ATF.*
The Garamond (Garamont, Garaldus) type families are among the most enduring and widely used. There are many variations, introduced by almost every important type foundry, and typophiles have strong preferences for this or that version. Claude Garamond was a 16th century French punch cutter and designer. His design was based on earlier designs of Aldus Manutius, a Venetian Renaissance publisher/designer. Many contemporary versions of the Garamond type derive from a variation of it designed by Jean Jannon in 1615.
Many type companies issued variations between 1900 and 1970. They include:
- *Deberny & Peignot issued versions from 1912 to 1928 which were based on a 1641 version of the Jannon cutting.*
- *ATF's 1917 version was derived from the original Jannon types, as were versions by Amsterdam Typefoundry, Linotype's Garamond No. 3, and Intertype Garamond.*
- *Lanston Monotype, in 1921, and later the Monotype Corporation, brought out a Garamont based on Jannon in the roman, and a design by Robert Granjon in the italic.*
- *Stempel released its Garamond in 1924, and Mergenthaler Linotype a heavier version a year later.*
- *Nebiolo's Garaldus (Garamond plus Aldus) appeared in 1956. It was designed by Aldo Novarese.*
- *Later versions were issued by Simoncini, Ludwig & Mayer, Grafotechna, Ludlow, Haas, Klingspor and ITC.*

abcdefghijklmnopqrstuv
wxyzABCDEFGHIJKL
MNOPQRSTUVWXYZ

*1915/**Goudy Old Style**/F. W. Goudy/ATF.*

abcdefghijklmnopqrstuv
wxyzABCDEFGHIJKL
MNOPQRSTUVWXYZ

*1918/**Goudy Modern**/F. W. Goudy/Lanston Monotype.*

abcdefghijklmnopqrstuvw
xyzABCDEFGHIJKLM
NOPQRSTUVWXYZ

*1919/**Cooper Old Style**/Oswald B. Cooper/Barnhart Brothers & Spindler.*

abcdefghijklmnopqrstuvw
xyzABCDEFGHIJKLM
NOPQRSTUVWXYZ

*1923/**Poliphilus**/Monotype.*
Poliphilus was derived from a type designed during the Italian Renaissance (1499) by Griffo for Aldus Manutius. The italic version, called Blado, is also shown here.

abcdefghijklmnopqrstuvwxyz
ABCDEFGHIJKLMN
OPQRSTUVWXYZ

*1923/**Blado**/Monotype.*

abcdefghijklmnopqrstuv
wxyzABCDEFGHIJKLM
NOPQRSTUVWXYZ

*1926/**Weiss Roman**/Emil R. Weiss/Bauer.*

abcdefghijklmnopqrstuv
wxyzABCDEFGHIJKL
MNOPQRSTUVWXYZ

*1928/**Granjon**/George W. Jones/Mergenthaler Linotype.*
Named after the French designer, Robert Granjon, it is considered an excellent adaptation of the Garamond design.

abcdefghijklmnopqrstuv
wxyzABCDEFGHIJKL
MNOPQRSTUVWXYZ

*1929/**Bembo**/Monotype.*
The 20th century version of a typeface designed by Francesco Griffo for Aldus Manutius in Venice. First used in Cardinal Bembo's De Aetna *in 1495 and named for him, it was a model followed by Garamond, and the ancestor of many European types through the 17th century*

abcdefghijklmnopqrstuv
wxyzABCDEFGHIJKL
MNOPQRSTUVWXYZ

*1935/**Electra**/W. A. Dwiggins/Mergenthaler Linotype.*

abcdefghijklmnopqrstuv
wxyzABCDEFGHIJKLM
NOPQRSTUVWXYZ

*1936/**Emerson**/Joseph Blumenthal/Monotype.*

abcdefghijklmnopqrstuv
wxyzABCDEFGHIJKLM
NOPQRSTUVWXYZ

*1938/**University of California Oldstyle**/F. W. Goudy/University of California.*

abcdefghijklmnopqrstuv
wxyzABCDEFGHIJKLM
NOPQRSTUVWXYZ

*1947/**DeRoos**/S. H. DeRoos/Amsterdam.*

abcdefghijklmnopqrstu
vwxyzABCDEFGHIJKL
MNOPQRSTUVWXYZ

*1950/**Palatino**/Hermann Zapf/D. Stempel AG.*

abcdefghijklmnopqrstuv
wxyzABCDEFGHIJKL
MNOPQRSTUVWXYZ

*1964/**Sabon**/Jan Tschichold/Stempel.*
*1967/**Sabon**/Jan Tschichold/Monotype/Linotype.*
Developed jointly by Stempel, Linotype and Monotype to meet the demand for a machine-composed face, this Sabon is fully compatible with a handset version. The roman is based on a Garamond design and the italic on a Granjon font, with both refined by Tschichold to meet the mechanical and stylistic needs of the day.

Reoi

Category: Old Style/Dutch

Features:

In the Netherlands the larger x-height, darker color, and greater contrast in stroke weight of the German black letter were melded with Aldine design traits. This style of type first appeared in the middle 16th century and later, as original designs, until the 18th.

abcdefghijklmnopqrstuvw xyzABCDEFGHIJKLM NOPQRSTUVWXYZ

*1913/**Caslon No. 3**/Mergenthaler Linotype Company. Several Caslons were introduced in this and later decades. One of the earliest was Caslon No. 3, shown. All were spin-offs from the Caslon Old Face designed by William Caslon in England in the 18th century. Earlier Caslons include Caslon Old Style, released in 1901 by Inland Type Foundry. ATF released Caslon 541 shortly thereafter. The earliest spin-off in the United States was Old Style, later renamed Caslon No. 471. It was first shown in 1822.*

abcdefghijklmnopqrstuv wxyzABCDEFGHIJKL MNOPQRSTUVWXYZ

*1913/**Plantin**/F. H. Pierpont/Monotype. This was the first modern revival of the work attributed to Christophe Plantin. It also served as a model for Times New Roman, one of the most popular typefaces created in the 20th century.*

abcdefghijklmnopqrstuv wxyzABCDEFGHIJKL MNOPQRSTUVWXYZ

*1932/**Times New Roman**/Stanley Morison/Monotype. Commissioned by* The Times *of London in 1931, and introduced by Monotype in 1932, Times New Roman is a widely used typeface today. It became available on the Linotype in London in 1932, in the United States in 1935, and versions were brought out by many others since. Stanley Morison supervised its design and provided the original specimens or type showings, which were used to draw the design. The designer, Victor Lardent, an artist on the Times staff, was appointed by Morison.*

abcdefghijklmnopqrstuvw xyzABCDEFGHIJKLM NOPQRSTUVWXYZ

*1937/**Janson**/C. H. Griffith/Mergenthaler Linotype. C. H. Griffith directed the design of this face based on the original cut c. 1690 by Nicholas Kis, a Hungarian working in Amsterdam. The face is named after Anton Janson, a Dutchman who worked in Leipzig, although he had nothing to do with it. Mr. Griffith did not know this in 1937. The data concerning Kis came to light more than a decade later.*

Reoi

Category: Old Style/Revivals

Features:

These are typefaces which, although they may display a predominance of old style design traits, are generally not patterned after any particular type of the period. Many times, in fact, they may share several design influences. As with other old style designs, character stroke is relatively conservative and weight stress is inclined.

abcdefghijklmnopqrstu vwxyzABCDEFGHIJKL MNOPQRSTUVWXYZ

*1905/**Windsor**/Stephenson Blake.*

abcdefghijklmnopqrstu vwxyzABCDEFGHIJKL MNOPQRSTUVWXYZ

*1914/**Souvenir**/M. F. Benton/ATF.*

abcdefghijklmnopqrst uvwxyzABCDEFGHIJK LMNOPQRSTUVWXYZ

*1921/**Cooper Black**/Oswald B. Cooper/Barnhart Brothers & Spindler.*

abcdefghijklmnopqrstuvw xyzABCDEFGHIJKLM NOPQRSTUVWXYZ

*1925/**Lutetia**/Jan van Krimpen/Enschedé.*

abcdefghijklmnopqrstu vwxyzABCDEFGHIJKL MNOPQRSTUVWXYZ

*1954/**Trump Mediaeval**/Georg Trump/Weber.*

Reoi

Category: Transitional

Features:

The style for these typefaces was established in the mid 18th century, primarily by the English printer and typographer John Baskerville. While the axis of curve strokes can be inclined, it is generally vertical. Weight contrast is more pronounced than in old style designs although serifs are still bracketed and head serifs are oblique. These typefaces represent the transition between old style and modern designs and incorporate characteristics of each.

abcdefghijklmnopqrstuv wxyzABCDEFGHIJKL MNOPQRSTUVWXYZ

*1907/**Scotch Roman**/Monotype. Based on an original version by Richard Austin.*

abcdefghijklmnopqrstuv wxyzABCDEFGHIJKL MNOPQRSTUVWXYZ

*1915/**Baskerville**/M. F. Benton/ATF. Baskerville, like Garamond, is a ubiquitous and enduring design. John Baskerville designed it in Birmingham, England. The ATF 1915 revival and the 1923 Monotype version are credited with its 20th century revival. Most foundries issued their versions in the 1920s and 1930s. Baskerville is a round letter. It is considered the first of the transitional faces because it has greater contrast between the thick and thin strokes than do Caslon or other old styles, yet less than is characteristic of modern faces (Bodoni, Didot, Torino, etc.).*

abcdefghijklmnopqrstuv wxyzABCDEFGHIJKL MNOPQRSTUVWXYZ

*1928/**Bulmer**/M. F. Benton/ATF. A recutting of an 18th century face originally cut by William Martin for William Bulmer of the Shakespeare Press. Martin was a pupil of Baskerville.*

abcdefghijklmnopqrstuv wxyzABCDEFGHIJKL MNOPQRSTUVWXYZ

*1928/**Perpetua**/Eric Gill/Monotype. The most popular roman designed by Gill, Perpetua was first used privately in a translation of* The Passion of Perpetua and Felicity. *The italic, cut later, was initially called Felicity. A titling version was also designed.*

abcdefghijklmnopqrstuv wxyzABCDEFGHIJKL MNOPQRSTUVWXYZ

*1930/**Perpetua Italic**/Eric Gill/Monotype.*

abcdefghijklmnopqrstuv wxyzABCDEFGHIJKL MNOPQRSTUVWXYZ

*1938/**Caledonia**/W. A. Dwiggins/Mergenthaler Linotype.*

abcdefghijklmnopqrstuv wxyzABCDEFGHIJKL MNOPQRSTUVWXYZ

*1939/**Fairfield**/Rudolph Ruzicka/Mergenthaler Linotype.*

Modern

The work of Giambattista Bodoni in the 18th century epitomizes this style of type. Here, contrast between thick and thin strokes is abrupt and dramatic. The axis of curved strokes is vertical and all serifs are horizontal with little or no bracketing.

Reoi

Category: Modern/Didone
Features:
These are typefaces created within the 18th century, or their direct descendants. Some designs have slight, but almost imperceptible, serif bracketing, and generally hairlines are not as thin as in 20th century moderns. In many cases, stroke terminals are "ball" shapes rather than the reflection of a broad edge pen.

abcdefghijklmnopqrstu vwxyzABCDEFGHIJKL MNOPQRSTUVWXYZ

*1908/**Didot**/Monotype.*
First cut by Firmin Didot in 1784, it became a standard model for French book type in the 19th century and versions of it were cut by several foundries in the 20th century. A face with pronounced contrast between thick and thin strokes.

abcdefghijklmnopqrstu vwxyzABCDEFGHIJKL MNOPQRSTUVWXYZ

*1908/**Torino** (also known as Romano Moderno)/Nebiolo.*

abcdefghijklmnopqrstu vwxyzABCDEFGHIJKL MNOPQRSTUVWXYZ

*1909/**Bodoni**/M. F. Benton/ATF.*
Bodoni is the archetypal modern typeface.

abcdefghijklmnopqrstuv wxyzABCDEFGHIJKL MNOPQRSTUVWXYZ

*1926/**Bauer Bodoni**/Bauer.*
The ATF version was adapted with variations by other foundries; the Bauer Bodoni however, is a distinctly different recutting of the original created by Giambattista Bodoni of Parma, Italy, in the 17th century. It is more delicate than the ATF recutting.

Reoi

Category: Modern/20th Century
Features:
These typefaces were created in the 20th century, and while they may share many design traits with Didones, they are generally not intended to be revivals of these earlier designs. They also tend to be more stylized than their predecessors.

abcdefghijklmnopqrstuv wxyzABCDEFGHIJKL MNOPQRSTUVWXYZ

*1929/**Corvinus**/Imre Reiner/Bauer.*

abcdefghijklmnopqrstuvw xyzABCDEFGHIJKLM NOPQRSTUVWXYZ

*1933/**Egmont**/S. H. DeRoos/Amsterdam.*

Clarendon

This is a style of type which first became popular in the 1850s. Like the Didones before them, Clarendons have a strong vertical weight stress, but this is where the similarities end. While they do have obvious contrast in stroke thickness, it is not nearly as dramatic as in the Didones. In addition, serifs are normally heavy, bracketed, and usually square cut.

Reoi

Category: Clarendon/19th Century
Features:
As the name implies these are the first released Clarendon typestyles. Their stroke weight contrast is least pronounced and their serifs tend to be short to medium length.

abcdefghijklmnopqrstuvwx yzABCDEFGHIJKLM NOPQRSTUVWXYZ

*1896/**Cheltenham**/Bertram G. Goodhue, Morris Benton/ATF.*
Designed for the Cheltenham Press of New York. 18 commercial versions of this face were created by Benton between 1904 and 1916.

abcdefghijklmnopqrstu vwxyzABCDEFGHIJKL MNOPQRSTUVWXYZ

*1904/**Cushing Antique**/F. W. Goudy/ATF.*
J. Stearns Cushing commissioned ATF in 1898 to design this face, which was redesigned by Goudy in 1904.

abcdefghijklmnopqrstuv wxyzABCDEFGHIJKL MNOPQRSTUVWXYZ

*1936/**Bookman**/Mergenthaler Linotype.*
This was originally cut as a bold face for Miller & Richard's Old Style, a 19th century face. A Ludlow version appeared in 1925.

abcdefghijklmnopqrstuv
wxyzABCDEFGHIJKL
MNOPQRSTUVWXYZ

1955/**Craw Clarendon**/Freeman Craw/ATF.

abcdefghijklmnopqrstuv
wxyzABCDEFGHIJKL
MNOPQRSTUVWXYZ

1955/**Fortune**/K. F. Bauer, Walter Baum/Bauer.

abcdefghijklmnopqrst
uvwxyzABCDEFGHIJK
LMNOPQRSTUVWXYZ

1958/**Craw Modern**/Freeman Craw/ATF.

Reoi

Category: Clarendon/Neo
Features:
These typefaces were first created in the 20th century. Contrast in character stroke weight is more obvious and serifs tend to be longer than earlier designs. Some versions also share design traits with other categories.

abcdefghijklmnopqrstuv
wxyzABCDEFGHIJKL
MNOPQRSTUVWXYZ

1900/**Century Expanded**/Morris Fuller Benton/ATF.
In 1894, Century was cut by Linn Boyd Benton in collaboration with Theodore Low DeVinne for the Century Magazine. *The objective was a darker, more readable typeface than the thinner type that was being used. It was also slightly condensed to accommodate the magazine's two-column format. Century Expanded, by Morris Fuller Benton, is a wider version of his father's, Linn Boyd Benton's, 1895 Century. The letters are expanded only in the sense that they are wider than the weak faces of the 19th century but not in relation to most contemporary typefaces.*

abcdefghijklmnopqrstu
vwxyzABCDEFGHIJKL
MNOPQRSTUVWXYZ

1906/**Century Old Style**/M. F. Benton/ATF.

abcdefghijklmnopqrstu
vwxyzABCDEFGHIJKL
MNOPQRSTUVWXYZ

1907/**Clearface**/M. F. Benton/ATF.

abcdefghijklmnopqrstu
vwxyzABCDEFGHIJKL
MNOPQRSTUVWXYZ

1915/**Century Schoolbook**/M. F. Benton/ATF.
This design was a result of Benton's research into vision and reading comprehension. It was conceived and widely used for setting schoolbooks. It was also the springboard for the many "legibility" designs that followed.

abcdefghijklmnopqrstu
vwxyzABCDEFGHIJKL
MNOPQRSTUVWXYZ

1952/**Melior**/Hermann Zapf/Stempel.

Reoi

Category: Clarendon/Legibility
Features:
This style of type was first released in the 1920s. Contrast in stroke weight is kept to a minimum in these designs; in addition serifs tend to be on the short side, and x-heights are usually large. These typefaces were designed to be highly legible and easy to read on less than ideal paper stock.

abcdefghijklmnopqrstu
vwxyzABCDEFGHIJKL
MNOPQRSTUVWXYZ

1925/**Ionic No. 5**/C. H. Griffith/ Mergenthaler Linotype.

abcdefghijklmnopqrstu
vwxyzABCDEFGHIJKL
MNOPQRSTUVWXYZ

1931/**Excelsior**/C. H. Griffith/Mergenthaler Linotype.
At this time newspapers were demanding typefaces that could be read easily on their newsprint, which was printed under the high speed letterpress printing conditions they had to live with. Excelsior was one of a number of so-called "legibility" typefaces introduced to meet this problem.

abcdefghijklmnopqrstu
vwxyzABCDEFGHIJKL
MNOPQRSTUVWXYZ

1940/**Corona**/C. H. Griffith/Mergenthaler Linotype.

abcdefghijklmnopqrstu
vwxyzABCDEFGHIJKL
MNOPQRSTUVWXYZ

1969/**Modern**/Walter Tracy/British Linotype.

Reoi

Category: Slab Serif
Features:
These typeface have very heavy serifs with no, or exceptionally slight, bracketing. Generally, changes in stroke weight are imperceptible. To many, slab serif typestyles appear to be sans serif designs with the simple addition of a heavy (stroke weight) serif.

abcdefghijklmnopqrst
uvwxyzABCDEFGHIJK
LMNOPQRSTUVWXYZ

1929/**Memphis**/Rudolph Weiss/Stempel.
The earliest modern revival of the Egyptian or slab serif typefaces. Mergenthaler Linotype released a machine version in 1935.

abcdefghijklmnopqrstu
vwxyzABCDEFGHIJKL
MNOPQRSTUVWXYZ

1930/**City**/George Trump/Berthold.

abcdefghijklmnopqrst
uvwxyzABCDEFGHIJK
LMNOPQRSTUVWXYZ

1931/**Beton**/Heinrich Jost/Bauer.

abcdefghijklmnopqrstu
vwxyzABCDEFGHIJKL
MNOPQRSTUVWXYZ

1931/**Karnak**/R. H. Middleton/Ludlow.

abcdefghijklmnopqrst
uvwxyzABCDEFGHIJK
LMNOPQRSTUVWXYZ

1931/**Stymie**/M. F. Benton/ATF.

abcdefghijklmnopqrstu
vwxyzABCDEFGHIJKL
MNOPQRSTUVWXYZ

*c. 1933/**Cairo**/Intertype.*

abcdefghijklmnopqrst
uvwxyzABCDEFGHIJK
LMNOPQRSTUVWXYZ

*1934/**Rockwell**/Monotype.*

Reoi

Category: Glyphic
Features:
Typefaces in this category tend to reflect lapidary inscriptions rather then pen-drawn text. Contrast in stroke weight is usually at a minimum, and the axis of curved strokes tends to be vertical. The distinguishing feature of these typefaces is the triangular-shaped serif design; in some faces this is modified to a flairing of the character strokes where they terminate.

abcdefghijklmnopqrstu
vwxyzABCDEFGHIJKL
MNOPQRSTUVWXYZ

*1932/**Albertus**/Berthold Wolpe/Monotype.*

abcdefghijklmnopqrstuv
wxyzABCDEFGHIJKLM
NOPQRSTUVWXYZ

*1951/**Augustea**/A. Botti and A. Novarese/Nebiolo.*

Sans Serif

Typefaces without serifs. Although stone cut versions of this style pre-date printing with movable type, the first typographic use of sans serif letters was in 1816 by William Caslon IV (a descendant of William Caslon, who designed the important serif typestyle bearing his name). Aside from their lack of serifs, the most distinctive quality of sans serif typefaces is their tendency toward an optically monotone stroke weight.

Reoi

Category: Sans Serif/Grotesque
Features:
These are the first commercially popular sans serif typefaces. Contrast in stroke weight is most apparent in these styles, and there is a slight "squared" quality to many of the curves. In some cases the R has a curled leg, and the G usually has a spur.

ABCDEFGHIJKLM
NOPQRSTUVWXYZ

*1901/**Copperplate Gothic**/F. W. Goudy/ATF.*

abcdefghijklmnopqrstuvwxyzAB
CDEFGHIJKLMNOPQRSTUVWXYZ

*1903/**Alternate Gothic**/M. F. Benton/ATF.*

abcdefghijklmnopqrstu
vwxyzABCDEFGHIJKL
MNOPQRSTUVWXYZ

*1904/**Franklin Gothic**/M. F. Benton/ATF.*
Originally issued in only one weight, the ATF Franklin Gothic family was expanded over the next several years to include an Italic, Condensed, Condensed Shaded, Extra Condensed, and finally a Wide. But, for reasons unknown to this day, no lighter or intermediate weights were created for this premier typeface.

abcdefghijklmnopqrst
uvwxyzABCDEFGHIJK
LMNOPQRSTUVWXYZ

*1908/**News Gothic**/M. F. Benton/ATF.*
Benton designed the light faces. The family became very popular and a machine version was designed under the direction of H. R. Freund for Intertype. In 1958-66, additional weights were developed for ATF by Frank Bartuska

abcdefghijklmnopqrst
uvwxyzABCDEFGHIJK
LMNOPQRSTUVWXYZ

*1948/**Trade Gothic**/Jackson Burke/Mergenthaler Linotype.*

Reoi

Category: Sans Serif/Neo Grotesque
Features:
Sans serif designs patterned after the first grotesques, but more refined in form. Stroke contrast is less pronounced than earlier designs, and much of the "squareness" in curved strokes is lost. These designs can be easily confused with their earlier counterparts however, and normally the most obvious distinguishing characteristic of these faces is the single bowl g.

abcdefghijklmnopqrstuv
wxyzABCDEFGHIJKL
MNOPQRSTUVWXYZ

*1896/**Akzidenz Grotesk**/H. Berthold AG.*
Also known as Standard, this is one of the typefaces widely used by Swiss typographic designers in the 1950's. The later and widely popular Helvetica and Univers families were based on this early sans serif typeface.

abcdefghijklmnopqrstu
vwxyzABCDEFGHIJKL
MNOPQRSTUVWXYZ

*1907/**Venus**/Bauer, Neufville.*

Reoi

Category: Sans Serif/Geometric
Features:
These are sans serif designs which are heavily influenced by simple geometric shapes. Strokes have the appearance of being strict monolines and character shapes made up of perfect geometric forms.

abcdefghijklmnopqrstuv wxyzABCDEFGHIJKL MNOPQRSTUVWXYZ

*1957/**Folio**/K. F. Bauer, W. Baum/Bauer.*

abcdefghijklmnopqrstu vwxyzABCDEFGHIJKL MNOPQRSTUVWXYZ

*1957/**Helvetica**/Edouard Hoffman, Max Miedinger/Haas.*
Edouard Hoffman of the Haas Type Foundry sensed the need for a new sans serif type and decided to refine the more than 50-year-old Akzidenz Grotesk. He collaborated with Max Miedinger, who drew the new design with a large x-height. Haas issued the face as Neue Haas Grotesk, but when Stempel produced it under license in 1961, the name was changed to Helvetica. It quickly became, and still is, a most popular type family. Helvetica is a large family, available in some form on all major typesetting systems. It was, and is, compatible with Swiss grid design, but is equally suited to a wide variety of typographic design problems. Hoffman and Adrian Frutiger (see Univers, next) were both students of Ernst Keller, the Swiss design teacher and practitioner (see Chapter VI). Both the Univers and Helvetica designs can be said to have their roots in Keller's discipline. He adopted a logical approach to type design, yet his own work, as for Parisian theater posters, was hand-lettered. He stressed beauty of letterforms and tight letterspacing long before the latter became popular. In Paris, often working with wood type, he spaced letters closely to save time in hand-setting (handling spacing material) and to save on spacing material.

abcdefghijklmnopqrstu vwxyzABCDEFGHIJKL MNOPQRSTUVWXYZ

*1957/**Univers**/Adrian Frutiger/Deberny & Peignot.*
Frutiger planned tne Univers family, its various weights, italics, degrees of condensing, before any of the faces were produced. Note the straight backed a, the pointed intersection of the diagonals on the K's, the long vertical stem and lack of a spur on the G. Univers is less of a monotone than Helvetica. There were 21 variations in the original Univers family. Shown here is the "normal" version, Univers 55.
Frutiger once wrote, "A letter is not an island...I must never forget that a letter exists only in relation to the others..." His Univers family, widely used to this day, is an outstanding example of not only relating every letter to every other, but of very carefully establishing the relationship of each face in the family to facilitate mixing them, and to enable them to set well in various languages having different letter frequencies. Like Helvetica, Univers was inspired by Akzidenz Grotesk and the feeling that a contemporary refinement of it was needed. Univers is less geometric and mathematically precise than the sans serifs of the 1920s and 1930s.

abcdefghijklmnopqrstu vwxyzABCDEFGHIJKL MNOPQRSTUVWXYZ

*1922-1930/**Erbar Book**/J. Erbar/Ludwig & Mayer.*
An early and popular new sans, Erbar was widely seen. Along with such other typefaces as Bernhard Gothic, Metro, Record Gothic, Stempel Sans, Vogue and the sans serifs of the 1900-1920 years, it cleared the way for today's popular sans serif designs: Helvetica, Univers, ITC Avant Garde Gothic, Antique Olive, as well as Eurostile, Folio, Microgramma, Optima, Peignot, Spartan, Tempo and Twentieth Century.

abcdefghijklmnopqrstu vwxyzABCDEFGHIJKL MNOPQRSTUVWXYZ

*1927/**Futura**/Paul Renner/Bauer.*
The Futura family, still widely used, is a classic design credited with popularizing the use of sans serif typefaces for both text and display. This is a no-nonsense "form follows function" face, stripped of serifs and frills, with essential curves. It has a relatively small x-height. Paul Renner created and drew Futura. According to authorities at the Bauhuas Archiv, some of the inspiration for the design came from a similar alphabet created, as a school project, by Ferdinand Kramer, a Bauhaus student. Kramer is presently an architect and industrial designer practicing in Germany.
The Futura family was released for machine setting by Intertype. Variations or imitations made by other manufacturers include: Airport Gothic (Baltimore Type), Twentieth Century (Lanston Monotype), Spartan (ATF and Mergenthaler), and Tempo (Ludlow). In addition to making minor design variations, each of these manufacturers added new weights or faces to the family.

abcdefghijklmnopqrstuvw xyzABCDEFGHIJKLM NOPQRSTUVWXYZ

*1927/**Kabel**/Rudolph Koch/Klingspor.*
Terminals of some letters are cut at an angle. The letterforms are humanistic rather than geometric. Some other names under which the Kabel design appeared were Sans Serif (Monotype) and Vogue (Intertype). Vogue also has some characters derived from the Futura design.

abcdefghijklmnopqrstuv wxyzABCDEFGHIJKL MNOPQRSTUVWXYZ

*1928/**Berthold Grotesque**/Berthold.*

abcdefghijklmnopqrst uvwxyzABCDEFGHIJK LMNOPQRSTUVWXYZ

*1928/**Stempel Sans**/C. W. Pischiner/Stempel.*

abcdefghijklmnopqrstuv wxyzABCDEFGHIJKLM NOPQRSTUVWXYZ

*1929/**Bernhard Gothic**/Lucian Bernhard/ATF.*
A popular typeface for several decades, Bernhard Gothic was available in light, medium, medium condensed, heavy and extra heavy versions.

abcdefghijklmnopqrstu vwxyzABCDEFGHIJKL MNOPQRSTUVWXYZ

*1929/**Metro**/W. A. Dwiggins/Mergenthaler Linotype. (Metrolite No. 2 of the family is shown here)*

abcdefghijklmnopqrstu vwxyzABCDEFGHIJKL MNOPQRSTUVWXYZ

*1929/**Vogue**/Intertype.*

abcdefghijklmnopqrstuv wxyzABCDEFGHIJKLM NOPQRSTUVWXYZ

*1930/**Tempo**/R. Hunter Middleton/Ludlow.*

abcdefghijklmnopqrstu vwxyzABCDEFGHIJKL MNOPQRSTUVWXYZ

*c. 1930/**Twentieth Century**/S. Hess/Monotype.*

abcdefghijklmnopqrst uvwxyzABCDEFGHIJK LMNOPQRSTUVWXYZ

*1951/**Spartan**/ATF, Mergenthaler Linotype.*

Reoi

Category: Sans Serif/Humanistic
Features:
Sans serif designs based on the proportions of Roman inscriptional capitals and old style lowercase letters. In many cases, contrast in stroke weight is also readily apparent.

abcdefghijklmnopqrst
uvwxyzABCDEFGHIJKL
MNOPQRSTUVWXYZ

*1918/**Johnston's Railway Type**/Edward Johnston/London Transport.*

abcdefghijklmnopqrstuv
wxyzABCDEFGHIJKLM
NOPQRSTUVWXYZ

*1928/**Gill Sans**/Eric Gill/Monotype.*
This design was commissioned by Stanley Morison for Monotype. It was the British counterpart of Futura and was intended to recover sales being lost to the new German designs, Kabel and Futura. Unlike Futura, Gill Sans is not basically geometric. Most of the characters are derived from classical serif designs. This may be why some people consider it the most readable and legible sans serif. The lowercase x-height is small by today's standards.

abcdefghijklmnopqrstu
vwxyzABCDEFGHIJKL
MNOPQRSTUVWXYZ

*1930/**Goudy Sans Serif**/F. W. Goudy/Lanston Monotype.*

abcdefghijklmnopqrstu
vwxyzABCDEFGHIJKL
MNOPQRSTUVWXYZ

*1958/**Optima**/Hermann Zapf/Stempel.*
A stressed, thick and thin sans serif. Strokes thicken toward the end. Note slightly splayed M, the heavy diagonal of the N. The lowercase counters are large and open and the ear of the g is parallel with the baseline. The E, F, and L are narrow as are the f and r. Variously described as a calligraphic roman and modified sans serif. Still among the widely used type families today. Optima, unlike most of today's sans serif typefaces, is essentially a classic roman design minus serifs

Reoi

Category: Sans Serif/Square
Features:
These designs are generally based on grotesque or neo grotesque character traits and proportions, but with a definite (and at times dramatic) squaring of normally curved strokes.

abcdefghijklmnopqrstu
vwxyzABCDEFGHIJKL
MNOPQRSTUVWXYZ

*1952/**Microgramma**/A. Butti, A. Novarese/Nebiolo.*
The family also includes condensed, extended, bold and bold extended versions. Caps only.
*1962/**Eurostile**/Aldo Novarese/Nebiolo.*
Eurostile complements Microgramma by offering a compatible lower case.

abcdefghijklmnopqrs
tuvwxyzABCDEFGHIJ
KLMNOPQRSTUVWXYZ

*1962/**Antique Olive**/Roger Excoffon/Fonderie Olive.*

Reoi

Category: Scripts
Features:
Typefaces that imitate cursive writing. Script typefaces come in all shapes and sizes; in the interest of expediency and efficiency we have grouped them all under this one category.

abcdefghijklmnopqrstuvwxyz
ABCDEFGHIJKLM
NOPQRSTUVWXYZ

*1937/**Coronet**/R. H. Middleton/Ludlow. A somewhat relaxed formal script.*

abcdefghijklmnopqrstuvwxyz
ABCDDEEFFGHH
IJKLLMNOPQR
RSSTTUVWXYZ

*1937/**Legend**/F. H. E. Schneidler/Bauer. An exceptionally dynamic calligraphic script with unusually large capitals.*

abcdefghijklmnopqrst
uvwxyzABCDEFGHIJKL
MNOPQRSTUVWXYZ

*1953/**Mistral**/Roger Excoffon/Olive*
An informed script with connecting lowercase letters.

abcdefghijklmnopqrstuvwxy
zABCDEFGHIJKLM
NOPQRSTUVWXYZ

*1966/**Snell Roundhand**/Matthew Carter/Linotype. A flowing script based on the hand of Charles Snell a 17th century British writing master.*

Reoi

Category: Graphic
Features:
These typefaces defy simple "pigeonholing." They can look like letters cut in stencil, imaged on computer terminal, or decorated with flowers. The only underlying design trait is that they have been constructed rather than appear to have been written.

abcdefghijklmnopqrst
uvwxyzABCDEFGHIJK
LMNOPQRSTUVWXYZ

*1901/**Britannic**/Stephenson Blake.*

abcdefghijklmnopqrstuvwxy
zABCDEFGHIJKLM
NOPQRSTUVWXYZ

1928/***Parisian***/*M. F. Benton/ATF.*

abcdefghijklmnopqrstu
vwxyzABCDEFGHIJKL
MNOPQRSTUVWXYZ

1937/***Peignot***/*A. M. Cassandre/Deberny & Peignot.*

Cassandre named this typeface for Charles Peignot, who had commissioned it for the French type foundry, Deberny & Peignot. Peignot was more than the manager of a type foundry: for more than half a century, he was the key figure in French typography, an arbiter of taste, an experimenter and an innovator in typeface design and in publishing. Peignot sensed the need for continual change so that typographic design could keep in tune with the times. He tried to accomplish in his field what his contemporaries (A. M. Cassandre, Jean Carlu, Paul Colin, Jean Cocteau, Le Corbusier, Francis Poulenc, André Gide and Erik Satie) were accomplishing in theirs. Peignot joined the Union des Artistes Modern, where he met many of the leading art innovators. Peignot felt a need to raise the consciousness of people in and out of the applied arts to contemporary ideas. In 1927 he founded the review, Arts et Metiers Graphics, *and edited it for ten of its 11 years. Its influence was worldwide and profound. Lester Beall (see Chapter VIII) cited the review as a major influence in his development. Not only its content, blending articles on the history of letterforms with Picasso etchings, but its daring layouts greatly stimulated creative minds and spirits. Many of its layouts were by the young Alexey Brodovitch (see Chapter VII), then working in Paris.*

Peignot advocated and practiced integrating the typographic arts with painting, sculpture and literature.

On the issue of order and vitality in typographics, Peignot felt that, "Functionalism pushed graphically to its extreme limit could not effectively be a source of inspiration for the future of typography." It was Charles Peignot who hired a young apprentice, Adrian Frutiger, to design the 21 variations of Univers (See Chapter XI). Peignot also was one of the first to realize that metal type would soon be extinct; he played a role in the development of one of the first significant phototypesetters, the Lumitype, known in the United States as the Photon.

Peignot also knew that typography would soon be in the hands of those not fully trained to handle it, and he foresaw the need for design education and for ways to prevent the typeface design piracy that would proliferate in the era of photographic typesetting. In 1956, he helped found the Association Typographique International (see Chapter XI) to control unethical copying of typeface designs. Charles Peignot died in 1983.

abcdefghijklmnopqrst
uvwxyzABCDEFGHIJKL
MNOPQRSTUVWXYZ

1940/***Radiant***/*R. H. Middleton/Ludlow.*

Category: Experimental

Features:

There have been a number of attempts to modify our alphabet in the 20th century. Some were aimed at simplifying our typographic language, others were attempts at answering both the needs of humanity and technology. Noteworthy experimental designs have been included in this category.

ABCDEFGHIJKLM
NOPQRSTUVWXYZ

1968/**OCRA**/*ATF.*

In the early days of reading machines, typefaces had to be specially designed to enable the mechanical readers to distinguish each letter and number readily. OCRA was designed to meet criteria established by the U.S. Bureau of Standards.

abcdefghijklmnopqr
stuvwxyzABCDEFGHI
JKLMNOPQRSTUVWXYZ

1968/**OCRB**/*Adrian Frutiger/Monotype.*

The European Computer Manufacturers Association (ECMA) recommended standards for character recognition systems. One of the designs it advocated was to "permit and encourage the widest possible use of optical character recognition by the use of character shapes which are as distinguishable as possible without undue sacrifice of the acceptability by the public as a general-purpose type font."

In 1925 Herbert Bayer designed and proposed a universal alphabet. It reduced the alphabet to a single set of geometrically designed letters.

abcdefghijklmn
opqrstuvwxyz

In Herbert Bayer's Universal typeface (above), each letter is distinctively different from every other in order to maximize legibility. A condensed bold and other weights were developed later. Capitals were eliminated. The face was developed from a minimum of geometric elements – several arcs, three angles, a vertical and a horizontal line.

In 1945 Bradbury Thompson offered Monalphabet. It was introduced in *Westvaco Inspirations*, No. 152. Mr. Thompson wrote of his experiment:

"The roman alphabet today has two different symbols for the majority of its twenty-six characters: for example, the large or capital A has no design similarity to the small or lower case a. Each layout in this issue is a typographic experiment in the interest of simplifying our alphabet to one graphic symbol for each character, regardless of size. This objective is based on the logic that each letter should retain the same design, just as the symbol for the Red Cross does not change, regardless of its size…

"Only small letters have been used without traditional capitalization. This usage is generally regarded as more readable, because of greater variation in the size and shape of different characters, than the use of all capital letters."

For the kind of emphasis that capital letters would normally supply one could use bold versions of the lower case designs, or use a larger size letter, as in these examples:

artist: **robert riggs**
art director: **leonard lionni**
advertiser: **felt and tarrant manufacturing co.**
agency: **n. w. ayer & son, inc.**
engraving: **silhouette halftone, 100 line screen**
printed by letterpress on piedmont enamel, 25 x 38 - 70

artist: fred and doris Wright
art director: Sture nelson
advertiser: american bosch Corporation
agency: Wm b. remington, inc.
engraving: 4 color process, 120 line screen
printed by letterpress on piedmont enamel, 25 x 38 - 70

WATER AND CELLULOSE FIBERS HAVE ALWAYS BEEN THE BASIC MATERIALS OF PAPER SINCE ITS INVENTION IN 105 A.D. THE MODEL EIGHTEENTH CENTURY PAPER MILL, LIKE THE LANGLÉE PLANT, WAS LOCATED NEAR A RIVER OR STREAM AND DERIVED CELLULOSE FIBERS FROM LINEN AND OTHER TEXTILE RAGS. THESE RAGS WERE SORTED BY HAND AND SENT TO VATS WHERE THEY WERE MOISTENED AND ALLOWED TO FERMENT FOR TWO MONTHS. THIS STEP AIDED THE DISINTEGRATION OF THE FIBERS.

Alphabet 26 was introduced by Mr. Thompson in *Westvaco Inspirations*, Nos. 180 and 213. The upper and lower case letters are the same design, but vary in size and color, thus reducing the number of designs to 26.

The Family Concept

Not only has the design of letters metamorphosized over the centuries, but so has the concept of what constitutes a typeface family. Highlights in the saga of the family are:

16th Century, second half: A given typestyle such as a Garamond or a Granjon is made available in a range of sizes from 5 to 42 points.

TYPOGRAPHIC COMMUNICATIONS TODAY

Chapter X: Typeface Milestones, 1896-1969

"The new school of typography was shifting the emphasis from what was said (copy) to how you say it (design)."

16th Century, second half: A companion oblique is designed to work with a roman (Granjon).

16th Century, late: Large x-height version of an existing design is introduced (Plantin, Granjon).

17th Century: Having one punch-cutter execute all versions of the growing family assures greater harmony of the letter forms.

18th Century, second half: Typefaces within a family vary by weight, proportions, x-height, and specific details (Bodoni).

18th Century, second half: Development of the point system by Fournier and Didot makes all type measurable and thus in Europe facilitates better alignment of letters when mixing faces in a family or when mixing families.

19th Century: Bold sans serif and slab serif faces available to complement, for emphasis, light romans and italics.

19th Century, late, and early 20th Century: Punch-cutting machine facilitates unification of letterforms in adjacent point sizes made from a single pattern master. First extensive typeface families appear (Century, Cheltenham). Some Century designs also add bold, bold italic, and bold condensed versions.

1930: A family now includes faces from different typeface categories. Jan van Krimpen's Romulus includes serif, sans serif and script typefaces.

1957: Large typeface families, such as Adrian Frutiger's Univers, are designed systematically.

1970: The concept of a full typeface family (usually four romans and four italics), with all faces introduced at the same time, is introduced and offered universally for all of its typeface families by International Typeface Corporation (ITC).

The family concept has matured since 1970 as the major manufacturers and distributors of typefaces regularly introduced full families at one time. But major changes were brewing rapidly. Technologies, more than art movements, were becoming the primary influences on typeface and typographic design.

1977: A two-part family (coordinated serif and sans serif faces, each in a range of weights) is developed by Gerard Unger. The typefaces are known as Praxis and Demos.

1982: One family has a range of weights in three different ascender/descender lengths. (Trinite, by Bram de Does).

1890-1970: A Bird's-Eye View

A decade-by-decade review of the typefaces introduced from 1890 to 1970 stimulates the following observations:

1890-1909: The turn of the century was a period in which type foundries in the United States matured, and the quantity and quality of their output fell into line with that of the long-established European type foundries. The American Type Founders (ATF), manufacturers of foundry type, was especially prominent in this respect. Formed as a merger of the major independent type founders operating in the United States in the late 1800s, ATF was a most influential force in the country's typesetting and printing industry through the first half of this century. With ATF, Morris Fuller Benton firmly established the concept of typeface families. He standardized and consolidated the thousands of type matrices which were acquired when ATF was formed, and he was a prolific designer of new typefaces as well as of revivals of classic designs.

What was New? Of the designs that, in one form or another, were important for several decades, or even endure to this day, the predominant categories were such long-accepted styles as the Venetians, Old Styles and Transitionals. These included the Century, Cheltenham, Cloister, Cushing and Clearface families shown earlier in this chapter. But it is worthy of note that some important Modern designs, such as Scotch Roman, Torino, and the revivals of Didot and Bodoni, were introduced early in this century, as were a number of sans serif faces, notably Alternate Gothic, Franklin Gothic, Venus, and News Gothic.

1910-1919: Although most of the typefaces introduced in the second decade of this century were revivals of either Old Styles or Transitionals, perhaps, in retrospect, the most significant was the typeface designed by the British calligrapher and type designer, Edward Johnston, for the London Underground Railways in 1918. It is considered the first of the 20th century sans serifs, despite the earlier appearance of the sans serif typefaces noted above. Known as Railway Type, or Underground, the type's letter proportions derive from faces even older than those of the 19th century. It opened the door for many later sans serifs.

Johnston's pupil, Eric Gill, later designed Gill Sans, a face still used and highly regarded today.

This period is also notable for a number of new designs by the prolific Morris Fuller Benton, and the emergence of Frederic W. Goudy as a major typeface designer.

The 1920s: There was a surge in the creation of new and redrawn classic typefaces in the 1920s. This decade witnessed the introduction of two sans serif type families that are still highly regarded, Paul Renner's Futura and Eric Gill's Gill Sans. In 1920 Goudy became an art director for Lanston Monotype Corporation. This not only brought his designs to a wider market, but enabled him to change the foundry's system of fixed widths for their characters. Under his guidance, proportions were adjusted to the requirements of the individual design. The first typeface produced by Monotype under this system was the Garamont, in 1921.

The 1930s: The introduction of Times New Roman in 1932 brought to market a readable, compact, visually pleasing type family that, more than 50 years later, has been made available on most equipment and at this writing is still widely used.

During this decade several new Egyptian type families reached the market, as did a few more sans serif types and several revivals of Old Style and Transitional designs that were well received.

The new school of typography was shifting the emphasis from what was said (copy) to how you say it (design). This battle is still alive today, but in the mid-1930s the emphasis on visual appearance and individuality in graphic design was something of a novelty. These were the years when such faces as Bernhard Gothic, Tango, Umbra, Mayfair Cursive, Mandate, Stellar Bold, Electra, Caledonia and Fairfield reached the market. Many were not influenced by Bauhaus concepts. Typographic individuality seemed impossible to achieve with just a few faces, so new faces flooded the market for many years. Today, although new faces are welcomed regularly, it is recognized that how the face is used is at least as important as just which face is used.

The mid-1930s also found typographic leaders calling for less ornament, less formal balance, more use of the new sans serif types, bleeds, type used in reverse, bold faces generously leaded, greater use of photography, large areas of striking color and freely arranged margins.

In the United States in the 1930s, designers were moving away from center axis symmetry and static balance. Their own comments made this clear.

In 1939 Paul Rand explained, "There should be a reason for the elements used."

Herbert Bayer, who came to the United States in 1938, believed that rules derive from the content of each task and are always suited to the specific purpose involved. Basic composition, he held, should be simple, dynamic, and one main form must dominate in it.

Emphasizing the need for constant change in typographic thinking, E. McKnight Kauffer said, "The problems that I worked on yesterday would be approached differently today...Advertising design cannot be disassociated from culture because it implies taste..."

McKnight Kauffer's statement, and Goudy's earlier statement emphasizing the need to consider style relative to the times, express the feeling of many professional communicators that there is an ongoing need for new typeface designs that capture the requirements of the period. Of course, sometimes revivals serve this purpose very well.

The 1940s and 1950s: The introduction of significant new typefaces fell off sharply in the early- and mid-1940s, the decade of World War II. A number of interesting designs were introduced in the late 1940s and the 1950s. Several faces that were to be widely popular and of enduring value made their debut. These included the Palatino, Melior, Helvetica, Univers, and Optima families.

The 1960s: In the 1960s, although few realized it at the time, the typographic world was moving away from the era of metal type and toward the phototypesetting and the digital world. It was in this decade that typefaces such as OCRA and OCRB were designed so they could be read by machines (although not so easily by people) and that a number of faces still of interest were introduced, including Antique Olive, Sabon, and Serifa.

Newspaper Text Typefaces

In the mid-1920s, typeface designer/manufacturers started to become sensitive to the special readability requirement of newstext typefaces. Printed at high speed on relatively poor quality paper, and often in small sizes, newspapers were not as easy to read, nor as attractive, as they should have been. From that time to the present, a number of typefaces have been designed to remedy this situation. Notable among these are the following, some of which are also shown in their proper design category in this and the next chapter.

abcdefghijklmnopqrstu
vwxyzABCDEFGHIJKL
MNOPQRSTUVWXYZ

*1925/**Ionic No. 5**/C. H. Griffith/ Mergenthaler Linotype.*

abcdefghijklmnopqrstu
vwxyzABCDEFGHIJKL
MNOPQRSTUVWXYZ

*1931/**Excelsior**/C. H. Griffith/Mergenthaler Linotype.*

abcdefghijklmnopqrstuv
wxyzABCDEFGHIJKL
MNOPQRSTUVWXYZ

*1932/**Times New Roman**/Stanley Morison/Monotype.*

abcdefghijklmnopqrstu
vwxyzABCDEFGHIJKL
MNOPQRSTUVWXYZ

*1940/**Corona**/C. H. Griffith/Mergenthaler Linotype.*

abcdefghijklmnopqrstu
vwxyzABCDEFGHIJKL
MNOPQRSTUVWXYZ

*1969/**Modern**/Walter Tracy/British Linotype.*

abcdefghijklmnopqrstu
vwxyzABCDEFGHIJK
LMNOPQRSTUVWXYZ

*1970/**Olympian**/Matthew Carter/Mergenthaler Linotype.*

abcdefghijklmnopqrstu
vwxyzABCDEFGHIJKL
MNOPQRSTUVWXYZ

*1972/**Times Europa**/Walter Tracy/Linotype Paul.*

abcdefghijklmnopqrstu
vwxyzABCDEFGHIJKL
MNOPQRSTUVWXYZ

*1980/**Nimrod**/Robin Nicholas/Monotype.*

Since 1970, phototypesetters, digital typesetters and computers have changed the way typefaces are designed and how they can be set and composed. What these technological advances mean to the typographic designer/specifier is the subject of Chapters XI and XII.

TYPOGRAPHIC COMMUNICATIONS TODAY

Chapter XI: Typefaces, 1969-

"Whereas painting, poetry and architecture greatly influenced typeface and typographic design in the early 1900s, the primary influences since the mid-1960s have come from bits and bytes, lasers and fiber optics, electronics, and even photonics."

FUTURE SHOCK hit the typeface and typesetting industries in the mid-1960s. Everyone was affected: users, vendors of machines and supplies, and typeface designers. Reverberations of the impact of computer and laser technologies swept through offices and data centers and changed the balance among the various sections of companies that were concerned with internal or external communications, with words, or with line or tone graphics in black-and-white or color.

As early as the mid-1960s some people foresaw the new directions and moved to take advantage of them. Others didn't fully grasp what was happening until the mid-1970s or later.

Whereas painting, poetry and architecture greatly influenced typeface and typographic design in the early 1900s, the primary influences since the mid-1960s have come from bits and bytes, lasers and fiber optics, electronics, and even photonics.

Although the full spectrum of the technological revolution in communications will be reviewed in the next chapter, in looking here at typefaces introduced in the '70s and '80s one should be aware of the following:

❧ Increasingly, through the '60s, '70s and '80s a full typeface family was introduced as a package, usually four weights of roman with corresponding italics.

❧ Non-exclusivity of design became a force. The same design and artwork was made available to all manufacturers to sell under the same name.

❧ The trend toward a larger x-height accelerated to the point that larger x-height typefaces now dominate the new designs.

❧ Tighter letterspacing was made possible by the new typesetting devices and now typeface designs take this into account.

❧ There is a new mathematics. Old designations of point sizes, for example, mean less now, since many machines can achieve almost any desired size (such as 8 3/16 point) and can slant, condense, expand, rotate and otherwise modify a given font.

❧ Computer programmed interpolations of middle weights are now common. Designers often draw only the lightest and boldest weights of a family and programs produce the in-between weights, subject, of course, to approval and editing.

❧ Typefaces can be completely created at a terminal. This practice exists today in limited areas and is not yet a commercial norm.

❧ Font complements have grown from under 100 characters in the early days of film strips, grids, and discs, to more than 250 for digital devices that serve an international market. (See illustrations in Chapter XII.)

❧ Typefaces are available for a variety of non-impact printers (such as laser printers, electro-erosion devices and thermal printers) and impact printers (such as dot matrix printers and printers using typeballs, thimbles, and daisy wheels.) For coarse resolution printers and some impact printers, a graphic design may be modified and sometimes a monospore version must be created. Not only are these output devices new to the world of typesetting, but impact devices have changed too. To satisfy the font needs of laser printer and computer manufacturers a new kind of type foundry has sprung up, the digital type foundry that converts existing analog font art into outline or bit map digital form.

❧ At the time of this writing we are in a wave of PC typesetting input. IBM PCs and Apple Macintoshes®, for example, dressed with appropriate software, can feed a text stream and typesetting instructions to the wide range of output devices noted above, as well as to fine resolution, high quality typesetters.

❧ Kerning, the nesting of adjacent characters (such as a To or Yo combination), was limited to a handful of character pairs in the days of metal type. It is now possible to kern over 1,000 character pairs in some digital systems.

❧ True italics, italics specifically designed to complement a roman font without any character distortion, are still preferred by designers and users who want the best quality typography. But for many of the less critical jobs, the slanted (or expanded or condensed) romans that can now be created on photo and digital typesetters are acceptable.

❧ Modern typesetting technology has the potential to create a revival in script and calligraphic typestyles.

❧ Some advantages of digital type are:

a. Does not degrade with use.
b. Can be set much faster than by earlier methods.
c. Greater exposure consistency across a page.
d. Sharp edge definition at high resolution, regardless of output size.
e. Very fine intercharacter spacing.
f. Anamorphic sizing.
g. Ability to rotate, displace, condense, stretch, screen, and reverse type.
h. Unlimited character kerning potential.

❧ A major problem with digital type is that jagged or saw-tooth edges of diagonals and curves are visible at low resolutions. As resolution decreases, so does typographic quality. The importance of this depends on the actual resolution, the nature of the job, and the output device.

The New Technologies and Typeface Design

In the era of metal and film fonts, type was stored in typesetting machines. Linotype, Intertype, and Monotype machines stored metal matrices for every character in the font. The machines set characters in lines and columns at the direction of the operators. The metal font matrices were analogs — full of real, tangible letters you could see and touch. This is also true of film fonts whether on strips, grids, discs or whatever.

But now we are in the digital era, and the master font is stored digitally. You can't see or touch it. The physical characters are not stored at all. What is stored is a description of each character in combinations of bits. The bits represent electrical impulses that are either on or off.

This comparatively new method of storing and generating characters has distinct advantages and disadvantages when compared to the metal and film analog systems. In this chapter we will review how digital typesetting affects typeface designs, and typesetting and typographic design, and we will examine the major typefaces introduced since 1970.

The New Look of Typefounding

One of the first to recognize that hot-metal typesetting machines were about to be superseded was Charles Peignot, key founder of the Association Typographique Internationale (A.TYP.I) and head of the French type foundry, Deberny & Peignot. As early as 1956 he foresaw that highly capable film typesetters, in which type fonts were stored and generated photographically, would change the nature of typefounding as an industry. Key changes over the next three decades were:

❧ The art of typeface design and of photography became increasingly controlled by entrepreneurs, electronic engineers, lens makers and computer specialists. Some of these people, while expert in their technological specialities, had little or no understanding of the subtleties of typeface and typographic design.

❧ These developments made it feasible and desirable to create new typeface designs for the new technologies. As noted above, the output characteristics of the new machines so changed the look of existing typefaces that it became desirable to redraw the best and most useful existing designs.

❧ It became much easier and less costly to make and sell unauthorized copies of type designs.

❧ To prevent the unethical copying of the new designs (since such copying would reduce the incentive to develop and market new designs), Peignot recognized the need for effective, international legislation to protect new type designs.

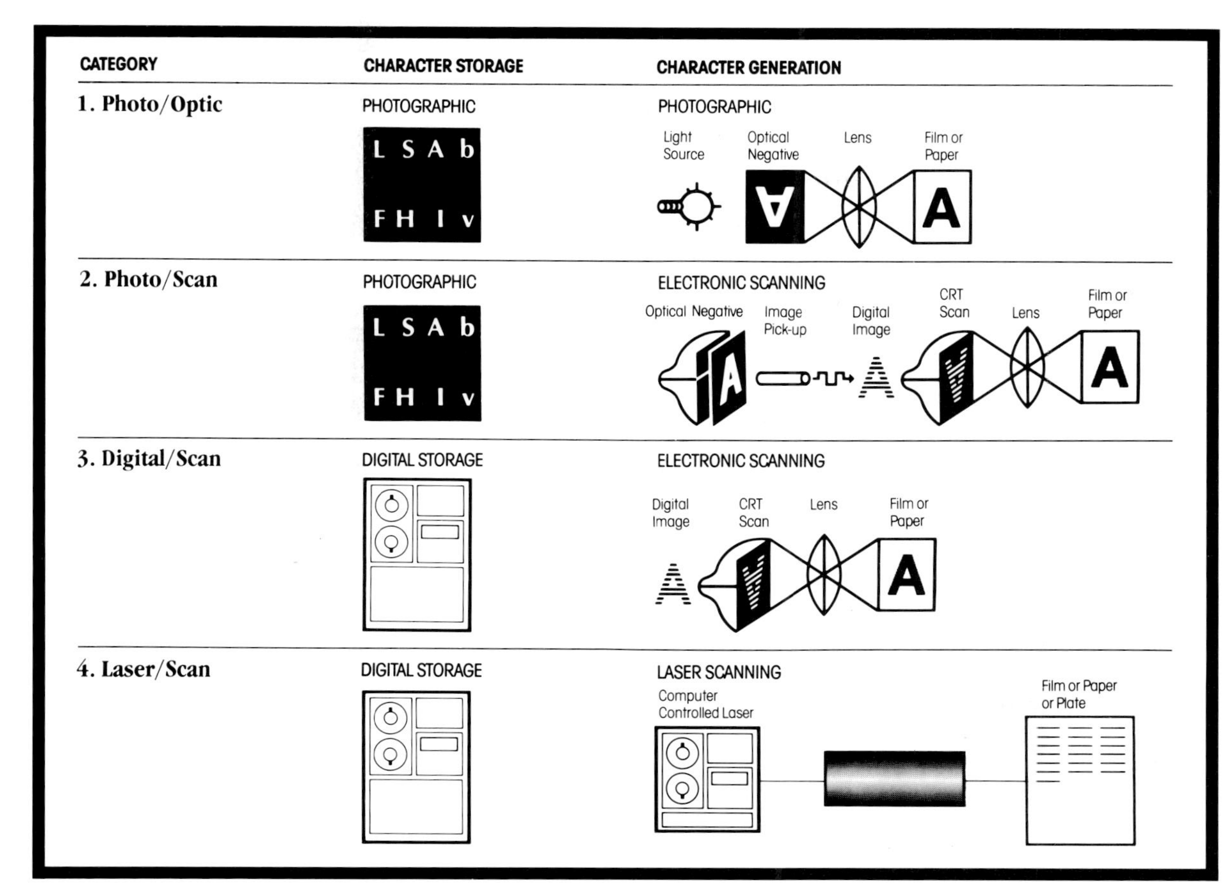

***The metamorphosis** of typesetters in the post-metal era.*

❧ Along with this he foresaw the need to educate users and the public to the desirability of such legislation.
❧ To this end, Peignot took the lead in establishing A.TYP.I in 1957. (The role of A.TYP.I and its achievements to date in typeface design protection are summarized at the end of this chapter.)
❧ The design of typefaces became no longer only the function of typefounders and manufacturers of typesetting machines, but also the province of independent designers and type design/marketing organizations such as the International Typeface Corporation (ITC).
❧ The development of new typeface designs was spurred by the realization of typesetting machine manufacturers that machine sales could be stimulated by offering better and more varied typestyles than those being provided by competitors.
❧ That understanding led to two seemingly contradictory developments.
1. Manufacturers designed and promoted exclusive designs.
2. As the offerings of companies like ITC became increasingly popular, most manufacturers made a point of including these non-exclusive designs in their libraries. This also assured that the same designs could be obtained on text typesetters, display setters, and artists' transfer and cut-out sheets.
❧ Some manufacturers realized that new typefaces not only enhanced machine sales, but became the basis for an additional profit center.
❧ The need for new type designs rested on several conditions:
1. The need to output to maximum advantage on the new typesetters.
2. Changing stylistic preferences.
3. The growing importance of offset lithography and the decline of letterpress printing.
4. In some environments, improved lighting conditions for reading.

❧ A growing awareness that stylistic differences are more important to readers than are functional criteria. This point was clearly expressed by John Dreyfus, honorary president and co-founder of the A.TYP.I, and a typographic advisor to Monotype Corporation Ltd. He wrote:

"The outcome of many experiments indicates there is no statistically significant difference between the legibility of a wide variety of text types, even between seriffed and unseriffed types. On the other hand, differences of real statistical significance were detected when readers were asked which styles they preferred. The fact that they were capable of reading a great many different styles of type with virtually no degree of difficulty did not prevent them from giving very firm opinions about the types which they preferred to read. This finding ought to be studied by those who decide in what types to compose the vast amount of printed matter that is intended to attract or to persuade, but which nobody is obliged to read. For it clearly matters quite a lot whether the right type is chosen to appeal to a potential buyer or voter – or to anyone else who becomes a target for persuasive as distinct from obligatory printed matter (like airline schedules or railway timetables which we all have to read from time to time). The truth revealed by careful experiments is that our remarkably adaptable nervous system is quite capable of decoding most typefaces without difficulty, but that it also leads us to develop quite strong personal preferences for a few particular types."

Typeface Design Systems

Although it is possible today to create a completely new typeface design at a computer controlled design station (such as the Metafont system developed by Donald Knuth, professor of Computer Science and Electrical Engineering at Stanford University), it is still the standard practice for independent designers to design and draw the basic characters and their weights by hand. The new design systems are used to create additional characters using elements from the core characters and to interpolate weights between the lightest and the darkest. The design systems are also used to convert the designer's analog art into digital form. These systems convert the details of the letterforms into a series of dots (also known as pixels, for picture elements). The dots are represented in the sytem by electrically on (for the black dots) or electrically off (white space) areas.

System Components; Input

Typeface design systems can be considered to have three front-end components. These are for input, for interacting with the system to facilitate editing the input, and for displaying the output.

The input component converts the drawing or analog art to digital form. Input devices can include cards, tape, an optical scanner, a tablet and electric sensor, a menu for selecting and executing functions, lightpen, cathode ray tube (screen monitor), keyboard, or a program describing the image.

***There is** an inverse relationship between the quality of the digital type image and the output resolution of the imagesetter. The first figure (top left) was set at 96 point/650 dpi and appears virtually analog to the naked eye. As the digital bit-map becomes coarser, however, more and more typographic detail is lost; the top-right figure was set at eight points/650 dpi, and the bottom-left figure was set at 12 points/300 dpi. At very low writing resolution, much of the detail in the analog design is lost (the bottom-right figure was set at six points/300 dpi). Photo courtesy of Mike Parker.*

***An outline** representation of letterforms interpolated by a high-order spline algorithm provides a high degree of data compaction while preserving typographic detail. A series of spline knots is defined by skilled lettering artists along the character's outline (left). The data can then be used to generate the stroke pattern of the filled letterform (right). The typeface is ITC Zapf Chancery® Light. Artwork courtesy of David Berlow.*

TYPOGRAPHIC COMMUNICATIONS TODAY
Chapter XI: Typefaces, 1969-

"Today, most commercial systems (but not all in-house systems) avoid optical scanning for input."

Letterform images are entered in one of two ways, as bitmaps or outlines. The bitmaps encode a pattern of pixels that represent the design, for example, of an A. The bitmap method requires a different bitmap for each size of the typeface. The outline method merely describes the shape of the character. In a later stage of manufacture, or in the actual typesetter or other printing device, the outline can be filled in and converted to a desired size.

In a typical procedure the typeface designer prepares the original characters manually. The analog characters are entered into the system one by one. They can be scanned by an optical scanner that passes a beam of light across the image in a series of fine, closely spaced parallel bands. The dark parts of the character create electrical signals that eventually print out as black pixels. The width of the laser scanning beam determines the high or low resolution of the resultant roster image. This method of entering data results in a variety of flaws or imperfections that must be cleaned up at an editing station.

Today, most commercial systems (but not all in-house systems) avoid optical scanning for input. They involve marking the character image with control points along the outside and inside edges of the character. The drawing of the character is positioned over an electronic grid in the tablet. The points are entered by specifiying their x-y coordinates on the grid. One variation of this input method uses a digitizer tablet with an electric sensor. The sensor has a set of selector buttons and a window encasing two crossed wires. The cross point of the wires is aligned with the control point to be entered and a selector button is pressed to enter the point in the system.

Imperfections still result and character editing at the interactive station is necessary. An alternate method of entering the control points uses a program that not only lists the coordinates of the control points but instructs the system how to connect the points, for instance by a straight line or a particular kind of spline (curve).

Interfaces

The better systems have interfaces that facilitate careful editing of the input, whether the encoding of existing analog letterforms or the modification of letters designed on the the system. The monitor screen permits visual interaction between the system and the operator/designer. Letters and elements of letters and characters can be stored for re-use on other characters so that the same elements, such as serifs and thick and thin strokes, do not need to be re-created unnecessarily.

Output Display

The edited characters can be output in analog form on paper or film or stored for use as digital information for such display devices as video screens or digital printers. Various output devices have different resolutions (pixels per inch). Some show only a rough approximation of the characters, while fine resolution devices capture and accurately portray the subtleties of letterforms.

Techniques for digitizing typefaces have been described and developed since the mid-1960s. The most widely used systems in the mid-1980s are Ikarus, Letter Input Processor, PM Digital Spiral, Metafont, Xerox Type Founder and Monotype's horizontal roster scan system.

Ikarus

Ikarus starts with an analog character; control points are entered on its outline. The system notes whether the point is a starting, edge, curve or tangent point. Points are then entered by pressing a button on the sensor, thus recording position and kind of point. Universal parameters such as height, width, horizontal and vertical alignment or slant can be adjusted for groups of characters. The consistency of characters throughout a typeface family is assured in this system. Characters can be individually modified. As noted above, weights between the extremes of light and bold can be interpolated by the system, which bypasses hand drawing. The system can also take input from an optical scanner and can perform a variety of clean-up operations. Manual editing, necessary because the system is not interactive, is minimized by procedures that can make all serifs and stems of a typeface match.

Ikarus facilitates the design of new alphabets, as well as the modification of existing ones. The system can also modify typefaces by enlarging, reducing, obliquing or slanting, expanding and condensing. It can create hybrid designs by interpolating between contrasting designs.

The Ikarus system is based on a format developed by Dr. Peter Karow of URW, Hamburg, West Germany. It is used in Europe, Great Britain, the United States, the USSR and Japan. It is also used in the drawing offices of Autologic, Compugraphic, Linotype and URW, among others.

Letter Input Processor (Letter IP)

Letter IP is an interactive font digitizing system. Its key components are a character digitizer, an interactive character editing system and a data base for storing letterform information. A high resolution vector display is connected to a digitizer tablet with a menu and a puck. A trained designer at the display terminal enters control points along the edge of the character by using the puck. The puck can also be used to select editing commands. Points entered are either curve, tangent or edge points chosen from a drawing or copy of the letterform. It is displayed as it is entered.

Letter IP was developed by Camex, Inc. Bitstream uses this system in its drawing office. Bitstream also offers an algorithm to convert outline data to bitmap data on the fly.

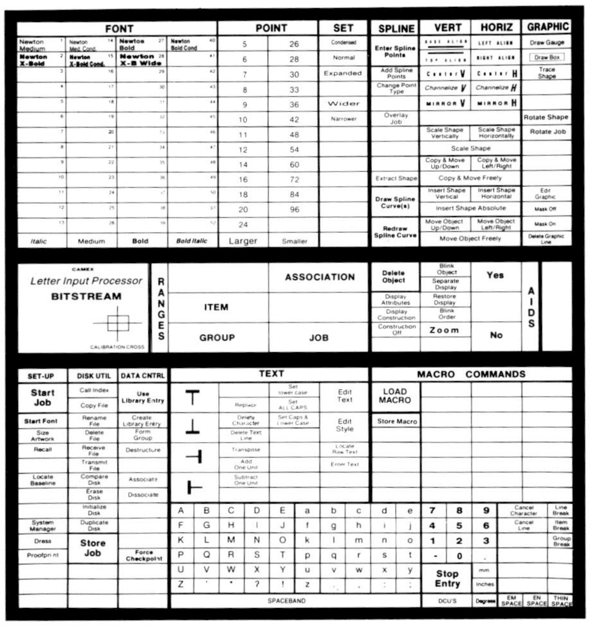

FONT
Newton Medium 1 | Newton Med. Cond. 14 | Newton Bold 27 | Newton Bold Cond 40
Newton X-Bold 2 | Newton X-Bold Cond. 15 | Newton X-B Wide 28 | 41
Italic | Medium | Bold | Bold Italic

POINT
5 26 | 6 28 | 7 30 | 8 33 | 9 36 | 10 42 | 11 48 | 12 54 | 14 60 | 16 72 | 18 84 | 20 96 | 24
Larger | Smaller

SET
Condensed | Normal | Expanded | Wider | Narrower

SPLINE
Enter Spline Points | Add Spline Points | Change Point Type | Overlay Job | Extract Shape | Draw Spline Curve(s) | Redraw Spline Curve

VERT / HORIZ
Base Align | Left Align | Top Align | Right Align | Center V | Center H | Channelize V | Channelize H | Mirror V | Mirror H
Scale Shape Vertically | Scale Shape Horizontally | Scale Shape
Copy & Move Up/Down | Copy & Move Left/Right | Copy & Move Freely
Insert Shape Vertical | Insert Shape Horizontal | Insert Shape Absolute
Move Object Up/Down | Move Object Left/Right | Move Object Freely

GRAPHIC
Draw Gauge | Draw Box | Trace Shape | Rotate Shape | Rotate Job | Edit Graphic | Mask Off | Mask On | Delete Graphic Line

CAMEX
Letter Input Processor
BITSTREAM
CALIBRATION CROSS

RANGES
ITEM | ASSOCIATION | GROUP | JOB

Delete Object | Blink Object | Separate Display | Display Attributes | Restore Display | Display Construction | Blink Order | Construction Off | Zoom | Yes | No
AIDS

SET-UP
Start Job | Start Font | Size Artwork | Recall | Locate Baseline | System Manager | Dress | Proofprint

DISK UTIL
Call Index | Copy File | Rename File | Delete File | Receive File | Transmit File | Compare Disk | Erase Disk | Initialize Disk | Duplicate Disk | Store Job

DATA CNTRL
Use Library Entry | Create Library Entry | Form Group | Destructure | Associate | Dissociate | Force Checkpoint

TEXT
Replace | Delete Character | Delete Text Line | Transpose | Add One Unit | Subtract One Unit
Set lower case | Set ALL CAPS | Set Caps & Lower Case
Edit Text | Edit Style | Locate Raw Text | Enter Text

MACRO COMMANDS
LOAD MACRO | Store Macro

A B C D E a b c d e 7 8 9 | Cancel Character | Line Break
F G H I J f g h i j 4 5 6 | Cancel Line | Item Break
K L M N O k l m n o 1 2 3 | Group Break
P Q R S T p q r s t - 0 .
U V W X Y u v w x y | Stop Entry | mm
Z ' • ? ! z , . : ; | Inches
SPACEBAND | DCU'S | Degrees | EM SPACE | EN SPACE | THIN SPACE

***The LIP menu** has nine functional areas:*
***Font, point, set and text commands** enable one to modify attributes of descriptive text associated with a character.*
***Spline functions** for creating an ordered series of spline knots and drawing the spline outline.*
***Vertical, horizontal and graphic functions** modify the data structure, position of character parts, or construction lines.*
***Ranges** allow selection of the level of data structure to act upon.*
***Secondary functions** in the design process are provided by the aids commands.*
***Set up functions** initialize various system parameters.*
***Disk utilities** perform local file manipulations.*
***Data control commands** allow the user to catalog character parts and alter the data structure.*
***Macrocommands** allow lettering artists to customize the LIP to their personal work habits.*

On Digital Spiral

PM Digital Spiral is a bitmap editing system developed by Peter Purdy and Ronald McIntosh. It is based on the concept that the crucial aspect of a character is its outline. As a corollary, it assumes that distortions on the outline are less tolerable than those inside it. A sharp edge is created by a designer, who traces the outline of digitized letters with a computer-stored spiral generated at a very high resolution. The tracing operation smooths away dropouts, pickups and other irregularities. The coordinates of key points of the smoothed outline are stored and can be called up later to re-create the sharp-edged image. The system allows for adjusting letter proportions and ascender/descender proportions for different sizes. Varityper is a major user of PM Digital Spiral.

December 17, 1987

Mr. Edward Benguiat
Photo-Lettering, Inc.
216 East 45th Street
New York, NY 10017

Dear Mr. Benguiat,

We thought that you would like to see how your design of ITC Souvenir® looks when output on a monospacing impact printer. This letter was printed out on an NEC Spinwriter with ITC Souvenir on its thimble image carrier.

Of course, one cannot compare it to proportionally spaced output on a fine resolution typesetter but the use of such typefaces in the office communications field, on impact or non-impact printers does offer this communications area an opportunity to achieve more impact, distinction, and memorability by widening the choices of available styles and the ways they can be used. We hope you like the look of this letter as much as we do.

Sincerely,

Edward M. Gottschall

Edward Gottschall,
Vice Chairman, ITC
Editor, U&lc

EG:kn

ITC Souvenir on a typewriter. *This letter was printed out on an NEC Spinwriter with ITC Souvenir on its thimble image carrier.*

Metafont
Metafont can be used to create new alphabets, not simply to convert analog characters to digital form. The user moves an electronic pen across a surface (a piece of paper or a terminal screen) and defines the parameters of the images. The user can specify the shape and width of the nib of the electronic pen, which can erase as well as create lines. The user specifies points by x and y coordinates and, with the selected pen, connects the resulting dots. After a basic font has been developed, parameters can be modified to create other typefaces for the same family.

As of this writing, Metafont is of limited commercial value. It requires a powerful computer and is very slow if quality output is desired. It also requires that the designer create a metafont program that mathematically specifies the desired letterforms. Perhaps, from the viewpoint of graphic arts quality typography, the big drawback to creating new typeface designs with Metafont, or with any system, or even with a pen or a brush for that matter, is that good design requires, above all else, a good designer. The best designers, for sound economic reasons as well as because of their training, are still designing typefaces with traditional tools.

Monotype
Monotype employs a horizontal raster scan of analog art of the letterforms. A large drawing of each character is scanned in relation to a grid made up of horizontal and vertical lines. Horizontal and vertical lines scan clearly, but curves and diagonals require editing, adding or removing pixels to achieve smooth lines. Monotype developed its own digitizer for its system. Trained typographers examine the original large drawing and assure its faithful reproduction in small print size. After satisfactory editing, including a check for compatibility with all other characters, the electronic impulses representing a character are stored on a floppy disc. Each point is derived by software from the master.

Many companies, in addition to creating digital fonts from analog art for use on their own equipment, offer a typeface digitizing service. Some companies are primarily digital font services. Major sources of digital fonts today include:
Adobe Systems, Inc.
Autologic Inc.
Bitstream, Inc.
Agfa Compugraphic Corporation
COPI
Digital Type Systems, Ltd.
Intran
Linotype Corporation
Linotype GmbH AG
Monotype
Nippon Information Sciences, Ltd.
URW Unternehmensberatung

Typefaces for Low Resolution Output
As personal or desk-top publishing proliferates, the demand for typefaces that can be output clearly is surging. What is low resolution with respect to typefaces? Although there is no formal and universal acceptance of the line separating low resolution typeface output from high resolution output, many people put that line at 700 dots per inch (dpi). Graphic arts quality typesetters generally output at resolutions finer than 1,000 dpi and as fine as 5,300 dpi. However, very clear, readable output that satisfies many publishing needs is being achieved at 300 dpi on a number of laser printers.

Can graphic art typefaces be successfully output by such printers? Should new typefaces be specially designed to optimize their output quality? The answer to both of these questions is a qualified yes.

Many graphic arts typefaces not only can be, but are being successfully output at 300 dpi. Some faces, especially those with extremely thin strokes or serifs, should be avoided for low resolution devices. Still other faces can be and have been successfully modified so that they can output clearly without losing or seriously compromising their essential character.

Of course, it is a good idea to design new typefaces that meet the requirements of low resolution devices, but that is not enough. Such faces should also have all the merits associated with a graphic arts quality typeface, including high legibility, a degree of individuality, esthetic appeal, good copyfitting characteristics and the ability to be developed as a full and useful family.

Monospace Typefaces
Some non-impact printers as well as daisy wheel, thimble and dot matrix printers, cannot output proportionally spaced fonts, nor fonts developed with a fine unit system. The finer letterspacing made possible by 54-unit phototypesetters and by digital typesetters cannot be approached by typewriters or word processors based on a nine unit system. However, the market is starting to ask for graphic arts typefaces. Such typefaces won't make typesetters of such devices, nor typography of their output, but they can give new distinction and personality to typewritten documents.

Some, but not all, existing graphic arts typefaces can be adapted for typewriters, word processors, and dot matrix printers.

For a more detailed discussion of the problems and special needs of low resolution printers, see "The Principles of Digital Type," by Charles Bigelow in *The Seybold Report on Publishing Systems*, Vol. 11, Nos. 11 and 12.

TYPOGRAPHIC COMMUNICATIONS TODAY

Chapter XI: Typefaces, 1969-

"It is becoming increasingly difficult to design a typeface that is distinctive enough to warrant introduction, yet not so novel as to be eccentric and of limited application."

New Technologies and Old Traditions

Approximately two-thirds of the typefaces in digital letterform libraries are derived from metal typefaces. One in four of our present day digital typefaces derive from sources 100 to 500 years old. Up to another 50 per cent trace their origins to designs of the recent past.

This poses two dilemmas. With so many designs now available, it is becoming increasingly difficult to design a typeface that is distinctive enough to warrant introduction, yet not so novel as to be eccentric and of limited application.

The other dilemma is that of fidelity to the original, whatever the original really was. The tendency today, epitomized by ITC typefaces, is to capture the spirit and essential skeleton of the letterform being revived, while taking into account the limits and freedoms of today's typeface design and typesetting technologies.

In several of the typefaces listed below, the original source or designer of the typeface is credited in addition to the modern artist. In some cases, because of an unclear background or space restrictions, an original designer may have been eliminated.

Typefaces 1969-1986

Old Style

These are typefaces which were originally created between the late 15th and mid 18th century. (Or are patterned after typefaces which were originally designed in this time period.) In these designs the axis of curved strokes is normally inclined to the left, and the contrast in stroke weight is not dramatic. Some versions, like the earlier Venetian old style designs, are distinguished by the diagonal cross stroke of the lowercase e. Serifs are almost always bracketed and headserifs are often angled.

Reoi

Category: Old Style/Revivals

Features:

These are typefaces which, although they may display a predominance of old style design traits, are generally not patterned after any particular type of the period. Many times, in fact, they may share several design influences. As with other old style designs, character stroke is relatively conservative and weight stress is inclined.

abcdefghijklmnopqrstuv wxyzABCDEFGHIJKLM NOPQRSTUVWXYZ

*1970/ITC **Souvenir**/Edward Benguiat, USA/ITC. (Based on M.F. Benton's Souvenir Light, c. 1914)*

abcdefghijklmnopqrstuv wxyzABCDEFGHIJKL MNOPQRSTUVWXYZ

*1972/**Garamond**/G. G. Lange, Germany/Berthold.*

abcdefghijklmnopqrstuv wxyzABCDEFGHIJKL MNOPQRSTUVWXYZ

*1974/ITC **Tiffany**/Edward Benguiat, USA/ITC. A blend of two earlier typefaces, Ronaldson (1884) and Caxton (1904).*

abcdefghijklmnopqrstuv wxyzABCDEFGHIJKL MNOPQRSTUVWXYZ

*1974/**Worcester Round**/Adrian Williams, GB/Fonts.*

abcdefghijklmnopqrst uvwxyzABCDEFGHIJK LMNOPQRSTUVWXYZ

*1975/**Belwe**/Alan Meeks, GB/Letraset.*

abcdefghijklmnopqrstu vwxyzABCDEFGHIJKL MNOPQRSTUVWXYZ

*1975-1977/ITC **Garamond**/Tony Stan, USA/ITC.*

abcdefghijklmnopqrst uvwxyzABCDEFGHIJKL MNOPQRSTUVWXYZ

*1976/**Poppl-Pontifex**/Friedrich Poppl, Germany/Berthold.*

abcdefghijklmnopqrstuv wxyzABCDEFGHIJKL MNOPQRSTUVWXYZ

*1977/**Caslon Buch**/G. G. Lange, Germany/Berthold.*

abcdefghijklmnopqrstu vwxyzABCDEFGHIJKL MNOPQRSTUVWXYZ

*1977/**Italia**/Colin Brignall, GB/ITC.*

abcdefghijklmnopqrstu vwxyzABCDEFGHIJKL MNOPQRSTUVWXYZ

*1977/**Raleigh**/Adrian Williams, GB/Fonts.*

abcdefghijklmnopqrstuv wxyzABCDEFGHIJKL MNOPQRSTUVWXYZ

*1977/**Seneca**/Gustave Jaeger, Germany/Berthold.*

abcdefghijklmnopqrst uvwxyzABCDEFGHIJK LMNOPQRSTUVWXYZ

*1978/ITC **Benguiat**/Edward Benguiat, USA/ITC.*

abcdefghijklmnopqrst uvwxyzABCDEFGHIJK LMNOPQRSTUVWXYZ

*1978/**Seagull**/Adrian Williams, GB/Fonts.*

abcdefghijklmnopqrstuv wxyzABCDEFGHIJKL MNOPQRSTUVWXYZ

*1978/**Stratford**/Freda Sack, GB; Adrian Williams, GB/Fonts.*

abcdefghijklmnopqrst
uvwxyzABCDEFGHIJK
LMNOPQRSTUVWXYZ

*1979/ITC **Clearface**/Victor Caruso, USA/ITC.*

abcdefghijklmnopqrstu
vwxyzABCDEFGHIJKL
MNOPQRSTUVWXYZ

*1979/**Quadriga Antiqua**/Manfred Barry, Germany/Berthold.*

abcdefghijklmnopqrstuv
wxyzABCDEFGHIJKL
MNOPQRSTUVWXYZ

*1979/**Vladimir**/Vladimir Andrich, USA/Alphatype.*

abcdefghijklmnopqrstu
vwxyzABCDEFGHIJKL
MNOPQRSTUVWXYZ

*1980/**Bramley**/Alan Meeks, GB/Letraset.*

abcdefghijklmnopqrstuv
wxyzABCDEFGHIJKLM
NOPQRSTUVWXYZ

*1980/**Brighton**/Alan Bright, GB/Letraset.*

abcdefghijklmnopqrst
uvwxyzABCDEFGHIJK
LMNOPQRSTUVWXYZ

*1981/**Weinz Kurvalin**/David Weinz/Itek.*

abcdefghijklmnopqrstu
vwxyzABCDEFGHIJKL
MNOPQRSTUVWXYZ

*1982/**Breughel**/Adrian Frutiger, France/Linotype.*

abcdefghijklmnopqrstuv
wxyzABCDEFGHIJKL
MNOPQRSTUVWXYZ

*1982/ITC **Galliard**/Matthew Carter, GB/ITC.*
This adaptation of Robert Granjon's 16th century design was drawn by Matthew Carter. It was originally designed for Mergenthaler Linotype.

abcdefghijklmnopqrst
uvwxyzABCDEFGHIJK
LMNOPQRSTUVWXYZ

*1983/**Edwardian**/Colin Brignall, GB/Letraset.*

abcdefghijklmnopqrstu
vwxyzABCDEFGHIJKL
MNOPQRSTUVWXYZ

*1983/ITC **Berkeley Oldstyle**/Tony Stan, USA/ITC.*
ITC Berkeley Oldstyle is based on Goudy's original design for the typeface he created for the University of California Press.

abcdefghijklmnopqrst
uvwxyzABCDEFGHIJK
LMNOPQRSTUVWXYZ

*1983/ITC **Caslon No. 224**/Edward Benguiat, USA/ITC.*

abcdefghijklmnopqrstu
vwxyzABCDEFGHIJKL
MNOPQRSTUVWXYZ

*1983/ITC **Weidemann**/Kurt Weidemann, Germany/ITC.*
ITC Weidemann was derived from the designer's Biblica typeface that was created for the German Bible Society.

abcdefghijklmnopqrstuv
wxyzABCDEFGHIJKLM
NOPQRSTUVWXYZ

*1984/**Magna Carta**/Vladimir Andrich, USA/Alphatype.*

abcdefghijklmnopqrstuv
wxyzABCDEFGHIJKL
MNOPQRSTUVWXYZ

*1985/ITC **Esprit**/Jovica Veljović, Yugoslavia/ITC.*

abcdefghijklmnopqrstu
vwxyzABCDEFGHIJKL
MNOPQRSTUVWXYZ

*1985/**Zapf Renaissance**/Hermann Zapf, Germany/Scangraphic.*

Reoi

Category: Transitional
Features:
The style for these typefaces was established in the mid 18th century, primarily by the English printer and typographer John Baskerville. While the axis of curve strokes can be inclined, it is generally vertical. Weight contrast is more pronounced than in old style designs although serifs are still bracketed and head serifs are oblique. These typefaces represent the transition between old style and modern designs and incorporate characteristics of each.

abcdefghijklmnopqrstuv
wxyzABCDEFGHIJKL
MNOPQRSTUVWXYZ

*1969/**Concorde**/G. G. Lange, Germany/Berthold.*

abcdefghijklmnopqrstu
vwxyzABCDEFGHIJKL
MNOPQRSTUVWXYZ

*1974/**Orion**/Hermann Zapf, Germany/Mergenthaler Linotype.*

abcdefghijklmnopqrstu
vwxyzABCDEFGHIJKL
MNOPQRSTUVWXYZ

*1975/**Concorde Nova**/G. G. Lange, Germany/Berthold.*

abcdefghijklmnopqrstu
vwxyzABCDEFGHIJKL
MNOPQRSTUVWXYZ

*1976/**Comenius**/Hermann Zapf, Germany/Berthold.*

abcdefghijklmnopqrst
uvwxyzABCDEFGHIJK
LMNOPQRSTUVWXYZ

*1977/ITC **Zapf International**/Hermann Zapf, Germany/ITC.*

abcdefghijklmnopqrstuv
wxyzABCDEFGHIJKL
MNOPQRSTUVWXYZ

*1978/**Leamington**/Adrian Williams, GB/Fonts.*

abcdefghijklmnopqrstu
vwxyzABCDEFGHIJKL
MNOPQRSTUVWXYZ

*1979/**Garth Graphic**/Renee LeWinter, Constance Robichaud, USA/Compugraphic.*

abcdefghijklmnopqrstu
vwxyzABCDEFGHIJKL
MNOPQRSTUVWXYZ

*1980/**Baskerville Book**/G. G. Lange, Germany/Berthold.*

abcdefghijklmnopqrstuv
wxyzABCDEFGHIJKL
MNOPQRSTUVWXYZ

*1982/**ITC New Baskerville**/ITC.*
(Licensed from Mergenthaler Linotype)

abcdefghijklmnopqrstu
vwxyzABCDEFGHIJKL
MNOPQRSTUVWXYZ

*1983/**Expert**/Aldo Novarese, Italy/Mergenthaler Linotype.*

abcdefghijklmnopqrst
uvwxyzABCDEFGHIJKL
MNOPQRSTUVWXYZ

*1984/**ITC Usherwood**/Leslie Usherwood, Canada/ITC.*

abcdefghijklmnopqrst
uvwxyzABCDEFGHIJK
LMNOPQRSTUVWXYZ

*1984/**Scenario**/Phil Martin, USA/Typespectra.*

abcdefghijklmnopqrstu
vwxyzABCDEFGHIJKL
MNOPQRSTUVWXYZ

*1985/**Cremona**/Vladimir Andrich, USA/Alphatype.*

Modern

The work of Giambattista Bodoni in the 18th century epitomizes this style of type. Here, contrast between thick and thin strokes is abrupt and dramatic. The axis of curved strokes is vertical and all serifs are horizontal with little or no bracketing.

Reoi

Category: Modern/20th Century
Features:
These typefaces were created in the 20th century, and while they may share many design traits with Didones, they are generally not intended to be revivals of these earlier designs. They also tend to be more stylized than their predecessors.

abcdefghijklmnopqrstu
vwxyzABCDEFGHIJKL
MNOPQRSTUVWXYZ

*1969/**Linotype Modern**/Walter Tracy, GB/ Mergenthaler Linotype.*

abcdefghijklmnopqrstu
vwxyzABCDEFGHIJKL
MNOPQRSTUVWXYZ

*1969/**Primer**/Colin Brignall, GB/Letraset.*

abcdefghijklmnopqrstu
vwxyzABCDEFGHIJKL
MNOPQRSTUVWXYZ

*1970/**Auriga**/Matthew Carter, GB/Mergenthaler Linotype.*

abcdefghijklmnopqrstu
vwxyzABCDEFGHIJKL
MNOPQRSTUVWXYZ

*1972/**Photina**/Jose Mendoza/Monotype.*

abcdefghijklmnopqrstu
vwxyzABCDEFGHIJKL
MNOPQRSTUVWXYZ

*1975/**Iridium**/Adrian Frutiger, France/ Mergenthaler Linotype.*

abcdefghijklmnopqrstu
vwxyzABCDEFGHIJKL
MNOPQRSTUVWXYZ

*1975/**Walbaum Book**/G. G. Lange, Germany/Berthold.*

abcdefghijklmnopqrst
uvwxyzABCDEFGHIJK
LMNOPQRSTUVWXYZ

*1976/**Franklin Antiqua**/G. G. Lange, Germany/Berthold.*

abcdefghijklmnopqrstu
vwxyzABCDEFGHIJKL
MNOPQRSTUVWXYZ

*1976/**Walbaum Standard**/G. G. Lange, Germany/Berthold.*

abcdefghijklmnopqrst
uvwxyzABCDEFGHIJK
LMNOPQRSTUVWXYZ

*1976/**ITC Zapf Book**/Hermann Zapf, Germany/ITC.*

abcdefghijklmnopqrst
uvwxyzABCDEFGHIJK
LMNOPQRSTUVWXYZ

*1980/**ITC Fenice**/Aldo Novarese, Italy/ITC.*
(Originally designed for Berthold)

abcdefghijklmnopqrstuv
wxyzABCDEFGHIJKL
MNOPQRSTUVWXYZ

*1981/**Tiemann**/Walter Tiemann, Adrian Frutiger, France/ Mergenthaler Linotype.*

abcdefghijklmnopqrstuv
wxyzABCDEFGHIJKL
MNOPQRSTUVWXYZ

*1981/**Else**/Robert Norton, GB/Robert Norton.*

abcdefghijklmnopqrst
uvwxyzABCDEFGHIJK
LMNOPQRSTUVWXYZ

*1982/ITC **Modern No. 216**/Edward Benguiat, USA/ITC.*

abcdefghijklmnopqrstu
vwxyzABCDEFGHIJKL
MNOPQRSTUVWXYZ

*1982/**Basilia Haas**/André Gürtler, Christian Mengelt, Eric Gschwind, Switzerland/Mergenthaler Linotype.*

abcdefghijklmnopqrstu
vwxyzABCDEFGHIJKL
MNOPQRSTUVWXYZ

*1983/**Bodoni Old Face**/G. G. Lange, Germany/Berthold.*

abcdefghijklmnopqrstu
vwxyzABCDEFGHIJKL
MNOPQRSTUVWXYZ

*1986/**Centennial**/Adrian Frutiger, France/Allied Linotype.*

Clarendon

This is a style of type which first became popular in the 1850s. Like the Didones before them, Clarendons have a strong vertical weight stress, but this is where the similarities end. While they do have obvious contrast in stroke thickness, it is not nearly as dramatic as in the Didones. In addition, serifs are normally heavy, bracketed, and usually square cut.

Reoi

Category: Clarendon/Neo

Features:

These typefaces were first created in the 20th century. Contrast in character stroke weight is more obvious and serifs tend to be longer than earlier designs. Some versions also share design traits with other categories.

abcdefghijklmnopqrst
uvwxyzABCDEFGHIJK
LMNOPQRSTUVWXYZ

*1974-1977/ITC **Korinna**/Edward Benguiat, USA; Victor Caruso, USA/ITC.*

Ed Benguiat enlarged the 1904 Berthold Korinna into a full family that included an italic, Korinna Kursiv.

abcdefghijklmnopqrst
uvwxyzABCDEFGHIJK
LMNOPQRSTUVWXYZ

*1975/ITC **Bookman**/Edward Benguiat, USA/ITC.*

abcdefghijklmnopqrst
uvwxyzABCDEFGHIJKL
MNOPQRSTUVWXYZ

*1975-1978/ITC **Cheltenham**/Tony Stan, USA/ITC.*

abcdefghijklmnopqrst
uvwxyzABCDEFGHIJK
LMNOPQRSTUVWXYZ

*1976/**Itek Bookface**/David Kindersley/Itek.*

abcdefghijklmnopqrstu
vwxyzABCDEFGHIJKL
MNOPQRSTUVWXYZ

*1982/ITC **Cushing**/Vincent Pacella, USA/ITC.*

abcdefghijklmnopqrstu
vwxyzABCDEFGHIJKL
MNOPQRSTUVWXYZ

*1984/**Allan**/Vladimir Andrich, USA/Alphatype.*

abcdefghijklmnopqrstuv
wxyzABCDEFGHIJKL
MNOPQRSTUVWXYZ

*1985/**Media**/André Gürtler, Christian Mengelt, Eric Gschwind, Switzerland/Autologic.*

Reoi

Category: Clarendon/Legibility

Features:

This style of type was first released in the 1920s. Contrast in stroke weight is kept to a minimum in these designs; in addition serifs tend to be on the short side, and x-heights are usually large. These typefaces were designed to be highly legible and easy to read on less than ideal paper stock.

abcdefghijklmnopqrstuv
wxyzABCDEFGHIJKL
MNOPQRSTUVWXYZ

*1971/**Rotation**/Arthur Ritzel/Linotype.*

abcdefghijklmnopqrstu
vwxyzABCDEFGHIJK
LMNOPQRSTUVWXYZ

*1970/**Olympian**/Matthew Carter, GB/Linotype.*

abcdefghijklmnopqrstu
vwxyzABCDEFGHIJKL
MNOPQRSTUVWXYZ

*1972/**Times Europa**/Walter Tracy, GB/Linotype Paul.*

abcdefghijklmnopqrstu
vwxyzABCDEFGHIJKL
MNOPQRSTUVWXYZ

*1975-1980/ITC **Century**/Tony Stan, USA/ITC.*
(Based on Century, designed by the Bentons for ATF)

abcdefghijklmnopqrstu
vwxyzABCDEFGHIJKL
MNOPQRSTUVWXYZ

*1980/**Nimrod**/Robin Nicholas/Monotype.*

abcdefghijklmnopqrstu
vwxyzABCDEFGHIJKL
MNOPQRSTUVWXYZ

*1983/**Clarion**/Robin Nicholas, Ron Carpenter/Monotype.*

Reoi

Category: Slab Serif
Features:
These typeface have very heavy serifs with no, or exceptionally slight, bracketing. Generally, changes in stroke weight are imperceptible. To many, slab serif typestyles appear to be sans serif designs with the simple addition of a heavy (stroke weight) serif.

abcdefghijklmnopqrs
tuvwxyzABCDEFGHIJK
LMNOPQRSTUVWXYZ

*1969/**Aachen**/Colin Brignall, GB/Letraset.*

abcdefghijklmnopqrst
uvwxyzABCDEFGHIJK
LMNOPQRSTUVWXYZ

*1974/ITC **Lubalin Graph**/Herb Lubalin, USA/ITC.*
This face was derived from Avant Garde Gothic with slab serifs added. It was drawn by Antonio DiSpigna and Joe Sundwall.

abcdefghijklmnopqrst
uvwxyzABCDEFGHIJK
LMNOPQRSTUVWXYZ

*1976/**Egyptienne**/Adrian Frutiger, France/Mergenthaler Linotype.*

abcdefghijklmnopqrstu
vwxyzABCDEFGHIJKL
MNOPQRSTUVWXYZ

*1977/**Serifa**/Adrian Frutiger, France/Mergenthaler Linotype.*
This face was originally issued by Bauer in 1967.

abcdefghijklmnopqrst
uvwxyzABCDEFGHIJK
LMNOPQRSTUVWXYZ

*1980/**Calvert**/Margaret Calvert, GB/Monotype.*

Reoi

Category: Glyphic
Features:
Typefaces in this category tend to reflect lapidary inscriptions rather then pen-drawn text. Contrast in stroke weight is usually at a minimum, and the axis of curved strokes tends to be vertical. The distinguishing feature of these typefaces is the triangular-shaped serif design; in some faces this is modified to a flairing of the character strokes where they terminate.

abcdefghijklmnopqrst
uvwxyzABCDEFGHIJKL
MNOPQRSTUVWXYZ

*1973/**Friz Quadrata**/Ernst Friz, Germany (Regular); Victor Caruso, USA (Bold)/ITC.*
(Based on a 1965 VGC design)

abcdefghijklmnopqrst
uvwxyzABCDEFGHIJK
LMNOPQRSTUVWXYZ

*1974/ITC **Serif Gothic**/Herb Lubalin, USA; Antonio DiSpigna, USA/ITC.*

abcdefghijklmnopqrstu
vwxyzABCDEFGHIJKL
MNOPQRSTUVWXYZ

*1974/ITC **Newtext**/Ray Baker, USA/ITC.*

abcdefghijklmnopqrst
uvwxyzABCDEFGHIJK
LMNOPQRSTUVWXYZ

*1977/ITC **Quorum**/Ray Baker, USA/ITC.*

abcdefghijklmnopqrst
uvwxyzABCDEFGHIJK
LMNOPQRSTUVWXYZ

*1979/**Romic**/Colin Brignall, GB/Letraset.*

abcdefghijklmnopqrst
uvwxyzABCDEFGHIJKL
MNOPQRSTUVWXYZ

*1980/**Congress**/Adrian Williams, GB/Fonts.*

abcdefghijklmnopqrstu
vwxyzABCDEFGHIJKL
MNOPQRSTUVWXYZ

*1980/**Icone**/Adrian Frutiger, France/Mergenthaler Linotype.*
Icone is an example of how a designer who derives inspiration from classical typefaces can take into consideration the reproduction capabilities of digital typesetters. Frutiger tried to create a design that could not be distorted objectionably. It is unusual in that it has very few absolutely straight lines.

abcdefghijklmnopqrst
uvwxyzABCDEFGHIJK
LMNOPQRSTUVWXYZ

*1980/ITC **Novarese**/Aldo Novarese, Italy/ITC.*
(Originally designed for Haas)

abcdefghijklmnopqrst
uvwxyzABCDEFGHIJK
LMNOPQRSTUVWXYZ

*1981/ITC **Barcelona**/Edward Benguiat, USA/ITC.*

abcdefghijklmnopqrstu
vwxyzABCDEFGHIJKL
MNOPQRSTUVWXYZ

*1982/**Versailles**/Adrian Frutiger, France/Mergenthaler Linotype.*

abcdefghijklmnopqrst
uvwxyzABCDEFGHIJKL
MNOPQRSTUVWXYZ

*1983/**Marbrook**/Leslie Usherwood, Canada/Berthold.*

abcdefghijklmnopqrst
uvwxyzABCDEFGHIJKL
MNOPQRSTUVWXYZ

*1983/**Poppl-Laudatio**/Friedrich Poppl, Germany/Berthold.*

abcdefghijklmnopqrstu
vwxyzABCDEFGHIJKL
MNOPQRSTUVWXYZ

*1983/**Proteus**/Freda Sack, GB/Letraset.*

abcdefghijklmnopqrstuv
wxyzABCDEFGHIJKL
MNOPQRSTUVWXYZ

*1983/**Pegasus**/Berthold Wolpe, GB/Linotype.*

abcdefghijklmnopqrst
uvwxyzABCDEFGHIJK
LMNOPQRSTUVWXYZ

*1984/**Bryn Mawr**/Joseph Treacy, USA/Mergenthaler Linotype.*

abcdefghijklmnopqrst
uvwxyzABCDEFGHIJK
LMNOPQRSTUVWXYZ

*1984/ITC **Symbol**/Aldo Novarese, Italy/ITC.*

abcdefghijklmnopqrstu
vwxyzABCDEFGHIJKL
MNOPQRSTUVWXYZ

*1984/ITC **Veljovic**/Jovica Veljović, Yugoslavia/ITC.*

abcdefghijklmnopqrst
uvwxyzABCDEFGHIJKL
MNOPQRSTUVWXYZ

*1985/ITC **Élan**/Albert Boton, France/ITC.*

Sans Serif

Typefaces without serifs. Although stone cut versions of this style pre-date printing with movable type, the first typographic use of sans serif letters was in 1816 by William Caslon IV (a descendant of William Caslon, who designed the important serif typestyle bearing his name). Aside from their lack of serifs, the most distinctive quality of sans serif typefaces is their tendency toward an optically monotone stroke weight.

Reoi

Category: Sans Serif/Neo Grotesque
Features:
Sans serif designs patterned after the first grotesques, but more refined in form. Stroke contrast is less pronounced than earlier designs, and much of the "squareness" in curved strokes is lost. These designs can be easily confused with their earlier counterparts however, and normally the most obvious distinguishing characteristic of these faces is the single bowl g.

abcdefghijklmnopqrstu
vwxyzABCDEFGHIJKL
MNOPQRSTUVWXYZ

*1977/**Video**/Matthew Carter, GB/Mergenthaler Linotype.*

abcdefghijklmnopqrst
uvwxyzABCDEFGHIJK
LMNOPQRSTUVWXYZ

*1980/**Haas Unica**/André Gürtler, Christian Mengelt, Eric Gschwind, Switzerland/Haas.*

abcdefghijklmnopqrst
uvwxyzABCDEFGHIJKL
MNOPQRSTUVWXYZ

*1980/ITC **Franklin Gothic**/Victor Caruso, USA/ITC.*

abcdefghijklmnopqrstu
vwxyzABCDEFGHIJKL
MNOPQRSTUVWXYZ

*1982/**Imago**/G. G. Lange, Germany/Berthold.*

abcdefghijklmnopqrstu
vwxyzABCDEFGHIJKL
MNOPQRSTUVWXYZ

*1984/**Akzidenz Grotesk Old Face**/G. G. Lange, Germany/Berthold.*

abcdefghijklmnopqrstu
vwxyzABCDEFGHIJKL
MNOPQRSTUVWXYZ

*1985/**Helvetica** (Numbered Series)/Linotype.
A refinement of Eduard Hoffman and Max Miedinger's original design.*

Reoi

Category: Sans Serif/Geometric
Features:
These are sans serif designs which are heavily influenced by simple geometric shapes. Strokes have the appearance of being strict monolines and character shapes made up of perfect geometric forms.

abcdefghijklmnopqrs
tuvwxyzABCDEFGHIJK
LMNOPQRSTUVWXYZ

*1970/ITC **Avant Garde Gothic**/Herb Lubalin, Tom Carnase, USA/ITC.*

abcdefghijklmnopqrst
uvwxyzABCDEFGHIJKL
MNOPQRSTUVWXYZ

*1975/ITC **Bauhaus**/Edward Benguiat, USA/ITC.
(Based on Universal by Herbert Bayer)*

abcdefghijklmnopqrst
uvwxyzABCDEFGHIJKL
MNOPQRSTUVWXYZ

*1976/ITC **Kabel**/Photo-Lettering Inc., USA/ITC.
(Based on the D. Stempel AG version designed by Rudolf Koch in 1927)*

"Manufacturers are more willing to introduce new typefaces, to introduce full families all at once and meet the fashion needs of the advertising segment of the market."

Reoi

Category: Sans Serif/Humanistic
Features:
Sans serif designs based on the proportions of Roman inscriptional capitals and old style lowercase letters. In many cases, contrast in stroke weight is also readily apparent.

abcdefghijklmnopqrstu
vwxyzABCDEFGHIJKL
MNOPQRSTUVWXYZ

*1969/**Syntax**/Hans Meier/Mergenthaler Linotype.*

abcdefghijklmnopqrst
uvwxyzABCDEFGHIJKL
MNOPQRSTUVWXYZ

*1976/**Frutiger**/Adrian Frutiger, France/ Mergenthaler Linotype.*

abcdefghijklmnopqrst
uvwxyzABCDEFGHIJK
LMNOPQRSTUVWXYZ

*1976/ITC **Eras**/Albert Boton, Albert Hollenstein, France/ITC. The slight forward slant makes a true italic unnecessary.*

abcdefghijklmnopqrstu
vwxyzABCDEFGHIJKL
MNOPQRSTUVWXYZ

*1977/**Souvenir Gothic**/George Brian/Typespectra.*

abcdefghijklmnopqrs
tuvwxyzABCDEFGHIJK
LMNOPQRSTUVWXYZ

*1979/**Praxis**/Gerald Unger, Netherlands/Hell.*

abcdefghijklmnopqrst
uvwxyzABCDEFGHIJK
LMNOPQRSTUVWXYZ

*1982/**Cosmos**/Gustav Jaeger/Berthold.*

abcdefghijklmnopqrst
uvwxyzABCDEFGHIJKL
MNOPQRSTUVWXYZ

*1982/**Shannon**/Janice Prescott/Compugraphic.*

abcdefghijklmnopqrst
uvwxyzABCDEFGHIJKL
MNOPQRSTUVWXYZ

*1984/**Vela**/Barbara Gibb, USA/Compugraphic.*

abcdefghijklmnopqrst
uvwxyzABCDEFGHIJK
LMNOPQRSTUVWXYZ

*1985/**Clearface Gothic**/Linotype. (Based on Clearface by M.F. Benton)*

abcdefghijklmnopqrst
uvwxyzABCDEFGHIJK
LMNOPQRSTUVWXYZ

*1985/ITC **Mixage**/Aldo Novarese, Italy/ITC. (Originally designed for Haas)*

abcdefghijklmnopqrstu
vwxyzABCDEFGHIJKL
MNOPQRSTUVWXYZ

*1985/**Signa**/André Gürtler, Christian Mengelt, Eric Gschwind, Switzerland/Autologic.*

Category: Scripts
Features:
Typefaces that imitate cursive writing. Script typefaces come in all shapes and sizes; in the interest of expediency and efficiency we have grouped them all under this one category.

abcdefghijklmnopqrstuvwxyz
ABCDEFGHIJKLMN
OPQRSTUVWXYZ

*1970/**Poppl-Exquisit**/Friedrich Poppl/Berthold.*

abcdefghijklmnopqrstuvwx
yzABCDEFGHIJKLM
NOPQRSTUVWXYZ

*1971/**Medici Script**/Hermann Zapf, Germany/ Mergenthaler Linotype.*

abcdefghijklmnopqrstuv
wxyzABCDEFGHIJKL
MNOPQRSTUVWXYZ

*1979/ITC **Zapf Chancery**/Hermann Zapf, Germany/ITC.*

abcdefghijklmnopqrstuv
wxyzABCDEFGHIJKL
MNOPQRSTUVWXYZ

*1984/**Sayer Esprit**/Manfred Sayer/Berthold.*

Reoi

Category: Graphic

Features:

These typefaces defy simple "pigeonholing." They can look like letters cut in stencil, imaged on computer terminal, or decorated with flowers. The only underlying design trait is that they have been constructed rather than appear to have been written.

abcdefghijklmnopqrst
uvwxyzABCDEFGHIJK
LMNOPQRSTUVWXYZ

1969/**Revue**/*Colin Brignall, GB/Letraset.*

abcdefghijklmnopqrst
uvwxyzABCDEFGHIJK
LMNOPQRSTUVWXYZ

1974/ITC **American Typewriter**/*Joel Kaden, USA; Tony Stan, USA/ITC.*

abcdefghijklmnopqrst
uvwxyzABCDEFGHIJKL
MNOPQRSTUVWXYZ

1979/ITC **Benguiat Gothic**/*Edward Benguiat, USA/ITC.*

abcdefghijklmnopqrstu
vwxyzABCDEFGHIJKL
MNOPQRSTUVWXYZ

1980/**LoType**/*Erik Spiekermann, Germany/Berthold.*

abcdefghijklmnopqrst
uvwxyzABCDEFGHIJK
LMNOPQRSTUVWXYZ

1981/ITC **Isbell**/*Dick Isbell, USA; Jerry Campbell, USA/ITC.*

abcdefghijklmnopqrst
uvwxyzABCDEFGHIJKL
MNOPQRSTUVWXYZ

1984/**Draco**/*Joffre LeFevre, USA/Compugraphic.*

abcdefghijklmnopqrstuv
wxyzABCDEFGHIJKLM
NOPQRSTUVWXYZ

1984/**Pictor**/*Henry Mikiewicz, Pam Grant, USA/Compugraphic.*

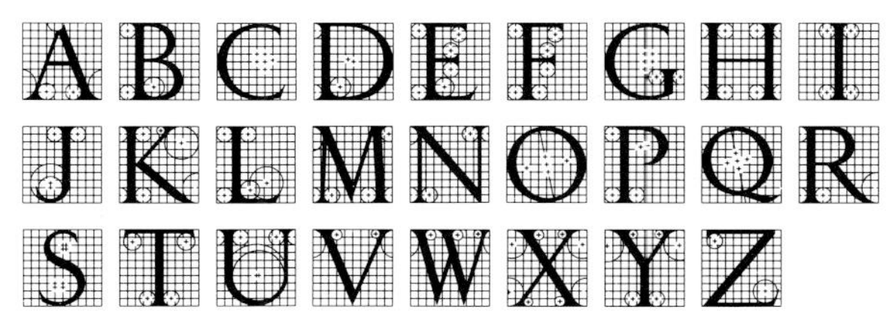

1985/**Champ Fleury**/*Jeffery G. Level, Bruce Frame, USA/Autologic.*

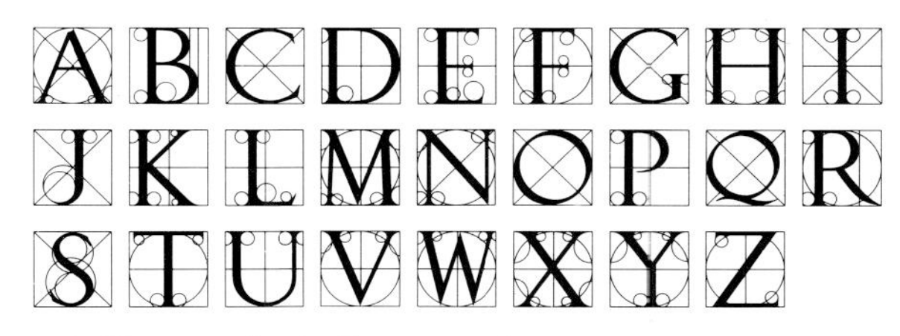

1985/**Geometrica**/*Jeffery G. Level, Bruce Frame, USA/Autologic.*

ABCDEFGHI
JKLMNOPQR
STUVWXYZ

1985/**Melencolia**/*Jeffery G. Level, Bruce Frame, USA/Autologic.*

The Influence of ITC

The International Typeface Corporation (ITC) was established in late 1969, just at the time the new technologies were beginning to affect the design of typefaces, typesetting methods, and what typographic designers could do and how they worked.

Recognizing the then-emerging new technological and typeface marketing climate, the ITC concept stressed:

❧ Non-exclusivity: Whereas typesetter manufacturers had been emphasizing the exclusivity of their designs and offering them, with rare exception, only to users of their own equipment, ITC offered all of its designs on equal terms to all manufacturers of machines and artists' materials.

❧ Royalty payments to typeface designers: In addition to an up-front lump sum for delivery of the art, ITC pays designers a percentage of all revenue earned by their designs. This applies to original designs as well as those adapted and licensed from other manufacturers.

❧ Payment of a low royalty for fonts at time of purchase. As of 1986, the royalty ranged from $30.00 to 5 cents per font, depending on the output capability of the machine or material on which it is used.

❧ In-family typography: All ITC typefaces are developed and introduced as a full family, most with four roman weights, plus matching italics. Some include condensed versions and alternate characters. This enables the user to achieve a full range of emphasis in a document while retaining a unified look throughout.

❧ A controlled approach to legibility: To achieve a satisfying blend of distinction and legibility, ITC typefaces feature a large lowercase x-height, refined character strokes to ensure even color, controlled intercharacter spacing to reduce unnecessary and disturbing visual gaps in typesetting, and controlled internal white space of characters to permit reducing and enlarging while retaining design character and legibility.

❧ Universality of art: The same art is given to all ITC Subscribers. Fine adjustments are made by manufacturers to tune a font to their equipment, but essentially an ITC typeface is the same on all fine resolution output devices. Today, coarse resolution devices and impact devices such as daisy wheel and thimble printers use the ITC faces. Obviously, the art is modified more for them, although it retains the essential look of the typeface.

If ITC took the lead in addressing the new typeface marketing environment, its lead was quickly followed by almost all other companies designing and releasing typefaces. Almost all major users of typefaces throughout the world are licensed to release ITC typefaces along with their own designs or those obtained from other sources.

The prime mover in developing the ITC concept was Aaron Burns, ITC's Chairman. In 1969 he and Herb Lubalin formed a partnership called Lubalin, Burns & Co., Inc. Shortly thereafter he approached Edward Rondthaler and Photo-Lettering, Inc. of New York City about his idea for the creation of an international typeface design and development company. Thus ITC was born, a jointly owned company of Lubalin, Burns & Co., Inc. and Photo-Lettering, Inc.

Since 1970, the cost of bringing a new typeface to market, though still considerable, has been dramatically lower than in days of hot-metal typesetting machines. As a result, manufacturers are more willing to introduce new typefaces, to introduce full families all at once and meet the fashion needs of the advertising segment of the market.

Typeface Marketers

A number of other typeface design companies have entered the market. These include TSI, Typespectra, Typsettra, Hardy/Williams, FONTS, World Typeface Center, Letraset, and Bigelow-Holmes.

TYPOGRAPHIC COMMUNICATIONS TODAY
Chapter XI: Typefaces, 1969-

"Geometry can produce legible letters, but art alone makes them beautiful."

***The Role of* A.TYP.I**

About two and a half decades after its founding in 1957, the Association Typographique Internationale (A.TYP.I) began to achieve its primary goal, referred to earlier in this chapter of TYPOGRAPHIC COMMUNICATIONS TODAY. In the early 1980s both West Germany and France wrote federal laws protecting the designs of new and original typefaces. A.TYP.I itself, in 1985, adopted a resolution defining what makes a typeface new and/or original and named an international panel of experts to give opinions when claims for registering a new typeface are challenged. A.TYP.I offers its resolution and its panel to litigants and courts when needed.

The German and French laws are essentially versions of a 1973 document developed by A.TYP.I in Vienna. To be truly significant, the Vienna agreement must be ratified by five countries. However, with two such major markets as Germany and France subject to the agreement, a great inhibition exists for those who would pirate typeface designs and offer them on the international market.

Aside from its work on typeface design protection, A.TYP.I meets annually and brings together typesetter manufacturers, typeface designers, teachers, students and others interested in the development and use of typefaces, to discuss matters of mutual interest and concern.

Thoughts About Typefaces

"The good type designer knows that, for a new font to be successful, it has to be so good that only a few recognize its novelty."
Stanley Morison in *First Principles of Typography.*

"All his typefaces are so designed that their basic novelty is scarcely noticeable. Perhaps that is the reason why his new creations have been accepted by the public."
Hans Rudolf Schneebeli writing about Adrian Frutiger in the introduction to *Type Sign Symbol.*

"...we best honor the achievements of the past when, inspired by their tutelage, we design for our own contemporary printing, alphabets suited to the industrial design of our century."
Hermann Zapf, in his introduction to *Manuale Typographicum.*

"Letters are symbols which turn matter into spirit."
Alphonse de Lamartine, *Cours familier de literature,* Vol. 6, Paris 1858, p. 406.

"Type gives body and voice to silent thought. The speaking page carries it through the centuries."
Friedrich Schiller, "Der Spaziergang," Lines 135-136 in *Schillers Werke,* Vol. II, Weisbaden 1952, p. 475.

"Type is one of the most eloquent means of expression in every epoch of style. Next to architecture, it gives the most characteristic portrait of a period and the most severe testimony of a nation's intellectual status."
Peter Behrens in his preface to the *Behrens-Schrift,* Offenbach am Main, 1902, p. 4.

"I am Type! Of my earliest ancestry neither history nor relics remain. The wedge-shaped symbols impressed in plastic clay by Babylonian builders in the dim past, foreshadowed me: from them, on through the hieroglyphs of the ancient Egyptians, down to the beautiful manuscript letters of the medieval scribes, I was in the making. With the golden vision of the ingenious Gutenberg, who first applied the principle of casting me in metal, the profound art of printing with movable types was born. Cold, rigid, and implacable I may be, yet the first impress of my face brought the Divine Word to countless thousands. I bring into the light of day the precious stores of knowledge and wisdom long hidden in the grave of ignorance. I coin for you the enchanting tale, the philosopher's moralizing, and the poet's phantasies; I enable you to exchange the irksome hours that come, at times, to every one, for sweet and happy hours with books—golden urns filled with all the manna of the past. In books, I present to you a portion of the eternal mind caught in its progress through the world, stamped in an instant, and preserved for eternity. Through me, Socrates and Plato, Chaucer and the Bards, become your faithful friends who ever surround and minister to you. I am the leaden army that conquers the world; I am Type!"
Frederic W. Goudy, reprinted in Melbert B. Cary, Jr.'s *A Bibliography of the Village Press,* New York 1938, p.179.

"Geometry can produce legible letters, but art alone makes them beautiful. Art begins where geometry ends, and imparts to letters a character transcending mere measurement."
Paul Standard, New York, *Manuale Typographicum,* Frankfurt am Main 1954, p. 63.

"The beauty of a type face lies in its restfulness and in the way it seems to extract light from the paper. This restfulness which makes a type beautiful has nothing lifeless or paralyzed about it, it might rather be described as organized life. As in the other arts, it consists of a balance of movement. This calm therefore has two components; life, and balance or rhythm."
Harry Graf Kessler in the catalog, *Ausstellung von Werken der modernen Druck-und Schreibkunst,* Weimar 1905.

Parts of a Character

The preceding pages illustrate and name most of the important typefaces of the 20th century. But not only typefaces have names. So do the parts of a letter.

"The thingamajig with the little bump" could describe an automobile shift lever, a record player turntable, the ear and bowl of a lowercase g, or any number of other things. Using correct nomenclature is vital to communication – especially technical communication; which is why most people who use automobiles and record players would choose the correct terms to describe a shift lever or turntable, it makes for simpler, more efficient communication.

For the same reasons, if you use type, it makes sense to use the correct terms in your type-related communication. There are not that many terms to learn, and most have simple and obvious meanings. The terminology of type is not difficult – but it is necessary. Since letters are the foundation of all typographic communication, they are the logical place to begin to build a typographic vocabulary.

Contrary to most typographic terms, the parts of a character can appear to have somewhat arbitrary names. The ear of a g could just as well be called a "knob" or "handle." The names of the different parts of a character, however, have a long and well-documented history. Reams of paper have been consumed describing and identifying the various parts of the letterform; written manuscripts exist which date back to the 15th century. Many of those terms, however, have become outdated or are too technical for normal use. What follows is a condensed version of many previous lists of letterform nomenclature. The twenty, or so, terms presented here will provide you with sufficient letterform vocabulary for all but the most erudite of typographic discussion and communication.

Arm A horizontal stroke that is free on one end.

Ascender The part of the lowercase letters b, d, f, h, k, l, and t that extends above the height of the lowercase x.

Bar The horizontal stroke in the A, H, e, t, and similar letters.

Bowl A curved stroke which makes an enclosed space within a character. The bump on a P is a bowl.

Counter The fully, or partially enclosed space within a character.

Descender The part of the letters g, j, p, q, y, and sometimes J, that extends below the baseline.

Ear The small stroke projecting from the top of the lowercase g.

Hairline A thin stroke usually common to serif typestyles.

Link The stroke connecting the top and bottom of a lowercase g.

Loop The lower portion of the lowercase roman g.

Serif A line crossing the main strokes of a character. There are many varieties.

Shoulder The curved stroke of the h, m, and n.

Spine The main curved stroke of a lowercase or capital S.

Spur A small projection off a main stroke, found on many capital G's.

Stem A straight vertical stroke, or main straight diagonal stroke in a letter which has no vertical stroke.

Stress The direction of thickening in a curved stroke.

Stroke A straight or curved line.

Swash A fancy flourish replacing a terminal or serif.

Tail The descender of Q or short diagonal stroke of the R.

Terminal The end of a stroke not terminated with a serif.

x-Height The height of the lowercase letters excluding ascenders and descenders.

Chapter XII: Bits, Bytes and Typographic Design

"...new terminals, output devices, networks, scanners and software have revolutionized the world of typesetting and given typographic designers a whole new set of tools, freedoms and restrictions."

As the preceding chapter explains, computer and laser technologies have changed the way typefaces are being designed and how the new typefaces look. Even more dramatically, wave after wave of new terminals, output devices, networks, scanners and software have revolutionized the world of typesetting and given typographic designers a whole new set of tools, freedoms and restrictions.

In the first half of the 20th century the driving forces that affected the look of typographic designs came from the new schools of painting, poetry and architecture. They continue to influence today's designers. But, since the late 1960s, the influence of the new technologies on typesetting and typographic design has been even greater. In this chapter we will summarize the current status and directions of these technologies and examine how they are affecting communication graphics.

A word of caution. What follows is only a summary report. It would take a multi-volume book to cover these developments in depth and, by the time such a book could be published, it would be partially obsolete, due to the rapid pace of significant technological advances.

The First Wave

Earlier in the 20th century, the first of the many technological waves that were to affect typographic design and the printing processes was being felt. Photography, and then color photography, were replacing illustration in editorial pages and in advertising. They were so eye-appealing, so powerful, so effective in making statements, that they even changed the role of text, in many cases supplanting it. Picture magazines such as *Life* and *Look* in the United States and their equivalents in England and Europe flourished. The spread of television reinforced the importance of the image in communication, as well as in entertainment. Photography's counterpart in printing was offset lithography; by mid-century, it was surpassing letterpress as the principal print reproduction process. By the 1970s the camera in phototypesetters was making metal typesetting obsolete, and, as outlined in the previous chapter, by the beginning of the 1980s digital typography was replacing devices and systems that stored fonts on film.

While considering the current state of the art one should realize that type and images today are no longer intended solely for the print media, nor even just for the human eye. Television, slide presentations, films, computer printouts, conversion to voice form, machine-readable images, signage, and electronic publishing such as videotext systems also require type, pictures and communication designers, and each of these media has unique mechanical requirements that must be met.

Today's Technological Spectrum

Every step of the process has been affected.

❧ Text originators – authors, editors, and copywriters have been keyboarding on terminals that relay the keystrokes to editing, makeup and output stations, bypassing re-keyboarding. The word originator keyboards, and sometimes specifies the type. Now, WYSIWYG terminals are simplifying this process.

❧ Images can be scanned into the systems, or created at an artist/designer terminal, sized, cropped, retouched, positioned, and merged with text. Even low-cost systems now handle halftone as well as line art; more sophisticated systems accommodate color art and permit the operator to separate and correct colors, and to instantly see the effect of their work on the screen. Manual work, including airbrushing and retouching, stripping elements in position, and even storing in a file, are all done electronically now.

❧ Electronic filing of text, images, or made-up pages is easy, fast, instantly accessible, compact, free of multiple copies, and cost-effective.

❧ Local networks for linking devices on one floor or in one building, and long-distance and satellite networks facilitate transmission of the digital information representing text, pictures, and typesetting and makeup instructions to one or more remote sites.

The following chart summarizes how the key steps in print communication have evolved in recent years:

	YESTERDAY	TODAY	TOMORROW
Writing a story, ad copy, a report, etc.	Pen, pencil, typewriter, dictation equipment	Conventional tools plus word processors and keyboard devices that key the copy for typesetter.	Voice input of text, data, and instructions will be more widely used. The same terminal, or any on line, used to originate a story will be used to edit it, create illustrations, make up pages or areas, set type, expose the pages, bypass platemaking, produce multiple copies (collated) in color and using both sides of the sheet. It will be able to communicate to remote sites and distribute itself electronically when so desired. While not everyone will need such an all-in-one machine, all sorts of combinations of multi-purpose devices will be possible and available. In sum, all steps will be digital/electronic, and the systems will be affordable across a wide budget range. Finer resolution printers, outputting on plain paper in a range of sizes, and with larger type libraries, are now foreseeable, at more widely affordable prices.
Illustration – art/photography	Brushes, pens, pencils, paints, inks, cameras, paper, board, etc.	As before, plus use of color terminals with electronic "pens" and graphic tablets. Also, scanners to digitize line or tone, b/w or color art, and to input them into the system.	
Design/layout	Drawing table, T-square, layout pad, pencils	Conventional tools plus electronic interactive input and makeup devices, as well as programmed formats.	
Typesetting, imagesetting	Foundry type, metal machine and phototypesetting	Photographic digital-CRT and digital-laser typesetting via typesetting services and in-office installations. Personal computers plus appropriate software programs to input and control typesetting specifications. Output devices now include coarse and medium resolution non-impact printers and fine resolution typesetters that can output pictures as well as text.	
Platemaking	Done by photo-engravers or printers	More platemaking done in-house or bypassed in a PC-to-laser printer system.	
Reproducing (printing, binding, etc.)	Commercial printers, binders, etc.	More printing done in-house on laser printers as well as offset presses, inkjet printers, etc.	

So much for an outline look at where the new technologies are taking us. Now, let's take a closer look at text and image input and editing devices and how they affect typesetting and typography, as well as at the impact of digital typesetters, imagesetters, and printers in the mid '80s. We'll also hazard a few guesses as to what the next major breakthroughs will be.

Electronic Manuscripts

Going fast, already gone in many places, is the marked-up manuscript. Authors, reporters, and copywriters are using word processors and personal computers to "type" their manuscripts. The result is usually a disk containing the text stream and sometimes codes representing typesetting markup commands. In addition to such author-generated manuscripts, micro and mainframe databases supply machine-generated data to the typesetter, and optical character recognition (OCR) devices scan paper manuscripts into the typesetting system to bypass re-keyboarding.

Database Typesetting

A database can be thought of as an electronic library. There, on mainframes usually, stories, data, and pictures can be stored digitally. For a newspaper, this comparatively compact system makes a vast amount of information instantly available. It replaces the huge, slow to access, paper files or "morgues." Such databases can be made available for a fee to subscribers. Special subject files such as Mead's Lexis (legal information) and Nexis (medical data), the Bibliographic Retrieval Service, and Lockheed's Dialog, compile, store, and sell data. They contract with information sources, such as magazines or newspapers, to obtain data. Users can search the database via key words, much as one would use a library card catalog. Data obtained can be for research, or the actual information received can be fed to a typesetting system without re-keyboarding. (For a more detailed description of database typesetting, see *The World of Digital Typesetting,* by John W. Seybold.)

Inputs, Front-Ends

The principal ways of keyboarding copy into a typesetting system are by:

1. Direct entry typesetters, in which the keyboard and typesetting output unit are part of a single device, as with Varityper Comp/Edits, Linotype CRTronics, Compugraphic Editwriters, Itek Quadriteks and Digiteks, for example. (As this was written, of the photo-optical direct input typesetters, only the Itek Quadritek was still in production. Digital direct-entry typesetters and slave typesetters driven by separate front-ends now dominate the market.)

2. Typesetter keyboards and front-end systems such as those offered by Quadex, Multiset, Xyvision, CCI, Penta, Atex, Bedford, and others. In these systems the copy is keyboarded and coded for setting on a "slave" typesetter. Here the input and output steps are in separate devices or systems.

3. Word processors by which the text stream is keyboarded and transported via a disk to a typesetter. An interface of some sort and proper coding are required to make such disks work on typesetters. In practice, the coding can be fully handled by the type shop referring to a marked-up hard copy of the manuscript, or the coding can be partially done by the word processor operator.

4. Personal computers with word processing and typesetting software are bringing considerable typesetting ability to offices, studios, advertising agencies and departments, and editorial staffs. The combination of a PC and software programs is making desktop publishing affordable and practicable. In fact, some of the same PC/software front-ends are so capable, they meet the needs of larger and more demanding users. For example, for about $10,000 you can buy an Apple LaserWriter Plus with PostScript® software, a Macintosh Plus with Aldus' PageMaker software, and JustText with Apple Talk, a local area network to link the system's components. This system includes spell check packages and the ability to select fonts and sizes from a growing library. It can produce special effects, such as sizing, rotating, stretching of letters. It includes kerning and hyphenation and justification programs, can draw boxes and rules, and can electronically make up pages with all elements in position.

MagnaType *offers what it calls a "complete front end typography system for the microcomputer." Its capabilities include automatic kerning, with 1,500 automatic kerning pairs per font and a 2,000 font capacity; automatic tracking, with four levels of white space adjustment; five methods of hyphenation and justification; and multi-tasking, that is output to a typesetter while you create and h&j another job. MagnaType drives all major typesetters and PostScript® devices.*

Chapter XII: Bits, Bytes and Typographic Design

"Electronic technology has made it possible to 'typeset' art."

MagnaType offers what it calls a "complete front end typography system for the microcomputer." Its capabilities include automatic kerning, with 1500 automatic kerning pairs per font and a 2,000 font capacity; automatic tracking, with four levels of white space adjustment; five methods of hyphenation and justification; and multi-tasking, that is, output to a typesetter while you create and h&j another job. MagnaType drives all major typesetters and PostScript devices.

AT&T's Unix operating system is used on many new wave PCs. Software written in such powerful languages as C or Pascal for Unix, when used in conjunction with systems that display typography, layouts, and images for composition, gives those systems considerable graphics capability. AT&T also has the TROFF typesetting program for pagemaking in the Unix environment.

Other features of PC composition are:

❧ Graphics – line or tone – can be handled by adding appropriate software and a printer or typesetter that can output them. Tone art can be entered into the system with a scanner. Low-cost ($2,500) scanners are expected to be on the market in the near future.

❧ Quality can be excellent – whatever you need and can afford. For example, you can output on low-cost dot matrix or daisy wheel printers, on a range of low to medium resolution laser printers, or on high quality, fine resolution typesetters. If a laser printer will satisfy most, but not all, of your needs for top-quality work, your system can be used for input – editing, makeup, and proofing, and the resultant disks sent to a typographic service for reproduction quality output.

❧ Production time is shortened, sometimes dramatically. This makes later closings possible.

❧ Full-time control. Corrections, page makeup, etc., can be done anytime and instantly.

❧ Production costs can be trimmed.

❧ Security of data can be assured.

As a result of all the above, the immediate future should witness a proliferation of desktop publishing, of typography replacing many typewritten documents and publications, of more work being done in-house. As a consequence of this and the touch screen, code-free, easy-to-use terminals now available, more executives and professionals are going to become computer literate. That in turn will further propel the trend to desktop and corporate electronic publishing.

Furthermore, the system can be used for other programs, such as those for spreadsheets, database publishing, and accounting.

Terminals to be used by artists, some professionals and executives are expected to be non-keyboard oriented. They will probably employ some combination of hierarchical menus, touch screens, and a mouse/graphic tablet unit.

PC-Typesetter Connections

At this writing, most major typesetting machines have linked their typesetters to PC or Macintosh input via an appropriate software. The following chart only indicates how pervasive the PC-typesetter linkage has already become.

Code explanation
A: Art/Design – facilitates visualization and composing of a full page using actual or simulated typefaces.
E: Editorial – word processing capability plus such typographic abilities as hyphenation, justification, special coding.
P: Production – input, storage, retrieval, editing as on a full typesetting device or system.

SOFTWARE SUPPLIER	SOFTWARE	CAPABILITIES	TYPESETTERS/PRINTERS	PC
Alphatype/Berthold	Multiset™	E,P	Alphatype CRS 8900, 9900	IBM
Aldus	PageMaker™	A,P	Apple LaserWriter	Macintosh
Allied Linotype	Wordset,™ Series 100	E,P	Linotron 101/Linotronic 300	Macintosh
	Series 200		Linotron 202	IBM
Bestinfo	SuperPage™	A,P	Most outputs	IBM
Compugraphic	PCS™	A,E,P	Compugraphic 8000, 8400, 8600 typesetters, and EP308 laser printer	
Horizon	G.O. Graphics	E,P	Compugraphic, Linotype, Varityper typesetters	IBM
Itek	PTW™	E,P	Digitek	IBM
PagePlanner	PagePlanner™	A,E,P	Linotron 202	IBM
Penta	Desktop Composition System™	E,P	Most typesetters	Data General
Software Studio	Do It™	A,P	Most digital typesetters and Apple LaserWriter	IBM
Varityper	Maxx™	E,P	Comp/Edit 6400, 6820	IBM

Note: Some systems, including those using a Macintosh for input, also feature Adobe's PostScript software for enhanced typographic capability. Linotronic 101 and Linotronic 300 typesetters are tied to Macintosh computers via Adobe's PostScript software and can utilize Aldus PageMaker software. Since the chart was compiled, PageMaker has become available for IBM systems and Ready-Set-Go 4 has become a major software offering for the Macintosh and will be available shortly to IBM users. Another major pagination program is Xerox's Ventura Publisher.

Text Coding

Today's electronic manuscripts eliminate rekeyboarding, with their attendant costs, error potential, and wastefulness of time, but they still have to be coded, giving, that is, in machine language, all the typographic and makeup instructions that one would have written on a paper manuscript. There are four ways this can be done.

Manual Coding

The customer supplies the computer disk and a conventionally marked-up paper manuscript. The type shop or department enters the necessary codes and makes any required text changes.

Generic Coding

The author enters a simplified code for typesetting instructions. Instead of using complicated mnemonics or computer language, the author simply keys in shorthand labels to identify each text element by its editorial role, rather than by its typographic parameters. For example, HDI could mean a particular style and size headline, or FO2, a kind of footnote. There is no universal generic code, although the Graphic Communication Association recommends its GenCode™ for generic coding. The coding must be agreed upon by author and typesetter for the machine to translate and execute it correctly.

Workstation Formatting

Some of the newer and more sophisticated author's terminals, such as the Macintosh Plus, offer touch screens. These enable the author to easily input many typesetting instructions, and permit him/her to choose typefaces and point sizes, and specify page makeup instructions. The terminals display the text instantly on a high-resolution screen. Thus, changes can be made and viewed instantly, so the author can control form as well as content.

Context Coding

Software programs can be written to automatically convert consistent electronic manuscripts for the typesetter. Such programs can be custom written for large or repetitive work, or both. Known as context codes, they are also useful for tabular work. Other programs are available on the shelf, such as SofType and Tplus typesetting software, that automatically convert IBM PC word processing files into typesetting format. This software also works for several other word processing systems and can be output on a variety of laser printers and typesetters.

There are also service bureaus, such as Technique Learning, a New York-based Media Conversion Service Bureau, that specialize in publishing applications. They take an electronic manuscript written on an Apple IIe, convert it to an IBM PC file for editing, and reconvert it to the Apple format to check it with the author. This can be done as often as necessary until both author and editor are satisfied. Then, using Media Conversion software, they input all the necessary typesetting commands so that they require no further manual intervention. They use several methods to embed these commands, but in any case, the resultant disk is ready to run on the typesetter with no further coding by the typesetter. The typesetting commands can be preserved, for example, for revised editions of books.

Inputting Images

Electronic technology has made it possible to "typeset" art. Until recently, interactive makeup terminals linked to typesetters, enabled the typesetter to output a page with all the type in position, and with holes or windows left for the insertion of illustrations. Today's imagesetters (successors to typesetters) and laser printers can accept digital information describing illustrations and then output the pictures in position. No more windows, no more manual stripping when such systems are used. How do the pictures get into the digital stream?

Typesetting expert and consultant John Seybold defines a picture or illustration as "anything to be reproduced that cannot be set in type." Two principal ways pictures get into a system are by an artist creating them at an electronic graphics terminal (described previously), or by scanning existing art. Scanning is still the more common method. There are a variety of scanning devices on the market. Some use the vidicon tube of a TV-type camera. Others use a flying spot scanner. And still others scan an entire line as a unit with an array of photo-diodes or CCDs (charged-coupled devices). There are flat-bed scanners and rotary scanners.

EXTRA! PROFITS LGS System

Linotype
"Over 100 Years of Service"

EXTRA! QUALITY Linotronic 300

True Output Versatility

Linotype® Graphic System

There are many systems that can do part of the job for you. But the real beauty of the Linotype Graphic System is that it integrates all the important pre-press functions, enabling you to go from idea to plate negative or plastic plate with the least work possible, while maintaining the high level of quality you need.

Layout: You won't be doing layouts by hand anymore. Because with the Linotype Graphic System you can create and store electronic layouts.

Camera: You know the camera process: make sure everything is clean and dust-free; shoot the line work; shoot the halftones; shoot the mechanical, opaque where necessary, etc.

Compare that with the Linotype Graphic System: you manipulate the graphics on the screen, send them to the Linotronic® 300 laser imagesetter, put them through the processor (no darkroom). That's it!

Stripping: if you've ever spent any time stripping a negative, you'll love this system. You simply combine the elements of your job — photos, line art and callouts on the Graphic System monitor, text on the input terminal and send it all to the Linotronic 300 laser imagesetter. There, your job will be output on film, RC paper or plastic plate, ready to go to press.

Typesetting: This is the area where you'd expect a Linotype product to shine. And the Linotronic 300 laser imagesetter won't let you down. With the ability to set high quality type from 1 point to 186 point; leading in 1/10 point increments; calculating in picas/points, inches or millimeters is truly a plus when it comes to setting computer forms; right/wrong reading; reverse video; tints and patterns; and page reduction, are some of the many features of the Linotronic 300.

Your text can be prepared on one of our Linotype terminals, or on most popular front end systems. Of course, you'll have the entire Mergenthaler Type Library™ at your disposal.

The Mergenthaler Type Library is the world's finest, with more than 2,000 typestyles, with new styles being added in the near future. Including the original designs of many of the world's most popular typefaces, such as Helvetica®, Optima® and Palatino®.

At Linotype, we regard past accomplishments as stepping stones to future growth. Our pride is tempered by a sense of responsibility that will keep us working harder to build on what we have already accomplished. Linotype is committed to improving the quality of our image and typesetting systems, designing newer typefaces, and serving the graphic arts industry with the finest support services for another 100 years.

EXTRA! EXTRA!

Output Direct to Plastic Plate!

Recently announced is the ability to output directly to plastic plates, using the new 3M Onyx™ Laser Plate material. This sample was prepared on the Linotype Graphic System and output on the Linotronic 300® with the image screened at 149 lines per inch, using a circle 45, dot.

The Linotronic 300 *can output, at high resolution, a fully composed page with all elements, type, drawings, halftones, in position.*

Resolution

Continuous tone scanners produce analog images, as for some facsimile devices, or to provide copy that will later be halftone screened. Here we are concerned with scanning that produces a digital image, a record of the image's tonal values in a pattern of "off" or "on" electronic signals that produce dots corresponding to every "on" signal.

The dots or image spots are known as pixels (for picture elements). The more pixels per horizontal and vertical inch, the finer the detail that can be recorded and the subtler the tone gradations that can be recorded. Very clean, readable type can also be output at 300 dpi, but graphic arts quality typography is considered to start at 1,000 dpi and run up to more than 5,000 dpi, to capture cleanly all the fine strokes and serifs in text size type, and to reproduce a fine screen halftone.

In reproducing type or line art, each pixel can represent a black dot or a white (non-image) space. When tone copy is reproduced, a byte (usually 8 bits) can represent a shade of gray. In an 8-bit system, 256 shades of gray can be represented.

It is possible to scan (input) at one resolution and output at another. Of course, enlarging from the input image makes the resolution more coarse. Doubling the image size would change a resolution of 1,000 dpi to 500 dpi. Considering that the enlargement of the image takes place horizontally and vertically, the resolution reduction is one-quarter of the dots or pixels per square inch, in this case from 1,000,000 (1,000 x 1,000) to 250,000 (500 x 500).

Color copy can also be scanned and digitized. Early systems separately scanned previously made color separations. Today's systems separate colors, digitize them, electronically color-correct them, compose them into pages with type and other pictures, and electronically do just about anything that used to be done manually or photographically. High resolution picture scanners store data as digitized continuous tone images.

A fine resolution output to film is done with a laser plotter. The plotter can also generate specified halftone dots and screen angles on the fly (instantaneously, as the system is running).

An early picture scanner (1975) was the ECRM Autokon. Advanced models are still widely used. Early typesetters that accommodated pictures included the Videocomp 500 (Information International Inc.), the Digiset (Hell), the APS 5 (Autologic), and the Lasercomp (Monotype). As these typesetters have improved their text-image merge capabilities, others such as the Camex Super-Setter, the Scantext (Scangraphic), the Linotronic 300, and Compugraphic's 8600 added this capability. Many laser printers and color systems such as those made by Scitex, Hell, Crosfield, Dainippon and Eikonix handle digitized images and merge them with text.

The typesetting of pictures is evolving from two directions, and two technologies are merging. Typesetters are now setting pictures and systems originally developed to process pictures now process type.

TYPOGRAPHIC COMMUNICATIONS TODAY
Chapter XII: Bits, Bytes and Typographic Design

"Just as there are electronic manuscripts and electronic text and input devices, there are electronic editing and composition systems."

Although the picture-text merge systems still tend to be at the middle and high ends of the market, at least for color pictures and halftones, as noted earlier, low-cost systems lack only a good low-cost scanner to bring the full text-picture merge capability to the whole spectrum of printing and publishing, corporate electronic and desk-top publishing included.

Electronic Paint Boxes

Not only can existing art be converted to digital form, but art can be originated digitally. Large image-text color composition systems have artists' stations for direct creation of illustrations and designs; these will be discussed later. Several personal computers have software giving them art creation abilities. There are also software packages and devices and systems dedicated to the electronic creation of color images. A paint system is a computer-controlled electronic graphics input station that can create a wide range of graphics – pencil, brush, charcoal, pen, etc., in a full range of colors.

Quantel, for several years maker of a very capable Paintbox for video, has introduced in the United States a 2,000 x 2,000 dpi version for print applications. The unit has been used in the United Kingdom since 1985 in packaging and advertising design. It interfaces to the Scitex, Crosfield, Hell and Dainippon for scanned input and four-color separation. It is priced at about $300,000. (Quantel, Ltd., Surrey, England)

Artronics/3M's paint system offers the artist paint or vector output. Paint software lets the artist paint with an electronic stylus on a digitizing tablet. The result is a medium-resolution graphic that is rich, subtle and usable for television, print and other applications, such as textile design. Vector graphics are less subtle tonally, but much higher in resolution. They produce crisp, sharp business-presentation graphics such as charts and graphs. The paint software comes in 512 x 512 dpi and 1,024 x 1,024 dpi versions. Artronics/3M systems offer a palette of 16 million colors, an electronic airbrush, and a package of vector-based charts, graphs, and type fonts that can be merged with paint images. (Artronics, Inc., S. Plainfield, New Jersey)

Quantel's Graphic Paintbox *(GPB) is a versatile tool. Both of these pictures were designed with it by Pepper Howard. "Siberia," an 85 x 85 mm transparency, was scanned into the GPB and all the type and typographic effects were produced on it, picking up background colors. The word "cowboys" was condensed and stretched and the typographic facility used to modify the typeface, with an outline and solid shadow dropped through. In the "GPB" piece a netting was scanned and the pencil was drawn on the system. Adrian Frutiger's Meridien typeface was outlined.*

This text slide *was generated on Artronic's turn-key Presentation Graphics Producer/PGP™ system. This slide was vector created. Artronics also offers paint software.*

Qolor

The Lightspeed Qolor System is a full-color interactive computer graphics paint system. It includes a monochrome monitor, a color monitor, and a graphics tablet with a pack. Images and graphics can also be entered via a high-resolution flatbed scanner of a high speed digitizing camera. It uses a resolution of up to 775 lines per inch for halftones and 1,550 lpi for line art. Images can be transparent or opaque, b/w or color, 2-D or 3-D. The scanned-in images can be sized, cropped, positioned, merged with other images, and color corrected. Artist-oriented, Qolor has options and menus that are self-explanatory and familiar to artists. A grid aids with electronic paste-up. The system can also store a library of reusable shapes. (Lightspeed, Boston, Massachusetts)

The Lightspeed *design system.*

Typical business graphic *from the Qolor system.*

And More, And More, And More...

New electronic tools and systems keep coming to the market, and older systems are being modified. Prices for some systems are as low as $13,000, and prices for some software are in the $2,000 to $3,000 range. On the market at this writing are Lumena (Time Arts, Inc., Santa Rosa, California); MacPaint and MacDraw (Apple Computer Corp., Cupertino, California); Mindset (Mindset Corp., Sunnyvale, California); Symbolics Color Graphics System (Symbolics, Inc., Los Angeles, California).

The above-named systems are, as of this writing, of particular interest to those concerned with printed communication graphics. There are also many devices and systems for other art/design applications, such as television, engineering, animation, cartography, and business graphics. Some of these, such as the Pixar, Robert Abel & Associates, and Magi packages also have applications in communication graphics.

Electronic Mechanicals

Just as there are electronic manuscripts and electronic text and image input devices, there are electronic editing and composition systems. Available systems vary widely in price, application and capability. Complete color pages, and, in some instances, complete press forms, are electronically assembled from electronic text and image files.

There are two forms of automated page makeup systems. Algorithmic pagination software generates pages automatically from a list of page parameters. Interactive pagination workstations enable a user to manipulate and merge text and graphic elements on a screen and to see changes take place as they are made. An interactive workstation can be an electronic paste-up station as well as an editing, color correction, and even a color art creation station.

Major typesetter manufacturers offer automated page makeup systems and preview terminals to team up with their output devices, many of which now output images as well as text.

Large systems for newspapers and magazines are offered by Atex (now a division of Eastman Kodak), Hastech, Chemco, and others. Interactive markup and composition terminals have also been developed by Camex, Raytheon, Harris, Xenotron, and others.

For full-color work on large publications and for large commercial service operations, there are systems from Scitex, Hell, Crosfield, Dainippon, and Eikonix. The accompanying picture and caption of a Scitex Response 530 system with designer's terminal explains the capabilities of such a system.

The system *can take input from color laser scanners of many manufacturers. Its manipulation features include cropping, sizing, rotating, collaging, thresholding (reducing the number of levels in the gray scale from the normal 256, as required by the output device), masking, airbrushing, color correction. Using Bitstream fonts, precomposed electronic text files are accepted from a front-end system. The display merges text and color images. The designer can manipulate the type as if it were art and changes in the text will be accommodated in the future. As this was being written, Scitex announced a full-capability system for approximately one-quarter of the price of its earlier system. The price for a reconfigured system starts at $285,000. It includes the Pre-sponse for scanner previewing, the Pixet (formerly the Response 100) for full-color page assembly, and the Astra console that combines full color page assembly capabilities with the layout and design capabilities of Scitex's Vista. Also available, at a higher price, is the Imager, a much faster page assembly unit than the Pixet. The Imager is the former Response 300 system.*

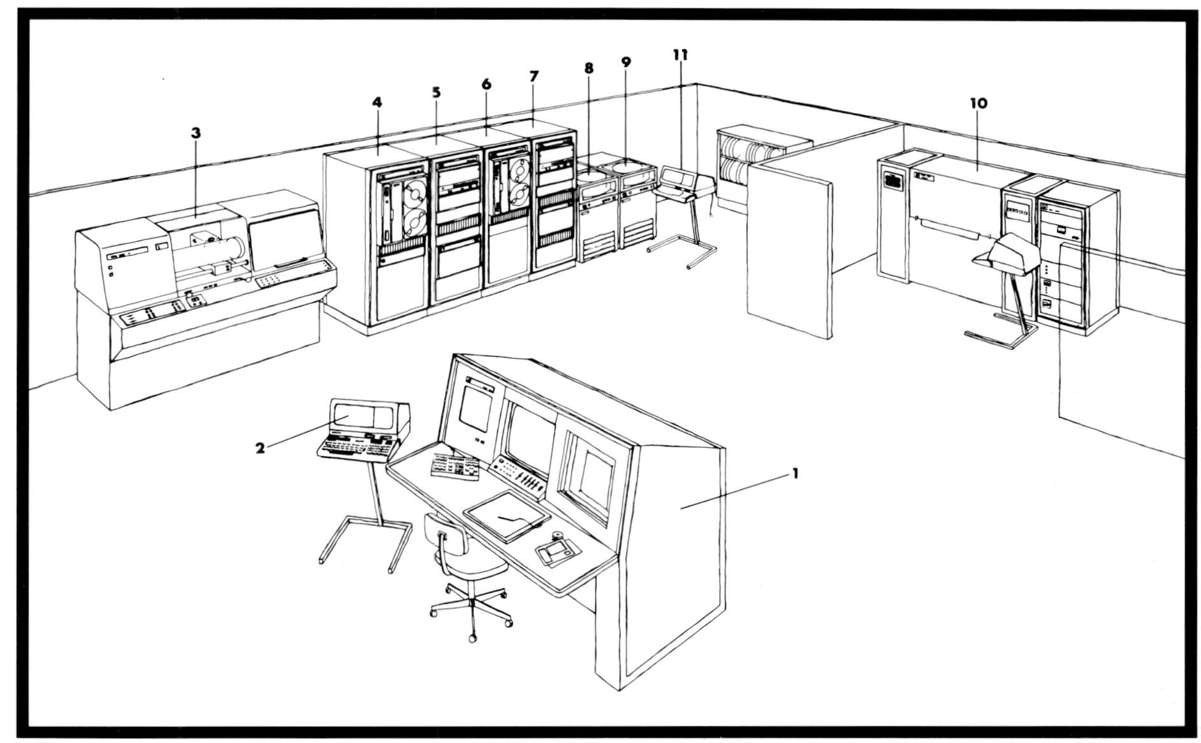

Sci-Tex Imager. *The system's eleven components are: (1) color design console, (2) video terminal, (3) electronic scanner for input, (4), (6) magnetic tape units, (5), (7) minicomputers, (8), (9) disc drives, (10) laser plotter for exposing output film, (11) video display terminal. System converts artwork to film, separates and corrects colors. Information is converted to digital form facilitating its manipulation. System can store information for later output and/or editing. Not only can pictures be edited, sized and cropped but type can be repaired (as broken letters). The Imager can do step-and-repeat work and can be used to create geometric designs, lines, even illustrations. Film up to 40" x 72" can be exposed with all elements positioned by the system. It also does electronic makeup. (Illustration courtesy of "Graphic Arts Monthly.")*

ImagiTex

ImagiTex markets a family of high-resolution, image capture, storage, and editing systems. The systems are interactive. Art and type can be scanned in, or type can be set on line. The data can be manipulated variously, cropped, composed, screened, and output to the printer as full pages in digital form.

The Interleaf electronic publishing system *is a WYSIWYG (What You See Is What You Get) system that combines writing, typesetting, and layout capabilities at the desktop in the office, rather than at the printshop. A laser printer is used for output, and a digitizing camera for inputting images (photographs, art, text) up to 8½" x 11". Images can be rotated, distorted, sized, cropped, positioned, and have their gray scales changed. Several actual type fonts can be shown on the screen; generic fonts are used for other typefaces. These fonts set to the same line width as the production fonts.*

Interleaf

The Interleaf electronic publishing system is a WYSIWYG (What You See Is What You Get) system that combines writing, typesetting, and layout capabilities at the desktop in the office, rather than at the printshop. A laser printer is used for output, and a digitizing camera for inputting images (photographs, art, text) up to 8½" x 11". Images can be rotated, distorted, sized, cropped, positioned, and have their gray scales changed. The system can also output to several major typesetters. Several actual type fonts can be shown on the screen; generic fonts are used for other typefaces.

These fonts set to the same line width as the production fonts so that line-endings will be exact. Color copy can be pre-separated and scanned-in as red, green, blue separations to allow for color correction by adjusting the gray scales.

TYPOGRAPHIC COMMUNICATIONS TODAY
Chapter XII: Bits, Bytes and Typographic Design

"It is two decades since metal line typesetters were being replaced by computerized photo setters... The next, and currently widely used, generation of typesetters stores a description of the characters as digital, rather than photographic information."

Texet

An interactive WYSIWYG system for merging text and graphics, Texet can accept pre-keyboarded text from the writer's PC or word processor. Stock designs can be created and stored for use and reuse. Typographic controls permit selection of word- and letter-spacing, kerning track, and pi characters for foreign language accents. Rules, boxes, and leaders can be composed. There is also a 110,000-word, user-expandable hyphenation lexicon. Line art can be created on the system. Photographs can be digitized and scanned. All elements can be edited, composed as per layout, stored, and output to a variety of printers or imagesetters.

Texet also facilitates setting multi-level math and tabular matter.

Texet monitor *displaying fully composed page, including halftones, composed on the Live Page workstation.*

The Star

The Xerox 8010 Star information system is designed to be used by professionals such as standards engineers, financial analysts, product engineers, accountants, personnel specialists, buyers, quality control specialists, market analysts, and consultants. It offers a video display terminal that can be used without code words. The user simply moves a small pointer to a symbol on the screen that represents a function. To access a file, for example, the user points to the symbol of a filing cabinet.

The Star can be used to create graphs and charts as well as documents. It can compose the elements of a page in position, and, with the proper software, convert input data into a pie chart or a bar chart. It can store and retrieve information and send and receive electronic messages. In short, it is a multi-purpose, easy-to-use terminal for the office professional.

The AT&T Personal Terminal 510 *can bring the full function and benefits of integrated voice and data communications to every manager in a company with an AT&T System 75 or 85 PBX. It provides immediate access to people, places and host computers by simply touching the appropriate spot on the screen.*

Star can create math equations and handle Greek letters and math symbols. It can output a variety of typefaces in sizes from 8 to 24 point and stores standard graphic symbols that can be called up and then positioned by using a "mouse" that controls the cursor for positioning elements on the screen.

A completed document, with text and graphics in position, can be printed out on the laser printer or distributed by electronic mail to a remote site.

Digital Typesetters and Digital Printers

It is two decades since metal line typesetters were being replaced by computerized photosetters. These were, in effect, mechanized cameras. They were directed by commands from on-line or off-line front-ends or keyboard input stations. Film strips, grids or disks contained the letterforms of the fonts. The desired character would be positioned, at high speed, in front of the light source and, via lenses, the correctly sized character would be exposed in position on photosensitive paper or film.

The next, and currently widely used, generation of typesetters stores a description of the characters as digital, rather than photographic, information. When properly activated, electron beams draw the characters onto photographic material.

These digital typesetters have been joined in the market by laser typesetters and laser printers. Laser typesetters use laser beams to expose the stored bits that describe the characters. Most digital typesetters store a description of the outlines of the characters. These master images can be exposed in the desired size, then the outline is automatically filled in by the typesetter or printer. Others, including laser typesetters, store a complete bit map for each size of the typeface and reproduce one size from each bit map. These laser devices generate the images with a raster image processor (RIP). The RIP positions the characters on the page. It can handle line art and tone art information when such is input to the system. Laser printers at present have lower output resolutions than do laser typesetters. Most printers are in the 240 to 400 dpi range, while typesetters usually run from 1,000 to 5,300 dpi. Most laser printers are also limited to 8½" by 11" or 8½" by 14" (or the European equivalent) output sizes. A few handle 11" x 17" size paper. Laser typesetters carry much larger type libraries and can output on film, whereas laser printers output on plain paper.

Raster Images

A raster image is produced on film, paper, or plate by a light source, usually a computer-directed laser beam that scans the recording surface at high speed at a given resolution. The laser beam is very fine. As it travels, it flicks on and off as directed by the computer. The computer, of course, is reacting to what has been put into it by a keyboard, input scanner or a graphic tablet and electronic pen. The on-off signals selectively expose the recording surface. Each on or off signal is known as a bit and, in this case, as a pixel. In an eight-bit system (more powerful systems are based on 16 or 32 bits to a byte), eight bits equal a byte. A byte is a collection of bits that are moved by the system as a unit. "Off" bits are usually represented graphically by a zero and "on" bits by a 1. The "off" bits represent non-image area, the "on" bits correspond to an image area. In this scheme a capital letter A could be represented as follows:

```
00000000010000000000
00000000111000000000
00000001101100000000
00000011000110000000
00000110000011000000
00001111111111100000
00011000000000110000
00110000000000011000
01100000000000001100
00000000000000000000
```

Scanned line or tone art, *converted to bits, is handled the same way. The letter above is represented by 200 pixels (10 rows and 20 columns). Fine resolution typography might require 500,000 pixels to reproduce a letter cleanly. The high-speed, large-memory 32-bit microcomputers that now make picture storing and processing feasible can also process type images more cleanly and rapidly.*

Vector Images

Vector data is created by a digitizer rather than a scanner. Line art or letters to be recorded are placed on a digitizing tablet. This has an electro-sensitive surface beneath which is a grid of closely spaced wires. The operator, using an electric pen or stylus, touches key points on the image. Every point touched records at an x-y coordinate position. The collection of points creates an outline of an image. (Remember the "connect the dots" art of your childhood?) The computer connects the dots. The more dots, the smoother the outline. But in any case, vector data takes up much less computer storage space than does raster data.

Most digital typesetters store font information as outlines and in vector form. The computer in the typesetter can convert typeface vector information to raster output and then merge it with its stored raster image data.

Image Processing

An editor at an editing terminal corrects errors or imperfections in an image by adding or removing pixels. Pixels, as noted above, are the very fine dots representing image or non-image areas. Pixels, as the creation of computer-controlled electronic impulses, can be part of a typeface or of line art or tone art. Thus, by manipulating pixels, the editor at the console can edit every image element in the job.

Image processors, unlike word processors, are designed for use by artists. Artists, as a rule, are not keyboard operators. Thus, to use a computer world term, the image processing terminal is made "user friendly" by requiring minimal use of the keyboard. Editing is primarily done with tools like those an artist is familiar with, such as a light pen or pointer. This can select commands from menus of options appearing on the screen or on a tablet. It allows the artists to draw art on the tablet and see the image form on the screen as it is being created, in so-called "real time."

Image processors can be used to size or reproportion images, or to crop, rotate, zoom, pan, outline, change details or tones or colors, or modify the gray scale. Image processors can also achieve posterized effects by thresholding (reducing to coarser steps) the gray scale contrast levels of tone art.

Image Recording

The major image recorders in this digital era are digitized typesetters and laser imagesetters, described above, and a variety of non-impact printers. Digitized type produced by vector-oriented typesetters sometimes shows a stairstep or jagged effect. (See Chapter XI)

These "jaggies" *appear when not enough vectors are used to produce the required diagonal or curve smoothly. Outputting at a finer resolution will not eliminate the jaggies unless the number of vector points used for storing the image is increased sufficiently. Careful editing in font preparation can minimize jaggies. Another way to avoid them when vector images are stored is to use a variably set arc, rather than a straight line, to join the vector points. (See the discussion of the PM Digital Spiral, developed by Peter Purdy and Ronald Macintosh, in Chapter XI.) Because digital typesetters use a CRT to draw images, they are line drawing devices and do not handle the raster data required for much pictorial reproduction. This is the realm of laser typesetters and laser printers.*

Recording Raster Information

High resolution (1,000 dpi or more) output devices for printing raster information use a beam of light for bit-by-bit exposure onto a photosensitive surface (film, paper, or plate). The light source can be a laser, a CRT, or an array of light-emitting diodes (LEDS). Laser typesetters often output to paper while laser platemakers burn offset plates. While laser devices can handle raster (tone as well as line) images, they expose one pixel at a time. LED devices with their array of lights can expose an entire raster line at once.

Laser and Other Non-Impact Printers

There are also low- and mid-resolution devices for recording raster images. Laser printers use a xerographic process to set type and art on plain (not photosensitive) paper. The laser beam exposes pixel by pixel on a photoconductor. Many of these devices are in the 300 dpi range, but Tegra's Genesis and Data Recording System's LaserScribe are in the 800 to 1,000 dpi range. Such laser printers are also capable of outputting each impression differently from the others. When so programmed, they are known as "on-demand" printers. Such printers are really a new kind of printing press. It is no longer necessary to print a run of paper documents and store them on shelves. One can print just the number needed immediately, then store and update the pages for later output, when and in the quantity needed.

In addition to laser printers, other non-impact devices, including LED (light-emitting diode) printers can record the composed raster image. Other technologies include ink-jet printers and electro-erosion printers. Systems that output to electronic media such as video are being developed. Videotext, for example, has yet to take hold in the United States, but, thanks to government support, is flourishing in France. Other systems specialize in producing 35mm slides, overhead transparencies and prints.

Impact Printers

Typewriters, and dot matrix, daisy wheel and thimble printers and band line printers, while not in the same segment of the typographic spectrum as typesetters and non-impact printers, are starting to use modified versions of some of the more popular graphic arts typefaces. This gives documents a new look and helps coordinate them graphically with a corporation's output on typesetters and printers.

There are other non-impact printing technologies, but as of this writing they are not of major interest for office printing or fine typography.

Typesetting Technologies, 1945-

The technological trend in typesetting since the mid-1940s might well be summed up by the key dates in the photo/digital typesetting era. They outline the progress from setting metal lines of type in galley form to outputting fully made-up pages, halftones included, on film, paper, or plates, or storing them for future use.

❧ 1945. René Higonnet and Louis Moyroud developed what later became the Photon 200. The innovation was stroboscopic character selection from a photographic typeface font on a continuously spinning disc.

❧ 1946. The Intertype Fotosetter was successfully field tested at the U.S. Government Printing Office. Essentially, it was like a hot-metal typesetter, a Linotype or an Intertype, in which the matrices carried the film images and a camera replaced the casting mechanism.

❧ 1965. The first digital typesetter was demonstrated at the TPG exhibition in Paris. It was the Digiset from Dr. -Ing Rudolf Hell.

❧ 1966. The PM (invented by Peter Purdy and Ronald Macintosh) Filmsetter 1001 was introduced. Typographic industry expert L. W. Wallis regards it as "The first CRT machine to have a major impact on the printing industry." This machine later became better known as the Linotron 505.

❧ 1968. Compugraphic Corporation introduced low-cost phototypesetters that brought the new technologies to a broad market.

❧ 1970. Minicomputer and typesetting technologies came together in the Linofilm VIP, the Fototronic TxT and the Linotron 505C.

❧ 1971. Direct entry phototypesetters had been around for a few years (H. Berthold's Diatronic, for example), but it remained for Compugraphic Corporation's CompuWriter IV to make a major impact on the market.

TYPOGRAPHIC COMMUNICATIONS TODAY

Chapter XII: Bits, Bytes and Typographic Design

"The typesetting input operator of the '80s will increasingly be neither a professional typesetter nor a secretary, but a typographist."

❧ 1972. MGD Graphic Systems Division of Rockwell International introduced the MetroSet. This was a digital typesetter that stored digital fonts as outlines. It eliminated the projection lens and produced a range of sizes up to 72 point from the outline master, so that it was no longer necessary to store a bit map for each size. The MGD technology was eventually taken over by Information International Inc.

❧ 1974. Direct-entry phototypesetters offered a full-size video display in the Comp/Set 500.

❧ 1976. The Monotype Lasercomp outputted both text and graphics in a raster scan device.

❧ 1977. Compugraphic Corporation introduced the EditWriter 7500 direct-entry phototypesetter. It permitted simultaneous operation of foreground (keyboard, screen, floppy disk drives) and background (photo-unit). One job could be printed while another was being keyboarded.

❧ 1978. The Linotron 202 brought digital typesetting to a broader market by cutting the cost of quality digital typesetting.

❧ 1979. The first desktop digital direct-entry typesetter, Linotype's CRTronic, was introduced.

❧ 1982. The era of image setting, foreshadowed by the first Lasercomp in 1976, became commercially significant when EOCOM introduced its EPIC system and Hastech Inc., its PagePro system.

Different historians might choose other milestones for this period, but these effectively outline the flow of technical progress. They were selected by L. W. Wallis and are elaborated on in a major study he has made. If I were to add a 15th date to Mr. Wallis' list, it would be the mid-1980s, when PCs are linked as front-ends to laser printers and typesetters for output, and much software is developed that brings many typesetting capabilities to the world of corporate electronic publishing.

Standards and Media Conversion Devices

The full potential for quality output from low-cost, easy-to-operate desktop systems, or even from the currently available high-quality output devices, depends not only on fine resolution output and the development of input scanners, input devices with text/graphics merge software, and imagesetter output devices, but on printing standards for computers and on media conversion devices. Such devices will enable documents created on a variety of computers or input terminals to be printed on different types of output devices, such as laser printers or typesetters, from different manufacturers. The need is for a common language among devices at every step of the process and regardless of manufacturer. Addressing this problem is Adobe's PostScript,™ a device-independent page description language, the Interpress™ page-description language developed by Xerox Corporation, and Imagen's DDL, as well as a number of media conversion devices.

PostScript

PostScript is a language for describing the appearance of text, graphics, and images on the printed page. Documents with integrated text and graphics can be printed on PostScript-equipped raster laser printers and typesetters. PostScript builds the pages at the resolution of the available printer or imagesetter. Since PostScript is device independent, documents can be created on a variety of front-ends, including personal computers. PostScript goes beyond electronic pasteup. The page, or portions of it, can be scaled and rotated to any angle for impact or emphasis. The program becomes an electronic stat camera capable of zooming in on, or magnifying, any portion of a page. A letter, word, or image can be placed anywhere on the page.

The program handles halftones. It also gives the user full control over font selection and sizing. Typeset-quality fonts are stored in outline form and output in the desired resolution and size. Under licensing agreements with Allied Linotype and International Typeface Corporation, Adobe Systems is converting established typefaces for use in PostScript programs.

ArchitecturalDesign | Issue #12 | Winter

Arch News

The Society of Architects
1400 New York Avenue
Washington DC 20018

Value is what the 1985 SOA National Seminar in Atlanta is about-- and it's what you'll find in greater quantity and greater quality than ever before at the convention's 1985 SOA Exhibit of New Technology and Products.

The biggest convention exhibit in SOA history will present you with a demanding challenge: Find a way to decide which products, services and technologies you want to learn more about:

Computer Technology
Software, Hardware
Contract Furniture
Interiors, Exteriors
Practice Systems

You'll find it all--plus a convention schedule that lets you see it all--at the 1985 SOA Display of New Products and Design.

The Art of the Dormer, a retrospective look at 19th Century dormers. At the Seattle Architectural Gallery through the 19th of the month.

This page was created with Hayden's Da Vinci, Aldus' PageMaker and the Apple LaserWriter.

"Architecture... has its own validity. It needs no reference to any other discipline to make it viable or to justify its value."
--Philip Johnson

Master Architect

The man featured in this month's issue may well be one of Vancouver's best kept secrets. You may not know his face, but if you live in Vancouver you know his work - that is, if you've ever visited Simon Fraser University, The Museum of Anthropology, Robson Square/The Law Courts, or any of a number of other governmental, commercial and residential buildings. The man is Arthur Erickson, Architect, and he has called Vancouver home for most of his life.

While the layperson may not recognize his face or name, during a remarkable and prolific career spanning more than 30 years, Arthur Erickson has received dozens of honorary degrees and virtually every major professional and personal award. To list them all would take pages, but they include the Man of the Year award, 1972; the Tau Sigma Gold Medal for excellence in Design,

Conferences, seminars, workshops:

May 21-25 25th Annual Meeting, The Society of Architects, 1400 New York Avenue, Wash. DC 20006.
June 10 Deadline, call for 500-word abstracts, "Designing and Managing Commercial Buildings: An Intensive Workshop."
June 25 American International Solar Conference and Exhibition. Thomas Convention Center, Dallas,TX.

Call (206) 555-1919 for details and register early for the 1985 SOA National Seminar, March 9-12, in Atlanta.

"Architecture aims at eternity; and therefore is the only thing incapable of modes of fashions in its principles."
--Christopher Wren

***Typical** LaserWriter® output using PostScript.*

Interpress

Interpress can be used to interface almost any type of document creation device with virtually any type of document printing device. It is specifically designed to support faster page-print engines, including those handling high resolution text and graphics. It has commands for describing text, graphics and pictures, as well as commands for creating various shapes and rotating and scaling them. It can handle multiple fonts, line and shaded graphics, halftones and continuous tone images, as well as instructions about the page image and the assembling and finishing of a document. It is also suited to commercial printing applications and can create signatures for folding and binding.

Interpress is a language that generates codes that can be interpreted by virtually all raster printers and by most microprocessor-controlled impact printers. It translates computer generated text and graphics into instructions for printers on how output should appear. When Interpress is implemented on a system, documents can be sent to any sufficiently programmed printer. No hardware configuration is required.

In effect, it allows the same output to be sent to printers featuring different capabilities. And it generates similar output at all printers.

This software protocol set makes it technically possible to link virtually any combination of computer systems and microprocessor-based printers. It also allows users to substitute printers much more easily as various printing technologies and application requirements evolve.

Interpress does not send a bit-mapped picture, or series of dots, to the printer. The Interpress language sends the printer's microprocessor controller a set of instructions for printing a specified image. This integrated set of page layout instructions and output data is called an Interpress master. The master, which is generated by the creator program (a text editor, graphics generator, etc.) actually serves as its own interface.

Interpress does not format text. Rather, it describes to the printer, in general terms, what the finished output document should look like. It does not specify how to format a paragraph or when to break a line. These formatting considerations are made during the text editing process, before the Interpress master is created.

DDL

DDL (document description language) has been developed by Imagen. Unlike PDLS, (page description languages), DDL describes the format of a full document to the printer, not simply a page at a time. In DDL, the contents of a page and the data defining page layout are separate, thus a document's format can be altered by changing the layout section only. With DDL, pages can be created in any order and easily positioned or repositioned. Images are automatically stored in a cache memory, without requiring that the user physically name and address the object for storage. The result is easy and automatic access for repeated use. DDL also enables bit map images to be reduced and enlarged without degradation in quality. The first use of DDL was by Hewlett-Packard for some of its printers. However, Imagen is making product-specific interpreters of it for other vendors on a licensee basis.

What Have the New Technologies Done to Typefaces and Typesetting?

The following is simply a list of changes that have taken place or are happening as a result of the ongoing electronic/digital revolution in typesetting design and manufacture, and the way typefaces are used.

❧ Typefaces and typesetting, and, to a lesser degree, quality typography, are migrating from the graphics arts industry to end-user offices, studios, and publishing departments.

❧ A much broader market is becoming typeface style-conscious, as corporate electronic and desktop publishers and in-office communicators become aware of type's superior ability to get attention, control emphasis, compact information, and be read, understood and remembered.

❧ Even in correspondence, businesses are starting to use what had been considered graphic arts typefaces. They are also using headlines and multi-column formats in correspondence and documents.

❧ A new kind of keyboarder is taking over. The typesetting input operator of the '80s will increasingly be neither a professional typesetter nor a secretary, but a *typographist.* She or he will work in offices, in studios, or at home, as well as in publications, typesetting services and printing operations.

❧ More fonts will include small caps and oldstyle figures, superior and inferior figures, foreign accents and pi characters and logos.

❧ Digital typesetters teamed with good front-end systems can automatically set, kern, and position fractions; automatically create characters similar to small caps (setting the cap letterform to the size of the lowercase x-height, or about 70 percent of cap height); automatically set underscores to a commanded length; automatically set horizontal and vertical rules; automatically set and position inferior/superior characters; and make chosen type styles condensed, expanded, or oblique. These extended machine capabilities, plus the enlarged fonts referred to above, will give designers new ways of achieving desired effects.

❧ Continued issuance of full-family fonts (such as ITC Cheltenham® or ITC Garamond®), as experienced designers prefer to design instantly for text and display, and less experienced in-office designers do so to be safe. However, for a while, new users of typefaces may be satisfied with a narrower range of weights within a family than is customary in the advertising and graphic arts markets.

❧ A new typesetting mathematics is with us. Interline spacing (leading) of 1/10 point is common on some machines, as is spacing that can be determined and specified optically, rather than mathematically, on electronic paginators. Sizes are no longer limited to such fixed steps as 6, 7, 8, 9, or 10 points, etc.

❧ Rule forms can be produced on typesetters, for uniform and precise continuous horizontal or vertical rules of almost any thickness and feasible length. Intersections of joining rules are clean.

❧ More sophisticated kerning and hyphenation/justification programs are commonplace.

❧ We also have more and better software programs for controlling typographic niceties such as letterfit. At the same time, more devices permit operator intervention, so that skilled operators can exercise the taste and judgment that a machine cannot apply in a customized situation.

❧ There may be some increase in script typefaces for machine setting, especially as typesetters and printers demonstrate their ability to connect characters, or to set them closer, and to cope with larger fonts containing the ligatures and alternate characters that give style and distinction to scripts and cursives.

International Typeface Corporation

2 HAMMARSKJOLD PLAZA
NEW YORK, NEW YORK 10017
(212) 371-0699

January 29, 1988

Mr. John Smith
Marketing Director
Smith Communications, Inc.
43 Penn Street
Smithtown, CN 30457

Dear Mr. Smith:

This is a preview of the letter of tomorrow. Its purpose is to introduce you to the important role typefaces will play in correspondence and internal communications in the near future. This letter demonstrates what the new look will offer.

1. Attention arresting power.
2. More and better ways of achieving *emphasis.*
3. More variable and flexible formats for better organization of the flow of information.
4. Approximately 40 percent more copy in a given space with resultant savings in paper, plates, printing, mailing (and note, no double line spacing is needed.).
5. Improved legibility and readability.
6. A wide choice of typestyles and sizes

In sum: increased communication effectiveness and reduced costs.

What this means to you.

The package of booklets accompanying this letter tells you how this trend toward using typefaces in correspondence, memoranda, reports and a wide variety of documents can communicate more information quicker and more effectively to help you **1.** sell more equipment and systems, and **2.** become a new profit center for you.

About this letter

Printer: This letter was output on an *Apple LaserWriter Plus®*, using fonts supplied by *Adobe®* an ITC subscriber. Adobe is one of the first to offer font description information to end users based on its *PostScript®* Page Description Language. Input of the document was done on an *Apple Macintosh Plus®* using the *Ready, Set, Go®* program distributed by *Letraset®*.

Resolution: 300 lines per inch.

Typeface: ITC Souvenir Light, *ITC Souvenir Light Italic*, **ITC Souvenir Demi**, ***ITC Souvenir Demi Italic***.

Very sincerely

Edward M. Gottschall

Edward Gottschall
Executive Vice President

Even in correspondence, *businesses are starting to use what had been considered graphic arts typefaces. They are also using headlines and multi-column formats in correspondence and documents.*

Chapter XII: Bits, Bytes and Typographic Design

"Digital picture transmission will play a leading part in the future of photographic typesetting techniques."

***A new** typesetting mathematics. These 136 different sizes of a Poster Bodoni capital H were set in 32 seconds on a Linotron 202. They include every half-point and full-point size from 4½ to 72 points. All sizes are automatically base-aligned and were set from one master font digitization. Input was paper tape. Setting time could have been reduced to about 24 seconds had the input device been on-line to the typesetter.*

The new typesetting mathematics will not only involve more half and full sizes than heretofore, but will eventually convert sizes to the metric system, provide for finer line spacing (now one-tenth point increments on some machines), and make possible optically selected sizes that may be as mathematically offbeat as 9⁷⁄₃₂ points.

❧ Typesetters and printers are able to modify fonts in many ways besides slanting, stretching, or condensing. Some can create outline or contour letters, add shadows, inlines and reverse type from black to white.

❧ Word- and letter-spacing can be expanded or reduced in infinitely fine degrees. Letters can be butted or overlapped.

❧ More ragged-right typesetting is possible as more users realize its advantages in controlling color in a text block and in avoiding distracting gaps in the text.

❧ The cost effectiveness of typeset versus typewritten copy is now widely appreciated. Savings are effected in presswork, plates, ink, paper, storage, and mailing and handling.

Type's New Look

Those who used and specified type in the 1960s and earlier will remember the constraints metal typesetting put on designers. Economically feasible mixing of text typefaces was usually limited to two versions, either a roman with a corresponding italic, or a lightface/boldface combination.

Automatic Modification of Typefaces

Although many digital and laser typesetters and printers can modify a typeface, for instance by slanting, condensing, or expanding characters, doing so sacrifices legibility, readability, and esthetics. The reasons for this are explained by designer Adrian Frutiger in his book, *Type Sign Symbol.*

```
Tremendous and far-reaching changes that are taking place
right now will accelerate and intensify in the immediate
future, with respect to the tools used by art directors,
designers, and writers and what effects they can achieve
while at the same time saving time and money.
```

Tremendous and far-reaching changes that are taking place right now will accelerate and intensify in the immediate future, with respect to the tools used by art directors, designers, and writers and what effects they can achieve while at the same time saving time and money.

***Compaction.** The typewritten copy has been set in the nearest comparable type size. Five lines of typewritten text have been compacted to five lines of less than half the width, and double-spacing has been eliminated, while appearance and readability have been improved.*

abcdefghijklmnopqrstuvwxyz
ABCDEFGHIJKLMNOPQRSTUVWXYZ
1234567890&1234567890$$¢£%
ĄÇĐĘŁØÆŒßąĉđęłøäẽôåfi
(:;,.!?•-–—“”’—/#*)[†‡§«»1234567890]

abcdefghijklmnopqrstuvwxyz
ABCDEFGHIJKLMNOPQRSTUVWXYZ1234567890
ABCDEFGHIJKLMNOPQRSTUVWXYZ1234567890

***More complete fonts.** Since digital typesetters can handle larger fonts than phototypesetters, we will see a resurgence of small caps, oldstyle figures, more foreign characters, as well as special superior figures in many new fonts. This ITC Fenice® font indicates the scope of fonts to come.*

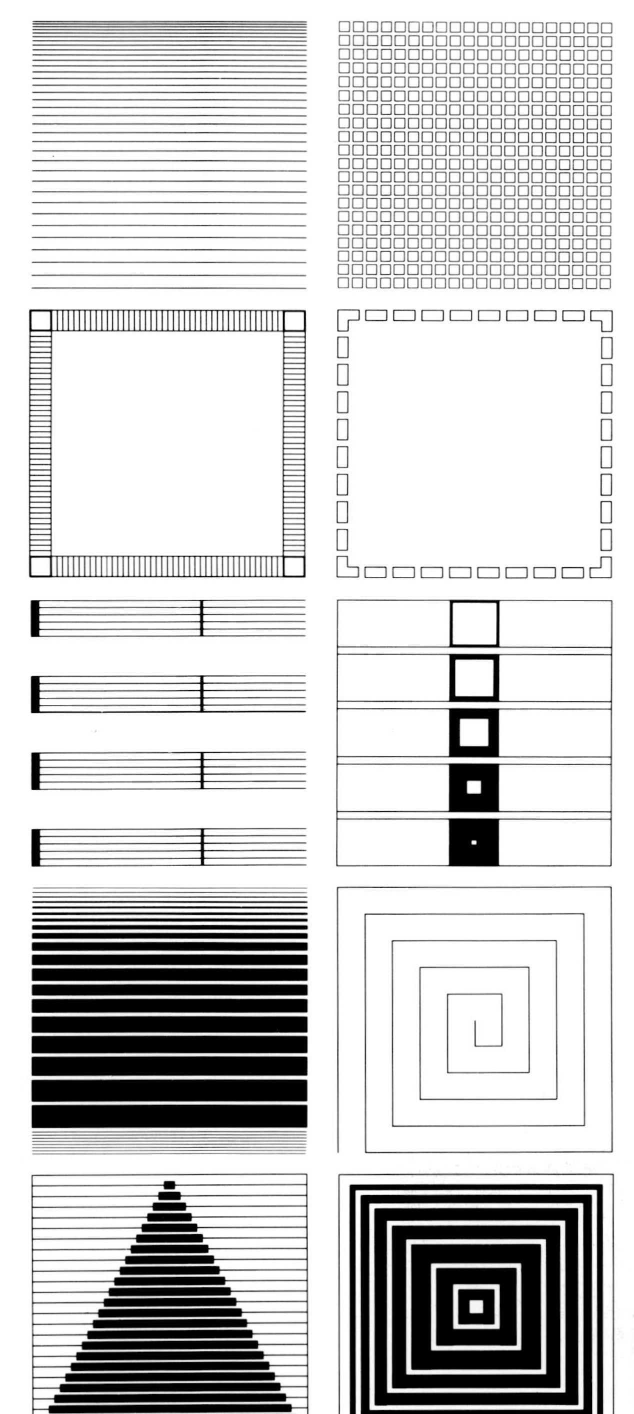

Electronic rules. *Few, if any, human hands could draw these rules, borders, boxes, grids, staffs, steps, or whatever, as precisely or as easily as they were set by Berthold's fps 2000.*

At their introduction, *duplexed type matrices facilitating mixing of two typefaces (such as a roman and an italic or a bold) were considered to offer a new freedom to designers. Such type required different matrices for each size and most machine-set text type was not made in sizes larger than 14 point. Today's digital typesetters can mix an almost unlimited number of styles and sizes quickly and easily. This is a far cry from the duplexed type of only a few decades ago, even from the "mixers" of the 1950s. Mixers were Linotype or Intertype machines that could work from two magazines at the same time, each containing different duplexed matrices.*

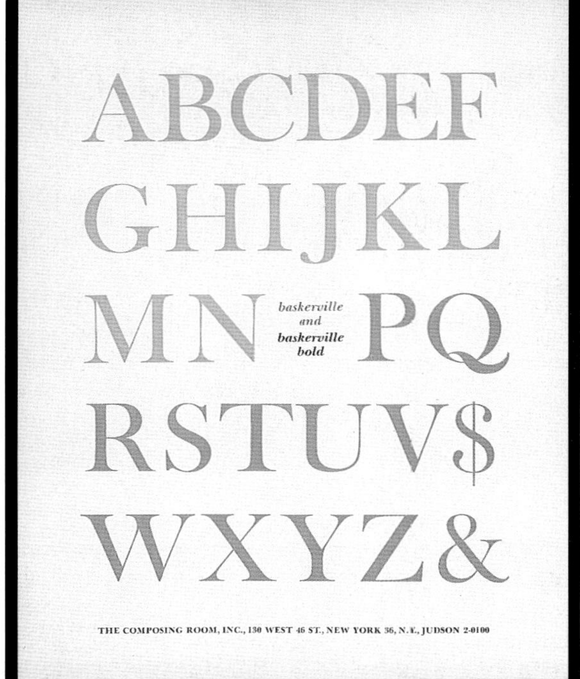

This cover *for a 1954 typeface specimen booklet shows how two weights of Linotype Baskerville, each in roman and italic, could be readily mixed on one job. To designers in the mid-1980s these new freedoms seem like severe restrictions. Aaron Burns*

On the left *is a showing of Bauer's Futura Light. All available metal typeface sizes are shown. Today one can create in-between sizes or, as the specimen on the right shows, one can set sizes beyond metal's maximum.*

Even the limited freedom of duplexing came at a price. Italics were forced to occupy the same space as the roman letters on the same brass matrix. This made some characters more upright than they should have been and inconsistent with the rest of the font. Today's technologies have removed these constrictions.

The Limits of the Automatic Modification of Typefaces

Digital picture transmission will play a leading part in the future of photographic typesetting techniques. This new technique makes it possible to distort the type image. The procedure corres-

TN-3 / SIMILAR TO NEWS GOTHIC BOLD

VERY TIGHT typography

TIGHT typography

NORMAL* typography

Tighter letterspacing, *judiciously used, today can make type more readable as well as save space. The bottom line was set in metal type, the top by film type. News Gothic Bold was used in all three lines.*

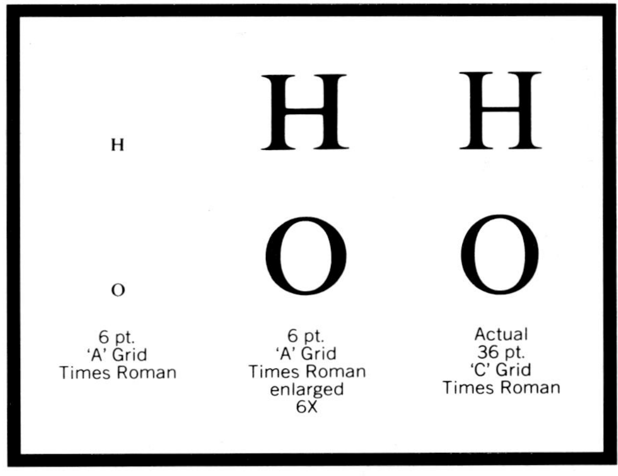

Most typesetters *and printers setting type today produce a full range of sizes from a small outline font master. In the days of metal typography, customarily each size was drawn differently so it would appear at its best. At left are two letters photographically enlarged from a 6-point master. The same characters at the right were intended to look like part of a specially designed 36-point font. Some machines today partially compensate for this spatial distortion by activating a white space reduction program on larger sizes. Others, outputting size for size from bit map masters, would compensate if each bit map were prepared from separately adjusted art.*

TYPOGRAPHIC COMMUNICATIONS TODAY
Chapter XII: Bits, Bytes and Typographic Design

"...we can expect systems that will do more, and at greatly increased speeds, be easier to use, offer better quality, and be more widely affordable."

The ampersand shown above *has been digitally set in resolutions of 200, 400, and 1,600 dpi at printout speeds of thousands of characters per second. Output quality, at any resolution, depends on factors other than resolution. Two important considerations are the fineness of the vectors used to describe the stored outline font master, and the fineness of the toner, ink, or other medium used to print the output.*

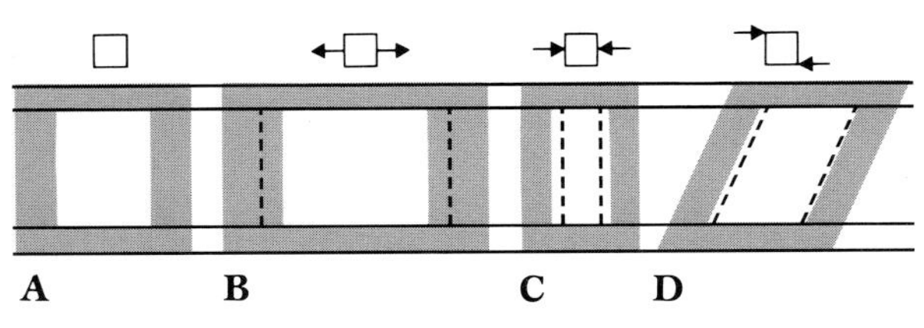

Schematic representation of the distortion process.
Figure "A" shows a simplified character, with normal proportions of stroke thickness and width of counter.
In "B" the character has been expanded to 150 percent: the weight of the horizontal strokes has remained the same, while the verticals have thickened by 50 percent, becoming bold strokes. The dotted line shows how a wide face should be drawn in harmony with the original form "A."
In "C" the original character has been condensed to 66 percent, making the vertical strokes thinner than the horizontal, a condition which can confidently be described as incorrect according to the elementary laws of legibility (a tree always *has a trunk thicker than its branches).*
In "D" the basic form has been sloped from upright to oblique. The purely mechanical pivoting process makes the vertical strokes thinner in this case as well, while the horizontals remain unaltered.

typography is to printing
as dramatics and elocution are to
the spoken word

Helvetica Medium, hand-set foundry type

typography is to printing
as dramatics and elocution are to
the spoken word

Helvetica Medium, Linofilm-set (normal)

typography is to printing
as dramatics and elocution are to
the spoken word

Helvetica Medium, Linofilm-set (minus one unit)

The top three lines *were hand-set in metal type. The middle three were set on a phototypesetter. The bottom lines were produced on a phototypesetter with a unit of space automatically removed. This ability to fit letters closely, even by minus letterspacing, can, when used judiciously, improve type's readability, legibility, and overall color and appearance.*

ponds to focusing on the television set, where the figures can be distorted into caricatures by turning a knob. The same thing happens in digital typesetting, which thereby offends against the elementary laws of legibility.

What's Next?

The fantastic pace of developments of the past two decades notwithstanding, we seem to be in for even more astonishing developments in the near future. Looking beyond the current state of the art and the rapid growth of graphics-oriented systems with increasingly versatile and powerful text and full-color image merge capabilities, we can expect systems that will do more, and at greatly increased speeds, be easier to use, offer better quality, and be more widely affordable.

Bigger Bytes

The trend is away from devices based on 8-bit bytes. The era of 16- and 32-bit bytes is arriving. This means greater computer speed, whether for storage or for processing.

Parallel Computers

Until now the need to meet the demand for more speed and power has been met by speeding up sequential processing through advances in electronic technology. The limits of that approach are being reached. One of the new approaches is parallel processing, whereby many calculations are performed simultaneously. Several parallel processors are already on the market. Machines offered by Floating Point Systems, Intel, and Bolt Beranck & Newman are known as coarse-grained processors. They feature between four and several hundred relatively powerful processors capable of simultaneous operation.

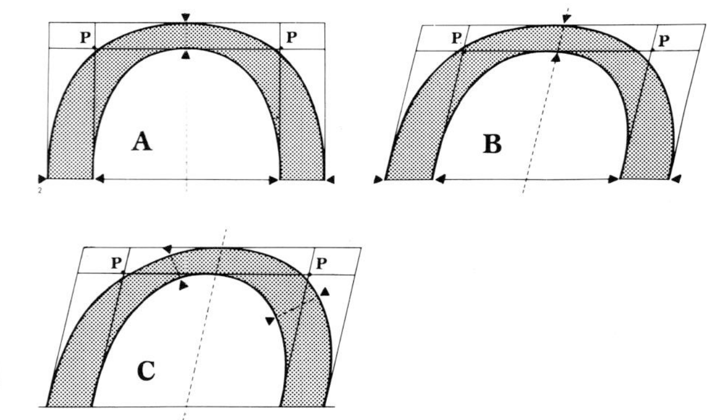

The sloping of round forms.
The original form "A" has been sloped purely geometrically by the cathode ray tube in "C" (see the comparison points P): one can see the distortion by which the bold/fine construction of the swellings in the strokes has fallen completely out of its axis. Drawing "B" shows the italic O produced by the artist. It is not distorted, but has a harmonious appearance as part of a face related to the roman version.

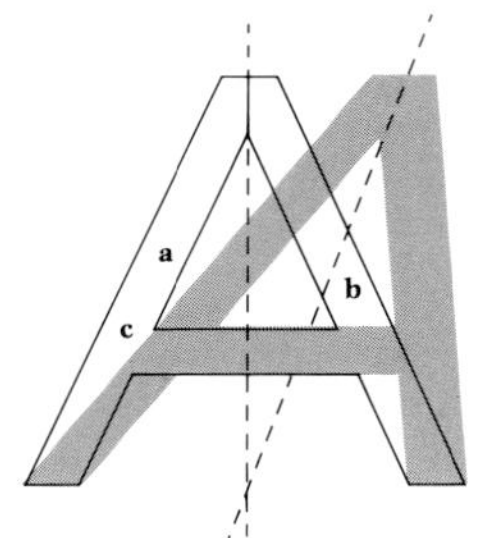

Characters with oblique strokes.
Distortion occurs most strongly in letters with oblique strokes, such as A, K, M, V, etc. In the upright A, the three strokes are very finely proportioned in relation to one another. Automatic sloping destroys this relationship: stroke a becomes thinner, b thicker, and c remains the same. The legibility of a typeface is based on extremely sensitive proportionings, which have been developed over the course of centuries. Automatic distortion presents a real danger, of which the user of automatic text-setting machines must be fully aware.

The Connection Machine, from Thinking Machines Corporation, is a fine-grained parallel processor. It contains 64,000 less powerful processors, each capable of handling one bit of information at a time. Such a machine can operate extremely fast, moving one billion calculations per second. It also has the potential to recognize and analyze digits. Conventional computers analyze pictures dot by dot. This makes it difficult for the computer to sensibly visualize the whole picture. A parallel computer can see the whole image at once and react accordingly. The last word is hardly in on parallel computers. Their limitations and potentials have yet to be fully explored.

VHSIC

The era of the superchip is upon us. Ultra-powerful silicon chips are operating at such high speeds they can tackle problems, such as radio waves, formerly considered too complex for computer technology. The new chips can translate speed of light signals almost instantaneously into digital pulses. They bring new power and precision to signal processing. Of course, this has great military significance, but eventually the new chips will affect the whole spectrum of activities using computers. Today's best chips pack thousands of transistors onto a tiny silicon square. Incredibly, the new chips store tens of millions in the same space. The chips are known as VHSIC (Very High Speed Integrated Circuits). A super-computer can perform many tasks. The new superchips are dedicated to a specific function. At present there are 36 kinds of superchips being produced for the Pentagon. By 1990 we may have chips four times as fast as VHSIC's, or about 100 times the speed of a present-day home computer. Along with increased speed comes increased accuracy.

Gallium arsenide chips are being developed to replace silicon chips. These chips will transmit electrons several times faster than silicon chips and will function as optical switches.

Photons Instead of Electrons

The optical computer seems to be the ultimate development in increasing the power, speed, and versatility of computers. It is not only envisioned by bold scientists, but is in the laboratory stage right now. The Optical Computing Department at AT&T Bell Laboratories hopes to create by the late 1980s a primitive prototype of an optical computer. It hopes to create a working, full-scale model by the early 1990s.

Computing with light instead of electricity would have these advantages:

❧ Raw speed. Although theoretically electrons can move at the speed of light, the world of silicon chips slows electrons down to less than one percent of their potential speed. Speed is being gained today by reducing the micro distances between electronic parts, but this approach is nearing its limit. Photons, on the other hand, always move at the speed of light, about 186,000 miles per second. Photon computers have the potential of operating from 100 to 1,000 times faster than is presently possible.

❧ Because photons have little effect on each other and can even pass through each other, photon computers would be able to handle multiple signals simultaneously without confusion.

❧ Electrons are either on or off, like a conventional light circuit. Thus, electron computers rely on bytes made up of a combination of on-off bits. Photons are analagous to a circuit with a dimmer instead of an on-off switch. Different degrees of laser brightness will expand the computer's logic system well beyond the present on-off or 0-1 binary system. Whole new and complex areas of computation will be handled by photon computers.

Although optical computers are clearly the wave of the future, one cannot predict when they will be commercially available and affordable. The driving force behind their development right now is the Defense Department and the obvious value of such computers for the Strategic Defense Initiative (Star Wars).

Optical Storage

In 1980 a 4K-bit RAM chip cost about $4. Today, for about the same price, or less, one can buy a 256K-bit chip. Today's storage disks, even the recent 3½" disk, can store 20-megabytes of data. But the big news for the near future is the optical disk. Its storage capacity is huge. One such disk, 5¼", holds 400 megabytes of data and, because it is much less likely to crash than are Winchester disks, it is more durable and reliable. The next breakthroughs needed to make optical disks widely useful is to increase their access speed (presently slower than Winchester disks) and to make them erasable. Laboratories are working on these goals now.

CD ROM, Hard Discs

CD ROM is the computer version of the audio compact disk. It can store large data bases and associated programs and can mix media. In an early demonstration, its developer, Microsoft, used it for a multi-media encyclopedia demonstration. The disk mixed text, music, speech, photography, graphics and animation.

The increased affordability of hard disks and their drives are making them more feasible for the desktop publishing and microcomputer markets and will bring to them the large and complex programs that only hard disks can handle.

Super Conductors

A super conductor is a material that conducts electricity, the flow of electrons, with no resistance. Until 1987 super-conductors could only operate at such extremely low temperature that they were commercially impractical. Early in 1987 a breakthrough occurred and now there is-a rush to develop super conductors for many applications. For computers they promise vastly increased speed, storage capability, miniaturization, and make it possible to handle more complex problems than presently handled. Super-conductors can now work at much warmer temperatures than formerly, but have not yet been developed at temperature levels that would make them commercially feasible. That final breakthrough is being worked on feverishly in many laboratories as of this writing.

Voice Input

Voice entry systems permit a person to talk to a computer. Such systems now exist, have a limited vocabulary and can perform certain functions, especially in automated manufacturing environments. Westinghouse and Intel, among others, have now developed improved systems. The new systems can be "trained" to recognize a user's speech patterns. Each user's voice pattern is stored on a template that is called up when an individual addresses the computer. Vocabularies are still limited to about 200 words, but each word can represent a code for a complex action so that considerable power is already available.

These systems are still primitive. Scientists in this field estimate that by the mid-1990s people will be able to talk with computers in a full conversational manner and without having to pre-train the machine. Just what voice input will mean to the world of computer graphics is only a matter of conjecture today.

Networking

Computer users in all areas are demanding that their PC or computer-controlled terminal, processor, or printer be able to talk to others from the same or a different manufacturer. Interface devices are available, but the trend is toward networks that both connect devices and enable them to talk a common language. Micro and mainframe links are being demanded. A number of LANS, (local area networks) are on the market already at a wide range of capabilites and prices. Also wanted are products that can link different LANS to each other. Many companies, including IBM and AT&T, Xerox, Wang and Apple are in this market and much progress can be expected in the near future.

Chapter XII: Bits, Bytes and Typographic Design

"...computers, systems, and software by themselves do not create/produce quality typography, nor effective, efficient communications. People do."

User Friendliness

Computers are becoming easier and easier to use. For graphic designers and artists complicated codes are already in the past. Prompts on the screen tell the user what to do next or offer a menu of options. And touch screens for the keyboard-shy enable them to just touch the option on the screen; the computer does the rest. Electronic pens and graphic tablets give the artist tools not too different from those used in precomputer times. The trend to more user-friendly devices will grow and as it does, will encourage more and more professionals and executives to use terminals. Also, as the years go by, more and more of the generation of artists and executives coming into the graphic arts will already have been computer-oriented.

Improved Output Quality

Finer resolution output and better inks and toners are expected to considerably upgrade the quality of printer output. As noted previously, two laser printers are already at the 800-1,000 dpi range. However, for graphic arts quality typographics, one must still output on a fine resolution typesetter.

X-ray chip etching.

A major breakthrough in vastly expanding chip power and speed is moving off the drawing boards and into the research labs. Presently chips can only be enhanced by reducing the space between the micron-thick circuits. Chip circuits are made by etching silicon with ultraviolet light waves. The etching pattern is driven by a large size master drawing that is drastically reduced in size and transferred onto a photographic negative or mask. The bright UV light shining through this mask etches the circuits atop the silicon. The shorter the wave length, the finer the etching. The plan is to shift from UV light to soft x-rays. Presently a chip can hold a million circuits. An X-ray etched chip might hold a billion. A minimum of $500 million would be needed to get this project off the ground. No one company, not even IBM or AT&T, is expected to handle this unaided. Government financing is needed.

Lower Costs

Costs of software, networks, chips, printers, terminals are still dropping. In the early '80s, 300 dpi printers fell from about $20,000 (for a low-cost printer) to $3,000. New printers may soon sell for $1,000 to $2,000. They will be slower, but for many users that won't matter. Some digital typesetter prices have also come down dramatically. Some are under $20,000 and going down. Of course, some require separate front-ends. The new affordability of printers and typesetters will expand the market for communication terminals and systems. As this happens, documents formerly typewritten will increasingly be typeset and illustrated and appear in multi-column format. There will be a growing demand for people who can create and execute effective layouts.

One immediate effect of the lowered cost and improved performance of these devices is to accelerate what is being called desktop publishing.

Desktop "do-it-yourself publishing" isn't just a new buzzword. It's a new way to write, edit, typeset, illustrate, makeup and print magazines, newsletters, newspapers, publishing manuals, instruction booklets, brochures and so on and on. It is a new way to manage and distribute information. It need not be poor quality type and pictures, but can be (depending on the software and hardware used) of very good to superb quality. Some of the key elements in a desktop publishing operation are a personal computer with word processing software, digital fonts and typesetting software, page/area makeup hardware/software, and a network to link the various elements in the publishing chain and permit PCs and printers from various manufacturers to function together and with output devices such as a laser printer or a typesetter. Desktop publishing can cut costs and improve communication effectiveness, and keep control in-house.

Typesetting Functionality

At the time of this writing, much publicity is being given to hardware and software that enables the so-called desktop publishing market to produce documents that are much more attractive, effective and efficient than the typewritten documents that formerly characterized this publishing segment. Personal computers and laser printers, coupled with appropriate software, such as Aldus' PageMaker, Xerox's Ventura Publisher, or ReadySetGo4, offer a great deal for an investment of less than $10,000. Some systems have graphics as well as text capabilities.

But for those who need letter quality output and finer resolution, a variety of page sizes and formats, and greater speed and volume of output, high performance corporate electronic publishing systems are available. These include text and graphics systems. They can use personal computers for text input. They often have multi-terminal workstations and a strong database capability, enabling many operators to work simultaneously. A LAN (local area network) converts the computers and CPU to artwork digitizers, laser printers, laser typesetters. The systems cost a minimum of $70,000, and go much higher. Suppliers include Angraf, Inc., Bedford Computer Corporation, Compugraphic (CAPS systems), Eastman Kodak, HTS (High Technology Solutions), Intergraph, Interleaf, OmniPage, Rise, Texet, Viewtech, Xenotron, Xerox (XPS system) and Xyvision.

Between the CEPS and desktop typesetting levels, in terms of price and capability, are a number of batch pagination oriented text systems and graphic workstations. The former link video terminals to a CPU, a previewing screen and other peripherals. Suppliers include Alphatype, Atex, Autologic, Compugraphic, Datalogics, Linotype, Miles, Penta, Rayport, and Varityper.

Apollo, AT&T, IBM and Sun offer hardware for self-contained graphics workstations. Interleaf and OmniPage offer bundled (hardware plus software) systems for self-contained graphics workstations.

Naturally, there are several levels of software available. Some software can give high performance capability to PC-based systems and is currently available for the more expensive and capable systems noted above. Other levels of software can upgrade considerably the output capability of moderate and low-priced systems. This is a rapidly changing, improving area; those interested in it must monitor new introductions regularly.

The Software Touch

Graphic designers, art directors, type directors, artists – users and specifiers of typefaces, typesetting, and typographic design by whatever job title – are not so slowly finding themselves surrounded by many software options for achieving the graphic effects they desire.

Of course, we are now in an era of digital type. Types are being designed digitally or with digital assistance. And type is stored and set and composed digitally. But that's just the tip of the iceberg. Consider the following type-related functions that are now or soon will be aided or accomplished by software that can run on a typesetter, a laser or LED (light emitting diode) array printer, a typesetting front-end or an IBM, IBM-compatible, or Macintosh computer.

❧ Storing a large type library on a CD (compact disk) or on an optical disk or a file of smaller disks.
❧ Setting a full range of type sizes from a stored outline.
❧ Page makeup, merging text with graphic elements either scanned into or created on the system.
❧ The ability to convert outline fonts to bitmap fonts on the fly.
❧ Design software offering graphic guidelines and options to raise the quality level of work output by people with minimal design training.
❧ Page description languages that offer such typographic refinements as kerning and hyphenation and justification, even to PC-based systems.
❧ Software to facilitate such typeface modifications as 3D-ing, outlining, reversing, curving, flexing, slanting, condensing, expanding – in short, to achieve the whole gamut of effects formerly achievable only with a camera and special lenses.
❧ A "library" of display/headline typefaces.
❧ Electronic clip art. The whole range of material, other than typefaces, formerly available only from print clip art sources.
❧ Algorithms for converting from one typeface format, such as Ikarus, to any page description language, such as Adobe's PostScript,™ Imagen's DDL,™ or Xerox's Interpress.™
❧ Copyfitting and cost-estimating software, such as National Composition Association's Alphacalc.

The effect of all the above and more to come is to increase the capability and quality level of corporate electronic publishing and office desktop publishing, narrowing the gap between them and graphic arts-quality output.

But computers, systems, and software by themselves do not create/produce quality typography, nor effective, efficient communications. People do. The training, the expertise, the taste and judgment of designers or of device operators are controlling factors. The new software, at least, makes it easier for more people to produce more work and often builds a higher floor under quality. Certainly it helps raise communications that had been typewriter-bound to new levels of attractiveness and effectiveness. At the same time, in the hands of design-sensitive operators, such software has the potential of making a designer more productive.

We should all be alert to typographic and design software in the immediate and near future. One can expect to see more of it, and see it being refined and improved. The items listed herein are the first opening wave in bringing the software approach to a broad spectrum of typesetting and typographic problems.

TYPOGRAPHIC COMMUNICATIONS TODAY

Chapter XIII: The Many Faces of Typography Today

"The graphic designer is first and foremost a communicator, and only within that framework an artist."

Typographic design of the last several decades reflects all the forces we have discussed in Typographic Communications Today. All the different ways of striving for vitality, or for clarity, or for some ideal blend of both, are alive today. All the influences of the art movements of the early decades of this century, of the subsequent design schools, and of the new and still evolving technologies have combined to offer today's graphic designers a vast arsenal of approaches with which to attack a communications problem, as well as finer tools with which to execute a chosen solution. The result today, evolving since the 1940s, is a broad spectrum of typographic design styles, if style is the correct term. In this chapter we will look at the work of leading designers from many parts of the world, to see how each approaches and solves a variety of graphic communications problems.

We don't see any dominating trends. Perhaps that is because we see so many trends. One way to understand and evaluate the graphic design of recent decades is to think of a graphic design grid – not the Swiss grid discussed in Chapter VI, but an analytical grid in which the horizontal axis runs from absolute focus on clarity to absolute focus on vitality, and the vertical axis represents the personality or style of a particular designer.

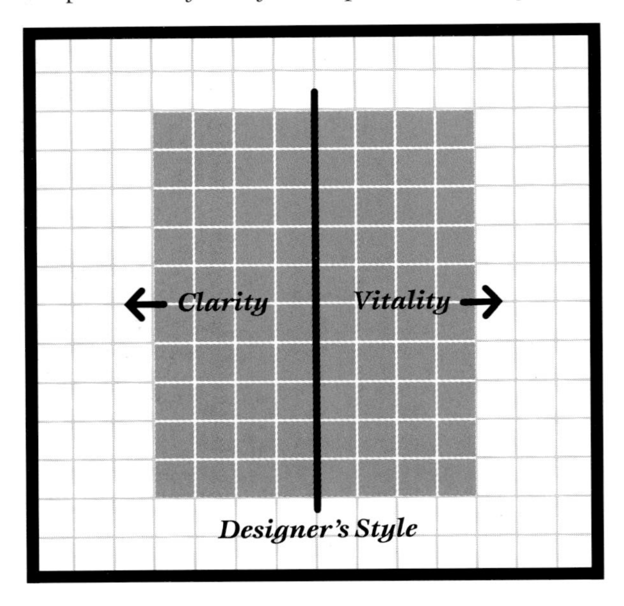

Of course, many graphic designers strive for the best of both worlds, for some ideal blend of clarity and vitality. And all good designers are flexible enough to embrace a segment of the clarity-vitality axis in their work, and to flow within that segment as each job requires. Consciously or subconsciously they seek the balance of clarity and vitality most appropriate to the problem at hand. In striving for communication effectiveness, appropriateness of style and of the clarity-vitality blend is crucial. An approach that is just right for one problem may be totally inappropriate for another.

An understanding of the crucial role of appropriateness in evaluating the communication effectiveness of a particular graphic design leads to an appreciation of why we have so many design approaches and styles today. Neither the Swiss grid nor the so-called "new wave" is the answer to all problems, nor is any other style or blend of styles. One should look at the work shown in this chapter with these thoughts in mind. Some are beautiful. Some are visually exciting. Some pieces are graphically quiet. Some are full of humor and personality, and others are dry and impersonal. But graphic designs, to be truly understood and appreciated, should be viewed in terms of how well they convey the intended message to the audience at which they are aimed. After all, that is their reason for being.

Typographic design is a vital force in visual communications. It does not exist for its own sake, and should not be evaluated as if it were design for design's sake. The sheer beauty of a piece of communication may contribute to its effectiveness, may distract or detract from it, or may merely be irrelevant. The graphic designer is first and foremost a communicator, and only within that framework an artist. He or she must manage not only graphic elements but often must involve both the message and graphic concept. Data, research, instinct, a knowledge and feeling for symbolism and the psychological aspects of graphic communication, all come into play before a design can be successfully executed in terms of its objective. The designer's role in the development of a printed communication is analogous to that of an architect or a composer in that he or she is responsible for the concept as well as its execution.

Corporate Design

Corporate design in the United States as we know it today was born in the late 1950s. Before then, corporate art/design departments focused on a letterhead, a trademark, an annual report, an employee publication, on this job or that, but with little thought to graphically coordinating them with each other and with every other visual impression made by a corporation. In the late 1950s and 1960s, the emphasis on corporate image design took off. It blanketed such diverse things as the sides of trucks, reception rooms, furniture, color standards, employee uniforms, logotypes, and, of course, typographics.

The goal was to present to the targeted audience a specifically desirable image (of reliability or modernity, for example) or a complex of images, and to do so in a way that the corporation's image, whether on an advertisement or on a letterhead or a product, a package, or wherever, would be readily identified with the corporation and easily distinguished from any other corporate image. Much market research was conducted to determine what a corporation's image was, what it should be, and how best to project it. Corporate design departments and directors became very prominent and very busy in the 1960s.

But before long advertising agencies and corporate design firms took over this function and that is still the general practice in the late '80s.

Designers like Paul Rand and Elliott Noyes played key roles in the incipient stages of corporate design, but great impetus also came from a few dynamic business executives who realized the importance of developing and presenting their corporation's image. These leaders included William Paley and Frank Stanton at CBS, Robert Anderson at Atlantic Richfield, and Walter Paepcke at the Container Corporation of America; the term "corporate image" may have been coined at Ciba Corporation in the 1950s under the design direction of James K. Fogleman, a corporate identity pioneer.

There are those who feel that corporate design is no longer the effective force it was in the '60s and '70s. Overall, corporate graphics may look good and, piece by piece, be effective, but the coordination of graphic impressions and their thorough integration with the nature of the corporation seems to be largely missing today. Corporate design manuals seem to be passé. Some, like West Coast design consultant and design teacher Louis Danziger, think that this may be a good thing since they tend to inhibit creativity and require frequent updating.

And there are others who don't exactly applaud the idea of corporate images. In 1984, Irving Miller received an AIGA medal for the Cummins Engine Company's contribution to good design, and he commented:

"Good design has nothing to do with image, which is a phony word if there ever was one. Image is basically an attempt to cover up, a cosmetic applied to make you look better than you really do. Good design at heart is simply honesty. It is an ingredient of character. Good design helps to form in any one part of the business an influence that affects all parts of the business. It sustains character and honesty in every aspect of the business. Good design, therefore, is very good business indeed."

Financial Graphics

Clarity certainly is a must in financial graphics and the focus on clarity has tended to keep innovative graphics out of annual reports and bank promotional materials. Swiss, or grid typographics traditionally make banking graphics conservative, easy to read, but often unexciting. Jack Odette, V.P. Communications Design, Citibank/Citicorp, however, notes that even a product that "doesn't come in different models, colors, flavors, or fragrances" can be made visually appealing.

Around 1970, influenced by young West Coast designers, corporate communicators started to question whether corporate gray was the best "color" for a growing corporation in this age. As a result, much financial advertising is more colorful, more graphically alive, more on the same wavelength as the young market it is often addressing. Banks no longer wait for customers to come to them. The marketing concept of locating and attracting customers is in full swing today, and graphics are among the tools now being used more aggressively and innovatively to beat the competition.

And the competition today isn't just other banks. It is money market funds, Sears, Greyhound, Gulf+Western, insurance companies, etc.; any of which can transfer funds out of a bank almost as fast as you can dial an "800" number.

Anything but dull is this 1984 Citicorp annual report cover. Type is in red and blue. Designer, Mike Focar, Art Director, Jack Odette.

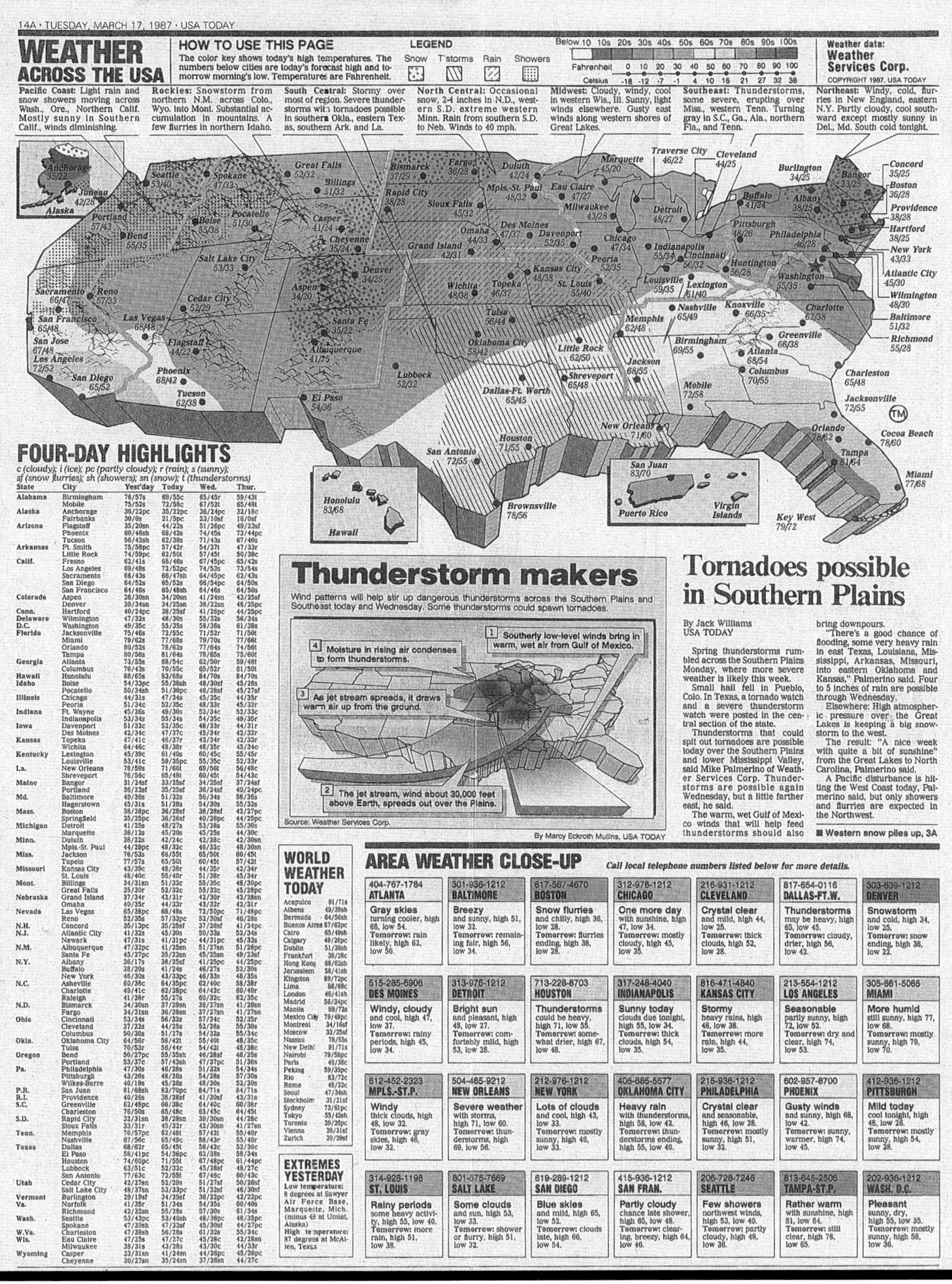

14A · TUESDAY, MARCH 17, 1987 · USA TODAY

WEATHER ACROSS THE USA

HOW TO USE THIS PAGE
The color key shows today's high temperatures. The numbers below cities are today's forecast high and tomorrow morning's low. Temperatures are Fahrenheit.

LEGEND: Snow · T'storms · Rain · Showers

Below 10 · 10s · 20s · 30s · 40s · 50s · 60s · 70s · 80s · 90s · 100s
Fahrenheit 0 10 20 30 40 50 60 70 80 90 100
Celsius -18 -12 -7 -1 4 10 16 21 27 32 38

Weather data: Weather Services Corp.
COPYRIGHT 1987, USA TODAY

Pacific Coast: Light rain and snow showers moving across Wash., Ore., Northern Calif. Mostly sunny in Southern Calif., winds diminishing.

Rockies: Snowstorm from northern N.M. across Colo., Wyo. into Mont. Substantial accumulation in mountains. A few flurries in northern Idaho.

South Central: Stormy over most of region. Severe thunderstorms with tornadoes possible in southern Okla., eastern Texas, southern Ark. and La.

North Central: Occasional snow, 2-4 inches in N.D., western S.D. extreme western Minn. Rain from southern S.D. to Neb. Winds to 40 mph.

Midwest: Cloudy, windy, cool in western Wis., Ill. Sunny, light winds elsewhere. Gusty east winds along western shores of Great Lakes.

Southeast: Thunderstorms, some severe, erupting over Miss., western Tenn. Turning gray in S.C., Ga., Ala., northern Fla., and Tenn.

Northeast: Windy, cold, flurries in New England, eastern N.Y. Partly cloudy, cool southward except mostly sunny in Del., Md. South cold tonight.

FOUR-DAY HIGHLIGHTS

Thunderstorm makers

Wind patterns will help stir up dangerous thunderstorms across the Southern Plains and Southeast today and Wednesday. Some thunderstorms could spawn tornadoes.

1 Southerly low-level winds bring in warm, wet air from Gulf of Mexico.
2 The jet stream, wind about 30,000 feet above Earth, spreads out over the Plains.
3 As jet stream spreads, it draws warm air up from the ground.
4 Moisture in rising air condenses to form thunderstorms.

Source: Weather Services Corp.

By Marcy Eckroth Mullins, USA TODAY

Tornadoes possible in Southern Plains

By Jack Williams
USA TODAY

Spring thunderstorms rumbled across the Southern Plains Monday, where more severe weather is likely this week.

Small hail fell in Pueblo, Colo. In Texas, a tornado watch and a severe thunderstorm watch were posted in the central section of the state.

Thunderstorms that could spit out tornadoes are possible today over the Southern Plains and lower Mississippi Valley, said Mike Palmerino of Weather Services Corp. Thunderstorms are possible again Wednesday, but a little farther east, he said.

The warm, wet Gulf of Mexico winds that will help feed thunderstorms should also bring downpours.

"There's a good chance of flooding, some very heavy rain in east Texas, Louisiana, Mississippi, Arkansas, Missouri, into eastern Oklahoma and Kansas," Palmerino said. Four to 5 inches of rain are possible through Wednesday.

Elsewhere: High atmospheric pressure over the Great Lakes is keeping a big snowstorm to the west.

The result: "A nice week with quite a bit of sunshine" from the Great Lakes to North Carolina, Palmerino said.

A Pacific disturbance is hitting the West Coast today, Palmerino said, but only showers and flurries are expected in the Northwest.

■ Western snow piles up, 3A

WORLD WEATHER TODAY

EXTREMES YESTERDAY

AREA WEATHER CLOSE-UP

Call local telephone numbers listed below for more details.

404-767-1784 **ATLANTA** — Gray skies turning cooler, high 68, low 54. Tomorrow: rain likely, high 62, low 50.

301-936-1212 **BALTIMORE** — Breezy and sunny, high 51, low 32. Tomorrow: remaining fair, high 56, low 34.

617-567-4670 **BOSTON** — Snow flurries and chilly, high 36, low 28. Tomorrow: flurries ending, high 38, low 28.

312-976-1212 **CHICAGO** — One more day with sunshine, high 47, low 34. Tomorrow: mostly cloudy, high 45, low 35.

216-931-1212 **CLEVELAND** — Crystal clear and mild, high 44, low 25. Tomorrow: thick clouds, high 52, low 28.

817-654-0116 **DALLAS-FT.W.** — Thunderstorms may be heavy, high 65, low 45. Tomorrow: cloudy, drier, high 56, low 42.

303-639-1212 **DENVER** — Snowstorm and cold, high 34, low 25. Tomorrow: snow ending, high 38, low 22.

515-285-6906 **DES MOINES** — Windy, cloudy and cool, high 47, low 37. Tomorrow: rainy periods, high 45, low 34.

313-976-1212 **DETROIT** — Bright sun and pleasant, high 48, low 27. Tomorrow: comfortably mild, high 53, low 28.

713-228-8703 **HOUSTON** — Thunderstorms could be heavy, high 71, low 55. Tomorrow: somewhat drier, high 67, low 48.

317-248-4040 **INDIANAPOLIS** — Sunny today clouds due tonight, high 55, low 34. Tomorrow: thick clouds, high 54, low 35.

816-471-4840 **KANSAS CITY** — Stormy heavy rains, high 48, low 38. Tomorrow: more rain, high 44, low 35.

213-554-1212 **LOS ANGELES** — Seasonable partly sunny, high 72, low 52. Tomorrow: dry and clear, high 74, low 53.

305-661-5065 **MIAMI** — More humid still sunny, high 77, low 68. Tomorrow: mostly sunny, high 79, low 70.

612-452-2323 **MPLS.-ST.P.** — Windy thick clouds, high 48, low 32. Tomorrow: gray skies, high 46, low 32.

504-465-9212 **NEW ORLEANS** — Severe weather with storms, high 71, low 60. Tomorrow: thunderstorms, high 69, low 56.

212-976-1212 **NEW YORK** — Lots of clouds and cool, high 43, low 33. Tomorrow: mostly sunny, high 46, low 33.

405-685-5577 **OKLAHOMA CITY** — Heavy rain with thunderstorms, high 58, low 42. Tomorrow: thunderstorms ending, high 55, low 40.

215-936-1212 **PHILADELPHIA** — Crystal clear and seasonable, high 46, low 28. Tomorrow: mostly sunny, high 51, low 32.

602-957-8700 **PHOENIX** — Gusty winds and sunny, high 68, low 42. Tomorrow: sunny, warmer, high 74, low 45.

412-936-1212 **PITTSBURGH** — Mild today cool tonight, high 48, low 26. Tomorrow: mostly sunny, high 54, low 28.

314-928-1198 **ST. LOUIS** — Rainy periods some heavy activity, high 55, low 40. Tomorrow: more rain, high 51, low 38.

801-575-7669 **SALT LAKE** — Some clouds and sun, high 53, low 33. Tomorrow: shower or flurry, high 51, low 32.

619-289-1212 **SAN DIEGO** — Blue skies and mild, high 65, low 52. Tomorrow: clouds late, high 66, low 54.

415-936-1212 **SAN FRAN.** — Partly cloudy chance late shower, high 65, low 48. Tomorrow: clearing, breezy, high 64, low 46.

206-728-7246 **SEATTLE** — Few showers northwest winds, high 53, low 40. Tomorrow: partly cloudy, high 48, low 36.

813-645-2506 **TAMPA-ST.P.** — Rather warm with sunshine, high 81, low 64. Tomorrow: still clear, high 78, low 65.

202-936-1212 **WASH. D.C.** — Pleasant sunny, dry, high 55, low 35. Tomorrow: mostly sunny, high 58, low 36.

***The weather map** in* USA Today *is an extraordinary achievement editorially, technologically and graphically. It also appears, with different data, in the European editions. The map appears daily. In each 24-hour cycle, data is gathered, edited, and poured into the format. Color plates are made, type is set, the page composed and, with the rest of the paper, transmitted as bits and bytes via satellite to numerous remote site printing plants for printing and nationwide and continent-wide distribution. Because the total press run is divided among printing plants, no one run is as long as the runs of other papers printed in a single plant. This makes later closings possible.*

Easy-to-understand codes in color and in patterns with clear legends show the day's weather across the USA. The map also gives four-day data (yesterday, today, the next two days) for many localities, as well as much other data. Telephone numbers are listed for 28 cities if more details are desired.

Charts and Graphs

In today's environment of message overload and the bombardment of the reader/viewer from electronic as well as print media, more and more designers and publishers recognize the value of presenting information graphically when possible. Swiss designer Karl Gerstner speaks of the urgent pressure to convey a message rapidly and with adequate means. Gerstner is an advocate of integral typography, where pictures, graphs, colors, shapes, etc. not only accompany the text but are integrated with it.

More and more information today is given in colorful and lively charts and other graphics utilizing symbolic and/or humorous icons. Graphic charts, compared to ordinary data tables, are better understood, make their points more rapidly, are better remembered. Symbolism and/or humor can build readership, but are at their best when they reinforce and do not distract from the message.

Magazine Design

In 1985 the *Journal of Graphic Design*, published by the American Institute of Graphic Arts (AIGA) published a symposium on the current state of the art of magazine design. Highlights from that report tell much about magazine design today and where it may be heading.

❧ *"Magazines today are timid... They put the whole ball of wax on the cover. The entire contents are given away... the well (the uninterrupted section of editorial content) has been relinquished to advertisers."*
Cipe Pineles.

❧ *"...there aren't any editors like* Esquire's *Arnold Gingrich around anymore. Today the advertising departments run the magazines."*
Henry Wolf.

❧ *"Something happened to the magazine in the Sixties; it was the loss of potency... television basically replaced the magazine in its dominance... the greatest handicap for vitality today is too much professionalism... everybody knows what sells, everybody knows about editorial balance, but this kind of methodology basically yields predictable results... What we've done in professionalizing the activity is protect the possibility of failure at the bottom and also cut the top off the imagination."*
Milton Glaser.

❧ *"...art directors today have too much impact... Editors are relying on design to sell lame ideas."*
Sam Antupit.

❧ *"...people do not get their primary source of visual information from magazines anymore... Since their primacy is diminished, magazines are changing in the way they apportion space... the quirkiness and serendipity of design is lost so that the Calvin Klein ads are more inventive than the editorial."*
Walter Bernard.

"The kids today, because they have no connection with the past, are out there reinventing the wheel."

TELLTALES OF TWO CITIES

Cost of living	New York City	Moscow
Hours worked per week	39.7	42
Manufacturing worker's earnings per week	$265.60	$56.54
Monthly rental 3-room apt.	$1,000	$37
Heat and electricity per month	$82	$4.50
Bus or subway per ride	50¢	8¢
Car	$6,200 (Citation)	$10,000 (Zhiguli)
Gallon of gasoline	$1.35	$1.25
Vodka (1 liter)	$6	$11
Dental checkup	$32	Free
Ballpoint pen	29¢	$1.50
1 lb. chicken	66¢	$2.55
Pack of cigarettes	75¢	52¢
Loaf of bread (1 lb.)	62¢	24¢
Jeans	$18.50	$45
Man's leather shoes	$42	$45
Vacation (2 weeks per person)*	$910	$120
Woman's dress	$90	$60
Sofa	$600	$260
Gold wedding ring	$75	$225
Hard-cover novel	$12.95	$3
Color television	$710 (25-in. screen)	$1,094 (24-in. screen)
Pantyhose	$1.50	$10
Newspaper	25¢ (Daily News)	5¢ (Izvestiya)
Woman's leather shoes	$33	$40

All figures are typical current prices.

*** Vacations: the New York figure represents a peak season cost with meals at a major Florida resort city; 70% of the Moscow figure is paid by the worker's union.**

This table *shows the difference in the cost of living in New York and Moscow in 1980. It is a real tribute to the researcher's art of finding and checking compatible facts and figures from two sides of the globe. Note, for instance, that chickens are the same the world over, but bread in Russia simply doesn't come in the shape familiar to Western nations. By Nigel Holmes, © Time Inc.*

Mercredi : variable

PARISPRESSE

France Soir

D H

Paris, mercredi 3 décembre 1975 ● 1,20 F ● DERNIERE HEURE

Télé : trois films prévus ce soir Dernière page

Grève : la difficile journée des banlieusards Page 4

Depuis plusieurs jours, les policiers surveillaient l'appartement parisien où leur ennemi public n° 1 avait trouvé refuge

La capture de Willoquet

Aux premières images du film, il avait dû avoir un drôle de sourire. Regarder « Brigade antigang » à la télé devait paraître à Willoquet une sorte de défi. Le sourire s'est crispé avant la fin. Jean-Charles Willoquet a été arrêté à 21 h 20, lundi soir, 17, rue d'Oslo (18e).

Après 146 jours de cavale il s'est rendu en disant : « Chapeau, dans la rue vous ne m'auriez pas eu vivant »

CELUI que les policiers avaient baptisé l'ennemi public N° 1, qui avait claironné qu'on ne le prendrait pas vivant, s'est laissé prendre comme son ami Mesrine. Sans coup férir. Après une « cavale » de cent quarante-six jours.

Les hommes de l'antigang et de l'Office de répression du banditisme avaient mis le paquet. Depuis quatre jours et quatre nuits, cinquante policiers surveillaient les immeubles du 18e arrondissement où le gangster était susceptible de se cacher.

Tout a commencé par une filature, celle d'un prisonnier bénéficiant de larges permissions de sortie. Cet homme a amené les policiers à d'autres truands et, enfin, à Willoquet.

« Nous étions sur sa piste depuis plusieurs jours, explique M. Jean Ducret, directeur de la police judiciaire. Nous avions appris que Jean Moscone, détenu à la prison de Poitiers, avait obtenu des permissions de quatre jours par semaine pour se rendre à Paris pour raison de famille.

« Au cours de ces week-ends prolongés, il était susceptible de prendre contact avec des gens du milieu qui gravitaient autour de Willoquet. Nous l'avions donc pris en filature. Parmi les truands qu'il contactait, nous nous sommes intéressés à un appartement, 17, rue d'Oslo (18e) loué par Simone Renault et son ami, un ancien proxénète, Daniel Roy, 50 ans.

Pas de risques

« Dans ce logement un homme semblait se cacher, poursuit le directeur de la P.J. De la maison d'en face, à la lumière, nous avons eu la preuve qu'il s'agissait de Willoquet. L'opération de police a été décidée ce soir. Tous les immeubles contigus ont été investis, y compris les balcons, car on pouvait craindre une prise d'otages.

« Nous n'avons pas voulu prendre le risque de les appréhender dans la rue, ajoute le commissaire Broussard. Cela aurait pu tourner à la tuerie. »

Le 17 de la rue d'Oslo est un grand immeuble neuf, cossu, où les gens se connaissent encore mal. Les propos de palier se résument à « bonjour », « bonsoir ». C'est là, au quatrième étage, que Simone Renault, la quarantaine appétissante, tantôt blonde, tantôt rousse, tenancière d'un hôtel du quartier à Clichy, abrite le gangster traqué.

« Nous étions sur des charbons ardents, racontent les inspecteurs, car il n'est pas sorti de tout le dimanche. » M. Pierre Hauss, au cinquième étage, a tout suivi : « Toute la journée, je fus intrigué par le curieux manège de peintres dans un appartement de l'immeuble d'en face. Ces ouvriers, vêtus de combinaisons blanches, le pinceau à la main, semblaient, en fait, plus préoccupés de ce qui se passait dans notre immeuble que par leur tâche. »

Il ne se trompait pas : à 21 heures, on frappe à sa porte : « Ouvrez, opération de police ! » M. Pierre Hauss hésite : sa femme est déjà couchée. Le commissaire Le Bruchec lui glisse sa carte sous la porte. M. Hauss ouvre et des policiers prennent position, mitraillette au poing, sur sa terrasse et braquent le balcon du dessous. Le commissaire lui demande alors d'aller sonner chez ses voi-

Suite page 3

Ce « charmant » jeune homme, sagement assis, souriant, détendu, les cheveux un peu fous, c'est tout simplement Charles Willoquet, après son arrestation, dans un bureau de la Police judiciaire. Il s'est rendu comme un vulgaire voyou débutant. Il avait pourtant dit : « Avant de me faire prendre, je ferai la peau d'un flic. »

(Photo Cl. POENSIN-BURAT.)

PEANUTS par Schulz

Excédés d'être la cible des syndicats et des juges ils s'estiment incompris par le gouvernement

Cadres et patrons : c'est la grogne

La condamnation du responsable de l'usine d'emboutissage Berliet à Vénissieux, c'est (peut-être) une goutte de trop dans la coupe amère des patrons et cadres responsables.

Certes, M. Michelland, condamné à six mois de prison, dont trois avec sursis, par le tribunal correctionnel de Lyon à la suite d'un accident mortel du travail, n'est pas écroué. Son appel est suspensif et les magistrats de la Cour peuvent lui accorder le sursis. Comme les Chambres d'accusation de Douai, de Riom et de Rennes ont remis en liberté les chefs d'entreprise, que des juges d'instruction venaient de placer en détention préventive.

UN degré a été franchi dans l'escalade. Cette fois, c'est une juridiction de jugement qui a condamné à la prison un cadre responsable. C'est un tribunal ayant délibéré, et nul n'oserait prétendre qu'il a suivi les consignes du Syndicat de la magistrature.

On peut donc s'attendre à des réactions patronales à la mesure de l'éditorial au vitriol que la revue du C.N.P.F. publiait le 15 novembre sous le titre « Racisme anti-patrons ».

Les 30.000 numéros se sont arrachés comme des petits pains et on a immédiatement procédé à un tirage à part de 60.000 exemplaires.

Il y a trois causes essentielles au « ras-le-bol » des patrons :

1°) - Ils se considèrent comme les premières victimes de la crise. 30.000 patrons, souvent chefs d'entreprises petites ou moyennes ont été ruinés depuis deux ans.

Déconfiture

Souvent il y a eu, dans les faits, confusion entre les biens de leur société en déconfiture et leur fortune personnelle. Dans le même temps les attaques personnelles sont multipliées. *Ils ont donc le sentiment de plus en plus net de la précarité de leur situation, aussi bien sur le plan matériel que sur celui de la considération sociale.*

2°) - Ils financent le coût social de la crise en licenciant au minimum (la production industrielle a baissé de 12 %, alors que les effectifs n'ont été réduits que de 4 %), en finançant le chômage partiel, et le chômage total à hauteur de 9 milliards de francs.

3°) - Leurs entreprises deviennent de plus en plus difficiles à gérer. On leur demande d'embaucher et on les prévient qu'il leur sera de plus en plus difficile de licencier. Les contrôles des prix sont de plus en plus tatillons. Quand ils investissent, on dit qu'ils favorisent l'inflation ; quand ils hésitent à le faire, on les accuse de bloquer la relance.

Selon eux la France détient le record du monde des prélèvements sociaux obligatoires sur les entreprises. Quand un patron donne 100 F à un salarié, il rajoute 52 F pour les cotisations annexes.

« Mal aimés »

A ces facteurs s'ajoutent le sentiment que le patronat constitue désormais la cible privilégiée des partis de gauche, tandis que les Pouvoirs publics, y compris les ministres les plus au fait des problèmes industriels, se désolidarisent des soucis des chefs d'entreprise.

En privé, le ministre de l'Industrie lui-même trouve normal qu'un patron n'ayant pas appliqué les consignes de sécurité rappelés par l'inspection du travail soit mis en prison.

Et Jean-Pierre Fourcade, répondant lundi à la mauvaise humeur exprimée par les patrons d' « Entreprise et Progrès », déclarait que le malaise des patrons n'était pas grand-chose par rapport au malaise des Français, contraints de vivre dans le monde industriel que les chefs d'entreprise ont modelé depuis vingt ans.

« Si l'industrie française, a-t-il dit, est mal aimée, c'est

Suite page 3

Pièces roses pièces noires

On croyait assister à une pièce inédite. Or, voici que l'on reconnaît au passage des répliques familières et des mots déjà entendus. Voici des scènes qui ravivent de vieux souvenirs. Voici que réapparaissent, côté cour, des acteurs que n'éclairaient plus les feux de la rampe. Voici des airs connus et des tableaux rétrospectifs.

Sur le théâtre politique, on affiche « reprise ». Ou, du moins, on en a l'impression.

Malaise de l'armée... problème des appelés... subversion... Cour de Sûreté de l'Etat... Cela ne vous dit rien ?

Grève des transports... grève de la télévision et de la radio... débats sur la régionalisation... diatribes contre la gauche... Couve de Murville et Guichard sous les projecteurs. Et jusqu'au ministre de l'Intérieur qui se met à ressembler à Marcellin. Le passé frappe décidément ses trois coups.

L'UDR, qu'on croyait morte, ressuscite avec éclat, alors que le rideau se lève à peine sur le septennat giscardien. On parlait de réformes, d'ouverture, de libéralisme. Il n'est plus question, désormais, que de sauvegarde, de durcissement, d'autorité.

Après les pièces roses, les pièces noires.

Faut-il donc faire, avec certains socialistes, le constat d'une « gaullisation » du régime et d'un renversement des rapports de force entre les partis de la majorité ?

Ou bien, à l'inverse, est-ce Giscard qui satellisa l'UDR ? « Les gaullistes, a dit récemment André Bord, le secrétaire général de l'UDR, sont toujours là pour barrer la route aux actions qui mettent en péril les institutions fondamentales de la société. »

Les gaullistes ont vocation de jouer la tragédie : l'heure n'est plus à la féerie.

Pierre SAINDERICHIN

P. 5, nos informations.

Les emplois en banlieue, on les trouve dans « France Soir » le mardi et le jeudi
Petites annonces 233-44-31
Page 8

« Atchoum ! » « A votre santé... »

Depuis deux ans, un Anversois, Roger David, 34 ans, soignait en vain le rhume de sa femme, Marie, avec un produit de son invention. Elle ne guérissait pas. Elle n'en mourait pas non plus, ce qui peut paraître plus étrange, car « l'anti-rhume » du mari était à base de cyanure.

David n'avait trouvé que ce remède empirique pour se débarrasser d'une épouse encombrante. Mais Marie résistait à tout — comme son rhume — et c'est un médecin, venu la soigner pour un évanouissement, qui faillit « y passer » en reniflant le médicament conjugal.

Moralité : le mari-guérisseur comparaît devant les juges, pour tentative de meurtre.

Ils doivent démolir leur maison

Les époux Bourhis — un couple de septuagénaires bretons — devront payer 300 F par jour... tant qu'ils n'auront pas démoli leur maison. Cette dernière, édifiée à Locmaria-Plouzané (Finistère), ne respectait pas les règlements d'urbanisme de la commune. Le permis de construire avait été accordé en mars 1973, mais annulé par la suite. M. Alain Bourhis n'en avait pas moins poursuivi la construction.

Mais celle-ci constituait une gêne pour les voisins, et un procès s'ensuivit. Il vient de se terminer par une décision de la cour d'appel de Rennes : la maison devra être démolie dans un délai de quatre mois. Sous astreinte de 300 F par jour de retard.

Visual orchestration *(above and near right). "To design a so called 'Boulevard Newspaper' was to me one of the most fascinating tasks as a typographer. Because it doesn't contain all the news that are fit to print. But it creates the news by selection and visual orchestration. The typesize is the message. And in every issue it has to create the daily reality. Thus the typographer is obliged to create the elements and the rules." Karl Gerstner.*

❧ *"The proliferation of specialized magazines has contributed to the problem... many art directors don't have any particular interest in the subject matter ...The kids today, because they have no connection with the past, are out there reinventing the wheel..."* Will Hopkins.

❧ *"An art director should be an aestheticist, and should work within a span of personal taste, because that's the only way to do a good job. Taste is* the *specialization, but, within that, the a.d. is a problem-solver. First of all, one should know what kind of magazine it is and for whom and then determine the highest level of performance that can do justice to that subject. Then the art director should give it an identifiable form and, within that identifiable form, as much variety as possible. And always within that limited taste, one must be continuously innovative,*

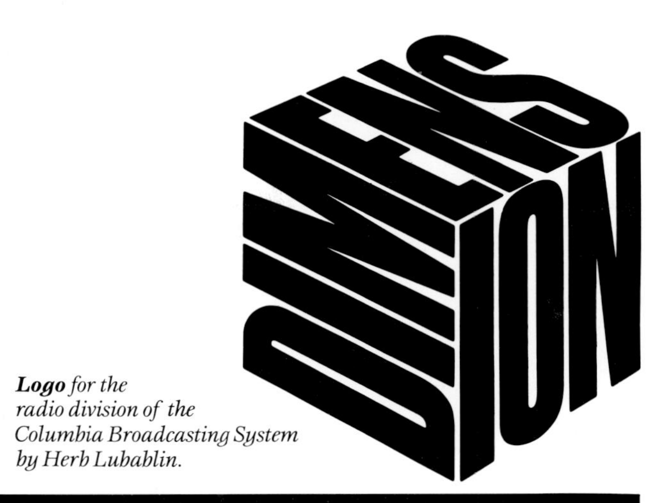

***Logo** for the radio division of the Columbia Broadcasting System by Herb Lubablin.*

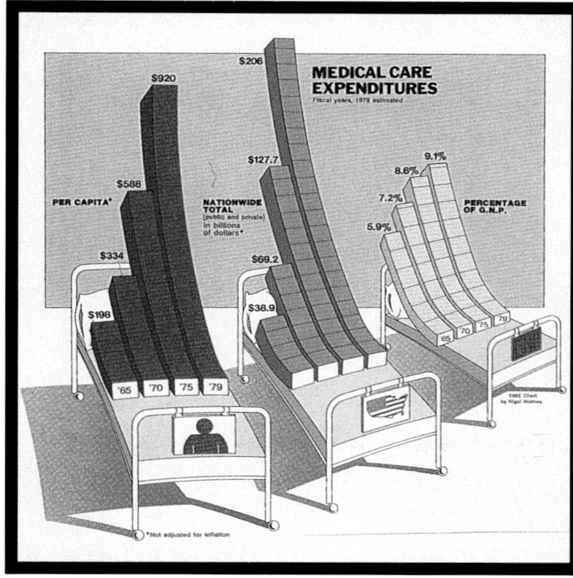

***With the bars** sitting up in bed, an immediate visual impression of hospital costs is given. The exact figures are printed at the top of each bar so that there can be no confusion about the bends in them. By Nigel Holmes, ©Time Inc.*

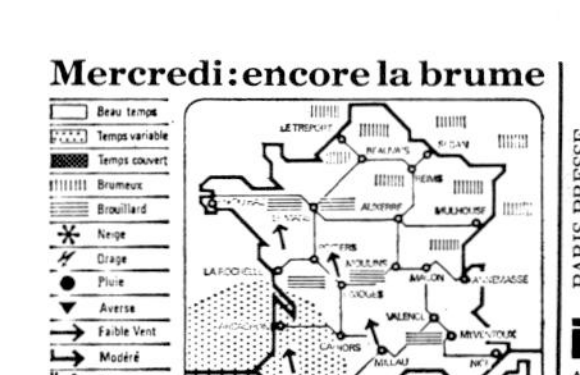

Mercredi : encore la brume

PARIS-PRESSE

France Soir

DERNIÈRE HEURE

Paris, mercredi 29 octobre 1975 ● 1,20 F

Football

Paris S.-G. : problèmes de sous

Trente ans après, Touvier...

Budget santé-urgences

L'esprit des rues

Priorité aux infirmières aux hôpitaux aux handicapés et aux personnes âgées

Simone Veil, ministre de la Santé, présente ce soir à l'Assemblée nationale un budget 1976 en augmentation de 15 % seulement sur celui de 1975.

Pour parer au plus pressé, elle a choisi une série de priorités : recrutement massif d'infirmières, modernisation de 40.000 lits d'hôpitaux, aide aux handicapés et personnes âgées, sauvetage de l'Institut Pasteur.

PEANUTS par Schulz

Creil (4.500 travailleurs à Paris) s'indigne :

Et la carte orange ?

Choux-fleurs contre E.D.F.

Elle tire sur son père trop sévère

France Soir Spéciales périphérie 77 - 78 - 91 92 - 93 - 94 95 vous propose DES EMPLOIS à proximité de votre domicile

Franco a reçu sa famille

Un résistant à la Une

L'honneur des juges

Par Henri NOGUERES

Il vole en dormant

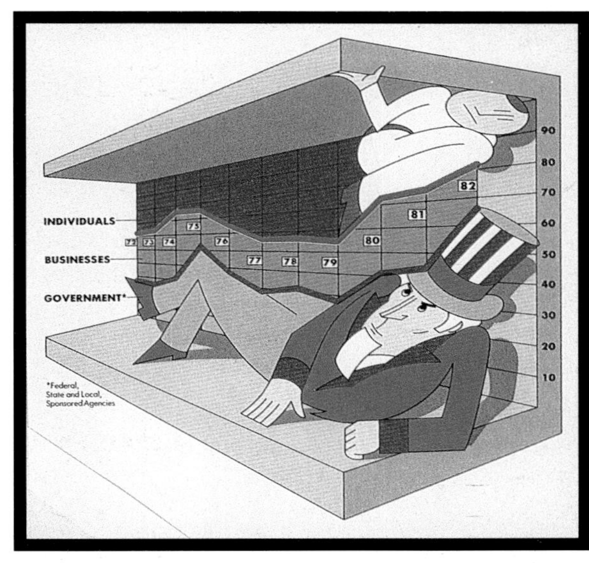

***This is** the complete four-color version of the fever chart whose overlays were shown on another page. It shows how government and business are using more and more of the available funds for borrowing, thus squeezing out the poor consumer shown in the uncomfortable position at the top. By Nigel Holmes, ©Time Inc.*

since that is the nature of the beast. The real challenge is to have unity with freedom.

"A magazine is not simply mise en page of type. It is a mise en page of meanings — expressed in type, photographs, illustration or all together."
Leo Lionni.

Symbolism in Communication

Around mid-century, advertising agencies, corporations, and publishers started to appreciate that a good art director was much more than a layout specialist. Slowly but surely, more and more art directors shared responsibility for developing message and campaign concepts as well as supervising graphic presentations. As art directors and graphic designers worked more closely with top management, their areas of involvement and their expertise grew. Many appreciated the psychological aspect of graphics, not only of obvious symbols but of the symbology inherent in a facial expression or in the body language of a model or in the beneath-the-surface meanings of various objects, odors, and shapes.

Chapter XIII: The Many Faces of Typography Today

"Each typeface, like each tone of voice or facial expression, conveys a mood and/or a meaning."

Today many communication designers consciously consider the symbolism in their designs and illustrations and make sure it is aimed to reinforce the intent of the message. One way to think of communication design is in terms of three dimensions: vitality, clarity, symbolism. It is the optimal blend of these qualities that attracts attention, presents a message understandably, and targets the message to make the desired impression on the selected audience.

Typeface/Typographic Symbolism

Each typeface, like each tone of voice or facial expression, conveys a mood and/or a meaning. When the typeface is properly chosen and used, its very personality subtly, often powerfully, reinforces the message. The symbolism of typefaces is not an absolute. One cannot arbitrarily rule that only bold typefaces should be used for advertising hard goods or major appliances, or only light faces or script should speak for perfumes. As much depends on how a face is used as on which face is selected. Experienced typographic designers either instinctively or consciously consider the symbolism of a typeface. It is not the role of TYPOGRAPHIC COMMUNICATIONS TODAY to dwell on this subject, but in this connection two points should be kept in mind:

1. There's more to choosing and using a typeface than considerations of legibility, readability, color, or copyfitting. A feeling for a typeface's psychological compatibility to a message problem can help maximize communication effectiveness.
2. In looking at the examples of typographic design shown in TYPOGRAPHIC COMMUNICATIONS TODAY, pause to consider how the designer has wedded the feeling of the type to the other graphic elements and to the message.

Today there is a heightened sense of the importance of symbolism in design that carries design past (but does not negate) the concern with graphic order and legibility of an Emil Ruder, an Armin Hoffmann, or a Ladislav Sutnar.

In printed communication, when the text clearly conveys the message, design can afford to, in fact often should, strive for novelty and visual vigor.

The danger in adding vitality to design is that such design can detract, compete with, confuse the message. Free-wheeling design is no more a virtue in itself than is grid-based design. Each must be skillfully applied to the problem at hand so as to make the message be:

- better noticed by the audience *at which it is aimed*
- read completely
- understood better
- more likely to be remembered
- more likely to be agreed with or favorably acted upon.

But readability, extent of readership and effective message transmission are no longer enough. Today, many competitive products and services

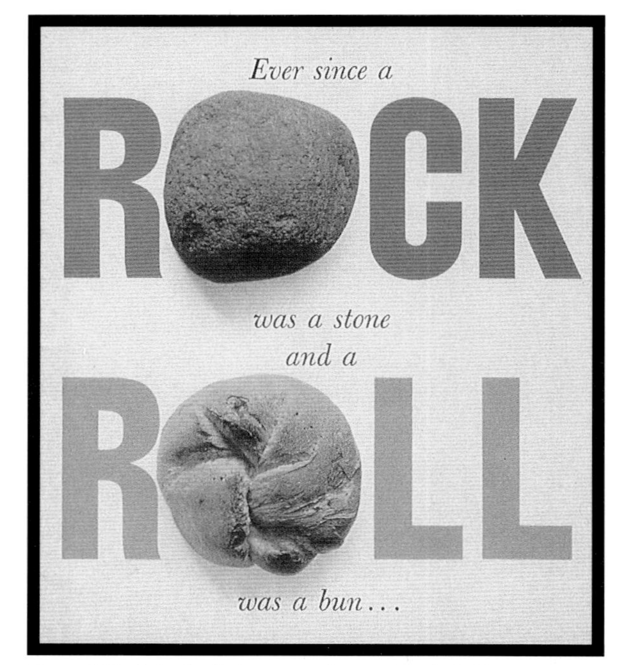

One of Herb Lubalin's *many pieces using the "O" as a receptacle for the illustration. 1957.*

are virtually indistinguishable from each other. To move a product, for example, advertising and promotional material must establish and impress perceived differences to replace the non-existent real differences. Advertisements must develop attitudes as well as convey information. In so doing, the role of the graphic elements, design, illustrations, the typefaces chosen, and how they are used can be crucial.

There are those who carry their advocacy of illusionistic images, as opposed to conceptual or realistic images, so far as to say that the presence of words, of verbal clarity, makes realistic images in pictures or sheer orderliness of design redundant. Like all theories, this concept is neither right nor wrong by itself. The choice of illustrations, of a design approach, or of a typeface, must be such as to enhance the communication, must be appropriate to the total message problem.

Conceptual images that make a full visual statement need fewer words to support them. Conversely, when the full statement is verbalized, the graphics should do more than merely repeat it. In viewing the work shown in this chapter, it is instructive to observe how different designers have coped with this challenge.

Expressive Typography

In the 1960s there was a surge of expressive typography, typography in which the type is physically positioned or modified so as to literally illustrate the primary statement. Many designers employed expressive typography very effectively. Most notable was the work done by Otto Storch in McCall's magazine and by Herb Lubalin. In

One in a series *of posters using winning typefaces in a competition sponsored by Visual Graphics Corporation. 1964. Herb Lubalin.*

An anti-war poster *for an exhibition sponsored by the American Institute of Graphic Arts by Herb Lubalin.*

some work a letter, or a word, or a block of copy would be reshaped to become an illustration of its own content. Sometimes an illustration was incorporated into the letters. And sometimes a simple line of type and an illustration were so positioned as to come alive. Here are some pieces by Herb Lubalin that show how effective this technique can be.

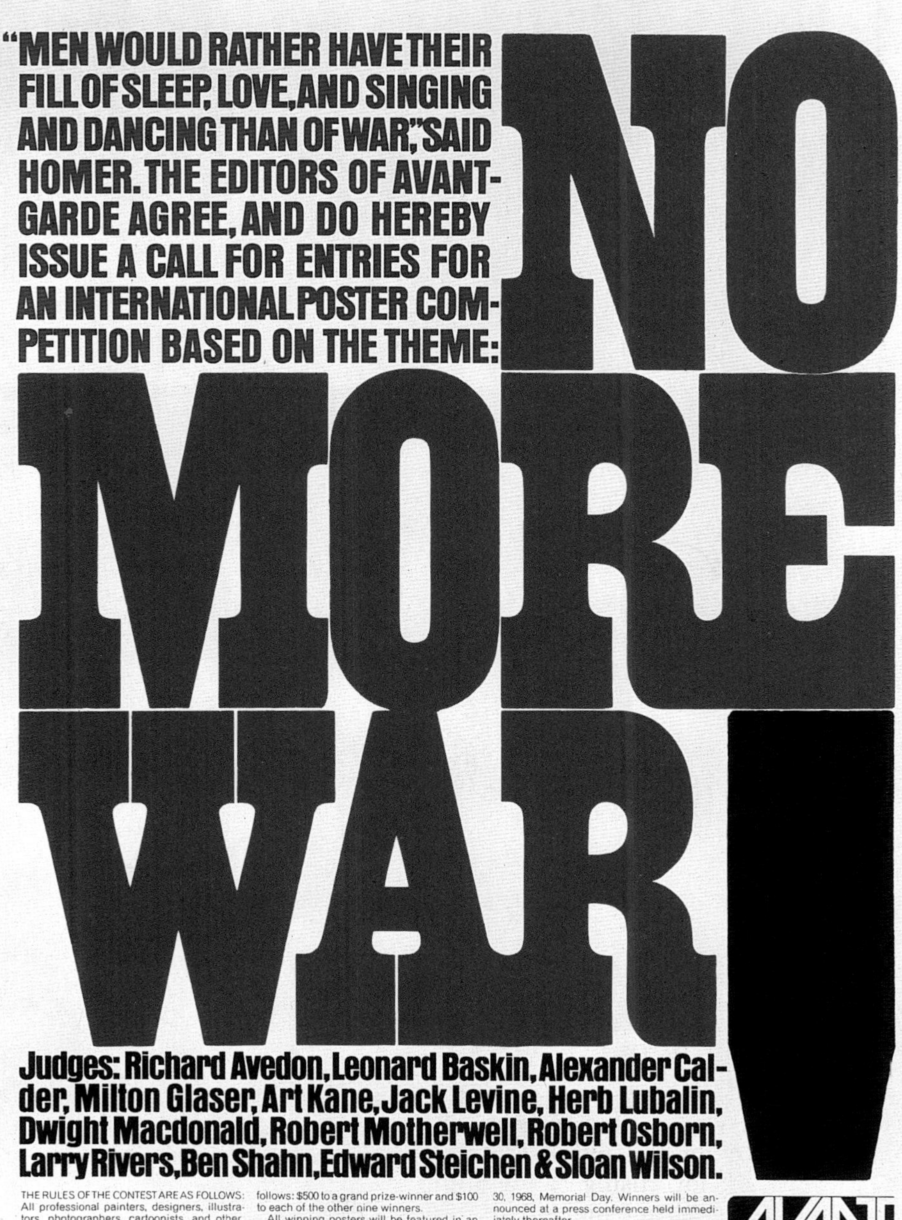

◀ ***Announcement*** *for* Avant Garde *magazine's anti-war poster contest. Herb Lubalin.*

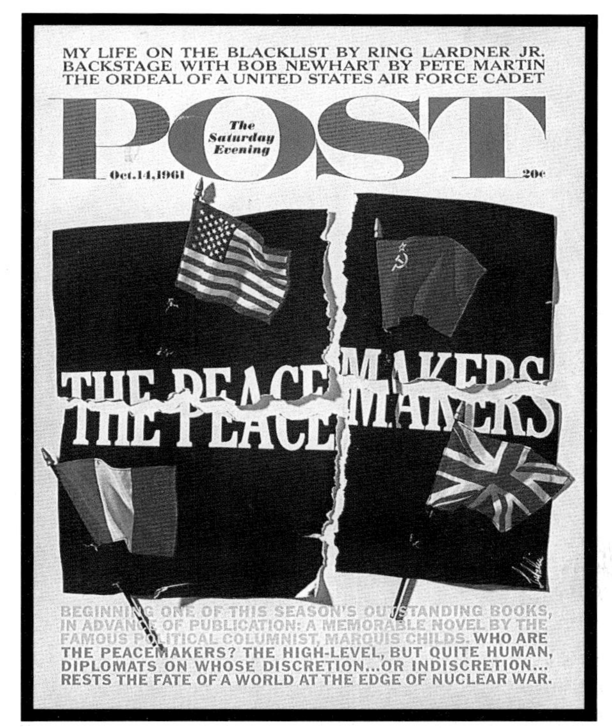

A 1961 cover *for* The Saturday Evening Post, *which had been redesigned by Herb Lubalin.*

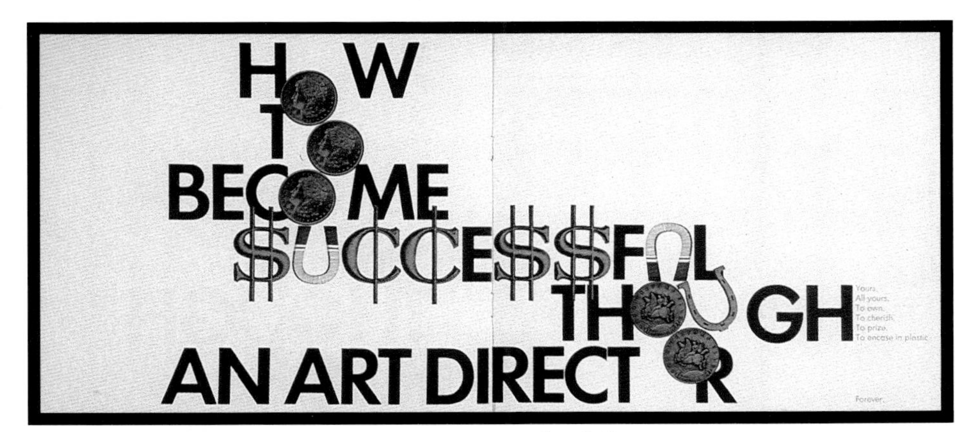

A promotion piece *for Sanders Printing Company. Herb Lubalin.*

A piece *produced by Bob Jones for his Glad Hand Press.*

TYPOGRAPHIC COMMUNICATIONS TODAY
Chapter XIII: The Many Faces of Typography Today

"Striving for something new often initiates a new chain of imitations."

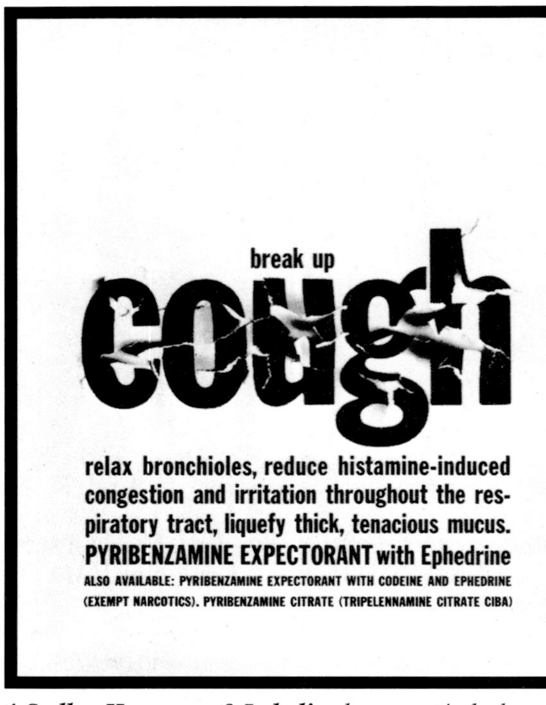

A Sudler, Hennessey & Lubalin *pharmaceutical ad. (See also, Herb Lubalin's treatment of "Marriage" and "Mother" in Chapter I.)*

It can be *a moustache (above)... or a parfait glass (below) ...or almost anything. By Otto Storch for* McCall's.

A classic example *of maximizing the transmission of the message while minimizing the graphics with just the right appropriate touch. This ad by George Lois for Coldene also illustrates the difference between a graphic gimmick and a device that truly enhances the message. The graphic device here is part of the primary statement.*

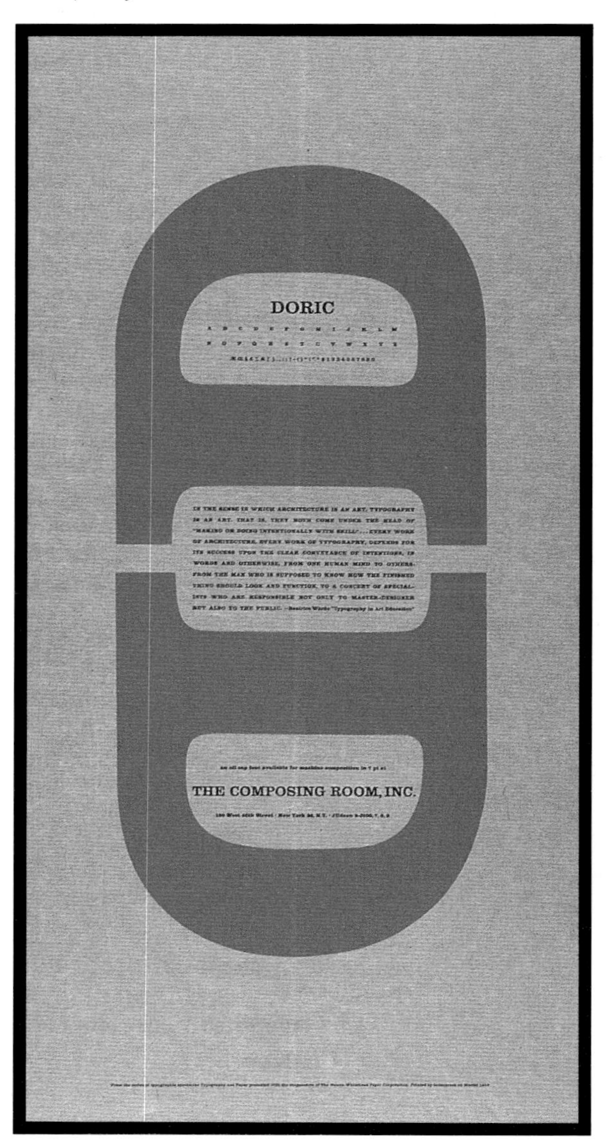

...or beautiful *in the simplicity of its own letterform magnified, as in this piece (left) by Aaron Burns for The Composing Room.*

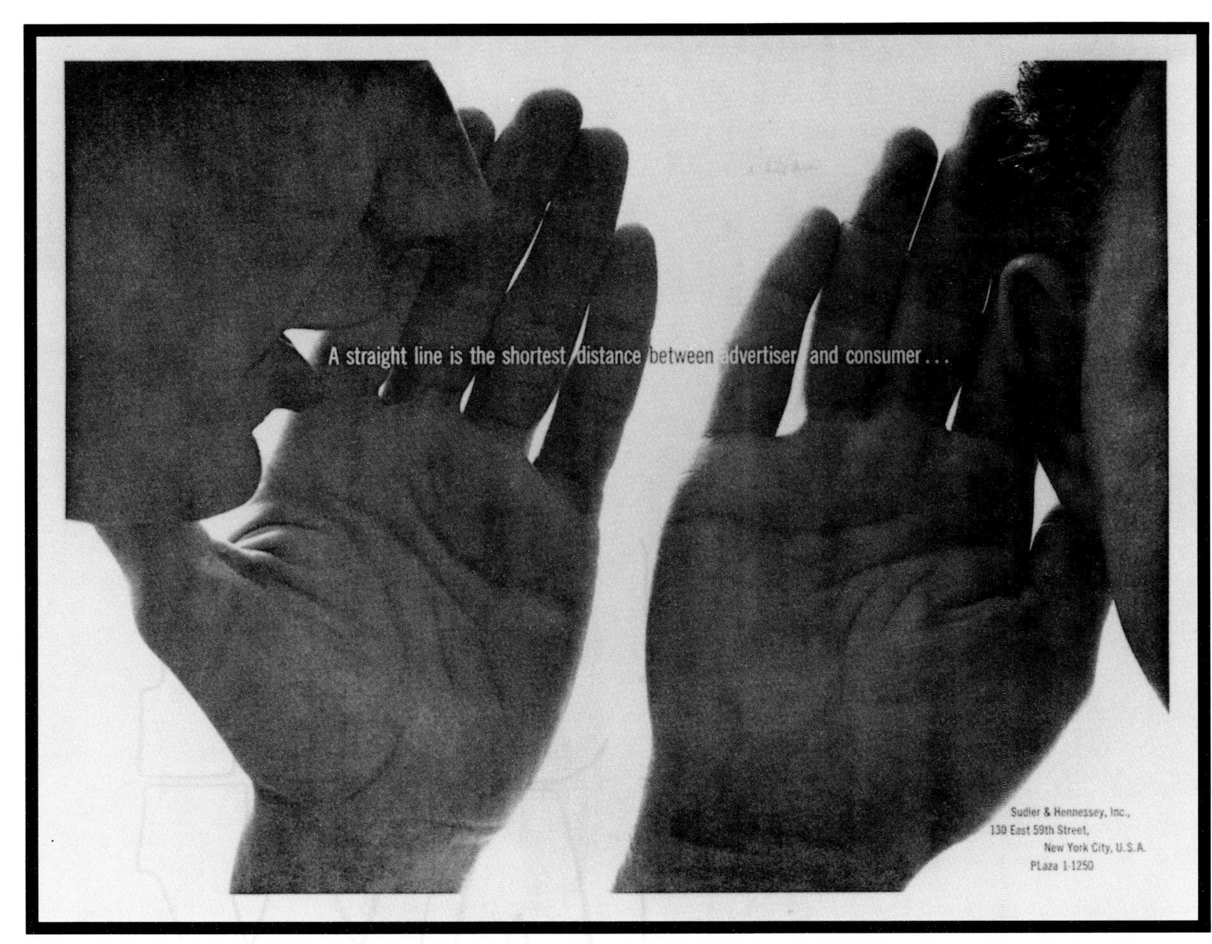

◀ ***A trade ad*** *for Sudler & Hennessey, Inc. Herb Lubalin.*

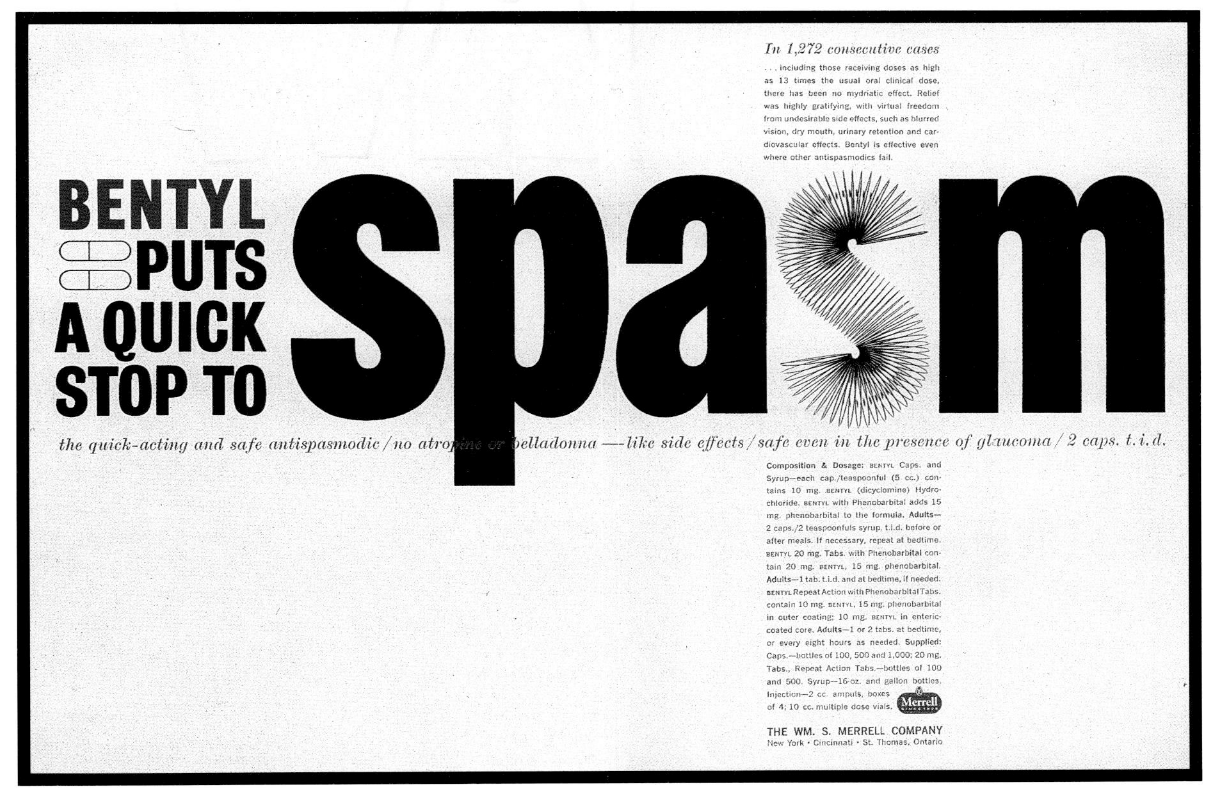

A Sudler, Hennessey & Lubalin *pharmaceutical ad.*

Commenting on expressive typography and other trends of the time, Allen F. Hurlburt suggests that striving for expressiveness and "something new" frequently initiates a new chain of imitations and clichés.

"Often what we like to describe as 'a new freedom' turns out on examination to be merely a new code of clichés. Like the rise and fall of the hemline, typography in our time has moved from the Swiss cheese to the sardine look. Not too many years ago, type designers were vying to see who could get the most letterspacing between the letters, and the most leading between the lines. Then we moved to the age of tightly stacked letters and compressed copy. The scissors and the camera made it possible to compress and interlock letters in a manner beyond the measure of mere type metal.

"Words that are not short enough can be cut into syllables or arbitrary letter groups, and with an assist from the scissors, we can set ten point type on a nine point body."

Of course, with today's technologies we can do all the above and a great deal more.

Today, thanks to digital devices and lasers, we can achieve either better or worse typography than was ever thought possible. And that is why, ideally, the marvelous computer and software and printer or typesetter should be coupled, at some stage, with a human being, a designer or art director, to couple their judgment and taste with the speed and versatility of today's systems.

The '70s and '80s saw a trend away from bouncy, expressive typography toward a quieter, more direct, more orderly typography. But nothing is forever. Today we are producing a broad spectrum of typographic designs. Enlivening the scene is the so-called "New Wave" typography.

The "New Wave"

The story line threading together the typographic decades described in Typographic Communications Today is about the ups and downs in emphasis on clarity versus vitality in communication graphics. In today's climate of neo-eclecticism, with many ways of solving problems accepted, and no one really dominant, the news and controversy center on new wave typography.

New wave typography has many names: Post-Modern, Swiss Punk, Pluralist, West Coast, Avant Garde, and Deco. What is it? Why is it? Where is it going?

In a sense it is old wave with a new twist. It is an attempt to achieve the vigor and explosiveness and element of surprise that futurists and dadaists gave to typographic design early in the century. When futurist and dada typographics seemed to confuse rather than propel messages, a reaction set in and De Stijl, constructivist, Bauhaus, and Swiss grid typographers focused on typographic clarity. Typography dealt with verbal information in a disciplined, organized manner. The best typography was the least visible, the quietest. It presented information clearly and vigorously without letting form upstage content. It was impersonal. Elements not essential to clear communication were out. We had a less-is-more kind of typographic minimalism.

As modernism in the '20s was a reaction to the staid, symmetrical typography in books, so today's new wave is a reaction to what some considered the sameness and dullness of the international or Swiss style. In a sense this new wave is a wave of designer subjectivity.

Architect Robert Venturi is credited with bringing vitality to buildings and interiors in a reaction against the stark functionalism, the ornamentless geometric forms of Mies van der Rohe and Walter Gropius. In a like manner, typographic designer and teacher Wolfgang Weingart shook up the world of the printed word. Early breaks with the neutral and objective typography in the Switzerland of the 1960s could be seen in the work of Rosemarie Tissi and of Siegfried Odermatt, and in Steff Geisbuhler's work for the Geigy pharmaceutical company.

Wolfgang Weingart

But the big shakeup came from Wolfgang Weingart. Weingart carried his revolt from objectivism further and had a great platform for spreading his point of view. He had been a student at the Basel School of Design, but, finding the teaching too dogmatic, he dropped the course after three weeks. Emil Ruder and Armin Hofmann recognized Weingart's drive and potential, and permitted him to stay at Basel and work freely. In 1968 Hofmann offered him a teaching

TYPOGRAPHIC COMMUNICATIONS TODAY

Chapter XIII: The Many Faces of Typography Today

"Typography must not be dry, tightly ordered or rigid."

Remember the Slinky toy? *Here the type literally adds bounce to the message and the ad, yet everything is perfectly readable. Otto Storch, for* McCall's.

the forty-winks reducing plan

This is a plan for growing slimmer and shapelier. It involves a diet—the only way to lose pounds is to take in fewer calories. It involves exercise—the most effective way to slough off inches is by toning muscles. But this plan has a third ingredient, which supplies what most plans lack—a feeling of comfort and well-being while you lose. The secret: a half-hour nap every afternoon. Your first reaction may be one of disbelief. You've probably always heard that sleeping puts *on* weight, but this is not true—nothing adds weight except eating. What rest can do for most people is reduce the compulsion to eat. Tired and tense, you feel you *need* the midmorning pastry or midafternoon sandwich for energy to keep going; rested and relaxed, you're less likely to want it. Perhaps a nap seems out of the question—you could never find the time, or you couldn't fall asleep in the middle of the day. These are common problems; but often, both can be solved. Some women may choose a time while the children are in school or while the baby, too, naps. Others may enlist the cooperation of another family member or exchange services with a neighbor. It may mean cutting down on the time you spend over coffee in the morning or perusing the newspaper, so your work gets done a little earlier. It will certainly take some juggling, and it won't be a cinch for most women, who are pretty overwhelmed with household chores; but for many, we believe it can be managed. As for your imagined inability to fall asleep, that can be remedied. The exercises on pages 78 to 81 should relax and just pleasantly tire your body, and the yawning trick described on page 80 is near magic. (No reason you shouldn't use it at night, too.) We know it's easy to prepare all sorts of plans and assume, impractically, that all women have the time to follow them. But we feel this plan has such special merit that we hope it can be tried out by a majority of our readers. Here's what we propose: At a given time each afternoon, muffle the telephone, and retire to your bedroom. Spend about twenty minutes doing the nonstrenuous exercises, and be sure to do them in order. Then pull down the shades; go through the yawning routine; and sleep or, at least, doze for the balance of the hour. Practice this for one week; at the end of that time, we predict you'll be noticeably slimmer and prettier, and you will have no gnawing hunger pangs as you follow the diet on page 192.

MCCALL'S BEAUTY DEPARTMENT / MIRIAM GIBSON FRENCH, EDITOR / NORMA CRAIG, ASSOCIATE / JOAN SANGER, ASSISTANT

One shouldn't use *a device simply because it's in fashion. Perhaps it takes even more courage to use a visual cliché, but to use it so very well. Perhaps the measure of how well it is used, of its communication effectiveness, is how well it fits the specific message and how well it is executed. Here, after years of shaping type blocks to pictures, is one of the very best. By Otto Storch for* McCall's.

position at the school, in the advanced program for foreigners, where he still teaches.

Although Weingart had associated with Ruder, Hofmann and Josef Müller-Brockmann, he found that the typography they taught had become too refined, too pervasive. He was 27 when he joined the Basel faculty and felt a need to revitalize typographic design. He replaced disciplined rationality with an expressiveness reminiscent of El Lissitzky and Piet Zwart. He rejected the right angle as the organizing device; he replaced grid or scientific-mathematically oriented division of space and positioning of elements with subjective, intuitive thinking. He challenged such typographic traditions as paragraph indentions. He did not hesitate to change type weights in the middle of a word. He would emphasize a word by reversing it into a black rectangle in the middle of a line. While others were setting type tightly, he letterspaced it widely.

Weingart modulated and warped type by overexposing, scratching and defacing it until it would be hardly legible. He juxtaposed images and textures, and used moiré patterns and enlarged halftone dots while others were trying to conceal both. He mixed type and tints with photography. He juxtaposed pictures in different scales, while others tried to maintain scale. What was he up to?

He felt that people were being bored by the spiritless orderliness of much work. He wanted to shock typographics to life. He seemed to agree with the Spanish painter, Francisco Goya, who had said, "Vitality! Ideal proportion and classical beauty be damned!"

Weingart's teachings have spread around the world as his students carried his thinking and his spirit back to their countries and as he traveled abroad. But he did not simply throw out all he learned about Swiss typography. In his own words, "Through my teaching, I set out to use the positive qualities of Swiss typography as a base from which to pursue radically new typographic frontiers.

"I try to teach students to view typography from all angles: type must not always be set flush left/ragged right, nor in only two type sizes, nor in necessarily right-angle arrangements, nor printed in either black or red. Typography must not be dry, tightly ordered or rigid. Type may be set center axis, ragged left/ragged right, perhaps sometimes in a chaos. But even then, typography should have a hidden structure and visual order."

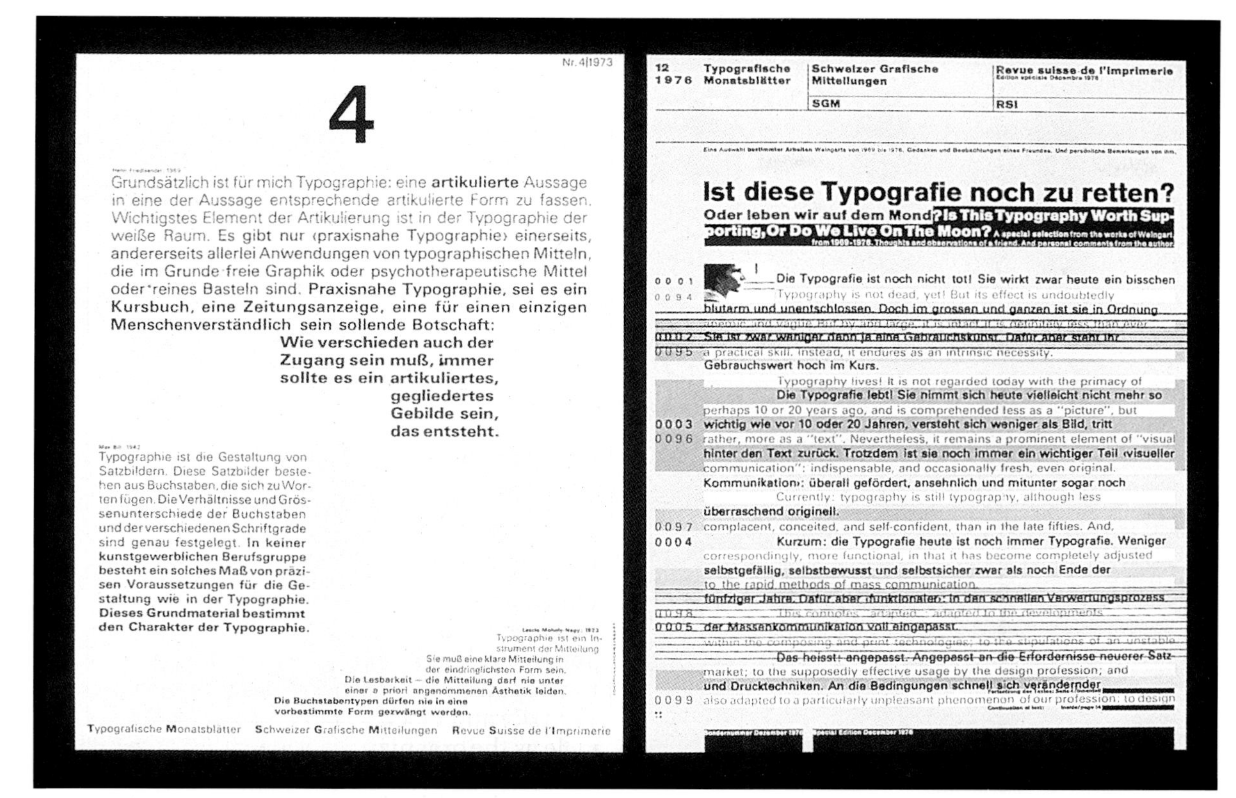

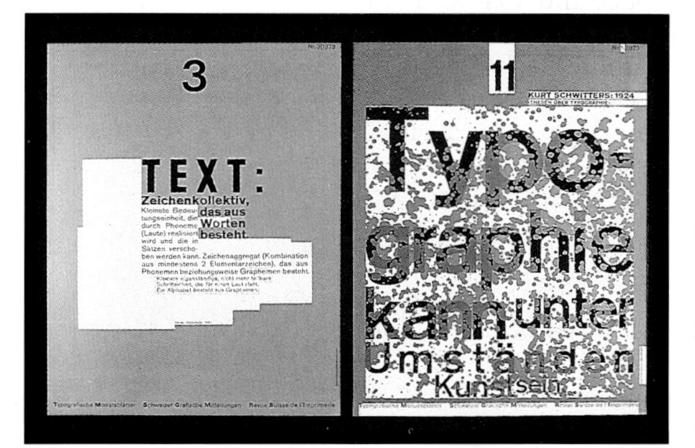

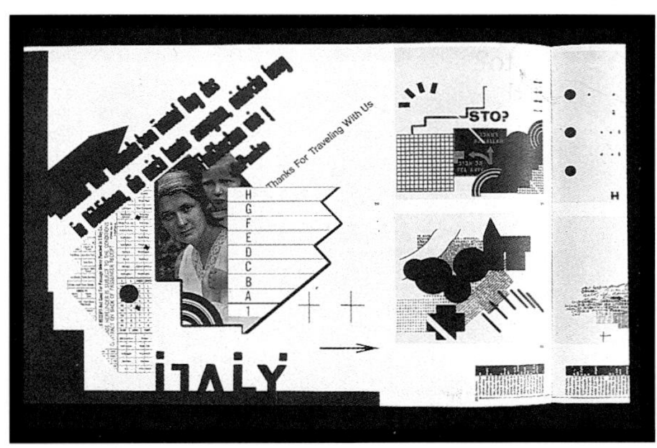

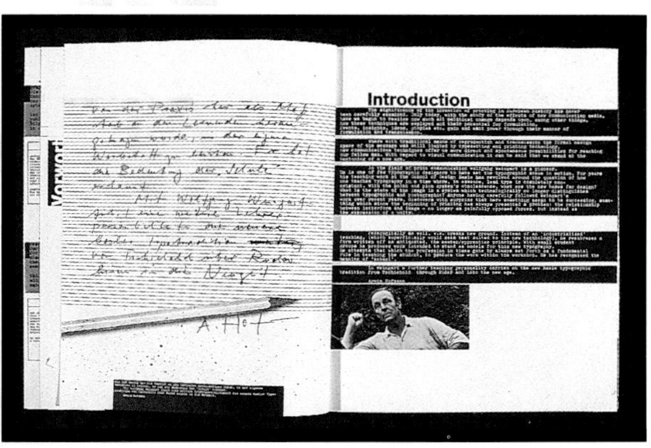

***Weingart's** work reflects his playful, inquisitive, experimental temperament and his strong reaction against classical Swiss typography. Six examples of his work are shown above.*

Wolfgang Weingart.

April Greiman

April Greiman, who studied with Wolfgang Weingart in Basel, blended some of his ideas with her own, and from her Los Angeles studio creates dynamic, intricate typographic designs. She brings a sense of depth to her graphics. Perspective is implied by overlapping elements and diagonal lines, and forms that throw shadows on other forms. Angled type is used with a mixture of illustrations, photography, and objects. The term "new wave" seems strange when applied to her

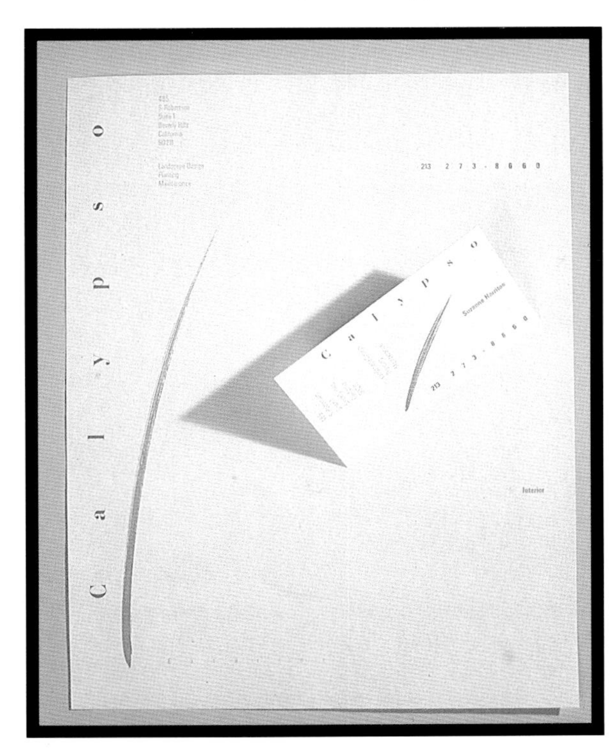

***Calypso** letterhead. April Greiman.*

Chapter XIII: The Many Faces of Typography Today

"Typographic design not only attracts but selects an audience."

California *Drop Cloth letterhead.*

California Institute *of the Arts bulletin, theater page.*

California Institute *of the Arts view book.*

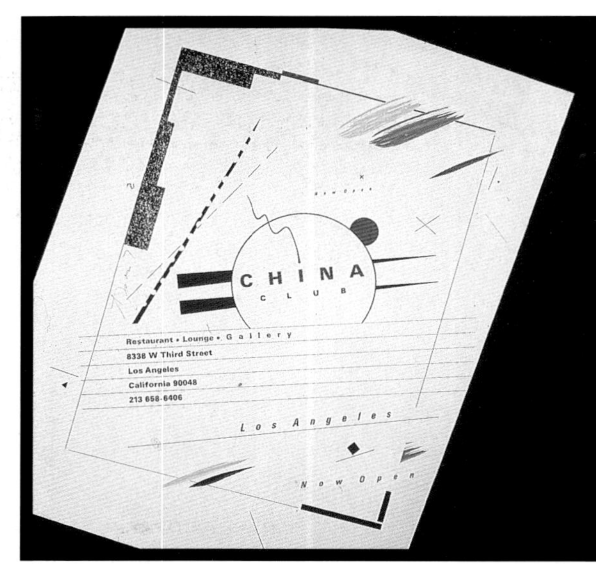

China Club, *ad.*

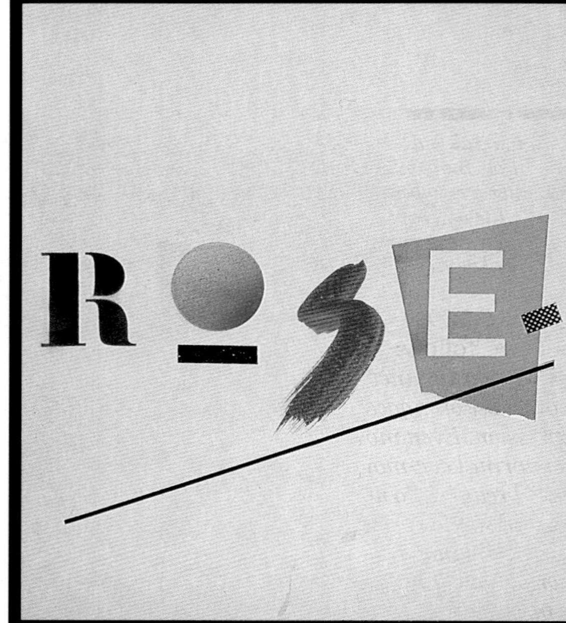

Logo *for Rose.*

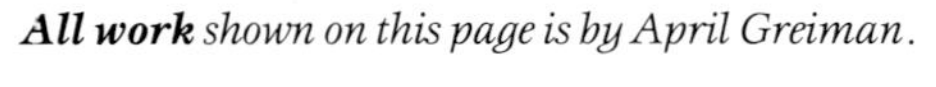

All work *shown on this page is by April Greiman.*

work and that of her followers. She handles typographic space much as El Lissitzky manipulated space in his Proun paintings. She uses textures, ruled lines, enlarged halftone screens and other long-existing graphic forms.

There are those who feel this is new and fresh when compared to the more conservative, orderly designs that abound today. Some feel it therefore is more of a standout and that once the viewer's eye has been captured, the handling and positioning of the elements moves the reader's eye along a design-suggested path. There are many other personal design approaches today, and they are

California Institute *of the Arts poster.*

the eye of a storm over whether they are truly effective communication vehicles or whether they confuse and compete with the message. It is suggested that one appraise such pieces individually, avoid generalizing, and try to understand the message/communication problem before evaluating the design.

It is not coincidence that alongside what some call punk typography we have punk clothing, punk films, punk music, punk illustration. Certainly, they bring energy and even shock to our eyes, our ears, our minds, and our spirit. Will they endure? What is their real value? What will they lead to? Presumed sages disagree when evaluating these movements. Bear in mind too that typographic design not only attracts but selects an audience. It is the responsibility of the buyer of design, where possible, to choose a designer in tune with the message and the audience. New wave design is intuitive and playful, subjective, often eccentric. These characteristics are neither good nor bad in themselves. How they are applied and how appropriate the design is to the message problem are the prime considerations.

Phrased Typography

Jan Tschichold's advocacy of asymmetric typography was concerned with attaining even color in text lines and blocks, in enlivening design while retaining order and clarity, and to improve both the beauty and readability of printed matter.

In more recent decades various designers have advocated what some called "thought unit typography" and others called "phrased typography."

By whatever name, its purpose was to make reading easier and more pleasant by breaking lines for sense or for reading rhythm, or for both where possible.

A cadenced form of the New Testament was designed by Morton C. Bradley. The original text is unchanged, but lines break at rhythmic points or at the end of a thought. This edition of the Bible was published by The Bradley Press, Arlington, Massachusetts. Compare the following cadenced and conventional settings from Saint Luke's account of the temptation of Jesus, and see for yourself how readability is eased. (See above right.)

AND Jesus, being full of the Holy Ghost, returned from Jordan, and was led by the Spirit into the wilderness, 2 Being forty days tempted of the devil. And in those days he did eat nothing: and when they were ended, he afterward hungered. 3 And the devil said unto him, If thou be the Son of God, command this stone that it be made bread. 4 And Jesus answered him, saying, It is written, That man shall not live by bread alone, but by every word of God. 5 And the devil, taking him up into an high mountain, showed unto him all the kingdoms of the world in a moment of time. 6 And the devil said unto him, All this power will I give thee, and the glory of them: for that is delivered unto me; and to whomsoever I will I give it. 7 If thou therefore wilt worship me, all shall be thine. 8 And Jesus answered and said unto him, Get thee behind me, Satan: for it is written, Thou shalt worship the Lord thy God, and him only shalt thou serve. 9 And he brought him to Jerusalem, and set him on a pinnacle of the temple, and said unto him, If thou be the Son of God, cast thyself down from hence: 10 For it is written, He shall give his angels charge over thee, to keep thee; 11 And in their hands they shall bear thee up, lest at any time thou dash thy foot against a stone. 12 And Jesus answering said unto him, It is said, Thou shalt not tempt the Lord thy God. 13 And when the devil had ended all the temptation, he departed from him for a season.

And Jesus, being full of the Holy Ghost, returned from Jordan,
and was led by the Spirit into the wilderness,
being forty days tempted of the devil.
And in those days he did eat nothing;
and when they were ended, he afterward hungered.

And the devil said unto him,
If thou be the Son of God,
command this stone that it be made bread.
And Jesus answered him, saying,
It is written that
Man shall not live by bread alone,
but by every word of God.

And the devil, taking him up into an high mountain,
showed unto him all the kingdoms of the world in a moment of time;
and the devil said unto him,
All this power will I give thee, and the glory of them,
for that is delivered unto me,
and to whomsoever I will, I give it.
If thou, therefore, wilt worship me,
all shall be thine.
And Jesus answered and said unto him,
Get thee behind me, Satan;
for it is written,
Thou shalt worship the Lord thy God,
and him only shalt thou serve.

And he brought him to Jerusalem,
and set him on a pinnacle of the temple,
and said unto him,
If thou be the Son of God,
cast thyself down from hence;
for it is written,
He shall give his angels charge over thee to keep thee,
and in their hands they shall bear thee up,
lest at any time thou dash thy foot against a stone.
And Jesus, answering, said unto him,
It is said,
Thou shalt not tempt the Lord thy God.

And when the devil had ended all the temptation,
he departed from him for a season.

***Conventional** and cadenced typesetting compared. Obviously, the cadenced version takes more space, is less economical, and is not for every job. But sometimes the improved readability justifies extra costs. Copy that is easier to read is more likely to be more widely read, better remembered and understood, and more favorably received.*

Other attempts to break lines for sense or rhythm include Square Span and Spaced Unit Typography. The former put thought units, even if they were not complete sentences, into small blocks. Spaced Unit Typography added word spacing within the line to create slight visual pauses at strategic points.

A strong advocate of ragged right typography with lines broken for sense was Max Huber. He spoke about this at the Type Directors Club 1958 world seminar, held at Silvermine, Connecticut. He said:

The typographic character today
should be employed with freedom
and nonchalance
and the same ease
with which American girl typists
handle their typewriters.
With this ease
and a sense of function,
they line up their text
on the left hand side of the page,
spacing only paragraphs,
just as Max Bill used to do.
Personally, I believe
that when the word falls at the end of the line,
it should not be separated.
A new line should be started
without breaks,
with simplicity
and a free ragged right composition.
Furthermore,
line lengths should vary
according to the meaning of the text.

Flush left and flush right (justified) typography causes many problems, including white spots scattered in a copy block and bad word breaks.

Some opinions on this subject, expressed in *Typographic Directions,* published by Art Direction Book Co., follow:

❧ *"...the main function of type is to be read...I think an overdose of ragged lines makes for a haphazard impression. Even more important, they play tricks with normal eye-movements. Studies show that experienced readers do not read one line at a time, but two, and sometimes three. Ragged right composition makes this kind of reading difficult and thus slows down speed of absorption. I wonder if the end justifies the means?"*
Stephen Baker, Baker & Byrne, Inc. New York.

❧ *"I think the concept is intellectually rational, but in operation has to live within a context of prior tradition, association, and experience on the part of the reader."*
Saul Bass, Los Angeles, California.

❧ *"To end each line where a thought ends or where a break of the line is logical I believe will ease reading."*
Herbert Bayer, Aspen, Colorado.

❧ *"...this is not primarily a typographical problem ...I agree with the notion of thought-unit composition but it is difficult to treat a text like this... Thought-unit composition needs more preliminary work from the writer. The visual rhythm must correspond with the cadence of words and their meaning. Not any text can be done this way. It needs a significant, if not to say poetical, language."*
Max Bill, Zürich.

❧ *"Flush left, ragged right typography versus justified setting, i.e.: flush left-flush right, is a subject that cannot be spoken of in general terms. Each solution to a problem will be governed by the problem itself; thus the layout of the typography of any one problem cannot be covered by an overall formula.*

This is an example	**of the square span**	**style of presentation**

Square Span

This is an example of the spaced unit style of presentation

Spaced Unit Typography

"However, we can speak in general terms about this kind of setting. First of all, it is obvious that for simple presentation of reading matter, a 'justified' block of text is simpler to read and possibly more pleasing to the eye than is ragged copy. This is probably due to the fact that we are more accustomed to reading text from a square page format, and have come to think of everything within that page as being arranged on a square module.

"From the purely esthetic point of view, setting type to a justified measure flush left and flush right always creates the problem of uneven word spacing. Whether or not this is objectionable depends on the size of type used, the type face and the width of the measure. The wider the measure, the less the problem of space between words is likely to occur, but the more difficult it becomes for the eye to retain a line over too long a length. There is no rule about when a line is too long...for this again must consider the size and nature of the type face.

"The case in favor of flush left, ragged right setting, rests chiefly on an esthetic factor, the evenness of color that occurs because of the ability to maintain a fixed amount of space between each word..."
Aaron Burns, New York.

TYPOGRAPHIC COMMUNICATIONS TODAY

Chapter XIII: The Many Faces of Typography Today

"The overriding consideration in good typography, which means readable typography, is legibility."

❧ *"Thought-unit typography is a good idea but it will never see the light of day except in brochure or jobbing printing where space is not a consideration. For normal book or continuous reading copy it would cost too much to produce. Remember, all the spaces have to be keyboarded. Remember also the additional amount of paper involved. You might be surprised to find how many people already use this method in commercial printing."*
Allan R. Fleming, Toronto.

❧ *"...sense of the copy and the goal of maximum reader understanding are vital questions. However, the question of thought-unit typography is one which is a literary rather than a typographic design problem.*

"In short copy or in headlines there is no question that thought-unit typography is not only useful but desirable and can be handled by designers. In longer text, thought considerations would be primarily the writer's problem and not the designer's. Thought-unit typography requires literary interpretation and I doubt that there are many designers who are capable of solving such problems.

"The overriding consideration in good typography, which means readable typography, is legibility. What is principally involved here as far as the designer is concerned is the proper selection of a typeface, proper word spacing, proper line spacing, the relation of type to paper, the relation of the size of type to the width of the line, and the relation of the size of type to the size of the format."
Paul Rand, Weston, Connecticut.

❧ *"The need is urgent – Yes, I am for 'thought-unit' typography. There was never a greater need for it as today. – In our time, life is governed by 'speed and intensity.' We travel faster, we produce faster, we also must communicate faster. All of the conventional and other non-functional visual design approaches prove inadequate when tested by the new need to speak to the mind rapidly. To fill this gap, new visual means to communicate directly has to come to speed up and to intensify comprehension. – Evaluated in this context, a dynamic concept of 'thought-unit' composition may open these avenues of approach to setting of text which suggest new potentials and refreshing discoveries in the typographic design aiming at fast perception...*

"'Thought-unit' typography must be planned – In order to achieve the desired impact and clarity of the text, the writing for 'thought-unit' setting must be planned from the beginning. – This means that the writer should not only master the techniques of type fitting for the clearly coined single or double line 'thought-units,' but it also requires that he should think in terms of an effective control over the continuity of a sequence of many lines, that, when set from type, must lead smoothly one into another. – In every task at hand, a sound 'thought-unit' typography planning implies control of visual flow. Such control may be accomplished only by integration of all 'thought-units' for the most efficient and continuous transmission of information."
Ladislav Sutnar, New York.

❧ *"Ragged right composition has been in my mind for many years. After some experimenting I found it far from foolproof. The good point about traditional composition is that it does not interfere between author and reader. Its lapses from logic are compensated for by general acceptance and do not draw as much attention as temperamental excursions into thought-unit writing might provoke. I have no craving to see Dickens, Balzac, or even Faulkner dissected into arbitrary showpieces, however memorable... on the other hand, advertising has everything to gain from any new approach to freedom... The notion of units might go a long way towards a clearer comprehension... but this calls for talent which is not evenly nor universally distributed."*
Maximilien Vox, Paris.

❧ *"I am in favor of thought-unit composition for advertising copy for two reasons:*
(a) Pungent copy, well loaded with meaning, needs and deserves the help of this 'little at a time' treatment, and
(b) feeble copy deserves the mortal punishment which thought-unit administers to it.

"Technically it is 'verse,' in the old original sense of the word. That is, something concentrated is offered as an entity (a 'line by itself') so that the reader can, so to speak, taste and swallow before consciously reversing his eye-movement. He then starts the next line-event with just enough sense of freshness to keep his attention taut...

"Apart from poetry, however, you have respectable precedents. Catholic and Anglican writers sometimes use the thought-unit style as a way of driving points home to readers who are too likely to slide over them.

"Any intensely written text, from high poetry to hard-sell copy, may benefit by being broken up by its author *into discrete lines..."*
Beatrice Warde, Epsom, England.

It is obvious from a reading of the above comments on thought-unit typography that typographers and writers all over the world and for many centuries have been concerned with the relationship of typographic design to communication understanding, emphasis, and retention.

It is equally obvious that there is no pat solution. But as the amount of money put into advertising grows, and as those who o.k. advertising and promotion budgets increasingly press for measured results, efforts will intensify to make every element of the ad contribute to its communication effectiveness.

A most fascinating and successful application of phrased typography appears in the Washburn Bible designed by Bradbury Thompson.

Mr. Thompson explains this use of phrased typography as follows:

"This NEW BIBLE, a Modern Phrased Version of the King James text, represents a new high in combining beauty and holiness. Here is beauty in thought enhanced by beauty in pictures and typography. This edition introduces the most revolutionary typographic concept in Biblical publishing since Johannes Gutenberg. It is most readable and understandable and brings beauty to the eye as well as to the mind and spirit. The setting of type is directed, not to rigid regularity in length of line and column, not to one person's notion of what makes a pleasing ragged right but rather to the rounding out of sentences and phrases so that the eye readily perceives and the voice readily conveys the meaning.

"Phrased typography facilitates reading out loud. No words are hyphenated at the ends of lines. Spacing between letters and words is consistent. Computer-controlled phototypesetting fits letters and punctuation marks more perfectly than is feasible with metal type. Although many of the typographic refinements are so minute as to be imperceptible to the average reader, the total creates a visual grace suited to the majesty of the text. The phrased typography also creates a cadence in the mind of the reader and literally makes reading a musical experience."

Contemporary Graphics Worldwide

Much beautiful and highly effective visual communication design is being produced today all over the world. Just as design excellence is not restricted to a particular style, so it is not confined to any one country or part of the world, as the examples illustrated in this chapter of TYPOGRAPHIC COMMUNICATIONS TODAY prove.

In his wonderful book, *Top Graphic Design,* British designer and design educator, F.H.K. Henrion, takes a look at the past several decades' work by designer members of the Alliance Graphique Internationale to survey recent design directions. He notes that in the 1940s we spoke of *commercial art.* By the 1960s the umbrella term for our area of concern was *graphic design.* Today we speak of *visual communication,* and communication effectiveness.

Genesis

1:1 In the beginning
God created the heaven and the earth.
2 And the earth was without form, and void;
and darkness was upon the face of the deep.
And the Spirit of God
moved upon the face of the waters.

3 And God said,
Let there be light:
and there was light.
4 And God saw the light, that it was good:
and God divided the light from the darkness.
5 And God called the light Day,
and the darkness he called Night.
And the evening and the morning
were the first day.

6 And God said,
Let there be a firmament
in the midst of the waters,
and let it divide the waters from the waters.
7 And God made the firmament,
and divided the waters
which were under the firmament
from the waters
which were above the firmament:
and it was so.
8 And God called the firmament Heaven.
And the evening and the morning
were the second day.

9 And God said,
Let the waters under the heaven
be gathered together unto one place,
and let the dry land appear:
and it was so.
10 And God called the dry land Earth;
and the gathering together of the waters
called he Seas:
and God saw that it was good.
11 And God said,
Let the earth bring forth grass,
the herb yielding seed,
and the fruit tree yielding fruit after his kind,
whose seed is in itself, upon the earth:
and it was so.
12 And the earth brought forth grass,
and herb yielding seed after his kind,
and the tree yielding fruit,
whose seed was in itself, after his kind:
and God saw that it was good.

***The entire** King James text of this Bible is set in lines of varying length, each a complete phrase, just as the words might be spoken. Text is set in 14 point Sabon Antiqua roman. Bradbury Thompson.*

This is not merely a semantic game. Graphic designers and art directors are still graphic designers and art directors. But today we "have... a much greater awareness of the process of communication and of visual perception; we also have a greater understanding of the different target publics to whom our messages are addressed. We know more about structure, theory and methodology on the one hand, and the mechanics of intuitive creativity on the other. Modules, grids and systems are all essential ingredients of the design process but they need not be used at the expense of intuition rather than in conjunction with it."

With these thoughts in mind let's look at some of the outstanding graphic designs over the past 40 or so years and from all around the world.

SWITZERLAND

The influence of Swiss designers and Swiss schools of design was reviewed in Chapter VI of TYPOGRAPHIC COMMUNICATIONS TODAY. The grid system, the emphasis on clarity and order in typographic design is still very much alive today and throughout the world. But the Swiss influence does not end there. Such designers and teachers as Wolfgang Weingart, Siegfried Odermatt and Rosemarie Tissi; Fritz Gottschalk, Hans Rudolf Bosshard, and Hans-Rudolf Lutz, to name just a few, as well as Karl Gerstner, Armin Hofmann, and Josef Müller-Brockmann who continue to design and to teach, are keeping the Basel-Zürich area a most influential center of graphic design. Some of their work, such as that of Wolfgang Weingart, shown earlier in this chapter, seems a radical departure from the earlier focus on graphic simplicity and obvious orderliness. Other work, notably that of the studio of Odermatt and Tissi, represents a brilliant blend of typographics with flare and clarity, with beauty and impact and readability.

Odermatt and Tissi

Siegfried Odermatt opened his design studio in Zürich in 1950 at the age of 24. He had studied photography and worked in photographic studios and advertising agencies. A self-educated graphic designer who did not study under the typographic designers at Switzerland's design schools, it is not surprising that he was one of the first to depart from their strictures. He blended the clear and effective presentation style of his contemporaries with dramatic use of color, imaginative cropping and lighting of photographs, and a fresh way of positioning graphic elements, and of dividing the space on a page or a spread. His work was

"A playful approach to typographic design with a respect for the message."

and is playful and uninhibited and represents the first significant departure from the International Typographic Style, as the Swiss grid approach came to be known.

In the early 1960s Rosemarie Tissi joined the studio and in 1968 became a partner. Tissi also couples a playful approach to typographic design with a respect for the message. She does not allow the message to be upstaged by the graphics. Richard Paul Lohse has described their work as "purposeful aesthetics."

Where grid typographic designs reduce graphic elements to those essential to an orderly presentation of a message, Odermatt and Tissi add, combine, build up elements to achieve drama, or power, or humor, or a mood that will enhance the message.

Writing in *Graphis 241,* Wolfgang Weingart cites two main streams in today's Swiss graphic design: the orthodox and the innovators. "Odermatt and Tissi," he writes, "have always been counted among the innovators. Their handwriting influenced the Swiss in the late fifties, the sixties, and well into the seventies... [it was] always a little more inventive, more imaginative, and above all, more subtle."

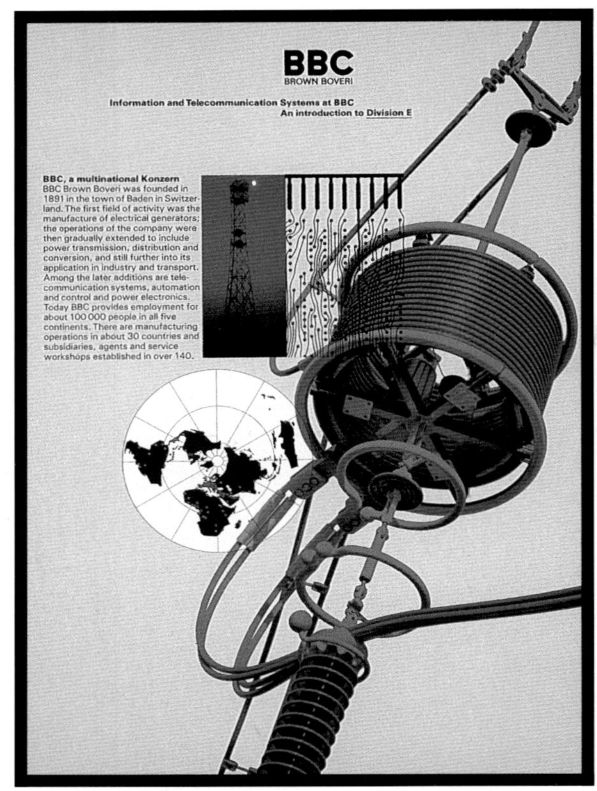

One of a series *of product information sheets for* BBC *Brown Boveri, manufacturer of electrical generators, power transmission equipment, telecommunication systems, automation and control and power electronics. Odermatt & Tissi.*

Poster project *for Prime Computer AG, Zürich. The figure 1 from the Prime logotype is used as a company symbol. Note the use of the figure 1 in place of the letter "i" in the word "Prime." Odermatt & Tissi.*

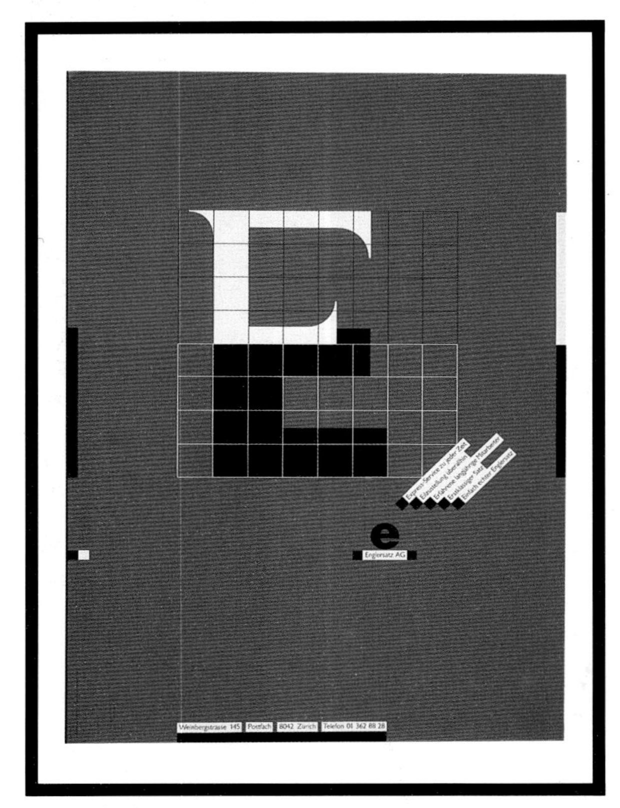

Poster *for the German Poster Museum in Essen announcing the 1985 exhibition of the Type Directors Club of New York. Odermatt & Tissi.*

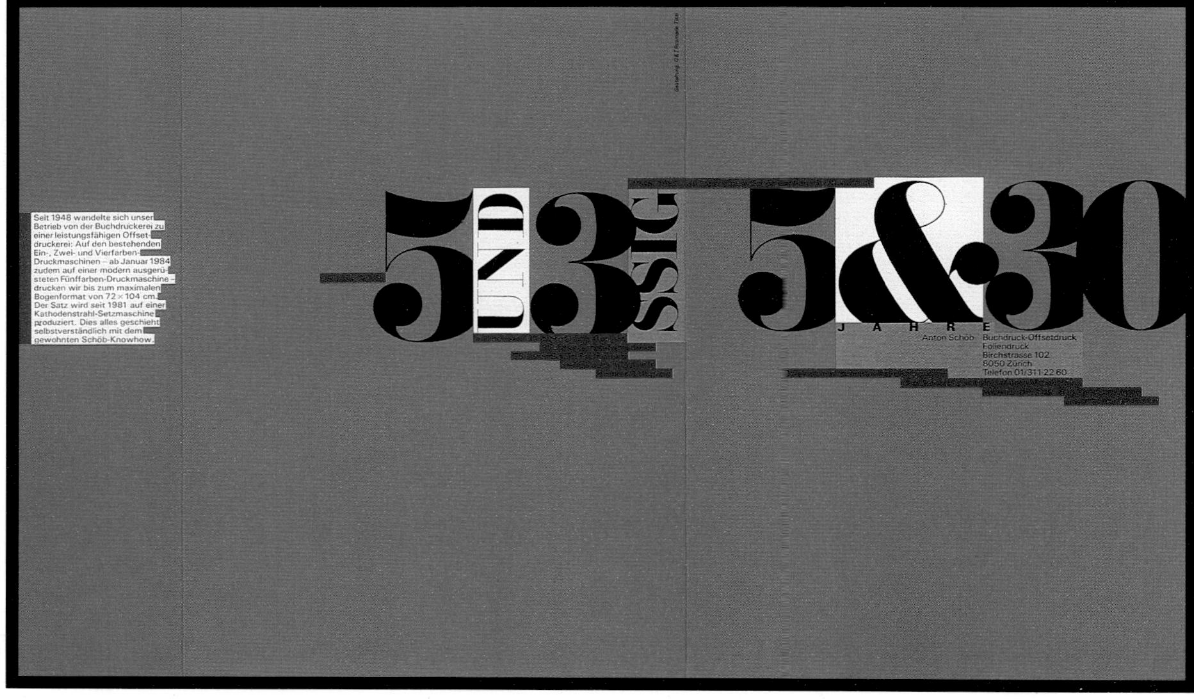

A portfolio cover *for sample of printing by the firm of Buchdruck-Offsetdruck Anton Schob. Odermatt & Tissi.*

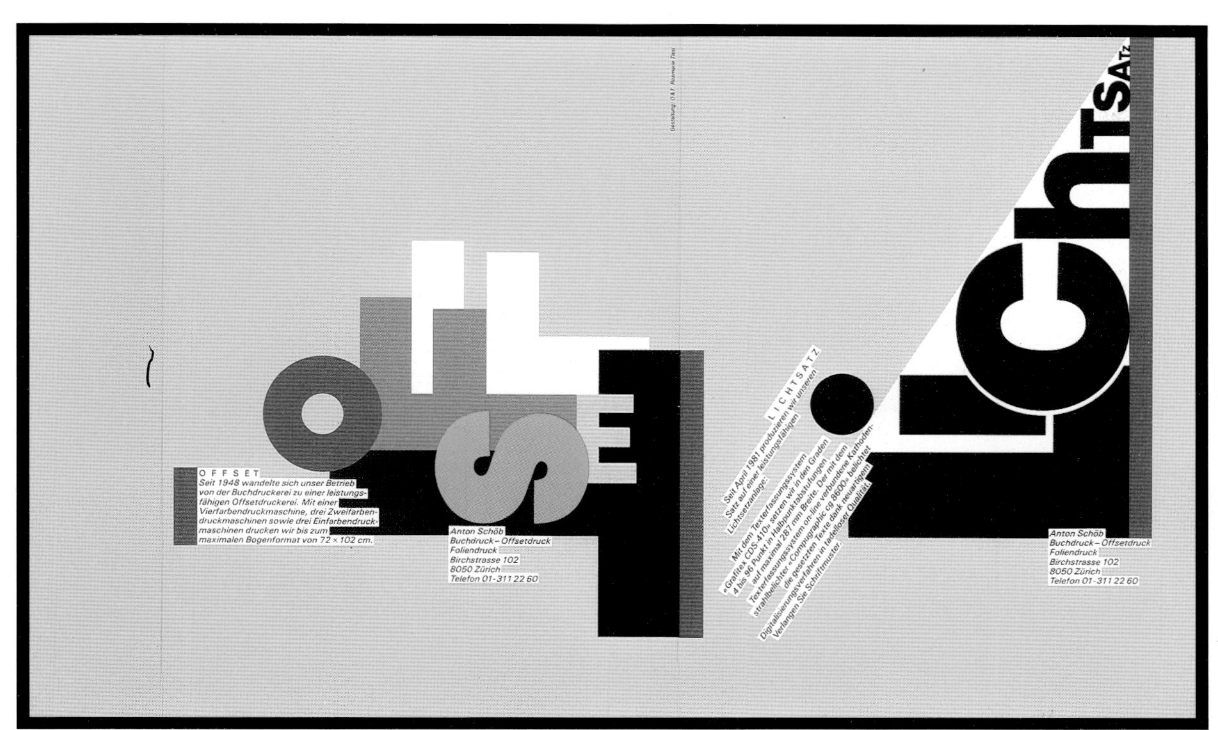

◀ ***A portfolio cover*** *for sample of printing by the firm of Buchdruck-Offsetdruck Anton Schob. Odermatt & Tissi.*

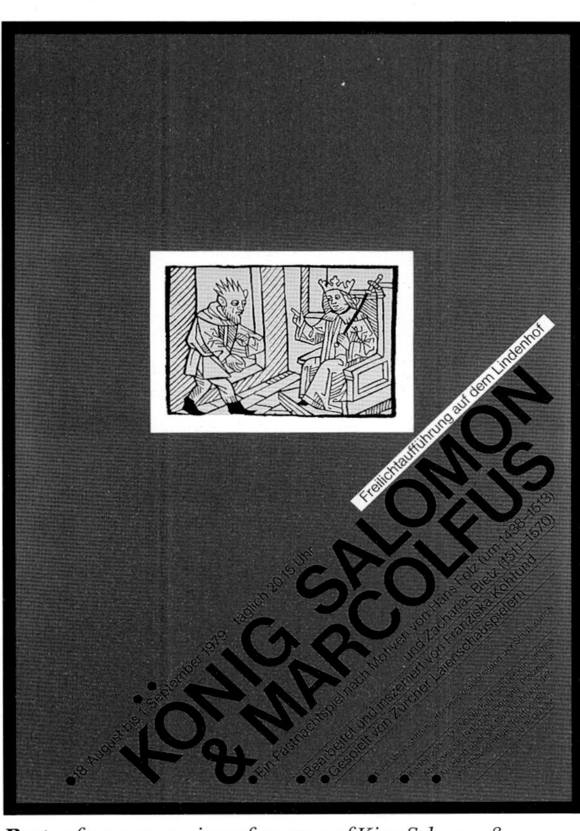

Poster *for an open-air performance of King Solomon & Marcolfus. The woodcut is from the era when the play was written. Odermatt & Tissi.*

Concert poster. *The central motif is an emblem designed for the theater. Odermatt & Tissi.*

Poster *for an exhibition of "Design from the Netherlands." The colors and form of the Dutch flag were used as an eye-catcher. Odermatt & Tissi.*

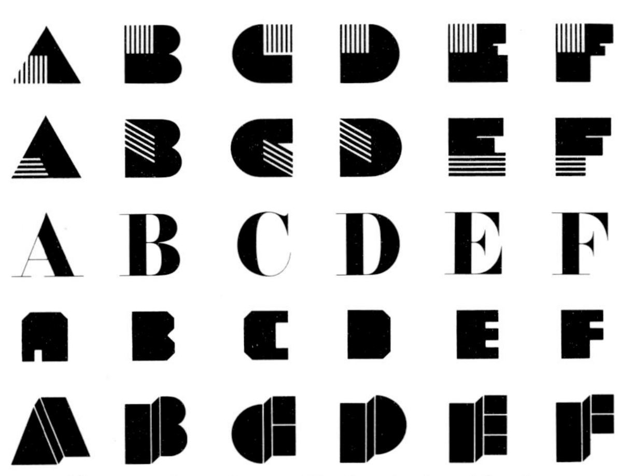

Headline typefaces *Sonora, Sinaloa, Antiqua Classica, Marabu and Mindanao, by Odermatt & Tissi.*

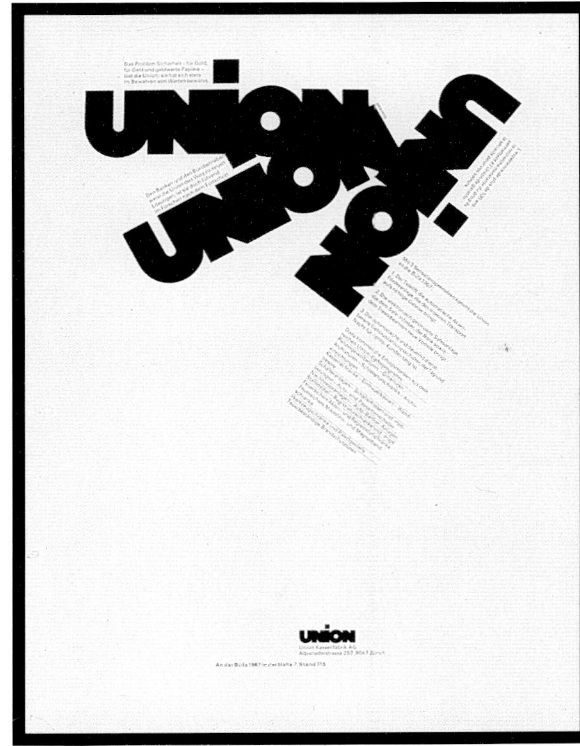

Newspaper advertisement *announcing the opening of a business equipment exhibition. Odermatt & Tissi.*

Hans-Rudolf Lutz

Typografische Monatsblätter, better known as TM, celebrated its 100th year as the verbal and visual voice of typographic design in 1981. TM is at once thoughtful and scholarly, yet visually vigorous and refreshing. It is a marvelous mirror of both the tried and true and the exciting and new. Rudolf Hostettler of St. Gallen was the editor of TM for many years. His contribution to typography during the 1950s and 1960s was significant.

Over the years, special issues of TM have been devoted to such typographic pioneers and leaders as Emil Ruder, Piet Zwart, Karl Gerstner, Jan Tschichold, El Lissitzky, Odermatt and Tissi, and Wolfgang Weingart, and its covers were designed by the featured designers or were in tune with their typographics. In 1979 the covers of all 12 issues were designed by Hans-Rudolf Lutz. He considers these "the most important work I did in my design career."

Lutz considers design as information. A magazine cover is not merely an eye-catcher, its design is not merely a dress for the content. To Lutz content is expressed in form (design) as well as in words. When a cover design, or any graphic design, is conceived and executed with this attitude, communication effectiveness is enhanced. Each of the 1977 issues contains a message inside linking the cover treatment to the theme or major point of the issue. For example, for the December issue, a *Playboy*-like cover is used with the following comment inside:

"It is not only the title copy of a magazine cover

"Cover designs create anticipation of specific magazine content."

which gives us information about its identity; design and image are also important.

"For the cover of this issue of 'Typografische Monatsblätter' we have 'imitated' the typographic and graphic concept of the Playboy magazine, but inserted the text of 'Typografische Monatsblätter' instead of the Playboy logotype.

"If you still recognized the cover of Playboy magazine (and even possibly mistook it for Playboy at the first moment), this would be evidence that the information conveyed by the title design and image concept is at least as compelling as the information expressed in the title copy.

"Making us typographers and designers more aware of this effect is the first aim of the concept of the 1977 series of covers for 'Typografische Monatsblätter.'

"We have a second aim:

"To show that cover designs create anticipation of specific magazine content.

"Imagine we were selling the 'Typografische Monatsblätter' 1977 at news stands (instead of by subscription only as at present). Most of the buyers would feel cheated on getting 'Typografische Monatsblätter' (instead of Playboy). And this in spite of the actual verbal message on the cover giving a true indication of the content.

"This is evidence that we cannot understand verbal information without being influenced (even sometimes misled) by the visual context within which words are placed.

"People in the advertising business seem to be much more aware of this phenomenon than typographers and designers. Consumers are often the victims."

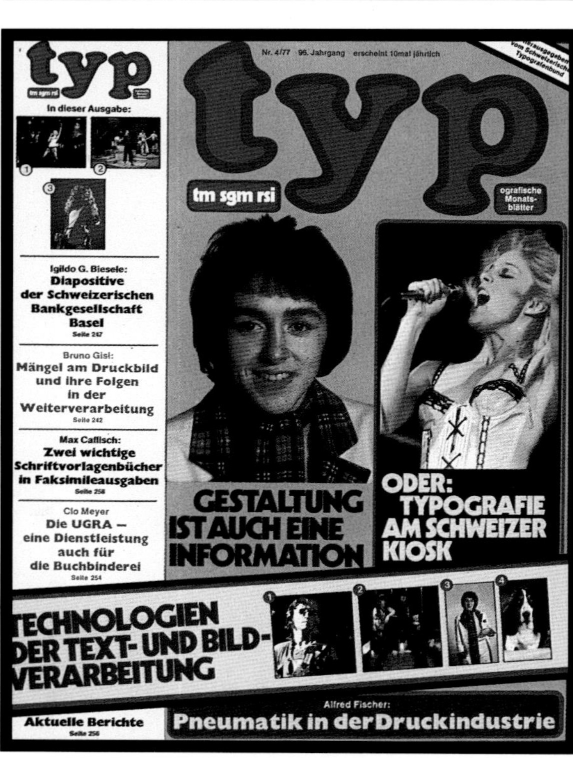

***Here are five** of Lutz's TM covers. If you consider these along with the work of Odermatt and Tissi, Wolfgang Weingart, and others whose work space does not permit us to show, you will realize that today Swiss typography, like typography in the United States, in Germany, in most countries, is not of one kind. It runs the gamut from the extremely conservative to the far out.*

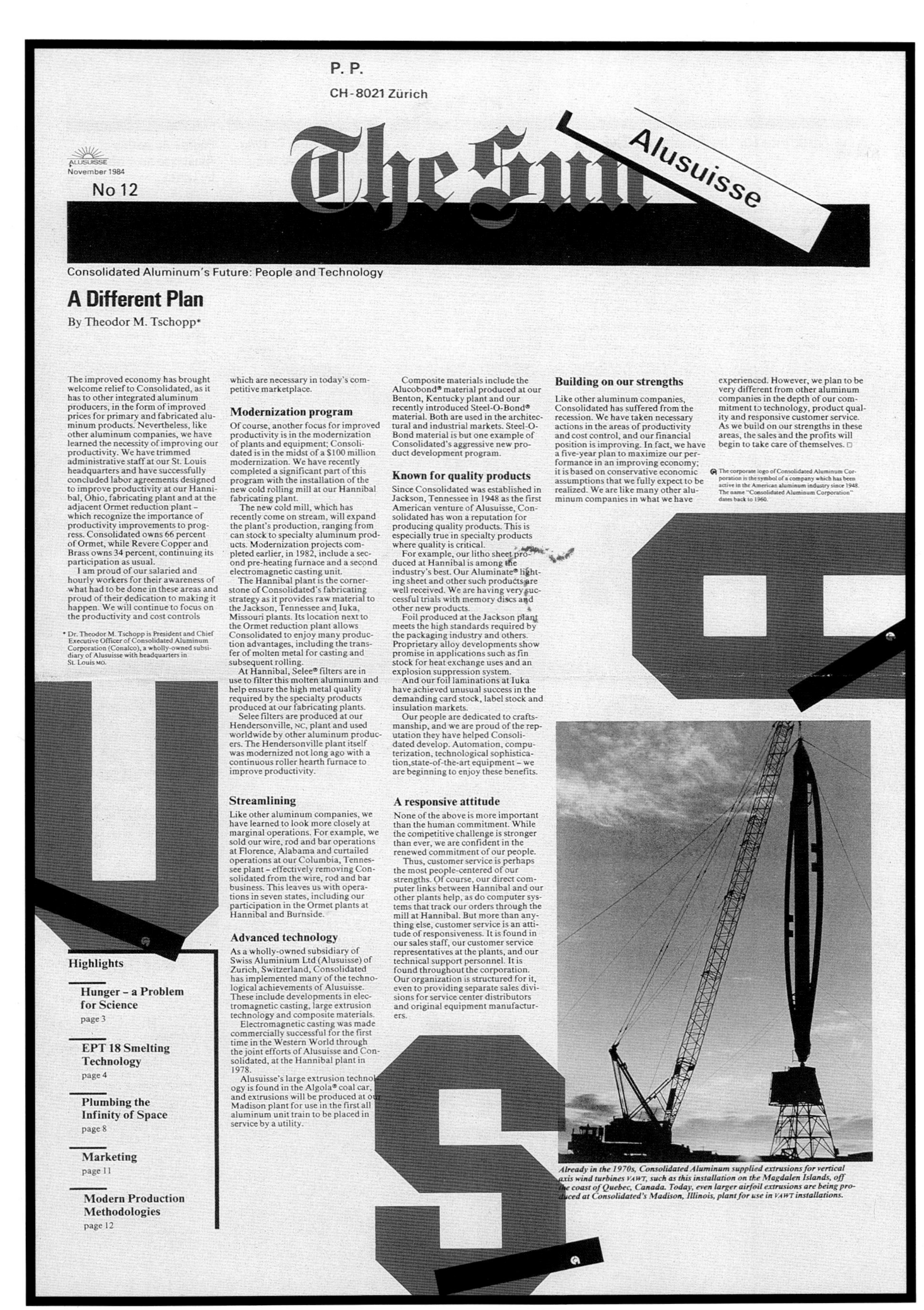

P. P.

CH-8021 Zürich

ALUSUISSE
November 1984

No 12

The Sun

Alusuisse

Consolidated Aluminum's Future: People and Technology

A Different Plan

By Theodor M. Tschopp*

The improved economy has brought welcome relief to Consolidated, as it has to other integrated aluminum producers, in the form of improved prices for primary and fabricated aluminum products. Nevertheless, like other aluminum companies, we have learned the necessity of improving our productivity. We have trimmed administrative staff at our St. Louis headquarters and have successfully concluded labor agreements designed to improve productivity at our Hannibal, Ohio, fabricating plant and at the adjacent Ormet reduction plant – which recognize the importance of productivity improvements to progress. Consolidated owns 66 percent of Ormet, while Revere Copper and Brass owns 34 percent, continuing its participation as usual.

I am proud of our salaried and hourly workers for their awareness of what had to be done in these areas and proud of their dedication to making it happen. We will continue to focus on the productivity and cost controls which are necessary in today's competitive marketplace.

Modernization program

Of course, another focus for improved productivity is in the modernization of plants and equipment; Consolidated is in the midst of a $100 million modernization. We have recently completed a significant part of this program with the installation of the new cold rolling mill at our Hannibal fabricating plant.

The new cold mill, which has recently come on stream, will expand the plant's production, ranging from can stock to specialty aluminum products. Modernization projects completed earlier, in 1982, include a second pre-heating furnace and a second electromagnetic casting unit.

The Hannibal plant is the cornerstone of Consolidated's fabricating strategy as it provides raw material to the Jackson, Tennessee and Iuka, Missouri plants. Its location next to the Ormet reduction plant allows Consolidated to enjoy many production advantages, including the transfer of molten metal for casting and subsequent rolling.

At Hannibal, Selee® filters are in use to filter this molten aluminum and help ensure the high metal quality required by the specialty products produced at our fabricating plants.

Selee filters are produced at our Hendersonville, NC, plant and used worldwide by other aluminum producers. The Hendersonville plant itself was modernized not long ago with a continuous roller hearth furnace to improve productivity.

Streamlining

Like other aluminum companies, we have learned to look more closely at marginal operations. For example, we sold our wire, rod and bar operations at Florence, Alabama and curtailed operations at our Columbia, Tennessee plant – effectively removing Consolidated from the wire, rod and bar business. This leaves us with operations in seven states, including our participation in the Ormet plants at Hannibal and Burnside.

Advanced technology

As a wholly-owned subsidiary of Swiss Aluminium Ltd (Alusuisse) of Zurich, Switzerland, Consolidated has implemented many of the technological achievements of Alusuisse. These include developments in electromagnetic casting, large extrusion technology and composite materials.

Electromagnetic casting was made commercially successful for the first time in the Western World through the joint efforts of Alusuisse and Consolidated, at the Hannibal plant in 1978.

Alusuisse's large extrusion technology is found in the Algola® coal car, and extrusions will be produced at our Madison plant for use in the first all aluminum unit train to be placed in service by a utility.

Composite materials include the Alucobond® material produced at our Benton, Kentucky plant and our recently introduced Steel-O-Bond® material. Both are used in the architectural and industrial markets. Steel-O-Bond material is but one example of Consolidated's aggressive new product development program.

Known for quality products

Since Consolidated was established in Jackson, Tennessee in 1948 as the first American venture of Alusuisse, Consolidated has won a reputation for producing quality products. This is especially true in specialty products where quality is critical.

For example, our litho sheet produced at Hannibal is among the industry's best. Our Aluminate® lighting sheet and other such products are well received. We are having very successful trials with memory discs and other new products.

Foil produced at the Jackson plant meets the high standards required by the packaging industry and others. Proprietary alloy developments show promise in applications such as fin stock for heat exchange uses and an explosion suppression system.

And our foil laminations at Iuka have achieved unusual success in the demanding card stock, label stock and insulation markets.

Our people are dedicated to craftsmanship, and we are proud of the reputation they have helped Consolidated develop. Automation, computerization, technological sophistication,state-of-the-art equipment – we are beginning to enjoy these benefits.

A responsive attitude

None of the above is more important than the human commitment. While the competitive challenge is stronger than ever, we are confident in the renewed commitment of our people.

Thus, customer service is perhaps the most people-centered of our strengths. Of course, our direct computer links between Hannibal and our other plants help, as do computer systems that track our orders through the mill at Hannibal. But more than anything else, customer service is an attitude of responsiveness. It is found in our sales staff, our customer service representatives at the plants, and our technical support personnel. It is found throughout the corporation. Our organization is structured for it, even to providing separate sales divisions for service center distributors and original equipment manufacturers.

Building on our strengths

Like other aluminum companies, Consolidated has suffered from the recession. We have taken necessary actions in the areas of productivity and cost control, and our financial position is improving. In fact, we have a five-year plan to maximize our performance in an improving economy; it is based on conservative economic assumptions that we fully expect to be realized. We are like many other aluminum companies in what we have experienced. However, we plan to be very different from other aluminum companies in the depth of our commitment to technology, product quality and responsive customer service. As we build on our strengths in these areas, the sales and the profits will begin to take care of themselves. □

* Dr. Theodor M. Tschopp is President and Chief Executive Officer of Consolidated Aluminum Corporation (Conalco), a wholly-owned subsidiary of Alusuisse with headquarters in St. Louis MO.

The corporate logo of Consolidated Aluminum Corporation is the symbol of a company which has been active in the American aluminum industry since 1948. The name "Consolidated Aluminum Corporation" dates back to 1960.

Already in the 1970s, Consolidated Aluminum supplied extrusions for vertical axis wind turbines VAWT, such as this installation on the Magdalen Islands, off the coast of Quebec, Canada. Today, even larger airfoil extrusions are being produced at Consolidated's Madison, Illinois, plant for use in VAWT installations.

Highlights

A fascinating blend *of lively yet orderly presentation by Gottschalk & Ash International, Zürich. This is page one of a tabloid newspaper format publication,* The Sun. *It is published by Alusuisse Information Services of Swiss Aluminium Ltd. The publication name and the large letters A, U, and S are in a dull orange color.*

Pierre Mendell/Klaus Oberer *designed this advertisement for Parke Davis & Co. 1963.*

FEDERAL REPUBLIC OF GERMANY

Graphic design, a major force in communications, no longer has national attributes. Like typographics in other countries, many styles now thrive. One can see there the influences of Swiss geometrics and of the more uninhibited graphics done in Switzerland and in the United States.

In 1953, the Hochschule fur Gestaltung opened in Ulm. Max Bill was a great force there. He designed the school's building and planned its curriculum. In some respects a successor to the Bauhaus, the HFG was at the center of new trends. New media included aircraft, balloons, rockets, television and radio. Experimental designs were created for film trailers, slide shows, appliance symbols, animated signs, symbols for exhibitions and sports events, many kinds of signage, textbooks, and three-dimensional displays. Bauhaus teaching influenced other art academies and schools in Germany, including the city art school in Frankfurt am Main as well as schools in Berlin, Breslau, Hamburg, Halle, Stettin and Kassel.

Typographic design in Germany today sees a number of styles flourishing. The Bauhaus style is no longer dominant. One also sees a less ornamental version of jugendstijl and some Victorian typography. Swiss influences are strong in German design. For some the Swiss grid style is not expressive enough for many products and messages. Clear, strong, conservative typographics are often modified by a striving for expressiveness, by a blending of type and pictures in a manner reminiscent of El Lissitzky, Kurt Schwitters or even Wolfgang Weingart. It is almost as if some designers are seeking a middle road between the exquisite craftsmanship, clarity and readability characteristic of the work of Max Caflisch and the often graphic explosiveness of Wolfgang Weingart. For the moment at least, there is a trend away from sans serif typefaces in advertising. One observer sees 80 percent of today's advertisements using classic roman typefaces. Gunter Gerhard Lange, director of typography for H. Berthold AG, views today's designer as a choreographer of all the elements in a printed piece (headlines, text, captions, pictures, etc.). Today's technology can accommodate this typographic choreography. On the other hand, Lange notes that the great abilities of the new typesetters and printers, their ability to mix styles almost without restrictions, can result in "mixing a kangaroo with an elephant."

Professor Kurt Weidemann of Stuttgart agrees with Herr Lange that the technology "is too good ... it needs a designer to control the output." Weidemann also finds too many contemporary designers too intrigued with technology at the sacrifice of maintaining high standards of typography. He says, "The more the machines can do, the better must be the typographer who works with them."

Some German designers cite as influences such American designers as Paul Rand, Alexey Brodovitch, William Golden, Herb Lubalin, Gene Federico, Henry Wolf, Saul Bass and Robert Gage, and designers from other countries, such as Wim Crouwel (Total Design, Amsterdam) and Odermatt and Tissi (Zürich). Younger designers find

Chapter XIII: The Many Faces of Typography Today

"Some see the so-called new wave a sophisticated visual language that addresses the younger market effectively."

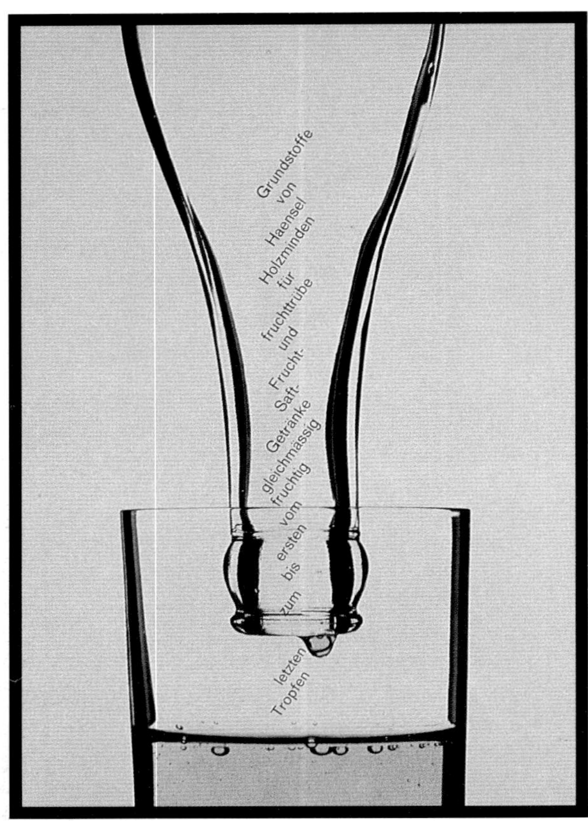

Advertisement *by Gerstner, Gredinger & Kutter for Henrich Haensel (Germany). 1962.*

the so-called new wave a sophisticated visual language that addresses the younger market effectively, and therefore is here to stay, as this market becomes a major buying force. A "good new wave" and a "bad new wave" is seen. These younger designers call for more feeling in design, more "direction and speed for type in space." Some studios, such as that of Olaf Leu Design and Partner (Frankfurt) have both activist and traditional designers in order to satisfy the needs and tastes of different clients.

Willy Fleckhaus and Twen

Book and magazine designer, Willy Fleckhaus, wanted to make an impact. Purposeful tension characterized his typographics. Fleckhaus, through *Twen* magazine (1959-1970) and his teaching, was a great influence in the German design community. He had studied with Max Bill and absorbed Bauhaus thinking. He became Professor of Graphic Design in Essen, and later in Wuppertal. He blended a contemporary sense of the need for visual vitality with his Bauhaus methodology, and one can see in his work for *Twen* the blend of drama, humor, and power with readability and careful organization of all typographic elements. Fleckhaus was co-founder and art director of *Twen*. The inventor of *Twen* was a brilliant German journalist, Adolf Theobold, then 29. He made *Twen* a wonderful marriage of copy and graphics. Fleckhaus also designed books for the Suhrkamp and Insel publishing houses and art directed the *Frankfurter Allgemeine Magazin*.

Olaf Leu

For over 30 years, Olaf Leu has been one of Germany's outstanding typographic designers. If you look at his work over this period, you don't find a Leu style so much as you find certain characteristics common to most of his work: clear, easily readable type, compelling colors, and imagery that is usually derived from, and reinforces, the message.

Anton Stankowski

Painter, photographer, graphic designer, Anton Stankowski's art and typographics have been a distinguished part of the graphics world since 1929. From 1929 to 1936 he worked in Zürich. After World War II he opened his studio in Stuttgart, where he is still painting and designing. Much of his typographic work is very clear and orderly, with judicious use of white space, color bars, and symbolic illustration contributing personality and eye appeal. Some of his typographic pieces employ large and even cropped letters, curved or angled words – yet all within an obviously ordered design.

The work *of the studio of Rombou Lienemeyer Van de Sand (Frankfurt) is camera-oriented and mostly in black-and-white. Simple, direct photography with visual illusions is employed to make a precise statement. For many problems, color is considered sentimental and too cosmetic, although this poster for the Berlin publisher, Rene Block, was in full color.*

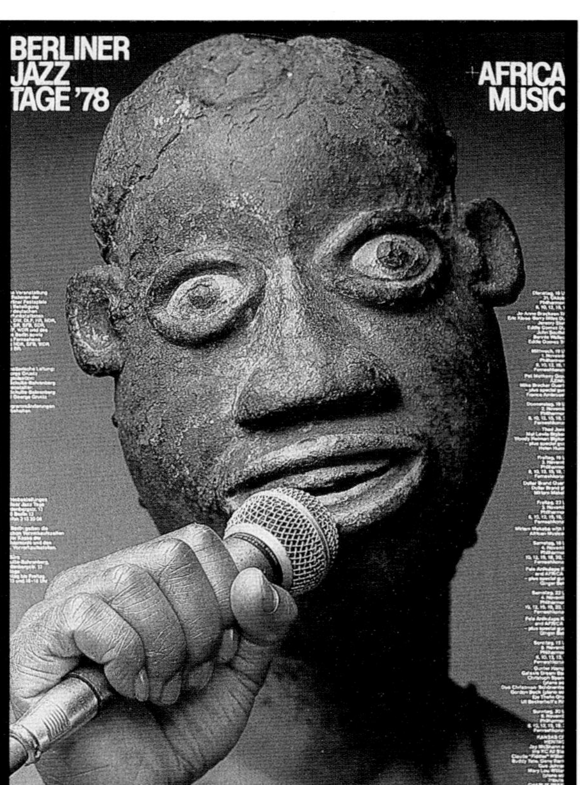

Guenther Kieser *achieves implausible effects with imaginative color photography and orderly typography.* FHK *Henrion considers him a 20th-century Hieronymous Bosch.*

A powerful example *of expressive typography by Gisela Cohrs of West Germany. This won the only prize in an open contest for posters against terrorism at the 1984 Warsaw Biennale.*

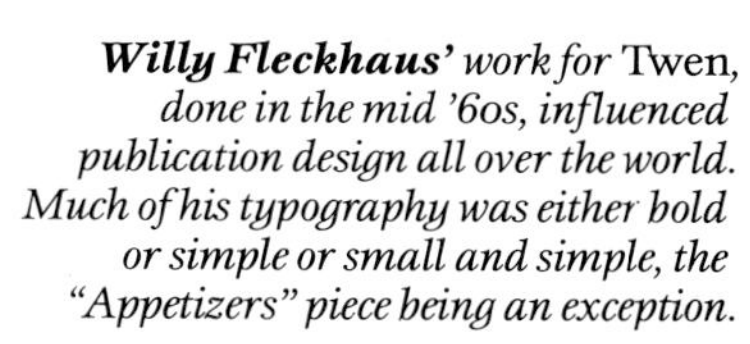

Willy Fleckhaus' *work for* Twen, *done in the mid '60s, influenced publication design all over the world. Much of his typography was either bold or simple or small and simple, the "Appetizers" piece being an exception.*

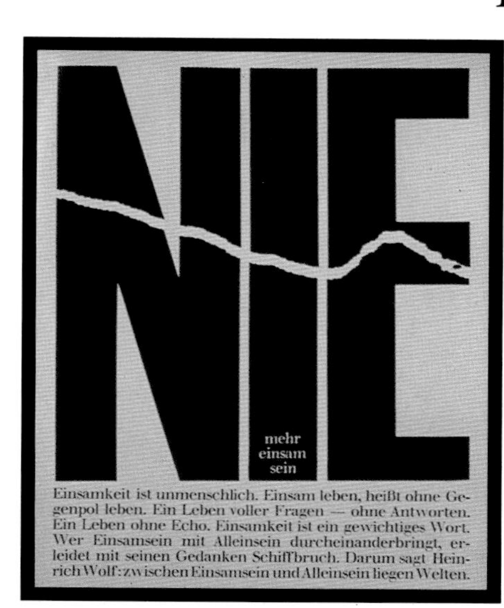

Frage an twen-Gourmet Karolus Koriander: Ei, Ei, was kochen wir heute? Seine Antwort: Bleiben wir ruhig bei diesem Vorschlag.

Hier kommen 19 Rezepte für

eier

Menschen, in deren Küche ich keine Eier finde, betrachte ich mit großer Skepsis. Was machen solche Leute um zwei Uhr morgens, wenn Gäste mit dem Ruf „Hunger, Hunger" in den Küchenbereich eindringen?

Sie haben völlig recht. Leute, die keine Eier im Haus haben, haben auch morgens um zwei keine Gäste. Solche Leute haben überhaupt keine Gäste, sie verdienen keine, denn sie sind von Grund auf ungesellig. Sehen Sie, so genau stimmt die Eiertheorie.

Noch eine Kostprobe davon: Ein Mädchen kann in der Küche so dumm sein, daß sie Koriander nicht von Kardamom unterscheiden kann — all das sei ihr vergeben, wenn sie in der Lage ist, aus vier Eiern fünf Gerichte zu zaubern. Um Abwechslung in die Eierküche zu bringen, folgen hier nicht nur fünf sondern 19 Eiergerichte.

Das hart gekochte (über fünf Minuten) und das weich gekochte (dreieinhalb Minuten) Ei seien hier ausgeklammert. Am Spiegelei allerdings werden wir uns nicht vorbeidrücken, vor allem nicht an seiner verfeinerten Abart, dem Setzei.

Das braten wir Ihnen auf Seite 118.

Der Mann mit kratzender Stahlstimme, Charles Aznavour, ist in wenigen Jahren ein Weltstar geworden. Wie er das gemacht hat, beschreibt für twen Pascal Bergues. Die Fotos machte Chadwick Hall.

MONETEN CHARLES

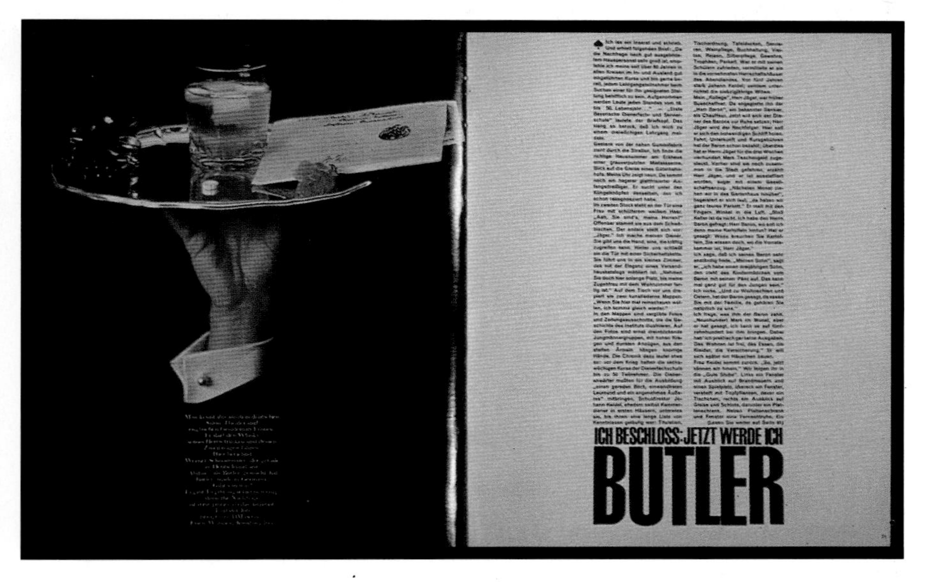

ICH BESCHLOSS: JETZT WERDE ICH BUTLER

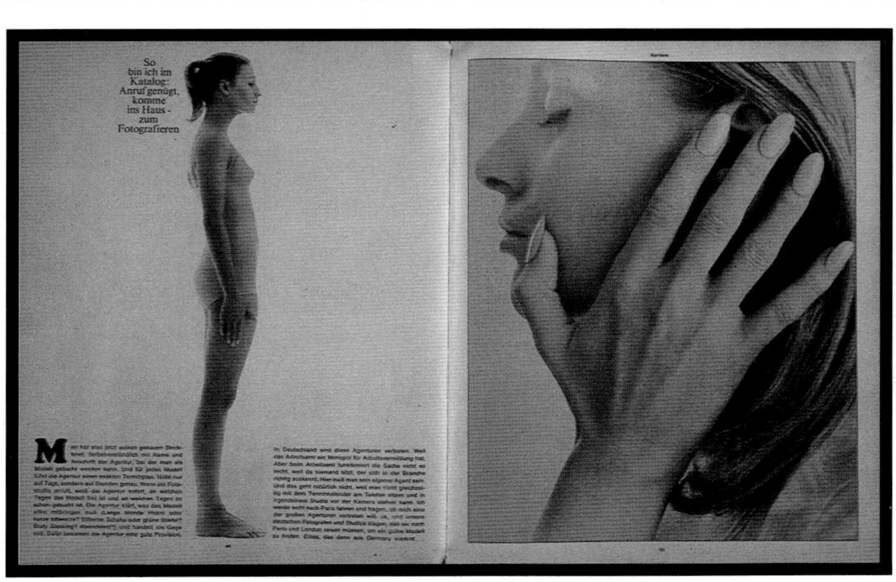

So bin ich im Katalog: Anruf genügt, komme ins Haus – zum Fotografieren

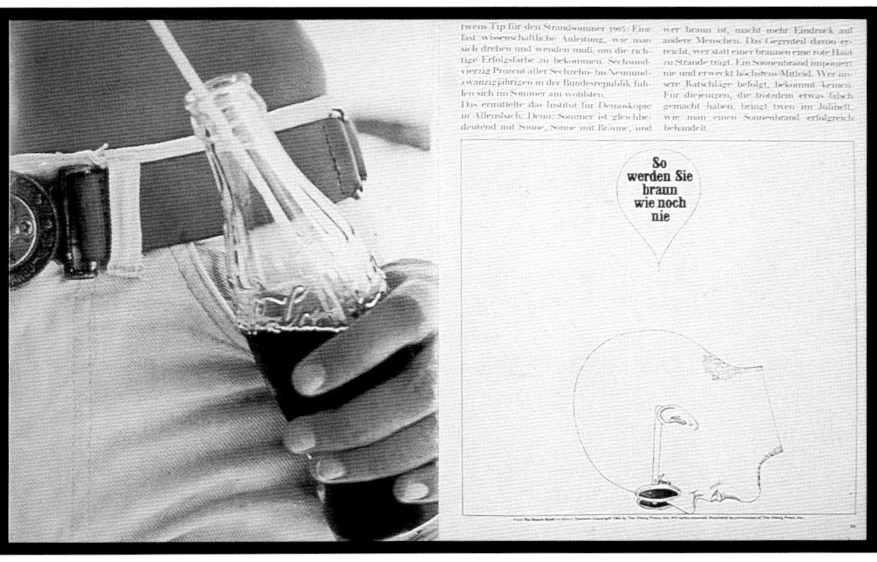

***Shown here** are several examples of the work of Olaf Leu.*

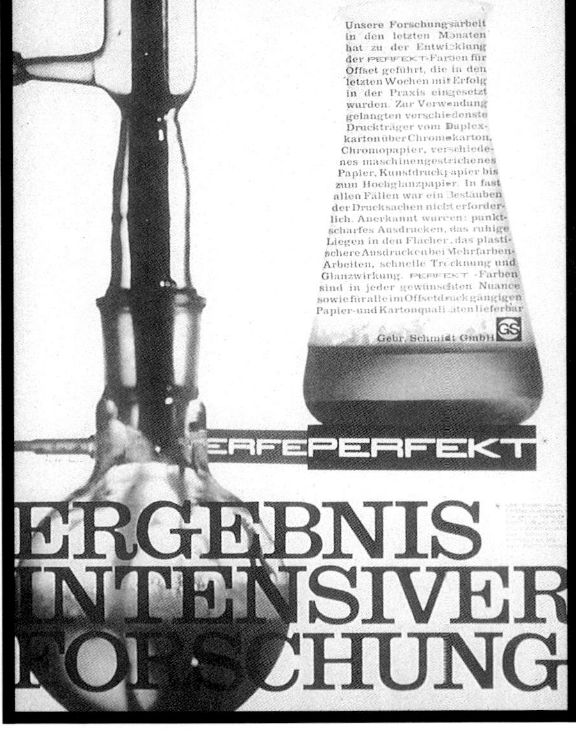

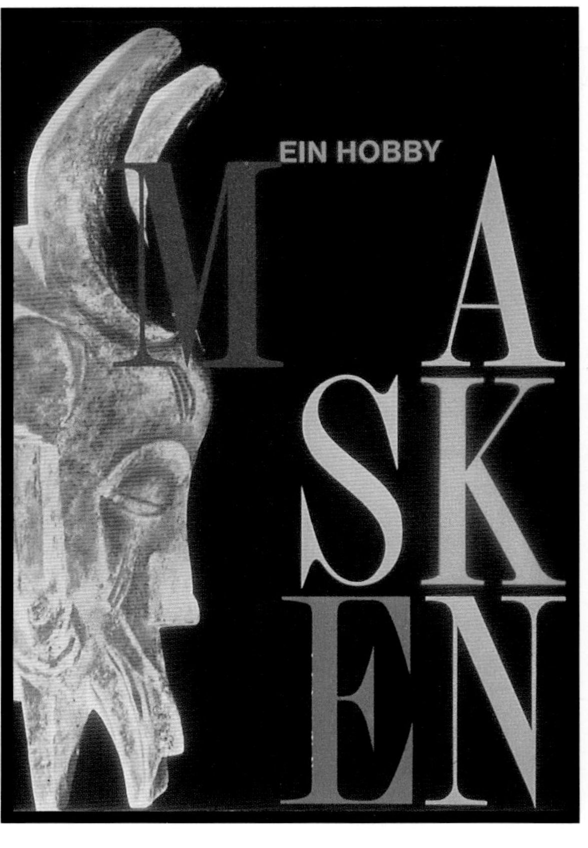

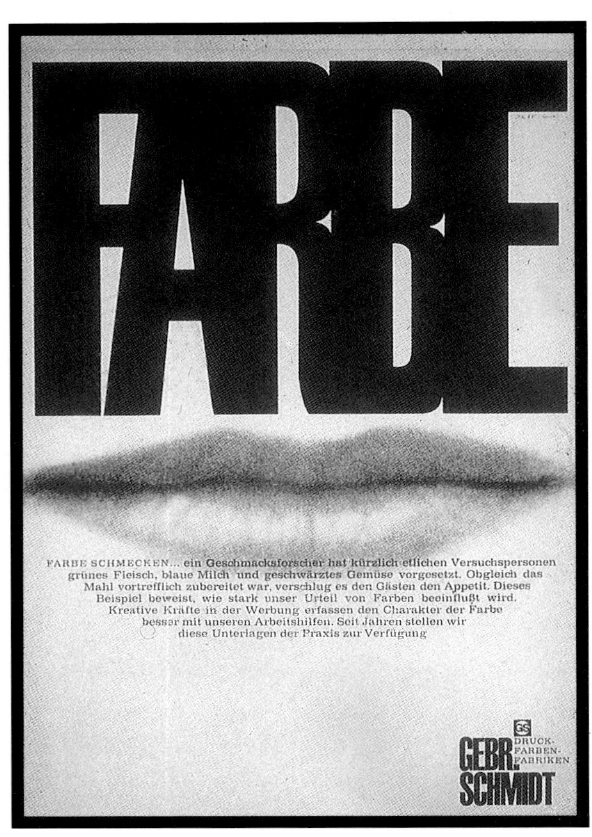

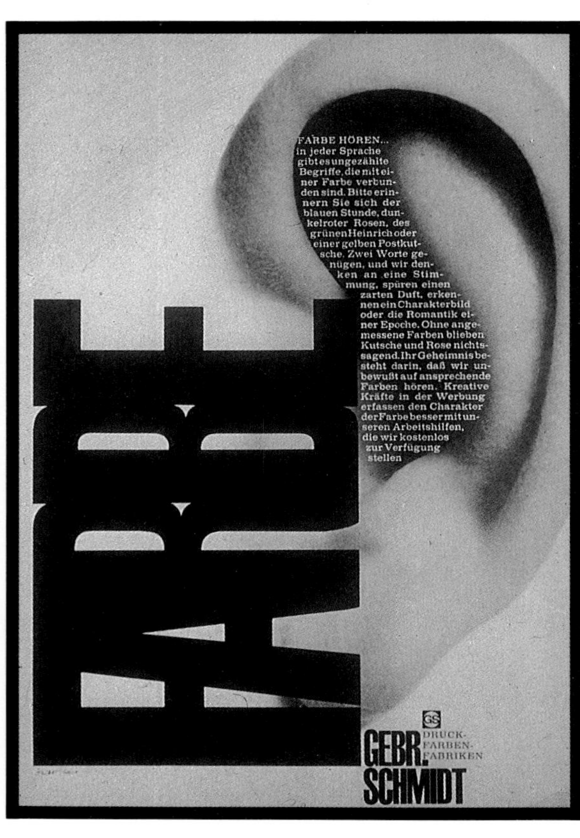

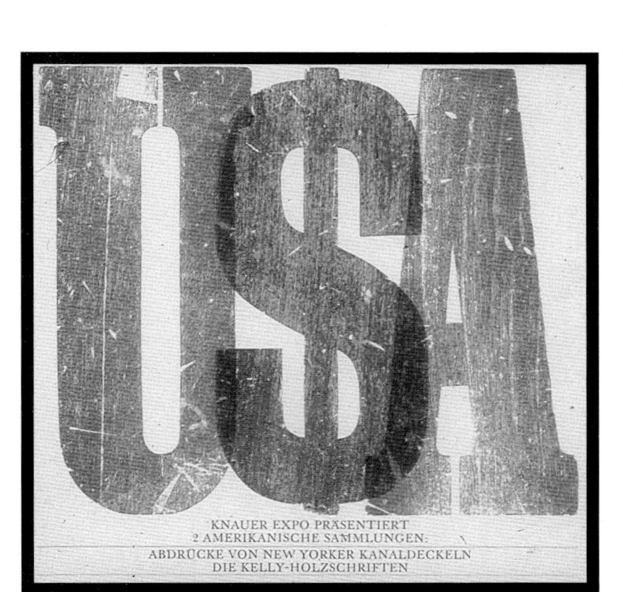

Another sample *of the work of Olaf Leu.*

Poster *concerning the returning prisoners of war, 1948. Anton Stankowski.*

Poster *for PH-Lampern, 1928. Anton Stankowski.*

Leaflet *for Hill Foodstuffs, 1929. Anton Stankowski.*

Public relations *advertisement for* IBM*, 1957. Anton Stankowski.*

Three advertisements *for Scherz, publishers. 1962-64. Anton Stankowski.*

Marktsituation

2

Diagnostische Studien dieser Art können mehr generell im Sinne von Basis- bzw. Strukturanalysen oder speziell auf die Belange eines Unternehmens und/oder eines Marktobjektes und/oder bestimmter Vertriebsformen ausgerichtet sein.

Je nach Umfang und Art der Aufgabenstellung erfolgt der Einsatz bzw. die Kombination von Schreibtisch-Forschung (Desk-Research) und Feld-Forschung (Field-Research). Besondere Bedeutung haben hier die abschließende Gewichtung und Aufbereitung der relevanten Daten ggfs. mit mathematischen Methoden sowie Modellvorstellungen.

Zur Markt-Diagnose gehören u. a. Feststellungen über Bestand, Bedarf, Angebot, Nachfrage, Vorstellungen, Absichten, Gewohnheiten, Interessen, Gefühle, Wünsche, Konkurrenz, Absatz- bzw. Beschaffungswege sowie Informationsquellen und Verhaltensweisen der Wirtschaftspartner im Hinblick auf Güter und Dienstleistungen jeder Art. Hierbei sind auch die wirtschaftlichen, sozialen, politischen, rechtlichen, technologischen und kulturellen Entwicklungen (Rahmenbedingungen) von Bedeutung, insbesondere unter mittel- und langfristigen Aspekten.

Wesentlich für die Qualität einer Marktuntersuchung ist zu Beginn der Zusammenarbeit zwischen Auftraggeber und Institut die Aussprache über die Gegebenheiten beim Auftraggeber und die speziellen Zielsetzungen der Marktuntersuchung. Nur dann kann das Institut optimal für den Klienten im Markt Erkenntnisse ermitteln. Sollten in den abgestimmten Voraussetzungen und Zielsetzungen noch Unklarheiten bestehen, so empfiehlt sich eine Vorstudie (»Pilot-Study«).

Marktkonzeption

3

Die prognostische Marktforschung liefert wichtige Beiträge für die Unternehmensplanung. Die Konzeptionsentwicklung für die Unternehmensplanung erfolgt sowohl in der Sicht der Marktentwicklung als auch unter Beachtung der materiellen, personellen und finanziellen Möglichkeiten des Unternehmens. Hierbei ist zu unterscheiden zwischen einer perspektivischen Trend-Prognose und einer innovativen Prognose; letztere berücksichtigt auch qualitative Veränderungen sowohl bei den relevanten Marktpartnern und -Segmenten als auch in den Entwicklungskapazitäten der Unternehmen.

Bei den Konzeptionen ist sodann zu unterscheiden zwischen solchen, die sich langfristig mit den Unternehmenszielen (z. B. Kapazitäten, Marktvolumen, Absatzzielen und -Organisationen, Markengestaltung) befassen, und solchen, die mittelfristigen Planungen (z. B. Produkt-Darbietung, Preisgestaltung, Absatzwege, spezielle Zielgruppen, Werbeaussagen) dienen.

Wesentliche Einsichten in das zukünftige Marktgeschehen werden gewonnen durch eine ganzheitliche Betrachtung der Feststellung relevanter Fakten, Verhaltensweisen und sozio-ökonomischer Meinungsbildungen im Bereich der für das Unternehmen heute und morgen bedeutsamen Marktpartner.

Für die Erfüllung dieser Aufgaben sind spezielle repräsentative Erhebungen im Markt sowie fachgerechte, unternehmensbezogene Interpretationen erforderlich.

Page *from a capabilities booklet for* GFM, *titled "*GFM *Knows the Market." The blocks are in a clear, medium blue. Anton Stankowski. 1982.*

Book jackets *(two above and three on the right) are by Heinz Edelmann. As is not uncommon with book jackets, the type is integrated with the illustration.*

Trademark *for children's sport shoes. Mendell & Oberer.*

LIBERO

A multi-volume dictionary. *The key to the contents is at the top of the spines of the volumes in a spectrum of colors. A bis Z (A to Z) reads across the set and is reversed on the black background. Mendell & Oberer.*

Mendell & Oberer

This graphic design studio in Munich combines strong imagery, innovative but appropriate typographics to create fresh, attractive, readable material.

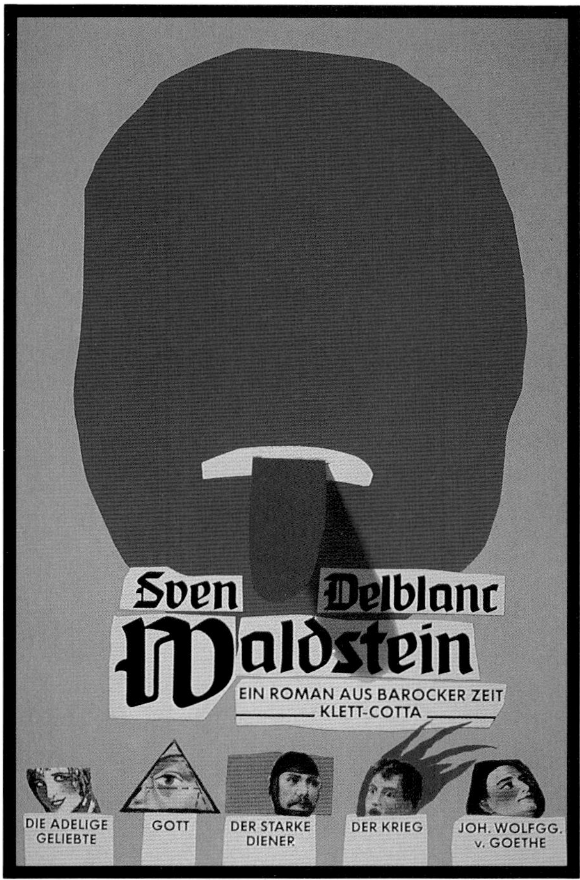

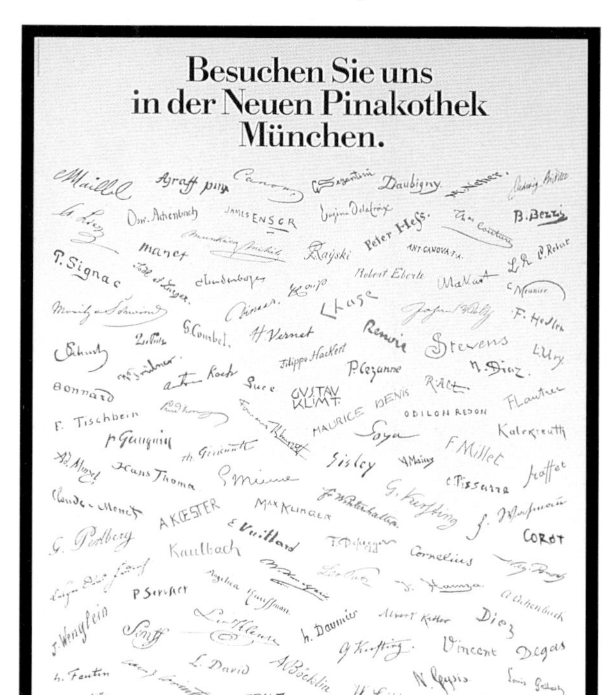

Poster *for the opening of the Neuen Pinakothek, the museum of modern art in Munich. Mendell & Oberer.*

Advertisement *for a drug to combat articular rheumatism. Mendell & Oberer.*

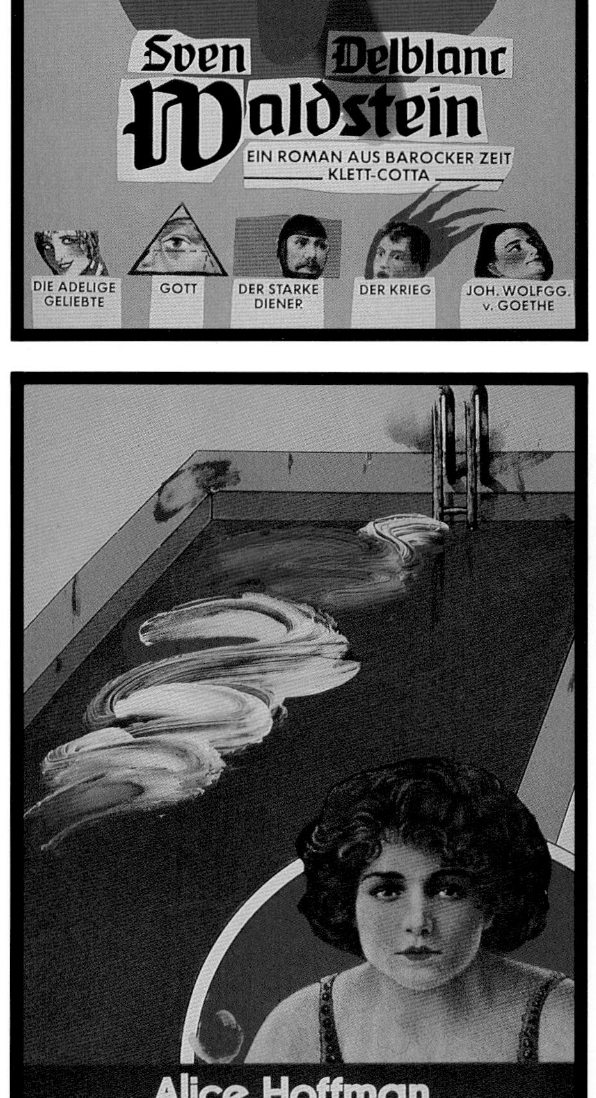

Poster *for an exhibition of Polish posters. Mendell & Oberer.*

"Sometimes the individuality and the flowing beauty of calligraphy is best suited to a piece."

Poster *for the museum of applied arts in Munich. "Design is art that makes itself useful." Mendell & Oberer.*

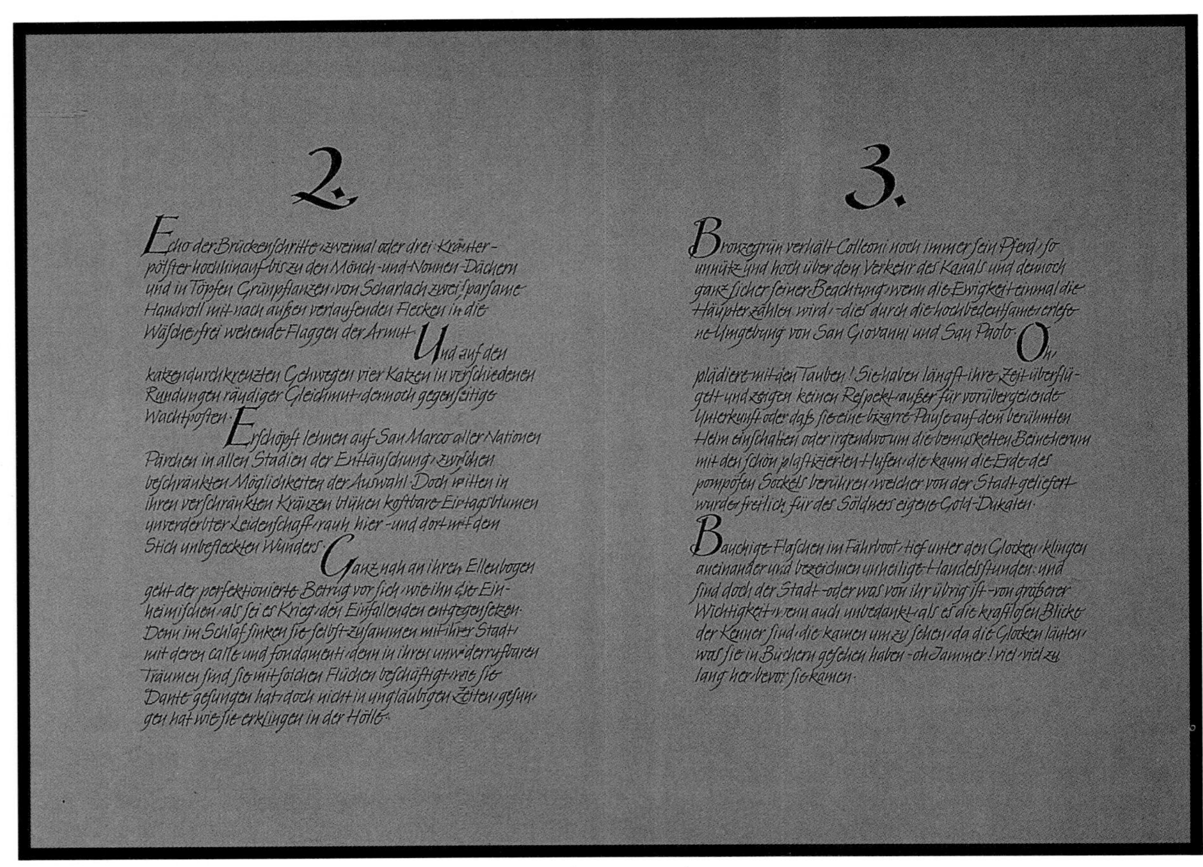

***For* A Last Ode to Venice.** *Calligraphy by Friedrich Neugebauer. Austria.*

GERMAN DEMOCRATIC REPUBLIC
Albert Kapr

Book *designed by Albert Kapr of the German Democratic Republic for* VEB *Verlag der Kunst.*

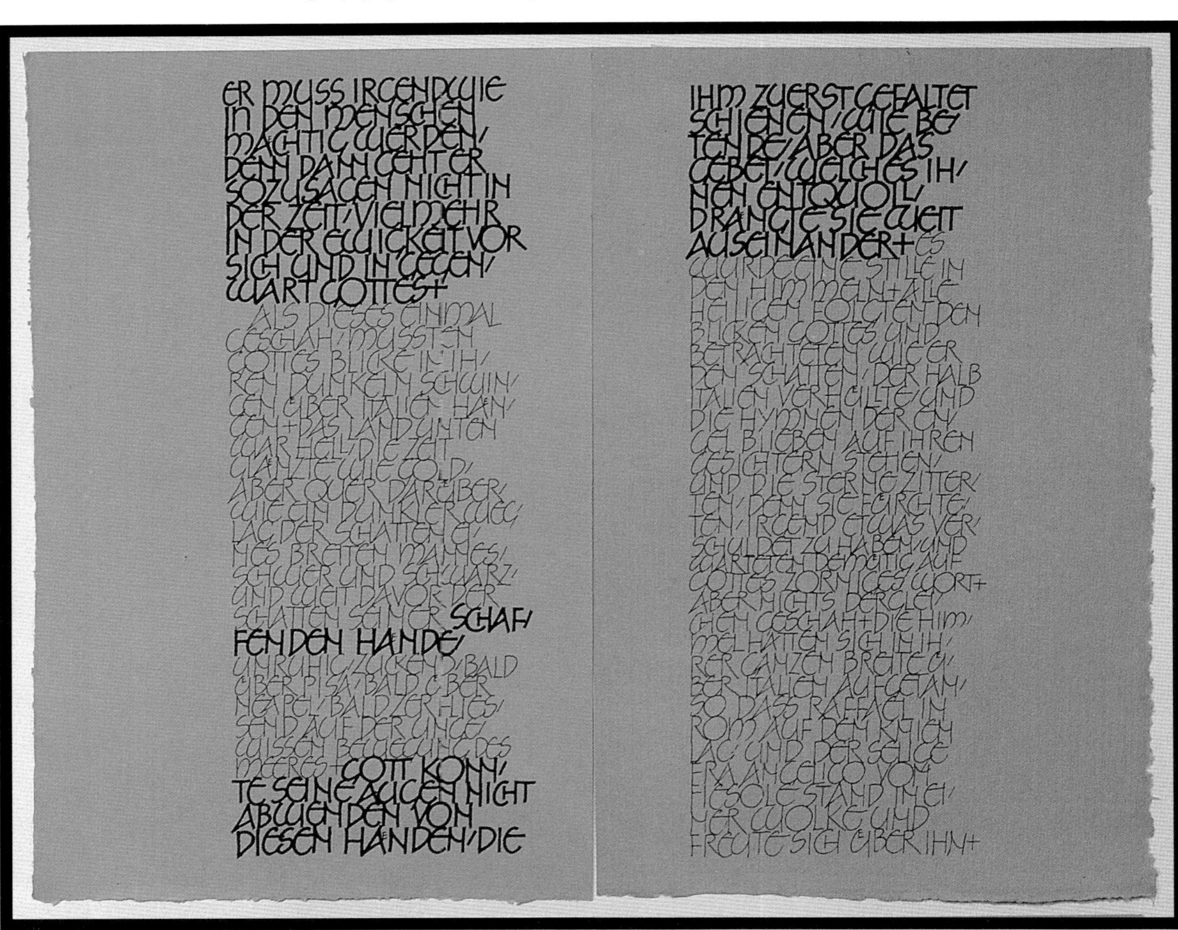

For a work *by R. M. Rilke. Calligraphy by Friedrich Neugebauer. Austria.*

Ispahan

Ispahan ***is an oriental fragrance;*** *the lettering was designed to evoke the tradition of the Arabian Nights. Carré Noir.*

BENEDICTINE

One of the oldest liqueurs, *Benedictine, was created by monks. The rising serifs evoke the tip of the Cross of Christ, the downward serifs the fork of the devil's tail. Carré Noir.*

Le Quartier de l'Horloge *is the "district of the clock," an old Parisian district near the Beaubourg Center. The hands of the clock are symbolized by the Q Logo by Carré Noir.*

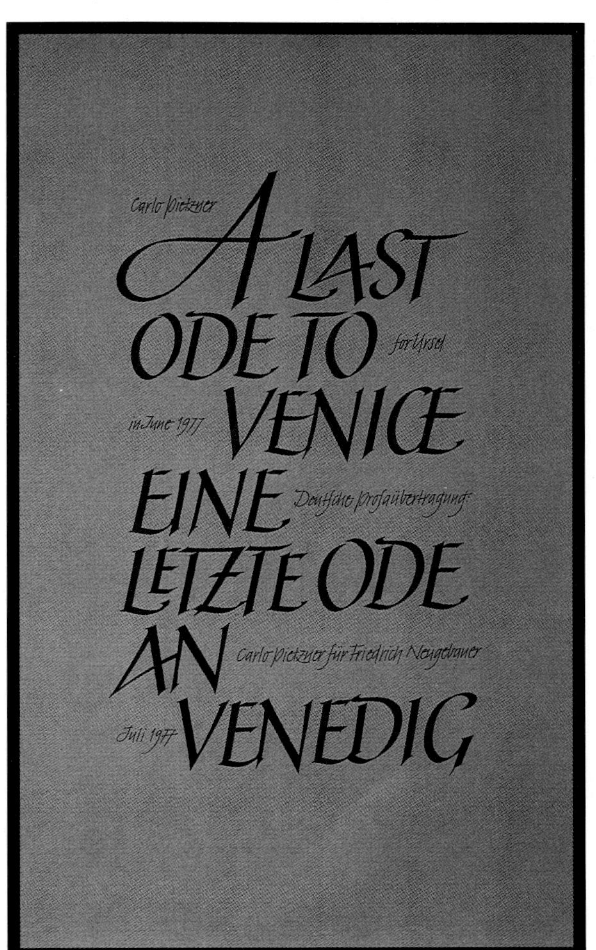

For A Last Ode to Venice. *Calligraphy by Friedrich Neugebauer. Austria.*

Carré Noir *developed these designs in the search for a logotype for Vichy. The second from the top in the first column was chosen.*

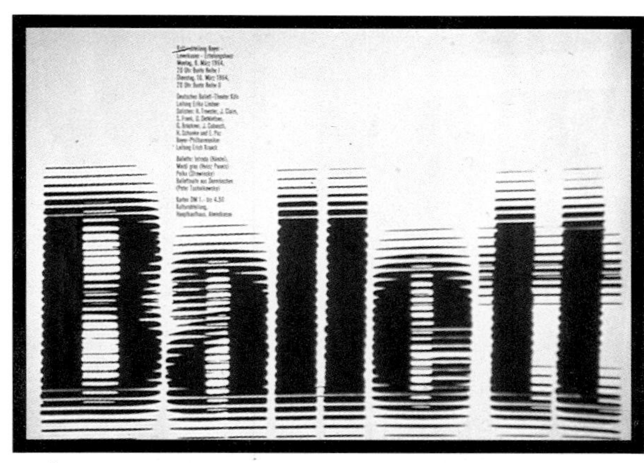

Poster *by Coordt von Mannstein for Kulturabteilung der Bayer AG. 1963.*

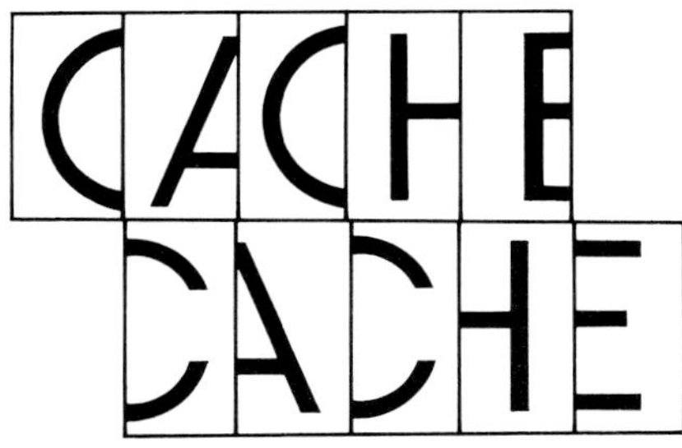

In English, *this means "hide-and-seek." Cache-Cache is the name of fragrance products for the young. The letters play hide-and-seek with themselves. Carré Noir.*

This logo *by Carré Noir for Pommery Champagne uses the typeface Boton, named after its designer, Albert Boton. Mr. Boton is also the designer of two ITC typefaces, ITC Elan® and ITC Eras.®*

AUSTRIA

Sometimes the individuality and the flowing beauty of calligraphy is best suited to a piece, not merely for a word or a headline, but even for text matter. The Austrian calligrapher Friedrich Neugebauer's work demonstrates how beautiful and effective calligraphy can be for full pages of reading matter. Just a few examples of his work are shown here.

FRANCE

Carré Noir and Grapus

Among the distinguished design studios in France are those of Carré Noir and Grapus. Carré Noir has done much work in the areas of package design, displays, corporate design, logotypes and trademarks. Some of their designs are shown here.

Grapus is a French design team. It was established in 1968 by three designers who had studied at the Warsaw Academy of Arts under Henryk Tomaszewski. They function as a design cooperative, rather than as individuals. Their concerns are with the environment, cultural events, and with helping to create a better world. Promoting soups or cigarettes is not for them. Although the messages they clothe are serious, they feel that entertainment and a light touch help put even the most serious messages across. Their work is distinguished by strong imagery and type-picture integration.

ABCDE
FGHIJK
LMNOP
QRSTU
VWXYZ
123456
7890&

A redrawing *of a Deberny & Peignot typeface adapted for use as initials in the* Encyclopaedia Universalis, *by Carré Noir.*

TYPOGRAPHIC COMMUNICATIONS TODAY
Chapter XIII: The Many Faces of Typography Today

A circus poster *by Grapus. France.*

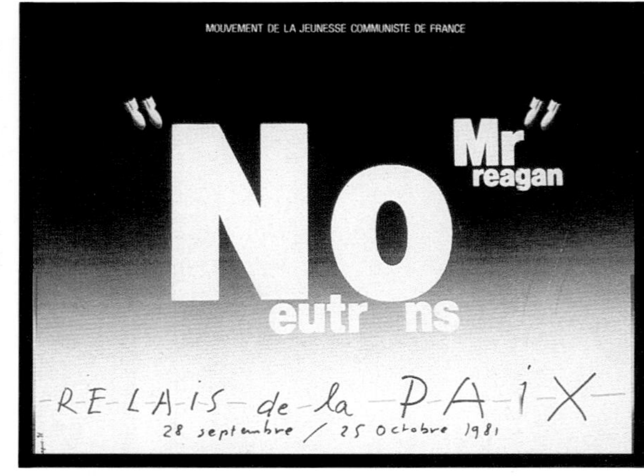

An anti-nuclear bomb poster *that says "No neutrons Mr. Reagan." Grapus. France.*

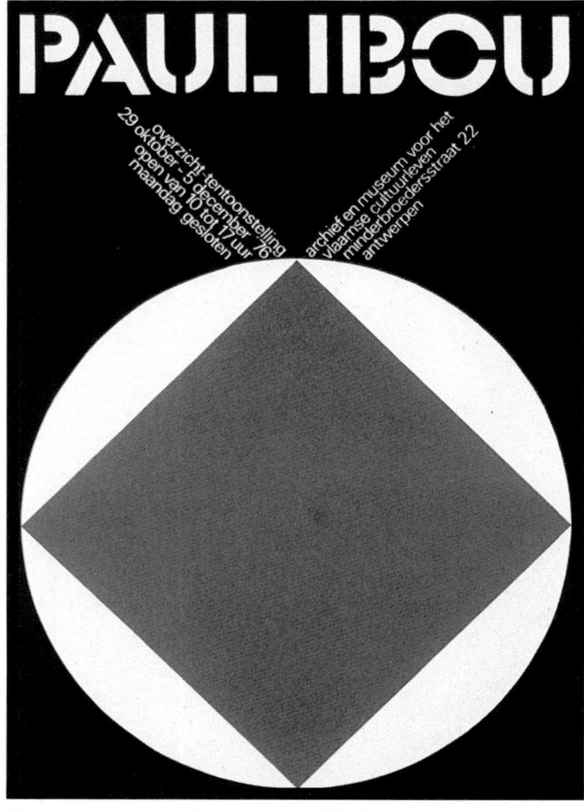

Poster *commemorating 15 years of freelancing. The square is in green. Paul Ibou.*

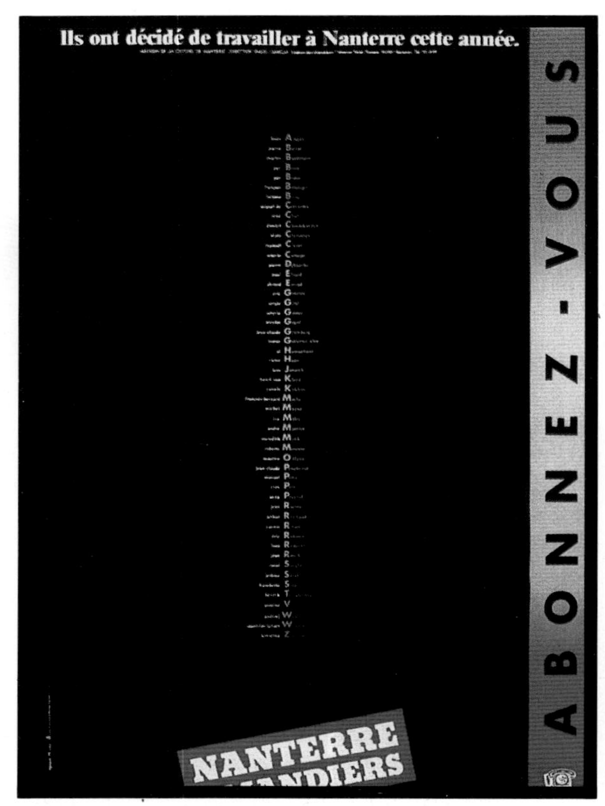

A poster *seeking subscriptions for the House of Culture in Nanterre. By Grapus. France.*

BELGIUM
Paul Ibou

Paul Ibou is one of Belgium's foremost, and most prolific, graphic designers. He started creating graphic designs in 1954, as an employee, at the age of 15. Since 1961 he has been a freelance graphic designer, typographer, painter and publisher. He has worked in many disciplines, including architectural graphics, geometric wood sculptures, newspaper design, logotypes, and film. Representative examples of his typographic designs for print media are shown here.

Poster *for the Ministry of Netherlands Culture. Paul Ibou.*

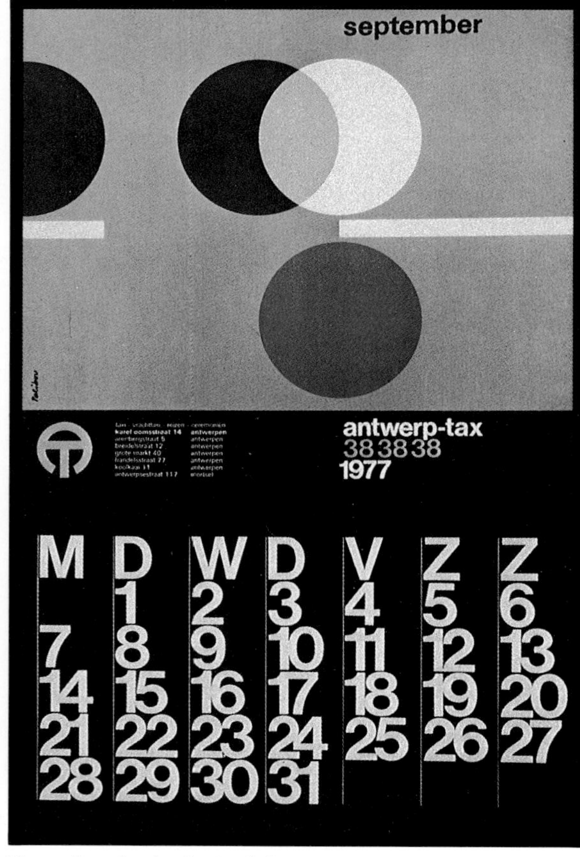

Page *of a calendar by Paul Ibou.*

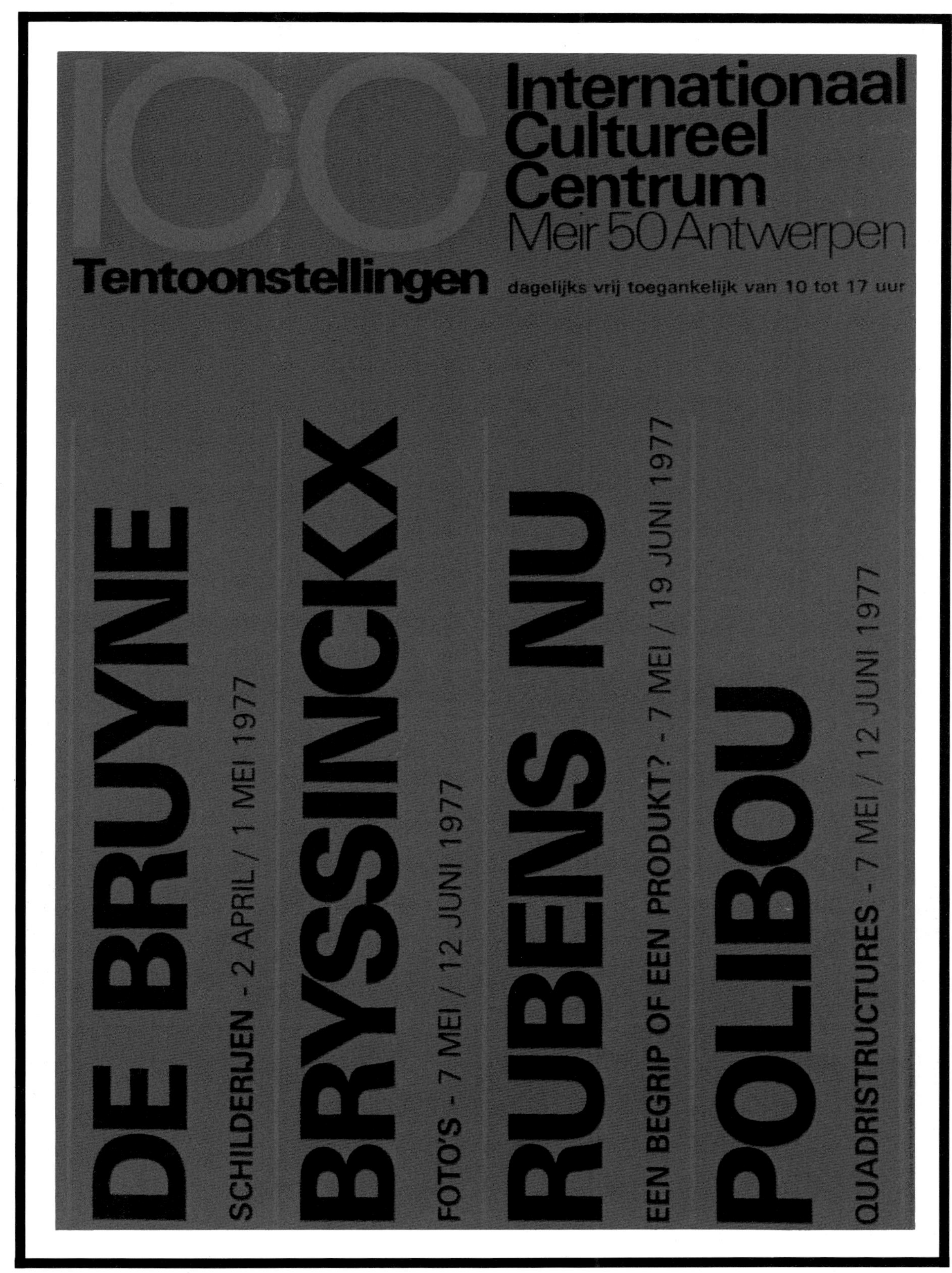

Poster *for the International Culture Center of Antwerp. Black type on medium blue blackground with "ICC" in light blue. Paul Ibou.*

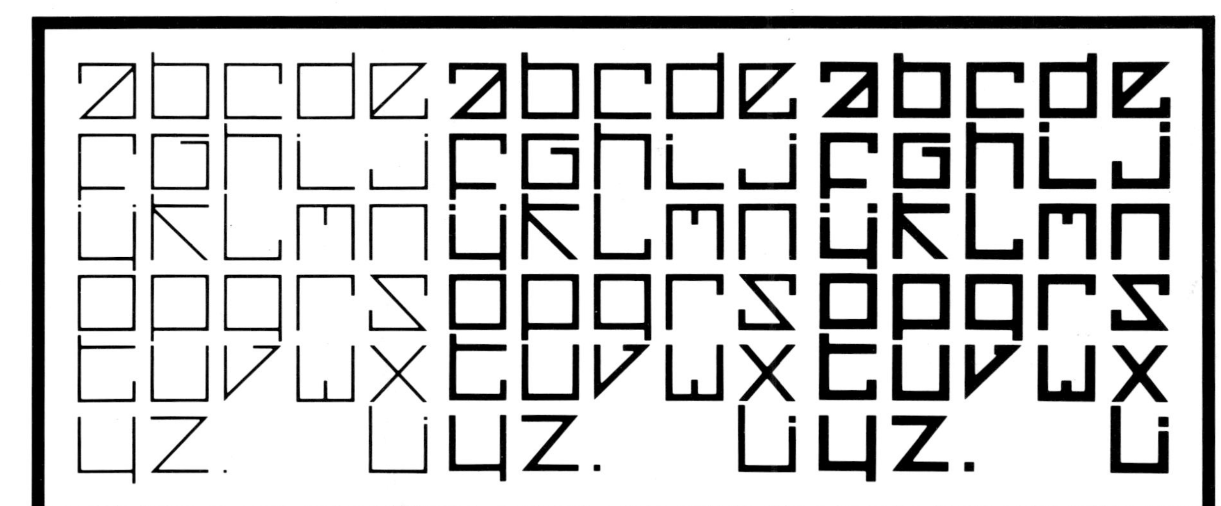

Square letter *design by Paul Ibou.*

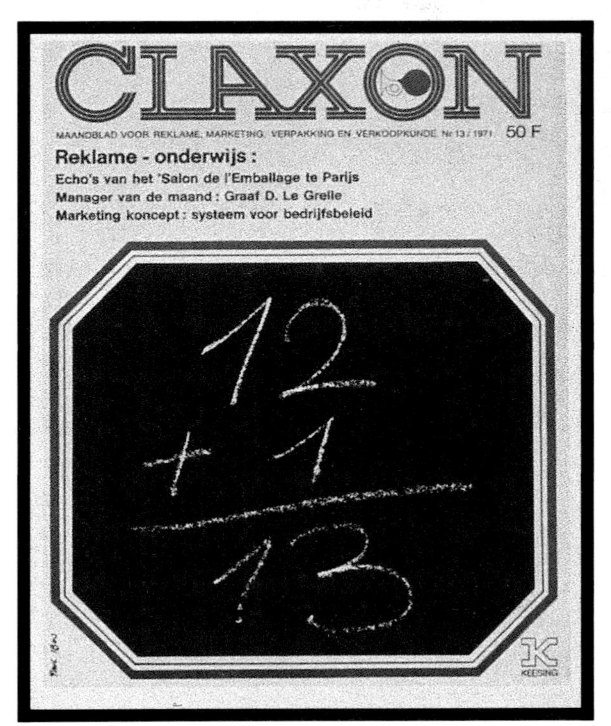

Designed *by Paul Ibou.*

"The grid evolved from its use by Renaissance and Gothic architects."

***Herman Lampaert,** Belgium*

***A record jacket** designed by Herman Lampaert in 1983. The lines of type blend colors from orange at the left through red, yellow, and green. Belgium.*

***A calendar** (above) and typographic design for an Antwerp financial newspaper (below). Paul Ibou. Belgium.*

De Financieel Economische TIJD

NIEUWS BINNENLAND

Benelux Ministers: Harde lijn tegen de GAULLE

Callaghan ruilt financien voor Binnenlandse zaken

BEURS

Verder in dit nummer

Mac Namara's benoeming tot president van Wereldbank uitgesteld

Wilson: geen associatie met EEG.

NIEUWS BUITENLAND

REY pleit voor eenheid tussen Zes

SIEMAG vereenvoudigt uwe ganse boekhouding

ADRESSOGRAFIE

Editoriaal

Staking in Gas en Elektriciteit neemt uitbreiding

De Londense goldpool

Jacques Richez

Belgian designer Jacques Richez, was born in Dieppe, France. He is internationally known for his experimental photography and exquisite craftsmanship, as well as for his powerful poster designs and other typographics. He often juxtaposes photographs and drawings and employs surrealist fantasies.

HOLLAND

Wim Crouwel and Total Design

Ever since the early days of Piet Zwart and of the De Stijl movement, Holland has been one of the centers where outstanding graphic design flourished (Pgs. 149–152). Total Design, in Amsterdam, is recognized internationally for its impactful, yet very orderly typographics, and for its multifaceted studio. A recent book, based on an exhibition of the work of Total Design, puts it this way:

"The Dutchman walking around with an open eye

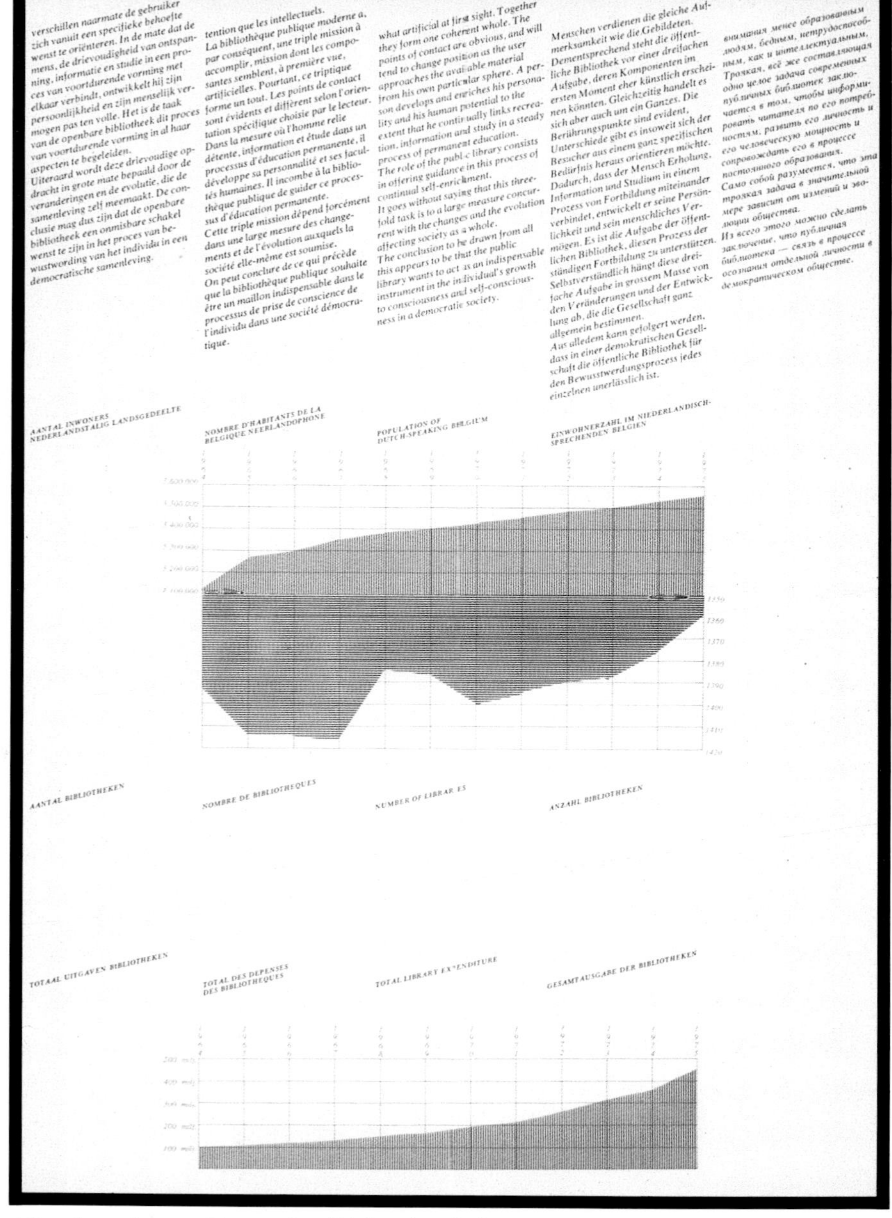

***A brochure** for IFLA (International Federation of Library Associations) at the 1977 world congress in Brussels. By Herman Lampaert. Belgium.*

will, sooner or later and whether he realizes it or not, come into touch with one of the many visual products of design-office Total Design of Amsterdam, here abbreviated to 'TD.'"

TD does interior design, environmental graphics, corporate design programs, the whole gamut of graphic design for print, film and electronic media.

Commenting on TD's frequent use of a fine grid to organize a design, Wim Crouwel explains that the grid evolved from its use by Renaissance and Gothic architects. Crouwel notes that the United States is geographically and historically further from the grid influence. The result is freer design that is often more appropriate to a particular problem than a European or grid approach would be. Americans, he feels, are problem-solvers first, while Europeans often impose a systematic solution on a problem. The European problem, as he sees it, is to develop a grid that suits the problem and then apply the problem to it. In the Netherlands the De Stijl influence is still strong; it is not applied literally, but it is studied in design schools and its sense of orderliness, carried over also from the Bauhaus and the constructivists, is still respected.

Both Wim Crouwel and Pieter Brattinga, of Form Mediation International, in Amsterdam, agree that alongside the De Stijl influence, today's designer is mindful of the work of Piet Zwart, which was organized yet graphically very vigorous. Brattinga also cites, as major influences on the development of typographic design, Stanley Morison, Jan Tschichold, Willem Sandberg, Karl Gerstner, Lou Dorfsman, Herb Lubalin, Wim Crouwel, Kohei Sugiura and Wolfgang Weingart.

A wide range of problems offered the opportunity for graphic experiments. Spatial design ranges from interior design recommendations and "monumental" input to show-window units in the branches, neon advertising and routing systems, and the build-up of a large graphic art collection. The task was always to keep the image clear and vital within a very inconstant urban environment, and this for a company whose rather abstract services are difficult to encompass in one single picture. Two posters for Randstad are shown (P. 151). One says "Apples for a Rainy Day," 1971. The other is a 1975 New Year's Day poster.

Gert Dunbar

Dunbar was born in Jakarta, Indonesia, in 1940, studied at the Royal Academy of Fine Arts in The Hague and the Royal College of Art in London. Since 1977 he has operated his own studio, Studio Dunbar. He works in two-dimensional and three-dimensional design areas and often uses photographic elements in unusual ways, and uses uncommon illustration techniques such as papier-mâché figures and perforations in paper. In the three posters shown, for exhibits of the work of Piet Zwart, De Stijl artists, and Mondrian, each artist is surrounded by elements of his work in surreal space. A departure from traditional exhibition posters, each employs readable yet actively angled and positioned type.

In his work for the corporate identity and sign system of the Dutch railways Dunbar's typography is clear and methodical, very utilitarian in the Swiss grid style. In much of his other work he prefers to bring in emotion and humor (P. 151).

Jurriaan Schrofer

Within TD both Wim Crouwel, TD's founder, and Jurriaan Schrofer have experimented with letterforms.

Poster *for an exhibition showing the folklore, history, culture and economy of a Belgian province. Jacques Richez. Belgium.*

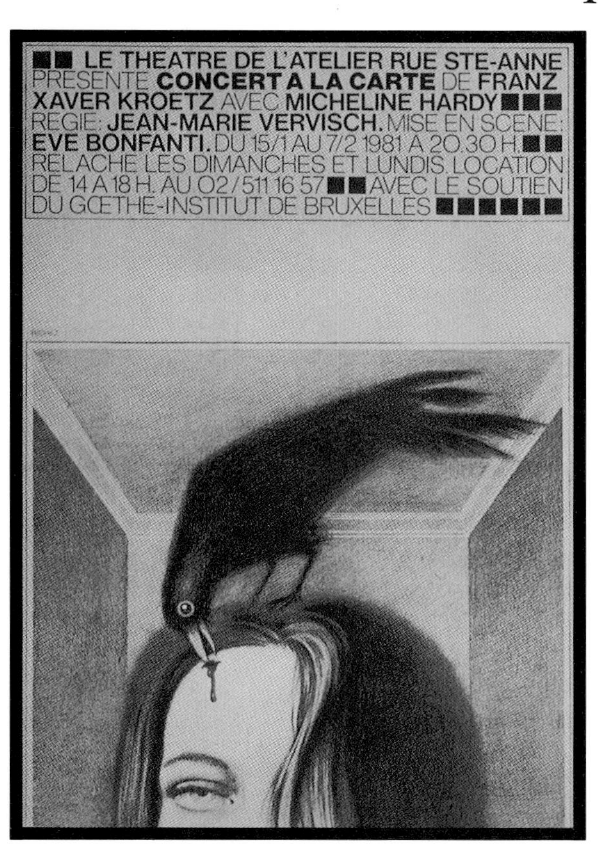

Theater poster. *Jacques Richez. Belgium.*

Theater poster. *Jacques Richez. Belgium.*

Nieuwe Amsterdamsche Courant
Algemeen Handelsblad
Stakende hoogleraren Politie bezet Sorbonne
Laatste nieuws Prijzen 3% hoger
Politie ontruimt Sorbonne
Motie van oppositie steekt Roolvink
Alleen regering onderzoekt optreden Indië
Sneeuw–Ajax
Hans vZ: alleen
Alleen regering onderzoekt militair optreden
Roolvink zeer ontstemd over motie
Wegen glad: ongelukken
Arbiter: sneeuw moet weg
Finale Europa Cup '70 in Rotterdam
abonneer nu
Toenemende vorst
Ursprungsland, die Schweiz.
PEUGEOT 504

Total Design *considers newspaper design a tailor-made challenge. Wim Crouwel and others at TD redesigned the* Algemeen Handelsblad *of Amsterdam in 1970. Shown here is a test page for further development. In this page and in the redesigned paper, superfluous flourishes were eliminated and articles were made easy to find, and to distinguish them from each other.*

Publication *for the Randstad Holland.*

TYPOGRAPHIC COMMUNICATIONS TODAY
Chapter XIII: The Many Faces of Typography Today

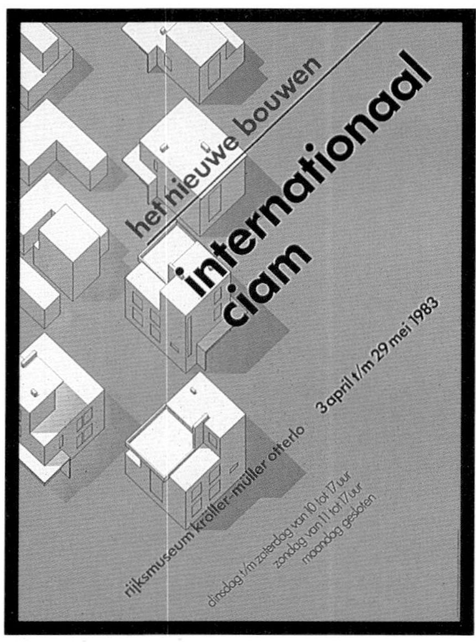

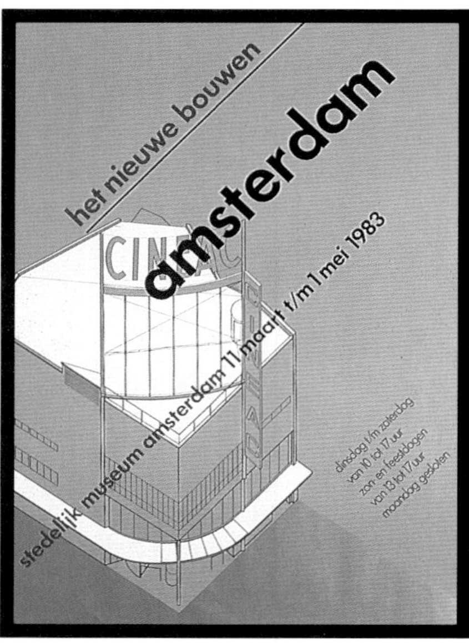

***TD designs** many posters for theaters and festivals, and these usually have a strong emotional appeal. For some serial posters, visual continuity and directness is preferred, as in the four shown here. All have a violet background with key parts of the display type in red. For such serial poster work TD develops preprinted basic layouts which can accommodate the text and illustrations for each event.*

de collectie moderne kunst
boymans-van beuningen
rotterdam

***Poster** for the Museum Boymans-van Beuringen in Rotterdam. Medium blue background with headline dropped out in white, the column of dates in black, and the tabular slashes in red. Total Design. Holland.*

***A 1973 calendar** for the printing office of E. van de Geer-Heirs, Amsterdam. "What should a calendar really be more than objective, useful and of esthetic level?" Wim Crouwel asked in 1958. That a calendar could be more he proved in a long series of calendars for printing-office E. van de Geer-Heirs of Amsterdam. A calendar can also be a terrain where the limits and possibilities of typography are surveyed. Here we see Crouwel experimenting with radical reduction of the main shape and with the relation between shape and color. In other calendars we find new, experimental letterforms on a systematic basis, creative use of the matrix and research in the relation of photography to text. Total Design. Holland.*

***A 1978 poster** for a folklore event. Total Design.*

FINLAND

Art and design are highly esteemed in Finland. The government supports cultural activity with regular awards and grants, as do many foundations. The Finns have their own design flair outside the international mainstream. This is true in many areas of design: product, industrial, graphic, for example. Furthermore, almost a quarter of Finland's foreign trade is design-related. This sampling of the work of just three of Finland's many fine typographic designers illustrates the vibrancy and freshness of their work (Pgs. 152–155).

__An example__ of an extensive house style developed by Total Design is the one for the employment agency, Randstad. For many years, the team of Ben Bos has designed almost all aspects arising within the framework of this house style. Two-dimensional objects (not shown) contain printed matter on which a double "r" creates the prominent trademark: posters, brochures, stationery, and forms; in addition, periodical printed matter like house journals Data *and* Revue *and annual reports and agendas.*

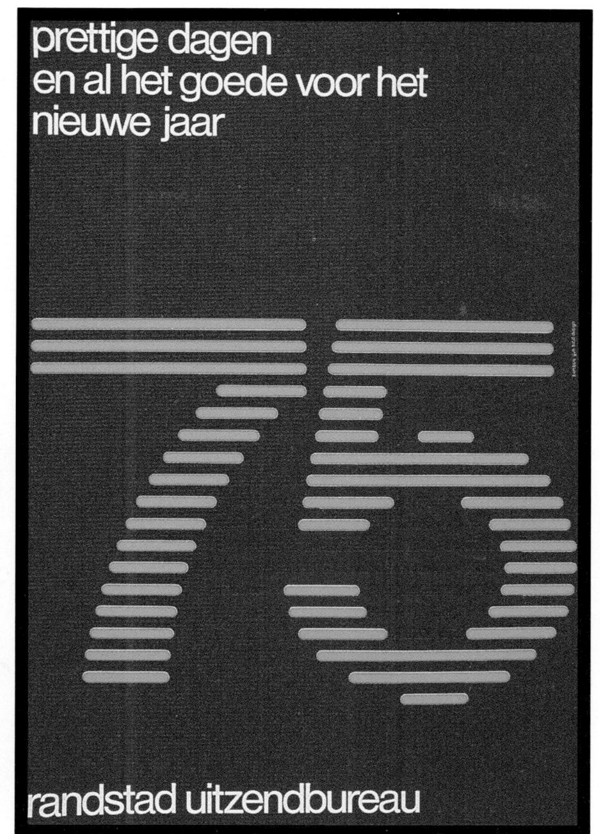

A wide range of problems offered the opportunity for graphic experiments. Spatial design ranges from interior design recommendations and "monumental" input to show-window units in the branches, neon advertising and routing systems, and the build-up of a large graphic art collection. The task was always to keep the image clear and vital within a very inconstant urban environment, and this for a company whose rather abstract services are difficult to encompass in one single picture. Two posters for Randstad are shown here. One says "Apples for a Rainy Day," 1971. The other is a 1975 New Year's Day poster.

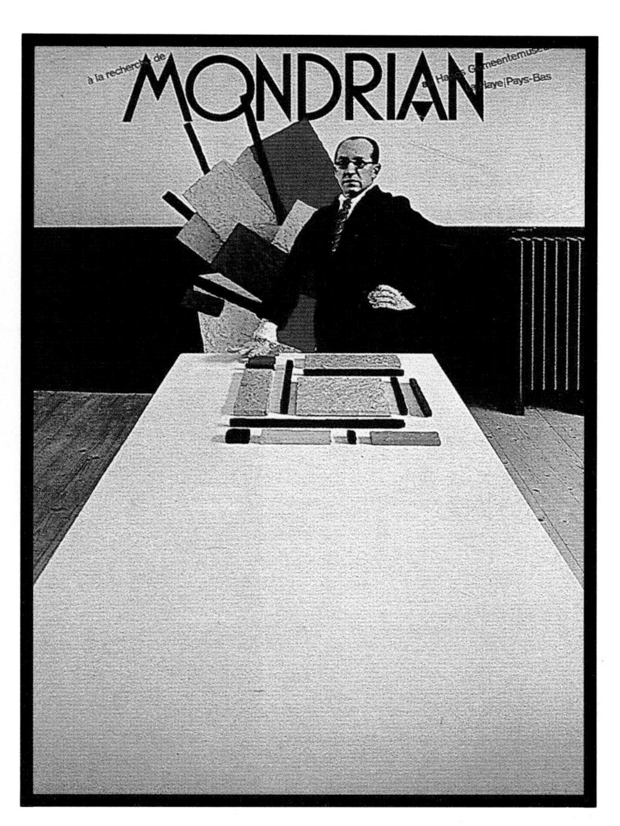

Gert Dunbar. *At left and above, three examples of the work of Dutch designer Gert Dunbar.*

SPAIN

José Pla-Narbona

In the past three decades, following the civil war, graphic design has been rejuvenated as young fine arts graduates traveled to design centers in Europe, subscribed to design publications, and pioneered the countries first professional association of graphic designers, Agrupación Grafistas FAD. One of its founders became one of Spain's outstanding artists and designers, José Pla-Narbona.

In a house built into a hill, some 37 km north of Barcelona and overlooking the Mediterranean, José Pla-Narbona has a multi-storied studio and home. Pla-Narbona is a multi-faceted artist: a surrealist painter of great vigor and a wild sense of humor; an engraver, a sculptor, and a graphic designer. His graphic designs are characterized by imaginative and unconventional yet symbolic illustrations, clear, very readable typography, and often an interweaving of text and illustration. Several examples of his work are shown here (Pgs. 156–157).

ITALY

Much of the most effective graphic design done in the past several decades in Italy is a stylistic continuation of the Swiss grid and visual vitality blend that Max Huber and others introduced to Italy in the 1940s. Selections from the work of six of Italy's leading graphic designers are shown here: Walter Ballmer, Giovanni Pintori, Franco Grignani, Albe Steiner, Heinz Waibl and Bruno Monguzzi (Pgs. 157–164).

Walter Ballmer

Ballmer studied at the Basel School of Applied Art. He has been resident in Italy since 1947, following an invitation from Studio Boggeri. He worked independently for some years, then began a long period of designing for Olivetti.

Chapter XIII: The Many Faces of Typography Today

A page from a book, Ik ga maar en ben, *by Dutch poet J. c. van Schagen, published by Nova Zembla, Arnhem. A sharp blade was used to slit the letters open. The letters were then bent back a little and the text was illuminated from behind and photographed. Printed in black on cream paper. Jurriaan Schrofer. Holland.*

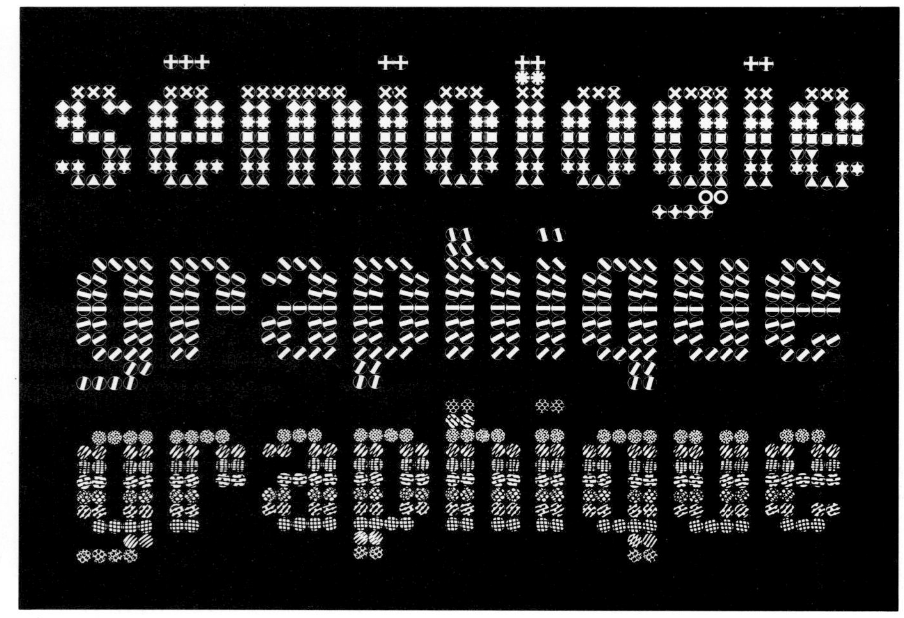

A detail *of the dust jacket for* Semiologie Graphique, *published by Mouton, The Hague. Illustrated are three of the six two-dimensional visual variables from the author's thesis. Jurriaan Schrofer. Holland.*

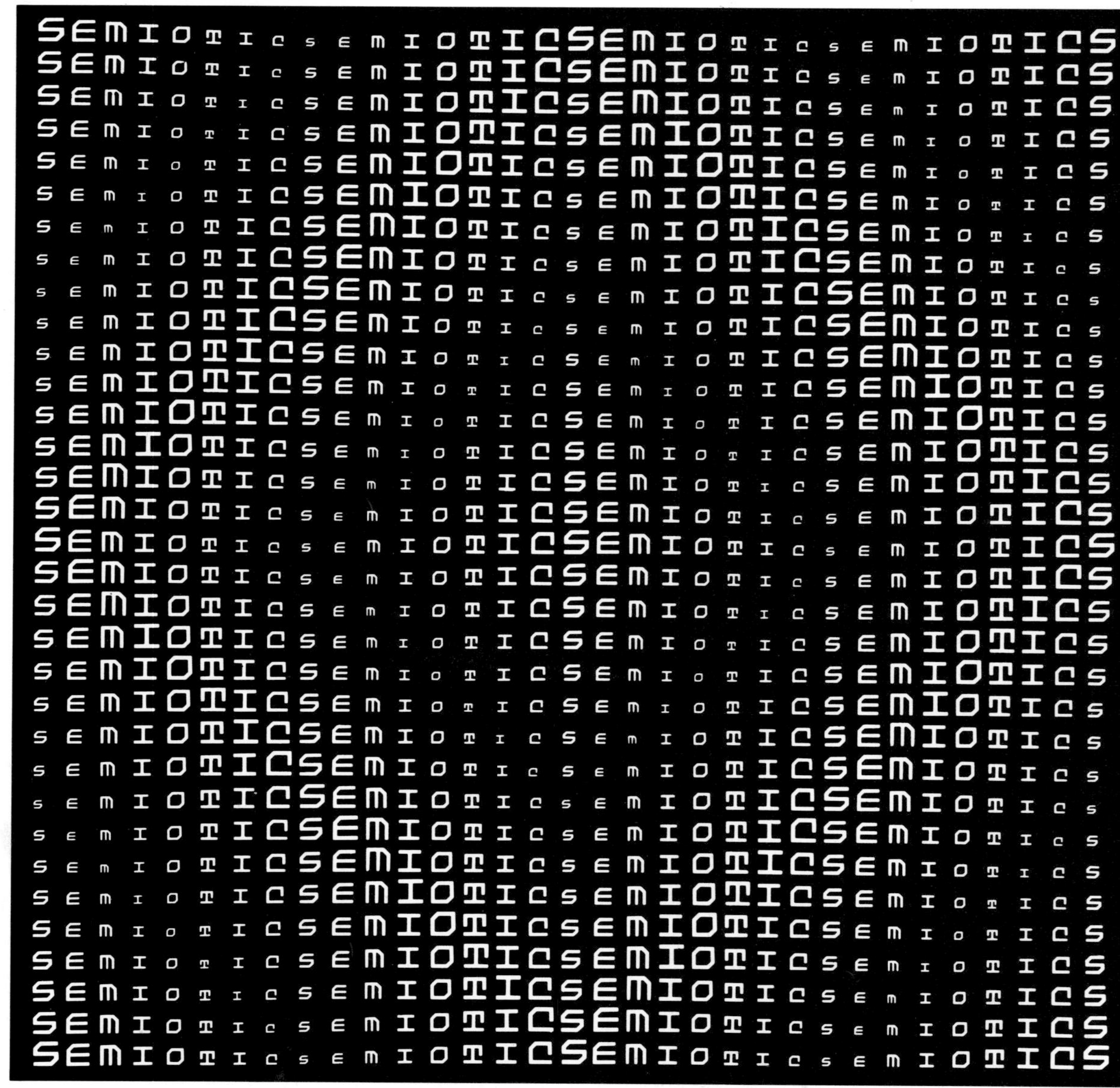

A poster *for* Semiotica, *a journal on semiotics, by Mouton publishers, The Hague. Jurriaan Schrofer. Holland.*

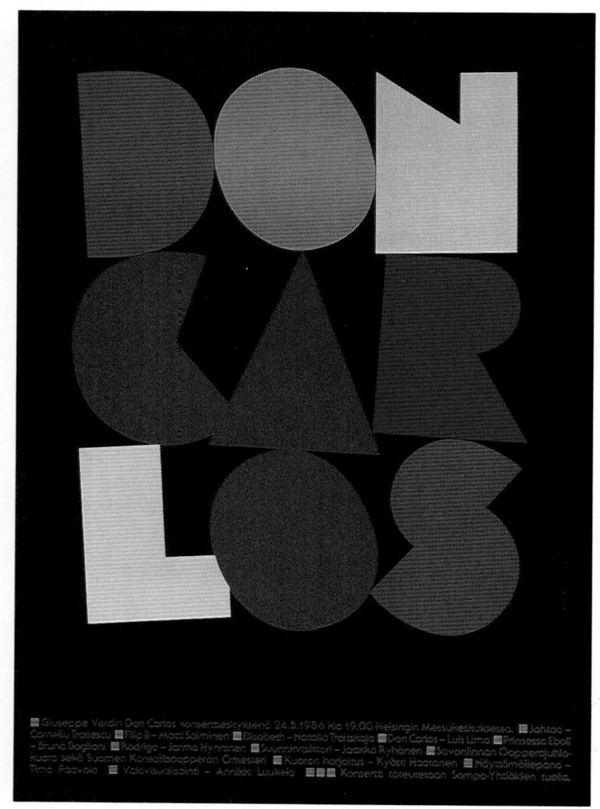

Poster *for the Don Carlos Concert in Helsinki, 1986. Erkki A. Ruuhinen. Finland.*

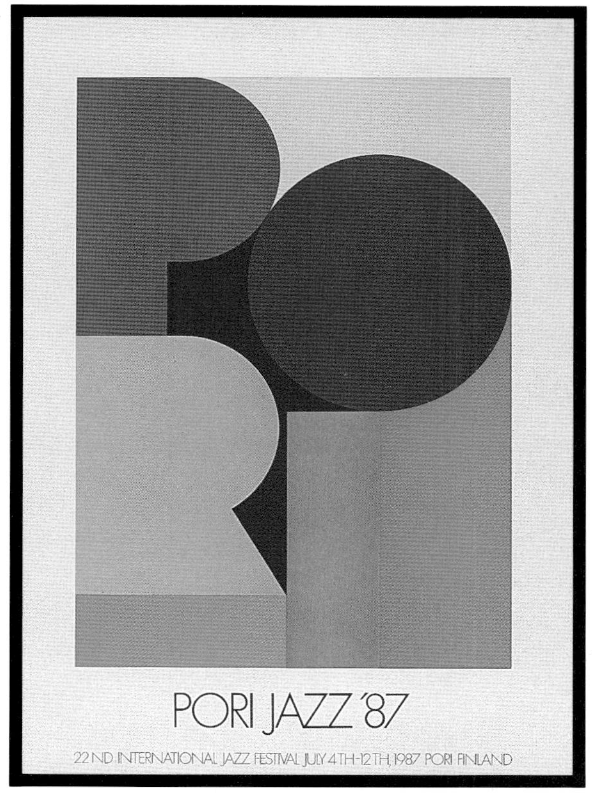

***Poster** for the Pori Jazz Festival, 1987. Errki Ruuhinen. Finland.*

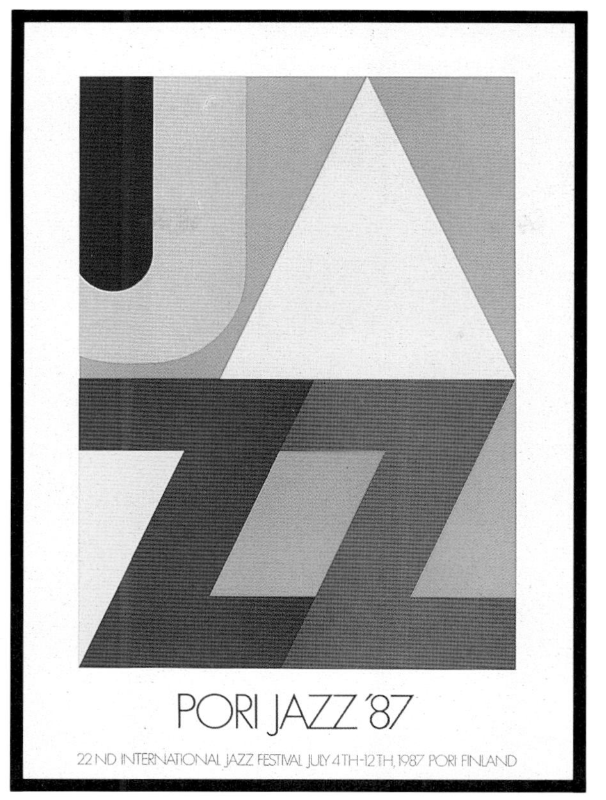

***Poster** for the Pori Jazz Festival, 1987. Errki Ruuhinen. Finland.*

***Poster** for the Pori Jazz Festival, 1986. Errki Ruuhinen. Finland.*

***Poster** for the Pori Jazz Festival, 1985. Errki Ruuhinen. Finland.*

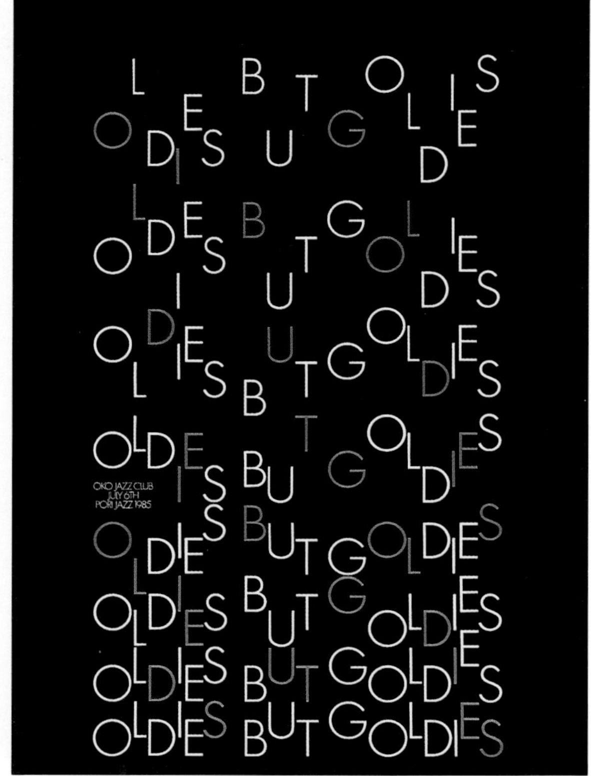

***Poster** for the Pori Jazz Festival, 1985. Errki Ruuhinen. Finland.*

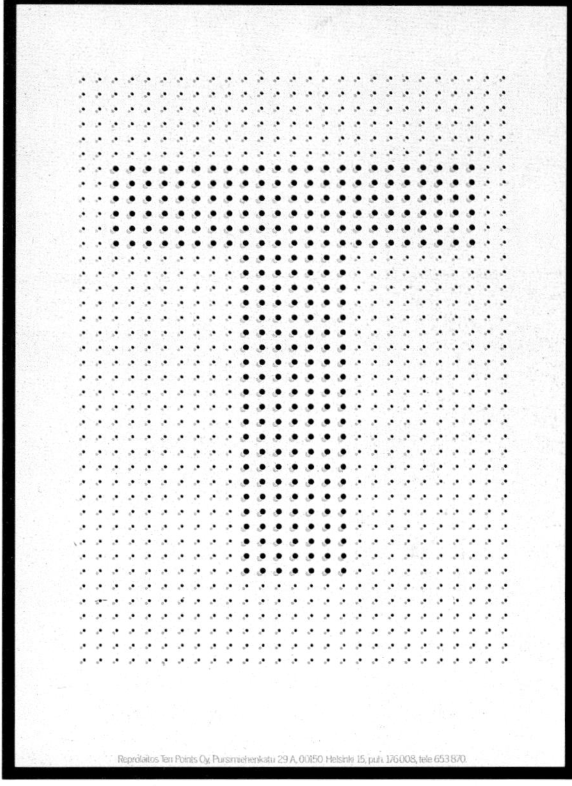

***Poster** for Ten Points Repro Ltd. 1984. Errki Ruuhinen. Finland.*

Franco Grignani

Early in his career, Grignani was a futurist. Later he realized the importance of research prior to starting an esthetic experience. He studied architecture, became a painter and an experimental photographer, as well as a graphic designer.

Albe Steiner

In 1977, two years after Steiner's death, FHK Henrion wrote of him: "He loved to experiment and innovate in two and three dimensions...He ran design as a way of life and as a way of influencing the environment through it...Design is an ordering activity...a way of reducing the chaos. You put a little order into it, through simplification and verification, and possibly by dramatic highlighting of things that matter...Design has gone a long way from being clever drawing, tasteful composition and new combinations. It is really an invitation to participation in creating new things and adding to the quality of life."

Bruno Monguzzi

Bruno Monguzzi, of Milan's Studio Boggeri, is Swiss, and commutes from the Italian-speaking area of southern Switzerland to Milan. He works within rigid grids, but his approach to a design problem is dual, to make it easily readable while achieving visual surprise by the way he mixes type, color, white space, and the sizing and positioning of the graphic elements. He also enjoys working with typographers in three-dimensional forms, as in exhibits and architecture. Antonio Boggeri observes that many designers are interested only in their own work and in ephemeral fashions. They are so immersed in visual communications that few are able to escape from the confines of a connection that accepts such fashions and accentuates their extravagances. "Bruno Monguzzi," he writes, "is one of those few. He belongs to the group of keen defenders of functional and constructive graphics...he recovers that geometric spirit that so strongly marked the appearance and structure of the new typography." But Monguzzi's work is not merely a realistic portrayal; it also contains his own conceptual interpretation.

Monguzzi says of his own work, "I never mediate. When I feel that there is no understanding, I drop out of the job immediately before getting into a nonsensical situation out of which no one can be satisfied...I try to keep out of fashion; to use what I consider the most appropriate tools, regardless of the current style. I consider styles dangerous

(continued on page 164)

I R K K U

SUUNNITTELUTOIMISTO
IRMELI SALMINEN OY
NEITSYTPOLKU 10 B
00140 HELSINKI
PUHELIN 90-661 705

ASIAKAS

TYÖ N:O MERKKI

LASKU N:O PÄIVÄYS

■ VISUAALINEN SUUNNITTELU

■ CASTING

■ TARPEISTO

■ NÄYTTELIJÄN/MALLIN PALKKIO

■ KULJETUSKULUT

■ NAAMIOINTI

■ KAMPAUKSET

■ MUU

■ PANKKI: STS PUNAVUORI 710027-2850 ■ KÄTEISALENNUS 8 PV 2%, 14 PV NETTO, VIIV.KORKO 16%

Elements *in a set of business forms and stationery for two stylists, Liti Wendelin and Irkku Salminen. They work in the same office, but run separate firms. They wanted the graphics to reflect both their relationship and their separate identities. Viktor Kaltala of Helsinki Oy. Finland.*

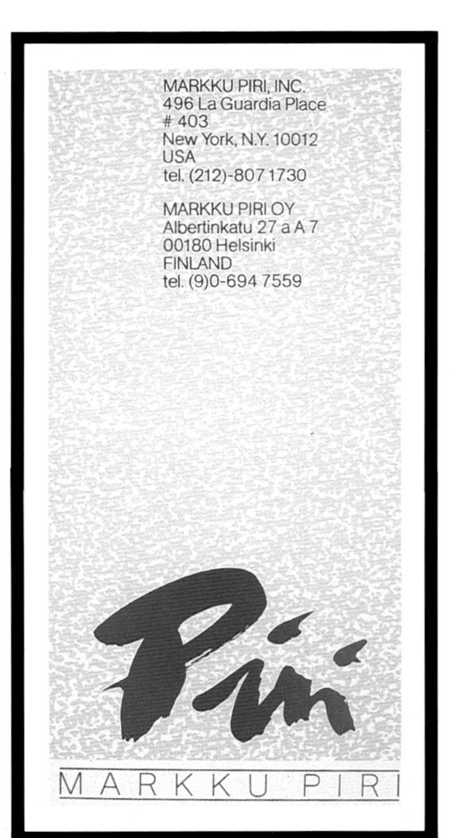

Business card *for Finnish textile designer Markku Piri. Mr. Piri works with shapes derived from his use of colors. Esa Ojala, Senior Designer, Alform Oy. Finland.*

From a brochure *for Marcello Kitchen by Viktor Kaltala of USP Helsinki Oy. Finland.*

The Waste Paper Basketball Club *is an active sports club for old team players who still want to enjoy the game. Letterhead by Viktor Kaltala of USP Helsinki Oy. Finland.*

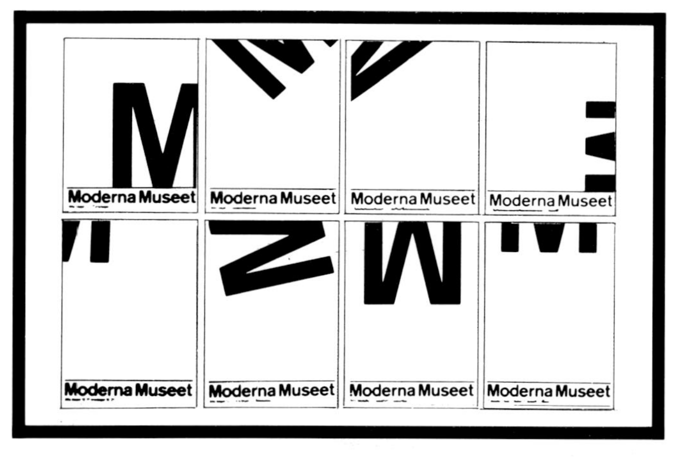

◀ ***Poster*** *for the Moderna Museet, 1961. Art Directors, John Melin & Anders Osterlin. Sweden.*

Of this poster *and business card, designer Viktor Kaltala writes, "My good friend, Mr. Ressi, is an experienced printing entrepreneur and a qualified graphic designer as well. One day he decided to return from the city environment of Helsinki to his original home town, Savonlinna. Savonlinna is a quiet town behind many woods and lakes in easternmost Finland. This fact inspired me to create something which I would call a typographic 'jungle.'" Finland.*

Advertisement *for Hasselblad Svensk, AB. Art Director, John Stern. Sweden.*

Advertisement for Byggproduktion. Art Director, Olle Mattson. Sweden.

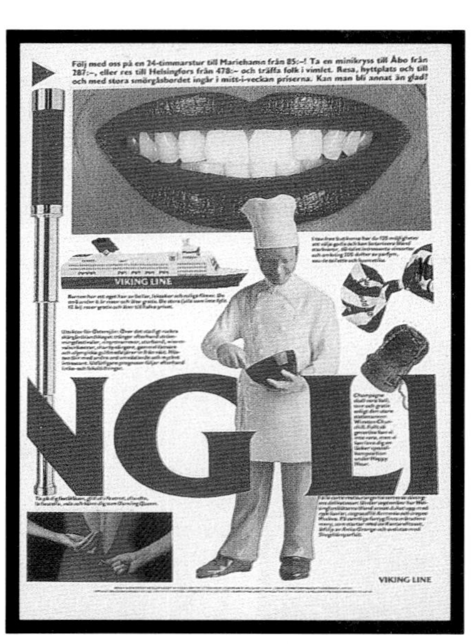

Advertisement for the Viking Line. Art Director, Lasse Liljendahl. Sweden.

Advertisement for the Viking Line. Art Director, Lasse Liljendahl. Sweden.

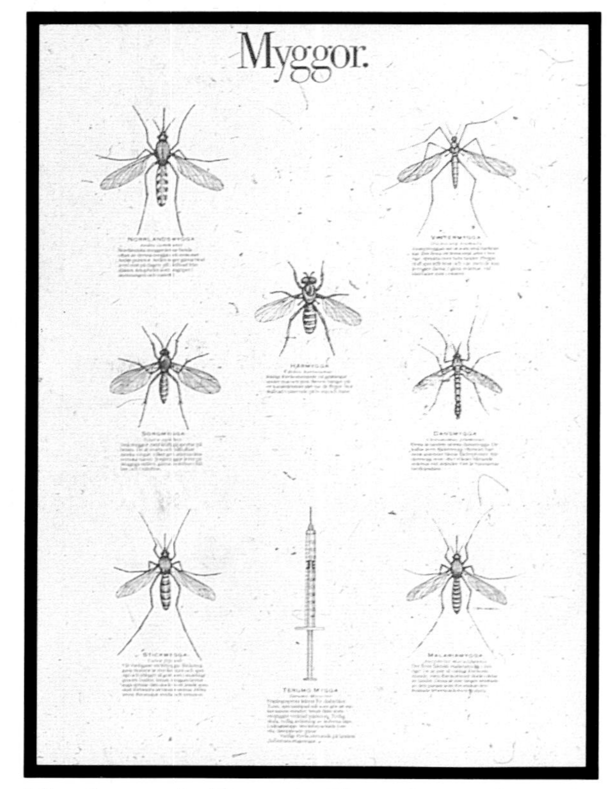

Advertisement for Myggor. Art Director, Lars Modin. Sweden.

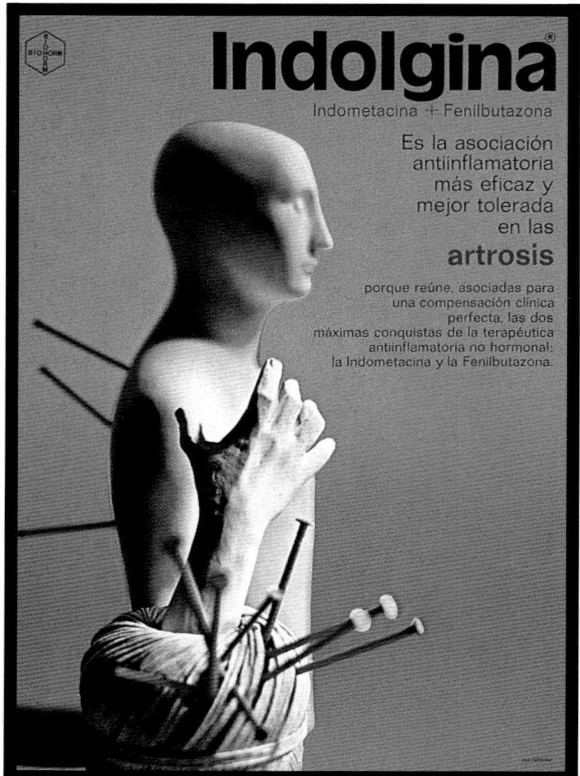

José Pla-Narbona. Spain.

Consumo cerebral de O_2 e HYDERGINA®

José Pla-Narbona. Spain.

José Pla-Narbona. Spain.

Advertisement for Klorin. Art Director, Wille Giesecke. Sweden.

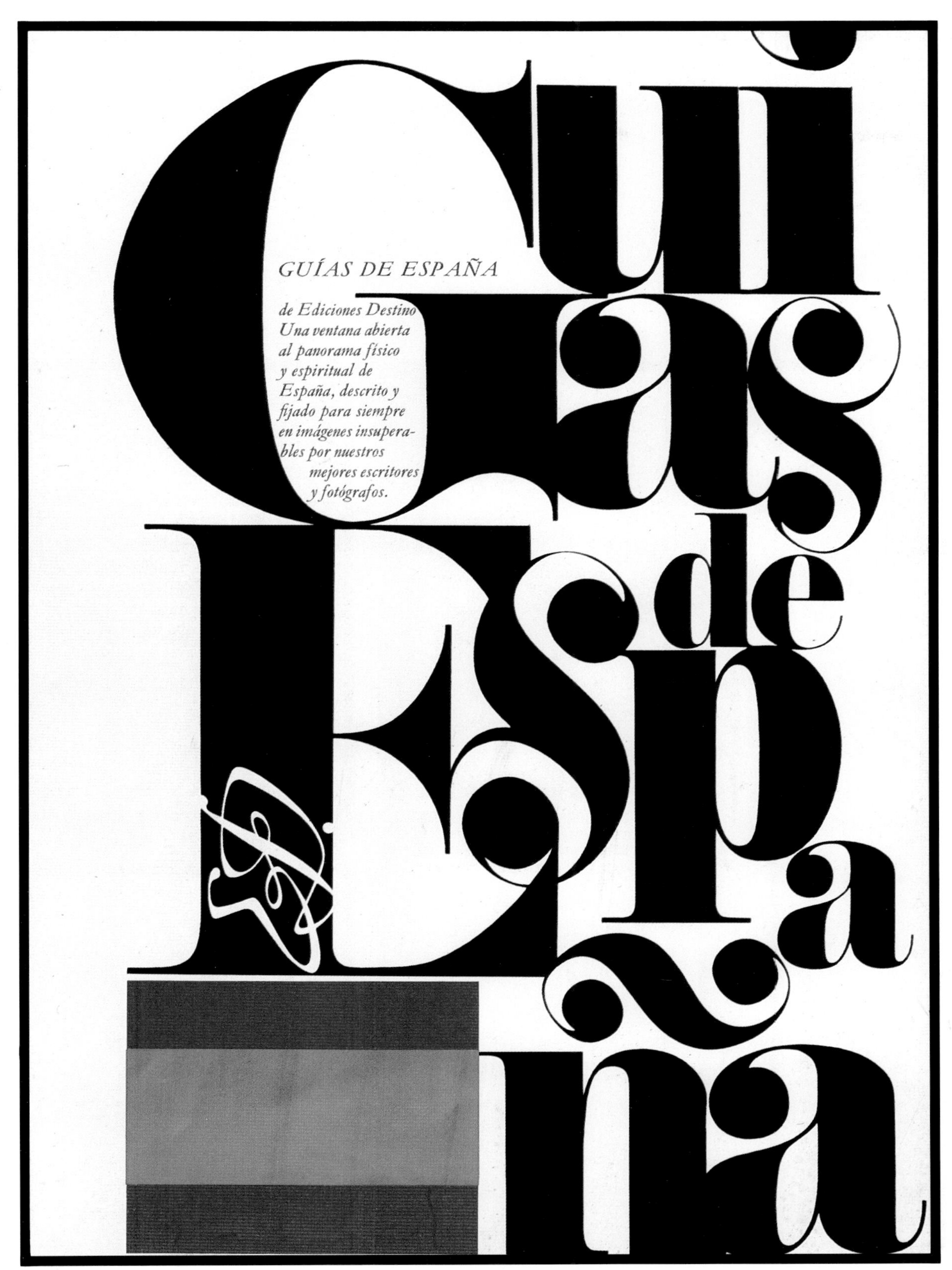

José Pla-Narbona. Spain.

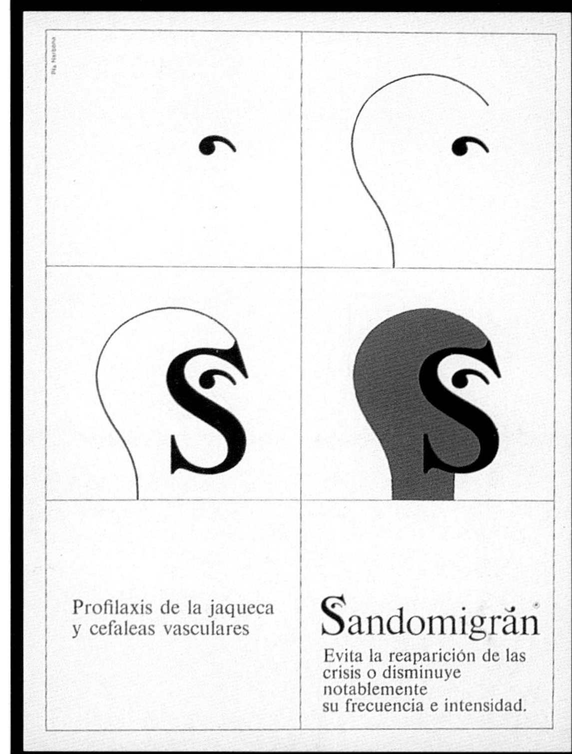

José Pla-Narbona. Spain.

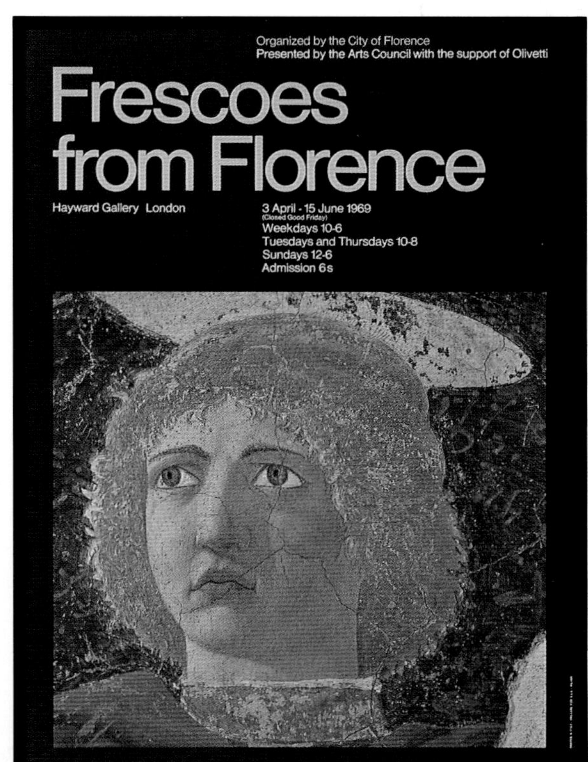

Walter Ballmer. Italy.

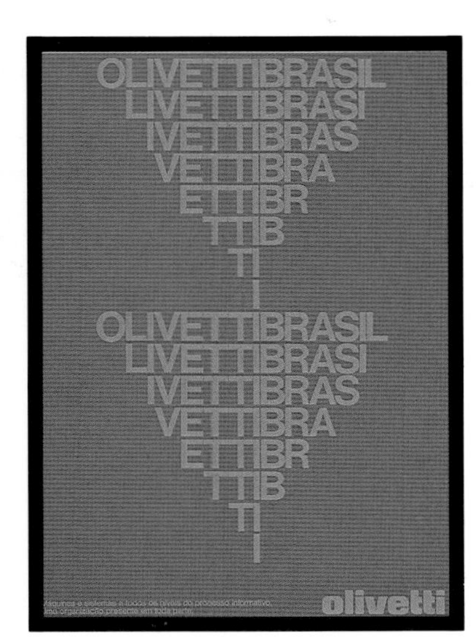

Three in a series *for Olivetti. Walter Ballmer. Italy.*

LOS PROFESIONALES UTILIZAN
MEDIOS ADECUADOS
PARA EJERCER SU PROFESION
LA ELECTRONICA OLIVETTI
ES ELECTRONICA PROFESIONAL
CALCULE ELECTRONICO
CALCULE OLIVETTI CALCULE LOGOS
Las calculadoras electrónicas impresoras Olivetti Logos son calculadoras profesionales. Con todas sus consecuencias: son calculadoras de gran calidad destinadas a funcionar sin reposo, dan todos los cálculos impresos con sus correspondientes símbolos y ofrecen un teclado cómodo, claro y racional. Todo esto no permite que las calculadoras Olivetti Logos sean máquinas diminutas. Pero ¿es necesario para el profesional que lo sean? Logos 240, Logos 245, Logos 250, Logos 270, para facturación, nóminas, costos, contabilidad, incidencias porcentuales, interés compuesto, liquidación de remesas, cambio de moneda, amortizaciones, media aritmética ponderada, media armónica, varianzas, coeficientes de correlación volumenes, polinomios, áreas y para cualquier tipo de trabajo capaz de impulsar su negocio.
olivetti
Organización comercial y asistencia técnica en toda España.

Walter Ballmer. *Italy.*

Giovanni Pintori, for Olivetti, in 1948. Italy.

***Giovanni Pintori,** for Olivetti, in 1963. Italy.*

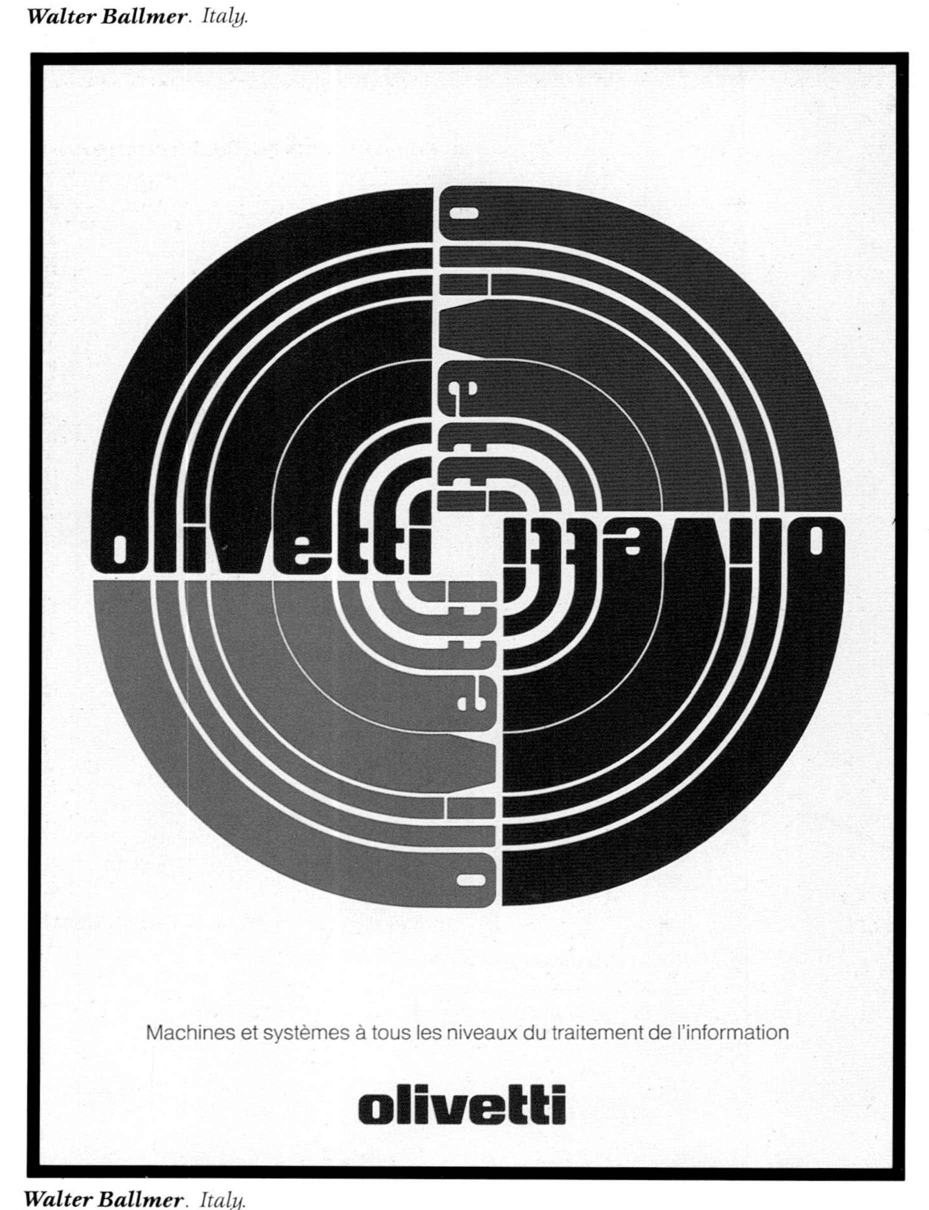

olivetti
Machines et systèmes à tous les niveaux du traitement de l'information
olivetti

Walter Ballmer. *Italy.*

***Giovanni Pintori,** for Olivetti, in 1957. Italy.*

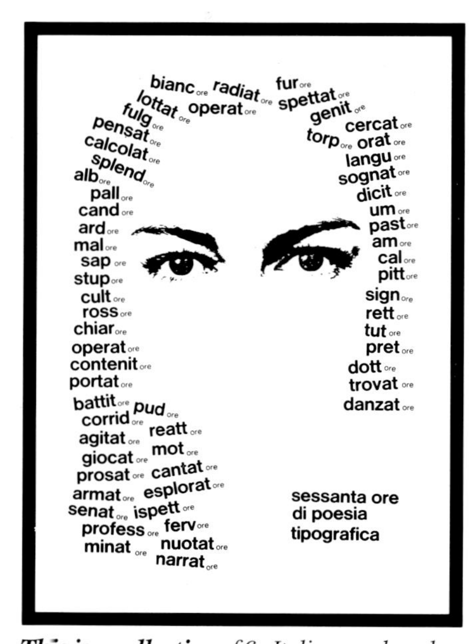

***This is a collection** of 60 Italian words ending in ore (time, hours), for 60 Hours of Typographic Poetry. Franco Grignani. Italy.*

***An advertisement** for the printing office of Alfieri & Lacroix. Text reads, "Speed changes the graphic design, the color, and the vision." 1957, Franco Grignani. Italy.*

DAPPERTUTTO

Dovunque si trattino numeri, parole, dati, informazioni. Nelle banche e nelle grandi industrie, nelle pubbliche amministrazioni e negli enti locali, negli aeroporti e negli alberghi, nei grandi magazzini e nelle stazioni ferroviarie, nelle poste e nei servizi. La nostra organizzazione tocca tutti i paesi del mondo.

olivetti

DAPPERTUTTO

Dovunque si trattino numeri, parole, dati, informazioni. Nelle banche e nelle grandi industrie, nelle pubbliche amministrazioni e negli enti locali, negli aeroporti e negli alberghi, nei grandi magazzini e nelle stazioni ferroviarie, nelle poste e nei servizi. La nostra organizzazione tocca tutti i paesi del mondo.

IN ITALIA

Siamo di casa. Abbiamo un'organizzazione commerciale con 103 filiali e centri di vendita, 345 concessionari esclusivisti, 73 distributori fiduciari, 521 centri di assistenza tecnica. I nostri specialisti sono a disposizione di chi utilizza le nostre macchine e desidera studiare con noi le soluzioni più razionali dei propri problemi, avere sicurezza in più.

olivetti

DAPPERTUTTO

Dovunque si trattino numeri, parole, dati, informazioni. Nelle banche e nelle grandi industrie, nelle pubbliche amministrazioni e negli enti locali, negli aeroporti e negli alberghi, nei grandi magazzini e nelle stazioni ferroviarie, nelle poste e nei servizi. La nostra organizzazione tocca tutti i paesi del mondo.

IN ITALIA

Siamo di casa. Abbiamo un'organizzazione commerciale con 103 filiali e centri di vendita, 345 concessionari esclusivisti, 73 distributori fiduciari, 521 centri di assistenza tecnica. I nostri specialisti sono a disposizione di chi utilizza le nostre macchine e desidera studiare con noi le soluzioni più razionali dei propri problemi, avere sicurezza in più.

NELLE MACCHINE CHE SCRIVONO

Siamo nelle macchine per scrivere da oltre un sessantennio. Alcuni dei nostri primissimi modelli potete trovarli ancora al lavoro. Costruiamo un'intera linea di macchine per scrivere, grandi e piccole, elettriche e manuali, per ogni destinazione, da quelle per la casa e la scrittura personale alle macchine per la scrittura professionale e degli uffici. Adesso questo annuncio vi presenta il nuovo

olivetti

DAPPERTUTTO

Dovunque si trattino numeri, parole, dati, informazioni. Nelle banche e nelle grandi industrie, nelle pubbliche amministrazioni e negli enti locali, negli aeroporti e negli alberghi, nei grandi magazzini e nelle stazioni ferroviarie, nelle poste e nei servizi. La nostra organizzazione tocca tutti i paesi del mondo.

IN ITALIA

Siamo di casa. Abbiamo un'organizzazione commerciale con 103 filiali e centri di vendita, 345 concessionari esclusivisti, 73 distributori fiduciari, 521 centri di assistenza tecnica. I nostri specialisti sono a disposizione di chi utilizza le nostre macchine e desidera studiare con noi le soluzioni più razionali dei propri problemi, avere sicurezza in più.

NELLE MACCHINE CHE SCRIVONO

Siamo nelle macchine per scrivere da oltre un sessantennio. Alcuni dei nostri primissimi modelli potete trovarli ancora al lavoro. Costruiamo un'intera linea di macchine per scrivere, grandi e piccole, elettriche e manuali, per ogni destinazione, da quelle per la casa e la scrittura personale alle macchine per la scrittura professionale e degli uffici. Adesso questo annuncio vi presenta il nuovo

SISTEMA ELETTRONICO DI SCRITTURA EDITOR S14

che realizza in modo completo e redditivo il processo della comunicazione scritta: ricorda i testi che scrive, li elabora, li integra e li stampa nel numero di originali desiderato, alla velocità di oltre 150 parole al minuto.

olivetti

***Walter Ballmer**. Italy.*

***This ad** for the printer, Alfieri & Lacroix, suggests that you choose your sugar-drop candy beginning with an A, as does Alfieri & Lacroix. 1960. Franco Grignani. Italy.*

***"Alfieri & Lacroix** takes lovely care of typography." 1964. Franco Grignani. Italy.*

***"Today you write** in the sky, on cement, on fabric, on pears... but the story and the quality of typography are made on paper." For the printer, Alfieri & Lacroix. 1965. Franco Grignani. Italy.*

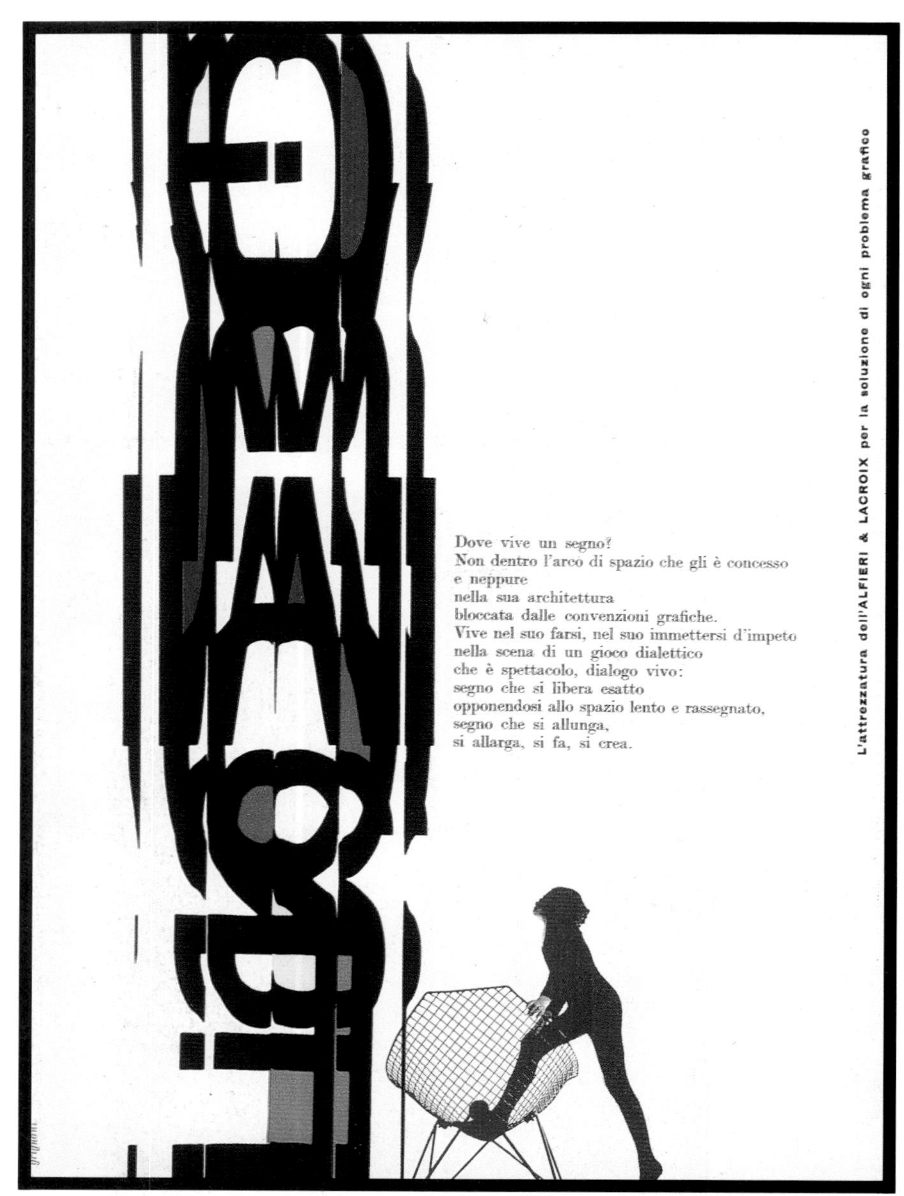

Dove vive un segno?
Non dentro l'arco di spazio che gli è concesso
e neppure
nella sua architettura
bloccata dalle convenzioni grafiche.
Vive nel suo farsi, nel suo immettersi d'impeto
nella scena di un gioco dialettico
che è spettacolo, dialogo vivo:
segno che si libera esatto
opponendosi allo spazio lento e rassegnato,
segno che si allunga,
si allarga, si fa, si crea.
L'attrezzatura dell'ALFIERI & LACROIX per la soluzione di ogni problema grafico

For Alfieri & Lacroix. *1959. Franco Grignani. Italy.*

While designing *this magazine cover, Franco Grignani became thirsty and decided to immerse the title in a glass of water. 1955. Italy.*

Cover *for the annual,* Advertising in Italy. *1964-65. Franco Grignani. Italy.*

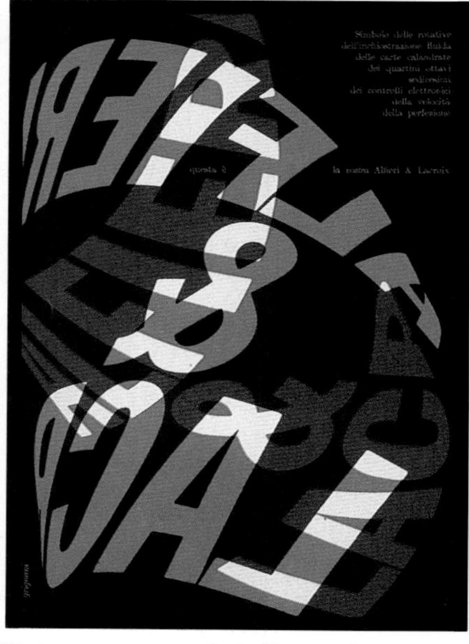

Rotary press *at work. Italian text is sweet, fluent, and oily to help the image. For Alfieri & Lacroix, printers. 1960. Franco Grignani. Italy.*

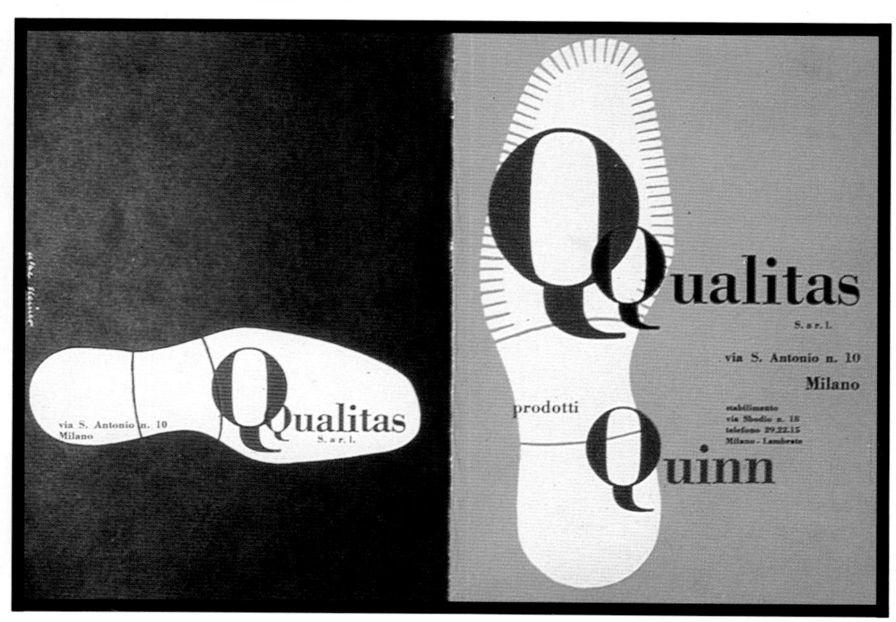

For Alfieri & Lacroix, *printers. 1960. Albe Steiner. Italy.*

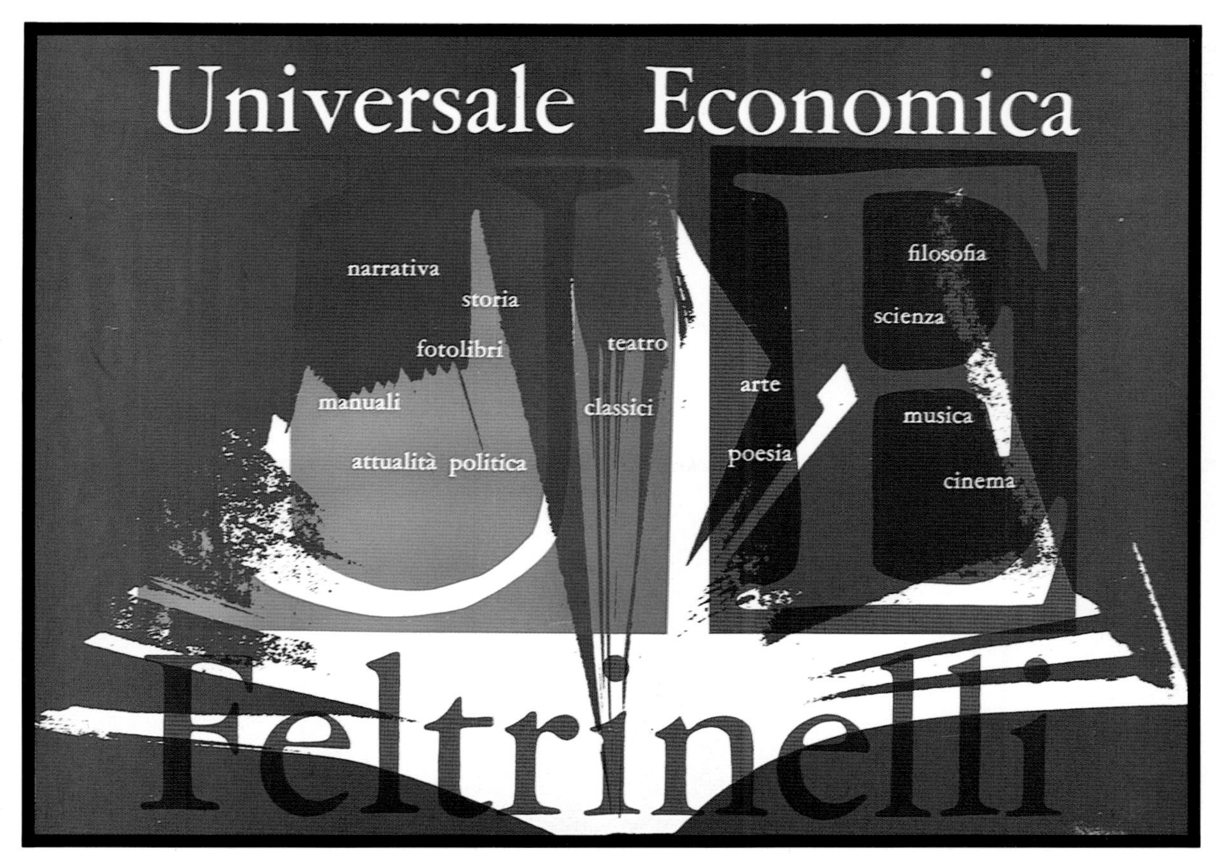

Comitato milanese di assistenza
della lega italiana
per la lotta contro i tumori.
Nei giorni 9, 10, 11, 12 dicembre 1969
fiera gastronomica
a prezzi di mercato
al Centro Ignis
Milano, Galleria Vittorio Emanuele.

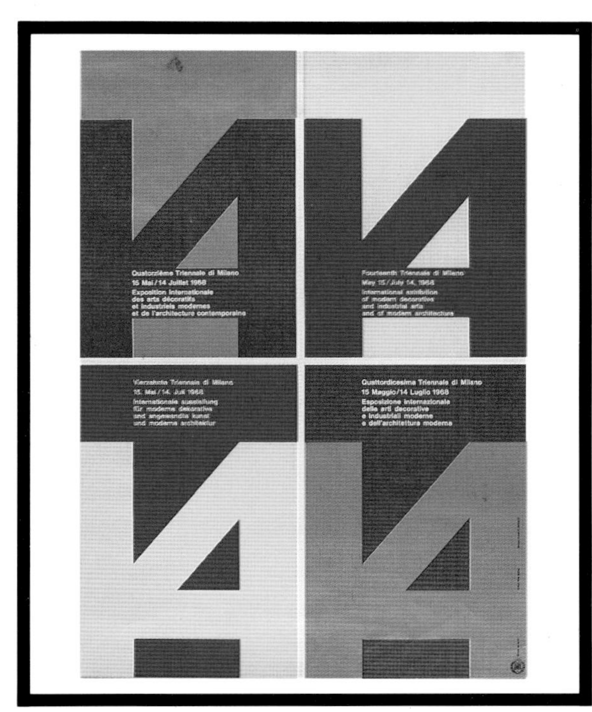

All work *shown on this page is by Albe Steiner. Italy.*

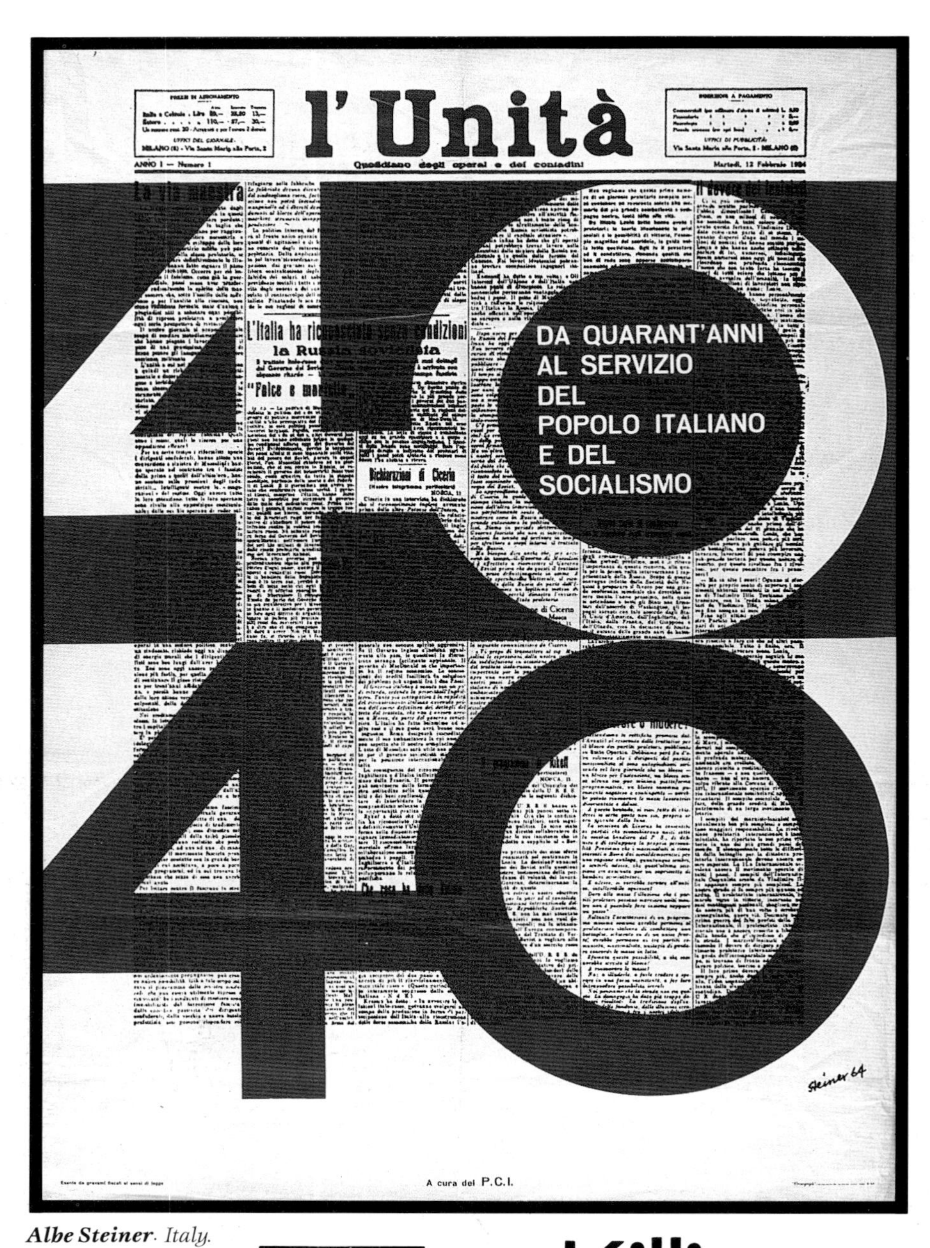

Albe Steiner. *Italy.*

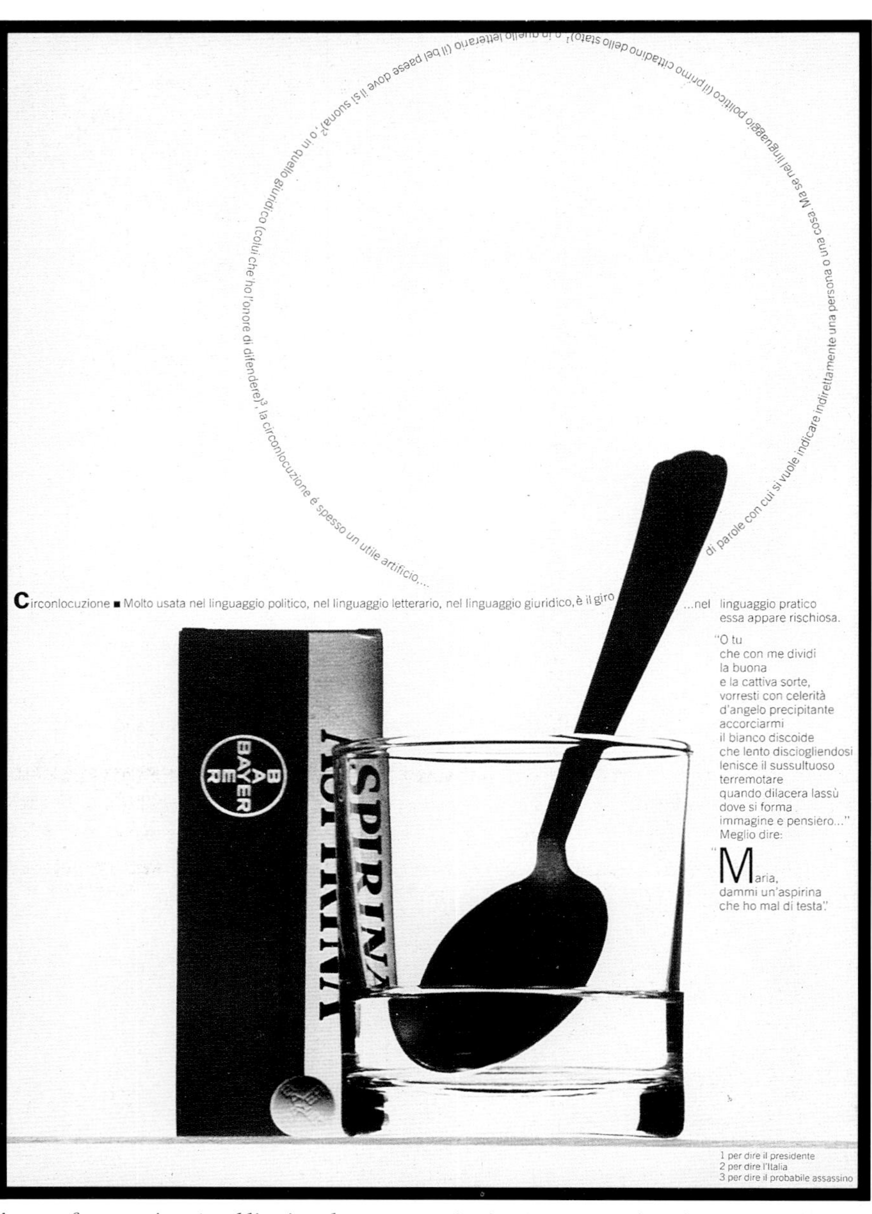

A page *from a printer's publication about communication. Every page describes a term. This page is about circumlocution and reads, in part, "il giro di parole" (the circle of words). Bruno Monguzzi, 1981. Italy.*

Centro Forme, *a furniture shop. 1973. Como, Italy. Heinz Waibl.*

For a department store, *Killian Corporation, in Cedar Rapids, Iowa, U.S.A. 1969. Designed for Unimark International. Heinz Waibl.*

Transunion Corporation. *1969. Designed for Unimark International. Heinz Waibl. Italy.*

Ceteco, *a manufacturer of copypaper. 1959. São Paulo, Brazil. Heinz Waibl. Italy.*

A graphic design magazine, *1961. Milan, Italy. Heinz Waibl.*

Officine Calabrese, *a manufacturer of industrial vehicles. 1963. Bari, Italy. Heinz Waibl.*

Pro Juventule, *a foundation for handicapped youth. 1983. Milan, Italy. Heinz Waibl.*

Skema Apredamenti *is a manufacturer of furniture for executive offices. 1982. Varedo Milan, Italy. Heinz Waibl.*

Two pages *from a printer's publication about communication. One deals with hyperbole, one with flashback. The typographic solution on the hyperbole page takes advantage of the two sentences given as examples: "I send you a million kisses" and "I send you a billion times to hell." Bruno Monguzzi, 1981. Italy.*

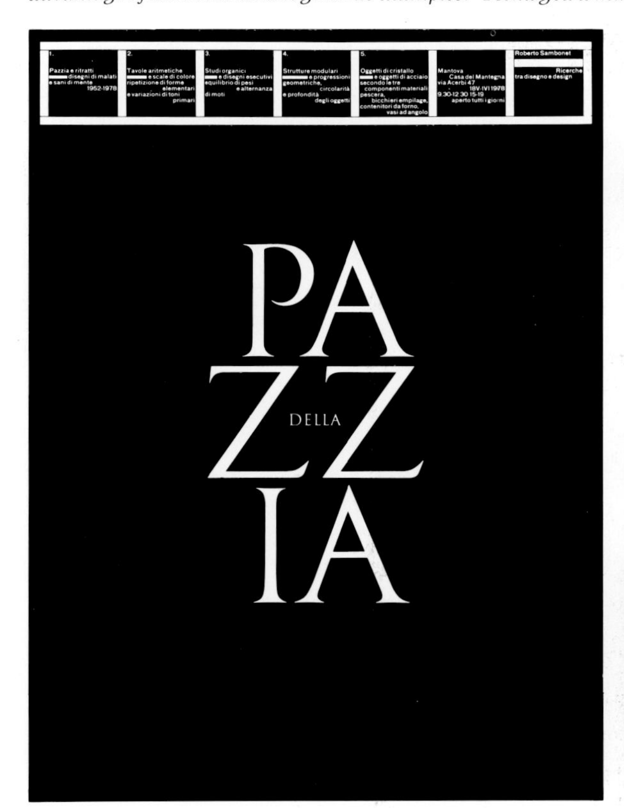

Poster. *Della Pazzia (on madness) avoids easy, dramatic tricks that might produce a superficial understanding of the subject matter. Bruno Monguzzi, 1978. Italy.*

An attempt *to reflect the spirit of the '20s in Russia for a poster announcing an exhibit of the work of Russian artists at the Sforza castle in Milan. There is a strong constructivist approach. The bars are black, red and gray, and establish a 45 degree grid. The grid design is carried out through the catalog also and gives its pages strong continuity. Bruno Monguzzi, 1975. Italy.*

The cover *of a printer's publication discussing communication. The logo is presented twice, once flat and the other curved to suggest an offset plate over a cylinder. Bruno Monguzzi, 1981. Italy.*

***A poster** for the zone councils of the city of Milan. It requests volunteer help immediately after the Inprima earthquake of 1980. It was, literally, designed overnight, but is one of Monguzzi's favorites. Here two squares and a rectangle overlap on a golden sector grid. The idea is in the gray rectangle. A covering ink lightens the black and slightly hides the dramatic scene in order to build psychological distance. Bruno Monguzzi, 1980. Italy.*

***Catalog cover** for an exhibition in Koln, Germany, dealing with Italian furniture design. A typographic cover, it is coordinated with all the printed matter related to the exhibit. Bruno Monguzzi, 1980. Italy.*

(continued from page 153).
because they define *a priori* the span of the possible solution...I think a designer involved with communication is supposed to be the instrument through which communication is correctly accomplished...As a student, I was first attracted by the fathers of modern typographic design, mostly Lissitzky and Zwart, and the early Swiss school, Bill, Lohse, Neuburg, Müller-Brockmann, Vivarelli, Gerstner. Then I became acquainted with Italian design and was particularly impressed with the work of Studio Boggeri, Huber, and Grignani, and later with what I call the New York typographic school of the late '50s, Gene Federico, Brownjohn, Lubalin, Dorfsman."

By his own admission, Monguzzi is an outsider among his design peers. He says, "I find our society a bit noisy. I just would like to contribute a little silence."

HUNGARY
Janos Kass

Janos Kass is a Professor at the Academy of Art in Budapest, and art director of the monthly magazine *Uj Iras* and the Kner Printing House. His work includes poster illustration, book design, stamp design, typography and book illustration. (P.165)

CZECHOSLOVAKIA

In early 1984 an exhibition, Typo &, was held at the ITC Center in New York. It reviewed the work of nine contemporary Czech designers and had previously been shown in Czechoslovakia. An introduction to the show by Bohuslav Holy summarizes the development of modern typography and graphic design there:

"During the period of Constructivism and Functionalism of the Twenties and Thirties, the essential characteristics of 'modern' Czech typography and graphic design were crystalized: they combined artistic inventiveness with stylistic unity, within the limitations imposed by mechanical production. Simultaneously, the rich heritage of classical typography maintained its vitality, especially in the area of book design. Among the seminal personalities of that period, Ladislav Sutnar deserves mention: a familiar figure to the American professional public, he worked in New York from 1939 until his death in 1976.

"After World War II, Oldrich Hlavsa's work was similarly influential. Through his work in books and advertising, where he constantly searched for new, expressive values in typography and graphics, he pointed to fresh directions for other Czech designers to follow. He enlivened the approach to design by demonstrating the possibilities that lay beyond the limits of strict adherence to classical or constructivist/functionalist doctrines. His influence, however, is proving to be far more fertile than that of a mere leader with disciples: he taught how provocative questioning can lead designers to develop their own personal interpretations and individual solutions.

"Today's Czech designers are concentrating their efforts on exploring typography as the basic means of graphic expression."

Three pieces *by Janos Kass. Hungary.*

Although each designer represented in Typo & has his or her own approach and mode of expression, Holy wrote, "One factor is common to them all: book design is a vital element in their work..."

Examples of the work of leading contemporary Czech graphic designers show a variety of approaches to blending graphic vitality, clarity, and excellent craftsmanship.

Commenting on influences on contemporary typography in Czechoslovakia, Oldrich Hlavsa writes:

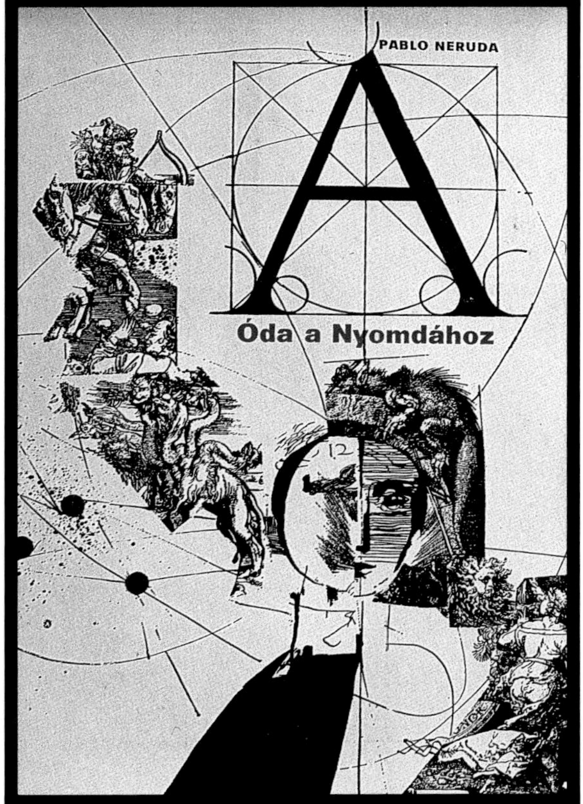

"Today's typography is influenced by art, particularly by the graphic arts. In the shops of today there is never time or space enough for art typography; that happens only in those rare cases where there is an art director with good will and courage... In July of 1966 I was a member of the International jury, Report 66, which judged the West German applied graphics. On that occasion, meetings with artists were organized and many times I asked them about the influence of American typography on the arts, specifically on the graphic arts in Europe. This question of American influence became clearer each day for any objective observer, except for the expert. That is why my opinion met with a lot of opposition, mostly by the experts who have educated German graphic artists in the post-war years, such as the directors of a variety of trade schools. Of course, there also were many who defended my side with great enthusiasm. I well remember the words a German friend used to express his agreement with my opinion: 'contemporary American typography has been exerting pressure on us for a number of years. Whether we like it or not, we repeat the principles of this typography without question, without sharp protests or diplomatic notes. In many cases, it means a certain freedom from strict rules of order which the tradition of our work has given us. Unfortunately, this freedom means too much unprofessional negation and violation of the principles of our profession due to a lack of understanding.'"

Besides Sutnar and Hlavsa, Czechoslovakian art and design was greatly influenced by Karel Teige. Teige was invited by Hannes Meyer to be a guest lecturer at the Bauhaus in 1930. In Prague, Teige brought back some of the Bauhaus design thinking. Josef Albers in 1928 and Hannes Meyer in 1930-31 lectured in Prague. Teige spread his ideas through journals he edited and a series of books he published. Teige believed that art should not be regarded as a luxury, but as a necessity of life. Further Bauhaus influence was felt in Czechoslovakia due to the many Slavic students studying at the Bauhaus, and when the magazine *Red* published a special edition on the Bauhaus (Czechoslovakian work, pgs. 165-175.)

Magazine cover. *Oldrich Hlavsa, 1964. Czechoslovakia.*

Magazine cover. *Oldrich Hlavsa, 1970. Czechoslovakia.*

Magazine cover. *Oldrich Hlavsa, 1970. Czechoslovakia.*

Oldrich Hlavsa, *1965.*

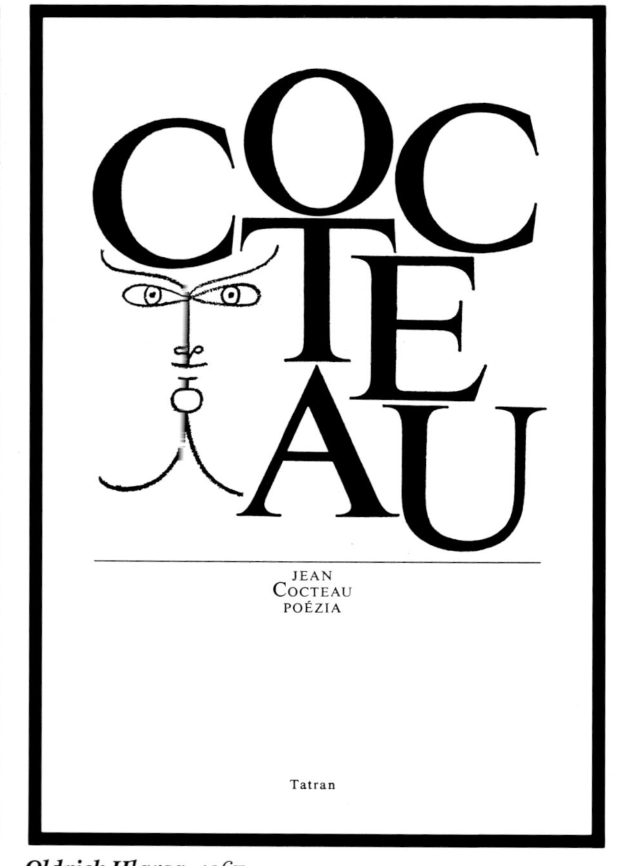

Oldrich Hlavsa, *1967.*

Oldrich Hlavsa, *1972.*

Oldrich Hlavsa, *1965.*

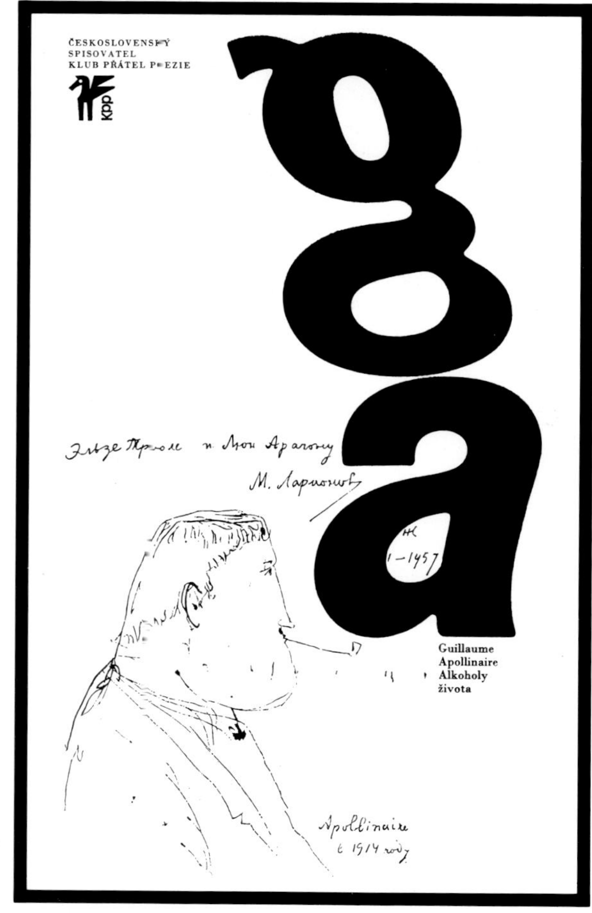

Oldrich Hlavsa, *1974.*

Oldrich Hlavsa, 1965.

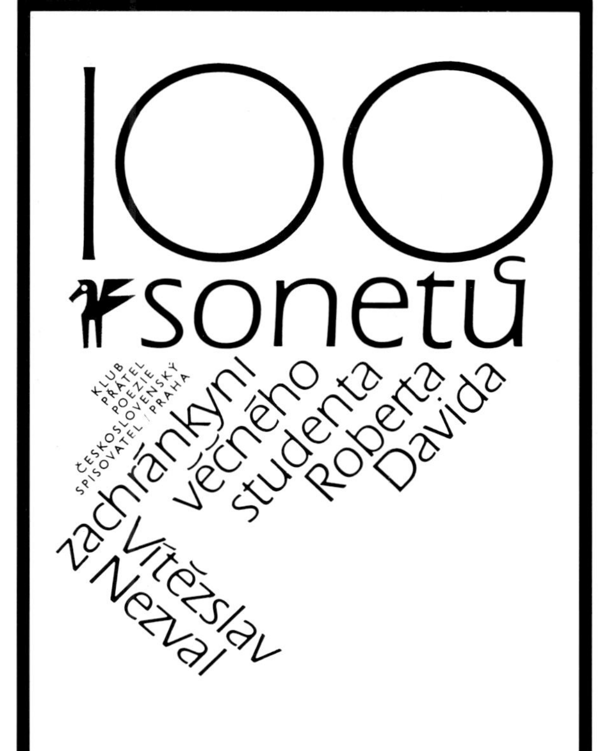

***Here the designer** "wanted to put together the name of the author and the title of the book to make one compact sign." Clara Istlerova, 1978-80.*

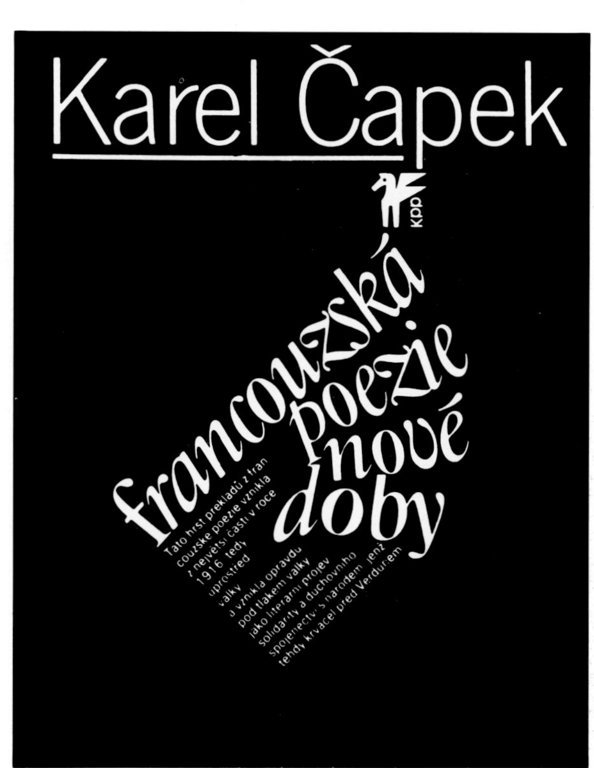

***A book of poetry** for a Czech poetry club. Clara Istlerova, 1980.*

***An edition** of Goethe's* Faust *in a calligraphic manner. Clara Istlerova, 1975-77.*

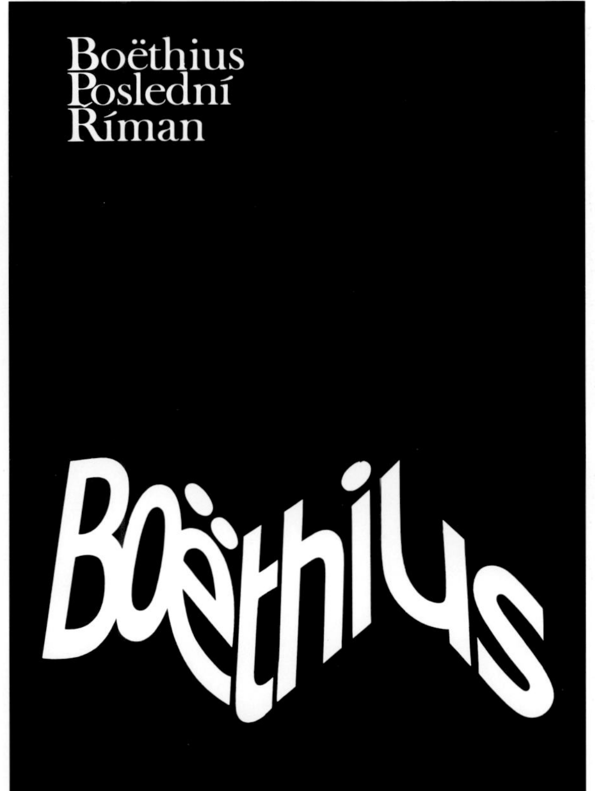

***One of several books** on philosophical literature done in black and white. Clara Istlerova, 1982-85.*

***A graphic linking** of the author's name and the title of the book. Clara Istlerova, 1978-80.*

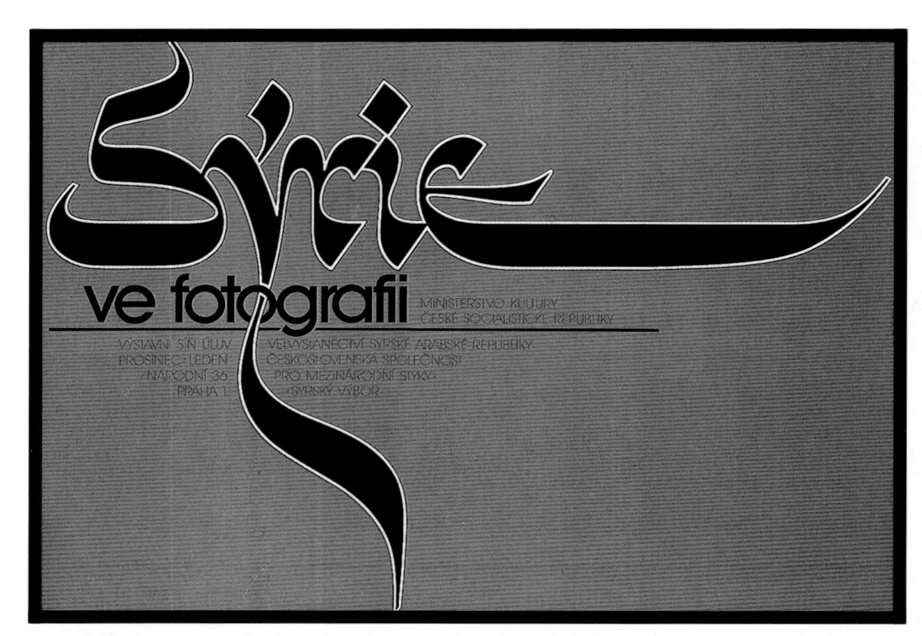

***An exhibition poster** for* Syria in Photographs. *The artistic form of Latin lettering has been adapted to the structure of the Arabic script. Jan Solpera, 1982.*

***Exhibition poster** for* Utility Glass. *The logotype,* SKLO *(glass), suggests the form of utility glass. Jan Solpera, 1983.*

Jan Solpera

Czech artist/designer Jan Solpera is primarily concerned with lettering in book design and in promotional and applied graphics, including architecture. He treats lettering as a pictorial element and believes that in so doing one can express much more than is conveyed by "the mere content of the communication." He believes that "Lettering can illustrate a certain period of history and a certain setting, express a mood, an atmosphere and further emotional moments. It enables an immensely rich compositional application in the rhythm of the surface, as well as spatial effects."

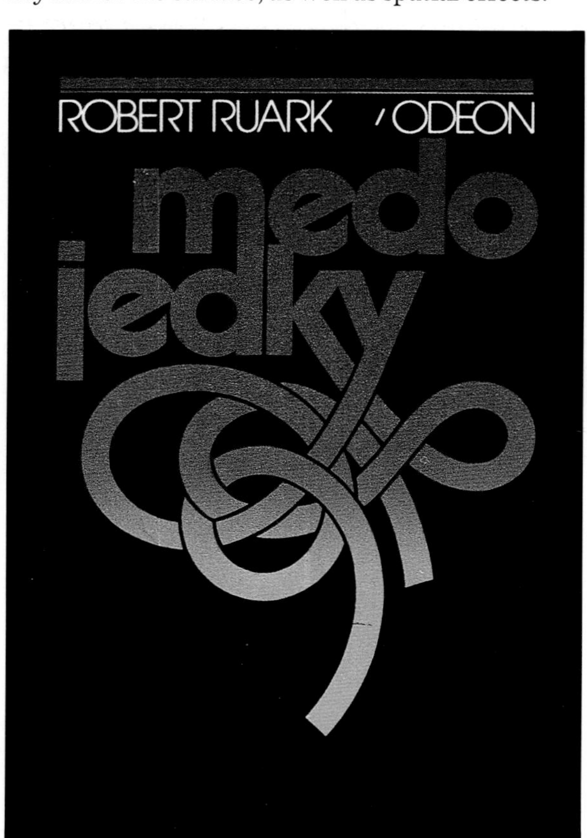

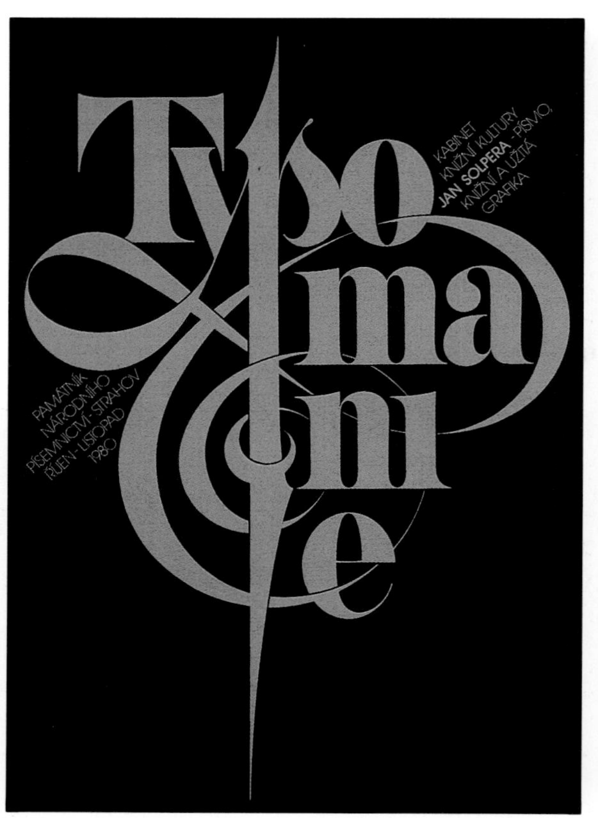

***A poster** for the designer's own exhibition. Typographic and calligraphic elements have been combined to show both poles of the artist's interests. Jan Solpera, 1980.*

***Book Jacket.** The typography and the calligraphic motif are designed to express the complexity of the story about a honey badger. Jan Solpera, 1979.*

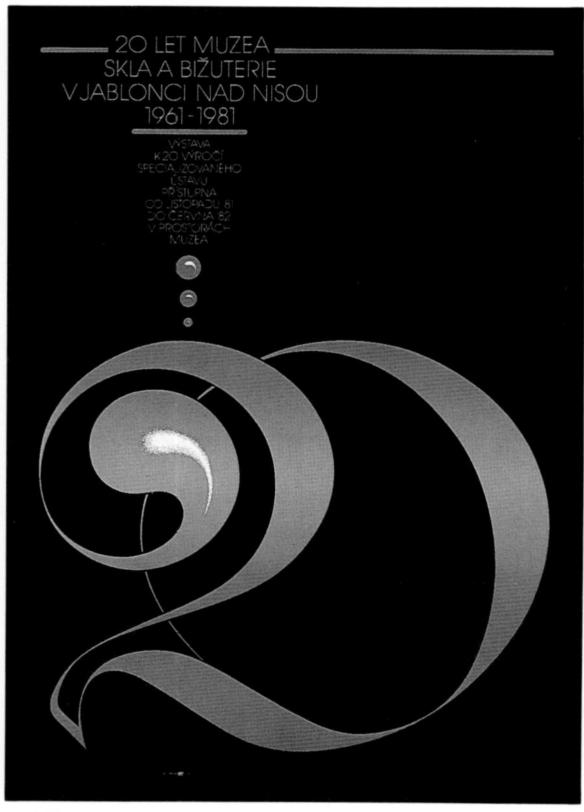

***Exhibition poster,** "20 years of the Museum of Glass and Fancy Jewelry." The shape of the figure evokes both a twisted metal strip and a drop of melted glass. The axial composition of the text aims to suggest the shape of an historical glass goblet. Jan Solpera, 1981.*

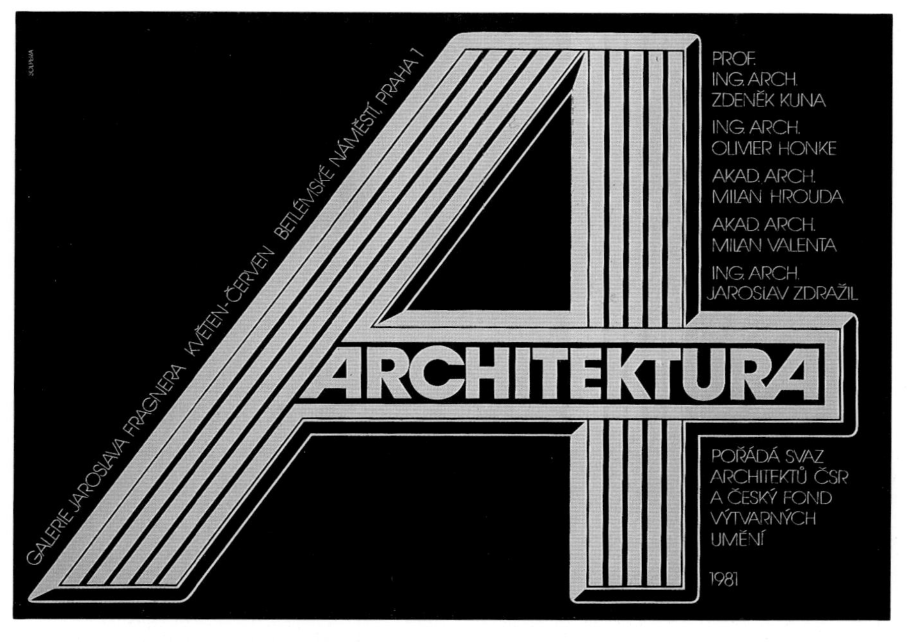

Poster *for exhibition of contemporary Czechoslovak architecture. The form of the letter A aims to evoke an architectonic element. Jan Solpera, 1981.*

Josef Tyfa

A Czechoslovakian graphic and book designer, Tyfa is also known for his typeface and trademark designs, a few of which are shown here.

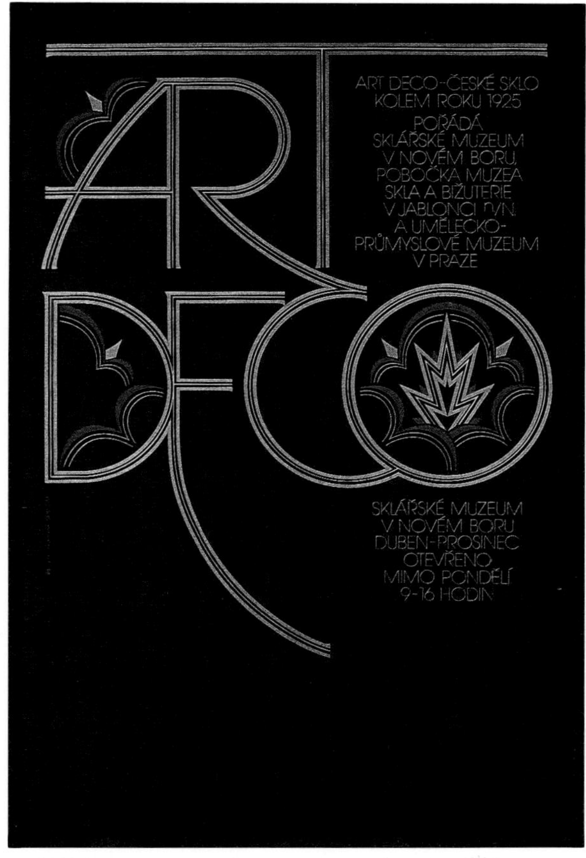

Exhibition poster *employs appropriate lettering and patterns derived from decor on glass from the art deco period. Jan Solpera, 1980.*

ÁBČĎĚFG
HÍJKĽMŇ
ÓPQŘŠŤÚ
VWXÝŽ&
1234567890
ábčďéfghij
kľmňôpqřš
ťůvwxyž*†

Týfova antikva/Grafotechna

ÁBČĎÉFG
HÍJKĽMŇ
ÔPQŘŠŤÚ
VWXÝŽ&
1234567890
ábčďéfghíj
kľmňôpqřš
ťůvwxýž†*

Týfova kurzíva/Grafotechna

Trademarks *for Gallery Hollor, Prague; for an edition of books; for Tepna Textile Trust; for the Jitex knitting factory. Josef Tyfa.*

ABCDÉFGHI
JKLMNOPQ
RSTŮVWXY
abčdéfghíjŽ
klmnopqrs
tůvwxyzß?
1234567890

ABCDÉFGHI
JKLMNOPQ
RSTŮVWXY
abčdéfghíjŽ
klmnopqrs
tůvwxyzß?
1234567890

ABCDÉFGHIJ
KLMNOPQR
STŮVWXYŽ
abčdefghíj
klmnopqrst
ůvwxyzß?
1234567890

Tyfa Antique *and Tyfa Italic (top) were designed in 1960. The designer aimed for a "contemporary antique typeface" with an unconventional fattening of some strokes.*

Juvenis Roman, *Demi-bold and Italic were designed in 1975 especially for children's books. The designer favored condensed letters and serifs with minuscules to facilitate joining of some letters.*

Zdenek Ziegler, *Czechoslovakia*
Much of Zdenek Ziegler's work is characterized by lively typography and lettering and integration of type and pictures. A few of his designs are shown here.

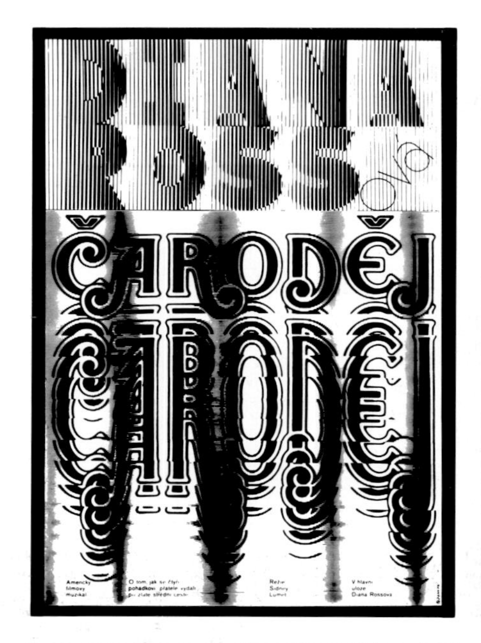

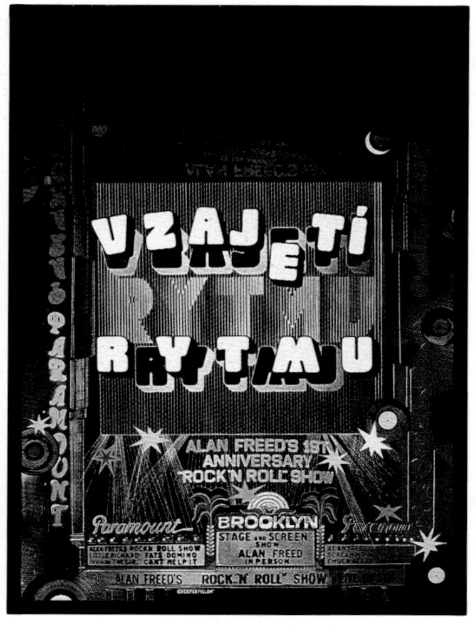

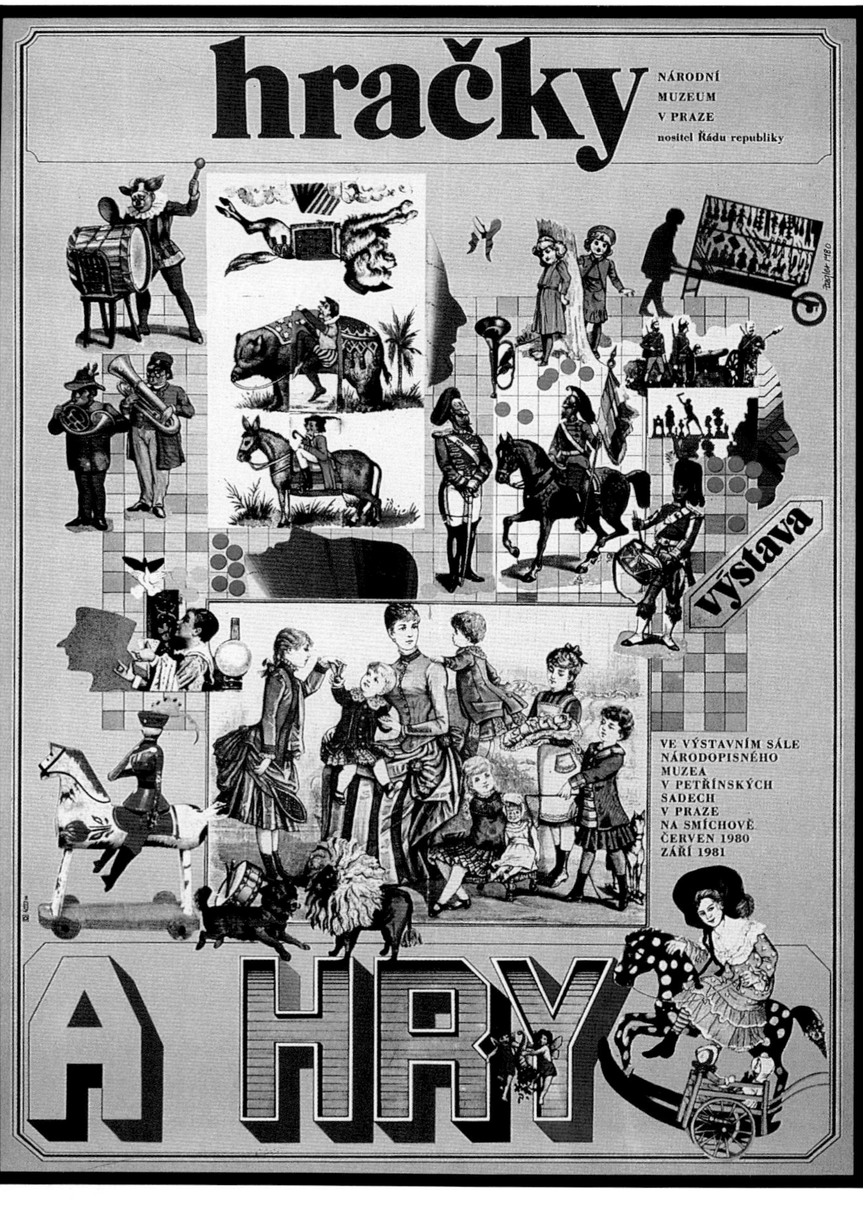

Typo portrait *of Kasimir Malevich. Jan Jiskra.*

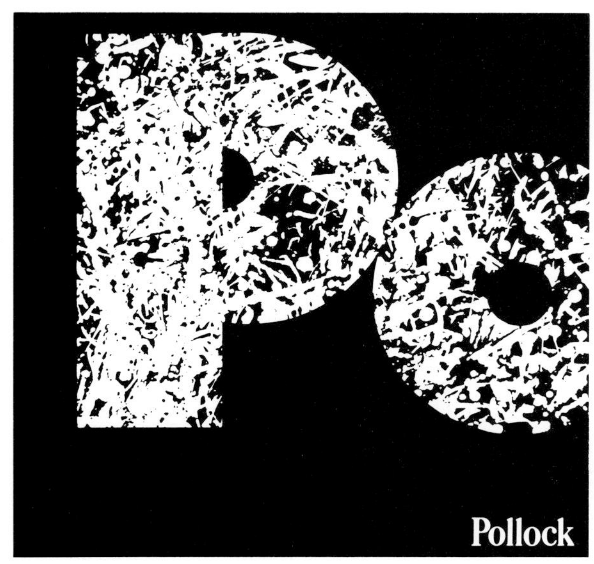

Typo portrait *of Jackson Pollock. Jan Jiskra.*

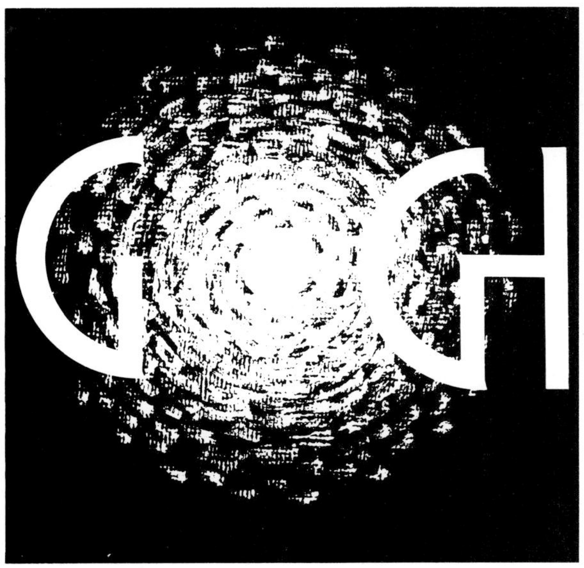

Typo portrait *of Vincent Van Gogh. Vaclav Kucera.*

One in a series *of books of poetry. Vaclav Kucera.*

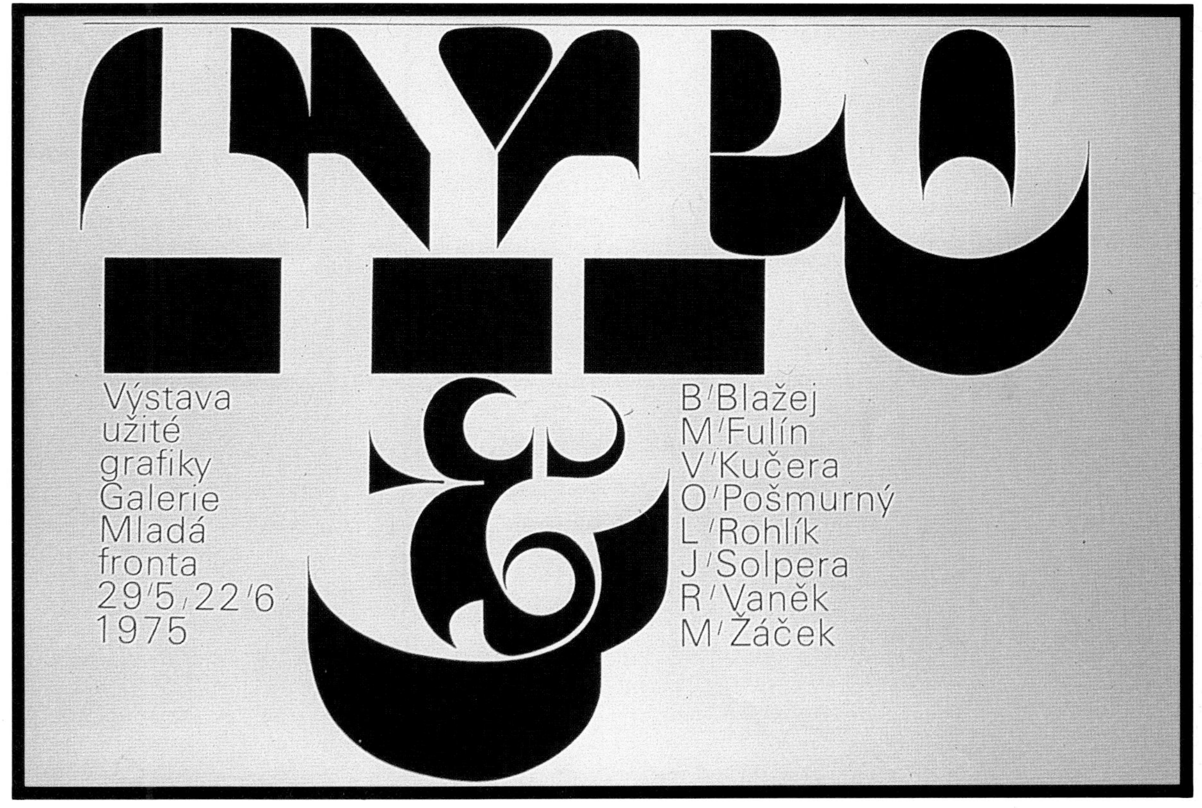

Poster *for the Typo & exhibition. Vaclav Kucera.*

TYPOGRAPHIC COMMUNICATIONS TODAY
Chapter XIII: The Many Faces of Typography Today

Oldrich Posmurny, *Czechoslovakia*

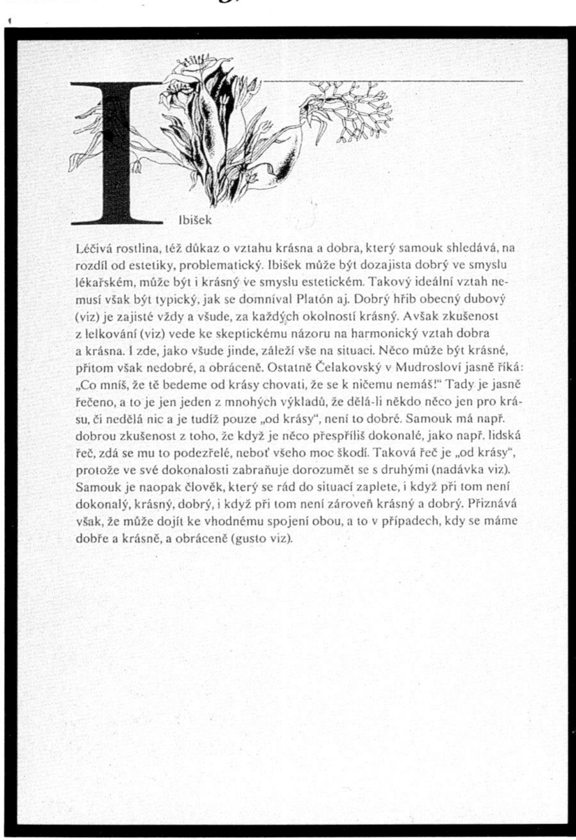

I

Ibišek

Léčivá rostlina, též důkaz o vztahu krásna a dobra, který samouk shledává, na rozdíl od estetiky, problematický. Ibišek může být dozajista dobrý ve smyslu lékařském, může být i krásný ve smyslu estetickém. Takový ideální vztah nemusí však být typický, jak se domníval Platón aj. Dobrý hřib obecný dubový (viz) je zajisté vždy a všude, za každých okolností krásný. Avšak zkušenost z lelkování (viz) vede ke skeptickému názoru na harmonický vztah dobra a krásna. I zde, jako všude jinde, záleží vše na situaci. Něco může být krásné, přitom však nedobré, a obráceně. Ostatně Čelakovský v Mudrosloví jasně říká: „Co mníš, že tě bedeme od krásy chovati, že se k ničemu nemáš!" Tady je jasně řečeno, a to je jen jeden z mnohých výkladů, že dělá-li někdo něco jen pro krásu, či nedělá nic a je tudíž pouze „od krásy", není to dobré. Samouk má např. dobrou zkušenost z toho, že když je něco přespříliš dokonalé, jako např. lidská řeč, zdá se mu to podezřelé, neboť všeho moc škodí. Taková řeč je „od krásy", protože ve své dokonalosti zabraňuje dorozumět se s druhými (nadávka viz). Samouk je naopak člověk, který se rád do situací zaplete, i když při tom není dokonalý, krásný, dobrý, i když při tom není zároveň krásný a dobrý. Přiznává však, že může dojít ke vhodnému spojení obou, a to v případech, kdy se máme dobře a krásně, a obráceně (gusto viz).

For Pablo Neruda's Ode to Typography. *Oldrich Posmurny.*

Promotional typography. *Oldrich Posmurny.*

Promotional typography. *Oldrich Posmurny.*

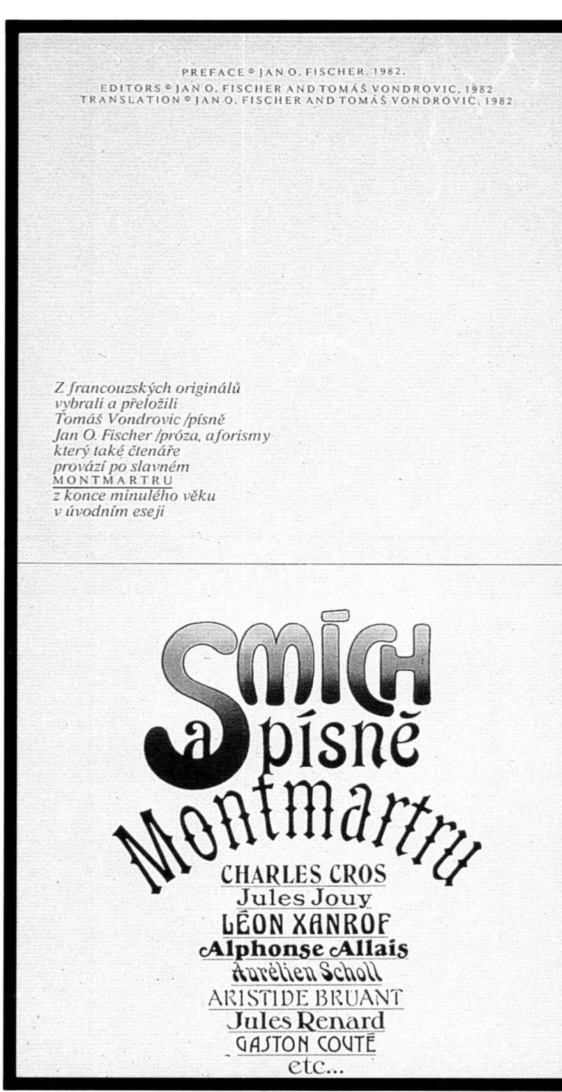

PREFACE © JAN O. FISCHER, 1982.
EDITORS © JAN O. FISCHER AND TOMÁŠ VONDROVIC, 1982
TRANSLATION © JAN O. FISCHER AND TOMÁŠ VONDROVIC, 1982

Z francouzských originálů
vybrali a přeložili
Tomáš Vondrovic /písně
Jan O. Fischer /próza, aforismy
který také čtenáře
provází po slavném
MONTMARTRU
z konce minulého věku
v úvodním eseji

Smích a písně Montmartru

CHARLES CROS
Jules Jouy
LÉON XANROF
Alphonse Allais
Aurélien Scholl
ARISTIDE BRUANT
Jules Renard
GASTON COUTÉ
etc...

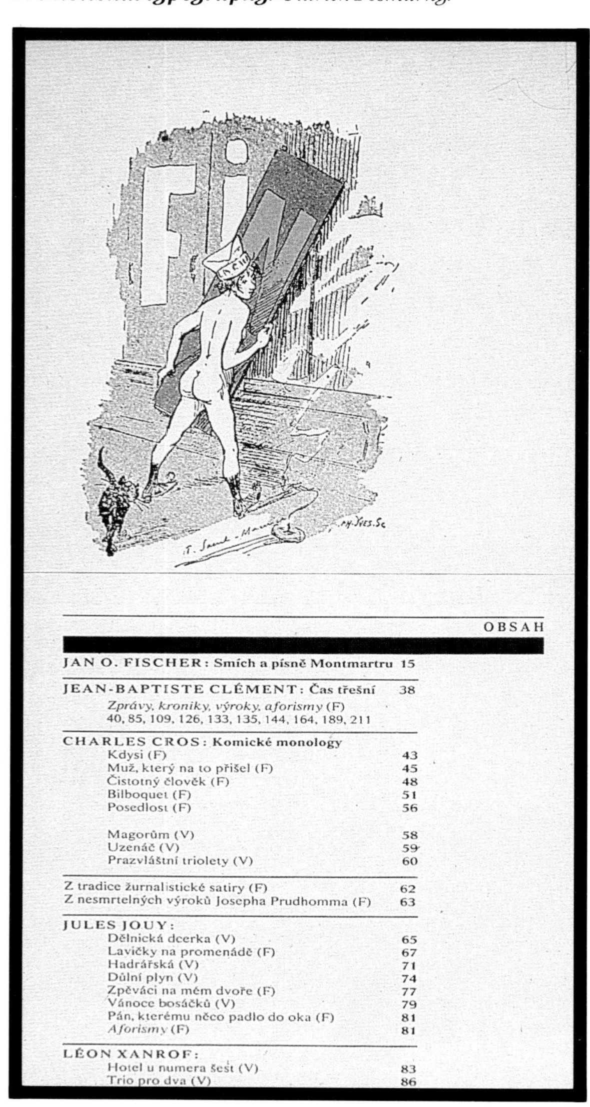

OBSAH

Double spreads *from the book,* The Laughter and the Songs of Montmartre. *Oldrich Posmurny.*

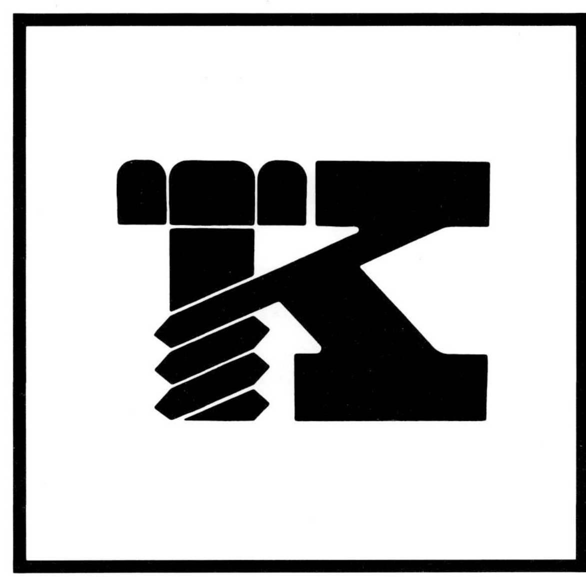

A sign. *Oldrich Posmurny.*

THE USSR

Contemporary typographic design in the USSR is characterized by several developments, including a new realism, a new freedom, and, yes, a new wave. These three trends are interrelated. Today an emphasis on deciding what is the most appropriate solution is taking precedence over the emphasis on personal style. The concern with *what* can be done is being replaced by a new freedom, partly due to the new technologies, to choose from many options what is best for the problem at hand. There is a new emphasis on this judgment by the artist, as well as on his or her talent and skill. Designers used to the grid and structured thinking are looking for a way back to a nostalgic and more emotionally appealing approach to design.

Typographic design in the USSR covers the graphic spectrum from the totally rational, orderly approach to the visually vital and exciting. Many of the examples shown here are of the latter kind. Some of them give the impression of a Soviet version of what the West calls new wave typography; some show type used to form lovely and pertinent illustrations.

Commenting on the design of typefaces, graphic designer, Maxim Zhukov, notes that an analogy has been drawn between high-speed highways and contemporary typography. Adrian Frutiger observed that highways are straighter and smoother than formerly, but smooth, straight roads encourage speeding, which results in more accidents. That is why, in entrances to parking lots and private roads, for example, artificial bumps are built into the road to slow drivers. Some type, too, has become simpler and prints more smoothly by offset than it did in the letterpress era. Too much smoothness, some say, can lull the reader. Zhukov feels that while bumps need not be introduced intentionally into typography, those natural imperfections built into letterforms might best be left in and that typographic "bumps" such as ragged right margins, irregular margins, subheads, stepped lines and initials, are often needed to jog or hold the reader's attention.

Many leading graphic designers in the USSR today make much use of graphic symbols to reinforce words and to help the text speak multilingually. Some typeface designers favor what they call a 3:2 approach: the size relationship between caps and lower case letters is 3:2, and the color between light and medium weights of the same face is also 3:2. This scientific/mathematical approach to typeface design is popular today in the USSR. Also, a typeface family is likely to be developed in serif, sans serif, and half-serif versions. Just a few type families in the Western world are developed in two or more design classifications, notably Trinité by Bram de Does, Praxis and Demos by Gerard Unger, Romulus by Jan van Krimpen, and in late 1988, ITC Stone by Sumner Stone.

CONTENTS
INTRODUCTION 1)
TECHNICAL DESCRIPTION 2)
AIRPLANE STRENGTH 3)
MASSES BREAKDOWN 4)
PERFORMANCE 5)
SERVICING AND MAINTENANCE 6)
OPERATIONAL CHARACTERISTICS 7)

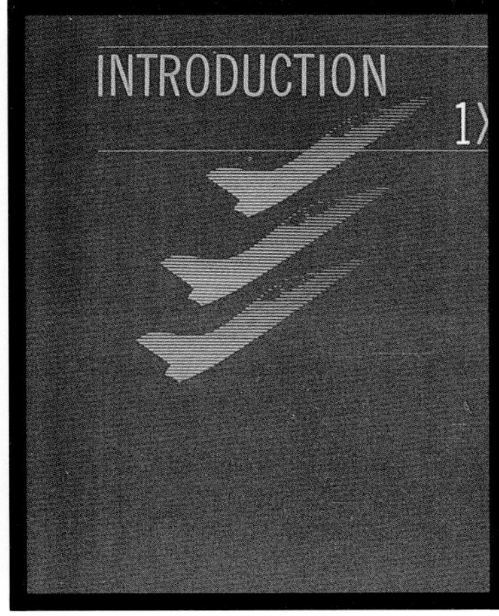

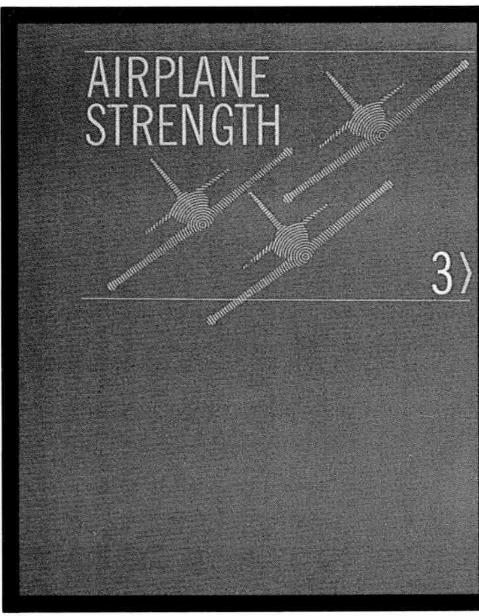

Contents page *and typical sectional title pages for a company booklet. Oldrich Posmurny.*

32

proslulého divadelního kritika Francisqua Sarceye; ten se vůbec stal oblíbeným terčem jeho satir a parodií (viz mistrnou parodii měšťáckého vztahu k umění v článcích Umění v soudech pana Francisqua Sarceye) apod. V řadě sbírek i roztroušeně po časopisech zanechal na sta anekdot, scének a krátkých povídek, improvizovaných (tu vtipně, tu poněkud násilně) na okamžitém nápadu, založených na nějakém paradoxu nebo objevujících v nečekaném závěru nejobyčejnější samozřejmosti. Po celkem všedním líčení všedních věcí bývá nečekaná pointa obsažena až ve zcela poslední větě (například ve známém monologu Bezesná noc červeného husara).
Vedle slovních hříček, anachronismů a tradičních humoristických motivů objevovali Jouy, Allais a další především nesmyslnost, absurdnost jako prameny humoru. (Přitom tu nešlo o absurditu jako bezútěšně zobecňující filozofii vševálného nesmyslu jako o sto let později třeba u Ioneska a v absurdním dramatu, ale spíše o poetické využití nesmyslného, absurdně komického nápadu.) Začínalo to nevinnými aforismy, založenými na básnivé fantazii a paradoxu, pokračovalo učenými definicemi samozřejmostí (zde nesporně sehrála svou úlohu tradice slavnostního hlupáka a výlupku šosáctví pana Prudhomma, jehož tvůrce Henri Monniera, 1799–1877,

vyhlásili humoristé Montmartru za jednoho ze svých předchůdců), tvrzeními založenými na nesmyslu a logické absurdnosti, nečekanými a nesmyslnými pointami anglického humoru. Crosovými monology či Jouyho nehratelnými, ale podrobně popsanými „bleskovými pantomimami" (pán vyjme jinému na požádání oko a odstraní z něho obrovský balvan) a končilo drastickým, krutým „černým humorem", který měl své předchůdce již v „malých romanticích" a „frenetickém žánru" a na Montmartru se stal přímo módou. Ze sérií karikatur a anekdot získal velkou proslulost cyklus o lékařích (například lékař piluje nohu úpícímu pacientovi: — Bolí vás to? — Ne, ale ta pila strašně skřípe!).
V jedné Allaisově povídce podává vynálezce podrobný chemický popis, jak mu věda pomohla přivést tchyni k výbuchu. (Vůbec absurdnost a černý humor se neustále spojují s motivy moderní techniky a vědy, s parodií reklamy atp.) Nebo se vypráví pohádka o zemi masa, kde po požáru lesa z uhořelých zvířat vznikla báječná vařená pochoutka. Či papoušek zaživa klovaný hejnem havranů křičí, jak se naučil v hospodě:

33

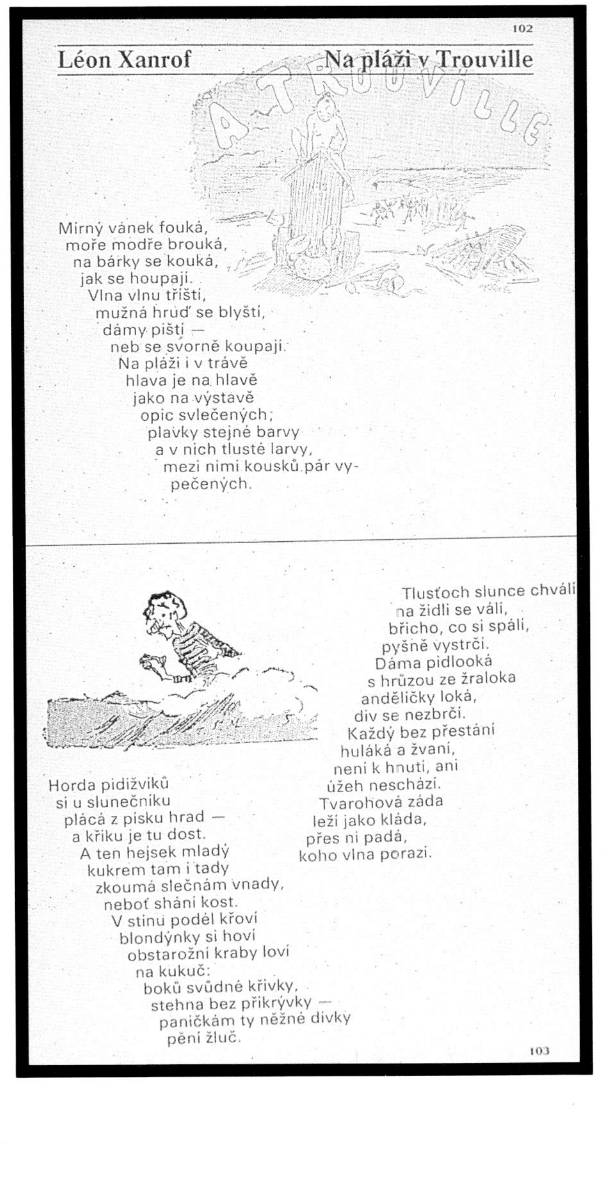
102

Léon Xanrof — Na pláži v Trouville

Mírný vánek fouká,
moře modře brouká,
na bárky se kouká,
jak se houpají.
Vlna vlnu tříští,
mužná hruď se blyští,
dámy piští —
neb se svorně koupají.
Na pláži i v trávě
hlava je na hlavě
jako na výstavě
opic svlečených;
plavky stejné barvy
a v nich tlusté larvy,
mezi nimi kousků pár vy-
pečených.

Tlusťoch slunce chválí
na židli se válí,
břicho, co si spálí,
pyšně vystrčí.
Dáma pidlooká
s hrůzou ze žraloka
andělíčky loká,
div se nezbrčí.
Každý bez přestání
hulákâ a žvaní,
není k hnutí, ani
úžeh neschází.
Tvarohová záda
leží jako kláda,
přes ni padá,
koho vlna porazí.

Horda pidižviků
si u slunečníku
pláčá z písku hrad —
a křiku je tu dost.
A ten hejsek mladý
kukrem tam i tady
zkoumá slečnám vnady,
neboť shání kost.
V stínu podél křovi
blondýnky si hoví
obstarožní kraby lovi
na kukuč:
boků svůdné křivky,
stehna bez přikrývky —
paničkám ty něžné dívky
pění žluč.

103

Double spreads *from the book,* The Laughter and the Songs of Montmartre. *Oldrich Posmurny.*

TYPOGRAPHIC COMMUNICATIONS TODAY

Chapter XIII: The Many Faces of Typography Today

The Second Wave

Today's typographic design in the USSR owes much of its vitality and orderliness to the avant gardeists of the 1920s, El Lissitzky, et al, and to what some call the second wave of the avant garde. Trained typographers, as well as architect Alexei Gan, sensitive to the graphic vigor of the avant garde typographers brought to it more discipline and visual clarity. Several examples of their work are shown here.

Alexei Gan

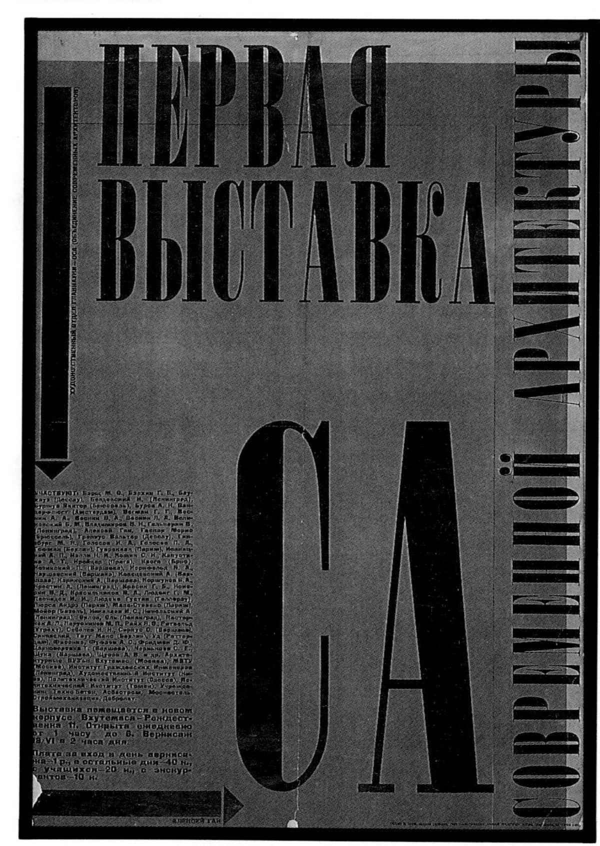

First Exhibition/Contemporary Architects/S.A. *1927. Letterpress, 42 1/2 x 27 3/4." © The Museum of Modern Art, New York.*

Gustav Klutsis

Book cover for: The Daily Life of Airplane Pilots, *by N. Bobrow. 1928. 8 15/16 x 12 1/4." © The Museum of Modern Art, New York.*

Promotional Brochure *for* CA *magazine. 1928. 11 3/16 x 15 1/16." © The Museum of Modern Art, New York.*

The Olympics and Typography

The 1980 Olympics held in Moscow affected typographic design by bringing typography into the street, making it public, not just book and publication-oriented. An evolution similar to that in the West followed. The need for an integrated look that blanketed several media became apparent. Increasingly, in the USSR, a specialist is employed to develop this family look that elsewhere is called the corporate image. In turn, book design is influencing street, or public, typography and environmental typographics which are still in their infancy. The resultant active public design should make it communicate more effectively.

The Russian avant garde artists, Rodchenko, Malevich and Lissitzky, for example, were talented in many media, and that is largely true of today's USSR designers. Few have become specialists in just one medium. Most deal with the full spectrum of design problems.

A Library Market

Most Soviet books are hardbound. The eye-catching paperback or dust jacket of the West is a rarity due largely to shortages of materials, equipment, and processes involved in its production and the absence of a commercial urgency to sell books. The USSR has a tremendous library system. People use libraries more than they buy books. The demand is for durable, rather than eye-catching editions.

Lettering and Type Design Today

Cyrillic is not the only alphabet in the Soviet Union, but is the one most used. In *The Art of Lettering in the Soviet Union,* author Yuri Gherchuk makes these points:

❧ In the sixties, and especially in the seventies, modern typography tended to supplant hand lettering wherever possible. (N.B. This was the post-Stalin era, when greater creative freedom was possible in the USSR.)

❧ Today there is greater interest in a variety of type styles.

❧ Display typography is being revived, although there is still much hand lettering in books and advertisements.

❧ An earlier uniformity of style is being replaced by the artist who "feels totally unfettered when facing a sheet of paper…He can transform a particular period style in his own way. He can give free rein to his fantasy, incarnating at his own risk highly sophisticated mathematical curves, streamlined contours of modern cars or living forms of plants or animals."

❧ Soviet designers not only fill specific assignments, but carry out design experiments for their research value or for exhibitions.
❧ Side by side with artists who "are hungry for unusual shapes and are not afraid of bizarre forms which may be almost illegible and unreadable" are those who are attracted by 19th century typography and its ornamentality.

The Western Influence
Among the forces stimulating Soviet design in recent decades is the uninhibited, individualistic art and design created in the United States and elsewhere in the West. Soviet designers have seen catalogs and exhibits of the work of Milton Glaser, Herb Lubalin, Seymour Chwast; many others were stimulated by the work of American and European designers shown in such magazines as *Graphis* and *Gebrauschgraphik.* Today's designers are expressing their own ideas and emotions, not only the State's.

Soviet Painting Today
The same post-Stalinist artistic freedom being exercised in graphic design is observable in Soviet painting. There is a wide range of styles, including much surrealism and, most recently, abstract expressionism, dadaism, conceptual art and minimalism. Soviet artists are aware of today's isms, but New York and Paris are not their guiding stars. The diversity of style and subject matter is much greater than is generally appreciated in the West. Soviet artists in recent decades work in styles ranging from conservative academicism and impressionism to art nouveau and photorealism, as well as the styles noted above. One might see half-breed and flying figures in the work of Alexander Sitmikov, or odd photographic perspective in that of Andrei Volkov. Some artists show the influence of such Americans as Grant Wood, Andrew Wyeth, Rockwell Kent. Wyeth, in fact, has been made an honorary member of the Soviet Academy of Arts.

The Art of Lettering
A selection from Yuri Gherchuk's *The Art of Lettering in the Soviet Union* illustrates the active way in which lettering and typefaces have been used in the 20th century.

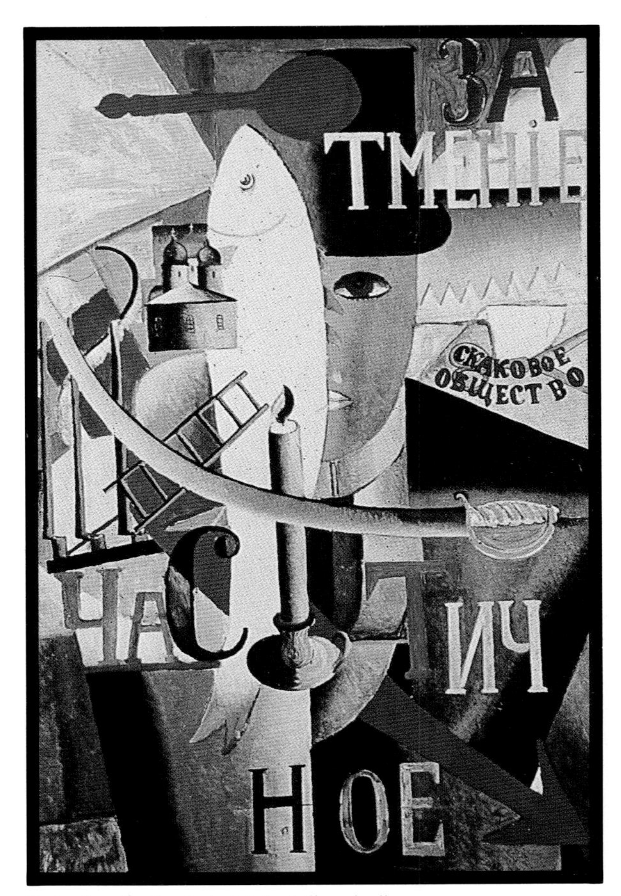

***Painting** by Kazimir Malevich, 1914.*

__Seal design__ by Sergei Chekhomin, 1919.

***Poster** by Vladimir Lebedev, 1920s.*

***Cover** by Vladimir Lebedev, 1925.*

***Cover** by Kazimir Malevich, 1913.*

***Poster** by Varvara Stepanova, 1922.*

TYPOGRAPHIC COMMUNICATIONS TODAY

Chapter XIII: The Many Faces of Typography Today

Calendar design *by Maxim Zhukov.*

Cover *by Alexander Rodchenko, 1925.*

Cover *by Alexander Deineka, 1930.*

Advertising typography *by Yuri Kurbatov, 1968.*

Cover *by Vladimir Favorsky, 1928.*

Poster *by Valentina Khodasevich, 1931.*

Alphabet study *by Dmitri Bazhanov, 1940s.*

Three-Chervonets Bill. *Goznak Banknote Company, Moscow. Designer unknown, 1937.*

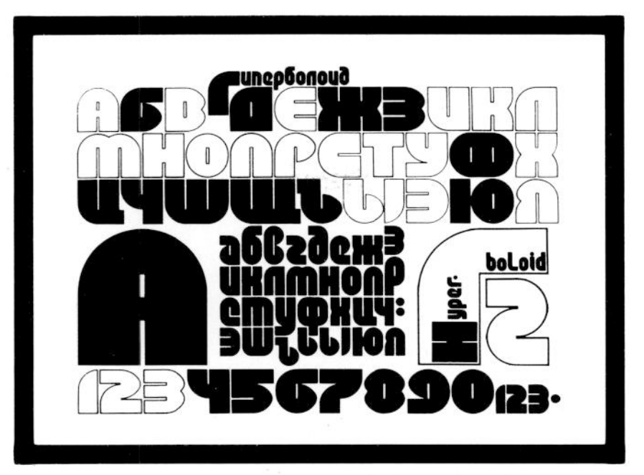

Hyperboloid Display, *solid and outline, Cyrillic version. Alexander Kononov, Kiev 1980.*

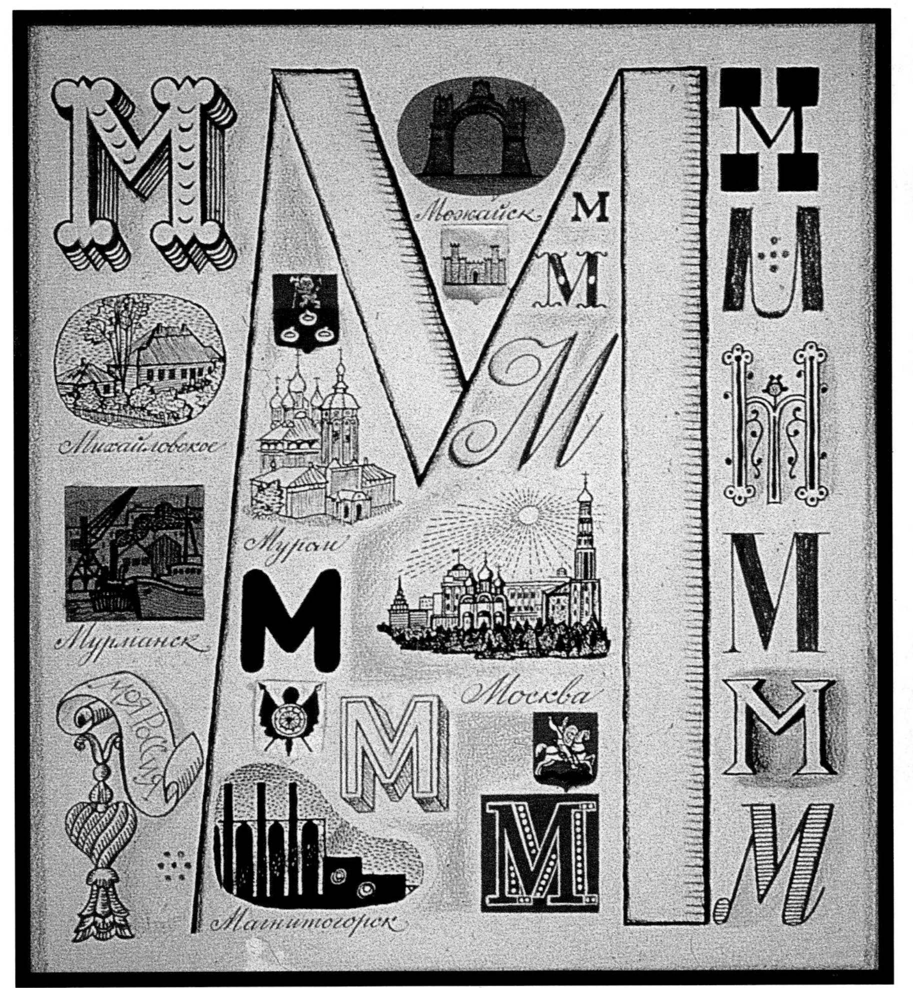

***Page from* Moya Rossiya** *["My Russia"], an* ABC *book by Serghey Pozharsky, Moscow 1967.*

Meander. *An attempt at systematization of the structural principles of letterform construction. Maxim Zhukov. Moscow 1972.*

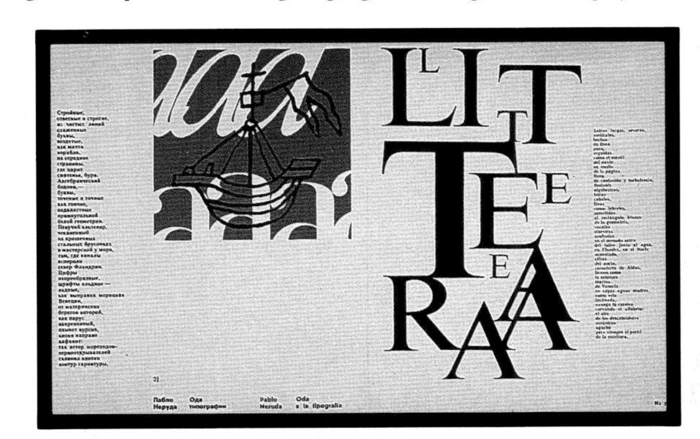

Double spread *from* Oda a la Tipographia *by Pablo Neruda. Yuri Markov, Moscow 1971.*

Invitation card. *Evgheny Gannushkin, Moscow 1973.*

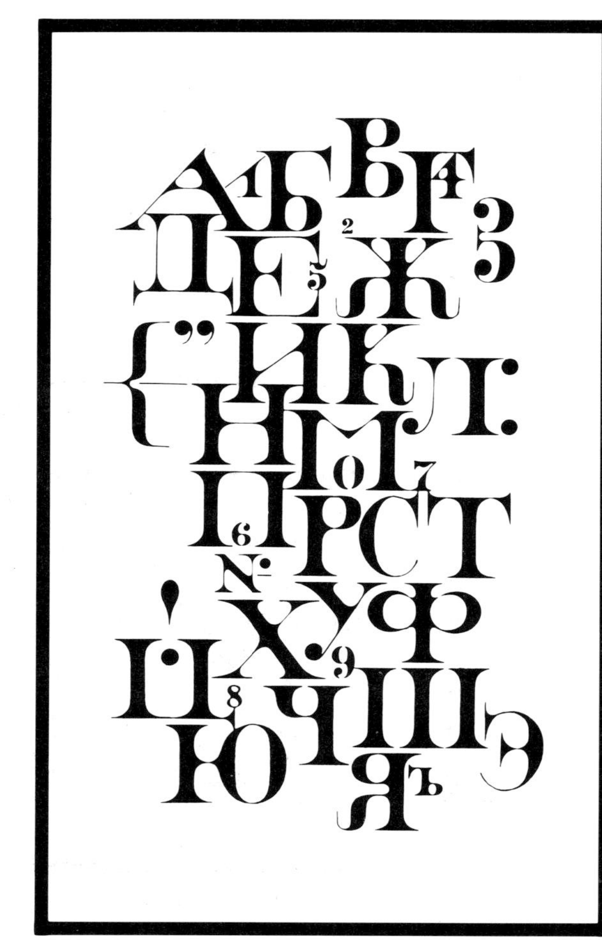

Alphabet study *by Boris Markevich, 1972.*

Typographica **USSR**

The exhibition Typographica USSR was held in New York at The Cooper Union in 1985. It was co-sponsored by the Artists Union of the USSR, Cooper Union and International Typeface Corporation. The following selections are from the exhibition.

Valery Akopov, *graphic and book designer, Moscow.*

Evgeni Dobrovinsky, *book, lettering, poster and graphic designer, Moscow. Three-dimensional poster.*

Yuri Bazhanov, *book designer, Moscow. Lettering study; gouache, 1977.*

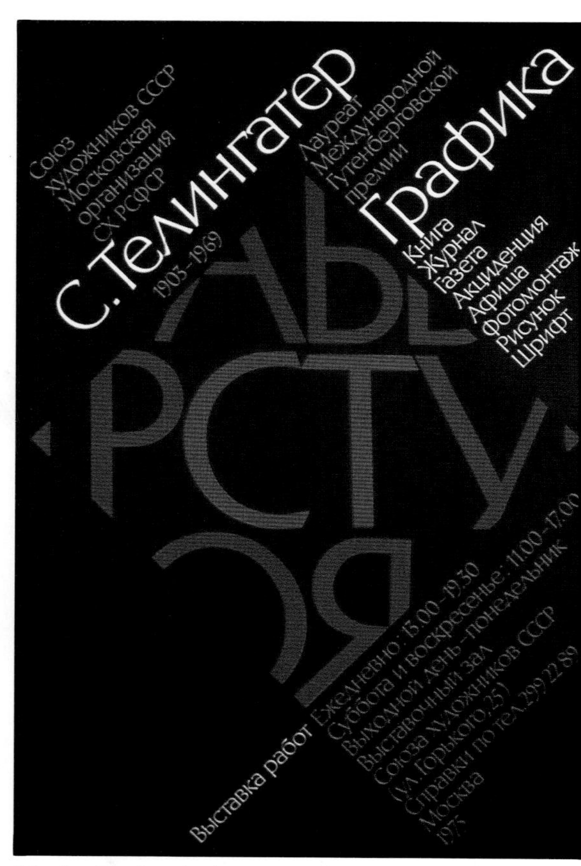

Maxim Zhukov, *book, poster and magazine designer, Moscow. Exhibition poster.*

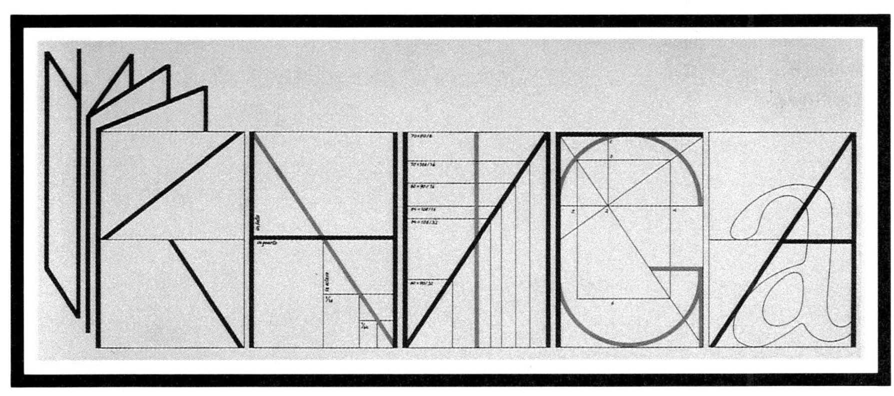

Arkadi Troyanker, *book and graphic designer, Moscow. Logotype for a book publisher.*

Victor Korolkov, *book and lettering designer, Moscow. Display type design; Cyrillic/Latin.*

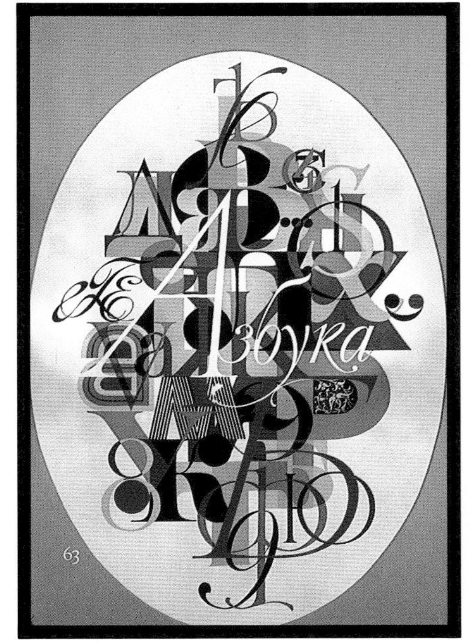

Yuri Kopylov, *book and lettering designer, Moscow. Alphabet study.*

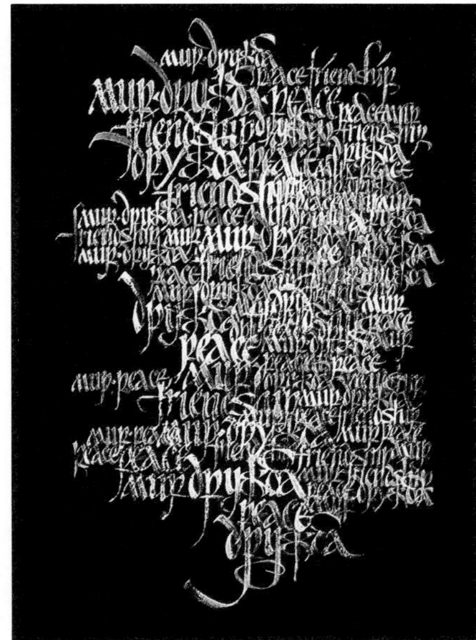

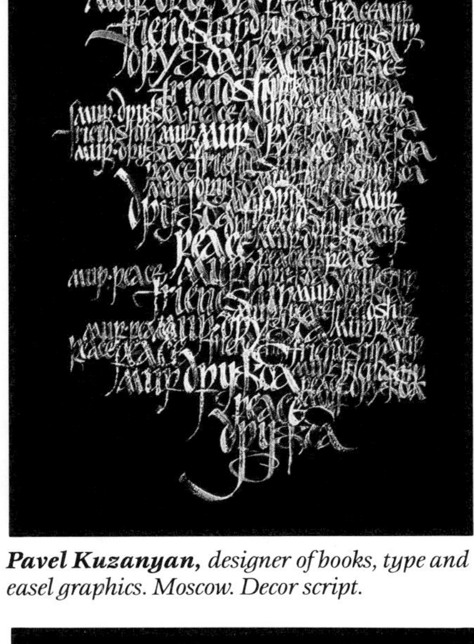

Pavel Kuzanyan, *designer of books, type and easel graphics. Moscow. Decor script.*

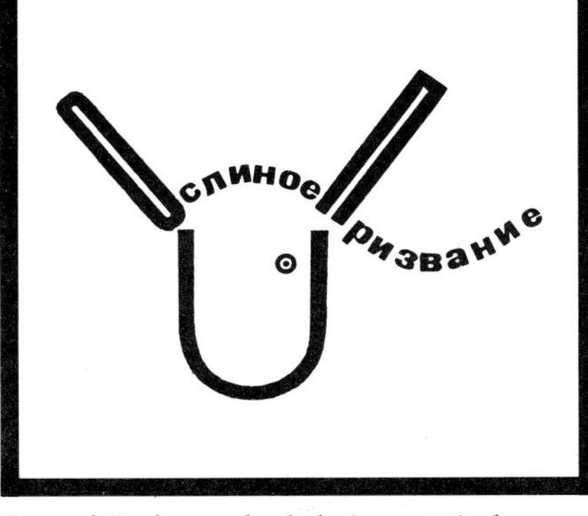

Evgeni Smirnov, *book designer, Minsk. Heading.*

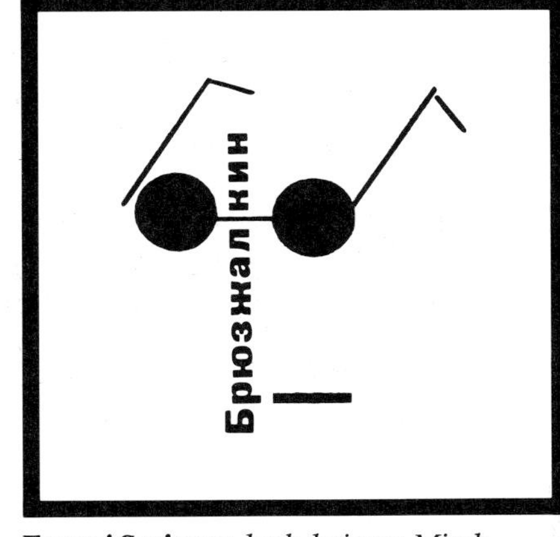

Evgeni Smirnov, *book designer, Minsk. Heading.*

Solomon Telingater, *book, lettering and magazine designer, Moscow. Cover.*

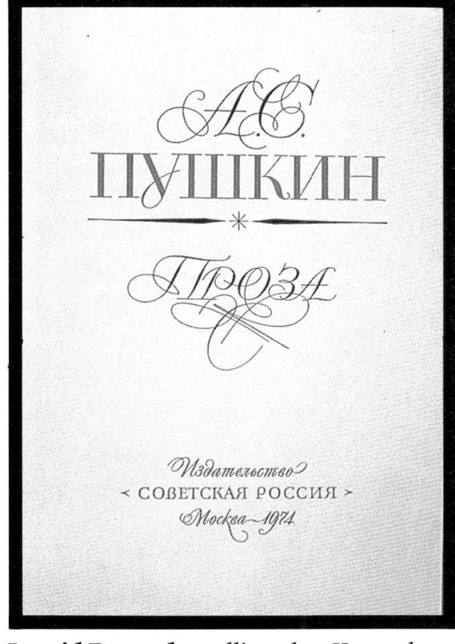

Leonid Pronenko, *calligrapher, Krasnodar. Calligraphic study.*

Alexander Laurentyev, *book designer, Moscow. "Book," a three-dimensional mobile in cardboard.*

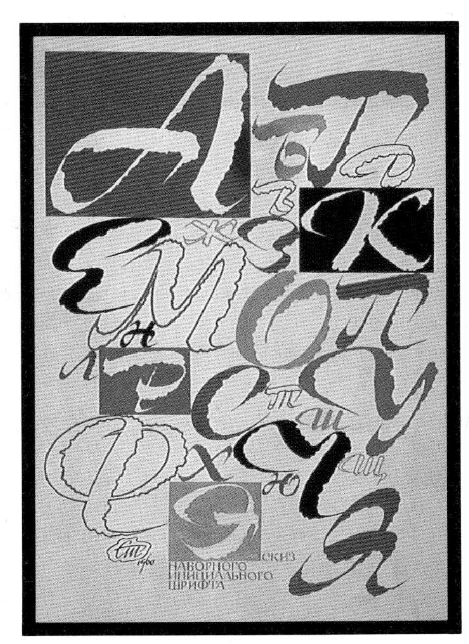

Solomon Telingater, *book, lettering and magazine designer, Moscow. Alphabet study.*

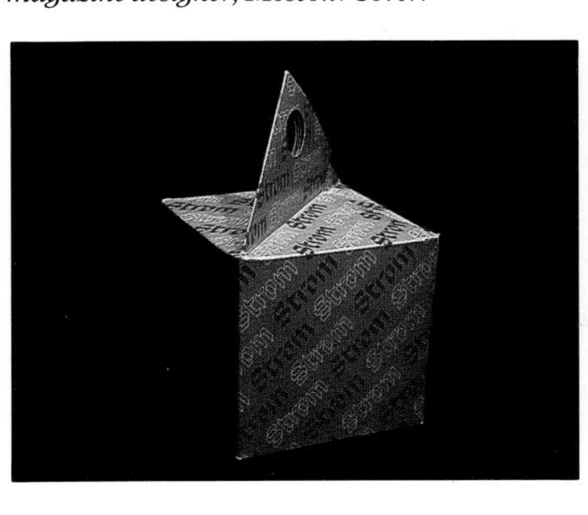

(Far left & left) ***Ramiz Guseinov,*** *graphic designer, Moscow. Elements of a corporate identity for v/o Stroymaterialintorg, a foreign trade company exporting building materials.*

TYPOGRAPHIC COMMUNICATIONS TODAY
Chapter XIII: The Many Faces of Typography Today

"Both the origins and the raison d'être of graphic design in the USSR are quite different from those of the Western world."

Typography Today in the USSR
The following thoughts and background information were contributed to Typographic Communications Today by Maxim Zhukov.

"Despite many obvious differences, at a first glance much of the contemporary Soviet typography appears rather familiar to a foreign professional. That visual similarity however must not lead us into confusion: both the origins and the raison d'etre *of graphic design in the USSR are quite different from those of the Western world.*

"Private enterprise and market competition are virtually unknown to the Soviet economy which is almost totally nationalized. Both products and services offered do not require heavy advertising and promotion by manufacturers, suppliers and retailers. Therefore, unlike the market-originated, market-oriented, and market-driven graphic design of the U.S. and West European countries, the basic philosophy of Soviet graphic design is dramatically different. Public service, information, identification, and education are among its first priorities. It is also catering to the political and propagandist needs of Soviet society. Only when it comes to the promotion of Soviet products and services offered to the foreign market, the objective need arises for Soviet designers to speak the esperanto of international graphic design and be up to the respective world standards. Incidentally, it is here where some of the most impressive designs are being produced, showing that the creativity and innovation that were trademarks of the Russian avant garde of the twenties, were kept alive throughout the post-Lissitzky decades of Soviet design history.

A Multi-Ethnic, Multi-Cultural Society

"Soviet graphic design being more a culture- than economics-oriented phenomenon, it is important to bear in mind the multi-ethnic and multi-cultural nature of the Soviet society where Russian culture and language serve as a cementing factor, an interface to a great number of cultures with their own origins, backgrounds and traditions – as different as Ukrainian from Uzbek, or Estonian from Armenian. Therefore, the Soviet Union being not as much a 'melting pot' as the U.S., its graphic design should be viewed in context with specific ethnic cultural environment…

"The fundamental multi-ethnic character of the Soviet culture and therefore, design, can explain, for example, the expertise of Soviet type designers in producing typefaces and type families covering several script systems at a time… That structure conscious approach leads them to develop typeface projects that not only transcend specific alphabets and scripts but also comprise entire type families (serif/sans serif/slab serif, etc.) their basic letter shapes being consistent and logical variations on the common theme.

"That basically structuralist and systematic way of thinking is very characteristic of many Soviet designers and their works. It strongly reveals itself not only in type design but in all fields of graphic design…

Book Design

"Book design holds a special place in Soviet graphic design. This is mostly due to the latter being more part of the cultural scene than of the business world. A majority of the leading Soviet designers were trained as book designers and are active in that domain. Modern Soviet book design was actually the first of the graphic design trades to be affected by the above mentioned functionalist-structuralist method, generated in part by the strong influence of the Swiss (Emil Ruder, Karl Gerstner, Josef Muller-Brockmann, Armin Hoffmann, et al.). The introduction of the layout grids to the Soviet book (and especially art and picture books) and magazine design goes back to the mid-sixties. The pioneers of the grid design in USSR – Yuri Kurbatov, Arkady Troyanker, Nikolay Kalinin, Mikhail Anixt, et al., including myself – later turned to developing more sophisticated structures (based on Golden Section, Le Corbusier's Modulor, Fibonacci Series, irrational numbers, and the like), than 'strictly-Swiss' equal unit grid systems … The traditionalist 'Art of the Book' according to Jan Tschichold, Raúl Rosarivo, Stanley Morison, Bruce Rogers, et al. was another source of inspiration to them. However they did not blindly follow the canons of classic book design but applied the same analytical structuralist method to studying it…

"It is rather surprising for a Westerner to watch the development of graphic design in USSR reconcile those methods which used to be considered antipodean, i.e. traditionalist axial typography vs. modern asymmetrical arrangement (also serif vs. sans serif, etc.). The reason is that the revival of interest in the heritage of classical typography, of which the tradition in Russia was practically lost, coincided with the upsurge of the structuralist method which was the leading trend in European design of the sixties ('less is more,' etc.), the latter having left a lasting impression on the whole course of modern Soviet design…

Orderliness vs. Spontaneity

"The point is that the very development of Soviet graphic design in modern times was driven by that incessant rivalry of two basic methods – orderliness vs. spontaneity – which were, still are, and probably will remain a universal motive power of all art and design evolution. The predominance of the realist, figurative art in USSR imparted special nuances to that competition.

"For decades hand lettering was considered to be superior to typography in its ability to 'faithfully communicate the subject matter,' and therefore, of a much stronger realist potential; meanwhile the most successful typographic experiments of the Soviet avant gardeists, their working hard on making type act and talk, were regarded as a formalist 'fetishization of printing material,' art for art's sake.

"Speculations on the alleged supremacy of hand lettering have given birth to nothing more purposeful and realist than typographics which fell into disgrace. Having succeeded in scaring designers off typography they actually resulted in yet another design style, *based on laborious hand lettering and ornamentation, hand-drawn as well…*

"That special art of the hand lettered typography had its masters – viz., Ivan Rerberg, Nikolay Ilyin, Yakov Yegorov, Solomon Telingater, Nikolay Sedelnikov, Yevgheni Kogan, Dmitri Bazhanov, et al. – of whom many were previously fervent champions of the 'new typography.' Even Lissitzky, the founding father of the Soviet avant garde typography, could not escape being affected by that evolution.

"That style of Soviet graphic design of the late thirties, which could be defined as kind of a neo-classicist revivalism, survived – with few variations though – till the mid-fifties when it was swept away by a stormy invasion of the free style graphics based on extensive use of brush scripts and matching line drawings, well blended together, light, elegant, free-

Sovietsky Khudozhnik 1985 *[Soviet Artist 1985]. A promotional catalog for an art publishing company. 1984. Cover (left) and double-spread (right). Michael Anixt, Valery Chernievsky.*

Promotional calendar *for an advertising agency. 1984. Valery Akopov, Vasily Dyakonov.*

spirited, sparkling with irony and wit. The partisans of a new wave – Lev Zbarsky, Mikhail Klyachko, Dmitry Bisti, Yuri Krasny, May Miturich, Boris Markevich, Ivan Bruni, et al. – were neither typographic nor graphic designers but illustrators inspired by their discovery of the Western modernist art (Matisse, Picasso, Miro, Klee), as well as of the early Russian avant garde (Goncharova, Larionov, Miturich, futurists and others), whose art started to regain its popularity within the Soviet art community.

Visual Parallels

"The pattern of the stylistic evolution has its close visual parallels in both American and European typographics, though with none of the above political connotations. They were all affected by the same trends: and extensive use of hand lettering in the thirties and forties and a craze for brush scripts in the fifties. And yet those design fashions by no means were conducive to, nor were they accompanied by, a decay of typography in the West, which was exactly the case in the Soviet Union.

"The wealth of type fonts once available for hand composition (complete in both Cyrillic and Latin versions) shrank to hardly a dozen of the bread-and-butter styles adapted for machine typesetting, many of them rather old fashioned designs and of doubtful aesthetic value. The craftmanship of composition, both body and display, gradually fell into decline, the very criteria of typographic quality having sunk into oblivion. Designers expert in typography were becoming an endangered species. Of them the foremost devotee of typography was Solomon Telingater, a friend of Lissitzky. Being an indomitable fighter for typographic quality, he was the author of the only book in the matter published in almost thirty years – Iskusstvo Aktsidentnogo nabora *[The art of display composition], issued by Kniga Publishers in 1965.*

"All that can explain that hand lettering, the proliferation of which was due to underestimation and mistrust of the visual features of the display typography, did finally become its surrogate, compensating for its virtual extinction. Hand lettering still holds key positions in poster design, environmental and architectural graphics, packaging design, and many other areas of graphic design. The top names in Soviet hand lettering of today are Pavel Kuzanyan, Vadim Lazursky, Yevgheny Gannushkin.

TYPOGRAPHIC COMMUNICATIONS TODAY
Chapter XIII: The Many Faces of Typography Today

"A great deal of pluralism and tolerance exists in Soviet graphic design, and it is difficult to single out specific trends..."

Paste-up Lettering
"Another substitute for typography which is still in heavy use today – paste-up lettering – was discovered and explored by my own generation of typographic designers arisen in the mid-sixties: Kurbatov, Troyanker, Valerius, et al. We were the first to introduce a practice of using the self-made Cyrillic versions of the better modern typefaces in designs. One of our first ventures of that kind was an attempt to 'cyrillize' Helvetica Medium (known to us as Neue Haas Grotesk), in 1963. Thus we opened Pandora's box: that endeavor proved very successful with fellow designers, and soon the graphic design market became inundated with paste-up typographics using home-made fonts, many of them of truly poor quality. That development was also enhanced and inspired by a wild boom in production of display typefaces for photolettering devices in the West in the late sixties and early seventies.
"With time the working conditions of Soviet designers showed signs of improvement, the advent of modern photo and digital typesetters giving them more room for creativity and providing a better quality composition than was previously attainable with hot metal. Another relief came with the spread of offset lithography, allowing for much more freedom in layout and for easier incorporation of paste-up display lettering into typeset body copy.
"The skills of designers far exceed the potential of domestic printing so that many projects have to be produced abroad to be adequately executed. Ironically, being ahead of their times and the current condition of the industry was another feature inherited by the Soviet design innovators from their avant gardeist forefathers of the twenties. Iskusstvo and other art publishers routinely had a sizable number of their books printed by the best available Soviet plants and many foreign vendors, that gave to the younger designers an opportunity to use better materials and more advanced technology for the proper realization of their concepts. However, some of today's more ambitious projects remain sketches and layouts as was the situation in the twenties. The same is true for those working in advertising and packaging, designing promotion materials, campaigns and corporate identity for major Soviet export companies, etc.

Design Pluralism
"There is one important detail (which is not really a detail) to be taken into consideration when discussing whatever aspect of the Soviet life. There are widespread beliefs that all spheres of Soviet culture exist and develop in a heavily centralized, thoroughly planned, tightly controlled pattern. These clichés are especially incorrect when applied to typographic design...
"One can tell for sure that Soviet designers are far from zusammen marschieren *(marching together). A great deal of pluralism and tolerance exists in Soviet graphic design, and it is difficult to single out specific trends...*

Soviet Art and Design Societies
"Until recently there was no single art society to encompass creative forces of all design areas. Book designers, logotype, visual identity and packaging designers were traditionally eligible for membership in the Artists Union, as well as poster designers. That society, however, was created by, and for the sake of, the fine art professionals and is heavily dominated by them. Some of the designers of architectural and environmental graphics are members of the Architects Union. Magazine and newspaper designers and photographers belong to the Journalists Union. Calligraphers, typographic and type designers do not really have a home of their own.
"The above situation is a clear reflection of a sizable professional dispersion of the Soviet graphic design. The recent formation of the Society of Soviet Designers does, however, offer a new hope for a better self-definition and self-determination of design in USSR, consolidation of its most creative forces, and the establishment of higher quality standards.

Calligraphic Revival
"After a long period of the dominance of hand lettering and a short-lived fashion for free style handwriting there is – parallel to the current typographical revival – a considerable rise of interest in calligraphy. It developed over the last two decades – which by yet another concurrence, coincides with the spreading of calligraphy in the U.S.. The leading role in promoting the art of penmanship in USSR belongs to the master scribes of Soviet Estonia. The historic heritage of calligraphy in Baltic Republics, based on the Latin script, makes natural part of the West European tradition. The acknowledged head of the Estonian School is Villu Toots whose oeuvre *enjoys wide international recognition...*
"Calligrapher's tools have changed from an orthodox flat pen, reed or a goose quill to a pointed pen or brush, a marker, a pencil, a stick, etc. Calligraphy has also changed its visual priorities, deliberately sacrificing readability to expressivity and sheer beauty, thus rejecting the built-in pragmatism of functionalist typography.

Spontaneity vs. Orderliness
"The above features now becoming a pride and essence of modern calligraphy is a graphic manifestation of a renewed search of spontaneity and fortuity, improvisation and extemporization in graphic design. This trend reveals itself in introducing bold, striking colors, textures and shapes (not necessarily geometrical), ornamental and decorative elements, images of all thinkable kinds, in nonorthodox combinations of type styles and sizes, in using 'mongrel' types, as well as with doing away with the fundamental rectangularity of the typographic layout and consistency in arrangement.
"That breaking of all taboos, present and past, is a perfectly natural and historically justified development, presenting a new turn of a spiraling path of the dialectical evolution of design. Having its close parallel in the Western post-modernist 'New Wave' movement, it also carries on the domestic tradition of the Russian avant garde's revolutionary mistrust to any tradition however respectable it appears.
"Young designers, post-graduates of the major art and design schools, make up a motive force of that movement. It is also visible in poster, packaging, stationery and ephemera design – and less so in book design...

A New Challenge
"The all out political and social renovation in the USSR with its trend to democratization, openness, focusing on popular needs, both spiritual and material – spells new obligations to society-oriented and culture conscious Soviet design. There is not only more room for creativity, expression, and competition, but also more public duties to fulfill, more needs to satisfy, more expectations to justify. For the design profession that presents one of the toughest challenges in Soviet design history since the Great Socialist Revolution of October 1917." Maxim Zhukov.

The following illustrations are of work by Soviet graphic designers since 1975.

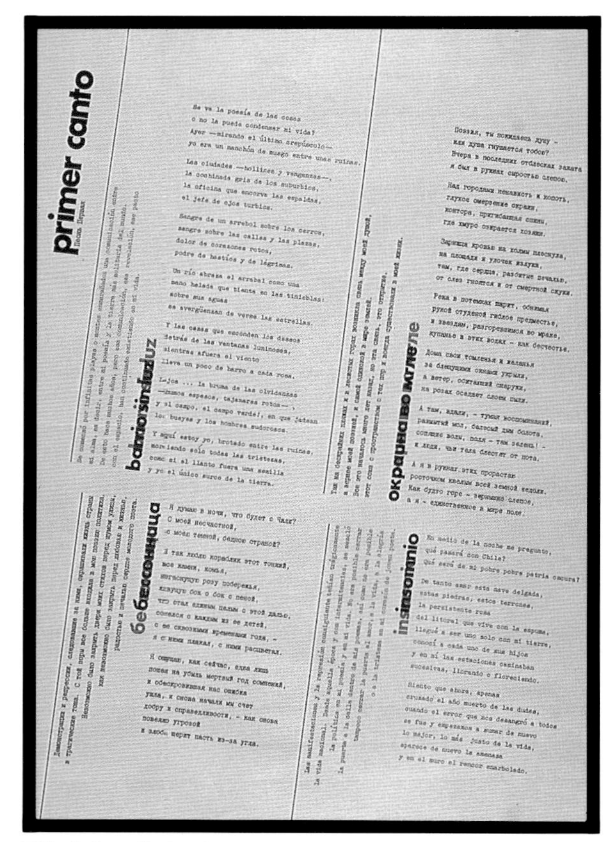

***Nikolai Kalinin,** book designer, Moscow. He designed Pablo Neruda's* Three Songs, *which was the gold medal winner in the 1977 typography competition at the International Book Design Exhibition in Leipzig, East Germany.*

Electrical
engineering
plants
promo
PROMOTION ACTIVITIES
V/O "Prommashexport"
renders technical assistance
in construction of electrical
engineering plants
manufacturing:
● power and communication cables
and enamel-insulated wires
● glass and porcelain insulators
● electrical equipment (electric heater
units, electric, furnaces, etc.)
● circuit-opening devices (circuit
breakers, switches, plugs, plug-sockets,
electric bells, etc.)
● power silicon rectifiers
● automobile storage batteries and
primary cells
Send all enquiries to:
Prommashexport, 18/1, Ovchinnikovskaya Emb.
Moscow 113324, USSR
Cable address: Prommashexport Moscow
Telephone: 220-15-05
Telex: 411932

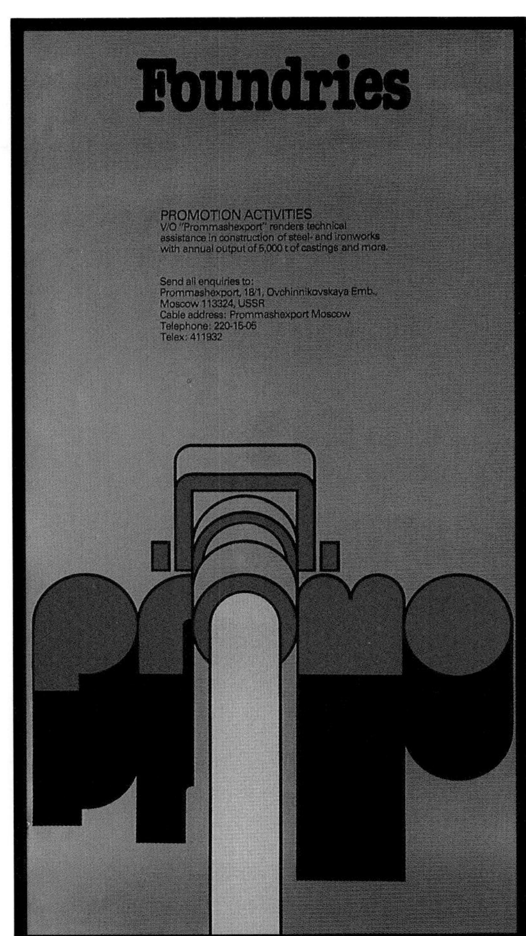

Foundries
PROMOTION ACTIVITIES
V/O "Prommashexport" renders technical
assistance in construction of steel- and ironworks
with annual output of 5,000 t of castings and more.
Send all enquiries to:
Prommashexport, 18/1, Ovchinnikovskaya Emb.,
Moscow 113324, USSR
Cable address: Prommashexport Moscow
Telephone: 220-15-06
Telex: 411932
promo

Three promotional posters *from an identity program for PromMash Export Group Companies. 1981-4. Valery Akopov, Michael Anixt, Vasily Dyakonov, Alexander Shumilin, Boris Trofimov.*

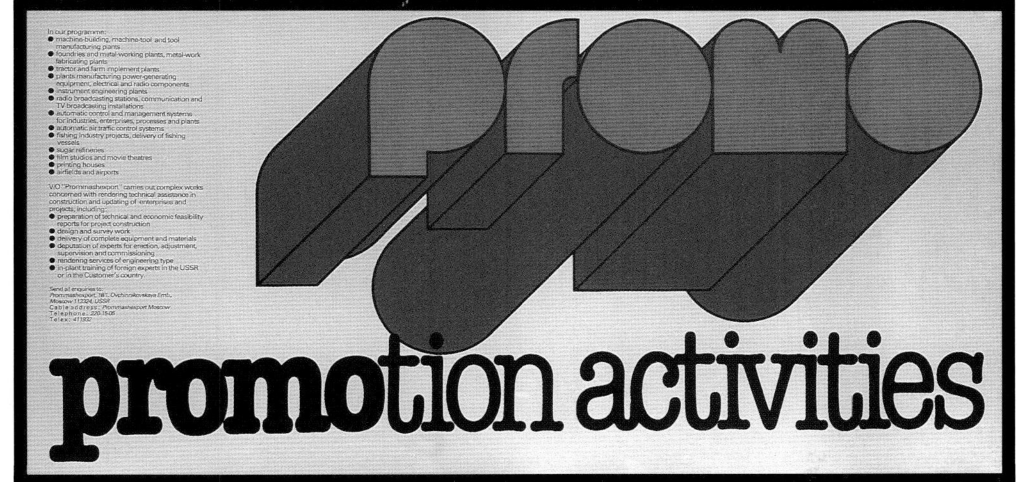

Vladimir Pertsov, *book and lettering designer, easel graphics, Moscow. Title spread.*

эстрадный сборник
ШУТИ И ПОЙ

Evgeni Smirnov, *book designer, Minsk. Title spread.*

Poster *for an exhibition of paintings for The Hong Kong and Shanghai Banking Corporation. Henry Steiner, Hong Kong.*

Package *for peanut oil for Amoycan. Henry Steiner, Hong Kong.*

HONG KONG
Henry Steiner

In Hong Kong designer Henry Steiner has created some excellent graphic designs since his arrival there in 1961 as Design Director for Asia Magazine. In 1964 he founded his own studio, Graphic Communication Ltd. Since then he has been active there as a designer and teacher. Steiner was born in Austria, studied in the United States at Hunter College and Yale University and at The Sorbonne in Paris.

IRAN
Morteza Momayez

Momayez faces not only the challenge of a bilingual society, he must contend with the Persian copy reading from right to left while the corresponding English copy reads from left to right. His work is colorful, lively, readable. A few of his posters are shown here.

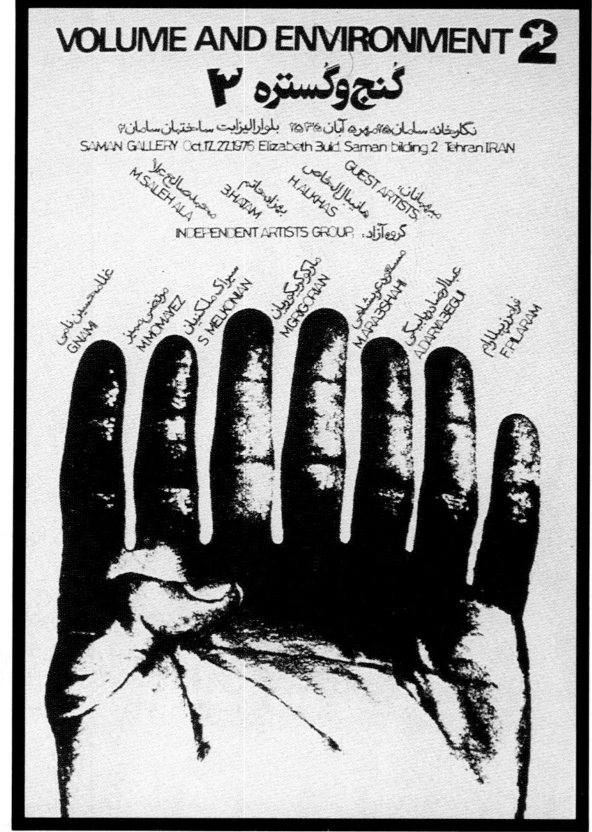

Poster *for an art exhibition. Morteza Momayez, Iran.*

Poster *for the Fifth Teheran Film Festival. Morteza Momayez.*

Concert poster. *Morteza Momayez.*

Poster *for the Farabi Film Center. Morteza Momayez.*

ISRAEL
Dan Reisinger

Reisinger works in environmental, graphic and three-dimensional design areas. His trademark is use of vivid color. His posters often require a blending of Hebrew (right-to-left reading) and English.

Poster *for a Jerusalem happening. Dan Reisinger.*

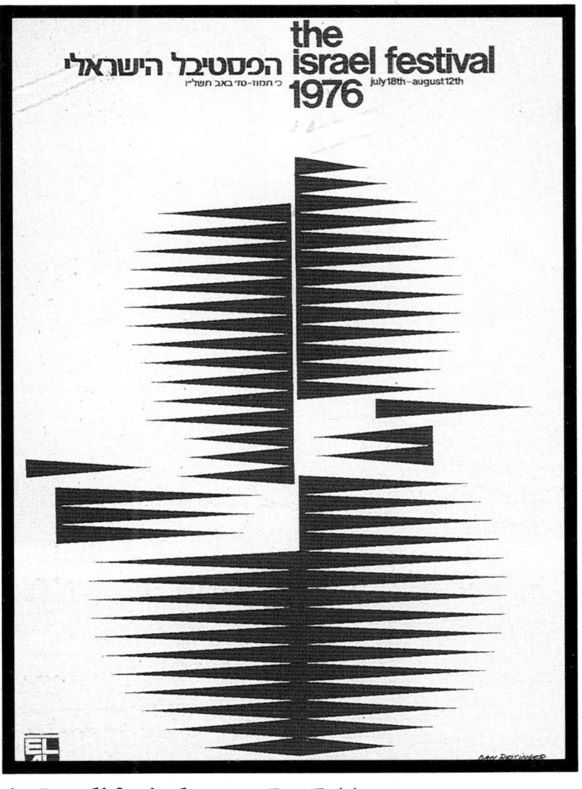

An Israeli festival poster. *Dan Reisinger.*

BRAZIL
Oswaldo Miranda

Oswaldo Miranda (Miran) is not only a graphic designer, he is a versatile illustrator and a calligrapher. His work is often characterized by a blending, rather than a mere assembling, of illustrations and typographic elements. While Miranda's work is not a copy of anyone's style, he has been particularly inspired by Herb Lubalin, Mo Lebowitz, Lou Dorfsman, Milton Glaser, Aaron Burns and Tom Carnase, all from New York, as well as by the work of Saul Bass and other West Coast artists. In *Novum Gebrauschgraphik,* German designer Olaf Leu wrote that Miranda is "a really necessary phenomenon in the graphic monotony of our time."

Cover *of a supplement to the magazine,* Raposa, *(the fox) dealing with the graphics of Herb Lubalin. Miran.*

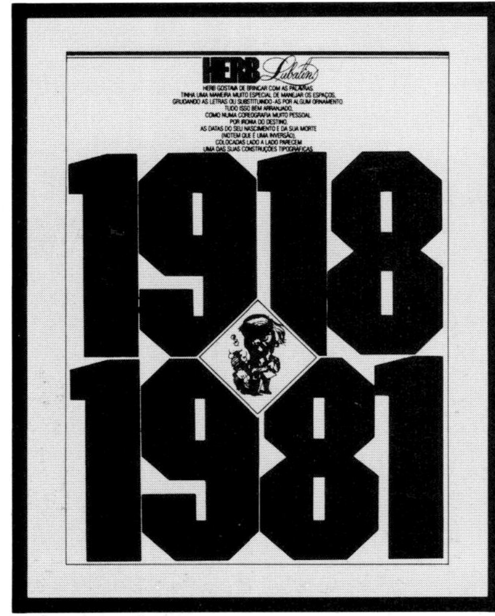

Pages _from_ Raposa _magazine on the occasion of the death of Herb Lubalin. Miran._

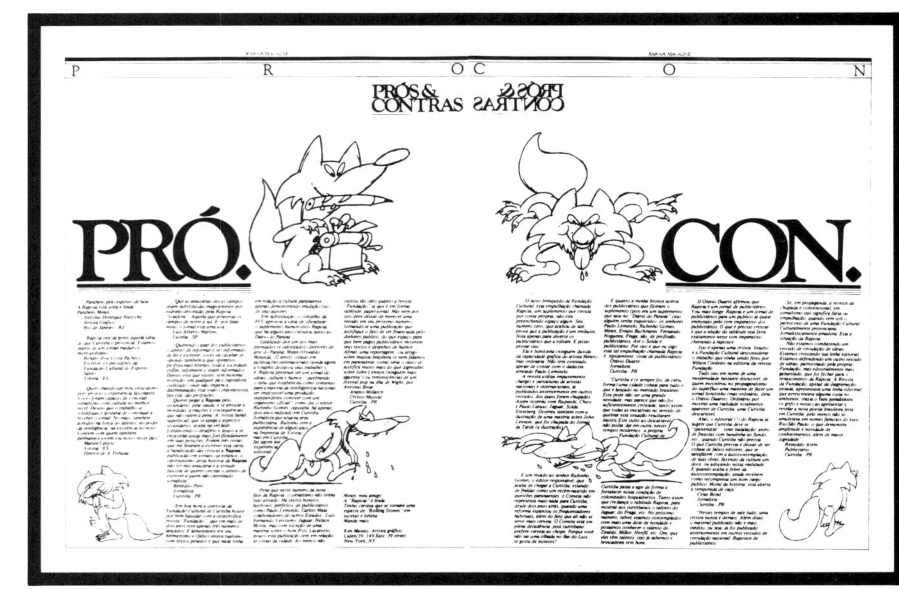

Editorial spread _from the magazine_ Raposa. _Art director, illustrator, Miran._

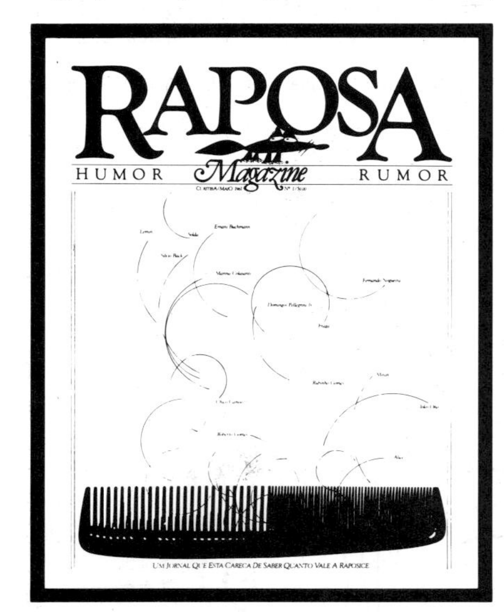

Three covers _for the magazine_ Raposa. _Art director, illustrator, Miran._

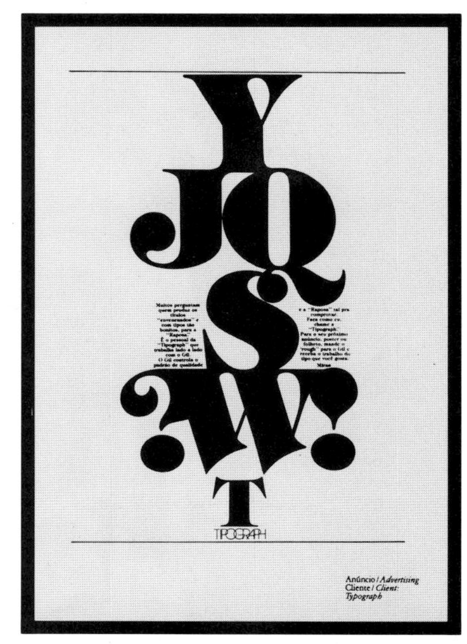

Advertisement _for a typographic service. Miran._

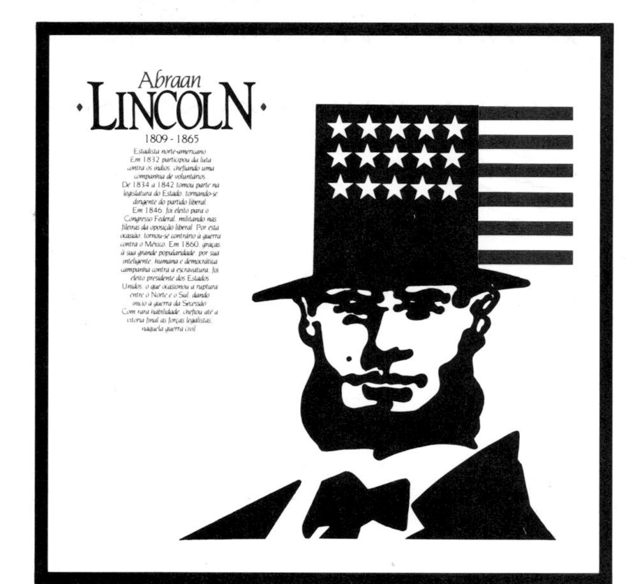

Editorial design _and illustration by Miran._

Design, _illustration, Miran._

Design, _illustration, Miran._

Editorial spread *from the magazine* Raposa. *Art director, illustrator, Miran.*

Editorial design *and illustration by Miran.*

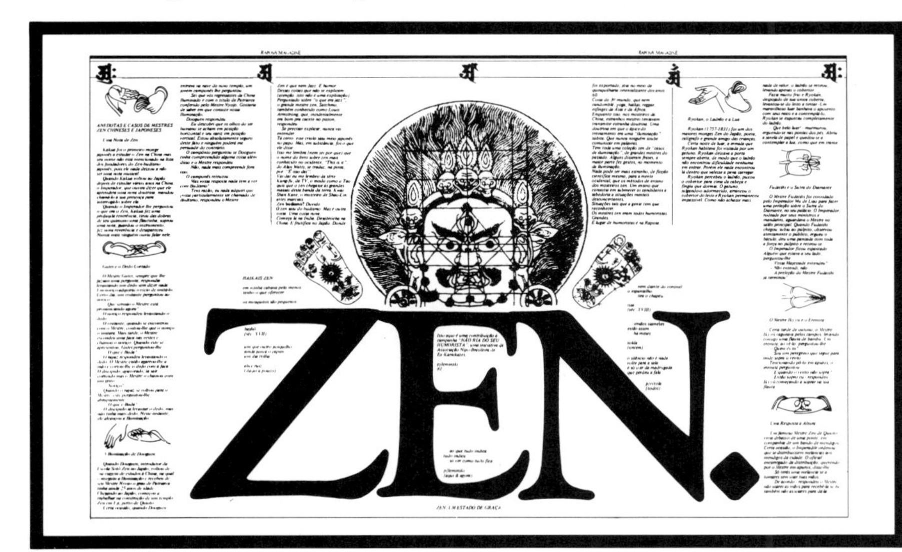

Editorial design *and illustration by Miran.*

Editorial spread *for* Raposa *magazine. Art director, illustrator, Miran.*

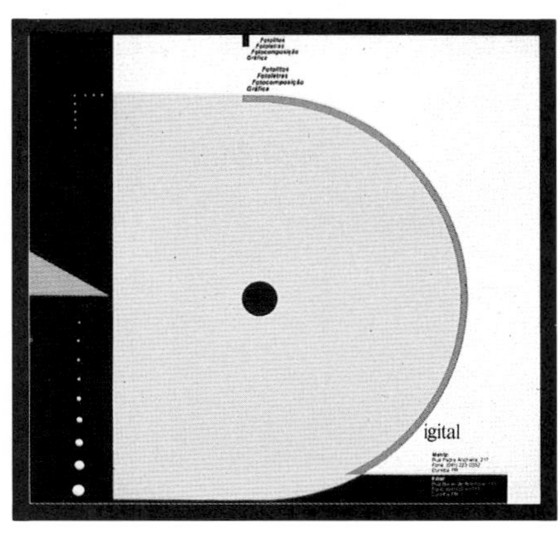

Design, *illustration, Miran.*

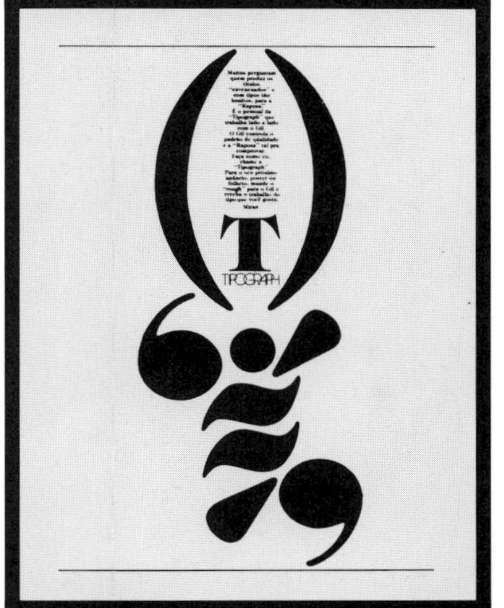

Advertisement *for a typographic service. Miran.*

Design, *illustration, Miran.*

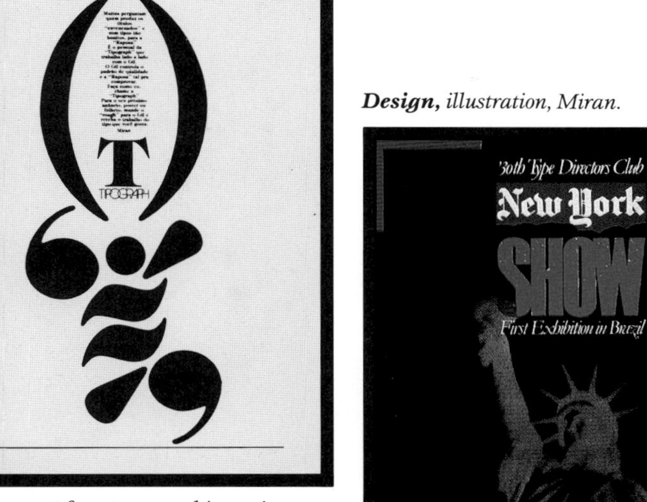

Editorial design *and illustration by Miran.*

Editorial design *and illustration by Miran.*

"The many roots of Japanese graphic design."

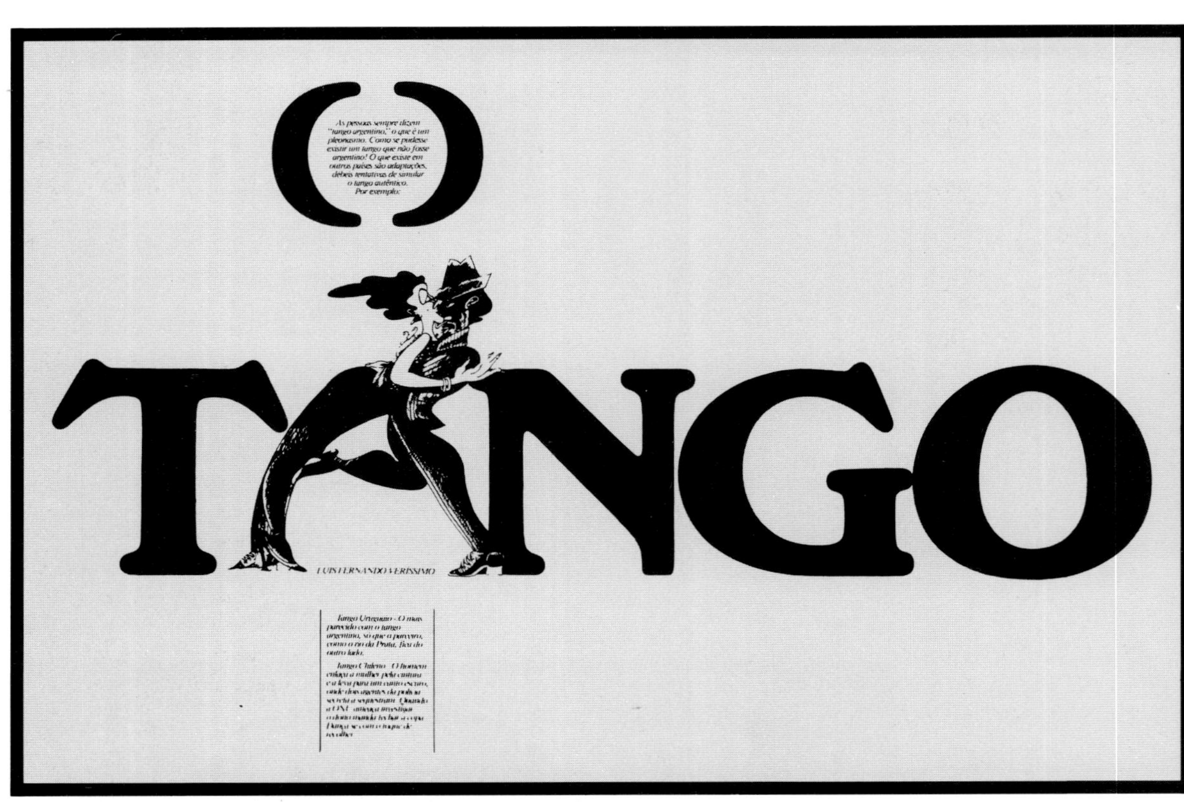

***Editorial spread** for* Raposa *magazine. Art director, illustrator, Miran, Brazil.*

***Editorial spread** for* Raposa *magazine. Art director, illustrator, Miran, Brazil.*

JAPAN

Contemporary typographic design in Japan has many roots, including traditional Japanese design, the Bauhaus, European constructivism, and the freer and often personal design approaches of such American graphic designers as Herb Lubalin, Lou Dorfsman, Bradbury Thompson and Gene Federico.

In the 1930s Bauhaus concepts made their way to Japan, where they influenced the curriculum at the Shin School of Design and Architecture in Tokyo. Japanese students at the Bauhaus practiced Bauhaus teaching when they returned to Japan. Works of the Bauhaus were exhibited in Japan in 1930 and books about the Bauhaus and Walter Gropius were published there.

But an even greater influence was the work of Yusaka Kamekura. His design leadership and influence might be compared in some respects to that of Paul Rand in the United States. His work as art director for several cultural magazines from 1937 to 1948 won him the title "Boss" in Japan. Under his influence, Japanese designers changed their belief that graphic communications had to be hand-drawn. Professional status was achieved by some graphic designers and the notion that such applied art was necessarily inferior to fine art was modified. Aside from his creative work, Kamekura influenced the development of the contemporary movement by helping found the Japanese Advertising Art Club, and in 1960, the Japan Design Center. In 1978, he became President of the Japan Graphic Designers Association.

The magazine *Brain,* through its articles, and especially the design contributions of Masuda Tadoshi, gave further impetus to the design movement. The simplicity and orderliness of the work of Kamekura and Tadoshi had its counterpart in that of Tadavori Yokoo. His work is the antithesis of constructivist or Bauhaus order. Yokoo captures the vigor of dada. He positioned elements dynamically, used pop art, fluorescent colors and mystical images.

Kamekura considers the Silvermine conference sponsored by the Type Directors Club a major influence in his work. Held in Silvermine, Connecticut, in 1958, it was called The Art and Science of Typography. It brought together leading designers from the United States and Canada, Europe and Japan. Here Kamekura met and mingled with Western designers. He was strongly influenced by the dynamism and personality in the work of Herb Lubalin and Lou Dorfsman. Before Silvermine, Kamekura observed, "Typography was not a key word. Now it is." At Silvermine he learned "typography in the Western sense." When he returned to Japan, Kamekura tried to combine the American design approach with Japanese design traditions.

In turn, younger design talents such as those of Ikko Tanaka and Kohai Sugiura were exposed to the work of American designers that Kamekura introduced to Japan.

Until this time, the 1950s and 1960s, Japanese advertising typography was essentially a way to label a product and convey simple "how-to" directions. But with the advent of the new typography, young Japanese designers learned how to use type to attract attention, convey ideas, establish a mood, manipulate degrees of emphasis, create a favorable image and make a memorable impression. During the past three decades, many Japanese designers have come to appreciate the importance of typography in typographic design and have produced beautiful and effective pieces.

Today, typographic design in Japan is on a par with the best in the world. In the '70s and '80s it has been driven by computer technologies and the vigorous work of the NAAC (Nippon Advertising Arts Council) and the Japan Typography Association. New typefaces include Miricho, similar to Roman, and a Gothic close to a Western sans serif. Designers have acquired considerable skill in blending the three indigenous scripts. Kanji (Chinese characters) is the traditional and formal script for ideographic communication. Katakana is simple geometric letterstyle used for imported words. Hiragana is a flowing syllabary (symbols for syllables rather than for letters) used for purely Japanese words. Contemporary typography is often a blend of these "alphabets" with roman characters.

Sentences are constructed by combining the three writing systems for a total of 8,000 characters. Some characters require 33 strokes. All Japanese characters are written in a square area, so they can be set and read horizontally or vertically. Much Japanese is read vertically and from right to left.

The poster is a major graphic communication form in Japan. A company's name or image is usually emphasized over a particular product so that its logo can endure in the public's mind. Beautiful art and design are considered to endow a message and a product or service with an aura of excellence, quality, desirability; graphic symbols from Japanese history and stylized patterns, rather than words, are often employed to attract readers and create a positive attitude. Japanese graphics also reflect aspects of nature and the seasons and often employ humor, even slapstick.

Thoughts About Typography

In 1982 a special issue of *Idea* magazine was subtitled "Typography in Japan." It included essays by leading designers. These excerpts from some of those essays, taken together, offer a composite picture of Japanese designers' attitudes toward type.

Typography: a New Meaning

"...the most important factor that distinguishes the graphic designer from many other specialists is the graphic designer's sharp sensibility to typography... the meaning of the word 'typography' has changed drastically since European modernization, in which the simple function of 'reading' types was enhanced to a new dramatic world of 'viewing' and 'feeling' types."
Yoshio Hayakawa.

Letters are Expressive

"Letters are beautiful in themselves. Just like the faces of human beings, some letters are intricately complex while others are blank and simple.

"It was toward the end of the 1950s or the beginning of the '60s...that the word 'typography' was coined in Japanese design circles. Until that time, this aspect of design was categorized as part of the layout planning and was not in itself considered to be a significant element of design. As a result of several international design conferences, the word 'typography' came to bear a very important meaning for designers, particularly from the perspective of those anxious for international recognition."
Kiyoshi Awazu.

Mr. Awazu also notes the influence of Swiss graphics magazines reaching Japan. He recalls it as "a rather shocking experience."

4,500 Characters Too Many

"Every press must have available for use at least 8,000 different characters, including kana *(Japanese characters), the Roman alphabet, and other various symbols, in order to meet the requirements necessary for a comprehensible newspaper. Out of these 8,000 characters, only 3,500 are sufficient to cover more than 99 percent of those included in an entire newspaper... We should all do our best to improve upon Japanese typography, perhaps the best way being to start making an attempt not to use those characters that are seldom used or too complicated to read."*
Tadasu Fukano.

The Influence of "Twen"

"A large portion of my virtually unfurnished room is occupied by my close 'buddies,' my books and magazines... In the indisputable position of utmost importance among these books is my collection of the German magazine, Twen."
Kenzo Nakagawa.

After discussing the influence of *Twen* and "the rich quality of graphic design produced in the United States," Mr. Nakagawa deplored the lack of creative typography in Japanese magazines and hoped for "a magazine filled with Japanese typography that animates with vivid expression the Japanese language."

Complexity Can Be a Virtue

"...in the early days of my career as a designer, I was very envious of European and American designers who were able to express themselves through orderly typography, intrinsic to Western languages.

"Now, however, it would appear that the very complexity of Japanese typography holds within it a driving force that transforms the essence of the traditional aesthetic sense into works of modern graphic design."
Kazumasa Nagai.

The New Typefaces

"A total of 42 new typefaces were marketed from 1977 to March, 1982. And they can be classified into two kinds – one that reflects new concepts and directions as a result of the recent diversification of typeface and the other that is based on existing typefaces. Shaken's 'Sutia' belongs to the Ming type family, but all its type are italic and are composed in horizontal lines. The same company's 'Gotia' belongs to the Gothic type family, but all its types are italic and are composed in horizontal lines. Moreover, its elements are quite different from those in the Gothic type family. The number of these new typefaces, including some fancy typefaces, is 15, or 35 percent of the total new typefaces. Those which belong to the Ming or Gothic type family number 24, or 56 percent of the total. And the remaining 4, (9 percent of the total) typefaces are classic typefaces such as Edo characters.

"How many of the total 42 new typefaces are creative in the true sense of the word? Even those which reflect new directions are basically Ming or Gothic typefaces. So they are never creative.

"One of the recent noteworthy trends in Japanese typography is that a new type family is planned and designed. In other words, several typefaces belonging to a new type family are marketed at one time. It takes by far more time and money to design a new type family than a single typeface. So the marketers of new typefaces see that all these new typefaces are usable and salable. The consequence is that very few of these new typefaces are sheer new ones. Furthermore, these new typefaces include both types for texts and typefaces for headlines, while the types for texts must be ones that do not make readers aware of their shapes, the types for headlines must be ones that have shapes interesting enough to attract readers' attention. So these new typefaces consist of two contradictory sets of types. Thus it has become very hard to design truly creative typefaces. I think, at the same time, this calls for the emergence of typographers who have foresight in additon to sharp sensitivity and wide experience."
Yasaburo Kuwayama.

The Stimulus of Letters

"To me letters and characters are communication symbols on one hand, and attractive objects that stimulate my sensitivity, on the other."
Takenobu Igarashi.

Soundsigns and Imagesigns

*"Japanese letters are soundsigns and imagesigns. The wit of the visual designs makes a letter whisper, makes a letter shout. Typography is the visual orchestration of a given text with an existing typeface. Except for the talking typography invented by Kohei Sugiura, Japanese designers are more concerned with the cosmetics of letters than the exploration of messages. Typography in Japan is more typo*graphy *than* typo*graphy."*
Helmut Schmid.

Of Tools and Designers

"Whether the designer's tool be a keyboard or whether it be a freshly cut bamboo brush pen, as long as he is continually aware of where he stands, through the medium of typography, the designer will be able to fulfill infinite possibilities in the communication between man and matter."
Kei Mori.

"An ability to combine logic and functionalism with individuality."

Yusaku Kamekura

Kamekura is best known for his posters, trademarks, and package designs, although he has also designed books, advertisements, and industrial products. Strong, simple graphic symbols characterized much of his early work. His more recent posters combine dramatic photography with type or lettering. His trademark designs are bold and free of extraneous decoration. The apparent simplicity of his designs can be deceptive. Ikko Tanaka, in *The Work of Yusaku Kamekura,* calls him "this greatest of Japanese designers." Tanaka particularly admires Kamekura's ability to combine logic and functionalism with individuality. At an early age Kamekura came into contact with the work of French poster designer Cassandre and in a bookstore he discovered the work of the Bauhaus and of Herbert Bayer. Although these and others from the United States and Europe influenced his work, Kamekura was an individualist. Yomosuka Natori, who studied photography and layout in Germany, returned to Japan and published the magazine *Nippon.* This was a high quality magazine, and the young Kamekura was a designer for it. Students of Kamekura's mature work find his greatness also derived from his ability to grasp the heart of an idea, the basic concept of the message, and then convey it most directly. Another aspect of his single-mindedness was his insistence on working as an equal with company executives. In an interview published in the magazine *Graphic Design* (No. 88), he said,

"No matter how much money I am offered, I will not do work that I am not convinced is right. This means that I refuse to do any work for political parties or religious groups, because I find that I usually cannot agree with their ideals and purposes....I simply cannot get an inspiration to do work that does not seem worthwhile and of interest to me...My work is only valid if I am involved in creating the image for the entire company in terms of logos and poster design and so forth, and I don't like to leave even a simple poster design in an ambivalent stage of development."

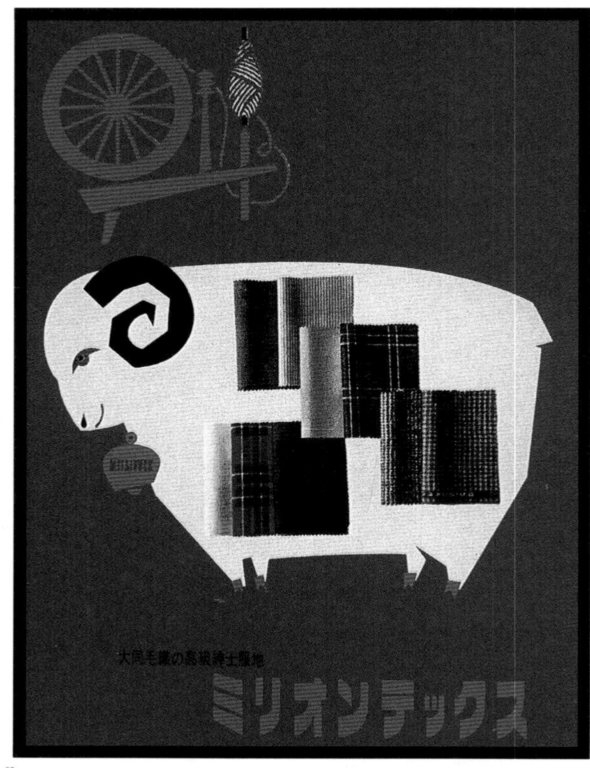

Poster *for Daido Worsted Mills, 1954. Yusaku Kamekura.*

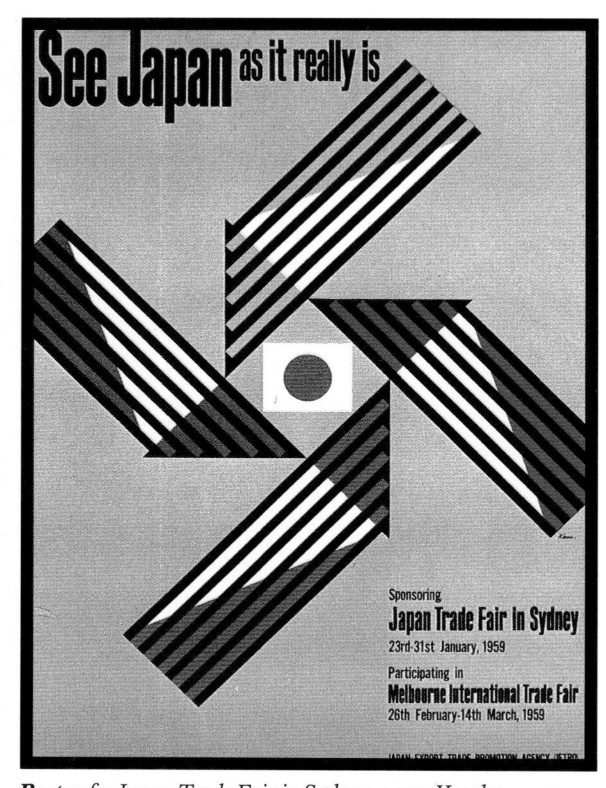

Poster *for Japan Trade Fair in Sydney, 1959. Yusaku Kamekura.*

Poster *for Japan Industry Floating Fair, 1958. Yusaku Kamekura.*

Poster *for 18th Olympic Games, 1961. Yusaku Kamekura.*

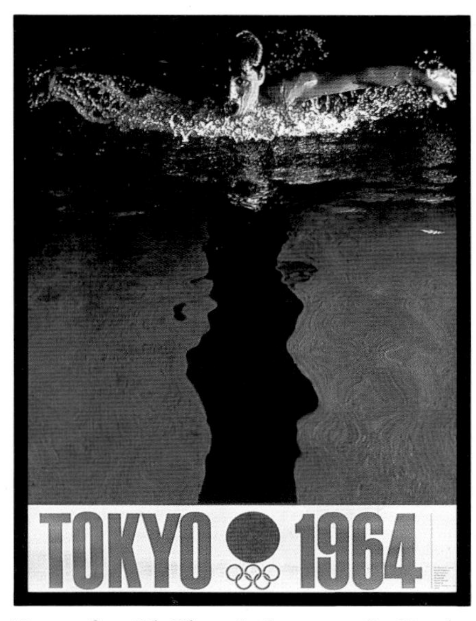

Poster *for 18th Olympic Games, 1963. Yusaku Kamekura.*

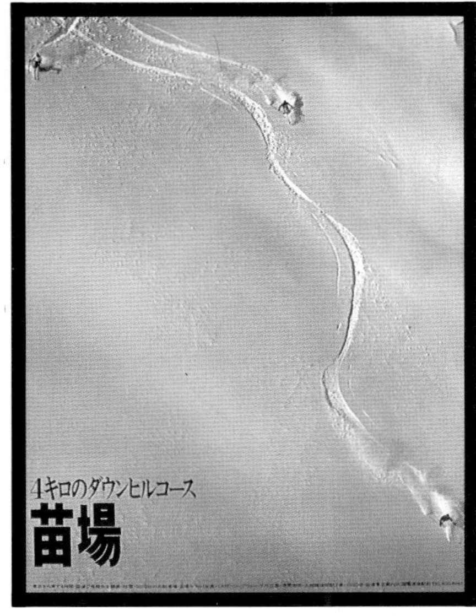

Poster *for Naeba Skiing Ground, 1968. Yusaku Kamekura.*

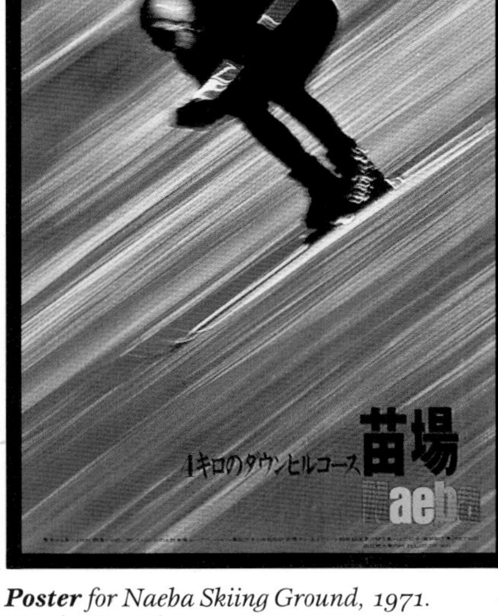

Poster *for Naeba Skiing Ground, 1971. Yusaku Kamekura.*

Poster *for the 10th Tokyo International Lighting Design Competition, 1983. Yusaku Kamekura.*

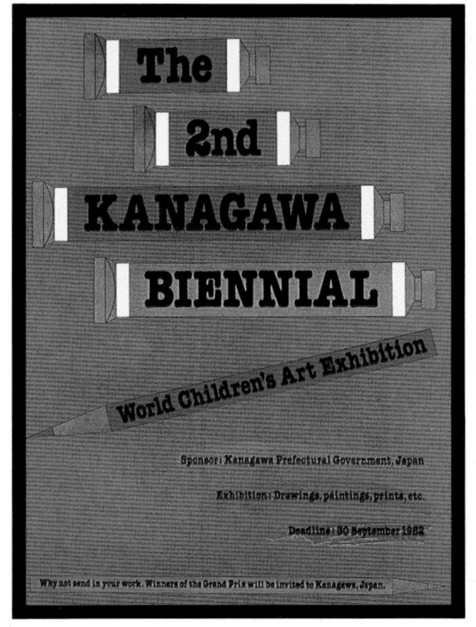

Poster *for World Children's Art Exhibition, 1982. Yusaku Kamekura.*

Poster *for Manza Skiing Ground, 1968. Yusaku Kamekura.*

Poster *(with symbol mark) for '81 FIS World Cup Furano, 1981. Yusaku Kamekura.*

Poster *for Hiroshima Appeals, 1983. Yusaku Kamekura.*

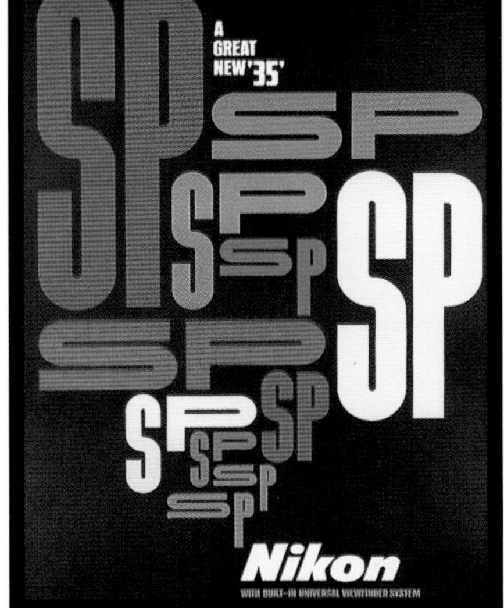

Poster *for Nikon SP camera, 1957. Yusaku Kamekura.*

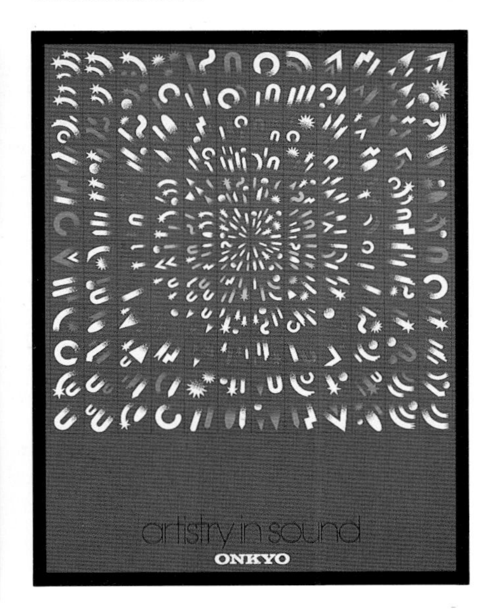

Poster *for Collection Series No. 4, Onkyo Audio Products, 1982. Yusaku Kamekura.*

Ikko Tanaka

Commenting on the work of Ikko Tanaka, American designer Lou Dorfsman writes:

"In the work of Ikko Tanaka one sees an amalgam of two design cultures. The reflections of the best of both worlds. Some of Ikko Tanaka's work displays the sensitive beauty and delicate use of space, color and line that one associates with the best of the East. Specifically – with Japan in spirit, texture and voice. On the other hand, his work has the bold graphic strength and drive one associates with the brashness and directness of the best of American or Western graphic design."

Tanaka's work is also distinguished by its effective blending of photography or illustration with calligraphy, for visual harmony of Japanese and English texts, and for its use of unusual colors. He designs books, trademarks, posters, advertisements, packages, signage, and a full range of commercial material.

Tanaka was a textile designer, then a graphic designer for Sankei Press in the early 1950s. In Tokyo he was an art director at Nippon Design Center and in 1963 opened his own design studio.

He does not have a style or a fixed approach to his work. Just as East or West are combined in his everyday life, so are they in his typographics. As Tanaka says, one may use a knife and a fork at lunch and chopsticks for dinner. About half of his Japanese typography is set vertically and half is set horizontally.

Tanaka's work has been influenced by American designers since 1950, Japanese brush calligraphy, and the Bauhaus and the Swiss grid system. He cites as major influences Karl Gerstner, Herb Lubalin, Lou Dorfsman, Paul Rand, and Josef Müller-Brockmann.

Kabuki No Hakken (Discoveries in Kabuki/Book on Kabuki), 1974. *Moved by the hieroglyphics of Lee period Chinese genre paintings, the designer thought of expressing the contrast between bold and light characters at its extremities. The Kanteistyle characters (bottom half: a form of writing Kabuki signs) for Kabuki were extended and condensed to make a bold composition. Above it, characters for the titles were laid out according to genre to create a mass made of characters. Because it was a sumi-ink print, the result was quite different from a hieroglyphic. Ikko Tanaka.*

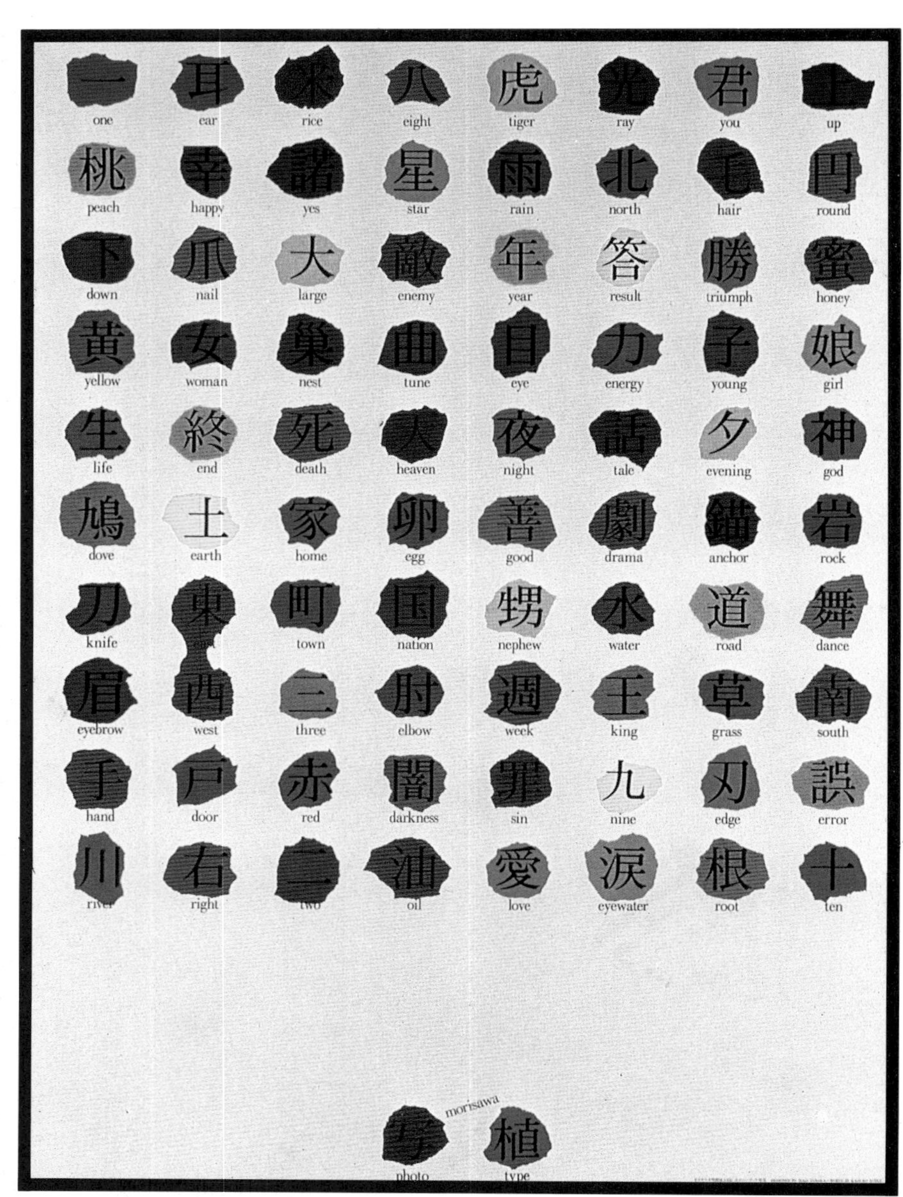

Morisawa Photo Typeset, 1973. *This is an "image poster" for Morisawa. It was created in an effort to better the understanding of Japanese characters by the English reader and also to publicize the beauty of phototypesetting. The last letter of each English word is the first letter of the next word, as in eight and tiger. Corresponding Chinese characters are written next to it. The copy is by Kazuko Koike. The background of each character is torn colored paper. It makes a colorful and decorative polka dot-like poster. Ikko Tanaka.*

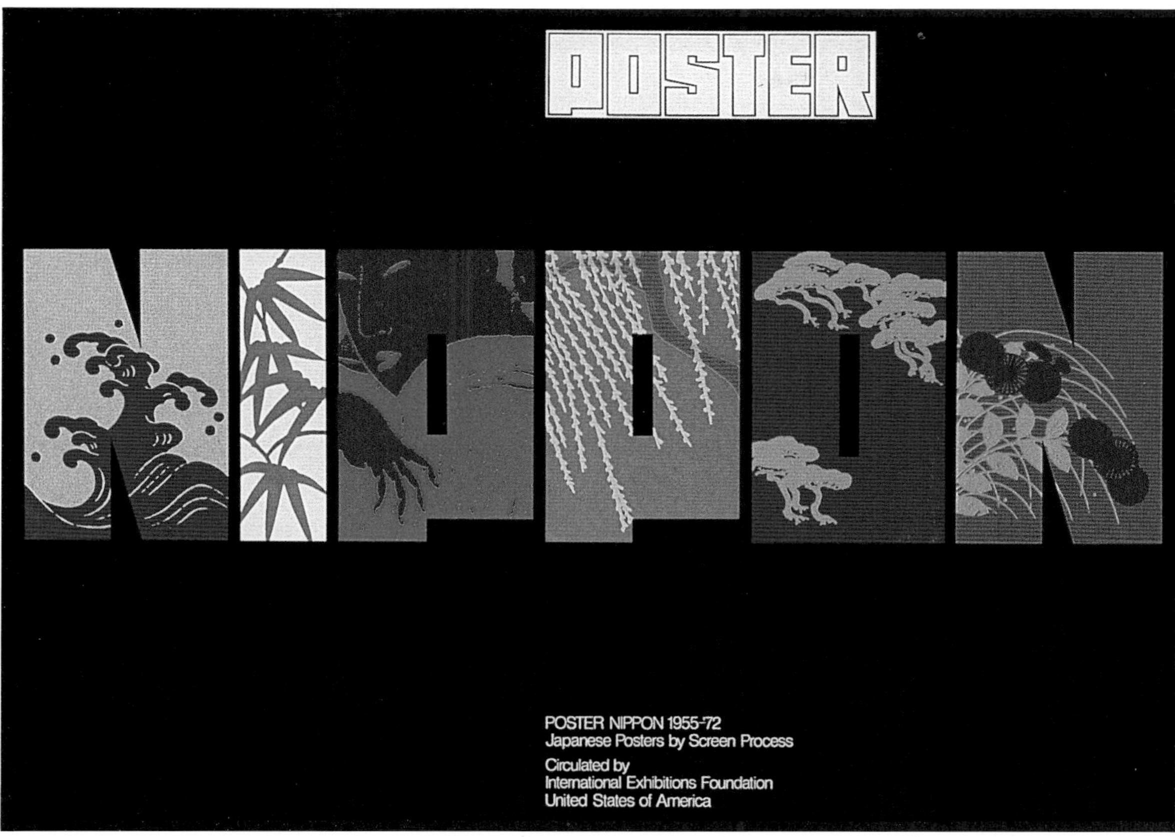

POSTER
NIPPON
POSTER NIPPON 1955-72
Japanese Posters by Screen Process
Circulated by
International Exhibitions Foundation
United States of America

Poster Nippon, 1972. *This is a poster for an overseas Japanese poster exhibition tour. It is an attempt to convert the European writing "Nippon" to a picture. The illustrations are mostly from Edo period (1603-1867) crafts: gold lacquer, dyes, weaving, wood block prints. Colors were changed and the designs were inserted into the letters. The outlines of the letters were thought of as picture frames and each design was trimmed accordingly. Care was taken to keep each illustration within the lettering. By closing-in the designs, it was thought it would be easy to recognize the letters "Nippon." The word "Poster" is in the same typeface. Ikko Tanaka.*

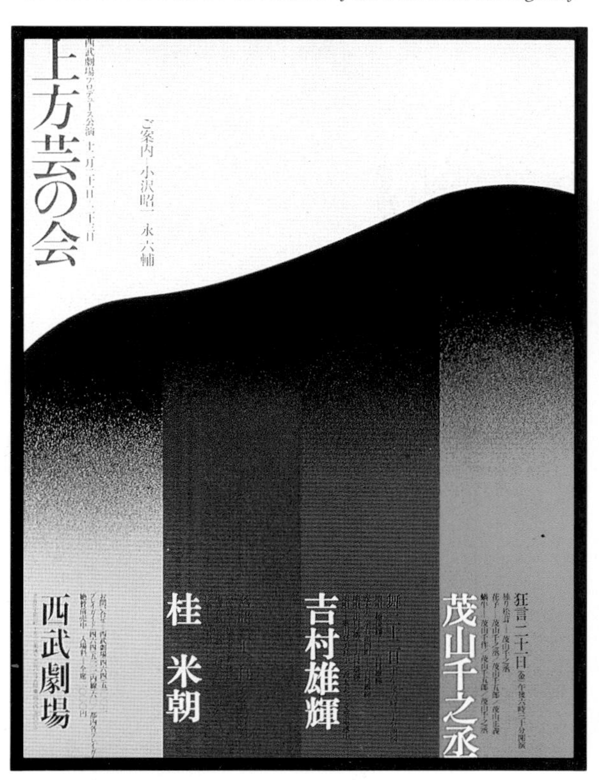

Kamigata Gei no Kai 1973. *This performance produced by Seibu Theater was conducted to have Kamigata performing arts such as Kansai (Western Japan) Noh Farce, dance and comic monologue enjoyed as much as possible. The names of those appearing is most important and they are separated into three colors (green, blue and red) to make the distinction between the different genres easier. The upper portion is cut with a hill-like pattern with a sand screen gradation. Ikko Tanaka.*

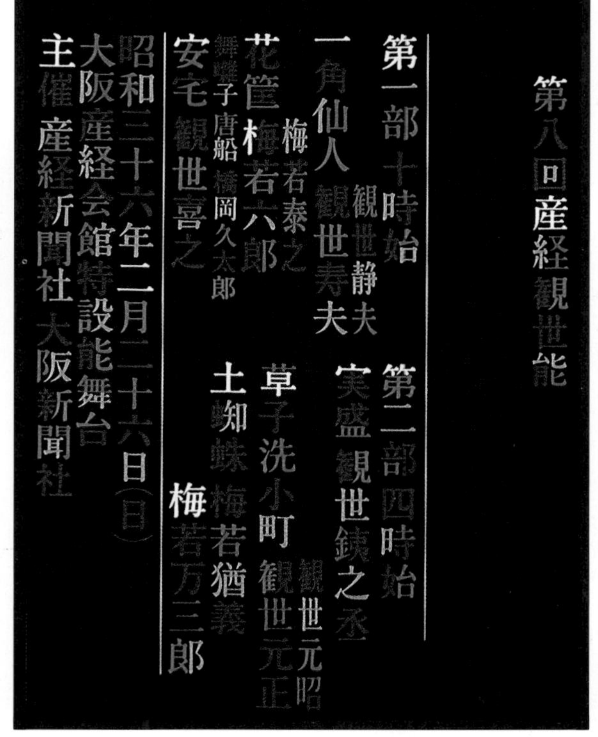

The Eighth Sankei Kanze Noh, 1961. *This poster was created to try and bring out the world of Noh simply with words which provide information such as time, place and program. The letters are not supplements to pictures and designs. The informative letters themselves are the main characters. The black Noh costume such as those seen in "Dojoji" was used as an image. The characters were separated into seven colors and the gorgeous image of the Noh play was shown. This poster was popular overseas and was reprinted several times. Ikko Tanaka.*

The 19th Sankei Kanze Noh, 1972. *As attempted in the eighth and ninth Sankei Kanze Noh, the informative letters have become the main character of the poster along with the colors. A strict layout is followed for the Noh performer rankings and programs. In other words, the name of the main character is placed on the left while the lesser characters are on the right. By the size and placement of the Kyogen and dance names, one can tell how they will perform and even their ranking. The designer always wondered if it would be possible to create a poster simply of letters and colors with such restrictions as mentioned above in mind. The colors of the curtain were used as a base and by creating a checked grid created the colors of Noh. Ikko Tanaka.*

"A blend of American emotionalism and Bauhaus and Swiss functionalism."

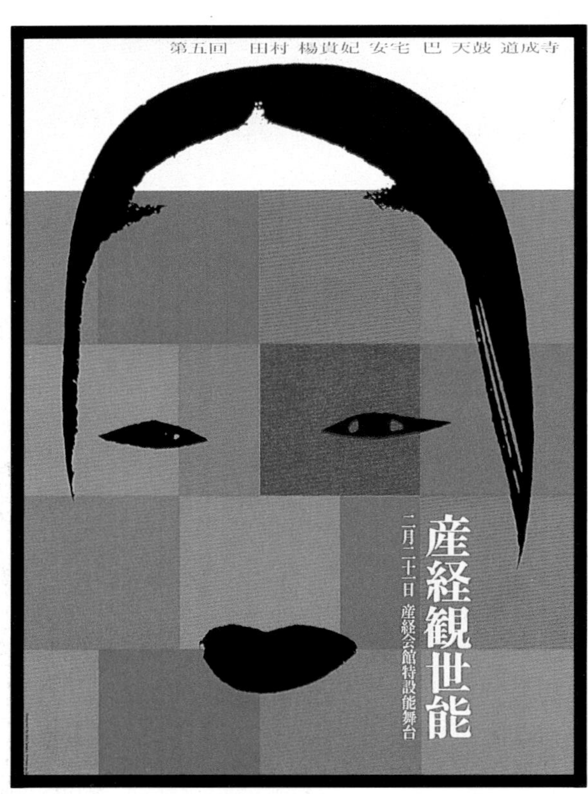

The Fifth Sankei Kanse Noh, *1958. A piece submitted to the Nissenbi exhibit. At this time, the designer was impressed by the Neue Grafik (New Graphic) movement in Switzerland. This was an attempt to see what would happen if the Noh mask was placed in a geometrical color composition. This method was relatively successful and the designer thought that the traditional image of Noh was blended into the modern design of the time. Though this piece came close to being selected, it was dropped. However, it can be said to be a very meaningful poster which allowed the designer to realize his style. Ikko Tanaka.*

Kazumasa Nagai

In 1960 Kazumasa Nagai joined the Nippon Design Center where he is now president. As with many other Japanese graphic designers, Nagai cites as major influences the Bauhaus, *Neue Graphik* magazine and, later, Herb Lubalin and Aaron Burns. He was also interested in the work and writings of Jan Tschichold. Nagai tries to blend in his work the emotionalism of American designers with the functionalism of Bauhaus and Swiss designers. In his cultural posters, for example, he employs symbolic patterns balanced with type for a unified impact. He strives for clear, but strong and beautiful typographics. Nagai feels the ideographic system is a handicap to designers and the Roman alphabet is easier to handle efficiently. He tries to bring something personal or warm into his designs through design, color and the way the type is handled.

Exhibit-announcement poster *for the Museum of Modern Art, Toyama. The designer explains that "This exhibition was to show artwork by primary school children and junior high school boys and girls. At each school, scores of children formed a team for painting what they liked on a huge-size sheet of paper. At this assignment all children must have experienced the pleasure similar to what they enjoy in putting chalk marks on walls, because they were allowed to doodle on a sheet as huge and spacious as a wall. The title of this poster (at the same time, the title of the exhibit) was expressed in the brush touch from what I perceived from the children's pictures. Every character is fairly visible and clear. The typesetting style in Japanese typography is tremendously flexible and in this poster the title consisting of nine characters runs vertically." Kazumasa Nagai.*

Poster *for an exhibition of George Rouault prints at the Museum of Modern Art, Toyama. The designer explains that Rouault's print,* Jesus on the Cross, *is centered in the big red cross in this poster. The title, "Rouault's Prints" is in Japanese in the arc arrangement on top. On the vertical bar of the big red cross, Rouault's name was imprinted in gold. Kazumasa Nagai.*

Poster *for the exhibition, Painting Toyama – The Hundred Landscapes by One Hundred Painters, held on the occasion of a Centennial Celebration of Toyama Prefecture. The designer explains, "Many golden suns symbolize the glory of each landscape and painters' names are scattered all over. Typography is a very important element in this poster." All the names of 100 painters are vertical. The main title centered in three lines also goes from the top downward. The first line means "A Centennial of the Establishment of Toyama Prefecture." The second line goes, "Painting Toyama – The Hundred Landscapes by One Hundred Painters." The third line states the exhibition period. On the left end of the poster there are two blocks of the statements in Chinese characters – the top is the Museum of Modern Art, Toyama, and below are the sponsoring organizations' names. Kazumasa Nagai.*

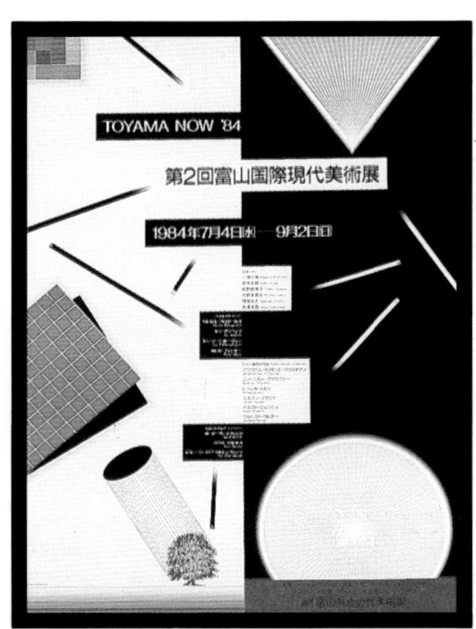

Poster *for The Second International Contemporary Art Exhibition at the Museum of Modern Art, Toyama. The exhibition was held by inviting works by contemporary artists in Japan, Benelux, West Germany and Scandinavia. The topmost horizontal line means "Toyama Now '84." The second line means "Art Exhibition in Toyama." The third line means "From April 7 (Wed) through September 2 (Sun)." Below these three lines there are four boxes in which the names of artists are listed. On the right side of the bottom, the statement lists the exhibition's sponsors. The designer said the typography blocks are centered to produce a contemporary sense effectively. Kazumasa Nagai.*

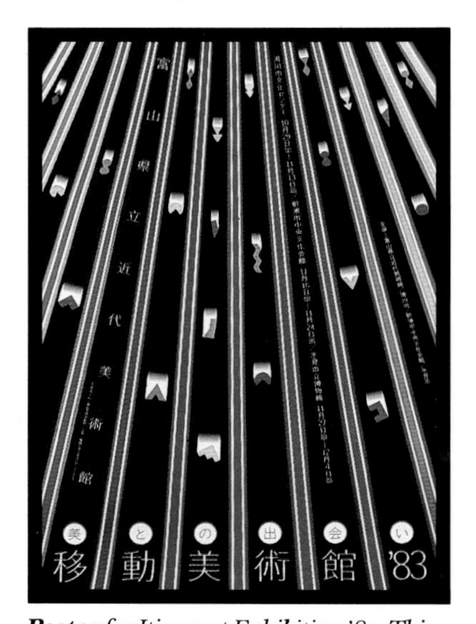

Poster *for Itinerant Exhibition '83. This project was planned and organized by the Museum of Modern Art, Toyama, together with Namekawa City, Culture Center of Shinminato City, and Himi City. Here, Japanese typography gives free swing to its flexibility. Three lines of the statement go from the top down toward the bottom, giving the who, what, where and when of the exhibition. The designer explains "all these are set in radiant angles, by which I mean to express the 'movability' of the Itinerant Exhibition." Kazumasa Nagai.*

Poster *inviting artists all over the world to join in the First Triennial Poster Contest. The designer explained that the contest was the first Japan ever held on a vast, international scale, and that the typography for the message required an arrangement on the bilingual basis – in Japanese and English. The Japanese typography is treated as the main elements. Kazumasa Nagai.*

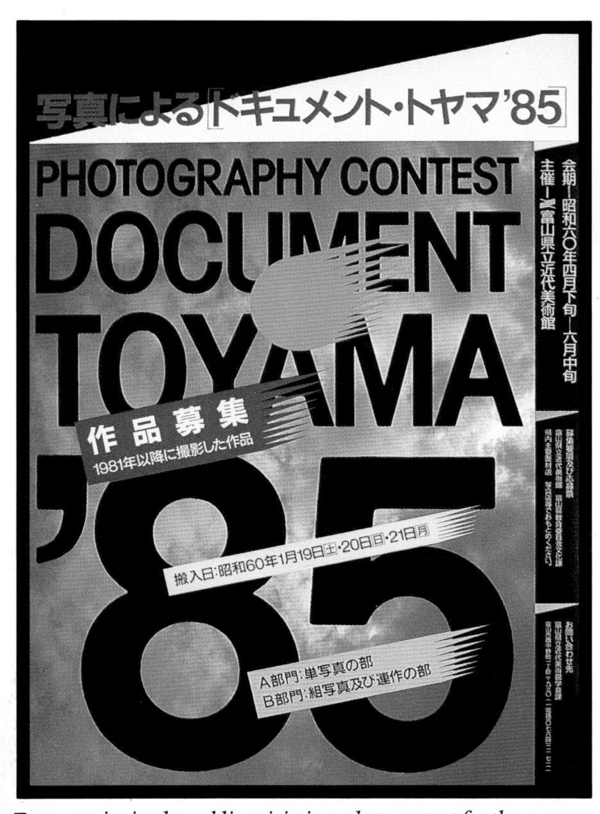

Poster *to invite the public to join in a photo contest for the purpose of securing documentary photos of Toyama Prefecture. The museum held an exhibition of the entry photos. The designer said, "For this poster, the photo of the blue sky with some clouds is employed as a background, over which boldface typography is used so as to give a strong impression or powerful documentary touch." Kazumasa Nagai.*

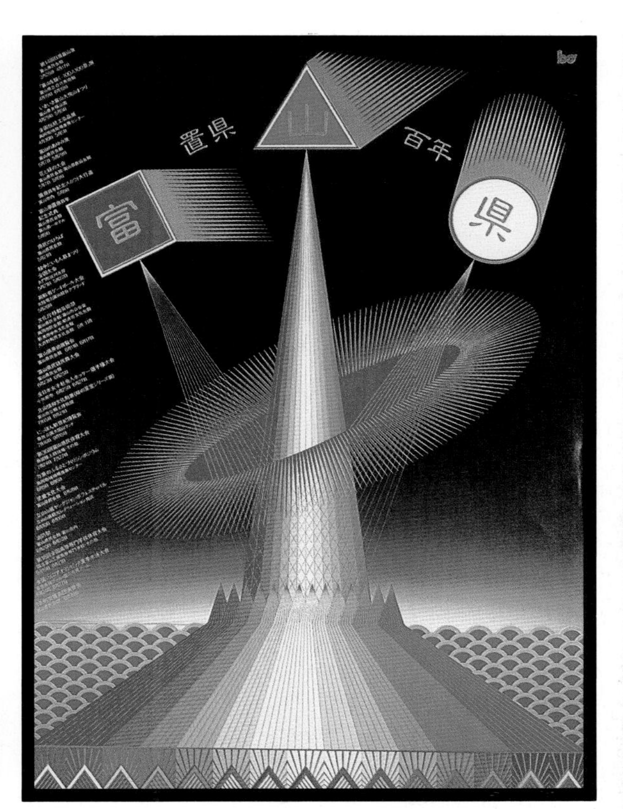

Poster *for a Centennial of the Establishment of Toyama Prefecture, announcing the various celebration events to be held, such as exhibitions, festivals, marches, and ceremonies. The three Chinese characters in three shapes – square, triangle and circle – mean* To, Yama *and* Prefecture. *The four Chinese characters placed above the three shapes mean* The establishment of the prefecture *(two left characters) and* A Centennial *(two right characters). All these characters are old-fashioned style. On the left side of the poster, all events to be held are listed. The designer said, "Toyama Prefecture faces the Japan Sea, and there's a mountain range of Tate-Yama, which is called the Japan Alps, behind. I tried to visualize the energy of Toyoma Prefecture for its future together with the Japan Sea and the mountain range of Tate-Yama." Kazumasa Nagai.*

Six Designers

Much Japanese communication design has dynamic graphics, graphic symbolism and a fresh approach to color. In Japan, as in other major graphic communication centers, there are many talented designers, each with a personal approach. The work shown here focuses on six of Japan's outstanding designers in the 1980s.

Japan's Annuals

For a thorough look at contemporary Japanese advertising graphics, see *'86 Annual of Ad Productions in Japan,* published by Rikuyo-Sha in Tokyo, and the *Japan Typography Annual,* published by Robundo Publishers, Tokyo.

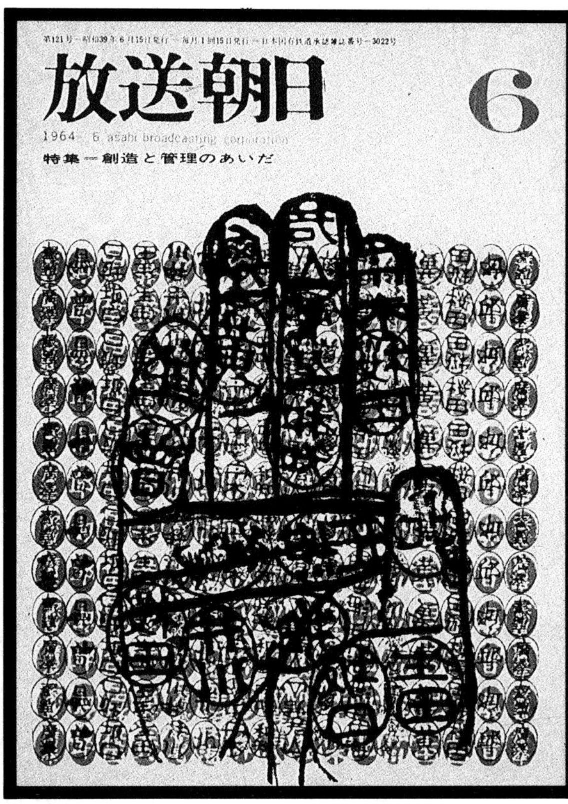

Magazine cover, *1964, for Asahi Broadcasting Corporation. Design and art direction, Kiyoshi Awazu.*

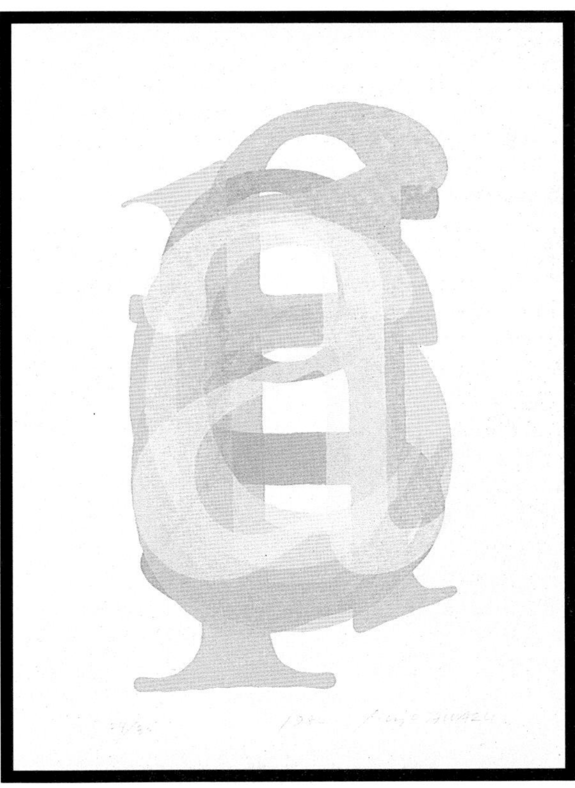

ABC logo, *1980. Kiyoshi Awazu.*

Old Japanese alphabet, *1980. Kiyoshi Awazu.*

Japanese alphabet, *1981. Kiyoshi Awazu.*

Poster *for desegregation campaign, 1977. Shigeo Fukuda.*

Logotype *for a polyester fiber's name. Ribbon style lines represent fashionable image. Tadasu Fukano.*

Symbol *for the centenary of the Japanese Red Cross Society. Tadasu Fukano.*

Opera poster, *1983, Shigeo Fukuda.*

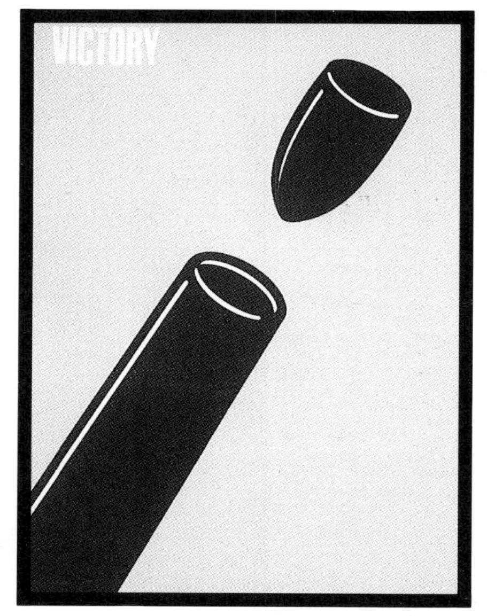

Poster *for the International Poster Competition at Warsaw commemorating the 30th Anniversary of Victory in War, 1975. Shigeo Fukuda.*

Opera poster, *1981, Shigeo Fukuda.*

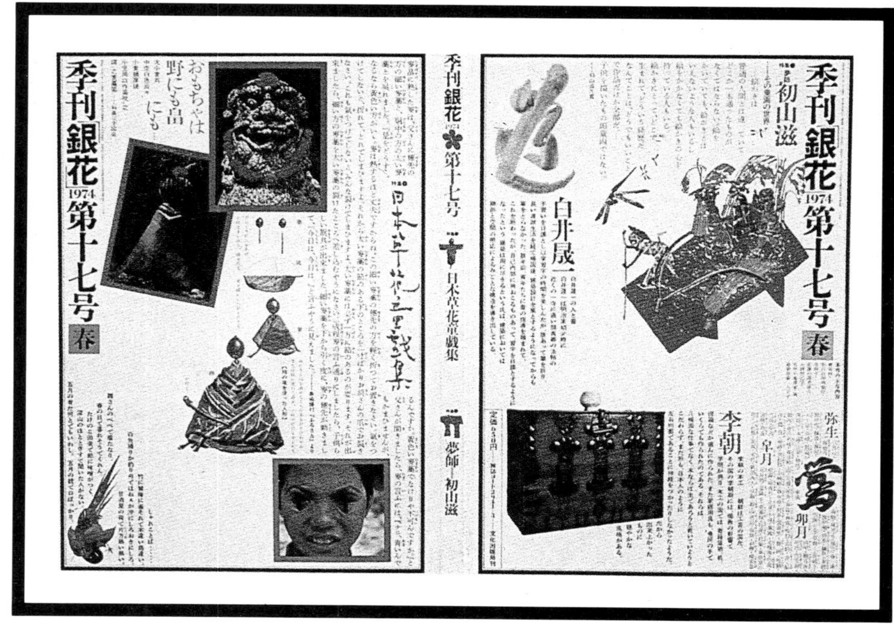

Magazine cover. *Kohei Sugiura.*

オートバイ

Title *of a motorbike magazine. Back slant style represents the riding form on the motorbike. Tadasu Fukano.*

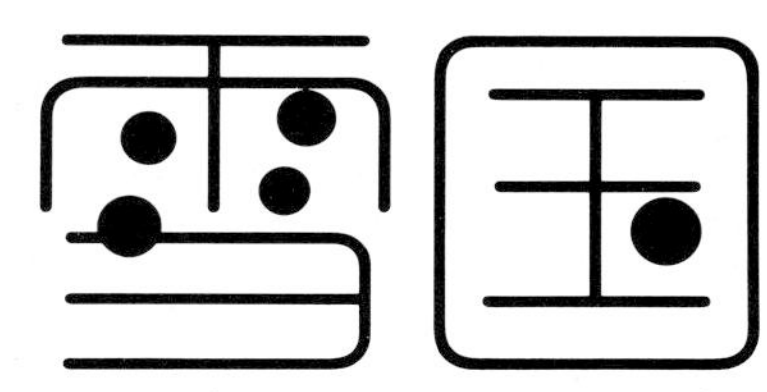

Logotype *for a Japanese restaurant. The name of the restaurant, "Yukiguni," means snow country. The charcoal balls were used as the eyes of a snowman in Japan; their irregular positions represent snow falling. Tadasu Fukano.*

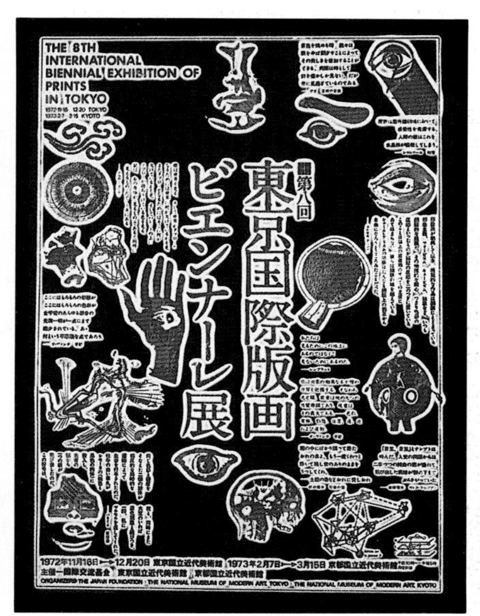

Poster *for an exhibition of prints in Tokyo, 1972. Kohei Sugiura, Shuhei Tsuji.*

Joy with letters. *The Igarashi Studio in Tokyo is concerned with communication design, environmental design, and "design for design." Takenobu Igarashi explains his sculptured aluminum letters, "My aluminum sculpture series,* AL *070783, was produced in 1983 and exhibited first at the Mikimoto Hall in Tokyo and then at the Reinhold Brown Gallery in New York. Each of the sculptures is made up of a number of thick and thin aluminum plates joined together by screws. For the first time I used a computer-controlled laser to cut the plates. A metal brush was used on the surface to give it more texture." These letters are about 5 1/2 inches tall. Some of Igarashi's giant letters are 12 feet high and 20 feet wide, and are intended for public or corporate environments, indoors and out.*

"The best designs are not wedded to a style but to optimally solving the communication problem."

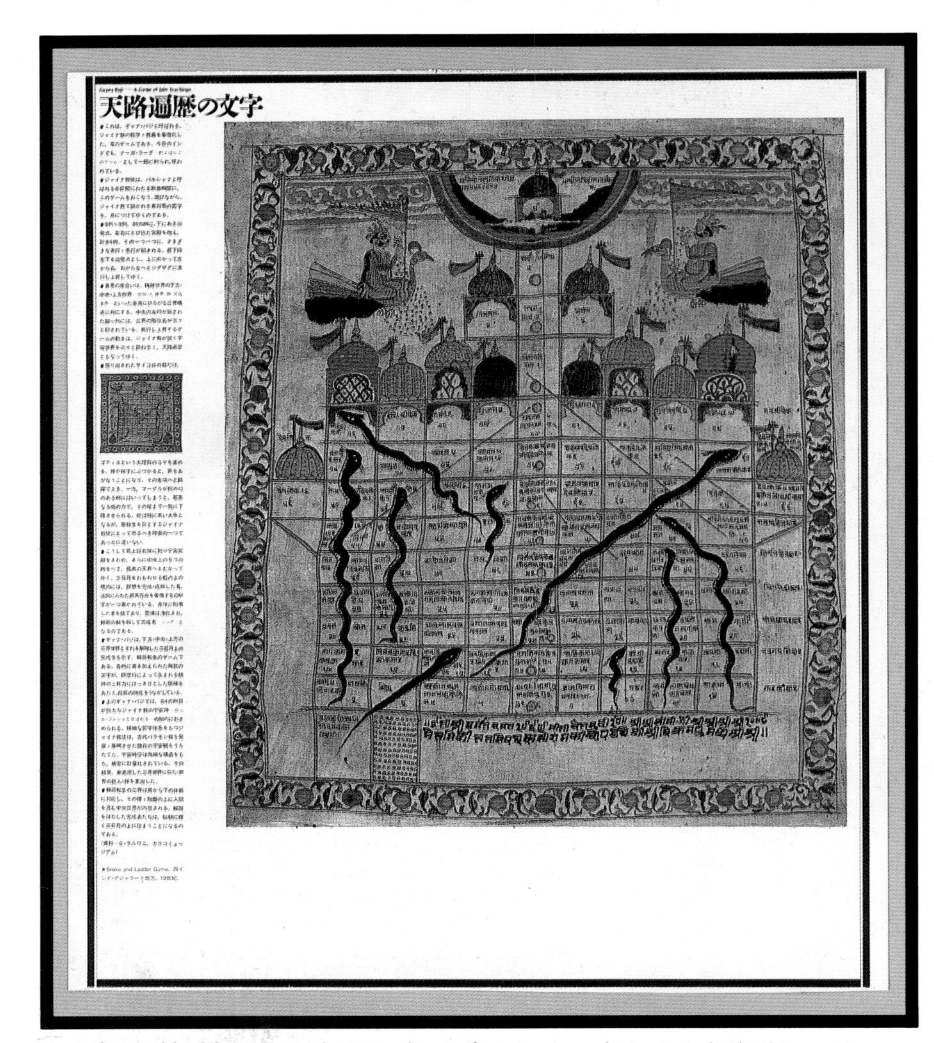

A snake and ladder game *of Jain teachings. (Jainism is a religion in India.) This was the illustration, plus explanation, for a page of a calendar designed by Kohei Sugiura.*

A mandala *is a concentric diagram with occult or spiritual significance. This mandala and the explanatory text were part of a calendar page designed by Kohei Sugiura.*

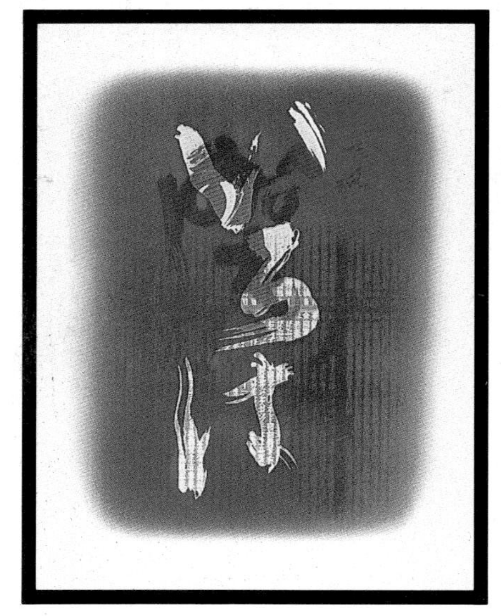

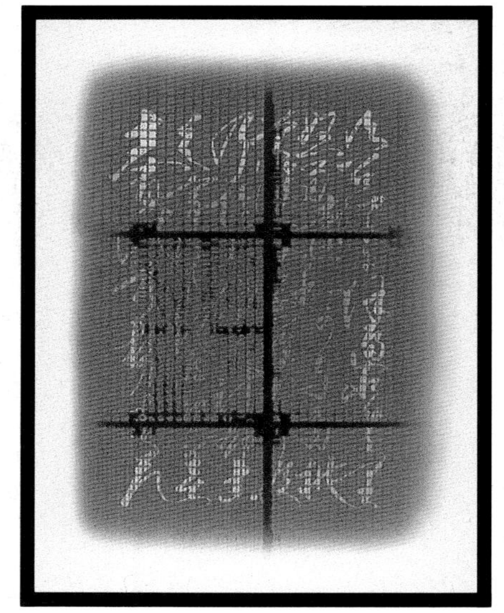

Eita Shinohara *incorporates type and calligraphy in his "Image Posters." Two of them are compositions of type and the Japanese syllabary. A poem poster blends calligraphy and typography. The snow poster is a composition of type and a Chinese character. Shinohara is one of a number of commercial graphic designers in Japan who create fine art and have their work exhibited. It is not suprising that artists and designers sensitive to the beauty of letterforms should incorporate type and calligraphy in their fine art and use them both sensitively and effectively in their commercial work.*

ENGLAND

The best and most stimulating typographic design in England since the 1960s displays a pragmatic blend of the clarity sought by the Swiss grid design and the graphic expressionism from New York. While observers and practitioners of graphic design cite many influences on contemporary typographics in the United Kingdom, collectively they emphasize the confluence of the intellectual Swiss approach and the more emotional work of the New York designers. The best designs are not wedded to a style, but to first understanding the communication and then developing an appropriate blend of clarity and vitality, tone and imagery.

Commenting on the roots of today's typography in the U.K., designer W. M. de Majo names many: Stanley Morison, Eric Gill, Beatrice Warde, John Dreyfus, Herbert Spencer, Ruari McLean, FHK Henrion, Ken Garland, the designers at Pentagram, Hermann Zapf, the Bauhaus, Max Bill, Richard Lohse, Karl Gerstner, Josef Müller-Brockmann, Adrian Frutiger, Armin Hoffman, Jan Tschichold, Jacques Garamond, Roger Excoffon, Deberny & Peignot, the De Stijl movement, Willem Sandberg and Total Design studio in Amsterdam. He cited as major influences from the United States Paul Rand, Ladislav Sutnar, Lester Beall, Will Burtin, Allen Hurlburt, Alvin Lustig, Saul Bass, William Golden, Lou Dorfsman, Herb Lubalin, R. H. Middleton, and Herbert Bayer.

Designer, editor, writer and teacher Herbert Spencer commented that the Bauhaus stress on the relationship between function and form is unfashionable today. There is now again greater use of decoration. Spencer, while not opposed to the introduction of decorative elements, insists that these should not impede transmission of the message. He believes that most great art reflects an economy of means – a concept that is currently too often disregarded. He cites the typography of El Lissitzky and Piet Zwart which, wild as it may sometimes seem, was always related to the message and designed to reinforce it graphically and not to obscure it. Too many of today's designers, Spencer says, are obsessed by the superficial pattern of graphics and pay scant regard to relating typography to the task of propelling the message. Such thinking, such a design approach, creates typography that is divorced from the message and establishes a communications barrier. Spencer draws an analogy between such typographic communications and a road linking site A with site B. One may embellish the sides of the road with trees, but trees scattered in the middle of the road create a hazard.

Pentagram

Perhaps the epitome of typographic design in England since the 1960s is Pentagram. It is large, diversified, has no house style, yet all of its designers blend vitality with a clear presentation of a carefully analyzed message. Each designer brings his or her own personal approach to the problem, but each seeks the most appropriate solution. The result is lively, effective graphics.

Pentagram's roots go back to 1962, when Alan Fletcher, Colin Forbes and Bob Gill formed the studio, Fletcher, Forbes, and Gill. In 1965, after Gill left, and architect Theo Crosby joined the firm, it was renamed Crosby, Fletcher, Forbes. With the addition of partners, the name was changed to Pentagram in 1972. Today Pentagram has three major studios and 12 designer partners: Crosby, Fletcher, Kenneth Grange, David Hillman, Mervyn Kurlansky and John McConnell in London; Forbes, Peter Harrison and Etan Manasse in New York, and Kit and Linda Hinrichs and Neil Shakery in San Francisco. In all there are over 70 artists and designers at the three locations, including the partners.

Commenting on some of the effects of computers on typographic design, Mervyn Kurlansky observes that the computer offers the designer a vast palette of typographic options, an amalgam of all preceding approaches, plus those offered by the new "restraint free" technologies. In a sense, Kurlansky says, our visual vocabulary uses clichés in new combinations. We must use known symbols and languages to be understood, yet achieve freshness via new arrangements. Some jobs, he observes, *require* that they be designed with a computer. This challenges the designer to use the resultant new tools to enhance communication and not merely to create a new look or a new distraction.

Fletcher expresses Pentagram's concern with blending clarity and vitality. "Designers have the opportunity, if not also the obligation, to offer a smack of connection between the objects we use, and the human gift for artful extremes. Function is fine but designers as the artists of our system must, as it were, provide the spice as well as the nutrition." He also notes that "a smile is worth a thousand pictures."

In *Living by Design,* a book published in 1978 by the partners of Pentagram, the partners reveal some of their thinking. Here are some key excerpts:

❧ Design can fulfill both a social and economic purpose.

❧ A design is not to be confused with its end purpose. The end purpose of design is not necessarily aesthetically pleasing; it can be so, it often is so, but it need not be so...A design is a plan to make something.

❧ Three main groupings of basic design are: *Product design,* which is generally three-dimensional and is often described as industrial design because the thing designed is often the end product of an industrial or manufacturing process; *Environment design,* which is nearly always three-dimensional and covers the design element of the work of architects, interior designers and town planners; *Graphic design,* which is almost always two-dimensional and covers those things which are drawn, painted, written or printed, and is traditionally related to printing, illustrating, advertising, promotion, packaging and so on.

❧ Peter Gorb, editor of *Living by Design,* notes that the graphic designer, especially, is concerned with communication, with "conveying information and signaling identity."

Pentagram's areas of activity include identity design such as trademarks and corporate programs; information design for many media, including posters, packaging, the whole spectrum of promotional graphics, exhibitions, office systems and exhibitions; and environmental and product design.

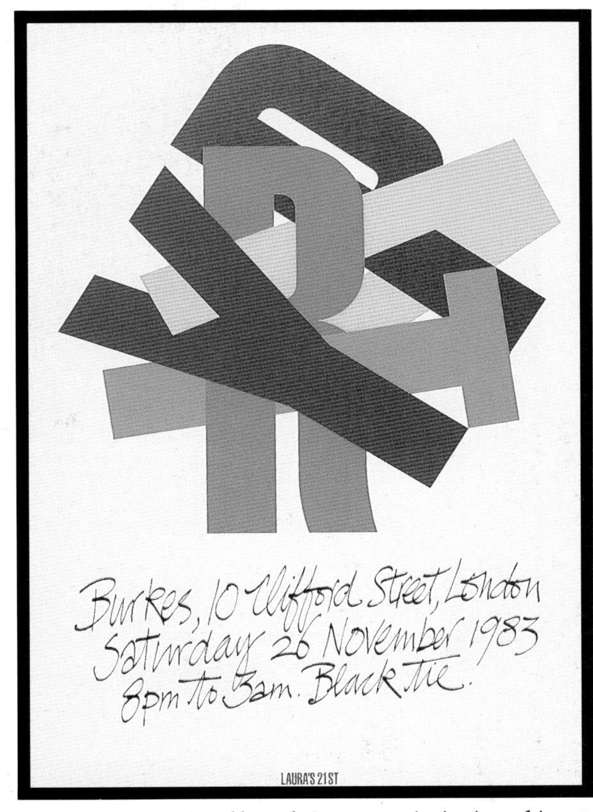

A poster *commissioned by Bob Gross as an invitation to his daughter Laura's 21st birthday party. The design was based on an arrangement of cutout letters. Designed by partner Alan Fletcher, Pentagram, 1983.*

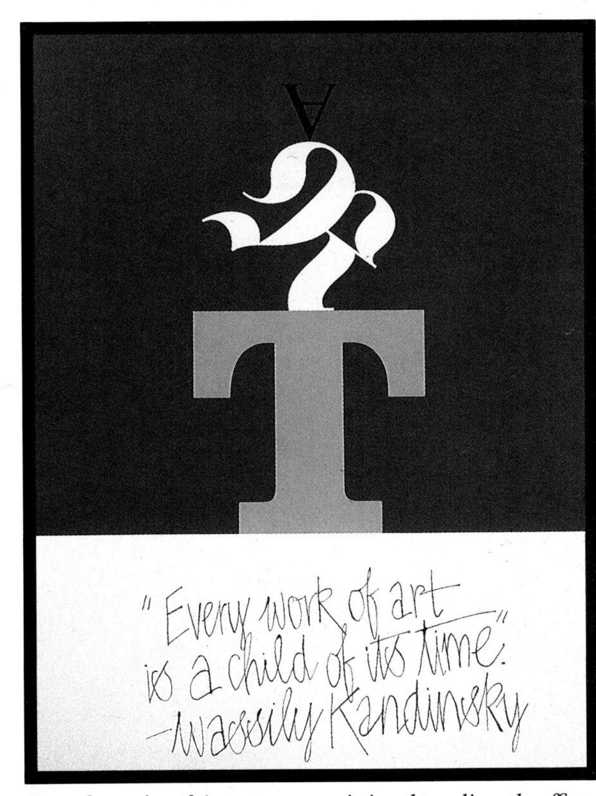

One of a series *of six posters commissioned to enliven the offices and corridors of IBM Europe's new headquarters in Tour Pascal, Paris. The posters were produced on a single theme, using different interpretive expressions of the word "Art," inspired by quotations from writers and artists. Designed by partner Alan Fletcher, Pentagram, 1983.*

Chapter XIII: The Many Faces of Typography Today

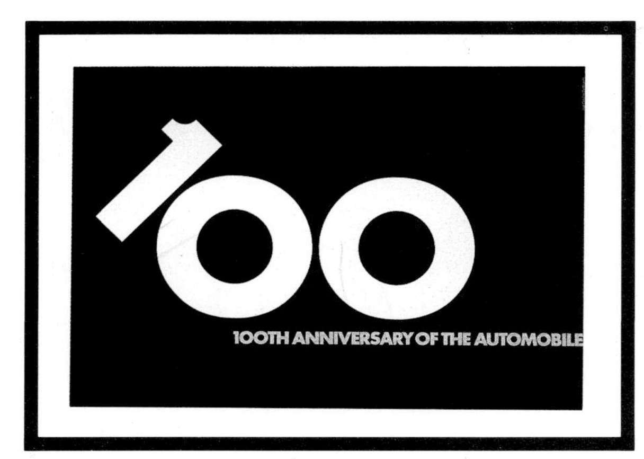

A poster *for Daimler-Benz to celebrate 100 years of the automobile. Designed by partner Alan Fletcher and Tessa Boo Mitford, Pentagram, 1985.*

A logotype *specially designed to celebrate the 50th anniversary of the Society of Industrial Artists and Designers in 1980. Designed by partner Alan Fletcher and Jennie Burns, Pentagram, 1980.*

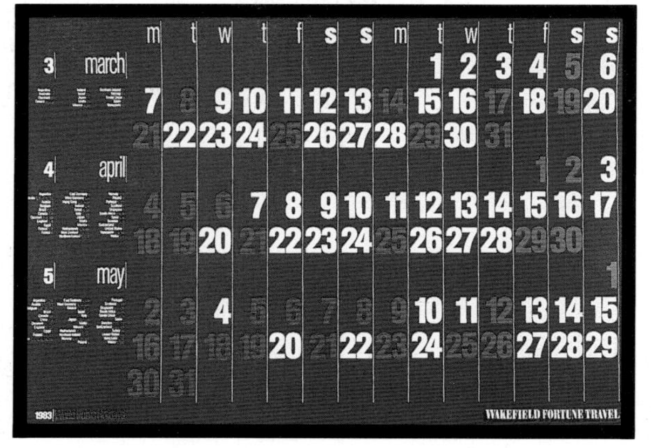

A 1983 calendar *for Wakefield Fortune Travel, showing public holidays around the world. Designed by partner David Hillman and Bruce Mau, Pentagram, 1983.*

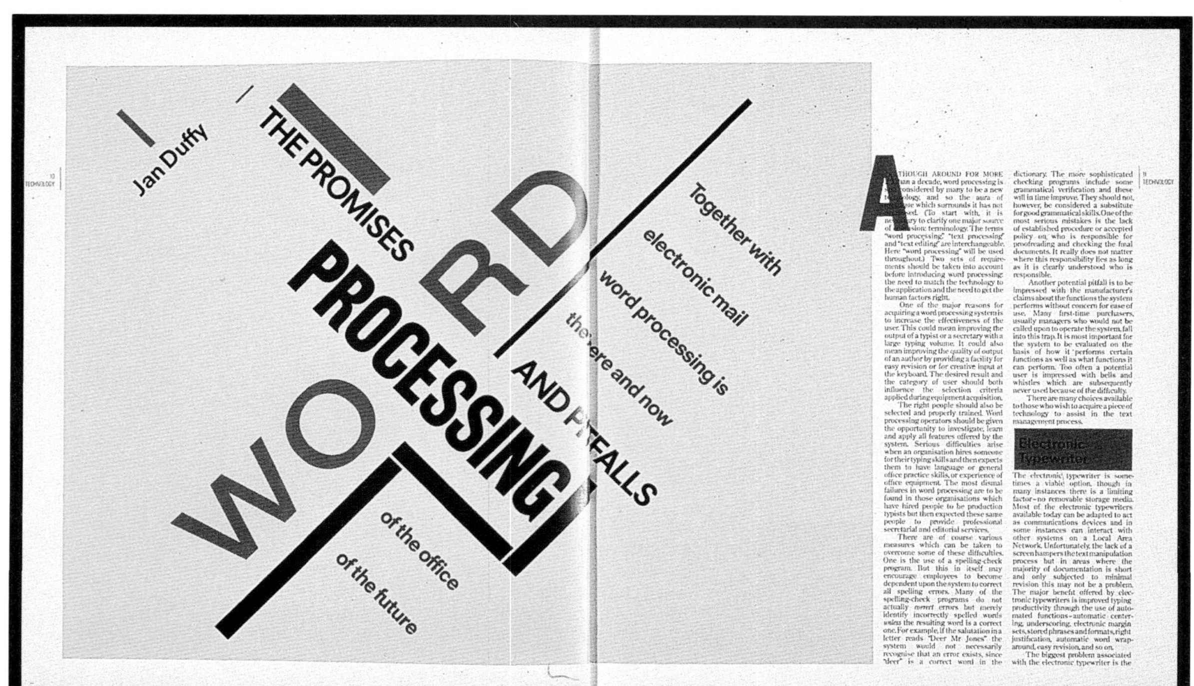

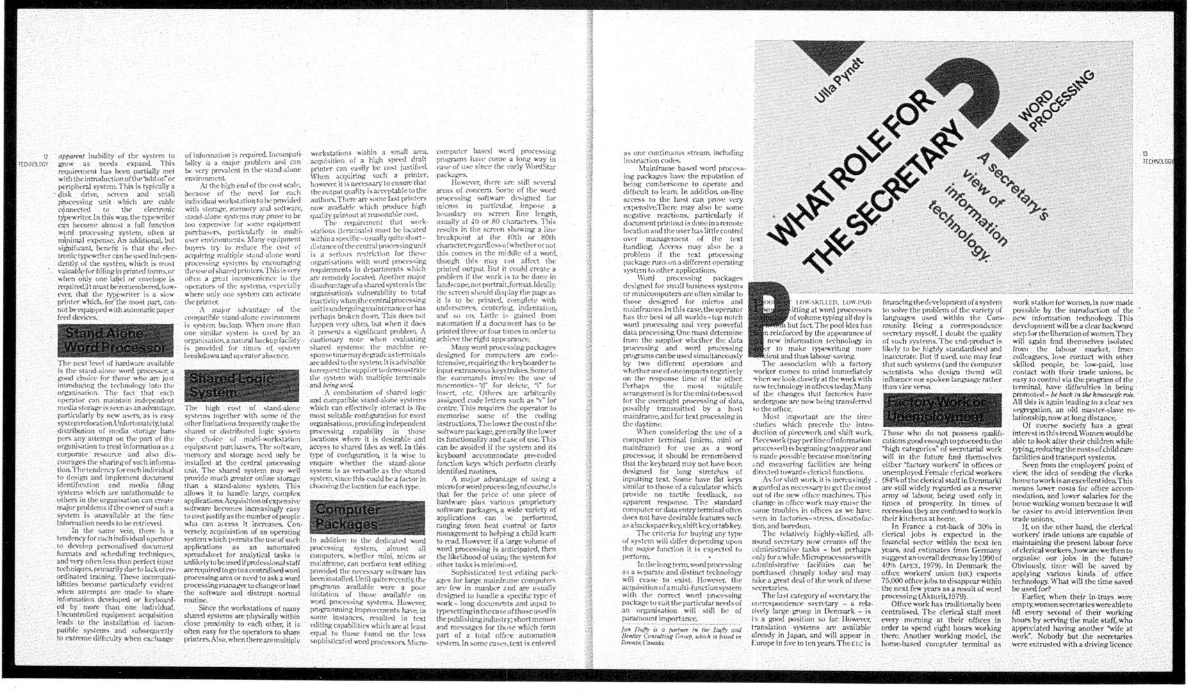

Information Resource Management (IRM) *is a quarterly magazine published by Ericsson Information Systems, a Swedish data processing and telecommunications company. The magazine is produced in English, French and German for international distribution. Designed and art directed by Pentagram partner David Hillman, the magazine deals with the whole range of information technology and its implications. Each issue has a design theme that reflects the nature of the editorial, whether through the work of one illustrator or a typographical treatment. 1983/4/5.*

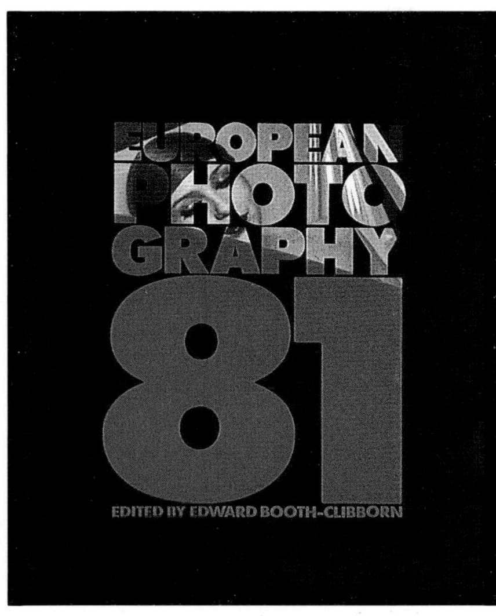

This first European Photography Annual *was published in 1981 as a reference guide for designers, photographers, illustrators and advertisers. Printed in hardback, it has had extensive circulation in Europe. Designed by partner David Hillman and Vicky Gornall, Pentagram.*

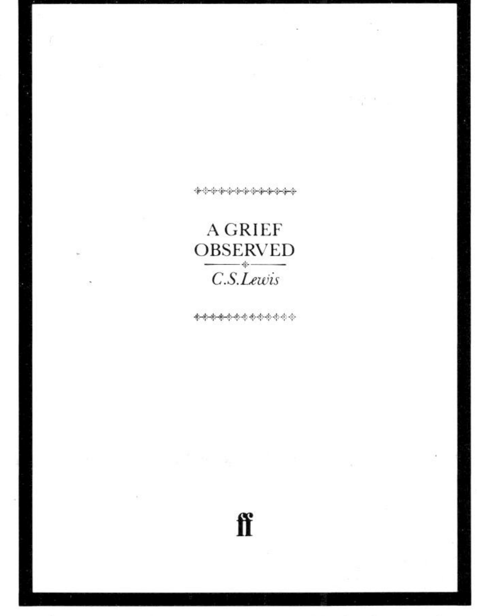

Faber & Faber *is a long-established British publishing house that has been undergoing important changes, including the promotion of a more adventurous book list. As part of the corporate identity program, two related ligatures were adopted as logotypes for the book publishing company and the music publishing company. In addition, Faber & Faber appointed Pentagram to plan and commission the jacket designs of over 200 new titles a year. The program is aimed at reestablishing the company's prestige and position, especially in the visually competitive paperback market. This jacket was designed in 1981 for* A Grief Observed, *by C. S. Lewis.*

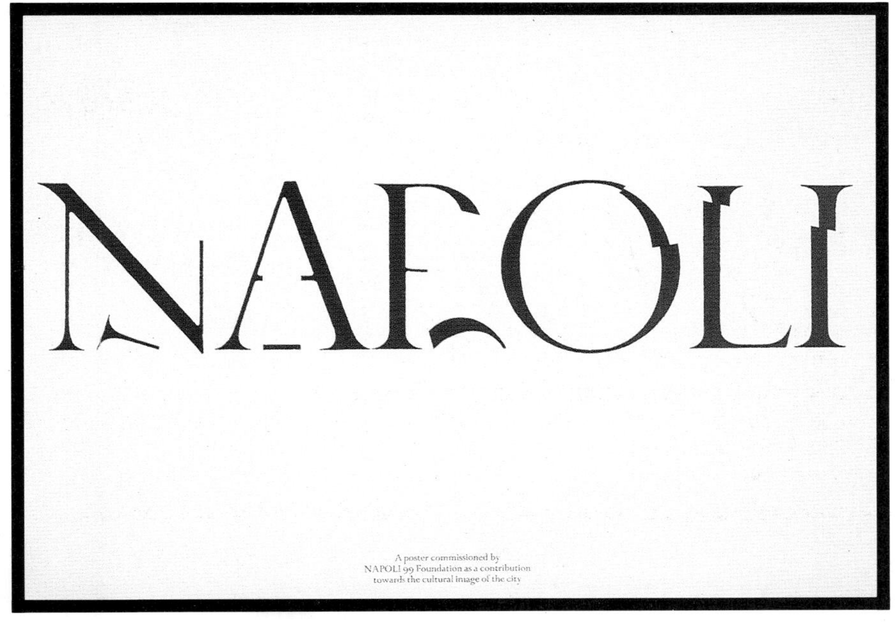

The Napoli '99 Foundation *was established in 1984 to draw attention to the present-day problems of Naples and to promote projects for the conservation of the city's cultural heritage. Pentagram partner John McConnell was one of those invited to design a poster for the Foundation's traveling exhibition. 1985.*

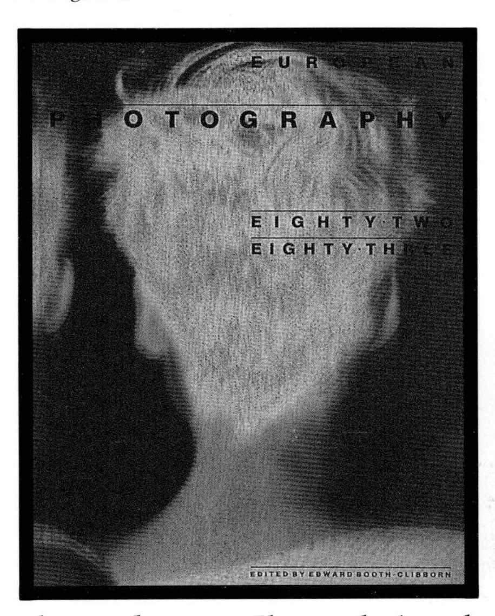

The second European Photography Annual *was produced in 1982 in a European, French and American edition. Designed by partner David Hillman and Bruce Mau, Pentagram.*

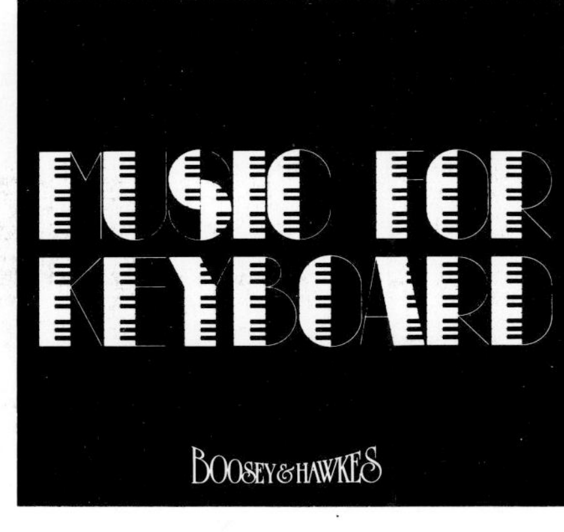

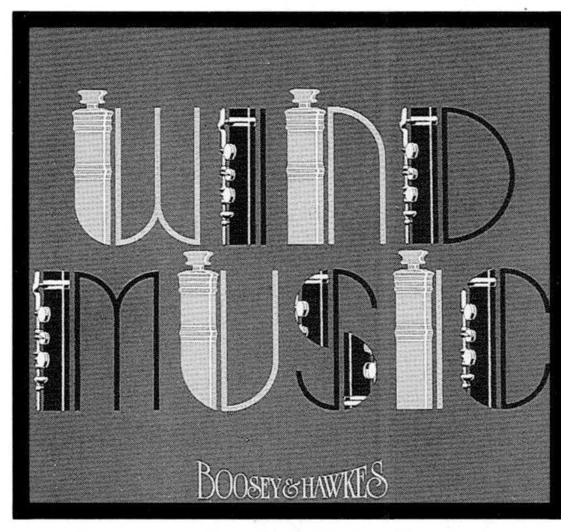

Two from a series *of music catalog covers for Boosey & Hawkes, the music publishers. These compositions show how, by investing the abstract letter with a pictorial device, the message can communicate content more effectively. Designed by Pentagram partner Mervyn Kurlansky, 1972-1980.*

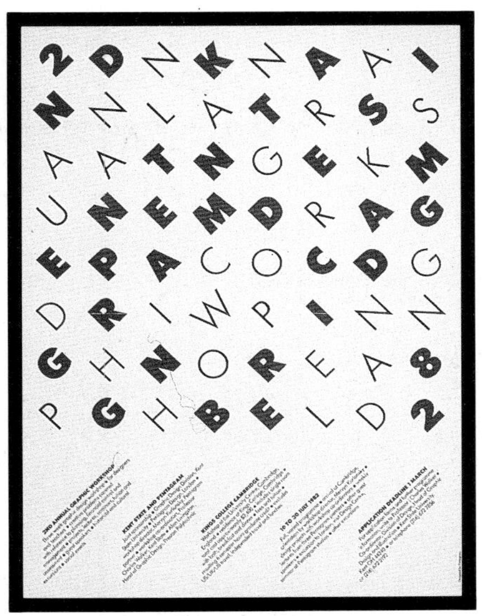

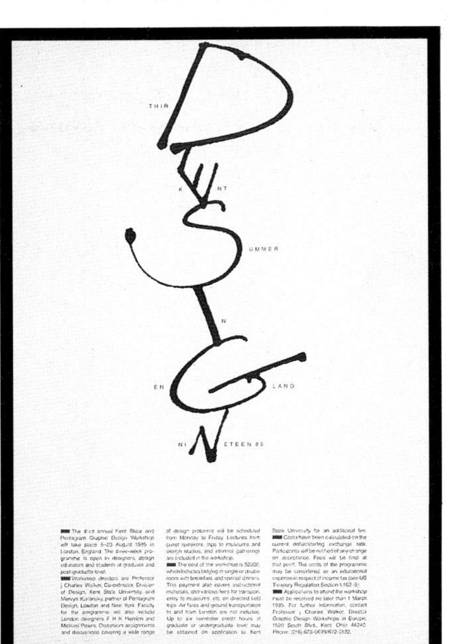

Three posters *designed to announce and invite applications to attend a graphic design workshop held each year at Cambridge University, England, and convened by Kent State University and Pentagram. The designs were constructed out of the title of the course, and reflected the workshop program, which focused on pictorial typographic problems. Designed by Pentagram partner Mervyn Kurlansky, 1972-1980.*

A poster design *to publicize an exhibition of work, Architects Celebrate Architecture, by members of the Association of Consultant Architects. The exhibition was held at the Royal Academy in London to celebrate the Festival of Architecture in 1984. Designed by John McConnell, a Pentagram partner.*

Chapter XIII: The Many Faces of Typography Today

"With few exceptions, our work has changed little in style over the years."

Tom Eckersley

Eckersley's posters feature polished, refined solutions. He strives for maximum graphic simplication.

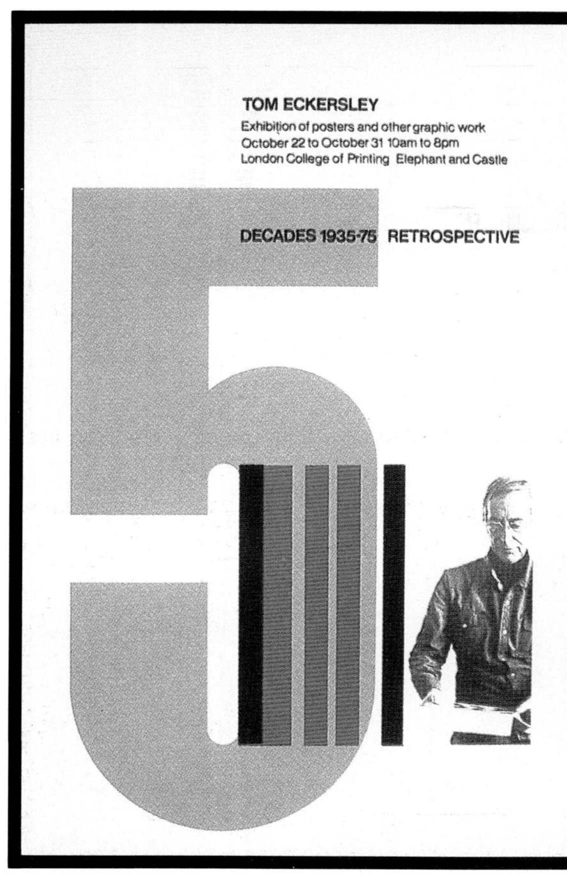

Exhibition poster *by Tom Eckersley.*

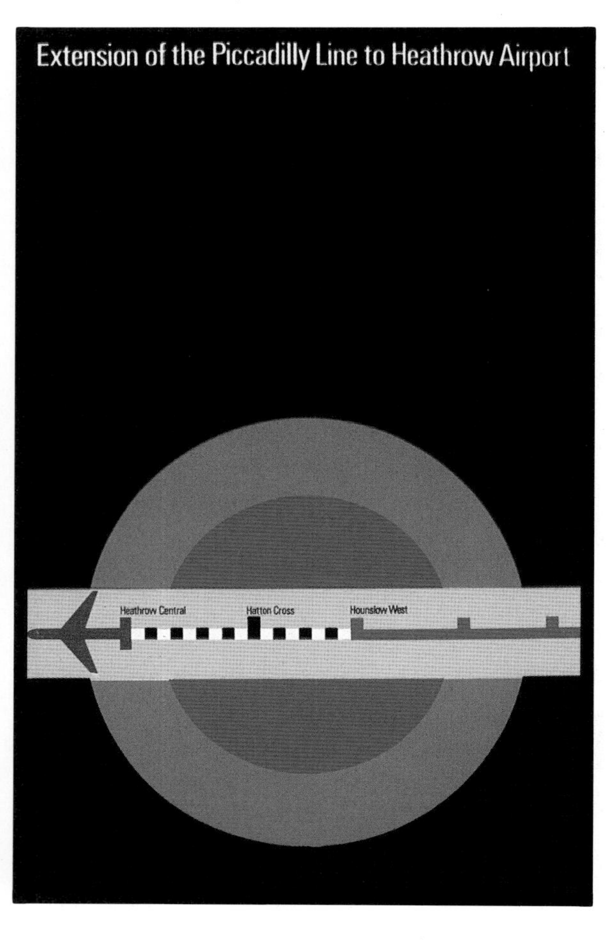

Posters *for London Transport by Tom Eckersley.*

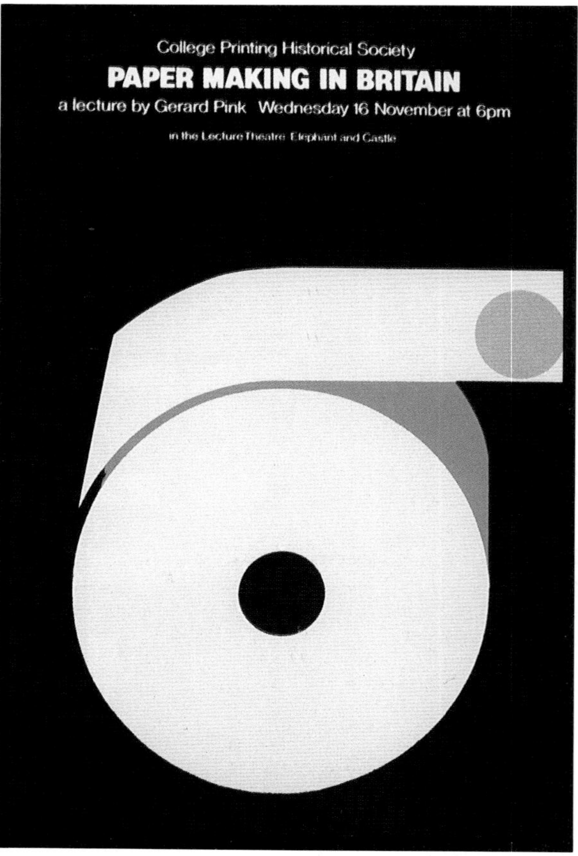

Poster *for London College of Printing, by Tom Eckersley.*

Ken Garland

In *Ken Garland and Associates: Designers, 20 Years Work and Play 1962–82,* Garland sounds off on designers' passing fancies and their debt to society. He wrote:

"I discover that, with few exceptions, our work has changed little in style over the years. True, there have been some passing fancies: we have long ago rejected our initial enthusiasm for the Univers series of sans-serif types – whatever did we see in that insensitive and pedestrian design? – and we've rediscovered the virtues of Garamond, Caslon and Bembo, but basically we've been Gill Sans and Baskerville persons all along, if you know what I mean. What's awkward about it is that I don't really believe that graphic design style should *be as unchanging as all that.*

"The sixties had become the scene of such a hectic, exuberant, optimistic, burgeoning economy that it seemed ungenerous and churlish to question the priorities involved in spending several kings' ransoms on the marketing and promoting of so many superfluous products – the wild bird seed, the electric carving knives, the heated loo-seats – when so many urgent tasks were waiting for our skills, if only they could be properly funded. However, I did. Looking back now, the 'First things first' manifesto I published in January 1964 and co-signed with 21 other designers and photographers reads a little self-righteously, but I still stand by every single word of it and I still say our priorities are completely crazy."

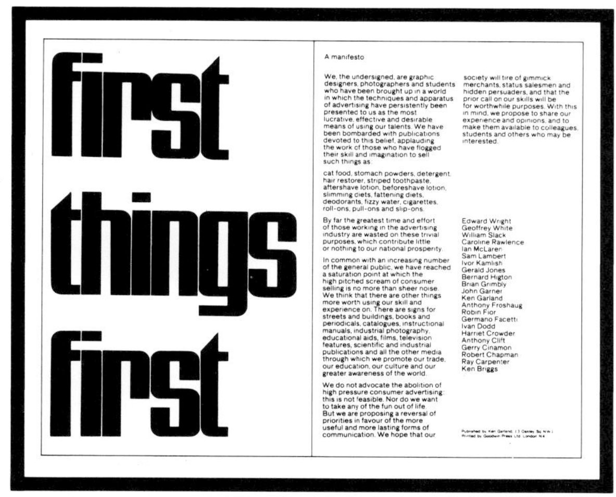

first things first

A manifesto

We, the undersigned, are graphic designers, photographers and students who have been brought up in a world in which the techniques and apparatus of advertising have persistently been presented to us as the most lucrative, effective and desirable means of using our talents. We have been bombarded with publications devoted to this belief, applauding the work of those who have flogged their skill and imagination to sell such things as:

cat food, stomach powders, detergent, hair restorer, striped toothpaste, aftershave lotion, beforeshave lotion, slimming diets, fattening diets, deodorants, fizzy water, cigarettes, roll-ons, pull-ons and slip-ons.

By far the greatest time and effort of those working in the advertising industry are wasted on these trivial purposes, which contribute little or nothing to our national prosperity.

In common with an increasing number of the general public, we have reached a saturation point at which the high pitched scream of consumer selling is no more than sheer noise. We think that there are other things more worth using our skill and experience on. There are signs for streets and buildings, books and periodicals, catalogues, instructional manuals, industrial photography, educational aids, films, television features, scientific and industrial publications and all the other media through which we promote our trade, our education, our culture and our greater awareness of the world.

We do not advocate the abolition of high pressure consumer advertising: this is not feasible. Nor do we want to take any of the fun out of life. But we are proposing a reversal of priorities in favour of the more useful and more lasting forms of communication. We hope that our society will tire of gimmick merchants, status salesmen and hidden persuaders, and that the prior call on our skills will be for worthwhile purposes. With this in mind, we propose to share our experience and opinions, and to make them available to colleagues, students and others who may be interested.

Edward Wright
Geoffrey White
William Slack
Caroline Rawlence
Ian McLaren
Sam Lambert
Ivor Kamlish
Gerald Jones
Bernard Higton
Brian Grimbly
John Garner
Ken Garland
Anthony Froshaug
Robin Fior
Germano Facetti
Ivan Dodd
Harriet Crowder
Anthony Clift
Gerry Cinamon
Robert Chapman
Ray Carpenter
Ken Briggs

The* first things first *manifesto *published by Ken Garland in 1964. It was signed by 21 other designers and photographers.*

Cover *of Galt Toys catalog. The theme of children supporting letters, sometimes misplaced, is carried out on the open pages inside the catalog. Ken Garland, 1969-1970.*

WHY CHANGE?

Countries using the metric system of weights and measures take more than half of our exports. The total proportion of world trade conducted in terms of metric units will no doubt increase. British industry recognises a change to the metric system as inevitable. This change is both supported and encouraged by the Government.

THE STANDARDS

The Government asked the British Standards Institute to provide metric British standards. The brief was not simply to convert existing standards to metric units, but to rethink these standards in the light of present industrial needs.

THE PROGRAMME

The timetable is published in:
Programme for the change to the Metric System in the Construction Industry – PD 6030.
Because of the change the opportunity is being taken to introduce the design concept of dimensional co-ordination. Details published in:
Dimensional Co-ordination in Building. Estimate of Timing for BSI work – PD 6249.
One of the great benefits of the decision to change is that manufacturers can take this opportunity to rationalize their product ranges.

WHAT AN ARCHITECT SHOULD READ

1 Programme for the Change to the Metric System in the Construction Industry PD 6030. 5s
2 A Guide for the Use of the Metric System in the Construction Industry PD 6031. 8s
3 Dimensional Co-ordination in Building. Estimate of Timing for BSI Work PD 6249. 5s
4 Conversion Factors and Tables Part 1 15s. Part 2 25s.
All obtainable from BSI Press office, 2 Park Street, London W1. 01-629 900
5 Building Metrication News A series of articles appearing in every fourth issue of 'Building'. From The Builder House, 4 Catherine Street, Aldwych, London WC2. 01-836 6251
6 RIBA The Architect and Change to Metric 3s6d
RIBA Metric Scales and Conversion Scales leaflet and price list available
A wall chart The Metric Look will be published by Sep 68
All publications available from RIBA Publication Sales Office 66 Portland Place London W1. 01-580 5533

WHAT BARBOUR INDEX IS DOING

We are explaining the programme to manufacturers; at the same time encouraging them to follow the timetable, and to provide technical information in metric terms now. Of course, during our normal visits to update your libraries, we will be bringing you new catalogues as soon as they are produced.

Cover *and side of metrication leaflet. Ken Garland. Michael Peters & Partners, Ltd.*

Michael Peters & Partners Ltd.

Joseph. *An elegant typographic logotype reflecting a very upmarket shop selling hi-tech products. Client, Joseph. Art Director/Designer, Maddy Bennett, Michael Peters & Partners, Ltd.*

A range of packaging *for Cordon Bleu, Private Label. The idea of a cookbook treatment was developed with an editorial typographic feel. Art Director/Designer, Glenn Tutssel, Michael Peters & Partners, Ltd.*

A special Victorian Christmas range *for Lyons, featured period hand-drawn lettering and metal set typography. Art Director, Glenn Tutssel; Designer, Carolyn Reed, Michael Peters & Partners, Ltd.*

Logotype *for Hayter, a company manufacturing grass-cutting machinery. A blade of grass forms part of the "Y." Art Director, Glenn Tutssel; Designer, Mark Wickens, Michael Peters & Partners, Ltd.*

Penhaligons Victorian *posy recreates an authentic-looking period identity across this product range, with a strong original typographic feel. Art Director/Designer, Maddy Bennett, Michael Peters & Partners, Ltd.*

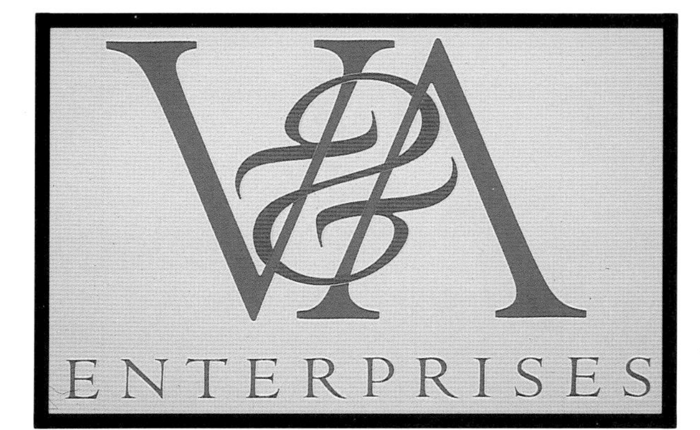

Logotype *for the Victoria and Albert Museum Shop. The V & A letterforms work both ways up – an advantage when stamped onto the base of a vase, etc. Art Director/Designer, Glenn Tutssel, Michael Peters & Partners, Ltd.*

"Functions can be vaguely defined or explicit, urgent, symbolic or decorative."

Design Showcases

There are many designers in England whose work is worth studying. It is not the purpose of TYPOGRAPHIC COMMUNICATIONS TODAY to present a comprehensive picture of the work in any country or by any designer or studio. However, those interested in seeing more of the work of contemporary British designers should look at *Graphics UK.'84*. This illustrated catalog of a national graphics exhibition held in London in 1984 was published by The Journeyman Press in London. Another good source is D&AD the annual catalog recording the best of British art direction, design illustration, copywriting, photography, film, and radio direction. Bulk copies are available from Internos Books, Colville Road, London, W3 8BL.

CANADA

The development of graphic design in Canada is recent. The pioneers were Raoul Bonin in the '30s and Clair Stuart, Allan Harrison, Carl Dair and Henry Eveleigh in the '40s. They were followed in the '60s by such Canadian-trained graphic designers as Theo Dimson, Allan Fleming and Jean Fortin. Some European designers came to Canada in the '50s and '60s, including Ernst Roch. Many other designers came to prominence in the '60s and later among whom were James T. Donoahue, Stuart Kish, Jean Morin, Ivan Laroche, Rolf Harder, Paul Arthur, Walter Jungkind, Pierre-Ives Pelletier, Gerhard Doerrie, Fritz Gottschalk (who has returned to Zürich) and Burton Kramer.

The recognition of the value of graphic design was enhanced by the growth and activities of Art Director's Clubs in Toronto, Montreal, Vancouver and Winnipeg, and, in 1956, by the founding of the Society of Typographic Designers of Canada, which changed its name in 1965 to Society of Graphic Designers of Canada.

Today, although there is no such thing as a Canadian style, much outstanding work is created in Canada. Major influences on Canadian graphic design are the work of American designers and the European designers who migrated to Canada. Representative work of today's Canadian typographic designers is shown here.

An expression of Canadian thinking about communication design is contained in this excerpt from the article, "Benchmarks," by Andrew M. Tomcik in the catalog for *The Best of the '80s*. The exhibition and catalog were sponsored by the Society of Graphic Designers of Canada.

"All design has some task to perform, usually many. Functions can be vaguely defined or explicit, urgent, symbolic or decorative. If our work didn't have such tasks, it would not be design but art, whose very uselessness helps make it the free and effective mirror and critic of society.

"That form follows function in some automatic causal sequence is doubtful. Even when we can identify function fairly explicitly and objectively, such as a stop sign, the form that is made is not necessarily the only one that need follow. What usually exists is a multitude of functions, humanly determined, of varying priority, and a plethora of possible forms, also humanly determined.

"The primary function or use need not be a measured, specific one. In fashion, for instance, the function of protection may be almost neglible in importance to the stylishness of form. To be seen and noticed supercedes warmth and protection, the visual symbol more important than the physical service.

"No matter how perceptive the skills of analysis, and no matter how skillful the creation of form, the crucial point in the process lies at the fulcrum between the analysis of needs and the synthesis of form. It is here where the designer begins to create a new form in response to a need.

"All design must be more than pure idea, it must have a visible, concrete embodiment. Only partly influenced by determined function, the resultant form is a response filtered through style, symbolic meaning, technology, operative formmaking systems and the designer's own personal fingerprints.

"The possibilities of form are endless, but designers have generally had the benefit of working within a tradition which they would modify and refine, leaving the next generation new models to modify and design. Tradition can be a platform for development or a wall against it.

"The Futurists of Italy wished to destroy their museums to remove what they saw as an obstacle to progress. The most advanced designers of Italy today use the very image and symbols that the Futurists wished to destroy. Each age selects according to its priorities – the discards of one age can be the forms of the next.

"Like some electronic attic, technology in its ability to miniaturize and store has relieved us of the necessity to select and limit. We have at our disposal the forms of many traditions simultaneously without the progression or the natural filtration. We are then forced to self-consciously limit our working possibilities practically or theoretically."

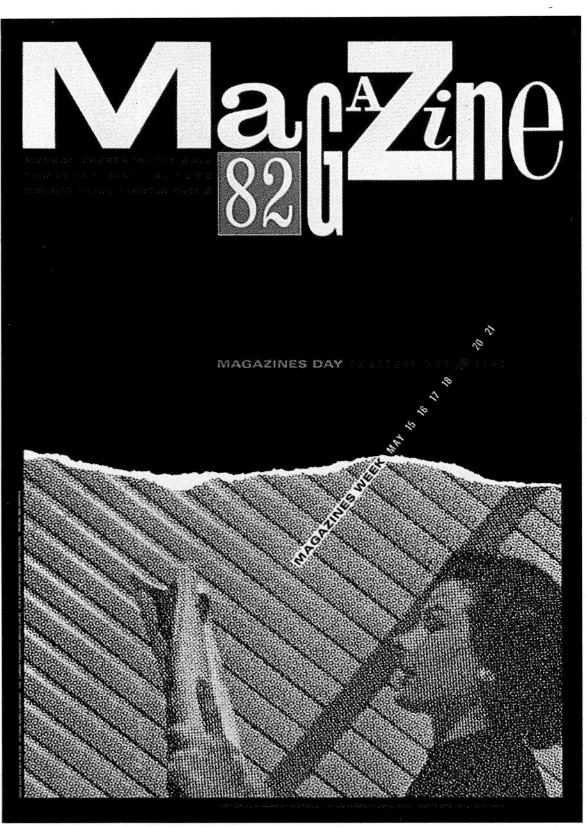

Poster *for the National Magazine Award Foundation. Art director and designer, Louis Fishauf.*

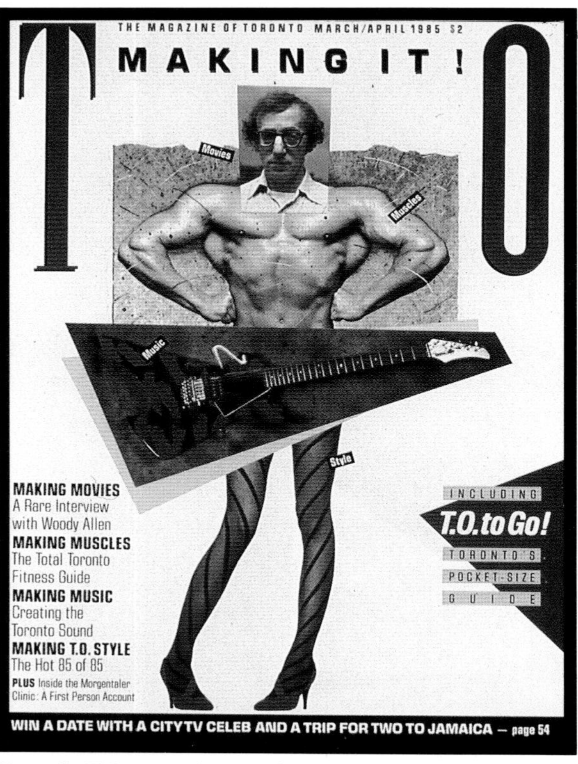

Cover *for* T.O. *magazine. Art director and designer, Louis Fishauf.*

1984 Annual Report *for Jannock Ltd. Art director and designer, Roslyn Eskind.*

Spread *for* Saturday Night *magazine. Art director and designer, Louis Fishauf.*

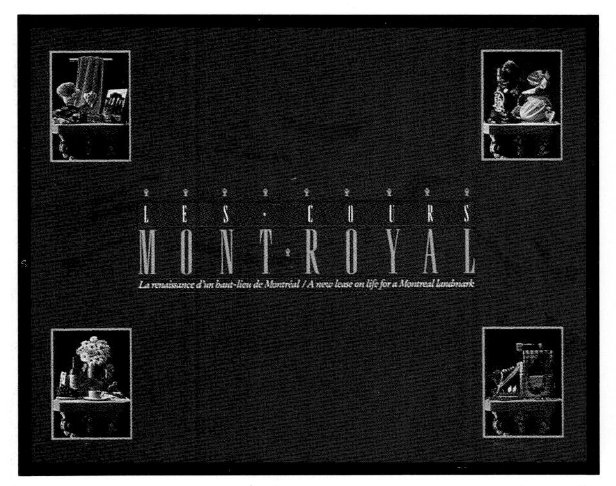

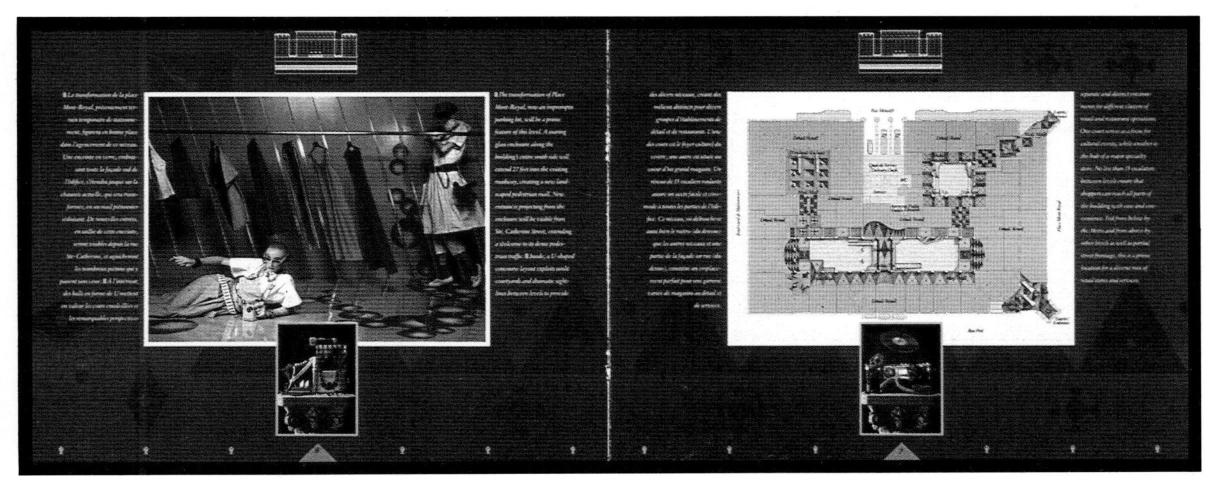

Cover and spread *for brochure, Les Cours Mont Royal. Art directors: Paul Browning and Scott Taylor. Designers: Paul Browning, Catherine Haughton and Joe Drvaric.*

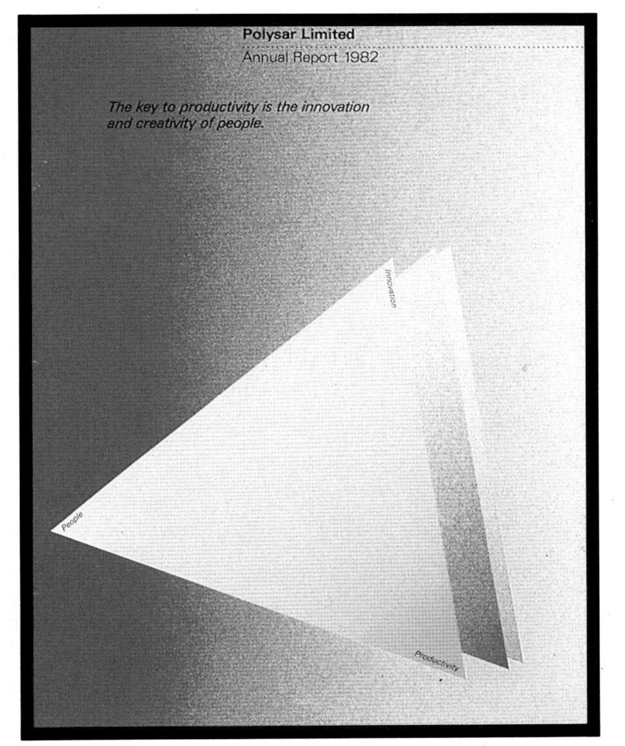

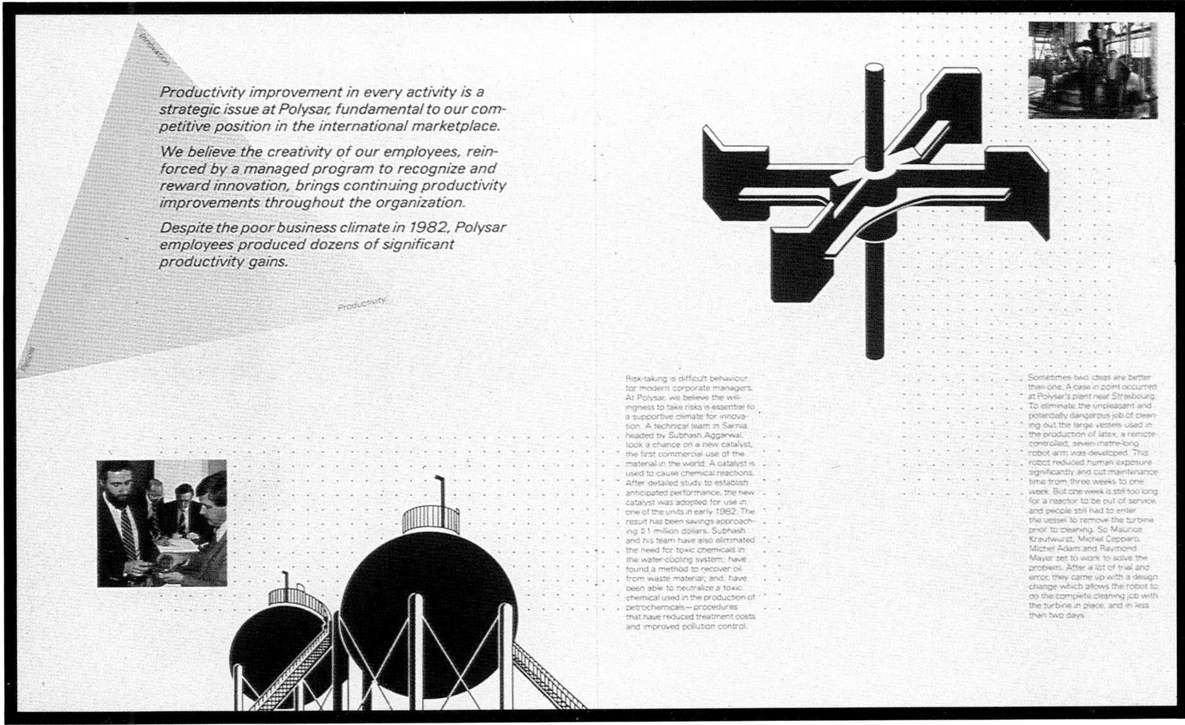

Cover and spread *of 1982 Annual Report for Polysar Ltd. Studio: Gottschalk and Ash International. Designer: Richard Kerr.*

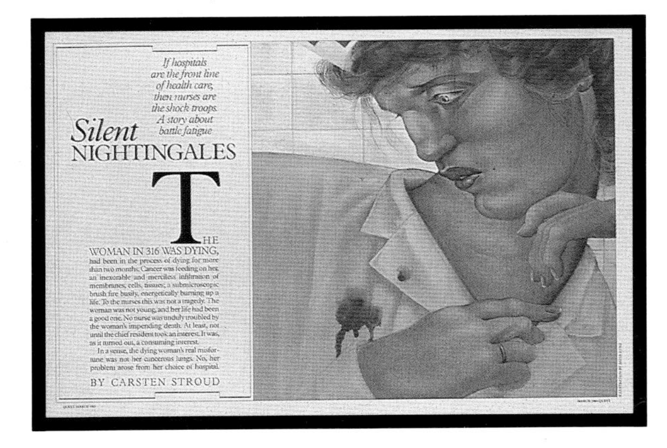

Spread for Quest *magazine. Art director and designer, Arthur Niemi.*

Jim Donoahue

Canadian-born, Donoahue formed Jim Donoahue & Associates, Ltd. in 1977. Among his steps between his studies at the Ontario College of Art in 1958 and the establishment of his studio was a period as assistant to Allan Fleming at Cooper & Beatty Ltd. Shown here are nine expressive and symbolic logos/wordmarks. Of the role of type in these designs, he says, "...without type to play with, I suspect I'd have been in a lot of trouble."

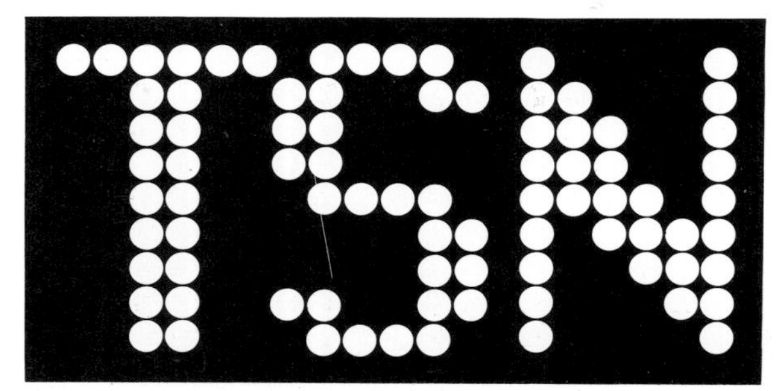

An invented typeface *from letters on a scoreboard. For The Sports Network. Jim Donoahue.*

A wordmark *for a bar in Hotel Newfoundland. The type becomes an illustration of a well-known narrow land mass in Newfoundland. Jim Donoahue.*

A wordmark *for a restaurant in a Toronto hotel with an interior space of glass, steel and light. Jim Donoahue.*

Mark *for the George R. Gardiner Museum of Ceramic Art. Mr. Gardiner's initial G becomes half a vase, illustrating ceramics. Jim Donoahue.*

The type becomes pasta *on a plate in this mark for an Italian restaurant in Toronto. Jim Donoahue.*

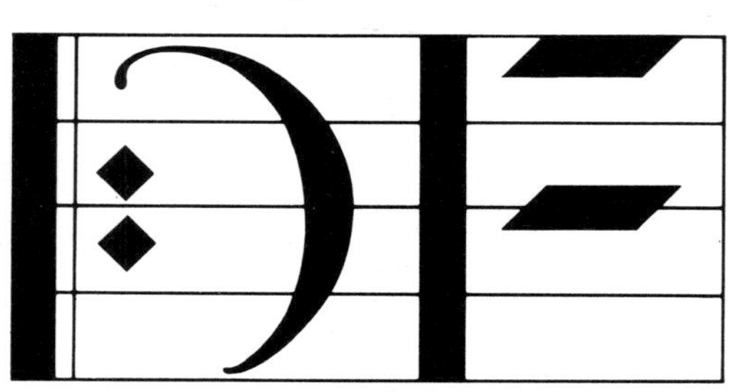

David Fleury *writes music for radio and television commercials. Jim Donoahue.*

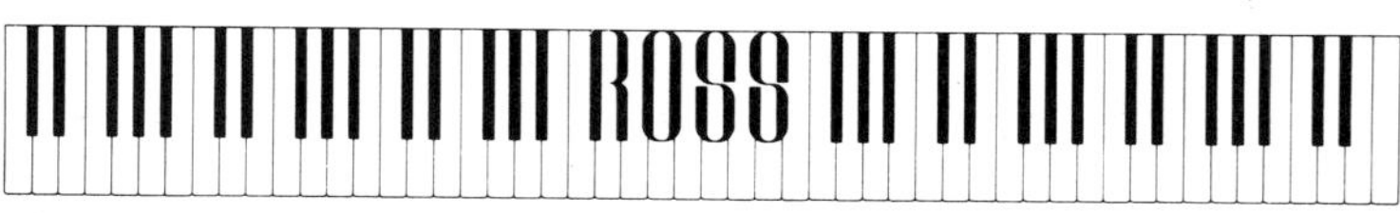

Mort Ross, *of Mort Ross Productions, writes music and plays piano. Jim Donoahue.*

Rolf Harder

Rolf Harder, of Rolf Harder & Associates, Inc., studied at the Landeskunstschule in Hamburg from 1948 to 1952. He opened a design office in Montreal in 1959 and has headed a studio there ever since. His designs include posters, books, symbols, advertising and promotional material.

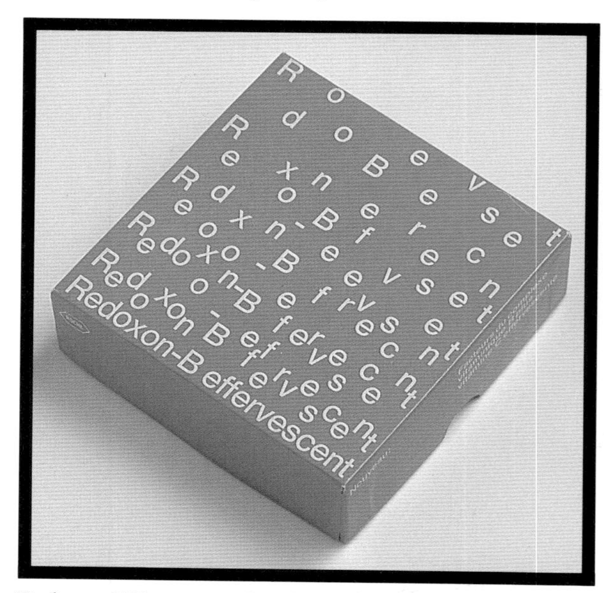

Redoxon Effervescent box. *The effervescent nature of this water-soluble vitamin tablet is reflected in the typographic treatment of this sample mailer. 1972, for Hoffman-La Roche Ltd. Rolf Harder.*

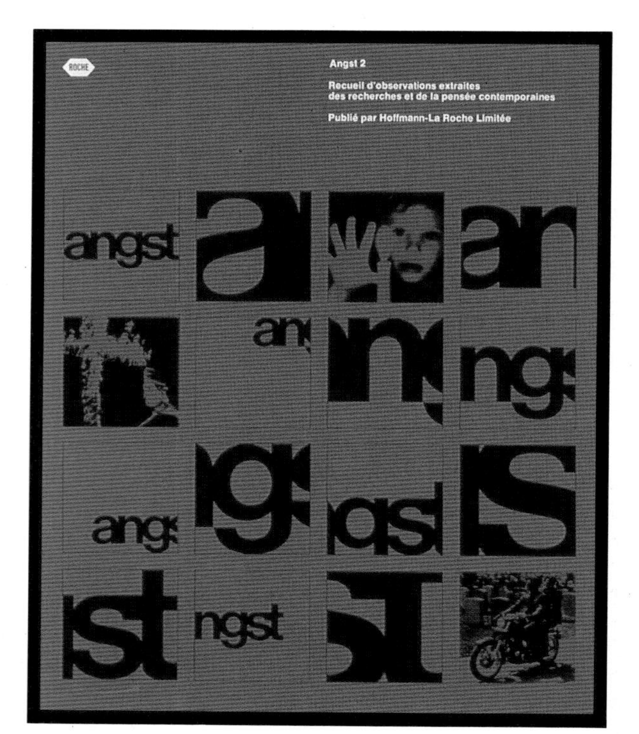

Angst *cover. One of a series of covers for publications on anxiety published by Hoffman-La Roche Ltd. The basic grid and typographic treatment remained unchanged throughout the series; only the photos and their positioning within the grid were changed from issue to issue, together with the background color. This concept permitted speedy production without sacrificing the identity of each individual issue. 1970. Rolf Harder.*

Advertisement *for graphic design magazine* Format. *The initial F is shown in different "formats" – a playful interpretation of the magazine's title. 1962. Rolf Harder.*

Librax advertisement. *Librax is for the control of gastro-intestinal disorders. Its dual (psychosomatic) effect is expressed by linking the product name with images of brain and stomach. 1975, for Hoffman-La Roche Ltd. Rolf Harder.*

Angst *logo was designed for a series of pharmaceutical publications published by Hoffman-La Roche Ltd. It expresses the threatening nature of anxiety. 1969. Rolf Harder.*

Party invitation. *Bilingualism is a constant challenge to the Canadian typographic and graphic designer. This invitation takes advantage of the fact that the French verb "joindre" contains the English "join" and both mean the same thing. 1978, Rolf Harder.*

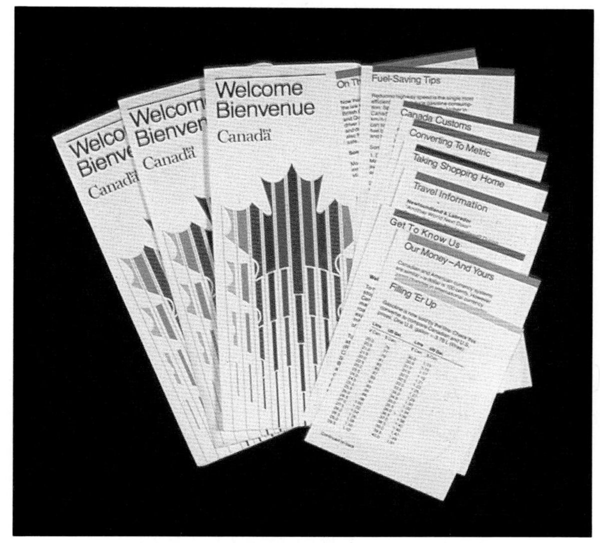

Welcome brochures *for Canada Tourism contain information for American tourists crossing the border by car. They are designed to be machine collated and contain a variety of color keyed, changeable elements. Art direction: Burton Kramer. Design: Burton Kramer and Karl Martins.*

Symbol and typographic treatment *for CentreStage visual identity, shown here applied to a van. The overall visual program encompassing CentreStage Theatre, Forum, Music and Company includes symbol, typographic treatment and use of color for stationery, advertising, promotion and signage. Art Direction: Burton Kramer. Design: Burton Kramer and Karl Martins.*

Poster *for a Mariposa Folk Music concert. Photographs of the two performers are integrated with their names. Art direction: Burton Kramer. Design: Burton Kramer and Sunil Bhandari.*

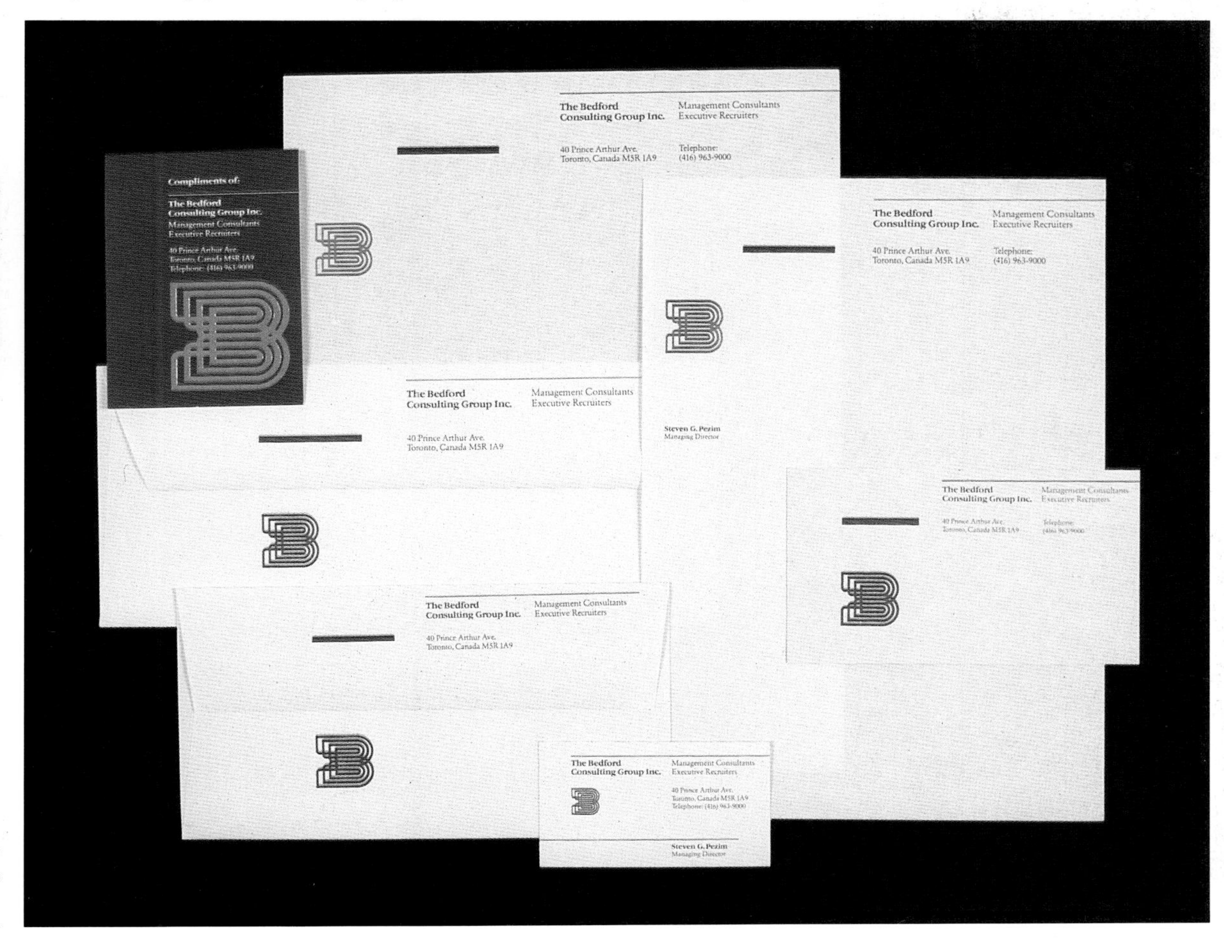

Symbol and stationery *for The Bedford Consulting Group, management consultants. Symbol design is a "kinetic" letter B, indicating activity, energy and the ability to respond quickly to varied client needs. Art direction and design: Burton Kramer.*

Burton Kramer

Burton Kramer studied design at the Institute of Design in Chicago, the Royal College of Art in London and Yale University. He practiced design in New York and Zürich before moving to Toronto in 1966, and has has headed his own design firm in Toronto since 1967. Kramer's work includes books, logos, promotional material, identity programs, posters, record covers – in fact, the gamut of graphic communications.

Typographic treatment *of a variety of forms and stationery for Boigen and Armstrong Architects. Design of symbol is based on interlocked letters B & A and conveys visually a sense of architectural space. Art direction and design: Burton Kramer.*

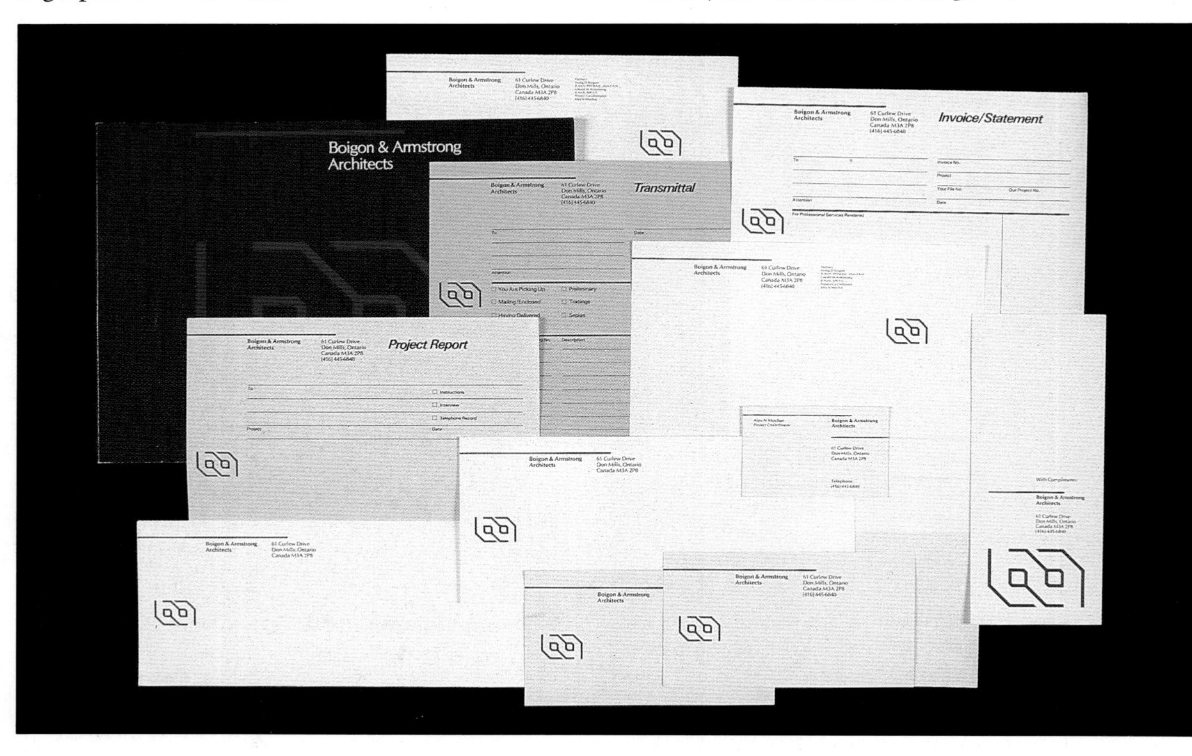

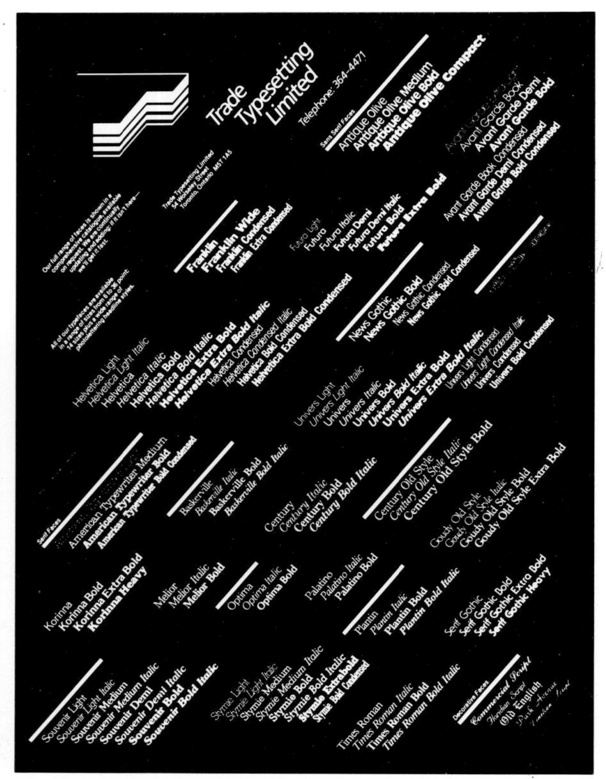

Poster *and one-line specimen broadsheet for a typesetter. Design of the symbol is based on the letter T for Trade Typesetting. The application to stationery, signs, etc. Art Direction: Burton Kramer. Design: Burton Kramer and Joe Gault.*

Ernst Roch

Ernst Roch was born in Yugoslavia, studied art in Graz, Austria, and moved to Montreal in the mid-1950s. His studio, Roch Design, designs identity programs, exhibits, trademarks, posters, postage stamps, packages and books.

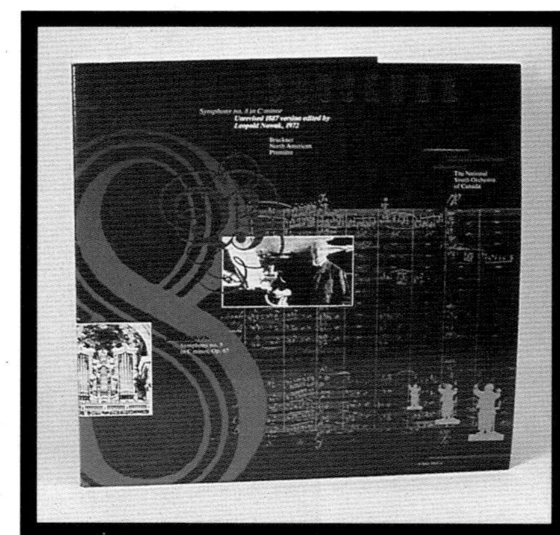

Record cover *for a Bruckner symphony performance combines type, illustration and color to convey a particular mood about the music and composer. Art direction: Burton Kramer. Design: Burton Kramer, Debbi Adams, Sunil Bhandari.*

Broadsheet/mailer *for the Shaw Festival in Stratford, Ontario. Typographic treatment of the name was used for all material for the season, such as programs, ads and posters. Color was chosen to give a festive look to all material. Art Direction: Burton Kramer. Design: Burton Kramer and Jeff Dawson.*

Poster *opposing Quebec's separation from Canada, 1979. Ernst Roch.*

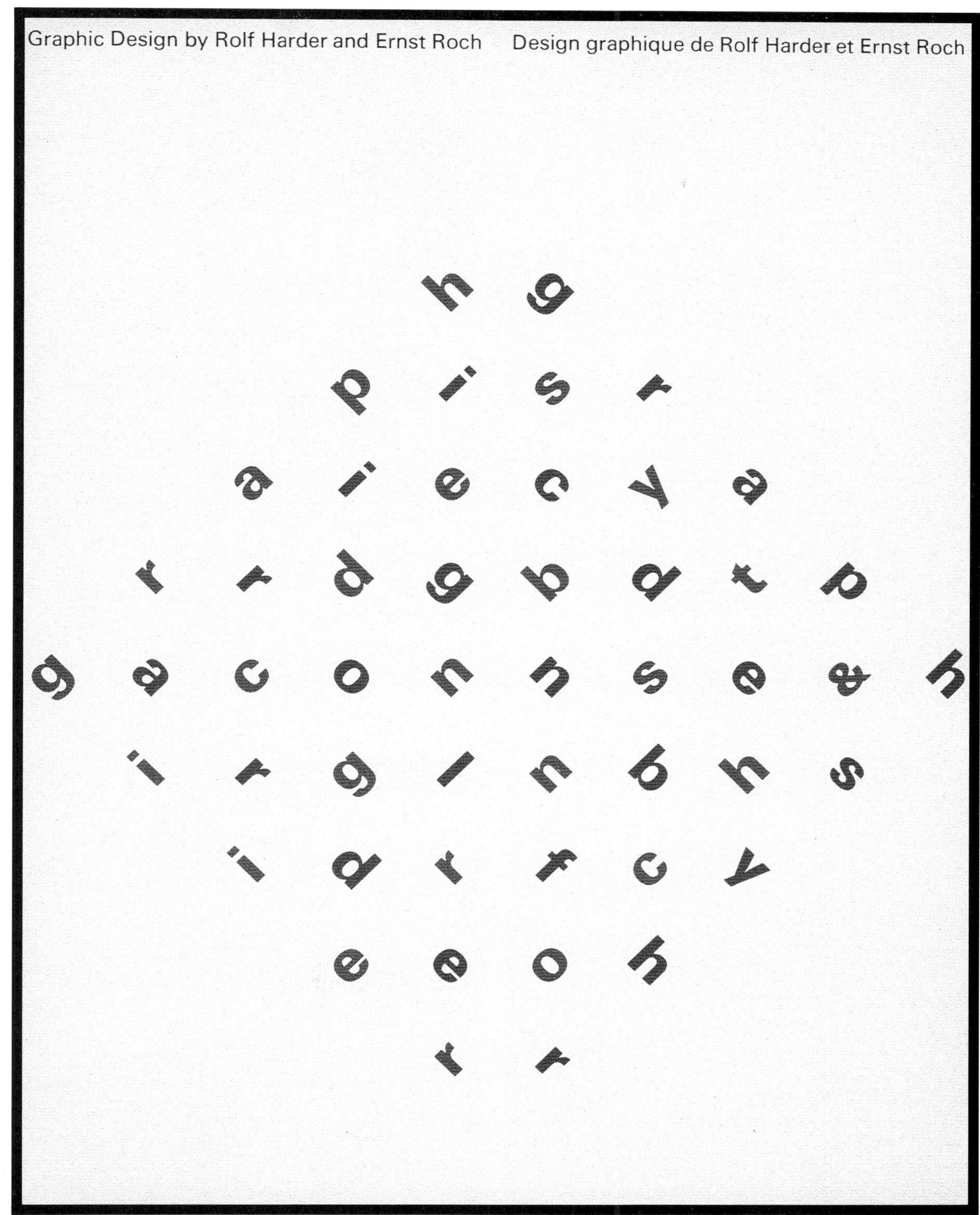

Graphic Design by Rolf Harder and Ernst Roch
Design graphique de Rolf Harder et Ernst Roch

Poster and catalog cover, *1977. Ernst Roch.*

Cover *for a special issue on education in the house publication of Imperial Oil Ltd., 1962, Ernst Roch.*

Advertisement *for industrial screw jacks for Quebec Steel Products Ltd., 1963. Ernst Roch.*

Cover *for a brochure on immigration to Canada. Ernst Roch.*

Annual report *for the Toronto Star Ltd. Theo Dimson. 1962.*

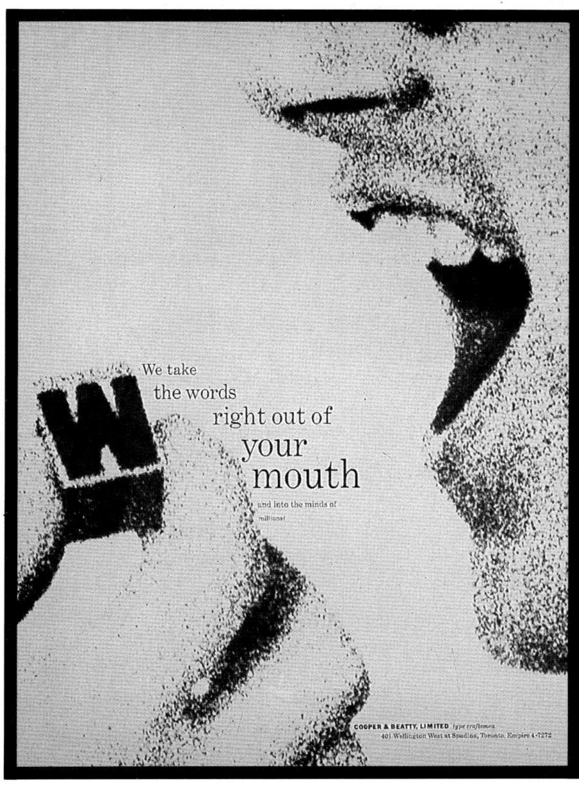

Advertisement *for Cooper & Beatty, Ltd. Canada, 1959. Allan Fleming.*

TYPOGRAPHIC COMMUNICATIONS TODAY
Chapter XIII: The Many Faces of Typography Today

"In the United States today, no dominating trend, due to the co-existence of many trends."

THE UNITED STATES OF AMERICA

As stated previously, the typographic scene in the United States since the mid-1940s has been one of no dominating trend, due to the development and co-existence of many trends. In the U.S.A. you can find strict and imaginative applications of the Swiss grid, admirers of the Bauhaus, new wave designers, designers who believe humor and personality in graphics enhance communication effectiveness, and those who feel design should be impersonal. In short, design in the U.S.A. today has many faces. The most successful designers and art directors learned long ago that they are primarily concerned with communication and that art and type and design are means to an end. However, one can generalize that many West Coast designers have more fun with graphics and take more risks to catch a reader's eye, evoke a smile, make a friend. The work shown on the following pages, along with that of April Greiman, Jack Odette, Nigel Holmes, Herb Lubalin, Bob Jones, Otto Storch, Aaron Burns, Bradbury Thompson and George Lois, shown earlier in this chapter, illustrates the great variety in contemporary U.S.A. design.

Perhaps because of this variety and the vigor of much graphics in the United States, designers in the U.S.A. today are influencing work abroad, much as in earlier decades European work stimulated designers in the United States.

Regional Design Centers Proliferate

In 1985 *Print* magazine's Regional Design Annual commented on the geographical redistribution of typographic design talent in the U.S.A. Some of its findings:

❧ Design buyers increasingly not only "want their print communications to be good; they want them to be different, even innovative."

❧ New York, although still a strong center of typographic design, no longer dominates the field as it once did, nor is it any longer the center of design innovation.

❧ Regional centers of growing design significance, and some of the key studios or designers, include: Minneapolis (Fallon McElligott Rice advertising agency and its design operation, the Duffy Group, headed by Joe Duffy); Dallas (Richards Brock Miller Mitchell agency, and designer Woody Pirtle); and Seattle (Rick Eiber; Hornall Anderson Design; Art Chantry; Wilkins Peterson); Phoenix, Albuquerque, Portland (Oregon) and Utah were also cited as growing design centers. Longer established design centers include Los Angeles, San Francisco and Chicago.

❧ In the Midwest, *Print* comments, "If new wave is not dead, it has ceased to be interesting, which many think is the same thing."

❧ In the East, according to Jim Eschinger of Nicki Adler Design, "More and more designers are realizing they've got to be business people."

❧ New York is called "a megaplex of all specialties plus a vast number of generalists who do it all," according to designer Richard Danne. "New York is totally eclectic; it will never have a style of its own, it's everything from A to Z."

❧ Designer Massimo Vignelli feels, however, there is a New York accent. He finds the Eastern and New York look more disciplined and less trendy compared with California, where the lifestyle and graphics are more colorful and playful.

The American School of Graphic Expressionism

Designer Herb Lubalin, in contrasting the American design touch to highly structured and theory-based European design, referred to "The American School of Graphic Expressionism."

The characteristics that Lubalin saw included intuitive designing, more informal organization of space, letting each problem lead to its own solution, novelty in seeking and presenting ideas and concepts, greater concern with the personal expression of the designer, a need to design each piece so that it contributes to establishing a product's or corporation's image.

Copy/art creative teams, headed either by a former copy chief or art director, became common in advertising agencies. The prototype for the creative team was the Paul Rand/William Bernbach co-development of advertisements at the Weintraub agency in the 1940s and early 1950s. Visual-verbal synergy as exemplified in advertisements for Ohrbach's department store opened the eyes of creative people to the added power that creative teams could give advertising messages.

Magazine and Newspaper Directions

The heyday of mass audience national magazines in the 1940s and 1950s brought exciting typographics to a wide readership. Key publication art directors included Otto Storch (*McCall's*), Henry Wolf (*Esquire, Harper's Bazaar, Show*), William Cadge (*Redbook*), Suren Ermoyan *(Good Housekeeping)*, Art Kane *(Seventeen)*, Cipe Pineles *(Glamour, Charm, Seventeen, Mademoiselle)*, Bradbury Thompson (*Mademoiselle, Westvaco Inspirations)*, Allen Hurlburt *(Look)*, Al Greenberg *(Gentleman's Quarterly)* and, of course, Dr. M. F. Agha *(Vogue)*, Paul Rand *(Apparel Arts)*, Alexey Brodovitch *(Harper's Bazaar)*, and Herb Lubalin's work for *The Saturday Evening Post* and *Eros*.

The demise of magazines, foreshadowed by the impact of television, did not occur, as feared, in the 1960s. True, many major national publications were discontinued, but many survived and were joined by smaller-format periodicals with specialized audiences. Such magazines continue to thrive. Magazine sections of newspapers also developed a new graphic vitality. Influential publication art directors of the 1960s and early 1970s include Peter Palazzo *(New York Herald Tribune, New York* magazine), Louis Silverstein *(The New York Times)*, Dugald Sterner *(Ramparts)*, Bea Feitler *(Ms.)*, Mike Salisbury *(West)* and *George Lois (Esquire* covers).

Lois' *Esquire* covers were not merely eye-catchers, nor simply dramatic statements of contents. They were powerful, visual editorial statements, often on controversial subjects.

Perhaps the most important newspaper design direction in the 1980s was the advent of the national daily, *U.S.A. Today*, which is distributed from its publishing source outside Washington, D.C. to satellite printing plants throughout the United States. Loaded with color, it is graphically bright and innovative. (See the illustration of its national weather map, P. 121).

For a comprehensive picture of recent and contemporary U.S.A. typographic design, one should look at such sources as the annual publications of the Art Directors Club of New York, the Type Directors Club, and the American Institute of Graphic Arts, the design annual editions of *Communication Arts* magazine, and *Print* magazine (especially the January-February 1964, January-February 1969, May-June 1977, May-June 1979 and July-August 1985 issues). Here we can only take a look at some of the design leaders whose work has helped set the pace or changed the face of typographic design.

Paul Rand and Bradbury Thompson

Poster *for IBM Corporation, 1980. Paul Rand.*

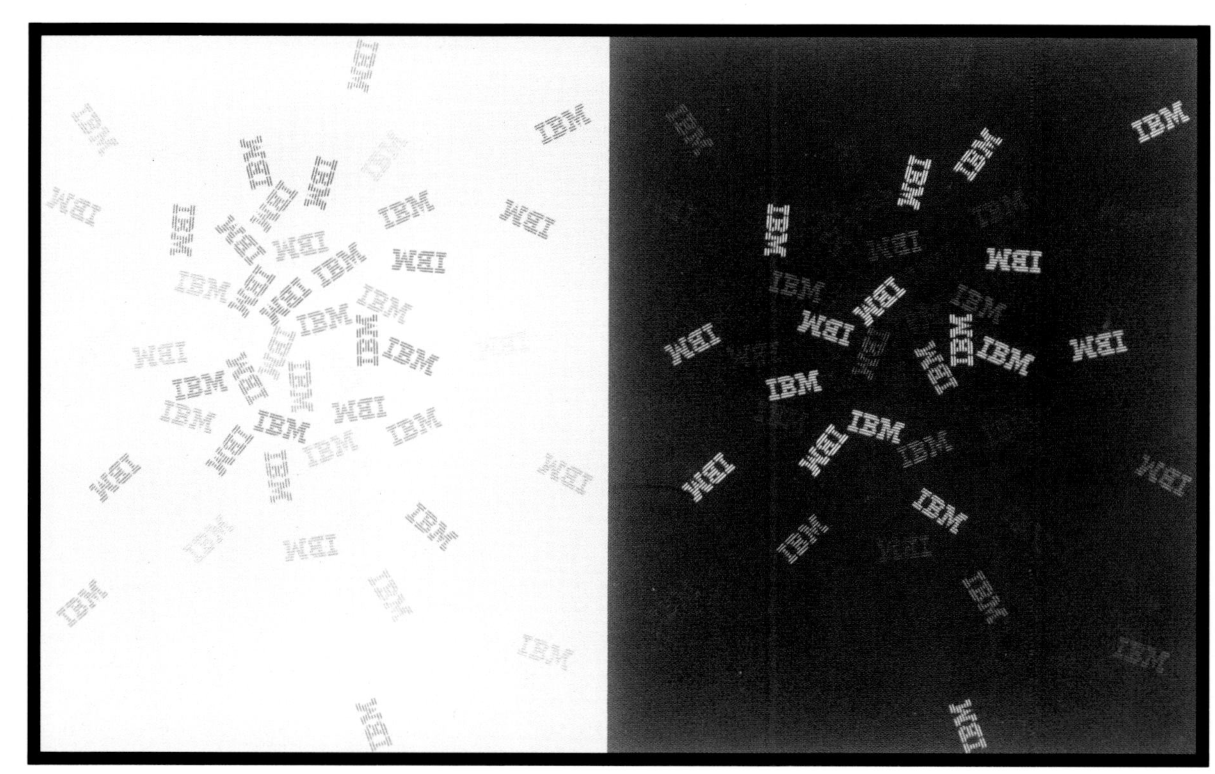

***Cover** design for* IBM *Corporation, 1982. Paul Rand.*

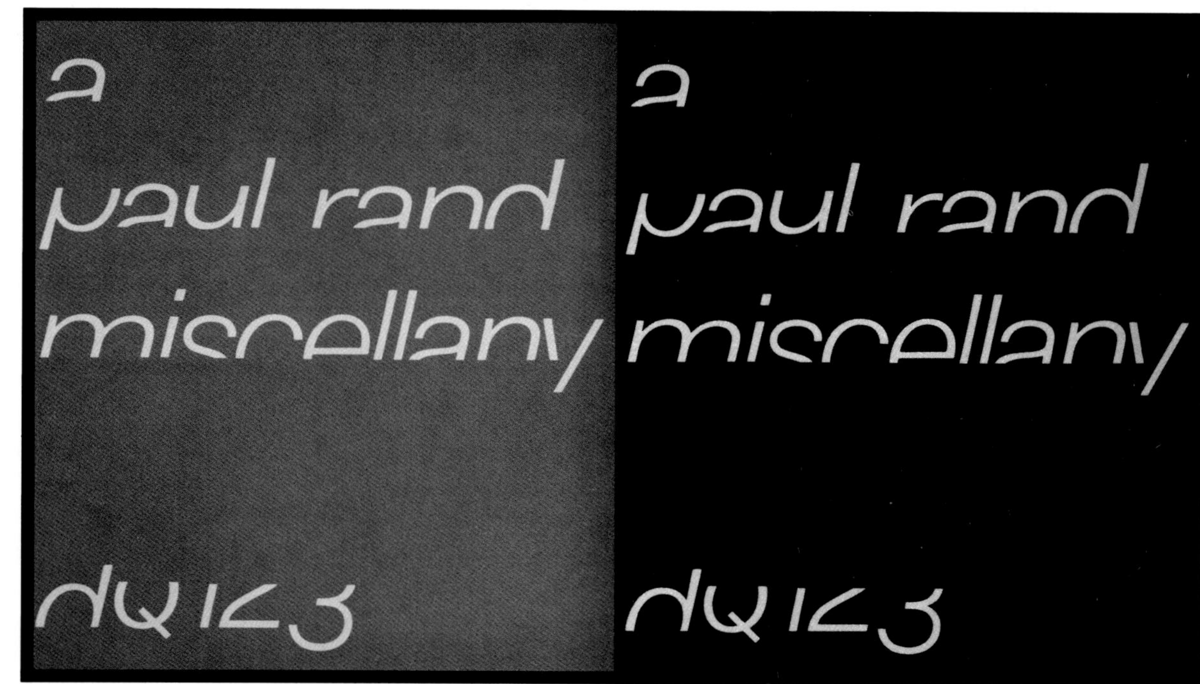

***Cover Design** for* Design Quarterly, *1984. Paul Rand.*

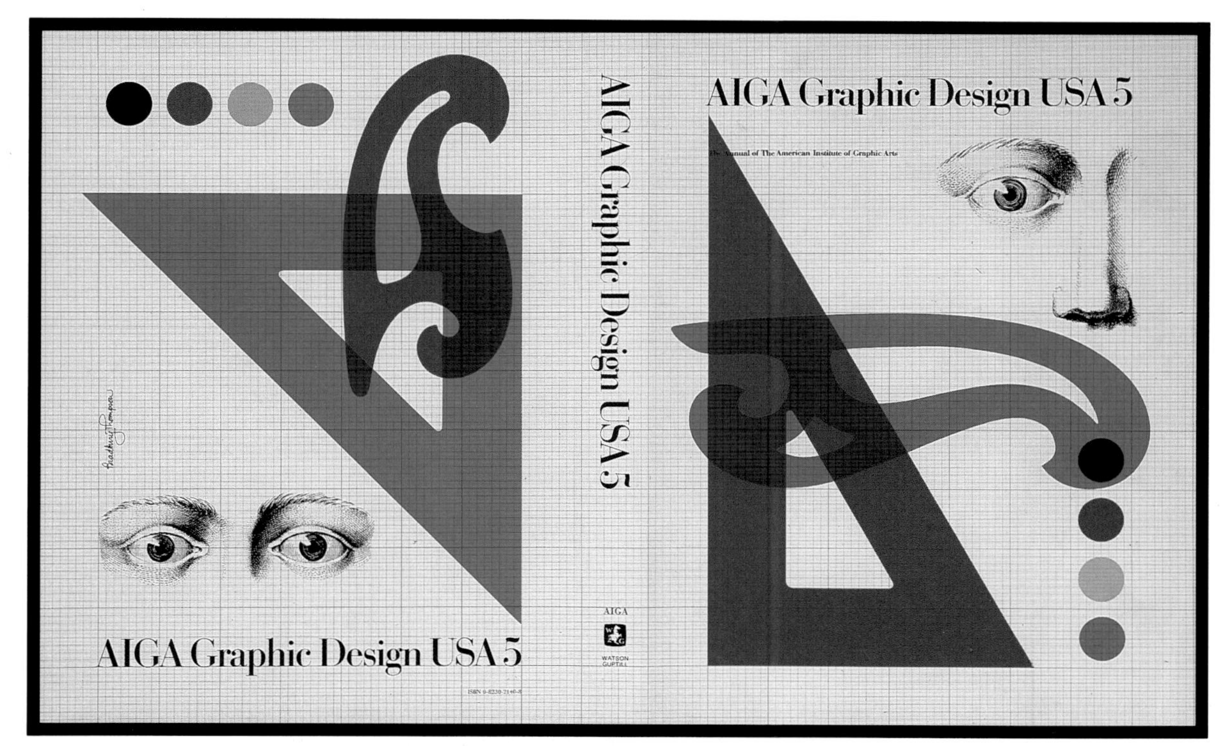

***Cover** for the* AIGA *annual book,* AIGA Graphic Design USA 5, *1984. Bradbury Thompson.*

Herb Lubalin

There's a wonderful book, *Herb Lubalin – Art Director, Graphic Designer, and Typographer.* Written by Gertrude Snyder and designed by Alan Peckolick, it has 360 illustrations, 166 in full color. The jacket really summarizes Lubalin's unique role in the typographic arts:

"The magnitude of Herb Lubalin's achievements will be felt for a long time to come... I think he was probably the greatest graphic designer ever," says Lou Dorfsman, Vice President, Creative Director, Advertising and Design, CBS Inc.

"For more than 40 years, Herb Lubalin expanded on the intricacies and elegance of typography-based design. He created new forms for communicating meaning, and new meaning for communication.

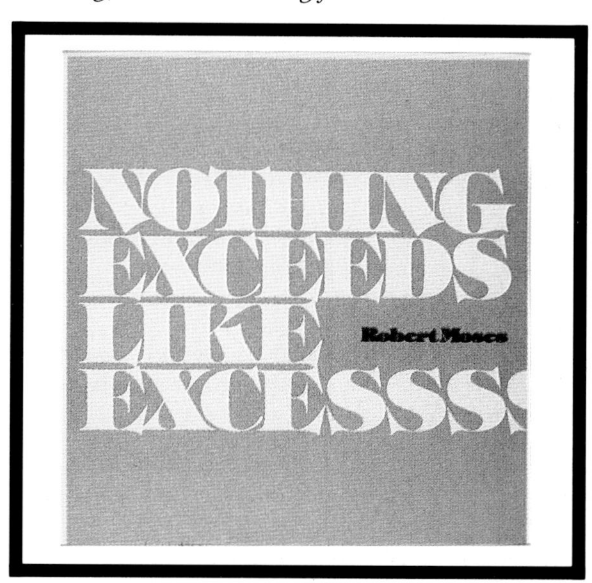

***In 1964** Herb Lubalin designed a series of posters for a typeface design competition sponsored by Visual Graphics Corporation. In 1978 he redesigned them using recently created* ITC *typefaces. Three of the redesigns are shown here. The new posters were not distributed, but appeared in* U&lc.

TYPOGRAPHIC COMMUNICATIONS TODAY
Chapter XIII: The Many Faces of Typography Today

"Where typography is considered an art form, there tends to be less concern with its communication power, and when it is viewed as a communication tool it tends to be less of an art."

"The typographics for which he is best known are as eloquent in their use of subtlety, character and individuality as words and language are themselves... For example, there is a child in his Mother & Child, (see Chapter I)...

"But Herb Lubalin's contribution to the graphic arts goes well beyond typography. As an agency art director, he pushed aside the established norm of copy-driven advertising and added a new visual dimension. As the publication designer for Eros, U&lc *and others, he broke through the boundaries that constrained existing magazines – both in form and content."*

Herbert Frederick Lubalin (1918-1981) was an agency, publication and studio art director before opening his own graphic design service in 1964. He was also co-founder of International Typeface Corporation and designer of several major typeface families, including ITC Avant Garde Gothic® (with Tom Carnase), ITC Serif Gothic® (with Antonio DiSpigna), and ITC Lubalin Graph® He also edited and designed *U&lc* magazine until his death in 1981.

In Europe, Japan and wherever else they speak of the American influence on graphic design, Herb Lubalin's work is always cited. Some of his work is shown earlier in this chapter, in the section dealing with expressive typography. A few other examples are shown here.

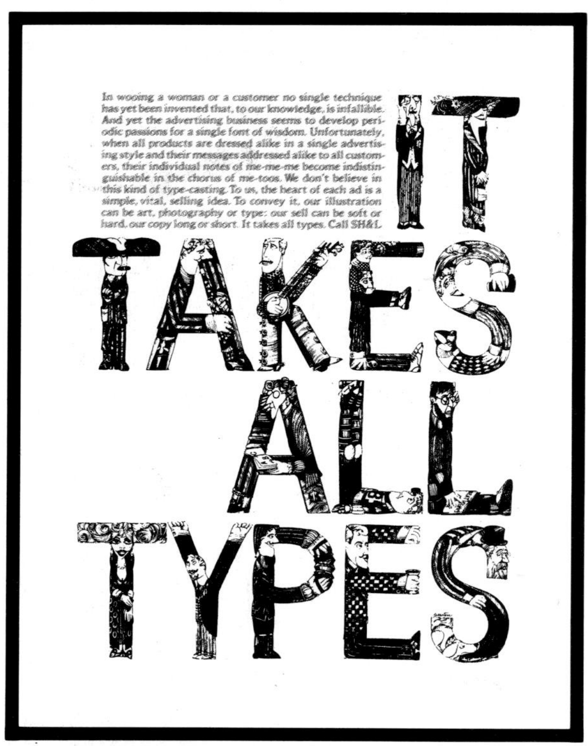

A trade ad *for Sudler & Hennessey, Inc. Herb Lubalin.*

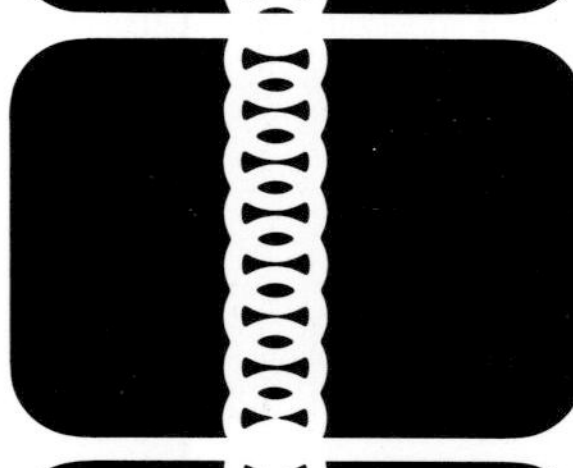

Animated sequence *for on-air television spot for* PBS. *Herb Lubalin.*

The March 1978 U&lc *carried a story on American jazz which Herb Lubalin designed using* ITC *typefaces. The article was a redesign of one that had appeared in* Der Druckspiegel *in 1960. One of a series of inserts* About U.S., *the original article was conceived, edited, typeset and produced under the sponsorship of The Composing Room, Inc., in New York. Percy Seitlin wrote the original text and Herb Lubalin designed it under the direction of Dr. Robert Leslie, Hortense Mandel and Aaron Burns.*

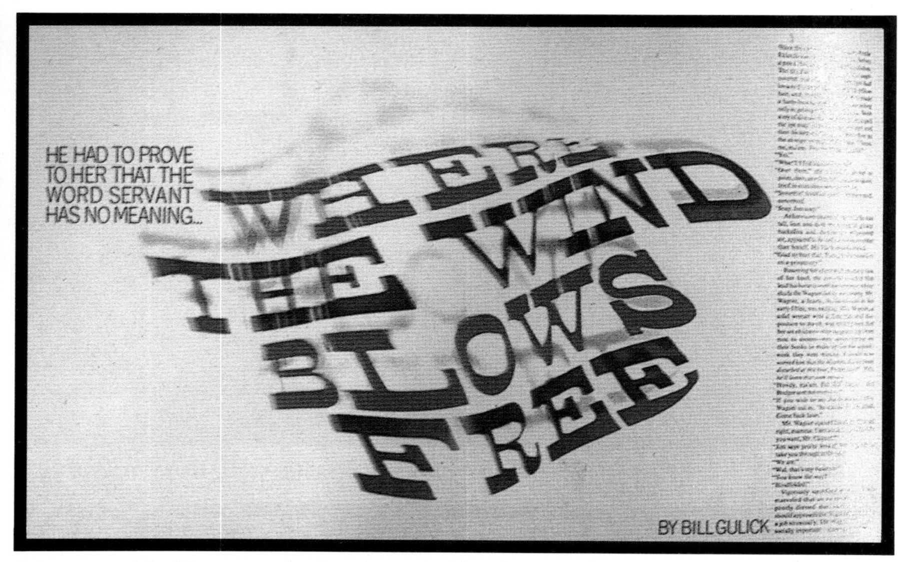

A typographically expressive *interior spread for* The Saturday Evening Post. *Herb Lubalin.*

Saul Bass

In the 1940s, New York born and educated Saul Bass started his career as a freelance graphic designer and agency art director. In 1945 he moved to California, and in 1952 established his own firm, Saul Bass Associates, in Los Angeles. In the print media and in film he has been a most innovative, creative, productive designer. He was one of the pioneers in the early days of corporate identity programs. Those who know Saul Bass also appreciate his ability to articulate his thoughts about design generally and about each project he develops. Some of his observations on the role of type in communications are expressed here.

❧ *"Typography is a tool, a component part of what I do. Where typography is considered an art form, there tends to be less concern with its communication power, and when it is viewed as a communication tool it tends to be less of an art."* Bass finds both positions valid, *"depending on the function of the piece, which approach or which mix is right."*

❧ *"Art is concerned with mood, feeling, and undefined* zeitgeist *(spirit of the times). When art plays the role of exploring directions and the hidden sides of life, it is more suggestive than realistic, more dense than clear. When type is used as an artistic form or to blend feeling into a message, it too tends to be less clear."*

Although Saul Bass experimented with type as an abstract entity early in his career, an interest in the other visual elements overwhelmed his concentration on type. Type became, in his new perspective, a supportive, rather than a central, element in a total design, important but rarely the dominant element.

Bass does not exclude the use of anything in the art spectrum. It all depends on the functional intent. He also views the art director as, among other things, a casting director, one who selects the artist, photographer, or designer most appropriate to the problem.

Saul Bass and Associates is known for its corporate identity programs, packaging design, theatrical film titles, and films for television. Here, to focus on work in which type was employed creatively, we will look at just a few of Bass package designs and posters, a magazine cover and an advertisement.

Shopping bag *for the Bell System Companies, for use in retail outlets in shopping centers. The design is related to the Bell System corporate identity program. Saul Bass.*

This Paul Harris shopping bag *ties into the company's design program. The type picks up the flavor of the illustration. Saul Bass.*

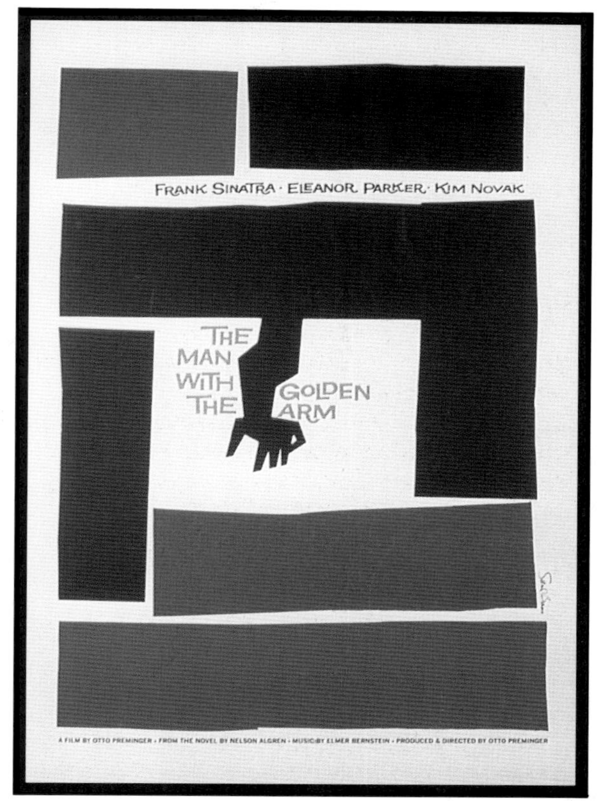

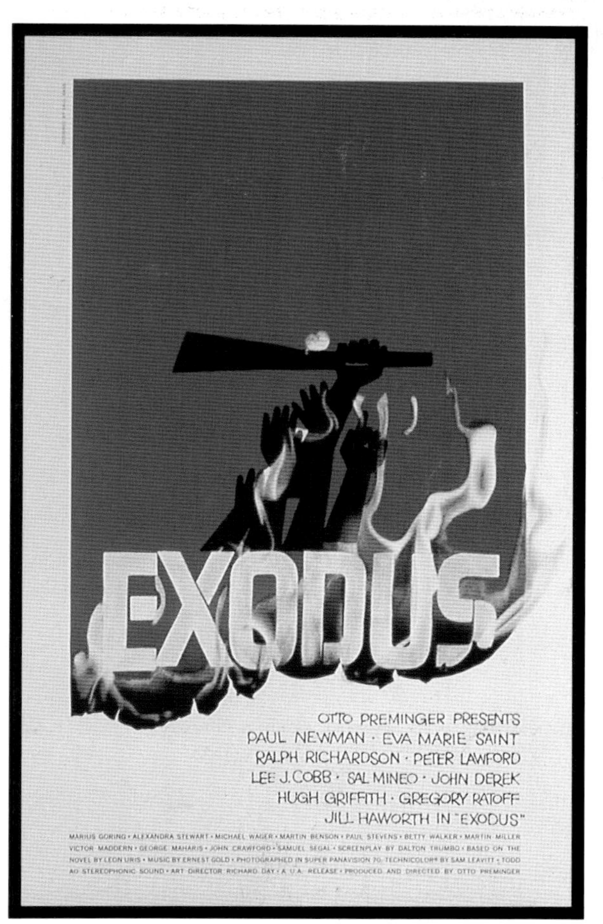

Film posters *by Saul Bass.*

TYPOGRAPHIC COMMUNICATIONS TODAY
Chapter XIII: The Many Faces of Typography Today

Poster *for the United Nations. Saul Bass.*

Cover *for* Environment *magazine. Saul Bass.*

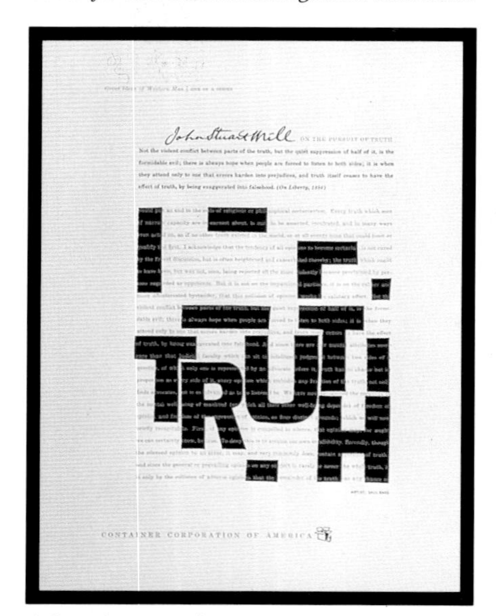

Advertisement *for Container Corporation of America's series on Great Ideas of Western Man. Saul Bass.*

Gene Federico

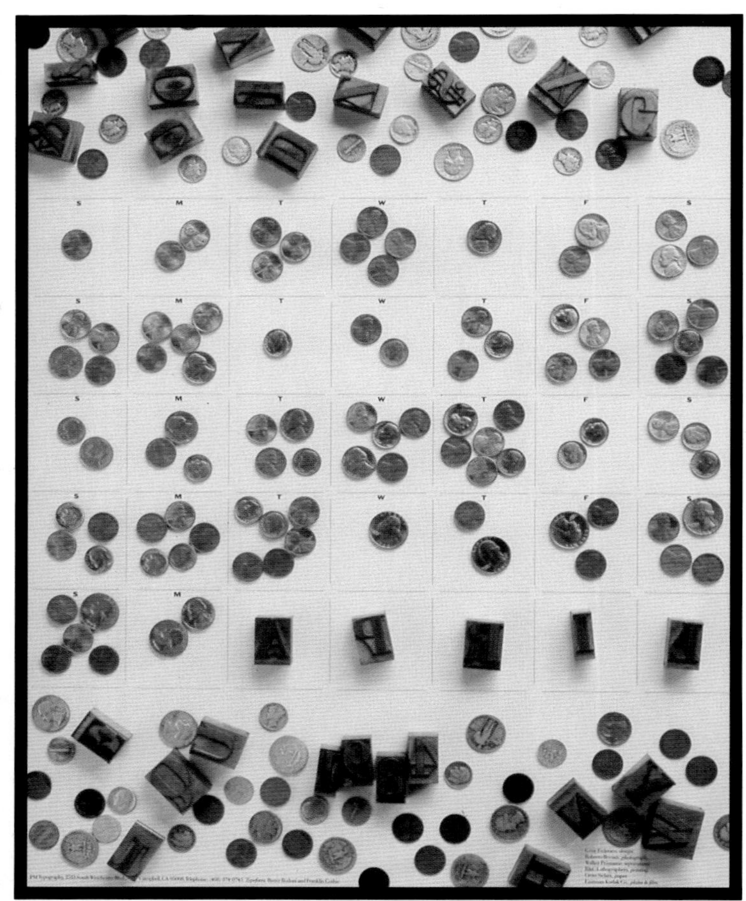

Not innovative *so much as a eulogy to metal type. The 96 pt. Bodoni Bold font used in the photograph was about to be sold for metal scrap. Federico acquired the font and kept it around for several years. One day he was asked to design a month in a 1984 calendar. The lovely metal type characters and many U.S. coins was his solution. Gene Federico.*

The **New Yorker** ***magazine campaign*** *grew directly out of the product to be advertised. The magazine page was enlarged two times its regular size to fit a* New York Times *page. Rules echo the three-column format, and 24 point Caslon 540 echoes the magazine's typeface. Gene Federico.*

This **Saturday Evening Post** ***spread*** *is an example of typography used as illustration. The piece was about a newspaper reporter. Typical tabloid typography was used in an illustrative sense to give the piece pertinent atmosphere without detracting from the story line. Gene Federico.*

Type and photography *express and illustrate the message.* Woman's Day *magazine. Bicycle wheels and Futura Light lower case are a perfect match. Gene Federico.*

The girl with dark hair was coming toward him across the field. With what seemed a single movement she tore off her clothes and flung them disdainfully aside. Her body was white and smooth, but it aroused no desire in him; indeed he barely looked at it. What overwhelmed him in that instant was admiration for the gesture with which she had thrown her clothes aside. With its grace and carelessness it seemed to annihilate a whole culture, a whole system of thought, as though Big Brother and the Party and the Thought Police could all be swept into nothingness by a single splendid movement of the arm.

1984
JFMA
MJJA
SOND

This piece *has only one reason for being: to indicate the designer/month relationship. Using 1, 9, 8, 4 and the initials of the 12 months, Federico created a square which he tilted at a 30/60 degree angle. To bring Orwell into the graphic, it being 1984, he reread 1984, found the only euphoric passage in the entire book and set it in Bodoni Bold. Except for a paragraph indent, it set itself into eight adjusted lines. Gene Federico.*

Written by Percy Seitlin, *this essay laments the disappearance of so many apples with such lovely names. Faking the photography of only three available apple types was the big burden in designing this piece. Typographically, it was a tour de force. Federico wanted to use the various title gothics then available in metal to stack and fit tightly and never use the razor blade. A few years ago a European colleague claimed this piece had been a great influence on him as a young designer. Gene Federico.*

Ladislav Sutnar

Book designed *by Ladislav Sutnar for Hastings House. 1961.*

TYPOGRAPHIC COMMUNICATIONS TODAY
Chapter XIII: The Many Faces of Typography Today

Robert P. Smith

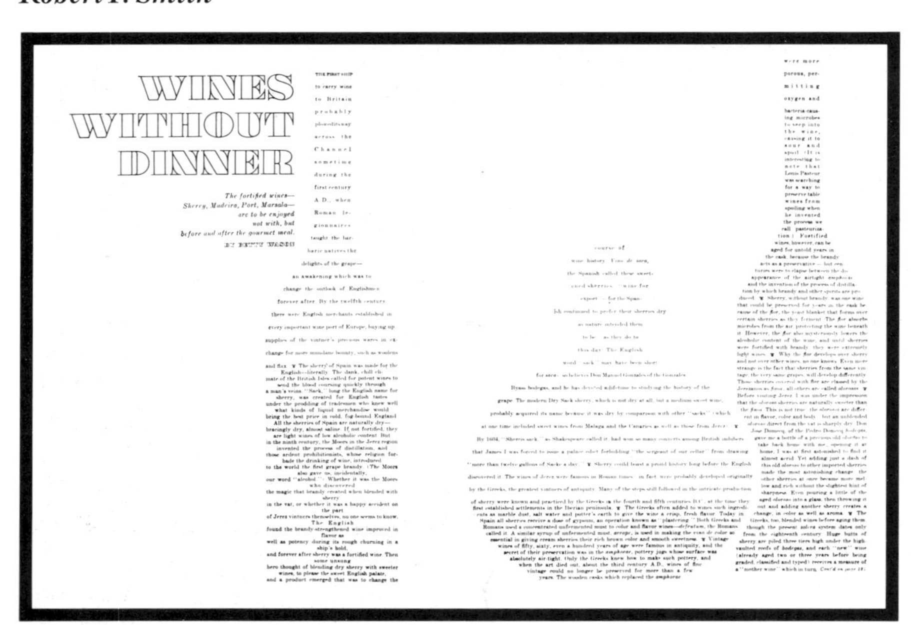

Spread *from* Gentleman's Quarterly *magazine. Robert P. Smith. 1963.*

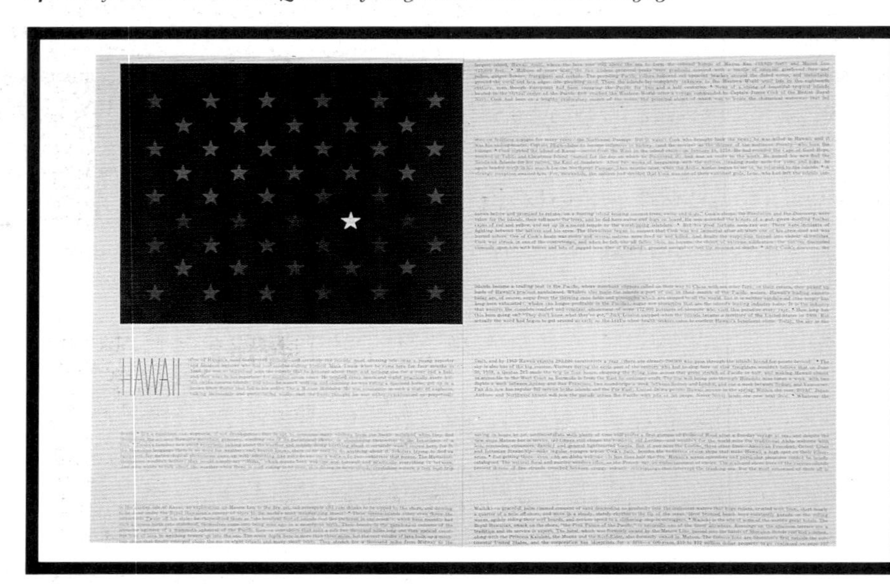

Spread *from* Gentleman's Quarterly *magazine. Robert P. Smith/Albert Greenberg. 1959.*

Aaron Burns

Poster *by Aaron Burns for The Composing Room, Inc. 1959.*

Donald Egensteiner

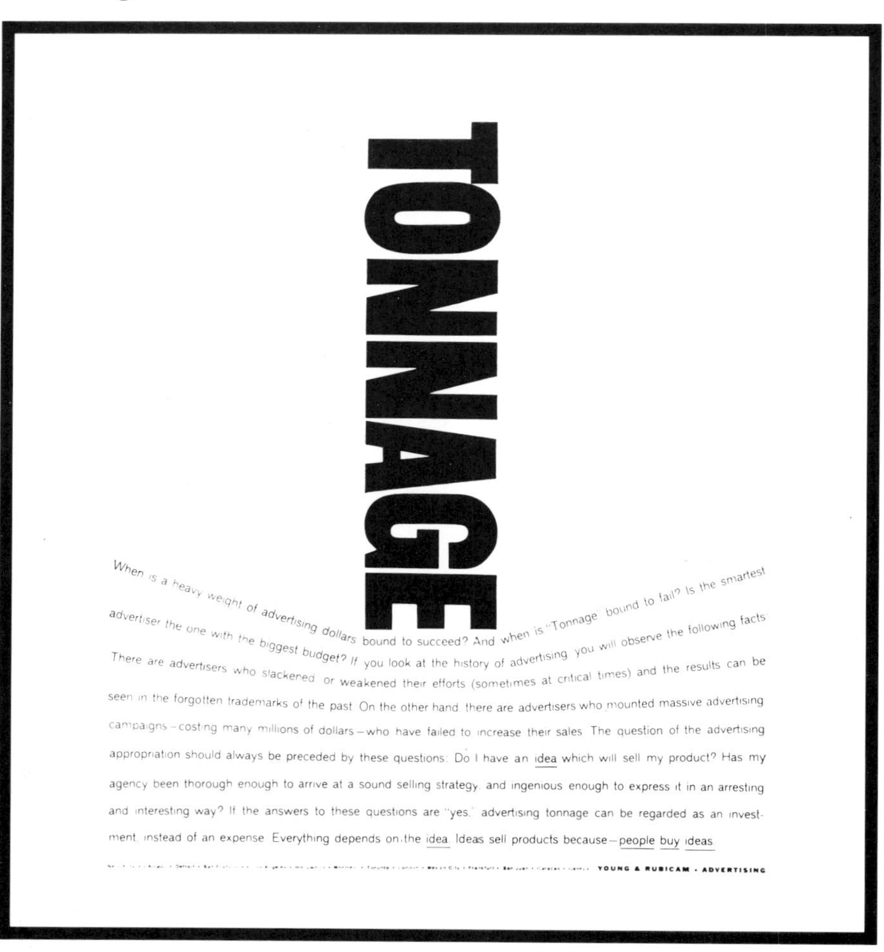

Advertisement *for Young & Rubicam, Inc. by Donald Egensteiner. 1960.*

Gollin & Bright

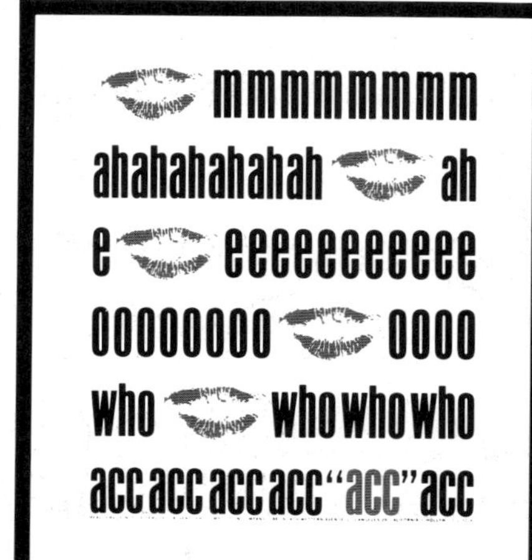

Advertisement *by Gollin & Bright, Inc. for Advertisers Composition Co. 1960.*

Dan Friedman

November calendar *for the Neuberger Museum, 1974. This was one of a series of monthly announcements created with the use of low budget means – typewriter, transfer type and hand-drawn elements. The design was adapted from an earlier experiment with the letter N, done as a student at the School of Design in Basel. Dan Friedman.*

WNYC stationery, *1980. Part of the visual identity created for New York's public radio and television station. The symbol emphasizes the initials NYC. Black-and-white was accepted as both an economy and as part of the visual identity. Dan Friedman.*

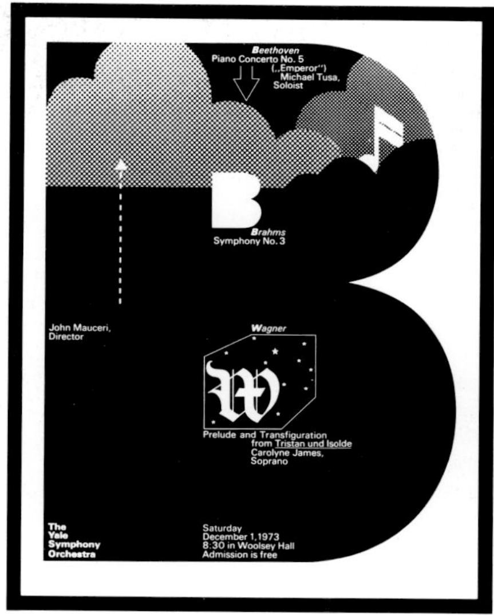

Concert poster *for the Yale University Symphony Orchestra, 1972. Dan Friedman.*

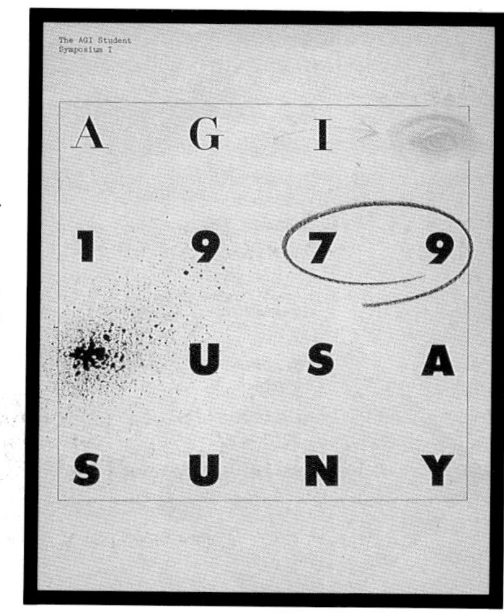

Booklet *for the AGI Student Symposium, 1979. This is another example of the use of low budget methods. The cover image was designed as a symbol to be used on other related print media. Dan Friedman.*

George Tscherny

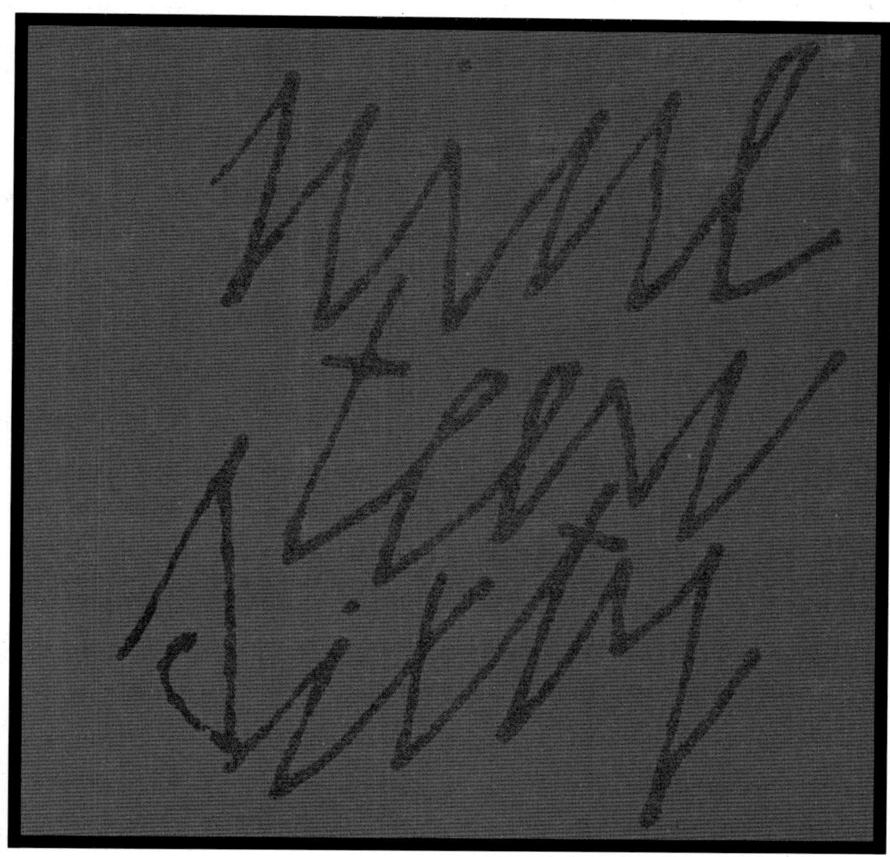

Of this calendar cover *for the Museum of Modern Art, art designer George Tscherny comments: "Type is for reading – except when it is not! As in the case of this calendar cover, where one has a whole year to decipher it."*

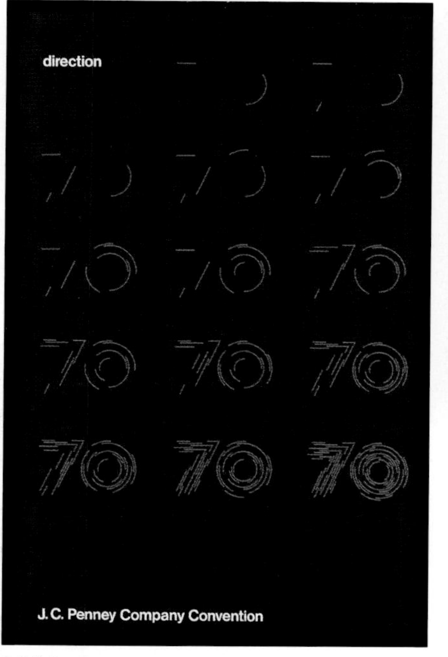

Of this 1969 poster *for J. C. Penney, George Tscherny writes, "Back in 1969 I tried to simulate and anticipate the use of the computer by graphic designers. Achieving an even progression, horizontally and vertically, was a tedious and time consuming job. Ironically, now that the computer is upon us and such design could be produced with ease and speed, I have less interest in this kind of programmatic play with letters."*

"As designers *we can only be as innovative and daring as our clients permit us to be. Corporate signatures are usually the most sacred of cows. Therefore, when a client permits you to 'touch the untouchable,' he deserves credit along with the designer for the solution." 1973, George Tscherny.*

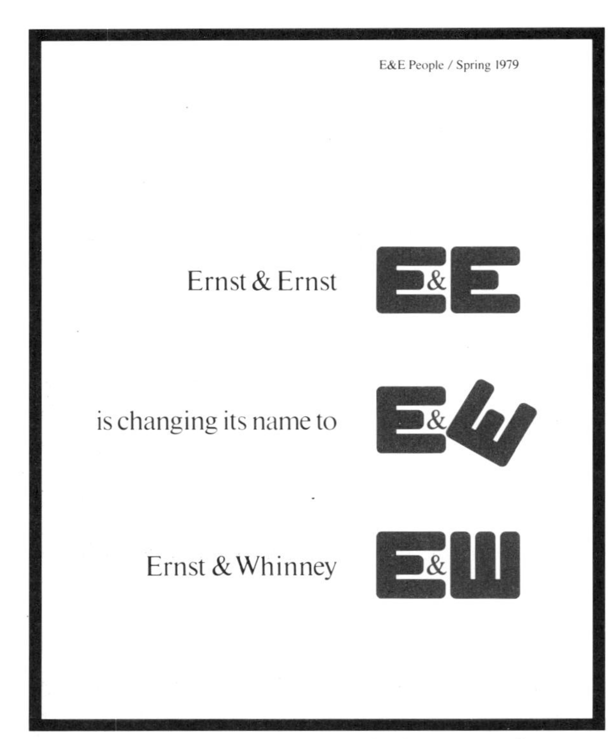

E&E People / Spring 1979
Ernst & Ernst
is changing its name to
Ernst & Whinney

*"**I am very fond** of the 'found object' school in typography. In other words, solutions which are found to be inherent in the material, and are utilized without much intervention or contrivance by the designer. The 'Air Canada' cover and 'Adhesive' in the Millipore typographic guidelines are other examples of this approach." 1979. George Tscherny.*

*"**The space** or frame surrounding typography is to me a significant consideration. The all-prevailing 8½" x 11" norm forced on designers by the graphic arts industry is hard to shed for economic reasons (i.e., the standard sizes of paper, press equipment, film, etc.). Specifications have to conform, unless the client is willing to buy his way out of it.*

"The worst aspect is that an already dull proportion turns even duller when such a brochure is opened to an 11" x 17" double page spread. How much more impact, when, for example, an 8½" x 8½" cover opens to an 8½" x 17" dimension. I have always been partial to the logic and potential drama the square format affords..." 1985, George Tscherny.

***A poster style sheet** for Millipore Corporation's advertising and promotion. One copy block states that "Illustrative and symbolic typography are not necessarily governed by the same rules that apply to conventional typography. Here, novelty, visual stimulus and impact are legitimate reasons for compromising legibility." 1984, George Tscherny.*

Henry Wolf

Esquire ***cover*** *on 1956 United States presidential election. Henry Wolf.*

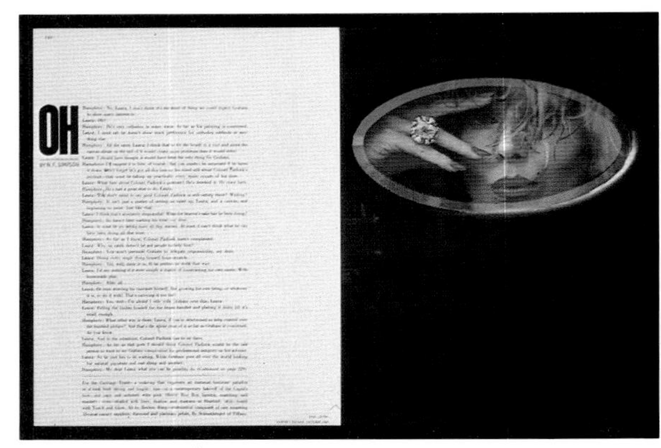

Harper's Bazaar *fiction spread. Henry Wolf.*

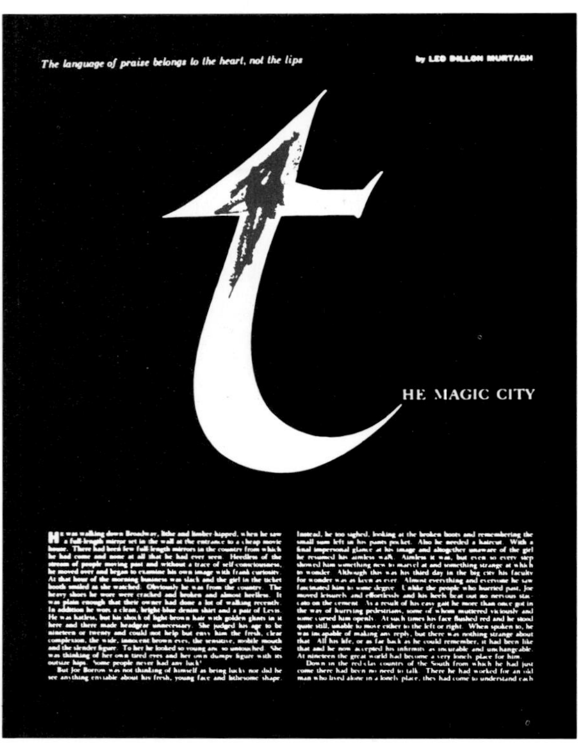

***Opening page** of an* Esquire *story. Henry Wolf.*

***Redesign** of cover format for* House Beautiful. *Henry Wolf.*

Call for entries *for a 1983 AIGA show. Henry Wolf.*

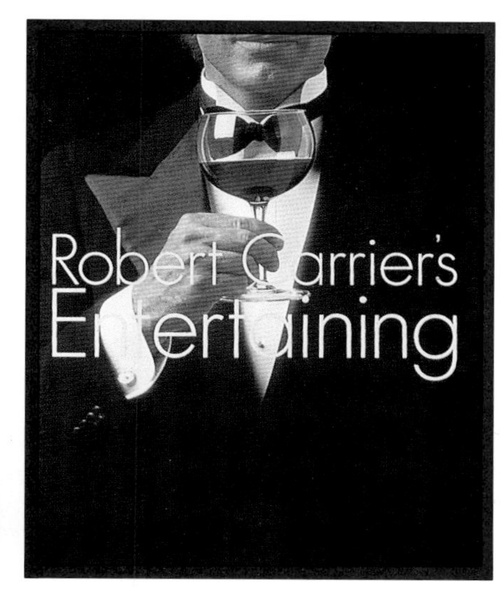

Book jacket *for a cookbook. Henry Wolf.*

Carl Zahn

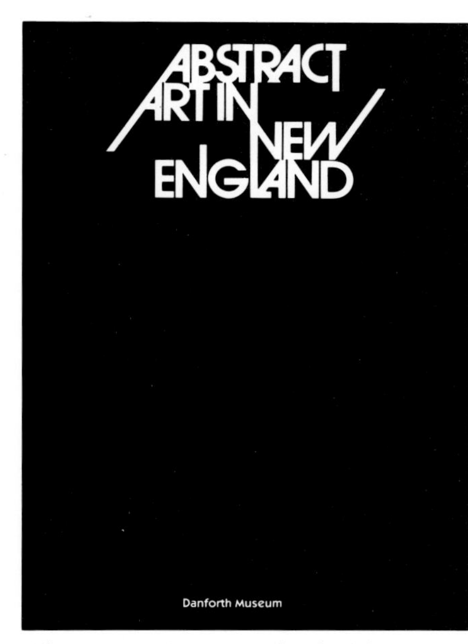

Abstract Art *in New England exhibition catalog. Danforth Museum in Framingham, Massachusetts, 1983.*

"I have long admired Herb Lubalin's Avant Garde Gothic for display type. This exhibition contained a number of metal sculptures executed in a geometric style of intersecting planes and rods. I have elaborated slightly on the ligatures, but I find the original assortment offers many structural possibilities." Carl Zahn.

The Trial of Six Designers. *Edited by Marshall Lee. Hammermill Paper Co., New York, 1968. "Marshall Lee asked six designers to redesign the original edition of Franz Kafka's* The Trial, *originally published by Knopf in 1937, with design by Georg Salter. I welcomed the opportunity and immediately called Marshall to reserve the endpaper of my choice, Grandee Black (we all had to use one color of the same paper). In the novel, the central figure is referred to only as 'K.' I picked this letter to furnish the illustration; it was set in Helvetica Extra Bold, and with each chapter half-title the K disintegrates a bit more. The text was set in Helvetica Linofilm 8/11 point, which I find easily readable, despite many statements by others to the contrary." Carl Zahn.*

Poster *for an exhibition of the graphic art of Jacques Villon at the Museum of Fine Arts in Boston, 1962.*

"I look to the characteristics of the work of each artist to try to discover a typographic equivalent. Villon's etchings make strong use of parallel cross-hatchings on the diagonal. I have always liked Frutiger's Univers; it is one of the most complete typographic designs of any time. Here I joined the l's and i's to create the pattern. The poster was printed silkscreen in dull black ink." Carl Zahn.

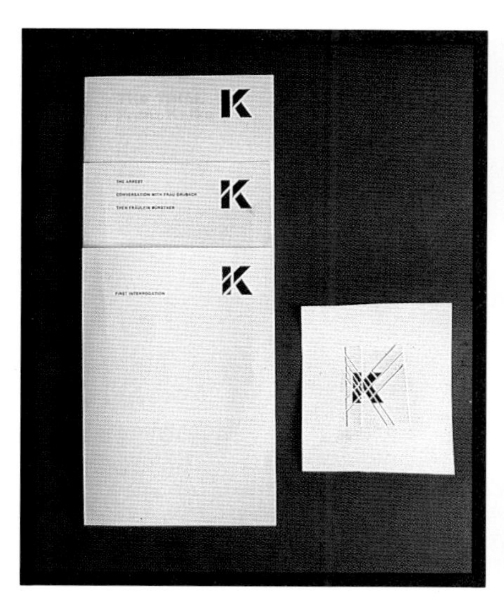

Matisse exhibition *subway car card. Museum of Fine Arts, Boston, 1966. "This advertised an exhibition made up mostly of Matisse paper cut-outs. I cut the letters out of paper and they were silkscreened. I draw letters when I can't find type that seems to fit the bill." Carl Zahn.*

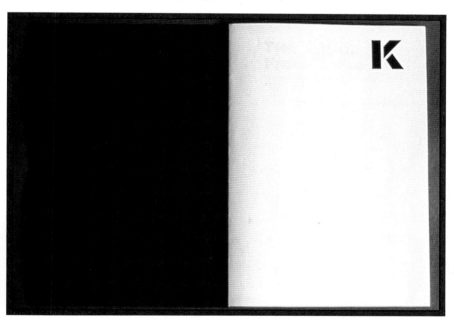

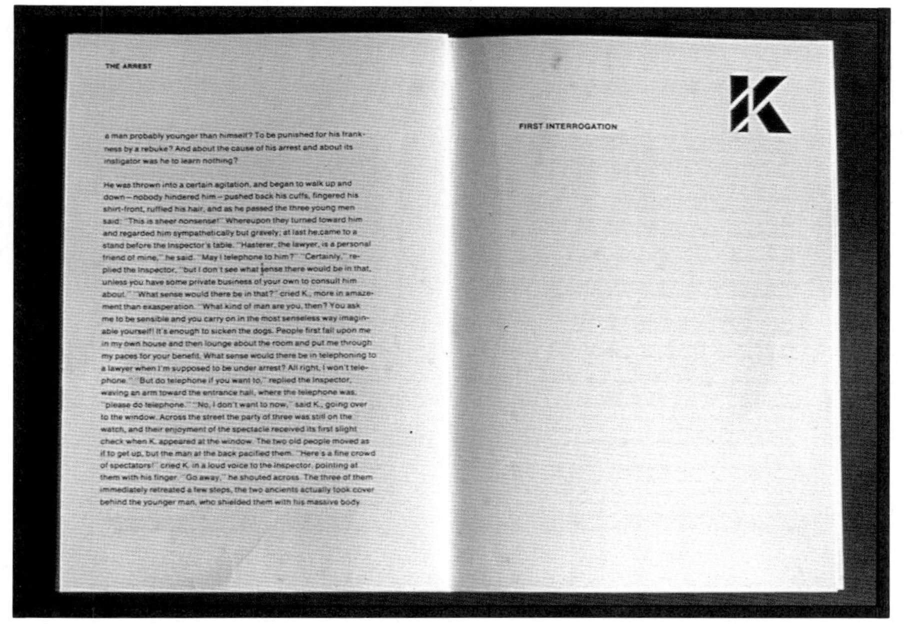

A Kind of Life: Conversations in the Combat Zone, *by Roswell Angier. Addison House, Inc., Danbury, New Hampshire, 1976. "The title is a direct quote from one of the 'exotic dancers' in Boston's 'Combat Zone.' I chose to treat it this way typographically. The book was set throughout in Futura." The cover die-stamp is "a G-string which I pasted up from sequins." Carl Zahn.*

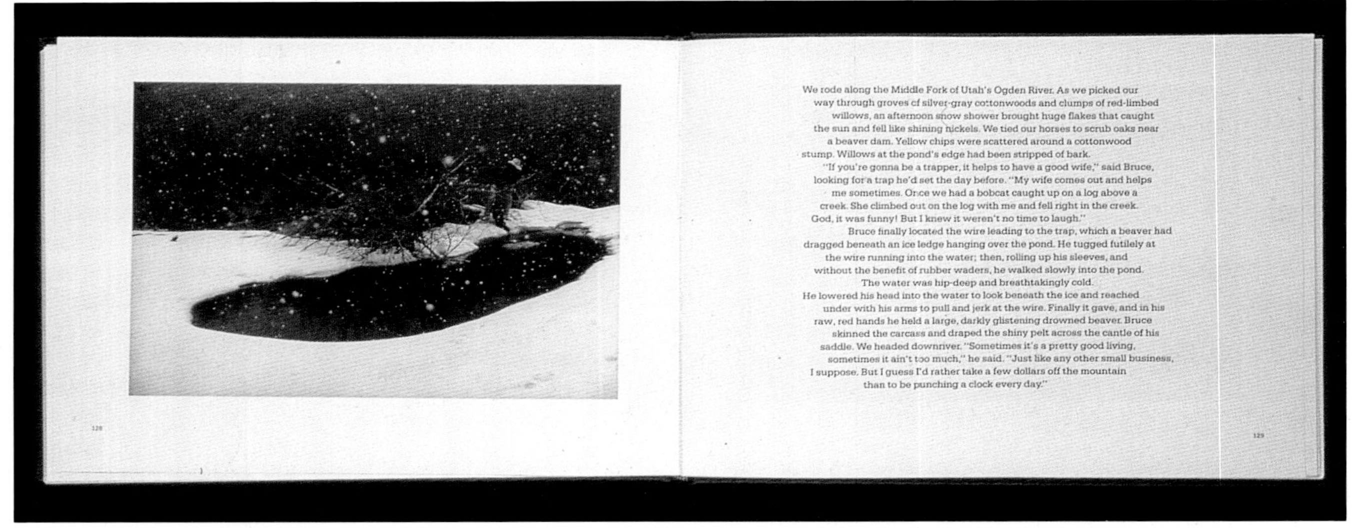

We rode along the Middle Fork of Utah's Ogden River. As we picked our
way through groves of silver-gray cottonwoods and clumps of red-limbed
willows, an afternoon snow shower brought huge flakes that caught
the sun and fell like shining nickels. We tied our horses to scrub oaks near
a beaver dam. Yellow chips were scattered around a cottonwood
stump. Willows at the pond's edge had been stripped of bark.
"If you're gonna be a trapper, it helps to have a good wife," said Bruce,
looking for a trap he'd set the day before. "My wife comes out and helps
me sometimes. Once we had a bobcat caught up on a log above a
creek. She climbed out on the log with me and fell right in the creek.
God, it was funny! But I knew it weren't no time to laugh."
Bruce finally located the wire leading to the trap, which a beaver had
dragged beneath an ice ledge hanging over the pond. He tugged futilely at
the wire running into the water; then, rolling up his sleeves, and
without the benefit of rubber waders, he walked slowly into the pond.
The water was hip-deep and breathtakingly cold.
He lowered his head into the water to look beneath the ice and reached
under with his arms to pull and jerk at the wire. Finally it gave, and in his
raw, red hands he held a large, darkly glistening drowned beaver. Bruce
skinned the carcass and draped the shiny pelt across the cantle of his
saddle. We headed downriver. "Sometimes it's a pretty good living,
sometimes it ain't too much," he said. "Just like any other small business,
I suppose. But I guess I'd rather take a few dollars off the mountain
than to be punching a clock every day."

Vanishing Breed *by William Allard. Little, Brown & Co., Boston, 1983. "This book of photographs on the vanishing American cowboy was combined with commentary from the photographer, based on interviews from his cowboying days," the designer explained. "The stories did not exceed one page, and were mostly dialogue. I had them set in Serifa Medium, another Frutiger type that I like very much. To avoid a blocky feeling, I had the pages set 'phrase style,' indented irregularly at the left, confirming to the sense of what was being said. I recalled some books by Victor Hammer where he had utilized an irregular margin on both sides of the type page to good effect." Carl Zahn.*

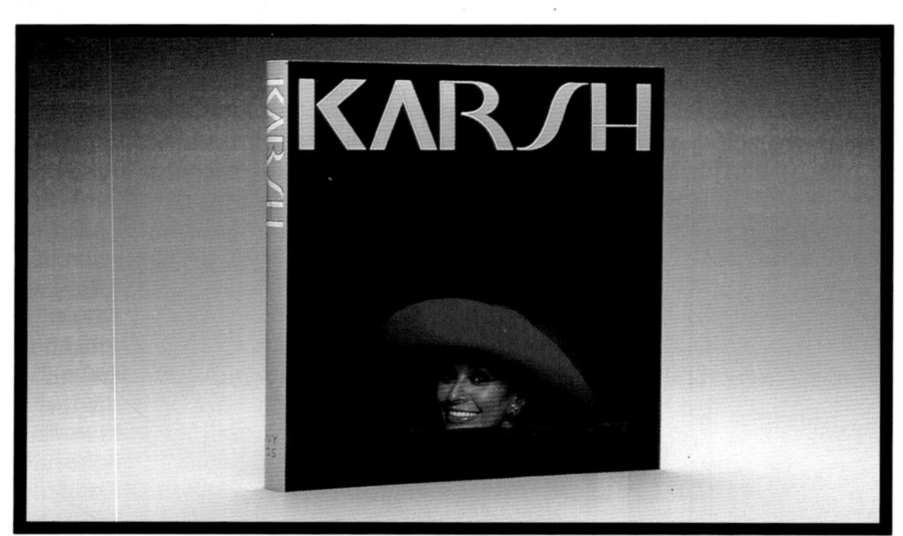

Yousuf Karsh. *Little, Brown & Co., Boston, 1984. "This is the jacket for a selection of Karsh's photographs to celebrate his seventy-fifth birthday," the designer explained. "The letters are a take-off from the maestro's letterhead which must date to the late '20s. The shading is printed in silver to go along with the art-deco feeling of the letters." Carl Zahn.*

Louis Dorfsman

***"A review** in the New York Times by the then TV critic was so positive and flattering to CBS that I felt the review was indeed 'worth repeating' in a full page. This straightforward, simple visual highlighted the statement to CBS' advantage." 1964, Louis Dorfsman.*

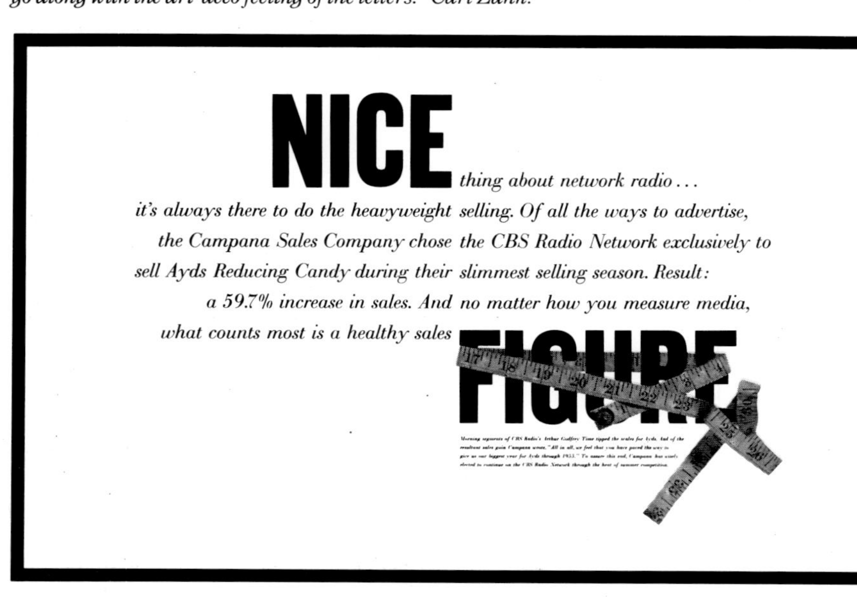

***One of a series** of trade advertisements in which typography is the major ingredient. The purpose of the series was to prove the selling virtues and strengths of CBS radio (in the early days of television) through the device of sales success of various products which were advertised on the CBS Radio Network. Louis Dorfsman.*

*“**When the new** Saarinen-designed CBS building reached the interior design stage, I noticed that the plan for cafeteria space had in it a 40′ by 8½′ empty white wall. I immediately suggested that I design a three-dimensional typography wall of words and objects dealing with food. Working together with Herb Lubalin, this is the result.” Louis Dorfsman.*

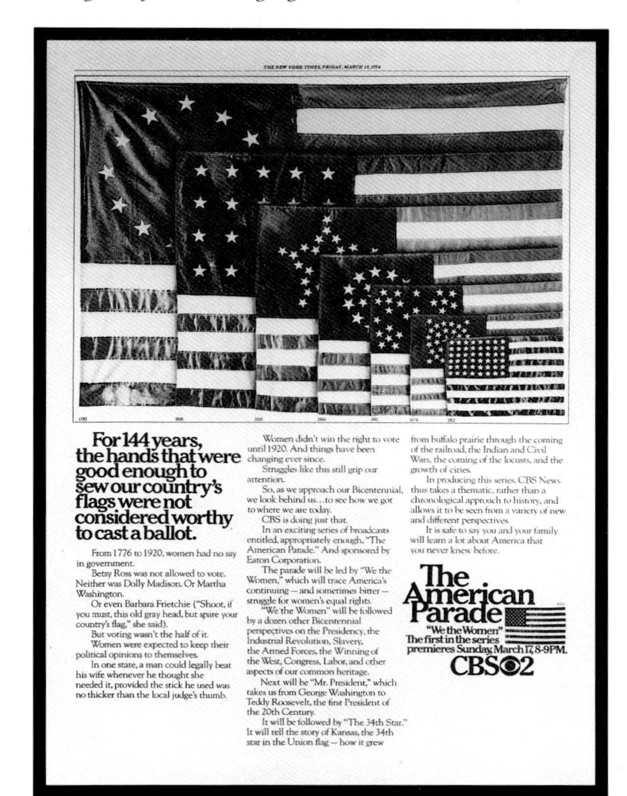

***American Parade:** This advertisement was conceived in celebration of the Bicentennial and special CBS programming for the event. The first CBS broadcast dealt with the contribution of women to the American Revolution. The copy is excellent; the headline especially so. This was the first ad of the series. Louis Dorfsman.*

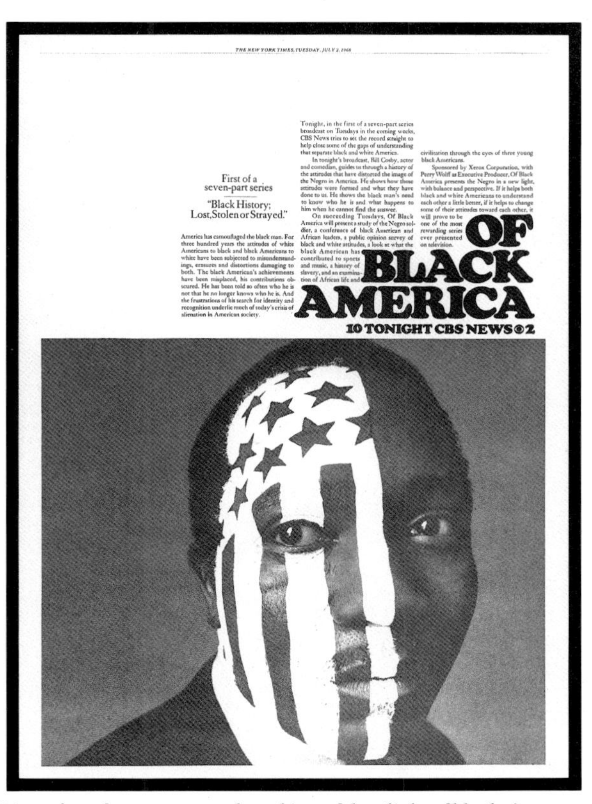

*“**A series** of programs on the subject of the plight of blacks in America. The treatment of the face is, to my mind, ‘typographic’ in its power and directness.” 1968, Louis Dorfsman.*

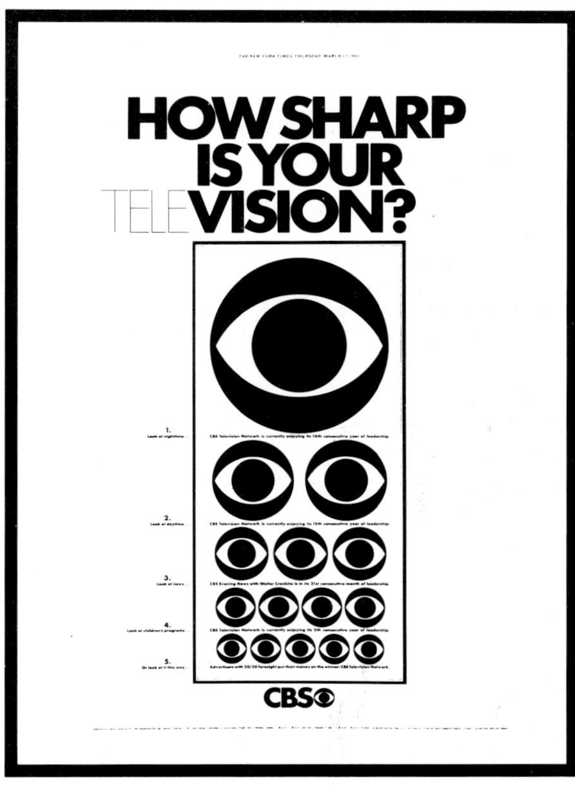

*“**Trick pun** of creating an eye chart to make the point of CBS TV leadership in audience viewing. The CBS eye logo is of course quite ‘typographic’ and thereby appropriate at several levels of the ad message.” 1969, Louis Dorfsman.*

***Advertisement** for CBS Television Network. Designed by Louis Dorfsman.*

***Advertisement** for CBS Television Network. Designed by Louis Dorfsman.*

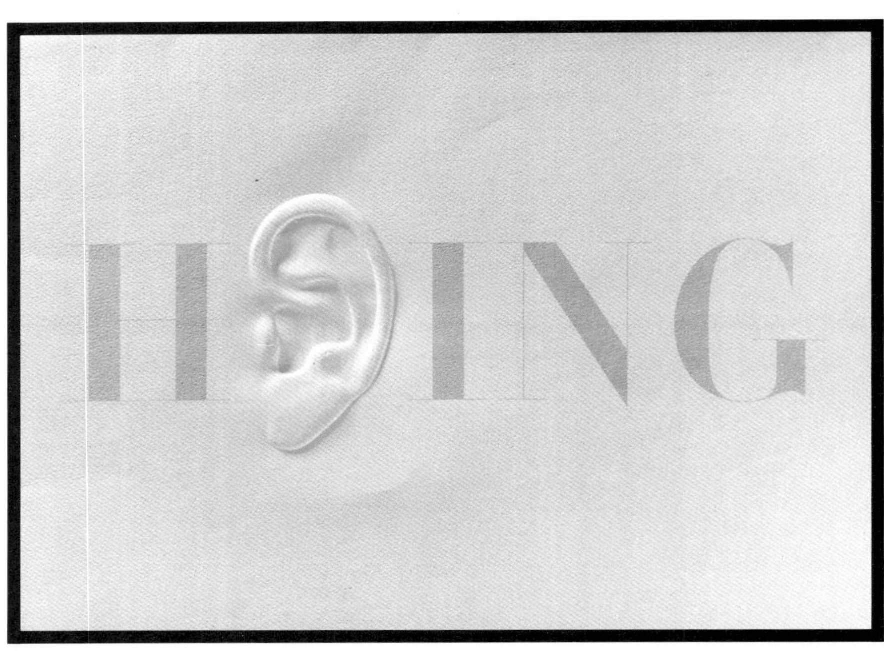

*"**This brochure** for the* CBS *Radio Network was designed in the early '50s to celebrate the strength and effectiveness of sound as an impactful force to deliver messages. The problem then, in the mid-'50s, was the sight and sound impact and competition of the new medium of television. The typographic treatment inside the book was quite innovative and unique at that time and indeed is still so." Louis Dorfsman.*

Rudolf de Harak

THE
INFORMATION
BANK

***Logotype** for* The New York Times, *1975. Rudolph de Harak.*

***Typeface design,** Quadra, 1970. Rudolph de Harak.*

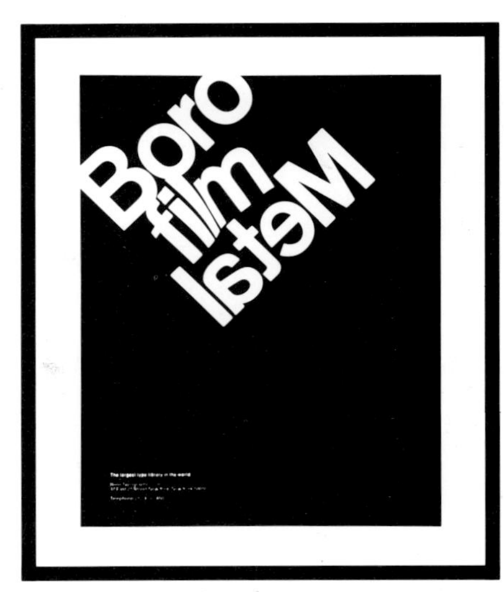

***Advertisement** for Boro Typographers, Inc., 1970. Rudolph de Harak.*

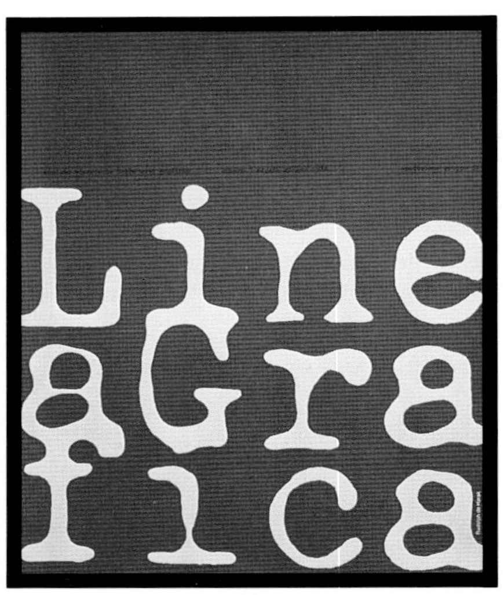

***Cover** for the Italian magazine,* Linea Grafica, *1976. Rudolph de Harak.*

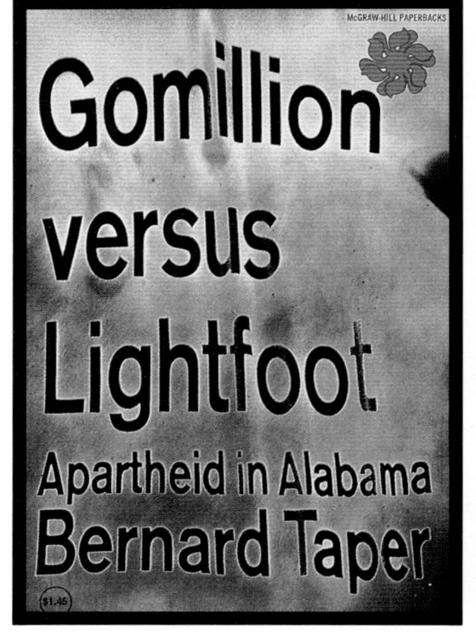

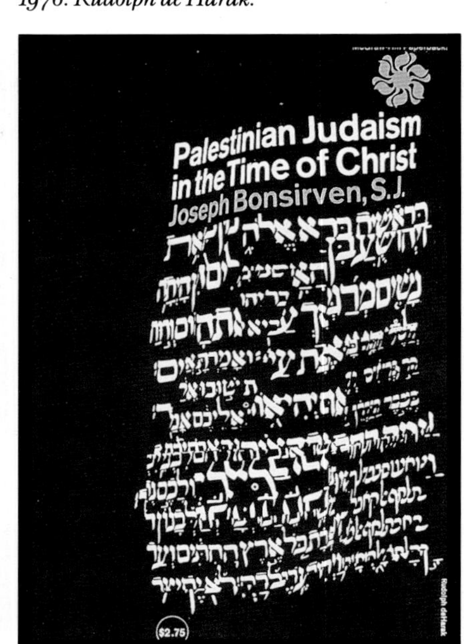

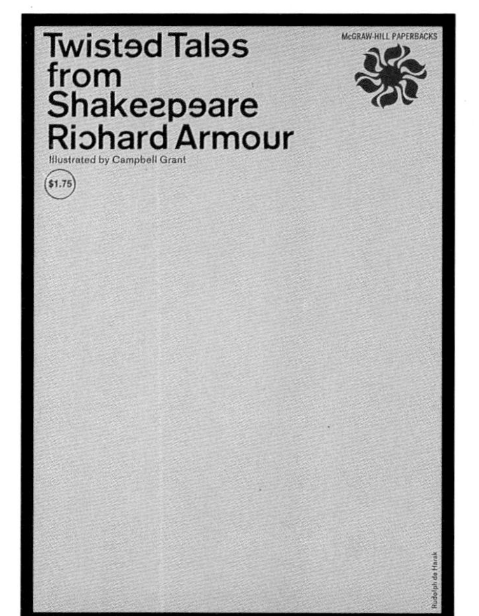

***McGraw-Hill book covers,** 1963-1965. Rudolph de Harak.*

Ivan Chermayeff

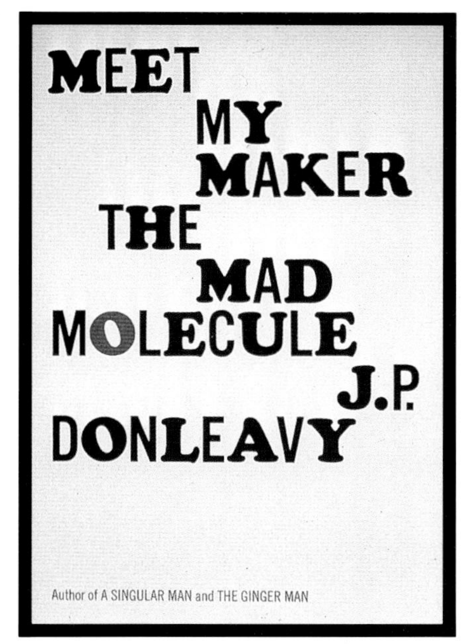

Book cover *designed by Ivan Chermayeff.*

Book cover *designed by Ivan Chermayeff.*

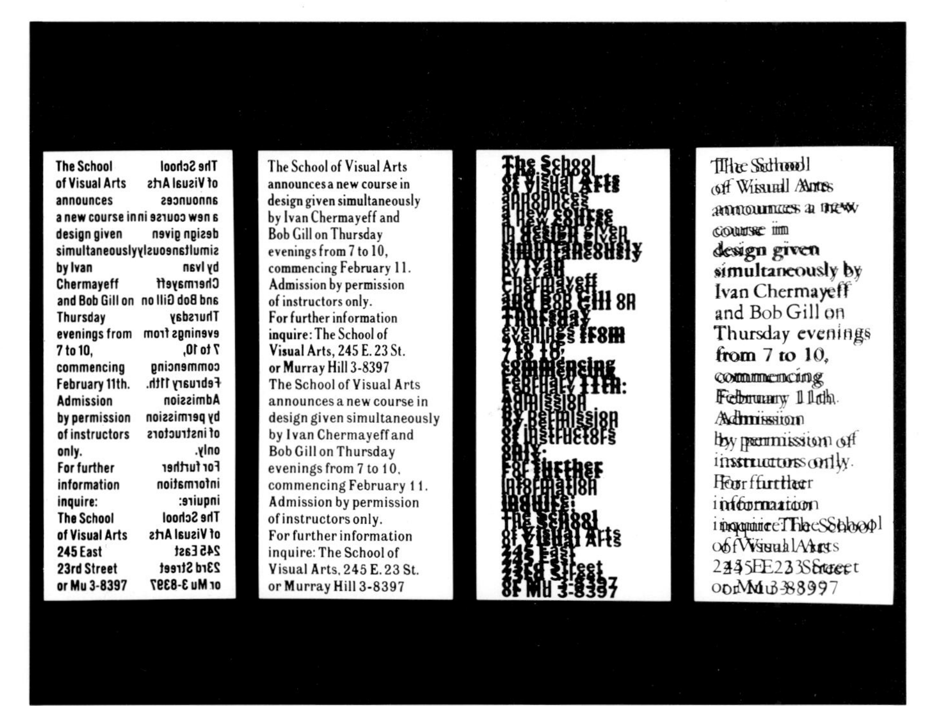

Announcement *of a new course in design at The School of Visual Arts, given by Ivan Chermayeff and Bob Gill. Design, Ivan Chermayeff.*

Book cover *designed by Ivan Chermayeff.*

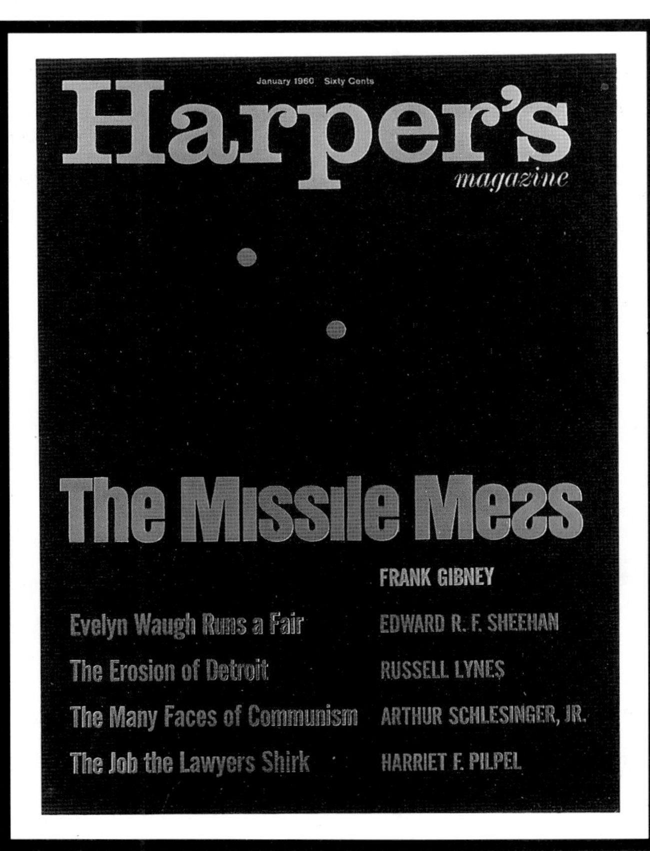

Harper's ***magazine cover,*** *1960. Ivan Chermayeff.*

Bob Farber

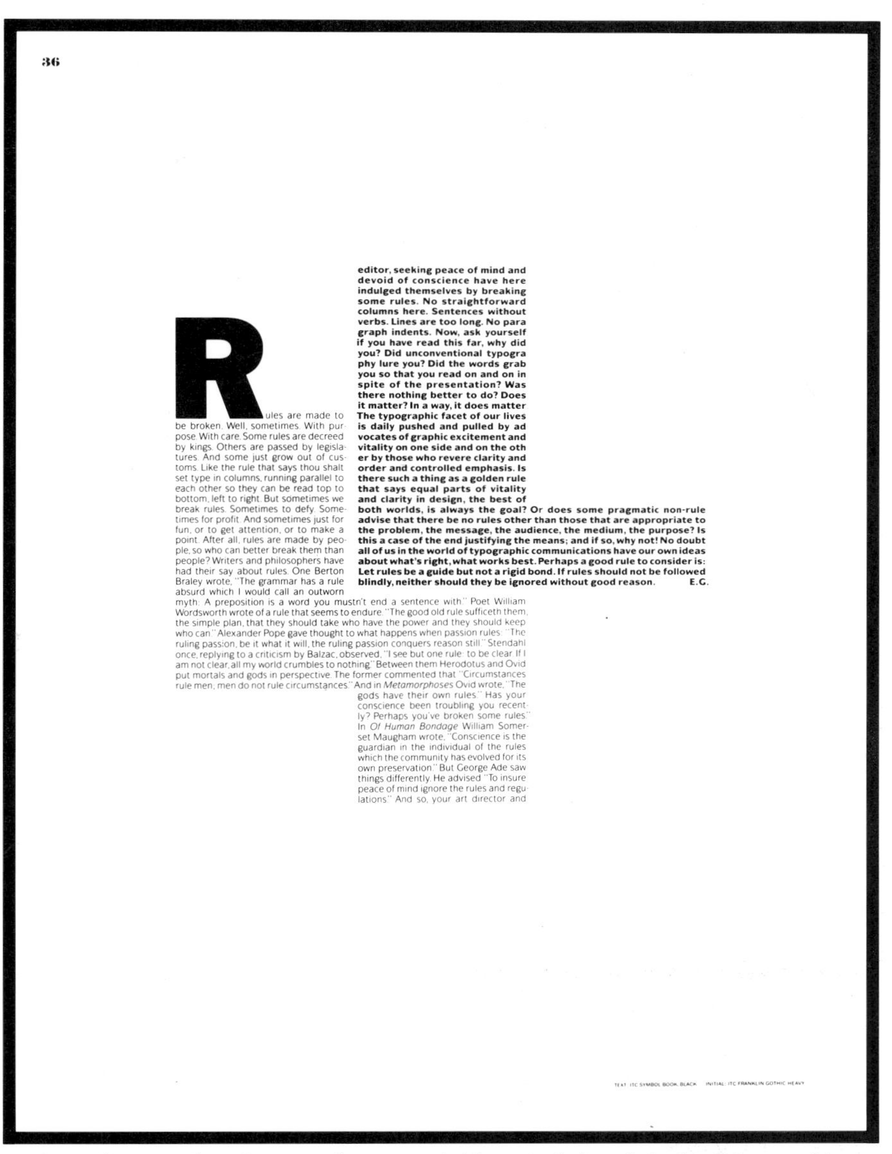

36

Rules are made to be broken. Well, sometimes. With purpose. With care. Some rules are decreed by kings. Others are passed by legislatures. And some just grow out of customs. Like the rule that says thou shalt set type in columns, running parallel to each other so they can be read top to bottom, left to right. But sometimes we break rules. Sometimes to defy. Sometimes for profit. And sometimes just for fun, or to get attention, or to make a point. After all, rules are made by people, so who can better break them than people? Writers and philosophers have had their say about rules. One Berton Braley wrote, "The grammar has a rule absurd which I would call an outworn myth: A preposition is a word you mustn't end a sentence with." Poet William Wordsworth wrote of a rule that seems to endure. "The good old rule sufficeth them, the simple plan, that they should take who have the power and they should keep who can." Alexander Pope gave thought to what happens when passion rules: "The ruling passion, be it what it will, the ruling passion conquers reason still." Stendahl once, replying to a criticism by Balzac, observed, "I see but one rule: to be clear. If I am not clear, all my world crumbles to nothing." Between them Herodotus and Ovid put mortals and gods in perspective. The former commented that "Circumstances rule men; men do not rule circumstances." And in *Metamorphoses* Ovid wrote, "The gods have their own rules." Has your conscience been troubling you recently? Perhaps you've broken some rules." In *Of Human Bondage* William Somerset Maugham wrote, "Conscience is the guardian in the individual of the rules which the community has evolved for its own preservation." But George Ade saw things differently. He advised "To insure peace of mind ignore the rules and regulations." And so, your art director and **editor, seeking peace of mind and devoid of conscience have here indulged themselves by breaking some rules. No straightforward columns here. Sentences without verbs. Lines are too long. No para graph indents. Now, ask yourself if you have read this far, why did you? Did unconventional typogra phy lure you? Did the words grab you so that you read on and on in spite of the presentation? Was there nothing better to do? Does it matter? In a way, it does matter. The typographic facet of our lives is daily pushed and pulled by ad vocates of graphic excitement and vitality on one side and on the oth er by those who revere clarity and order and controlled emphasis. Is there such a thing as a golden rule that says equal parts of vitality and clarity in design, the best of both worlds, is always the goal? Or does some pragmatic non-rule advise that there be no rules other than those that are appropriate to the problem, the message, the audience, the medium, the purpose? Is this a case of the end justifying the means; and if so, why not! No doubt all of us in the world of typographic communications have our own ideas about what's right, what works best. Perhaps a good rule to consider is: Let rules be a guide but not a rigid bond. If rules should not be followed blindly, neither should they be ignored without good reason. E.G.**

U&lc *art director Bob Farber wanted to set some bold type in the lap of a book weight type of the same face. He made the layout before the text was written.* U&lc *editor Ed Gottschall then wrote appropriate copy on the theme of "rules are made to be broken – but not without good reason."* 1985.

In a fun-with-type exercise, U&lc *art director Bob Farber created a series of designs for the March 1983 issue. Editor Ed Gottschall wrote the copy after seeing the designs. Several of the pages are shown below and on the following page.*

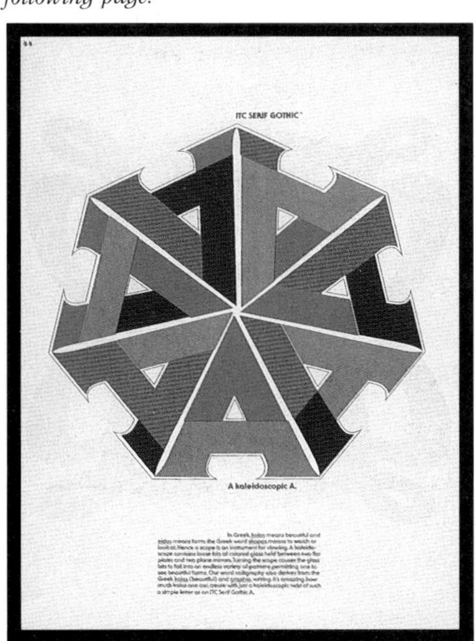

ITC ***Serif Gothic.®*** *Bob Farber.*

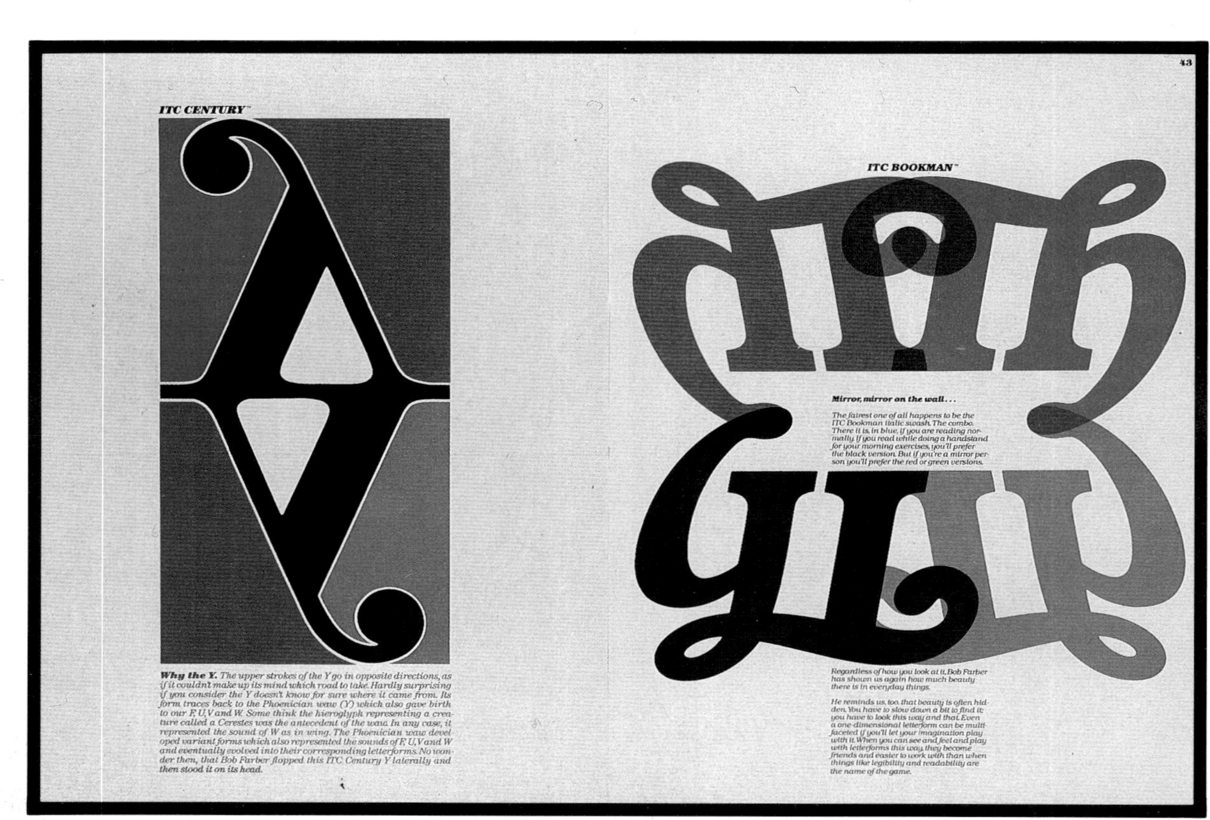

43

ITC CENTURY™

Why the Y. *The upper strokes of the Y go in opposite directions, as if it couldn't make up its mind which road to take. Hardly surprising if you consider the Y doesn't know for sure where it came from. Its form traces back to the Phoenician waw (Y) which also gave birth to our F, U, V and W. Some think the hieroglyph representing a creature called a Cerestes was the antecedent of the waw. In any case, it represented the sound of W as in wing. The Phoenician waw developed variant forms which also represented the sounds of F, U, V and W and eventually evolved into their corresponding letterforms. No wonder then, that Bob Farber flopped this ITC Century Y laterally and then stood it on its head.*

ITC BOOKMAN™

Mirror, mirror on the wall. . .

The fairest one of all happens to be the ITC Bookman italic swash. The combo. There it is, in blue, if you are reading normally. If you read while doing a handstand for your morning exercises, you'll prefer the black version. But if you're a mirror person you'll prefer the red or green versions.

Regardless of how you look at it, Bob Farber has shown us again how much beauty there is in everyday things.

He reminds us, too, that beauty is often hidden. You have to slow down a bit to find it; you have to look this way and that. Even a one-dimensional letterform can be multifaceted if you'll let your imagination play with it. When you can see and feel and play with letterforms this way, they become friends and easier to work with than when things like legibility and readability are the name of the game.

ITC **Century**.® *Bob Farber.*

ITC **Bookman**.® *Bob Farber.*

38

To hex people is to put an evil spell on them, to bewitch them. One sect of the Pennsylvania Dutch, the Mennonites (unlike the Amish), use hex signs on their barns and elsewhere to ward off the evil forces, a kind of witch insurance. They also have an expression that appeals to Bob Farber: "Just for pretty." When in southeastern Pennsylvania one day, he sought the reason for a colorful pattern on a local artifact and was told, "It's just for pretty." That's what Bob's exercise with the (ITC Tiffany) X's here is all about. Not to be read. Not to be analyzed. Just enjoyed. Just for pretty.

X, as in hex

ITC TIFFANY

39

This gracefully ornate ITC Barcelona™ ampersand is as full of curves as the origin of the symbol. The symbol, today, represents the word "and." But, once upon a time, our language was less direct, less concise. In certain circumstances, people used the expression "and per se and." Literally this meant "and by itself and." This mouthful was represented by space- and time-conscious people as &, and the expression tightened to the word "ampersand." The convoluted phrase not only became an efficient, function-oriented symbol but a point of fascination for typeface designers. The range of ampersand designs runs the gamut from streamlined to highly ornate. Ed Benguiat created two ampersands for ITC Barcelona.™ Both are graceful and totally curvilinear. ***U&lc art director Bob Farber chose the alternate or more elaborate one for this page.*** *He found it so beautiful, he just enlarged it, dressed it, like Joseph, in a coat of many colors, and let it float free for all to admire.*

The ampersand and its multicolored coat.

ITC BARCELONA™

ITC **Tiffany.** *Bob Farber.*

ITC **Barcelona**.® *Bob Farber.*

Otto Storch

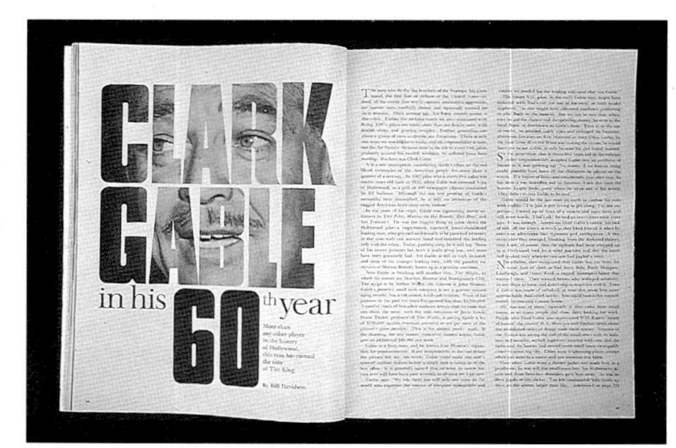

"I have always believed *that there is some kind of magic attached to some names and some words. It is a combination of the way the words look, their sound and the reinforcement of the image behind the words. In this layout it seemed only logical to put the man himself into his magical name." Otto Storch, art director,* McCall's *magazine.*

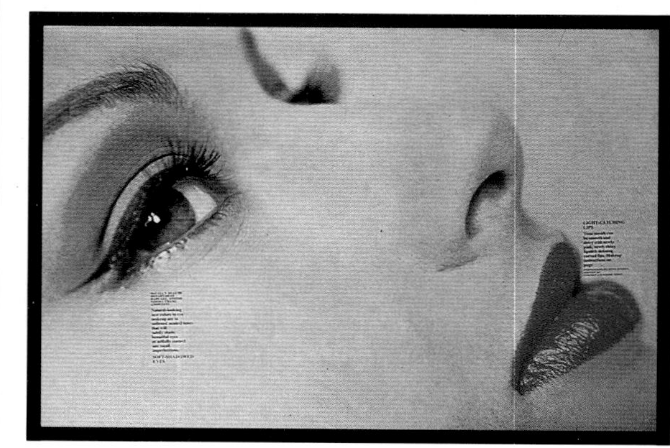

"The opening spread *of a cosmetic article. The make-up on eyes and lips is so 'eye-catching' visually, I decided that there would be greater impact and quicker reader assimilation if the picture were allowed to dominate the type." Otto Storch, art director,* McCall's *magazine.*

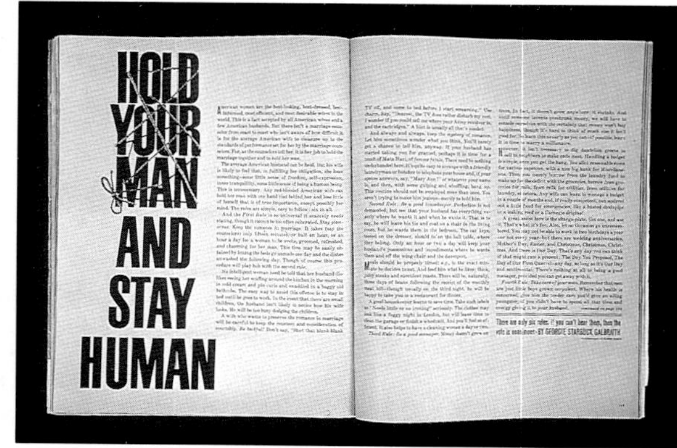

"At McCall's *I not only tried to pick the appropriate typeface for a particular article, but then we tried graphically to make it say more. I always thought of it as talking type." Otto Storch, art director,* McCall's *magazine.*

George Lois

The previous ad *in this campaign featured the Wolfschmidt bottle and a tomato. Art director George Lois explains, "Just one week after the Wolfschmidt bottle romanced the tomato, it got down to serious banter with an orange. This ad did something else that was unusual: it referred back to an ad that ran the week before, proving that one and one make three. Sam Bronfman, that sweet tyrant, looked at this ad crosseyed, not quite sure what to make of it. 'We're saying Wolfschmidt has taste,' I argued. 'We're saying oranges taste better when mixed with Wolfschmidt. We're saying people drink to have fun.'"*

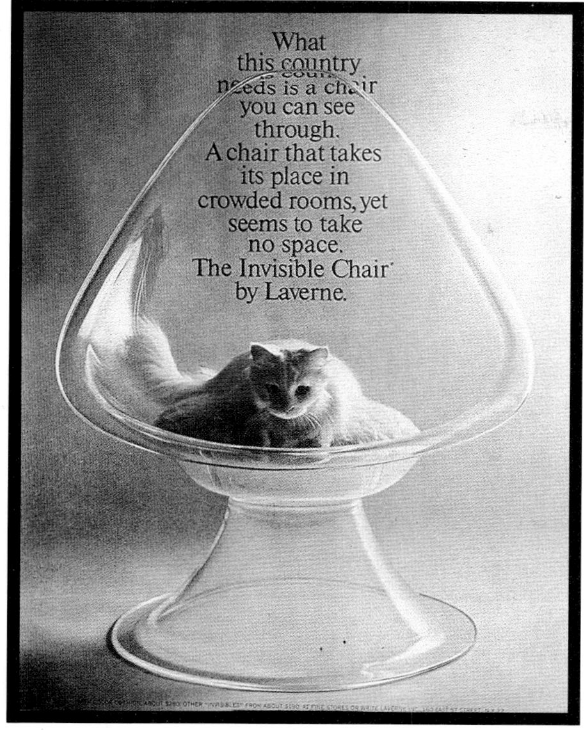

What better way *to illustrate a chair's transparency than to let the type be read through it? Typography at the heart of the message concept. Art director, George Lois.*

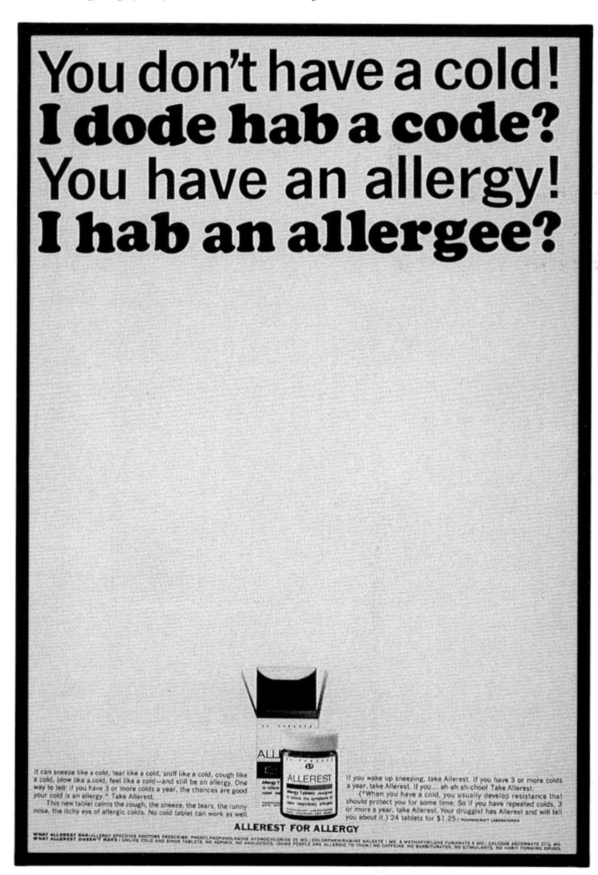

George Lois' advertisements, covers, etc., *are famous for their strong, crisp presentations of the message's primary statement. Often the art/photography carries the message, sometimes the headline does, sometimes both do. His handling of type is usually not tricky, but supportive of the message.*

Jacqueline Casey

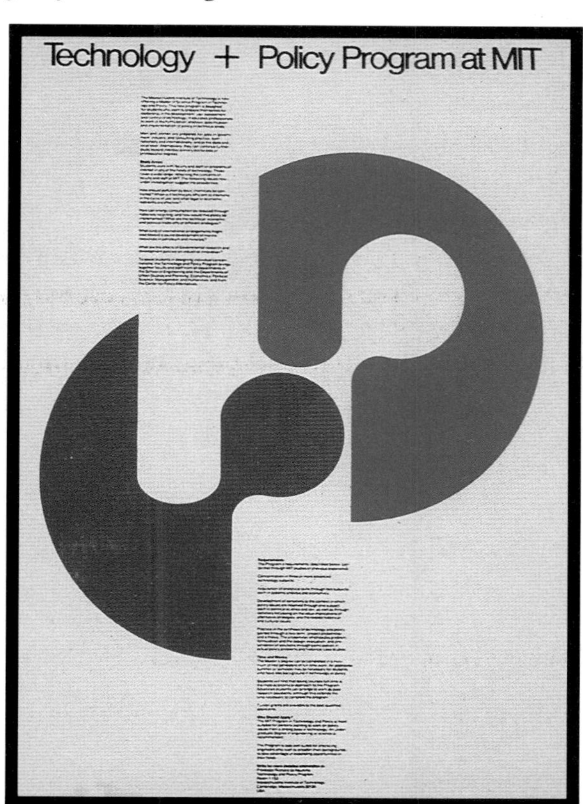

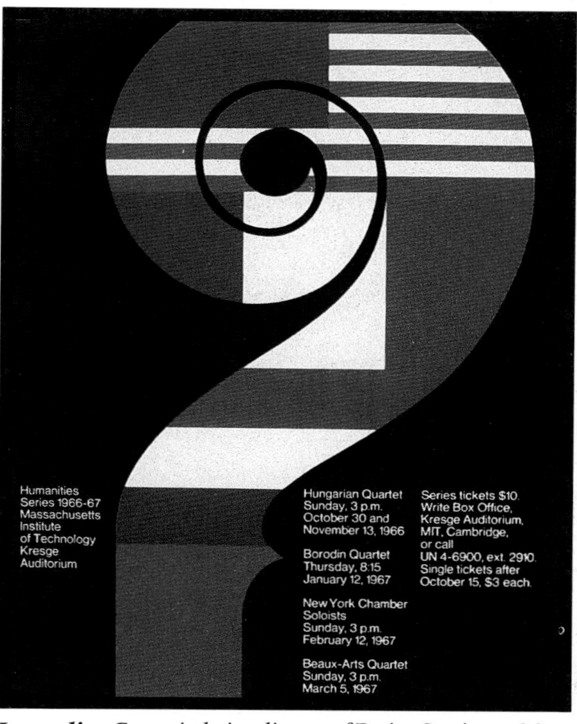

Jacqueline Casey *is design director of Design Services at Massachusetts Institute of Technology. These two examples of her work there, each using strong, solid colors, illustrate her search for graphic strength, directness, and simplicity.*

Seymour Chwast

This alphabet *was done for a book celebrating the 300th anniversary of Bach's birth, and is just for fun. Seymour Chwast.*

TYPOGRAPHIC COMMUNICATIONS TODAY
Chapter XIII: The Many Faces of Typography Today

***This piece** was done by Seymour Chwast and Chris Austopchuk for the Disaster issue of the* Push Pin Graphic. *The letterforms illustrate the meaning of the words and are a visual interpretation of the particular disasters.*

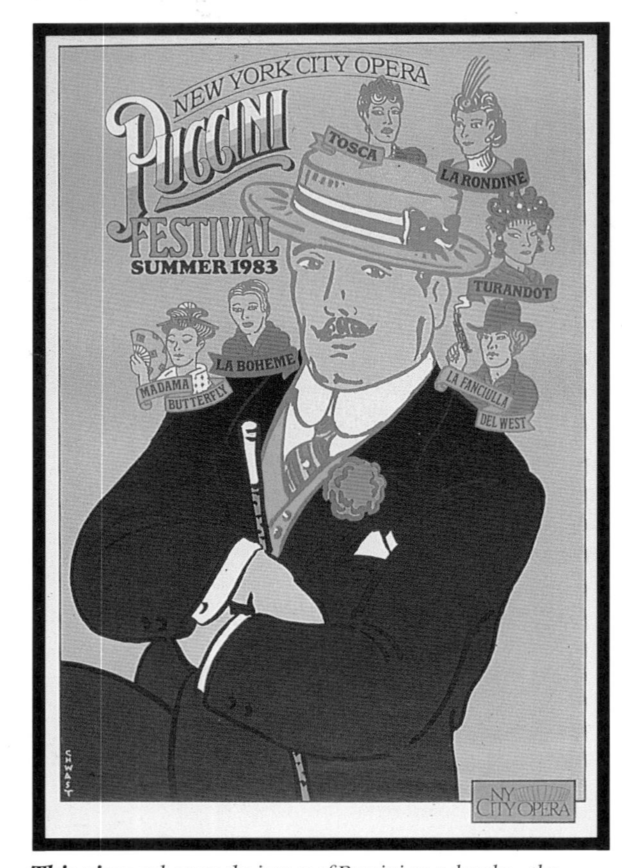

***This piece** enhances the image of Puccini as a dandy – the type is flourishy, and makes a visual note of the operas to be performed. Seymour Chwast.*

***The type styling** here is a combination of art deco influence and Russian constructivism. The O in Nitespots functions as both an O and an illustration of the product. Seymour Chwast.*

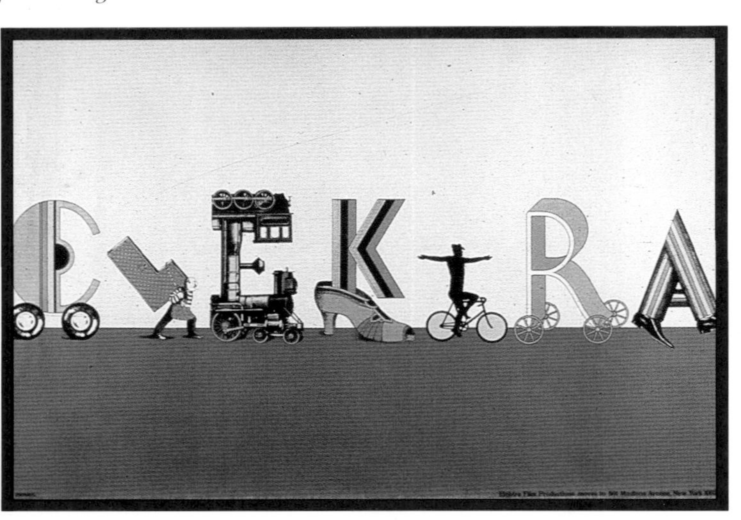

***This series** of letterforms was done for Elektra Films as a moving announcement poster. Each letterform is an illustration of a different type of locomotion, and each is one of an assortment of objects, as the contents of a move so often are. Seymour Chwast.*

Steff Geissbuhler

***Butazolidin** piece for J. R. Geigy, Switzerland. Steff Geissbuhler.*

***A capability brochure** cover for the J. R. Geigy propaganda department. Steff Geissbuhler.*

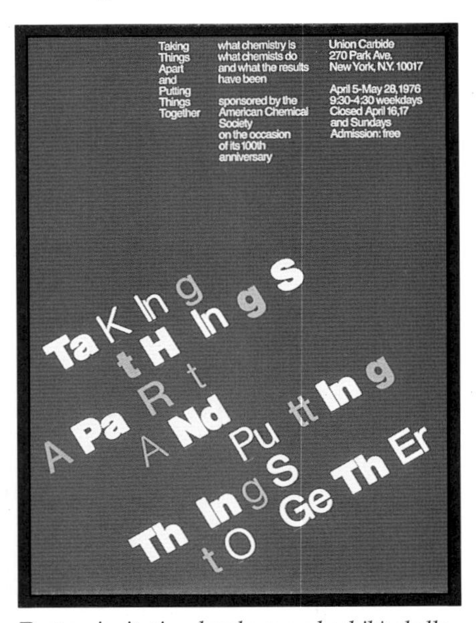

***Poster,** invitation, brochure and exhibit shells for the American Chemical Society 100 Year Anniversary exhibit. "Playing around with the title, quite by accident the words were taken apart and became chemical formulas. In a way it illustrated the title as well as the essence of chemistry." Steff Geissbuhler.*

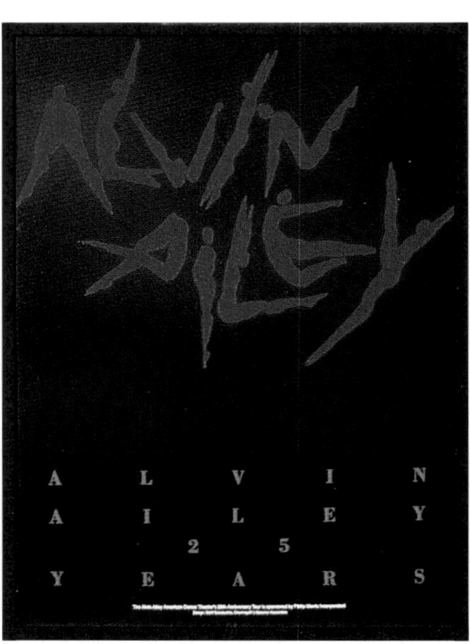

*"**The client** was looking for an identity for the group, rather than an image of a single dancer. The name Alvin Ailey was written figuratively with brush strokes, thus creating the identity of name and group. The bottom type suggests an audience and static order as opposed to dance." Steff Geissbuhler.*

Alan Peckolick

IBM Office Furniture Catalog. *On the cover, the five sections of the catalog are represented by overlapping and fragmenting the numbers, as if one could see through the book. Each section divider shows the same configuration as the cover, but only highlights the specific number and section in color. The fragmentation of the numbers reminds one of floor plans, office configurations, furniture details, fitting together of parts, etc. Various sequential progressions in gray and color make the image each time different and playful. Steff Geissbuhler.*

"This poster *was designed as a preface to a portfolio of posters done by Herb Lubalin, to be used as a fund-raiser for the Lubalin Study Center. I wanted to do something with very clean, contemporary looking typography, that would be arresting but in keeping with the posters in the portfolio, which were done in various type styles." Alan Peckolick.*

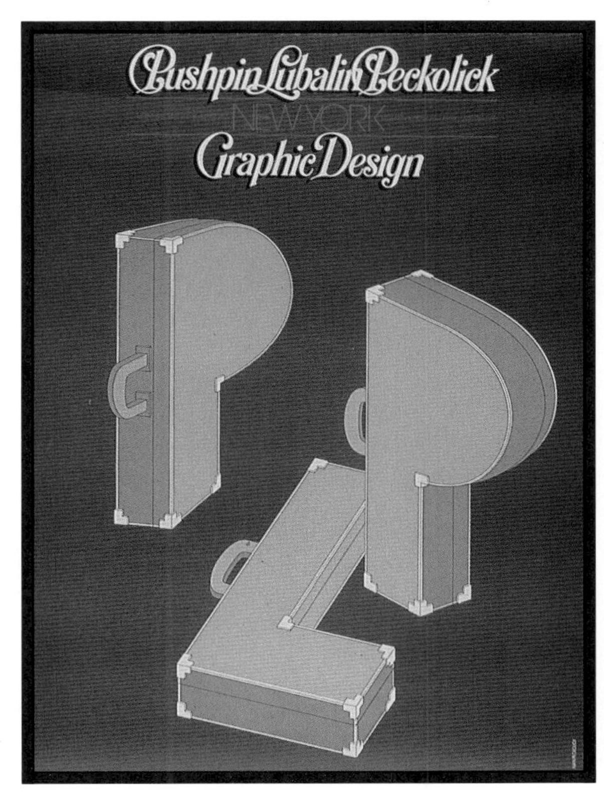

"This poster *was done to announce a show of work by Pushpin Lubalin Peckolick in Wiesbaden, Germany. I chose to use the initials of the company and turn them into luggage to reinforce the company name and to convey the idea of this being a show of work from a New York firm which had traveled to Germany." Alan Peckolick.*

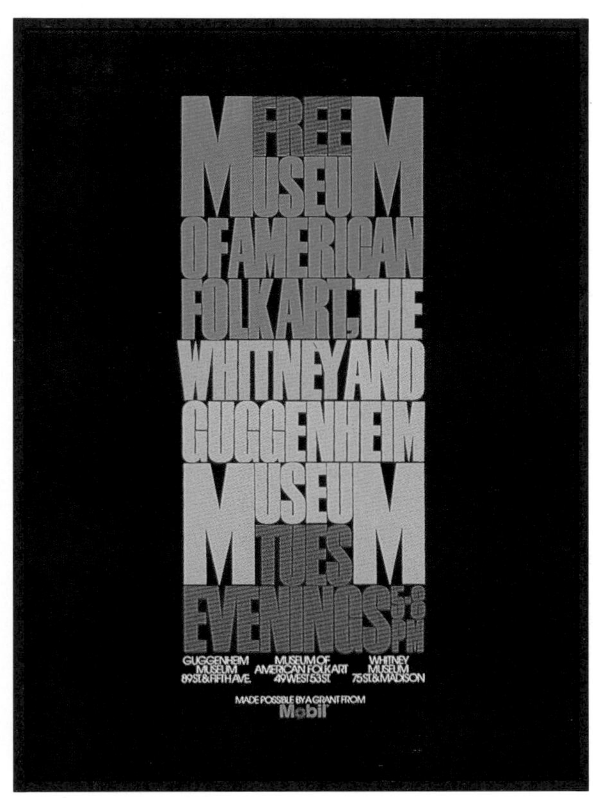

Free Tuesdays bus shelter poster. *"This was to announce Mobil's support of keeping museums open in the evenings. I chose to do a typographic poster that would convey all the necessary information regarding which museum, and which hours, etc., but would also represent a piece of art that might hang in one of the museums. The use of color and the elongated shapes suggested by the letter forms are reminiscent of a hard-edged modern art piece." Alan Peckolick.*

All For Love poster. *"This bus shelter poster was done as an announcement for a series of plays on Masterpiece Theatre. The plays all dealt with the theme of love, but showcased different kinds of love: i.e., parental, romantic, etc. I chose to utilize the dictionary definitions for all the words in the series title to express the idea of the variety of possible interpretations of a single word or concept, in this case, love." Alan Peckolick.*

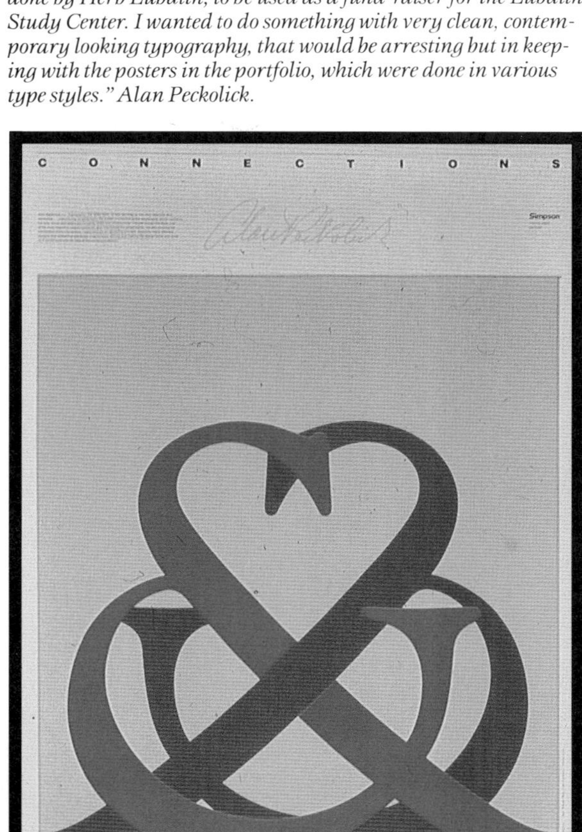

"This poster *is one of a series of posters done by various designers on the theme of 'connections.' I interpreted the word typographically with the ampersand, which is the connector of words and ideas." Alan Peckolick.*

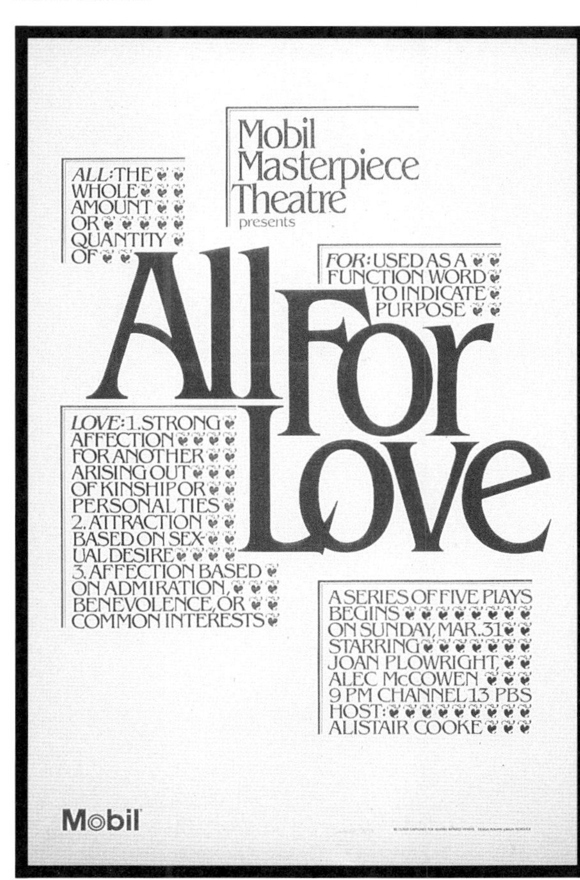

Mo Lebowitz

CBS
OWNED
STATIONS
WE POINT WITH PRIDE & THINK YOU'LL BE INTERESTED IN:

Television Stations' "Project Working"

Among the CBS Owned Television Stations' most successful demonstrations of commitment to their communities have been yearly "station projects." These projects focus on a single social issue through special public affairs broadcasts, public service announcements and editorials, even, when warranted, reports in regularly scheduled news broadcasts. Projects have included such topics as crime, parenting, the family, education, the First Amendment and aging.

"Project Working" is this year's project, focusing on all aspects of employment: how to find a job; how to keep it; how to get a better one; job satisfaction and dissatisfaction; training programs for youth; how to choose the right career; women in the work force; and careers for people over 65.

Journalists Prefer CBS AM Operations

The special credibility of the CBS AM Group's five all news stations was recently underscored when working journalists in each market were asked what stations they turned to most for news. The journalists favored the CBS AM news operations by an average 2 to 1 margin in the surveyed cities of Boston, New York, Chicago, San Francisco and Los Angeles.

The Roper surveys also picked up a number of

All Five Television Stations Honored

Once again this year the CBS Television Stations have received top honors.

A Peabody Award went to WBBM-TV for its investigative series "KILLING CRIME: A POLICE COP-OUT" (see story on page 7).

Among other first place honors for outstanding

- Frisco Rocker Unemployed. P. 11
- Getting Ticketed Means Getting Help. P. 3
- Governor Kean Visits. P. 6
- Health Fair Helps Children. P. 1
- Hispanic Media Skills Bank. P. 13
- Hitradio = Community Radio. P. 10
- In Praise of Heroes and Heroines. P. 14
- Hunter Citizen of the Year. P. 10
- Kids 2 Kids. P. 14
- KMOX-AM Breaks Sex Barrier. P. 10
- KNX-FM Documentary Honored. P. 13
- KNX-FM vs. Unemployment. P. 14
- "Kup" Salute. P. 8
- Los Angeles Station Contacts. P. 14
- Magazine Radio. P. 12
- New Jersey Office Opened. P. 4
- New York Station Contacts. P. 4
- Penny Vote for Multiple Sclerosis. P. 5
- Philadelphia Station Contacts. P. 6
- Probe of Police Gets Results. P. 7
- Rock + Frisbee = Blood. P. 11
- San Francisco Station Contacts. P. 12
- St. Louis Station Contacts. P. 9
- Talking to Ten. P. 5
- THURSDAY'S CHILD Gets Results. P. 3
- 'St. Louis' Voice' = 1,400 Answers. P. 9
- Washington Contacts. Back Cover
- WHTT: A New Voice in Boston. P. 2

CBS owned stations. *"An 19-page newsletter that the client wanted to look, and be, full of news. The use of the ruled format, the ITC American Typewriter Bold Condensed with the 10 point Century Expanded on a narrow measure and set flush left, help give the page snap with readability." Mo Lebowitz.*

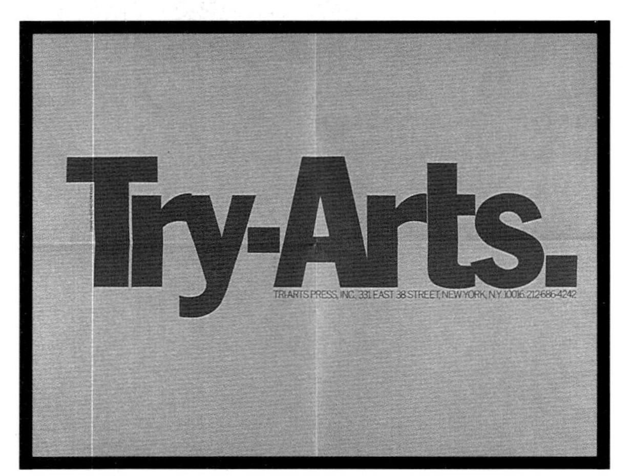

Try-Arts. *"The simplest thing I can ever remember doing. The copy, concept and typographic treatment are one and the same. Because of the type size, letter and word spacing were of even more importance than usual." Mo Lebowitz.*

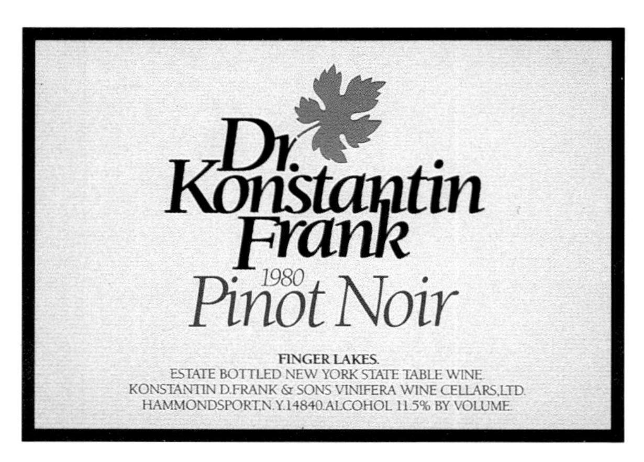

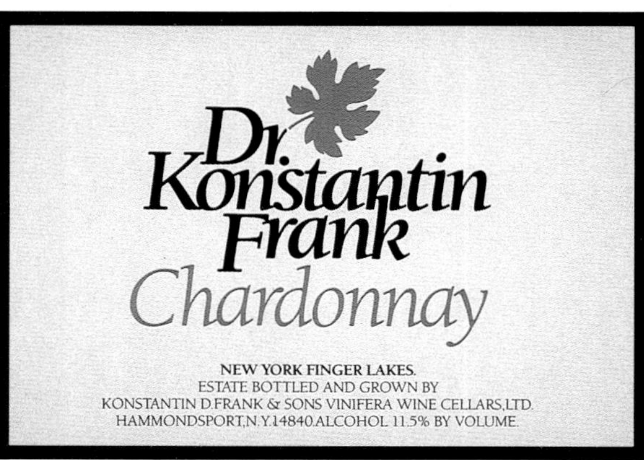

Dr. Frank Wine labels. *"Good wine label typography is usually simple. The size limits placed on the designer by the state and national governments make doing a label even more difficult, so simplicity is a must. These labels were meant to update an old name and to give the wine good shelf attention, as well as to look good on a restaurant table. I used only one typeface: ITC Berkeley Oldstyle, which seems to have the nice combination of looking classic as well as modern." Mo Lebowitz.*

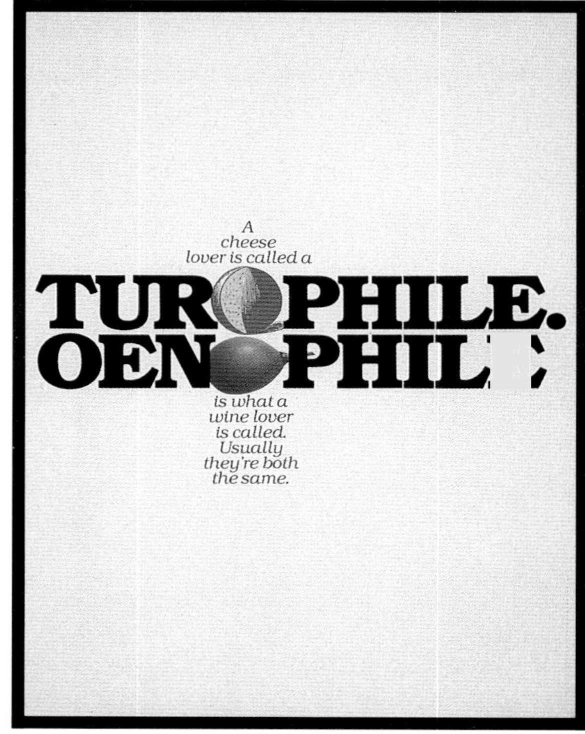

***"A 16-page brochure** used to show how ITC Bookman looks in actual settings. Big type, small type, narrow and wide margins, columns of copy, reverses, overprints and more, were needed to demonstrate the face." Mo Lebowitz.*

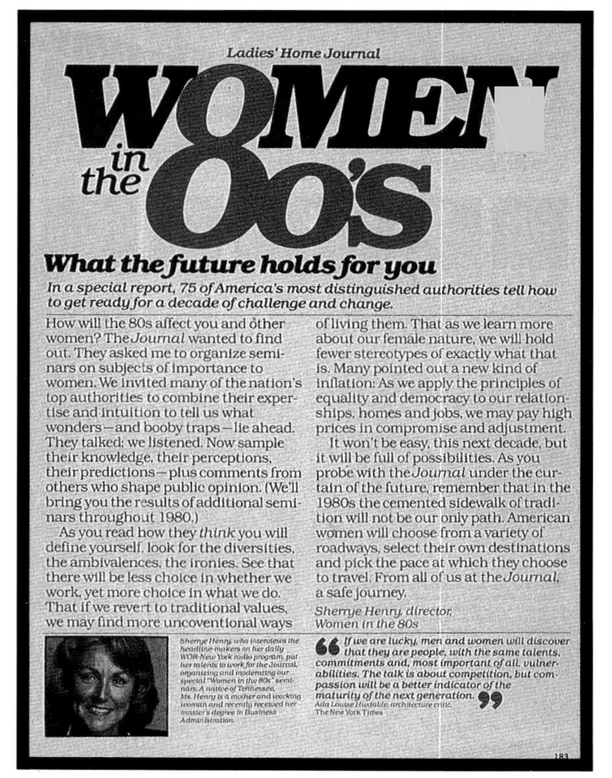
Ladies' Home Journal

in the 80's

What the future holds for you

In a special report, 75 of America's most distinguished authorities tell how to get ready for a decade of challenge and change.

How will the 80s affect you and other women? The *Journal* wanted to find out. They asked me to organize seminars on subjects of importance to women. We invited many of the nation's top authorities to combine their expertise and intuition to tell us what wonders—and booby traps—lie ahead. They talked; we listened. Now sample their knowledge, their perceptions, their predictions—plus comments from others who shape public opinion. (We'll bring you the results of additional seminars throughout 1980.)

As you read how they *think* you will define yourself, look for the diversities, the ambivalences, the ironies. See that there will be less choice in whether we work, yet more choice in what we do. That if we revert to traditional values, we may find more unconventional ways of living them. That as we learn more about our female nature, we will hold fewer stereotypes of exactly what that is. Many pointed out a new kind of inflation: As we apply the principles of equality and democracy to our relationships, homes and jobs, we may pay high prices in compromise and adjustment.

It won't be easy, this next decade, but it will be full of possibilities. As you probe with the *Journal* under the curtain of the future, remember that in the 1980s the cemented sidewalk of tradition will not be our only path. American women will choose from a variety of roadways, select their own destinations and pick the pace at which they choose to travel. From all of us at the *Journal*, a safe journey.

Sherrye Henry, director,
Women in the 80s

Sherrye Henry, who interviews the headline-makers on her daily WOR-New York radio program, put her talents to work for the Journal, organizing and moderating our special "Women in the 80s" seminars. A native of Tennessee, Ms. Henry is a mother and working woman and recently received her master's degree in Business Administration.

"If we are lucky, men and women will discover that they are people, with the same talents, commitments and, most important of all, vulnerabilities. The talk is about competition, but compassion will be a better indicator of the maturity of the next generation."
Ada Louise Huxtable, architecture critic,
The New York Times

Women in the '80s. *"An 8-page magazine insert for* The Ladies' Home Journal. *Again, only one typeface: ITC Bookman. But it has all the necessary variations to answer the problem. Lots of quotes, blurbs and photos had to all hang together and make some visual sense. Most important here are the spaces not filled with words." Mo Lebowitz.*

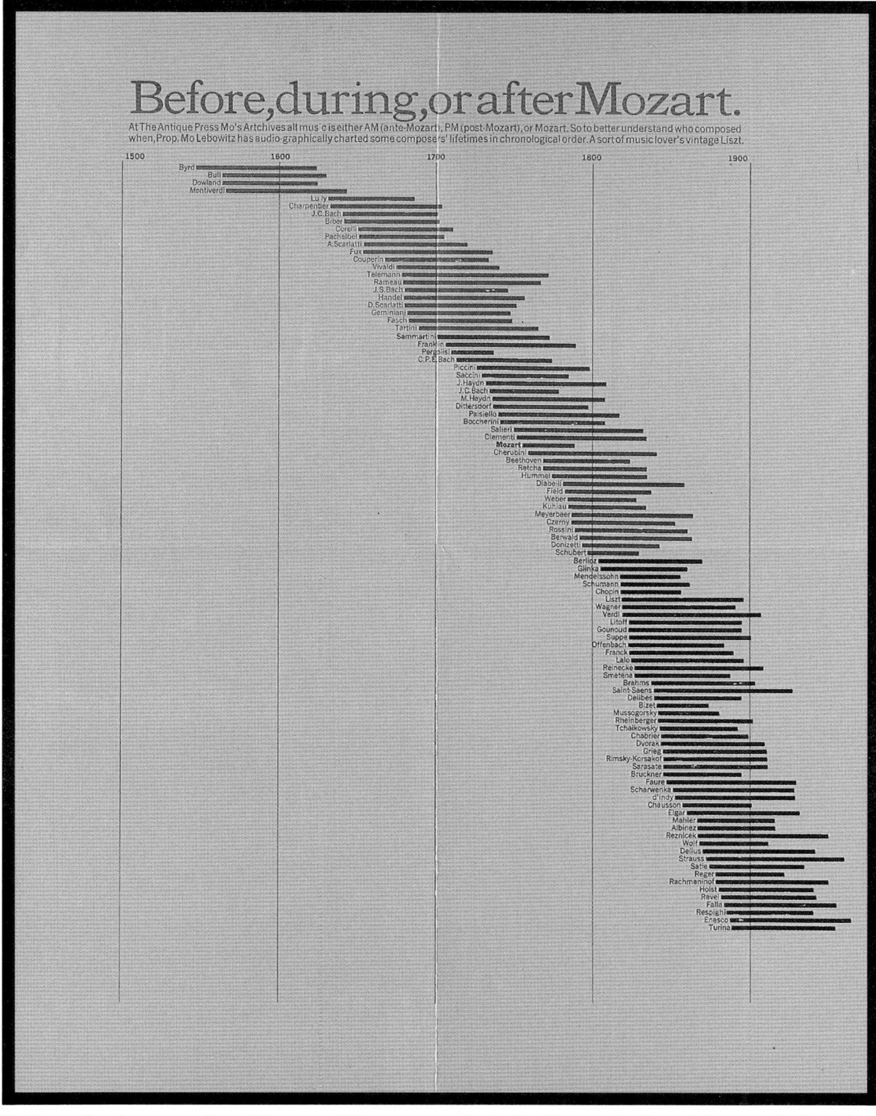

Before, during, or after Mozart. *"The typography is the illustration here. The use of rules is most important so the reader can scan the poster from top to bottom and see how the composers' lives overlapped. This was produced on a proofpress using metal types and rules." Mo Lebowitz.*

"This design, *to coordinate all graphics for the Piccolo Teatro di Milano, tends to reach an expression of identity through a highly organized structure of information, using only red and black as color identity. It is the beginning of the definition of our 'style,' defined by the consistent use of thick bars to separate bands of information." Massimo Vignelli.*

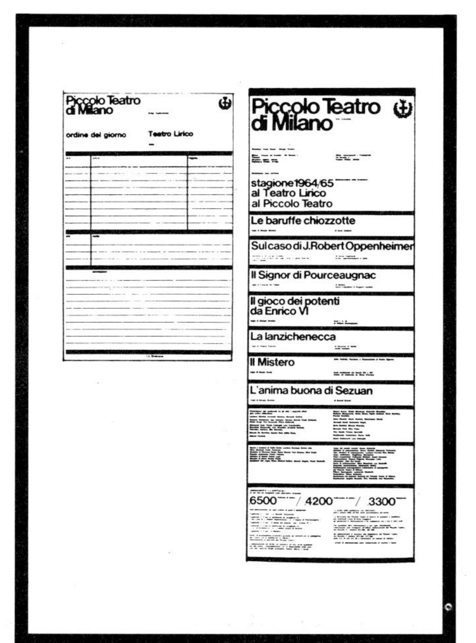

Parsons School of Design Exhibition announcement. *"The type is set in a classical rhetorical way – all centered, all caps, all Bodoni. The paper is tissue, crumpled after the printing, and was mailed that way. By this gesture, the rhetoric becomes more ambiguous and the balance is restored." Massimo Vignelli.*

Massimo Vignelli

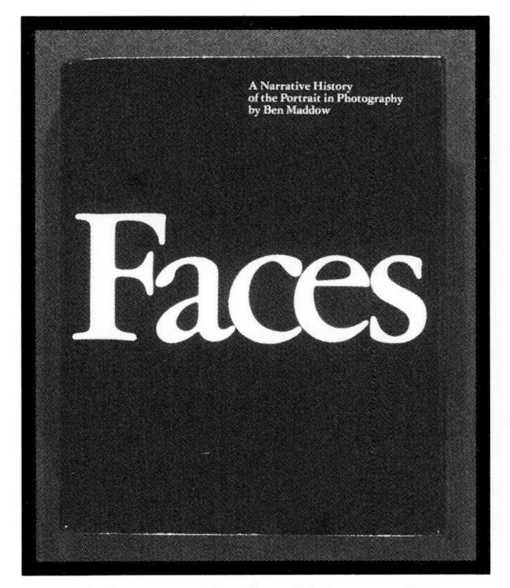

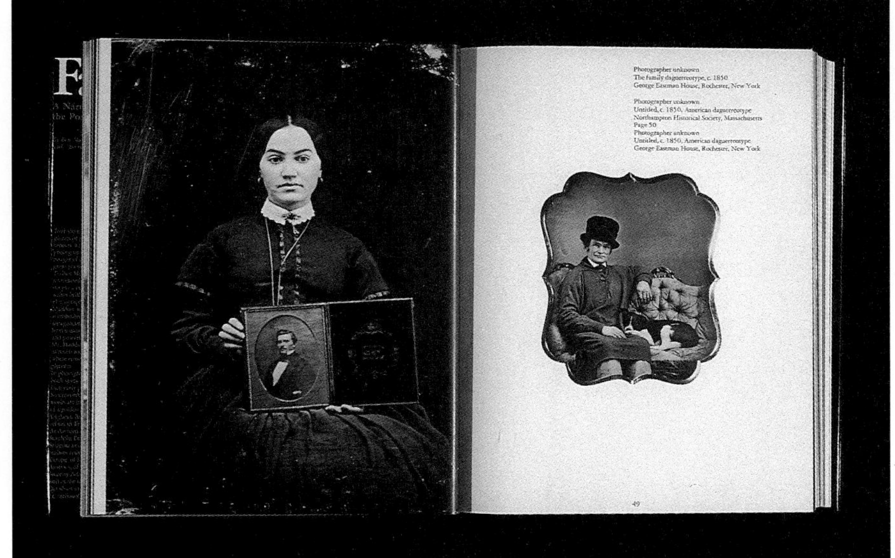

"One of the many books *which exemplify our approach to book design: simple, forceful, and unobtrusive layouts. On the cover the title has been simplified to increase its impact: from* A Narrative History of the Portrait in Photography *to* Faces, *which allows the designer to play with type and get the message across fast and powerfully. The inside layout is simple: full pages, spreads, and little pictures at the center of the pages, A Vignelli hallmark." Massimo Vignelli.*

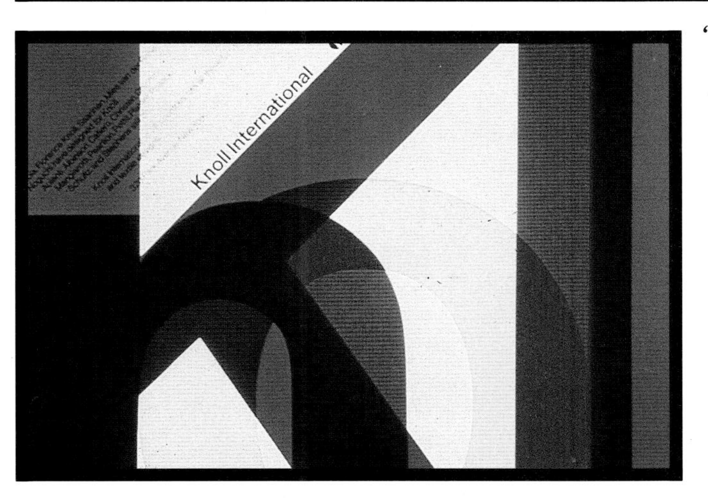

"The overlaying *of the color of the letters of the word 'Knoll' creates a colorful message related to the extensive use of primary colors in the Knoll products." Massimo Vignelli.*

*"**The design** of this monthly paper of architecture expresses structure and impact through its forceful layout and strong use of black lines and large headline typesizes. The covers stress identity and diversity." Massimo Vignelli.*

*"**This poster** for the New York Institute of Architecture and Urban Studies (IAUS) reflects the overall graphic style we designed for them. (*Skyline *was one of their publications, too.) This poster organizes the text in horizontal bands and four columns to force the message. The scale of images creates the contrast that gives impact to this poster." Massimo Vignelli.*

B. Martin Pedersen

Images. *"I received some splendid photographs from Anne and David Dubilet. I wanted to capture the readers' attention with them. On the subsequent spreads, I featured the photos large with the typography playing a secondary role to complement the photos." B. Martin Pedersen.*

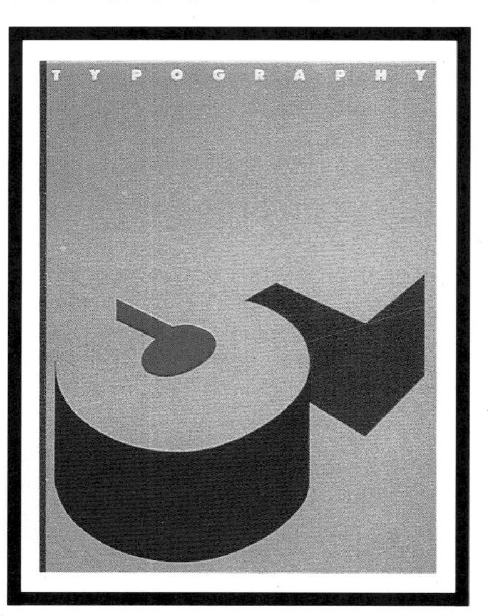

Typography 5, *the annual book of the Type Directors Club exhibition. "I felt that by three-dimensionalizing the numeral 5 and then laying it on its side and applying different colors to the shadow areas, I could achieve an interesting poster-like effect for the cover." B. Martin Pedersen.*

U&lc *flight cover.* *"For a tabloid whose main function is to display type, I thought it would be interesting to attempt to integrate the eagle with the typography and cause tension by having the eagle's talon grasping the type as if it were prey." B. Martin Pedersen.*

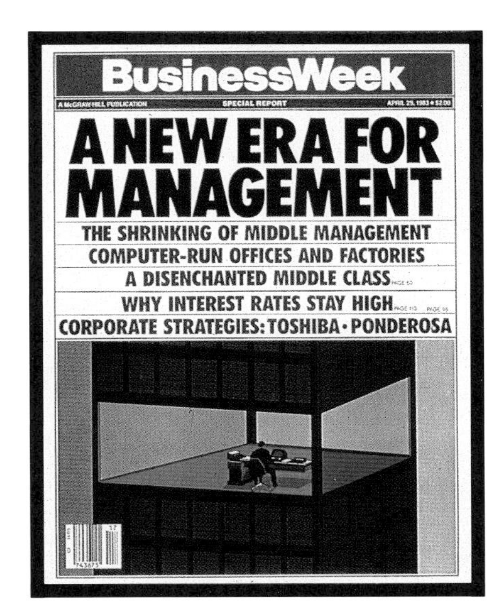

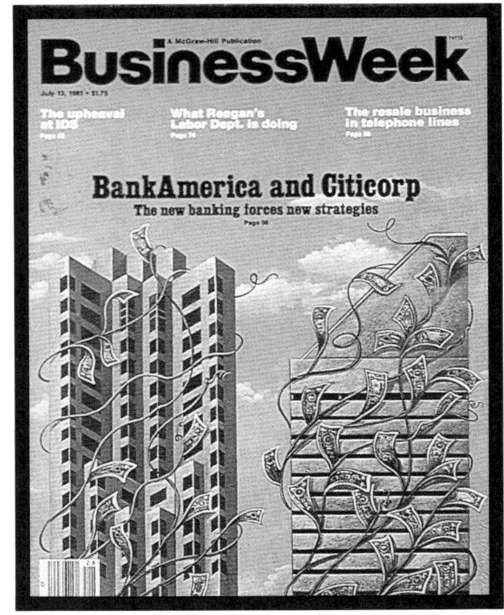

BusinessWeek. *"The problem, given to me by Lew Young, editor, was to give* BusinessWeek *high visibility on the newsstand. Their present cover was totally lost due to both mediocre art, which was partially a budget problem, and also the cover art director's preference for dark colors. My analysis of newsstands was that most magazines were 4-color bleed art all vying with each other for attention. What struck me as the most visible 'sell' from a distance was* The Daily News *and* The Post. *I thought, therefore, to apply a tabloid approach with b/w headline type for contrast, thus reducing the size and responsibility of the art on the cover, resulting in a greater emphasis to the editorial sell." B. Martin Pedersen.*

U&lc *spread*, *The Wright Stuff. "An attention-getting headline used with typefaces that were chosen to complement the art." B. Martin Pedersen.*

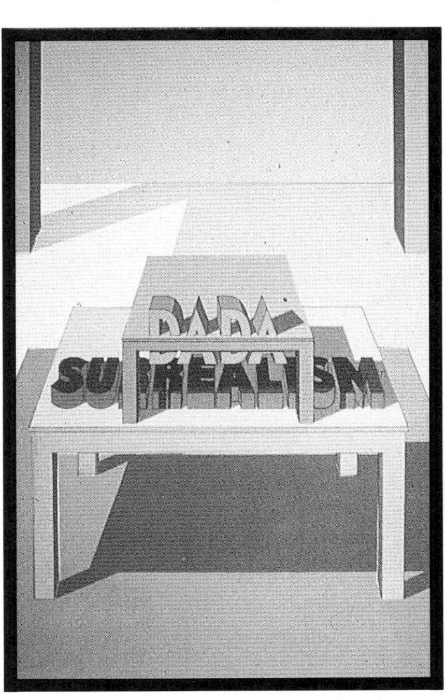

Poster *for an exhibition at MoMA (NY). Poster was never used. Milton Glaser.*

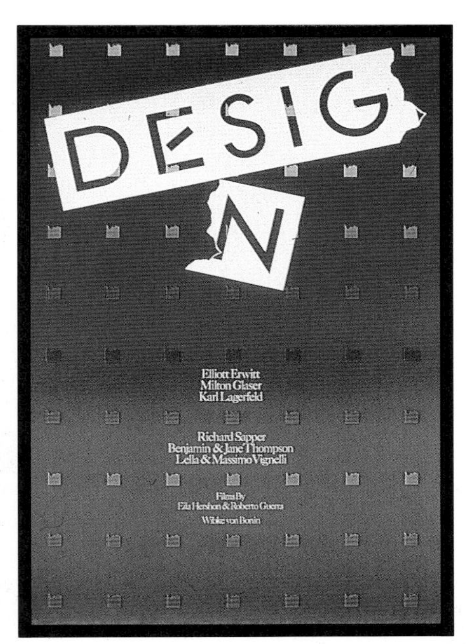

Poster *for Cable TV series on designers, 1983. Milton Glaser.*

Milton Glaser

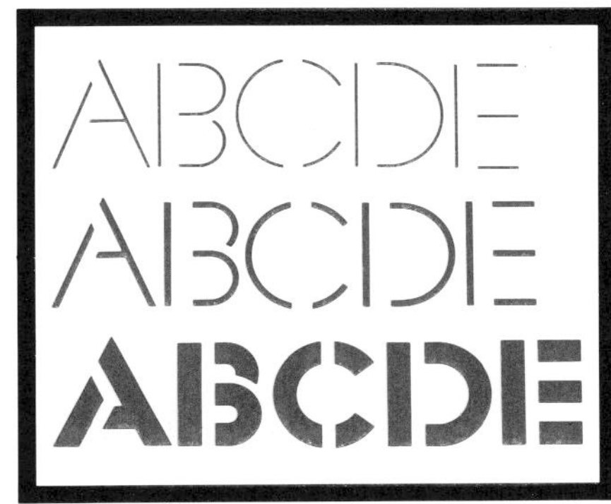

Page *of Neo Futura type from the* Milton Glaser Graphic Design Book.

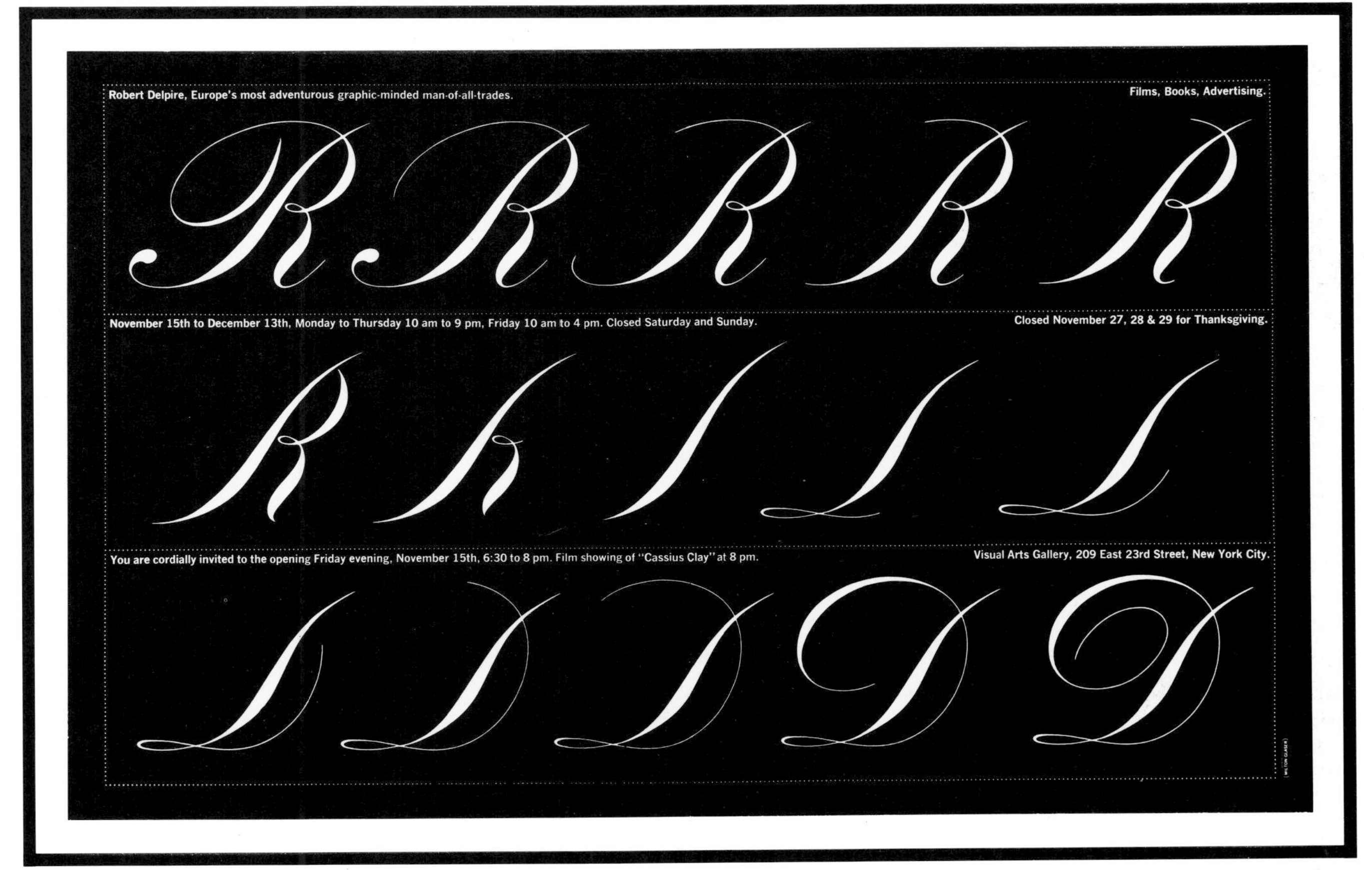

Poster *publicizing an exhibition of the work of Robert Delpire at the School of Visual Arts Gallery. Milton Glaser.*

TYPOGRAPHIC COMMUNICATIONS TODAY

Chapter XIV: Thoughts About Yesterday, Today, and Tomorrow

"It is this writer's position that despite all the wonders a computer can perform, it cannot and will not replace designers."

TYPOGRAPHIC COMMUNICATIONS TODAY is primarily concerned with communication graphics and the role of typography in it. But communication has many facets. We may want to communicate facts, ideas, attitudes, ethics or moods. We may want to convince, to sway, to entertain, to calm, to enrage. We may want to communicate some combination of these. The art/science of effective communication is a blend of languages: words, symbols, graphics, sounds, the body/facial language of the performing arts, the structure of drama or of opera or ballet, for example.

In printed communication the portion carrying the words relies on typography, the choice and use of typefaces, to enhance the information conveyed by the words, to clothe the words most appropriately and most effectively, so that they will accomplish their assigned mission. Of course, non-verbal elements (illustrations, charts, tables, etc.) and the design combine with the typographic elements to achieve the communication goal. Ideally all the elements, verbal and visual, will serve to reinforce each other.

Throughout this work we have frequently used the term typographic design. We consider the designer, like an architect, to be one who conceives and develops the master plan or concept and oversees its execution. "Typographic design," as we have used the term, refers to the creation, selection and arrangement of graphic elements to form an effective piece of communication in which typography plays an important role.

A Panoramic View

A panoramic view of the past 100 years of typography reveals the ebb and flow of designers' relative emphasis on vitality or clarity in their work. No doubt most designers feel that what they do is best suited, most appropriate, to the message problems they handle. This writer has a bias toward typographic design that captures the best of both worlds, that is both vigorous and lucid.

True, it is impossible not to notice the unexpected. But attracting attention is only the first step in the communication process, and if confusion or obscurity follow, then the eye-stopping devices have overpowered the message they were designed to empower. On the other hand, clarity and order alone are rarely enough. If a piece is boring or indistinguishable from many others, it may lack the power to attract maximum readership or make a deep and memorable impression.

Just as speakers and writers have tones of voice and style that can be modified as necessary, so typographic designers have a wide range of design devices to choose from. They can be whimsical, dramatic, fashionable, analytical, bold, subdued, stylized or stylistically neutral, research-focused or intuitive, as the occasion demands. All these and many other visual tones of voice are employed today. They co-exist with the full spectrum of emphasis on clarity and/or vitality in visual communications. In that sense one might say there are no trends because so many seemingly different design approaches flourish together. But there are some developments or trends worth noting.

Design as a Profession

Until early in the 20th century, graphics were created by specialized craftsmen such as layout artists, letterers, printers, engravers, typesetters, illustrators, all administratively coordinated by a manager. It was in the 1930s that industrial designers such as Walter Dorwin Teague, Norman Bel Geddes, Raymond Loewy and Henry Dreyfuss sold American business executives on the concept that the eye-appeal of a product affects its success in the market. It was around this time, too, that groups such as New York's Art Directors Club and the American Institute of Graphic Arts made their influence felt. They focused management's attention on high standards of art, on the importance of art and design in effective communication, and on the key role of art directors and designers. Conferences such as the International Design Conference in Aspen, organizations such as ICOGRADA and AGI (Alliance Graphique Internationale) and the outstanding design work of several major corporations and advertising agencies gave impetus to the recognition of design as a profession. Professional societies for industrial designers, package designers, art directors, type directors and others, proliferated.

Today we have large consulting firms handling corporate identity programs, studios of all sizes providing a wide range of services, and advertising designers and art directors working independently or in advertising agencies and corporate departments.

Design today is an established corporate department alongside marketing, accounting, legal, and other operational departments. And in recent decades design schools have proliferated in the United States, adding to the number and caliber of young designers entering the job market.

While design and designers are now accepted and highly regarded in business circles, design, unlike architecture, medicine, or law, is not a licensed profession.

Aimed Design

Today's typographic design, more than ever before, is carefully aimed to achieve targeted objectives. Designer Vance Jonson writes that what we once called "commercial art or design" and later called "marketing or communications design" should now be thought of as "strategic communication design." Visual and verbal symbols are at least as crucial to a message's impact as is the literal, obvious message. Jonson regards typographic communication today as "an art and a science. It is combative" and multi-sensory, not just verbal/visual. Paul Rand, and many after him, saw the artist caught between esthetics and the need to sell. He wrote, "There is nothing wrong or shameful in selling...Long range, the interests of business and art are not opposed."

Today's designer has not only computers and lasers and software as tools, but also the new science of marketing. Aimed design is a must today, and today's designer must use it along with the new technologies and esthetic knowledge, taste and judgment to produce the most effective communications.

Random Thoughts

TYPE IS TO BE READ

(Excerpts from "Lettering is a Visual Presentation of Language," a speech by Otl Aicher at the Type Directors Club Silvermine Seminar, 1958.)

"Modern typographers usually organize lettering in a planelike fashion, and it is looked upon as a painting. Rarely is any attention paid to the linear process of reading."

"We are inclined to forget that the reading process goes from left to right and that we should have a precise point of reference for the eye at the left rather than at the right. It is hard to find another explanation for the bad habit of flush right lines."

"We tend to forget that we usually read at arm's length distance. How else could one explain the great confusion of different sizes of type on one page?"

"Very little is known about the optimum speed of reading. Some texts today may have to be spelled out, whereas others are understandable at a slight glance."

"We have forgotten the fact that we do not read single letters, but conceive images of words and of groups of words. We have forgotten that we read sections of sentences, which require a certain length of line."

Tradition v. Traditionalism
(Excerpt from a speech by Herbert Spencer at the Type Directors Club Silvermine Seminar, 1958)

"To the artist, the architect, the writer or the composer, I believe tradition is vital to his creative activity.

"But excessive respect for tradition becomes traditionalism. And traditionalism kills the tradition.

"What then, is tradition? Tradition is a living, active, and vital force in creative activity. It consists not of a code of rigid conventions, but of principles based on accumulated experience. Those principles we inherit, make use of in our work and codify in the life of our own experience, and then hand on to succeeding generations. Tradition is an inheritance we cannot avoid but which we can easily misinterpret and abuse. It imposes obligations and restrains our formal innovations, yet I do not think we can regard tradition as a prison. It is, I think the only sound basis of growth.

"But it is vitally important that we should clearly distinguish between tradition, *which may exercise a healthy restraint upon our innovations, and* traditionalism, *which is indeed a prison, or perhaps more accurately, a cemetery – a graveyard of dead ideas and decaying conventions.*

"Traditionalism is the negation of tradition. It is the real enemy of healthy tradition. Traditionalism is the product of men devoid of creative ability and incapable of original thought who fail to grasp and to understand the essence of tradition, and who seek therefore to arrest and petrify and preserve the formal expression of tradition at a particular moment. Traditionalism is tradition mummified. It is tradition reduced to a collection of lifeless conventions.

"Traditionalism is fostered by men who do not understand tradition but who are awed by it. The creative artist and designer must always and inevitably oppose traditionalism and those who engender it."

Thesis, Antithesis, Synthesis

One way of looking at the past century is to view the flow from one school of art or design as a form of Hegelian dialectics. This force is still at work today, as this writer suggested in a U&lc editorial, excerpted here.

"Dialectic is a process of change whereby an entity (thesis) is transformed into its opposite (antithesis) and preserved and extended by a blending of thesis and antithesis into a higher form, synthesis.

"This Hegelian concept applies to all of life – to politics and to economics, to law and to ethics, to science and religion, and to art.

"Some of the current shock being encountered by artists and designers is nothing more than dialectic at work. In our dynamic society, periods of harmony, tranquil periods when dialectic clash is muted, are static pauses, periods of little change or growth.

"Dramatic evidence of dialectic forces in graphic design is in the effects of bits and bytes, electronic pens and lasers, hardware and software, upon art and design, creativity and productivity, talent and thinking.

"Struggle, history and Hegel tell us, is the law of growth. Change is the cardinal principle of life. Nothing great in life is accomplished without passion. The great artists and designers of tomorrow will be those who can passionately embrace both the thesis of personal creativity and the antithesis of computer-enhanced tools to reach new and higher esthetic levels: a new synthesis that in turn will be a thesis to another generation and the platform for the next round in the dialectical evolution of esthetics."

The century-long struggle between the demands of clarity and vigor for communication effectiveness is an example of the endless flow of thesis, anthithesis, and a synthesis that often becomes the thesis for the next Hegelian round.

So – what is right or best? Where is the end? As observed earlier, unique problems demand customized solutions. Appropriateness, not fashion, not style, is the first consideration.

In appraising a work of typographic communication (and the emphasis here is on communication) one must evaluate it in terms of its success in achieving its purpose.

The burden of achieving an appropriate solution rests primarily on the buyer of the design. He/she should know the various design approaches to a problem and what the style and touch of each available designer is, and then select one in tune with the nature of the problem.

One must also distinguish between appropriateness and graphic clichés that superficially address a problem. For example, some years ago Doyle Dane Bernbach prepared an advertisement for the then-fledgling El Al Airlines. El Al was small and new, and the campaign needed a primary statement that was both strong in its appeal and unique to El Al. The airline's new plane, for a brief period, offered on its trans-Atlantic route the fastest flight available. To dramatize this, the agency ran full-page newspaper ads dominated by a bird's-eye view of the ocean with one-third of the picture raggedly torn off and the terse message that El Al had shrunk the ocean by one-third.

This graphic device was not only appropriate but at the heart of the message. Such an appropriate device is not a gimmick. A gimmick is a device, often a cliché, that is not at the heart of the message and is little more than an eye catcher. Following the El Al ad, which won an Art Directors Club award, there was a flurry of ads with torn photographs. In most of these the tearing of the picture was graphic gimmickry, the use of a visual device momentarily in fashion to get attention.

Taste, Judgment, and Computers

It is this writer's position that despite all the wonders a computer can perform, it cannot and will not replace designers. The human beings bring intuition, initiative, taste, judgment and decisiveness to the solution of a problem, while the computer's strength is in number crunching and analytical thought within given parameters. This will be true even when Artificial Intelligence (AI) is available. This point of view is supported by such existentialist philosophers as Martin Heidigger and Hubert Dreyfus. They believe the mind (and thus design creativity) solves problems holistically, not step-by-step, nor by sequentially analyzing possibilities, as does a computer.

The Vocabulary of Form...

Here are some comments by Paul Rand on the relationship of art and craft in design:

"There is an old romantic idea that intuition and intellect do not mix. There is an equally erroneous belief that inspiration takes the place of industry. Fortified with such misconceptions, it is understandable that we tend to minimize the importance of learning the rules, the fundamentals which are the raw material of the artist's craft.

"In graphic design, as in all creative expression, art evolves from craft. In dancing, craft is mastering the basic steps; in music, it is learning the scales. In typographic design, craft deals with points, lines, planes, picas, ciceros, leads, quads, serifs, letters, words, folios, pages, signatures, paper, ink, color, printing and binding.

"The vocabulary of form (art) includes, among others: space, proportion, scale, size, shape, rhythm, repetition, sequence, movement, balance, volume, contrast, harmony, order and simplicity.

"Just as there is no art without craft and no craft without rules, so too there is no art without fantasy, without ideas. A child's art is much fantasy but little craft. It is the fusion of the two that makes the difference."

The Designer as Problem Solver

Ivan Chermayeff offered these comments on the designer as a problem solver.

"Design comes from a combination of intelligence and artistic ability. A designer is someone who should solve problems. He is a borrower, co-ordinator, assimilator, juggler, and collector of material, knowledge and thought from the past and present, from other designers, from technology and from himself. His style and individuality come from the consistency of his own attitudes and approach to the expression and communication of a problem. It is a devotion of the designer to the task of fully understanding the problem and then expressing those ideas which come from this search in its appropriate form that makes him a professional.

"There is a large body of designers, clients and consumers who don't really care very much about very much. The joy and pleasure of doing a good job for its own sake has not been discovered by enough people."

TYPOGRAPHIC COMMUNICATIONS TODAY

Chapter XIV: Thoughts About Yesterday, Today, and Tomorrow

"...the new typographic technologies that are being developed for office communications and electronic publishing mark the beginning of a new era of printed communications."

Of Licentious Typography

Max Caflisch made these comments on the value of experimentation:

"The notion that typography, in order to be contemporary, must *have an experimental character is misleading, even grotesque. The typographer must learn to distinguish between good and bad, meaningful and unmeaningful, disciplined and licentious typography. He has to make his decision with the reader in mind and in the best interest of the reader, who as the final link in the chain determines the value or lack of value of a printed piece by being attracted by it, by reading it, or by passing it unmoved and throwing it into the always present wastepaper basket."*

Symmetry as Ornament

"Symmetry is antithetical to the functional and integrated character of typography. Symmetry is an ornament, a mode, or a fashion like any other." Max Huber, at the Type Directors Club Silvermine Seminar, 1958.

Of the Readability/Excitement Tradeoff

(Excerpt from a speech by Herb Lubalin at the Type Directors Club conference, Typography USA, 1959.)

"Through typographic means, the designer now presents, in one image, both the message and the pictorial idea. Sometimes, this 'playing' with type has resulted in the loss of a certain amount of legibility. Researchers consider this a deplorable state of affairs but, on the other hand, the excitement created by a novel image sometimes more than compensates for the slight difficulty in readability."

Trying Too Hard to Be Different

(Excerpt from a speech by Allen F. Hurlburt at the Type Directors Club conference, Typography USA, 1959.)

"At its best, American typography features a clarity of expression and an overall integration of design that is in the finest tradition of typography and its related arts. At its worst, it represents a sacrifice of clarity and true personal expression in favor of a preoccupation with typographic fads.

"Like the automotive stylists, we are frequently all trying too hard to be different together, creating shallow style that can have little lasting effect on the mainstream of typographic design. We move from the ornate to the starkly plain and back again, and from wide leading to tightly stacked type lines, as though each new method were the only true way.

"This twisted path to conformity is strewn with the tortured reminders of the vagaries of our typographic taste: Broadway, Agency Gothic, Cartoon, Corvinus, Neuland, Signal and Slim Black, to name but a few."

The Bauhaus Non-Style

(Excerpt from a speech by Herbert Bayer at the Type Directors Club conference, Typography USA, 1959.)

"While the aspirations of the Bauhaus were to discover and formulate principles of design and not to create a style, the term Bauhaus-style was coined in complete misunderstanding of the aims which were pursued there. Furthermore, style cannot be trends of taste devoid of inner substance and structure, applied as a cultural sugar-coating. To solve the demands of visual communication, the designer has at his disposal an infinite variety and multitude of means; not those which conform to the stamp of a style, but the more timeless methods of creativity and tools which enable him to meet taste. Design of which I speak here is not for design's sake. If 'style' becomes predominant, it overshadows its own purpose. It becomes an obstacle in the perception of the specific problem which it is supposed to serve. Formalism and the straitjacket of a 'style' will eventually lead to a dead end, while the nature of things is the self-changing pulse of life with its unlimited forms and ways of expression; thus, one must see clearly and not make new clichés out of old formulas."

Typographic Cunning Has Its Place

(Excerpt from a speech by Louis Dorfsman at the Type Directors Club conference, Typography USA, 1959.)

"Typography, obviously, deals with controlling and distributing both type and space to aid to the maximum *the reader's understanding of the text. It is therefore primarily utilitarian and only secondarily esthetic. The enjoyment of patterns is rarely the reader's chief aim (although it may conceivably be, and often is, the designer's chief aim).*

"Any disposition of printing material which (whatever the intention) has the effect of coming between author and reader is wrong. *It follows logically that design and printing materials meant to be read leave little room for 'affected' typography. Even dullness and monotony in the typographic sense are far less disturbing to a reader than typographic eccentricity or pleasantry.*

"Cunning of that sort may, however, be desirable or even essential in the typography of certain forms of communication in our society – material not intended so much to be read as to be noticed. *The endeavor we call advertising design is particularly susceptible to distortion or trickery in typography to achieve 'freshness,' and thus survive inattention in a highly competitive environment. This is not, therefore, to be taken as a condemnation of such type design; it serves an important function in a society where advertising is a major economic force."*

A Statement of Strength

(Excerpt from a speech by Lester Beall at the Type Directors Club conference, Typography USA, 1959.)

"...In appraising the influence of the typographical design of the dadaists and the pioneers of 'die neue typographie' on American typographical design, as it unfolded in the early thirties, it would be a serious mistake not to also evaluate the influence of American political, county fair, and recruiting posters of the Civil War, and American and English children's books. For the American political posters, the recruiting posters of the Civil War and 'die neue typographie' all had one factor in common... a statement of strength! *In the early thirties, the desire to meet the challenge of a new period in our economic and social history was reflected by the designer's search for forms that were* strong, direct, and exciting!*"*

The Era of New-Think

(Excerpt from an article by Vance Jonson in the AIGA Journal of Graphic Design, Vol. 4, No. 4, 1986. Jonson is a principal of Jonson Pirtle Pedersen Alcorn Metzdorf & Hess, with offices in New York City, Stamford and Dallas.)

"A perfect example of leading edge creative New-Speak is Manhattan Graphics' Ready,SetGo!3, currently the most sophisticated personal computer system on the market. With it, one can experience the liberated feeling of creative focusing, because it manifests our ideas easily, quickly and accurately. It transforms the screen into a super drawing board on which we can organize the pictures and words into any vehicle we choose. The user of this new software controls both form and content and is limited in output only by creative stamina. Using any popular typeface, the author can change size, leading, measure and form (centered, flush left or flush right, justified) instantly. Also, the author can do complicated run-arounds, kerning (either manually, letter by letter, or automatically), move an arbitrary character or group of characters up, down, left, right and insert it anywhere because the text will automatically reflow throughout the entire piece with real-time hyphenation occurring automatically at word-wrap speed. The author may also import graphics from a number of different sources including MacPaint, MacDraw, MacDraft and the clipboard feature. Continuous tone photos can be converted to halftones by a scanning process called 'Digitizing' and color can be reproduced electronically.

"The implications to the design industry are vast. Massive economic savings are projected, and alert individual designers can profit instantly from intelligent applications of these new tools."

Just Fads in the Future?

Focusing a critical eye on the future of typographic communications, Young & Rubicam vice president Klaus Schmidt envisions a continuance of many of the current approaches to graphic design, those that are both compelling and functional. Within this framework an infinite number of specific additions to communication problems are possible. Mr. Schmidt sees this broad framework remaining viable while various design fads come and go. He sees no new true movement since such a broad range of approaches has already been developed, just fads, as young designers get bored and "innovate" by reinventing the wheel.

Creativity – Liberating and Harnessing

If art history in the 20th century is the history of the liberation of creativity, modern typographic design history is the history of harnessing creativity to the solution of visual communication problems.

Type and Society

(Concluding remarks by Will Burtin, program chairman, Art and Science of Typography, April 26, 1958.)

"The body of knowledge which we utilize daily has been doubling in volume every ten years since 1800. It is a problem of staggering proportions to keep up with this growth in terms of making knowledge enrich *society instead of confusing it. It has been observed that this growth is not equalled yet by a better knowledge of the communication field – its techniques, its potential for the common good, its inherent potential toward better understanding of ideas through the visualizing process.*

"Obviously we cannot consider design by itself alone because its progress stems from the ideas of a society as a whole. But if through the better use of the tools of design – among them typography – an easier access to knowledge develops, design has a vital role to play. From this follows that designers are facing a challenge unprecedented in the history of the arts. This is what (Sandberg and) others call the 'the new art' – the art of reaching out further and further – to more and more people – to bring enjoyment of the new and to reevaluate and enjoy the old.

"The arts are essential for the understanding of others and of ourselves. They are equally essential in the integrating process of technological and scientific advances into the general body of a civilization. They are most essential, however, in the establishing of a sense of balance and harmony within our environment, in the pursuit of progress and peace."

Technology Modifies Design

Looking to the future of typographic communications, Aaron Burns, writing in the November/December 1986 issue of *Print* magazine, reviewed changes made in the 1970s and 1980s and those now emerging. Here are some of his observations:

❧*"For example, the ability to set type photographically in point sizes larger than could previously be done with metal-set processes made it economically possible to design a full-page newspaper advertisement set entirely in 36 point or 72 point type."*

❧*"Intermixing several weights of a type family in varying sizes; setting type with less space between characters and/or between lines to achieve a variety of type colors and textures; setting characters closer together without having to notch or mortise metal type (a laborious, time-consuming and costly process) are just a few of the many technological features of phototypesetting that designers were able to take advantage of in creating new typographic design solutions."*

❧*"I believe the new typographic technologies that are being developed for office communications and electronic publishing mark the beginning of a new era of printed communications.*

"Correspondence, memos, documents, reports, material customarily set in typewriter faces, are already being set in typefaces such as Helvetica, Times Roman, Optima, ITC Avant Garde Gothic, and ITC Souvenir – typefaces formerly used only in the graphic arts.

"Typographic arts quality, not typewriter quality, is what electronic publishing portends for the 'Office of the Future,' which is already being called the 'Office of Today.' And most assuredly, this revolution in office communications will have its effect on the future of every professional graphic designer and typographer."

❧*"At first, the limited range of type families, of type sizes, the often lower resolution and inferior quality image produced by the toners used in non-impact printers are likely to slow the development of this typographic communications revolution. But as output quality improves and costs of equipment decrease, sophisticated typography, with all of its communications advantages, will pervade every area of graphic communications, as it now does advertising, publishing, and commercial printing."*

❧"Typographic quality, *not* typewriter quality, *is what we can look for in the typographic communications world of tomorrow.*

"I believe that the new typographic communications machines that will pervade the office and home environments will lead to more typographically produced communications than would ever have been produced on a conventional typewriter using standard typewriter typefaces.

"Much of the work that will be produced in the office environment will be done, not by typists or secretaries, but by a new generation of 'typographists.' These typographists will become the 'general practitioners' of typography. The knowledgeable and experienced designers and typographers of today will be the specialists – the internists – the surgeons of typography. There will be room and need for both.

"Already, the new technologies have made possible new typeface designs – designs on a scale never before affordable under the old methods."

The Thread, the Fabric, the Spirit and the Mind of Man

It is an old story, perhaps as old as man, that as times passes, artists in various forms of expression find the existing and accepted ways of doing things too limiting. What was once stimulating and exciting becomes trite, clichéd and confining.

This thread weaves through time in waves that crest in innovation after innovation. One might think of many of these threads as weaving into a kind of ever-changing fabric of our culture and society. While the periods of greatest experiment and innovation do not precisely coincide across the arts, for example, there is a mutually beneficial interplay that results in a cultural synergism in which the effect on the spirit and mind of man is greater than the mere sum of the interwoven elements.

TYPOGRAPHIC COMMUNICATIONS TODAY
Chapter XIV: Thoughts About Yesterday, Today, and Tomorrow

"...the message problem: just what is being said, to whom, by whom, and with what objective."

The 1890s and Early 1900s

Literature & Theatre	*Visual Arts*	*Music*	*Science & Technology*
Henrik Ibsen	Claude Monet	César Franck	Guglielmo Marconi
Leo Tolstoi	Paul Cézanne	Sergei Prokofiev	Thomas Edison
Émile Zola	Vincent Van Gogh	Richard Strauss	Henry Ford
Walt Whitman	Edgar Degas	Peter Tschaikovsky	Louis Jean and Auguste Lumière
Feodor Dostoyevsky	Henri Matisse	Claude Debussy	Pierre and Marie Curie
George Bernard Shaw	Henri de Toulouse-Lautrec	Gustav Mahler	Wilhelm Roentgen

Cultural Synergism in the 1900s

The accompanying table lists just a handful of the painters, composers, authors and poets, and scientists whose innovations changed the face of their art or science.

This minuscule list does not pretend to cover even the major developments and figures in each field. Its sole purpose is to suggest that we look not just vertically at our own discipline, but horizontally across our cultural spectrum to begin to grasp how the waves of discovery and experiment and innovation move together and interact on each other and on intellects and attitudes and spirits.

While more and more writers were examining how society affected the lives of individuals and how psychological drives affect human behavior, painters were looking more carefully at aspects of everyday life and seeing colors and details in new ways; composers were developing new sounds by using new chords and moving toward atonality, and scientists were discovering and inventing such things as wireless telegraphy, mass-produced automobiles, cinematography, phonograph records, radium, x-rays, electrons and helium.

The cultural threads of the 20th century wove their way from representationalism in painting through the various movements reviewed in Chapter II to total non-representationalism. In music, the tonality and regularity of Bach gave way to the dynamism of new chords as epitomized by Richard Wagner, then Richard Strauss and Claude Debussy. Perhaps the aural impressionism of Debussy or Maurice Ravel can be compared to the visual impressionism of Claude Monet or Camille Pissaro and the later paintings of Wassily Kandinsky and Jackson Pollock to the atonality of Arnold Schoenberg, Alban Berg, or even John Cage; and these in turn to the evolution from Charles Dickens to James Joyce, Thomas Wolfe, e e cummings, Gertrude Stein and today's concrete poets.

The threads have moved from a long-accepted way of achieving order, as in the standard tonal scale, to a 12 note atonal scale, each with its own rules and parameters, and to the freer, seemingly rule-less music of Philip Glass or John Cage.

The Threads of Typographic Communications

If all this has a bearing on directions in typographic communications, it is that they should be seen and appreciated not as isolated or unique or strange developments, but in the context of concurrent cultural threads and fabrics.

Fads and fashions have their place for adding spice and variety to our lives, but they do not endure. Directions that endure add real value to our lives, to our ways of hearing, seeing, thinking, feeling, communicating.

One test for survival, the line of distinction between a fad and an innovation that endures, is the measure of its appropriateness to the purpose it serves. As observed throughout Typographic Communications Today, the past century has woven a complex fabric of choices for typographic designers to work with. The challenge is not merely to innovate or to come to terms with new technologies, but to never lose sight of the need to choose from these threads those that best suit the problem at hand. If this century has blessed the designer with many options, it has simultaneously challenged the designer's taste, judgment and analytical ability.

Tomorrow and Tomorrow and Tomorrow

One of the oldest and truest of clichés is that the only constant is change. Of that and little else we can be sure. Typographic designers need to be, and by their very nature are, sensitive to what is new: new in design directions, in technology, in the whole cultural, socio-economic environment. It is this obligation to try to distinguish between momentary fashions and what is new and durable, and to move with the times to look fresh while applying their new knowledge selectively, how and where it fits the communication need. The first challenge always was, still is, and always will be to thoroughly understand the message problem: just what is being said, to whom, by whom, and with what objective. Only then can the typographic tone of voice be determined and the elements that comprise it be specified. In a constantly changing world, if there is another constant besides change, that challenge is it.

A Time of Pluralism

One way to sum up today's communication design directions its many tones of vision, is to understand its rejection of past styles as "the" way to design. This rejection of regarding previous styles as sacred is coupled with the acceptance, in the design community overall, of virtually all styles. Today, therefore, attitudinally, we have a design pluralism that, for any given problem or challenge, seeks the most appropriate blend of clarity and vitality.

TYPOGRAPHIC COMMUNICATIONS TODAY
Acknowledgments, Permissions

Typographic Communications Today was made possible by the considerable assistance of very many designers, design historians and design teachers from many countries. The author is also indebted to the many authors and publishers whose works, listed in the bibliography, supplied crucial information, and from which I have quoted numerous thought-stimulating passages.

First and foremost I must thank Aaron Burns. As President of International Typeface Corporation, he, one day in late 1983, proposed that a work such as this be written. The general idea was his and he gave me, to the fullest, all the ingredients one needs to do a project well: an open-ended schedule, an adequate budget and a free hand, plus his confidence, encouragement and frequent suggestions.

It was my privilege to travel around the world and interview many of today's outstanding typographers and designers, and to speak with them not only about their own work, but about the tides and waves in graphic design during the past century. Their insights, generously shared, add depth to this study and helped mold its point of view, so that it is more than reportage. Just a few, who could not be visited personally, painstakingly answered my detailed questionnaires. And still others, not listed here, kindly sent samples of their work for inclusion herein.

Each and every one of those in the following acknowledgments list was a major help in the development of Typographic Communications Today. On some subjects different and contradictory opinions were expressed. Since this is not intended as a formal academic study, I have rarely attributed the opinions expressed and take responsibility for the overall theme and the opinions I have chosen and/or espoused.

Edward M. Gottschall.

Bass, Saul
Baudin, Fernand
Bayer, Herbert
Bill, Max
Bosshard, Hans-Rudolf
Brattinga, Pieter
Burns, Aaron
Caflisch, Max
Crouwell, Wim
Danziger, Louis
De Majo, Willie
Droste, Dr. Magdalena
Frutiger, Adrian
Gabor, Peter
Garland, Ken
Gerstner, Karl
Gürtler, André
Haley, Allan
Herdeg, Walter
Hlavsa, Oldrich
Hoffmann, Armin
Huber, Max
Kamekura, Yusaku
Kurlansky, Mervyn
Lampaert, Hermann
Lange, Günter Gerhard
Laufer, Roger
Leu, Olaf
Martin, Noel
Miranda, Oswaldo
Monguzzi, Bruno
Müller-Brockmann, Josef
Nagai, Kazumasa
Odermatt, Siegfried
Olyff, Michel
Pfäffli, Bruno
Rand, Paul
Remington, R. Roger
and The Graphic Design Archive on Videodisc
at Rochester Institute of Technology
Schmidt, Klaus
Spencer, Herbert
Spindler, Victor
Tanaka, Ikko
Thompson, Bradbury
Tomaszewski, Roman
Weidemann, Kurt
Weingart, Wolfgang
Wolf, Henry
Zapf, Hermann
Zhukov, Maxim

The following were most helpful in the production, picture gathering, proofreading and critiquing of the text:
Miriam Bensman
Janice Brunell
Laurie Burns
Pat Krugman
Carl W. Smith
Ilene Strizver
Katrina Swendseid
Sid Timm
Juliet Travison
Theresa Turco
Kim Valerio

TYPOGRAPHIC COMMUNICATIONS TODAY
Select Bibliography

THIS IS A LIST of only those books, magazines and other writings that have been of considerable help in the writing of TYPOGRAPHIC COMMUNICATIONS TODAY. Readers wishing more information or a different point of view would do well to start with these works, some of which contain bibliographies that can lead more deeply into the study of typography, typefaces and graphic design.

In the interest of facilitating reading, I have rarely cited works in the text. Also in the interest of readability, I have avoided footnotes and a bibliography that includes all available works on the subjects. On the other hand, I have consulted many authoritative sources, interviewed knowledgeable people all over the world, and had the final text checked by several outstanding scholars. In sum, although the work is not addressed to scholars, a considerable effort was made to assure its correctness.

This select bibliography is arranged as one list, alphabetized by the authors' or editors' names. For books, the information, when relevant, is arranged as follows:

Name of the author or authors, the editors, or the institution responsible for the writing of the book; *Full title of the book,* including the subtitle, if any
"Title of series," if any, and volume or number in the series
Volume number or total number of volumes of a multi-volume work
Edition, if not the original
City of publication
Publisher's name (sometimes omitted)
Date of publication

For articles in periodicals, the relevant information is arranged as follows:

Name of the author
"Title of the article"
Name of the periodical
Volume number (sometimes issue number)
Date
Pages occupied by the article

Other sources, such as booklets, catalogs, encyclopedias and portfolios are identified as such.

Every effort has been made to research the copyright owners of the materials quoted in this text. Omissions brought to our attention will be credited in a subsequent printing.

Alliance Graphique Internationale
12 Grafici dell'AGI
1984

American Institute of Graphic Arts (AIGA)
Journal of Graphic Design
Vol. 1, No. 1 – Vol. 4, No. 3
June 1982 – July 1986

Amstutz, Walter
Editor
Who's Who in Graphic Art, Vol. 2
Dübendorf, Switzerland
De Clivo Press
1982

Association Typographique Internationale (A.TYP.I)
Index of Typefaces
Munchenstein, Switzerland
A.TYP.I
1975

Barker, Nicolas
Stanley Morison
Cambridge, Massachusetts
Harvard University Press
1972

Barrett, Vivian Endicott
Kandinsky at the Guggenheim
New York
Abbevill Press
1983

Barron, Stephanie and Maurice Tuchman, Editors
The Avant-Garde in Russia, 1910-1930: New Perspectives
Cambridge, Massachusetts
The MIT Press
1980

Belloli, Prof. Dr. Carlo
Italian Pioneers of Graphic Design, 1905-1937
Neue Grafik
October 1959
2-26

Bennett, Paul A.
Books and Printing: A Treasury for Typophiles
Cleveland and New York
The World Publishing Co.
1951

Berman, Felix
Posters – Odermatt & Tissi, 1959-1980
A reprint from Typographische Monatsblätter

Boggeri, Antonio
Max Huber in Italy
Typographica, New Series No. 2
41-51

Bos, Ben and others
Total Design (Exhibition catalog)
Amsterdam, The Netherlands
Total Design
1983

Boyle, Richard J.
American Impressionism
New York Graphic Society
Boston, Massachusetts
1982

Broos, Kees
Piet Zwart
The Hague, The Netherlands
Haags Gemeente Museum

Burns, Aaron
Typography
New York
Reinhold Publishing Corp.
1961

Burns, Aaron
Typography Today
Print
January/February 1964
11-95

Burns, Aaron
Typography Today – and Tomorrow
Print
November/December 1986
37-39

Burns, Aaron and others
Typomundus 20
New York
Reinhold Publishing Corporation
1966

Burns, Laurie
Typographica USSR
Print
May/June 1985
86-95

Butorina, Evgenia, compiler
The Lettering Art: Works by Moscow Book Designers 1959-1974
Moscow
Kniga
1977

Caflisch, Max
Typography Needs Type, booklet
Lausanne, Switzerland
Association Typographique Internationale
1977

Carter, Rob and Ben Day and Philip Meggs
Typographic Design: Form and Communication
New York
Van Nostrand Reinhold Company
1985

Cave, Roderick
The Private Press, 2nd edition
New York and London
R. R. Bowker Company
1983

Cohen, Arthur A.
The Avant-Garde in Print
A series of portfolios documenting 20th century design and typography.
The five visual portfolio titles are:
Futurism
Lissitzky
Dada
Typographic/Master Designers in Print 1
Typographic/Master Designers in Print 2
New York
AGP Matthews, Inc.
1981

Cohen, Arthur A.
Herbert Bayer
Cambridge, Massachusetts
The MIT Press
1984

Davis, L. Mills
Toward the Electronic Studio
Washington, D.C.
Davis, Inc.
1986

Droste, Magdalena, catalog editor
Herbert Bayer, Das Künstlerische Werk 1918-1938
West Berlin
Bauhaus-Archiv
1982

Finsler, Hans
Alfred Willimann
Neue Grafik
June 1962
2-15

Fox, Martin
Editor
Great Graphic Designers of the 20th Century
Print (A special issue)
Vol. 23, No. 1
January/February 1969

Friedman, Mildred
Editor
A Paul Rand Miscellany
Design Quarterly
No. 123
1984
3-32

Frutiger, Adrian
Type Sign Symbol
Zürich, Switzerland
ABC Verlag
1980

Garland, Ken
Ken Garland and Associates: Designers
London
Graphis Press
1982

Gerdts, William H.
American Impressionism
New York
Abbeville Press
1984

Gerstner, Karl
Compendium for Literates, A System of Writing
Cambridge, Massachusetts
The MIT Press
1974

Gerstner, Karl and Markus Kutter
Gerstner & Kutter 1959
Gerstner & Kutter 1960
Gerstner & Kutter 1961
Gerstner & Kutter 1965
Basel, Switzerland

Gerstner, Karl
Typographisches Memorandum
TM (Typographische Monatsblätter)
February 1972
2-35

Gherchuk, Yuri
The Art of Lettering in the Soviet Union
Moscow
Sovietsky Khudozhnik Publisher
1983

Gorb, Peter and partners of Pentagram
Living by Design, Rev. edition
London
Lund Humphries
1979

Gordon, Robert and Andrew Forge
Monet
New York
Harry N. Abrams, Inc.

Gottschall, Edward M.
Graphic Communication '80s
New York
Prentice-Hall
1981

Gottschall, Edward M.
Editor
Typographic Directions
New York
Art Directions Book Company
1964

Goudy, Frederic W.
The Alphabet and Elements of Lettering
New York
Dover Publications, Inc.
1963

Goudy, Frederic W.
Typologia
Berkeley, California
University of California Press
1940

Grannis, Chandler B.
Editor
Heritage of the Graphic Arts
New York
R. R. Bowker Company
1972

Gray, Camilla
Alexander Rodchenko: A Constructivist Designer
Typographica, New Series No. 11
2-19

Grunigen, B. von and others
Emil Ruder
Typographische Monatsblätter
March 1971
174-232

Guerman, Mikhail
Art of the October Revolution
Leningrad
Aurora Art Publishers
1979 (First English language edition)

Gürtler, André; Christian Mengelt, Erich Gschwind
From Helvetica to Haas Unica
Typographische Monatsblätter
July/August 1980
189-202

Haley, Allan
Phototypography
New York
Scribner's
1980

Harris, William H., and Judith S. Levey
The New Columbia Encyclopedia
New York and London
Columbia University Press
1975

Hauschofer, Heinz
Paul Renner – Ein Eindruck
Munich
Typographische Gesellschaft München
1978

Henrion, FHK
Top Graphic Design
Zürich, Switzerland
ABC Verlag
1983

Hill, Anthony
Max Bill
Typographica 7
21-28

Hodik, Barbara and Roger Remington
Editors
The First Symposium on the History of Graphic Design
Rochester, N.Y.
Rochester Institute of Technology
1983

Hofmann, Armin
Thoughts on the Study and Making of Visual Signs
Design Quarterly 130

Holmes, Nigel
Designer's Guide to Creating Charts and Diagrams
New York
Watson-Guptill Publications
1984

Holmes, Nigel
Designing Pictorial Symbols
New York
Watson-Guptill Publications
1985

Hostettler, Rudolf
Editor
Odermatt and Tissi
Typographische Monatsblätter
Fall 1978 (Special issue)

Hostettler, Rudolf
Editor
Jan Tschichold
Typographische Monatsblätter
April 1972
288-322

Hostettler, Rudolf
Editor
Wolfgang Weingart
Typographische Monatsblätter
December 1976
725-756

Hurlburt, Allen
The Design Concept
New York
Watson-Guptill Publications
1981

TYPOGRAPHIC COMMUNICATIONS TODAY
Select Bibliography

Hurlburt, Allen
The Grid
New York
Van Nostrand Reinhold Company
1978

Igarashi, Takenobu
Design, 1970-1982
Tokyo
Takenobu Igarashi Design
1982

Igarashi, Takenobu
Space Graphics
Tokyo
Takenobu Igarashi Design
1983

Ishihara, Yoshihisa
Editor
Articles by Helmut Schmid, Wolfgang Weingart, Wim Crouwel, Kohei Sugiura, Franco Grignani, John Cage, Emil Ruder
Typography Today, Idea, Special issue
1980

Jaspert, W. Pincus and W. Turner Berry and A. F. Johnson
The Encyclopedia of Typefaces
London
Blandford Press
1970 (4th edition)

Johnston, Priscilla
Edward Johnston, 2nd edition
New York
Pentalic Corporation
1976

Kery, Patricia Frantz
Art Deco Graphics
New York
Harry N. Abrams, Inc.
1986

Khan-Magomedov, Selim O.
Rodchenko: The Complete Work
Cambridge, Massachusetts
The MIT Press
1987

Koch, Rudolf and others
The Little ABC Book of Rudolf Koch
Boston, Massachusetts
David R. Godine
1976

Lawson, Alexander and Archie Provan
100 Type Histories, Vols. 1, 2
Arlington, Virginia
National Composition Association
1983

Lewis, John
The 20th Century Book, 2nd edition
New York
Van Nostrand Reinhold Company
1984

Lissitzky-Küppers, Sophie
El Lissitzky
London
Thames and Hudson, Ltd.
1968

Lubalin, Herb
The Graphic Revolution in America: 40 Years of Innovative Typography, 1940-1980
Print
May/June 1979
41-104

Luke, John
Bradbury Thompson
Gutenberg & Family
January 1985
5-11

Mason, Stanley
Lester Beall
Graphis
No. 144
350-361

Massie, Suzanne
Land of the Firebird
New York
Simon and Schuster
1980

Meggs, Philip B.
A History of Graphic Design
New York
Van Nostrand Reinhold Company
1983

Müller-Brockmann, Josef
The Graphic Designer and His Design Problems
Niederteufen, Switzerland
Verlag Arthur Niggli AG
1983

Müller-Brockmann, Josef
Grid Systems in Graphic Design
Niederteufen, Switzerland
Verlag Arthur Niggli AG
2nd Rev. edition 1985

Müller-Brockmann, Josef
A History of Visual Communication
Niederteufen, Switzerland
Verlag Arthur Niggli AG
1971

Museum of Modern Art (New York)
De Stijl
Bulletin: Vol. XX, No. 2
Winter 1952-1953

Neuburg, Hans
Graphic Design in Swiss Industry
Zürich
ABC Verlag
1965

Neuburg, Hans
30 Years of Constructive Graphic Design
Neue Grafik
October 1959
27-35

Neumann, Eckhard
Henryk Berlewi and Mechano-faktura
Typographica, New Series No. 9
21-28

Neumann, Eckard
Typography, Graphic Design and Advertising at the Bauhaus
Neue Grafik
February 1965

Ogawa, Masataka and Ikko Tanaka and Kazumasa Nagai
The Works of Yusaku Kamekura
Tokyo
Rikuyo-sha Publishing, Inc.
1983

Passuth, Kisztina
Moholy-Nagy
London
Thames and Hudson Ltd.
1985

Perfect, Christopher and Gordon Rookledge
Rookledge's International Typefinder
London
Sarema Press
1983

Pirovano, Carlo
Editor
Max Huber Progetti Grafici 1936-1981
Milan
Electa
1982

Pirovano, Carlo
Editor
lo Studio Boggeri 1933-1981
Milan
Electa
1981

Propper, Robert A.
Typography of the Right and Left
Print
May/June 1977
45-52

Rand, Paul
A Designer's Art
New Haven, Connecticut
Yale University Press
1985

Rand, Paul
Thoughts on Design
New York
Van Nostrand Reinhold
1970

Réalité editors
Impressionism
Secaucus, New Jersey
Chartwell Books, Inc.
1973

Rehe, Rolf F.
Typography: How to Make It Most Legible
Carmel, Indiana
Design Research International
1974

Richez, Jacques
Recent Belgian Graphic Design
Graphis
No. 144
290-309

Rogers, Bruce
Paragraphs on Printing
New York
Dover Publications, Inc.
1979
Rotzler, Willy
Art and Graphics
Zürich
ABC Verlag
1983
Ruder, Emil
Typography
Niederteufen, Switzerland
Verlag Arthur Niggli AG
1967
Ruuhinen, Erkki
Erkki Ruuhinen Design
Helsinki, Finland
Erkki Ruuhinen Design
1985
Sakamoto, Noboru
Saul Bass and Associates
Idea
Special issue
Sakamoto, Noboru
30 Influential Designers of the Century
Idea
Special issue
Sandberg, W. and H. L. C. Jaffé
Pioneers of Modern Art
New York
McGraw-Hill Book Co.
1961
Sandberg, W. J. H. B.
Sandberg
Lelystad, The Netherlands
1986
Schapiro, Meyer
Van Gogh, Rev. edition
New York
Harry N. Abrams, Inc.
1982
Seitlin, Percy and Robert Leslie
PM (renamed *AD* in 1940)
1934-1942
Seybold, John W.
The Seybold Report on Publishing Systems
Vol. 1, No. 1 – Vol. 16, No. 2
Seybold, John W.
The World of Digital Typesetting
Media, Pennsylvania
Seybold Publications, Inc.
1984
Snyder, Gertrude and Alan Peckolick
Herb Lubalin
New York
American Showcase, Inc.
1985
Society of Graphic Designers of Canada
The Best of the 80s (Exhibition catalog)
Toronto, Canada
Spencer, Herbert
Pioneers of Modern Typography
London
Lund Humphries Publications Ltd.
1969
Spencer, Herbert
H. N. Werkman, Printer-Painter
Typographica 11
19-26
Spindler, Victor and Klaus Schmidt
Typographic Refinements in Phototypesetting
Direct Advertising (DA)
Vol. 60, No. 3, 1974
9-17
Stedelijk Museum
Kurt Schwitters, catalog 152
Amsterdam, The Netherlands
1956
Stedelijk Museum
Werkman, A Selection of Prints and General Printed Matter
Amsterdam, The Netherlands
1977
Stedelijk Museum
Piet Zwart, Typotekt (Exhibition catalog No. 257)
Amsterdam, The Netherlands
Stella, Frank
Working Space
Cambridge, Massachusetts
Harvard University Press
1986
Stern, Anatol
Avant-garde Graphics in Poland Between the Two World Wars
Typographica, New Series No. 9
3-20
Sutnar, Ladislav
Visual Design In Action
New York
Hastings House
1961
Tanaka, Ikko
The Work of Ikko Tanaka
Tokyo
1975
Tomaszewski, Roman
Typographia '72
Projekt (Warsaw)
June 1972
2-10
Tschichold, Jan
Asymmetric Typography
(Translated by Ruari McLean)
New York and Toronto
Reinhold Publishing Corporation and Cooper & Beatty, Ltd.
1967
Tschichold, Jan
El Lissitzky
Typographische Monatsblätter
December 1970
1-24
U&lc
Pro.Files: The Great Graphic Innovators
Agha, Dr. M. F., Vol. 5, No. 4, Pages 4, 8
Bass, Saul, Vol. 4, No. 3, Pages 8, 12
Bayer, Herbert, Vol. 4, No. 4, Pages 12, 16
Brodovich, Alexey, Vol. 4, No. 1, Pages 8, 16
Burtin, Will, Vol. 7, No. 1, Pages 28-30
Chermayeff, Ivan, Vol. 8, No. 2, Page 4
Chwast, Seymour, Vol. 8, No. 3, Pages 4-7
Dorfsman, Louis, Vol. 5, No. 4, Pages 6, 9
Federico, Gene, Vol. 5, No. 1, Pages 4, 8
Fletcher, Alan, Vol. 5, No. 1, Pages 6, 9
Geismar, Thomas, Vol. 8, No. 2, Page 6
Glaser, Milton, Vol. 4, No. 1, Pages 12, 17
Golden, William, Vol. 4, No. 4, Pages 14, 17
Krone, Helmut, Vol. 6, No. 2, Pages 12, 16
Lois, George, Vol. 4, No. 1, Pages 14, 17
Lubalin, Herb, Vol. 8, No. 1, Page 3
Müller-Brockmann, Josef, Vol. 6, No. 2, Pages 14, 17
Pineles, Cipe, Vol. 5, No. 3, Pages 6, 10
Rand, Paul, Vol. 4, No. 1, Pages 10, 16
Sandberg, Willem, Vol. 7, No. 3, Page 4
Thompson, Bradbury, Vol. 4, No. 3, Pages 10, 13
Wolf, Henry, Vol. 5, No. 3, Pages 8, 11
Wallis, L. W.
Type Design Developments 1970 to 1985
Arlington, Virginia
National Composition Association
1985
Weingart, Wolfgang
My Typography Instruction at the Basle School of Design
Design Quarterly 130
Wingler, Hans M.
The Bauhaus
Cambridge, Massachusetts
The MIT Press (English adaptation)
1969
Wolfe, Tom
From Bauhaus To Our House
New York
Farrar, Straus & Giroux, Inc.
1981
Yorke, Malcolm
Eric Gill, Man of Flesh and Spirit
New York
Universe Books
1981
Zapf, Hermann
Manuale Typographicum
Frankfurt au Main
Z-Presse
1968
Zhukov, Maxim
Books Now and Forever
Grafik (Budapest)
April 1982
14-21

Index

PAGE NUMBERS for text references are set in roman type. Page numbers referring to illustrations are set in italic. Typefaces with full alphabet showings appear in Chapters X and XI and are listed in this index alphabetically under, "Typefaces, full alphabet showings."

Index

TYPOGRAPHIC COMMUNICATIONS TODAY

Colophon

Designer
Mo Lebowitz

Composition
Characters Typographic Services Inc.

Type family
ITC Esprit,™ designed by Jovica Veljović

Printer and binder
Dai Nippon Printing Co.
Japan

Paper
86 lb. Royal Art Matt

Jacket design
Julie Simms
Designer, The MIT Press